Language and Thought

World Anthropology

General Editor

SOL TAX

Patrons

CLAUDE LÉVI-STRAUSS
MARGARET MEAD
LAILA SHUKRY EL HAMAMSY
M. N. SRINIVAS

MOUTON PUBLISHERS · THE HAGUE · PARIS
DISTRIBUTED IN THE USA AND CANADA BY ALDINE, CHICAGO

INTERNATIONAL CONGRESS OF ANTHRO-POLOGICAL AND ETHNOLOGICAL SCIENCES, 9TH, CHICAGO, 1973.

Language and Thought

Anthropological Issues

Editors

WILLIAM C. McCORMACK
STEPHEN A. WURM

MOUTON PUBLISHERS · THE HAGUE · PARIS
DISTRIBUTED IN THE USA AND CANADA BY ALDINE, CHICAGO

General Editor's Preface

None of the sciences of man has excited more philosophical and psychological discussion among its participants — and interested on-lookers — than linguistics. To the intellectually curious person, no part of this discussion is more stirring than that relating language to human thought and culture. This book deals anew with the fundamental problems of cognitive anthropology, with empirical evidence and theory from scholars of many cultures who reported their findings to a large international Congress.

Like most contemporary sciences, anthropology is a product of the European tradition. Some argue that it is a product of colonialism, with one small and self-interested part of the species dominating the study of the whole. If we are to understand the species, our science needs substantial input from scholars who represent a variety of the world's cultures. It was a deliberate purpose of the IXth International Congress of Anthropological and Ethnological Sciences to provide impetus in this direction. The *World Anthropology* volumes, therefore, offer a first glimpse of a human science in which members from all societies have played an active role. Each of the books is designed to be self-contained; each is an attempt to update its particular sector of scientific knowledge and is written by specialists from all parts of the world. Each volume should be read and reviewed individually as a separate volume on its own given subject. The set as a whole will indicate what changes are in store for anthropology as scholars from the developing countries join in studying the species of which we are all a part.

The IXth Congress was planned from the beginning not only to include as many of the scholars from every part of the world as possible, but also with a view toward the eventual publication of the papers in high-quality volumes. At previous Congresses scholars were invited to bring papers which were then read out loud. They were necessarily limited in length; many were only summarized; there was little time for discussion; and the sparse discussion could only be in one language. The IXth Congress was an experiment aimed at changing this. Papers were written with the intention of exchanging them before the Congress, particularly in extensive pre-Congress sessions; they were not intended to be read aloud at the Congress, that time being devoted to discussions — discussions which were simultaneously and professionally translated into five languages. The method for eliciting the papers was structured to make as representative a sample as was allowable when scholarly creativity — hence self-selection — was critically important. Scholars were asked both to propose papers of their own and to suggest topics for sessions of the Congress which they might edit into volumes. All were then informed of the suggestions and encouraged to re-think their own papers and the topics. The process, therefore, was a continuous one of feedback and exchange and it has continued to be so even after the Congress. The some two thousand papers comprising *World Anthropology* certainly then offer a substantial sample of world anthropology. It has been said that anthropology is at a turning point; if this is so, these volumes will be the historical direction-markers.

As might have been foreseen in the first post-colonial generation, the large majority of the Congress papers (82 percent) are the work of scholars identified with the industrialized world which fathered our traditional discipline and the institution of the Congress itself: Eastern Europe (15 percent); Western Europe (16 percent); North America (47 percent); Japan, South Africa, Australia, and New Zealand (4 percent). Only 18 percent of the papers are from developing areas: Africa (4 percent); Asia-Oceania (9 percent); Latin America (5 percent). Aside from the substantial representation from the U.S.S.R. and the nations of Eastern Europe, a significant difference between this corpus of written material and that of other Congresses is the addition of the large proportion of contributions from Africa, Asia, and Latin America. "Only 18 percent" is two to four times as great a proportion as that of other Congresses; moreover, 18 percent of 2,000 papers is 360 papers, 10 times the number of "Third World" papers presented at previous Congresses. In fact, these 360 papers are more than the total of ALL papers published after the last International Congress of Anthropological and

Ethnological Sciences which was held in the United States (Philadelphia, 1956).

The significance of the increase is not simply quantitative. The input of scholars from areas which have until recently been no more than subject matter for anthropology represents both feedback and also long-awaited theoretical contributions from the perspectives of very different cultural, social, and historical traditions. Many who attended the IXth Congress were convinced that anthropology would not be the same in the future. The fact that the next Congress (India, 1978) will be our first in the "Third World" may be symbolic of the change. Meanwhile, sober consideration of the present set of books will show how much, and just where and how, our discipline is being revolutionized.

Besides its three companion volumes, *Language and man, Language and society*, and *Approaches to language*, readers of this book will be especially interested in others published in this series on evolutionary, cognitive, and psychological anthropology; on folklore; and on the cultures of many regions in all parts of the world.

Chicago, Illinois   SOL TAX
September 8, 1976

Preface

A general session on "Language in Anthropology" at the IXth International Congress of Anthropological and Ethnological Sciences (Chicago, Fall 1973) was organized by McCormack at the invitation of Professor Sol Tax, president of the Congress. It evolved over more than a year on the basis of relevant papers volunteered to the Congress, plus an equal number of papers solicited by McCormack, notably at international linguistics congresses in Europe in 1972, under gratefully acknowledged travel support from The Canada Council of Ottawa and The Wenner-Gren Foundation for Anthropological Research of New York City. What started out as a single session ended up as several subsessions, of which four major topical ones have yielded the volumes in the *World Anthropology* series entitled *Language and man*, *Language and thought*, *Approaches to language*, and *Language and society*.

Wurm joined this undertaking at the invitation of Professor Tax upon the recommendation of McCormack and he assumed full responsibility for the conduct and written summaries of the session discussions based on precirculated papers. Wurm chaired essentially all subsessions of this general session, i.e., an opening informal subsession, the four formal topical subsessions, a fifth one on language in anthropology at large, and four *ad hoc* gatherings of self-selected membership. At his invitation, he was accompanied by Dr. Nguyen Dang Liem of The University of Hawaii, who acted throughout as his assistant and discussion coordinator. Wurm's subsequent written summaries of discussions were aided by the prepared texts of the formal discussants and tapes of most of the proceedings.

For three years, from mid-1972 until finalization of the resultant books,

Anna Pikelis McCormack acted as administrative and editorial associate to McCormack. All operations behind the scenes have carried the stamp of her extraordinary competence. For further and efficient assistance, she joins McCormack in thanking Mrs. Charlotte Stewart, secretary for the Department of Linguistics of The University of Calgary.

The subsession on "Language and Thought" had for its discussion theme "semantic probabilities in human cognition and symbology." As only an hour of time was available for it, discussion was restricted to its four formal discussants and the authors of papers in the subsession. However, all Congress members were explicitly free to contribute additional comments, verbally or in writing, on other occasions.

Editorial discretion for the present volume on *Language and thought* rested solely with McCormack. Some papers included for discussion at the subsession have found publication in other volumes of the *World Anthropology* series. No paper which was not included in the subsession has been added to this book.

The University of Calgary   WILLIAM C. MCCORMACK
Calgary, Alberta, Canada
January 15, 1975

Table of Contents

SECTION ONE

Introductory

Introduction

WILLIAM C. McCORMACK

This volume of papers, presented at the IXth International Congress of Anthropological and Ethnological Sciences, is composed of papers focusing on cultural semiotics as well as papers exemplifying current research in the related fields of ethnosemantics, ethnoscience, and ethnophilosophy. They were aggregated into a subsession with the idea that participants might through discussion explore the validity of descriptive semiotic models for cultural analysis, but time proved to be far too short for the emergence of any group orientation fully inclusive of the topics offered for discussion.

What did emerge was chiefly an advance in critical judgment regarding the "Sapir-Whorf hypothesis" of linguistic-cultural determinism and relativity of unconscious thought patterns as revealed by linguistic fieldwork in anthropological settings:

The latent content of all language is the same — the intuitive SCIENCE of experience. It is the manifest form that is never twice the same, for this form, which we call linguistic morphology, is nothing more nor less than a collective ART of thought (Šapir 1921:233).

The background linguistic system ... is not merely a reproducing instrument ... but rather is itself the shaper of ideas, the program and guide for the individual's mental activity, for his analysis of his impressions, for his synthesis of his mental stock in trade (Whorf 1956:212).

The Sapir-Whorf hypothesis has long been of interest in anthropology, and here receives renewed attention from some authors of papers in Section 2 on "Linguistic Models."

In early writings on the Sapir-Whorf hypothesis, issues were for the most part stated nebulously (see Henle 1958:24; or Osgood and Sebeok 1965:192–195), and scholars such as Bidney (1953:112–116, 440) contended that the prevailing logic was false in substituting an overobjectivized culture process for the individual culture-bearer's perception of relevancies. Generalizations came the more into question as a result of the burgeoning sociolinguistic studies of grammatical variation within speech communities (e.g. Labov 1972), multilingualism, specialized jargons, and social stylistics of language use (e.g. Hymes 1966), as well as studies on syntactic-semantic universals (e.g. Silverstein 1972). The classic "strong" statements of the hypothesis gave way to weaker statements characterized by caution and moderation, for example:

Language is one of the factors influencing perception and the general organization of experience. This influence need not be primary or unique or compelling, but neither is it negligible (Henle 1958:18).

Nowadays the Sapir-Whorf hypothesis is neither wholly accepted nor wholly rejected, and it features in the present volume as a touchstone for problems of proof and validity. The problem of proof may be insoluble, because of the alleged untestability of propositions relating language and thought (see Herriot 1970). Certainly it is vexing. Haugen's constructively offered criticism of such adherents to the hypothesis as are guilty of "pure and simple speculation based on superficial acquaintance with exotic languages which have so far not produced native linguists who could check the foreign analyst's intuitions" (p. 23) is countered in the *World Anthropology* series by a paper on "Clauses and cases in Southeast Asian languages and thought," by the Vietnamese linguist Nguyen Dang Liem. In the *Approaches to language* volume to he subscribes the linguistic world-view ideas of Sapir. But after enumerating several critics of linguistic relativity, Haugen himself predicts that, "Even if his [Whorf's] ideas may be out of favor now, they are certain to reappear in one guise or another, as they have over the past two centuries" (p. 11).

Currently, dominance in linguistic scholarship does appear to rest in the contrary position that, if any causal model is assumed, thought serves as the independent variable, and the apparently correlated linguistic expression as the dependent variable. Scholars among whom the Sapir-Whorf hypothesis is now out of favor are many; in addition to those named by Haugen, they include Black (1959), Diebold (1965), Herriot (1970), Adams (1972), and Penn (1972). In the present volume, data in Schveiger's examination of Romanian time concepts contrast with Whorf's claim for linguistic relativity of time concepts (see Houston 1972:193–194), and thus indirectly support an anti-Whorf position. More direct variations on an anti-Whorf theme occur here in the papers by the Cartesian philosopher Vendler, with his relatively mechanistic and universalist conceptual psycho-semantics; by the ethnosemanticist of color terminology Heinrich, with his implicitly Lockean epistemology; and by the social anthropologist Gregersen, with his adduced social functionalism. Each of these is in his way critical of any "kingly" role for language as a model for perception or thought. Even Whorf himself, in a remarkable text provided by Haugen (p. 26), once qualified the value of language as "in some sense a superficial embroidery upon deeper processes of consciousness which are necessary before any communication, signaling, or symbolism whatsoever can occur."

Nevertheless, Haugen's prediction that in one guise or another Whorf's ideas are here to stay is evidenced in the views of some notable philosophers of science (e.g. Kuhn 1962); students of proxemics (e.g. Hall 1966); students of cultural contributions to visual pattern perceptions — themselves interesting as relatable by neurophysiology to the homeostatic areas of the brain engaged by linguistic operations and various sensory discriminations (e.g. Segall, Campbell, and Herskovits 1966; Pribram 1973:136–138); and certain anthropological linguists who, like the empiricist philosopher Quine (1969:89–90) and the psychologist Pribram (1972:19–20), incline to the "weak" version of Whorfian theory in claiming that habitual ways of speaking influence but do not determine thought or knowing (see Boas 1938:211–221; Hoijer 1954; Bright and Bright 1965:257–258; Hymes 1966). In the present volume, sympathy for Whorfian intuitions — which in their holistic focus, like the structural anthropology of Claude Lévi-Strauss, partly overlap the phenomenologist's program (see Spiegelberg 1965) — comes notably from the phenomenologist and linguist Verhaar. Overtly dissatisfied with the apparent inability of standard linguistic theories to show connections between Indonesian speech and the richness of culture-specific cognitions engaged by the act of speaking Indonesian, his attitude is one that might be rendered as, "Why NOT the world-view hypothesis?"

This present volume does reflect substantial consensus on one point, namely, that no definitive and standardized techniques for semantic analysis have yet been forthcoming from the discipline of linguistics, and for this reason even the most formalized of analyses in cognitive anthropology make only partial use of linguistic models. Disenchantment with linguistics in this regard was voiced by Silverstein (1972) in a review for anthropologists of current issues in linguistic semantics; it is echoed here by Verhaar. Indeed, in the present volume, Ikegami directs his paper to an argument that effective research in cognitive anthropology must proceed from a distinction between "meaning" for the linguist, as paradigmatic in the widest sense, and "meaning" for the anthropologist, which must be heuristic.

In keeping with this negative consensus on a negative conclusion most papers in the present volume are discrete analytic forays into the research area of cultural perceptions and cognitions. They draw variously on linguistic techniques and/or anthropological concepts but, after Section 2, without any great regard for which label befits what. Essentially each author sets his own problem and resolves it in his own way, therefore the organization of the volume is an artifact of the editor's thought.

Section 3 on "Ethnoscience" groups together papers with a programmatic perspective by Knight and Werner, papers by Scheffler and Tanaka on kin nouns, and papers by Lebeuf and Lemaitre on ethnobiology, which create cognitive models from lexical field inventories, segregated in various ways to serve as objects of analysis.

The papers in Section 4 on "Ethnohermeneutics" reach conclusions of pragmatic value for the field anthropologist. Ferguson and Khare show that concepts from comparative sociology may at times "fit" local meanings. But Lehman and Yotsukura show how mistranslations can result from scientific bias; Bellman illuminates how they can result from neglecting the performance concomitants to a text; and Derrett elucidates how imitation of the hermeneutics of a foreign culture can distort local culture.

Section 5 on "Oppositions" pertains to classification of cultural knowledge by bipolar connotative meanings of lexical items, arbitrarily systematized — e.g. as by numerology, in the paper by Kamau — and, as Lévi-Strauss has maintained, isomorphic with constraints set by the human mind as a naturally coding divinatory tool. Whether this viewpoint of Lévi-Strauss is accepted, as it is here by Dumont and Rossi-Landi, or questioned, as it is here by Ekvall and Fischer who show modification of meaning by local cultural styles, the relevance of systematizing connotative meaning for cultural analysis is not likely to be challenged by anthropological fieldworkers today.

Finally, in Section 6 on "Functions, Structures, and Values," there are grouped together three papers which bring matters full-circle back to the disenchantment with linguistic semiotics expressed in Section 2. Winner criticizes theorists of language other than members of the Prague school for failing to include study of aesthetic functions of communication in their apperception of linguistic semiotics. Welte asserts that linguistic abstraction fails to capture features of human values such as to make them analytically available for comparative study. Haydu concludes that significant, culturally transmitted, growth-points in individual

---

development are not discoverable through the semantic or grammatical features which linguists can abstract, i.e. "Culture conceived only as a semiotic realm is dead" (p. 477).

An overall object of the IXth International Congress of Anthropological and Ethnological Sciences was to reflect accurately the contemporary state of worldwide anthropological understanding of topics thematic for its component sessions and conferences. The subsession on "Language and Thought" conveyed the idea that thought is not "inner speech," and provided many examples of studies of human nature through the media of folk, scientific, and symbolic classifications drawn from a variety of world cultures. Several papers show that the aesthetic/valuing functions and processes in human nature can be distinguished from other patterning revealed in language, thought, and culture, and establish the possibility that these value entities may form an underlying, universal, deep structure for human experience.

REFERENCES

ADAMS, P., *editor*
  1972 *Language in thinking.* Harmondsworth: Penguin Books.
BIDNEY, D.
  1953 *Theoretical anthropology.* New York: Schocken Books.
BLACK, M.
  1959 Linguistic relativity: the views of B. L. Whorf. *Philosophical Review* 68:228–238.
BOAS, F.
  1938 *The mind of primitive man.* New York: Macmillan.
BRIGHT, J. O., W. BRIGHT
  1965 Semantic structures in northwestern California and the Sapir-Whorf hypothesis. *American Anthropologist* 67:249–258.
DIEBOLD, A. R., JR.
  1965 "A survey of psycholinguistic research, 1954–1964," in *Psycholinguistics.* Edited by C. E. Osgood and T. A. Sebeok, 205–291. Bloomington: Indiana University Press.
HALL, E. T.
  1966 *The hidden dimension.* Garden City, N.Y.: Doubleday.
HENLE, P., *editor*
  1958 *Language, thought, and culture.* Ann Arbor: University of Michigan Press.
HERRIOT, P.
  1970 *Introduction to the psychology of language.* London: Methuen.
HOIJER, H.
  1954 "The Sapir-Whorf hypothesis," in *Language in culture.* Edited by H. Hoijer, 92–105. American Anthropological Association Memoir 79. Chicago: University of Chicago Press.

HOUSTON, S. H.
  1972   *A survey of psycholinguistics.* The Hague: Mouton.
HYMES, D.
  1966   "Two types of linguistic relativity (with examples from Amerindian ethnography)," in *Sociolinguistics.* Edited by W. Bright, 114–158. The Hague: Mouton.
KUHN, T. S.
  1962   *The structure of scientific revolutions.* Chicago: University of Chicago Press.
LABOV, W.
  1972   *Sociolinguistic patterns.* Philadelphia: University of Pennsylvania Press.
OSGOOD, C. E., T. A. SEBEOK
  1965   "Psycholinguistics: A survey of theory and research problems," in *Psycholinguistics.* Edited by C. E. Osgood and T. A. Sebeok, 1–192. Bloomington: Indiana University Press.
PENN, J. M.
  1972   *Linguistic relativity versus innate ideas.* The Hague: Mouton.
PRIBRAM, K. H.
  1972   "Neurological notes on knowing." Mimeographed manuscript. Center for Advanced Study in Theoretical Psychology, University of Alberta, Edmonton.
  1973   The comparative psychology of communication: the issue of grammar and meaning. *Annals of the New York Academy of Sciences* 233:135–143.
QUINE, W. V. O.
  1969   *Ontological relativity and other essays.* New York and London: Columbia University Press.
SAPIR, E.
  1921   *Language.* New York: Harcourt, Brace.
SEGALL, M. H., D. T. CAMPBELL, M. J. HERSKOVITS
  1966   *The influence of culture on visual perception.* Indianapolis: Bobbs-Merrill.
SILVERSTEIN, M.
  1972   "Linguistic theory: syntax, semantics, pragmatics," in *Annual review of anthropology*, volume one. Edited by B. J. Siegel, A. R. Beals, and S. A. Tyler, 349–382. Palo Alto, California: Annual Reviews.
SPIEGELBERG, H.
  1965   *The phenomenological movement: a historical introduction* (second edition). The Hague: M. Nijhoff.
[WHORF, B. L.]
  1956   *Language, thought and reality: selected writings of Benjamin Lee Whorf.* Edited by J. B. Carroll. New York and London: M.I.T. Press and John Wiley.

SECTION TWO

Linguistic Models

Linguistic Relativity: Myths and Methods

EINAR HAUGEN

A perennial topic of discussion in American linguistics has been the so-called "Sapir-Whorf hypothesis," or in Benjamin Whorf's own words "linguistic relativity," though it would be better named "linguistic determinism." One hears less of it today, partly on account of the severe and reasoned critique of its more extreme forms by Eric Lenneberg (1953), Joseph Greenberg (1954), Robert Longacre (1956), Joshua Fishman (1960), Robert Miller (1968), etc. Another reason may be merely the bandwagon effect of the current search for universals and a corresponding disinclination on the part of some linguists to study real languages. The purpose of this article is not to pound another nail in the coffin of linguistic relativity, but to suggest some approaches to the problem of thought and language.

Linguistic relativity stresses the validity and importance of each language as a determinant of its speakers' thinking, while the current universalism stresses the common human features and plays down the "surface" features that characterize each language and language variety. There is much to be said for each of these complementary views, but a one-sidedness that claims truth for only one of them is misleading and intellectually dangerous. I would like to consider the problem of where Whorf's insights went wrong and why they did so. Even if his ideas may be out of favor now, they are certain to reappear in one guise or another, as they have over the past two centuries.

For those who are still learning about linguistics it might be well to recall that Benjamin Whorf was an insurance adjustor who came under the influence of Edward Sapir and made a name for himself by relating the grammatical and lexical structures of certain Indian languages (chiefly Hopi and Navaho) to the supposed modes of thinking of their speakers and by contrasting these with the structures and thinking of English (and other non-Indian) speakers. In the late forties and early fifties he was sponsored by such noted figures in American linguistics and related fields as George Trager, John Carroll, and Harry Hoijer. In 1954 a special conference was organized under Hoijer's direction to discuss Whorf's ideas (Hoijer 1954). At this meeting, leading linguists found themselves thrusting in thin air, as anyone can see by reading the lengthy discussion and Weinreich's perceptive review. Whorf's works were diligently quoted in the writings of the disciples of Korzybski, founder of the "General Semantics" movement, e.g. S. I. Hayakawa. Similar ideas were propounded by Dorothy Lee on the basis of her studies of the Wintu language. A major project of empirical research to confirm or disconfirm Whorf's ideas was launched under the direction of John Carroll, the so-called "Southwest Project in Comparative Psycholinguistics," which resulted in little more than a decent burial by the participants of the ideas they had come to study (Hymes and Bittle 1967). More recently, attempts have been made to reinterpret the research results of the Project by students of socio-linguistics, chiefly Dell Hymes (Hymes 1966).

It was Whorf's merit to take ideas that had been part of virtually every linguist's stock-in-trade for more than a century and try them out on the newly investigated languages of the American Southwest. As the outcome proved, the attempt failed, and few would defend the basic ideas advanced by Whorf today. His eloquence and enthusiasm were infectious enough to excite a number of linguists with anthropological interests, especially American Indianists, as well as a wide circle of laymen and scholars in other fields.

It will be the purpose of this paper to outline (1) some reasons for the failure of the Whorfian hypothesis, then (2) to sketch in some of the motivation and background of Whorf's ideas, and finally (3) to propose how the study of bilingual behavior might enable us to put his ideas into perspective.

THE PITFALLS OF RELATIVITY

Let us review with some attention a few of the more striking examples of Whorf's contrastive analysis of English (as a representative of "Standard Average European") and certain American Indian languages.

In a comparison with Shawnee, Whorf ([1941] in Carroll 1956: 233–

245) provides two English sentences which (he claims) have nothing in common but the present tense and the subject pronoun "I": (a) "I pull the branch aside" and (b) "I have an extra toe on my foot." Then he produces Shawnee translations of these and finds that they are "closely similar; in fact, they differ only at the tail end": *ni-l'Ɵawa-'ko-n-a* and *ni-l'Ɵawa-'ko-Ɵite*. "Shawnee logicians and observers would class the two phenomena as intrinsically similar." As this is hardly more than a guess on Whorf's part (in that he offers no informant's word for it) and is based on a purely surface similarity of the two sentences, we are justified in asking just how valid his analysis is.

Basing our inquiry only on the information Whorf provides, the sentences are morphemically analyzable as: (a) "I-fork-tree-by hand-cause" versus (b) "I-fork-tree-on toes-[have]." Sentence (a) is transitive, with "fork-tree" as the object of a movement by the hand as instrument, while (b) is possessive, with "fork-tree" attributed to the toes as locative. The only common element in the two Shawnee sentences is actually the phrase *l'Ɵawa-'ko*, in which Whorf claims that *l'Ɵawa* is a common term denoting "a forked outline" and that *-'ko* may be a form of a word denoting "tree, bush, tree part, branch, or anything of that general shape." The meaning of the sentences offered shows (whatever analysis one may make of its parts) that *l'Ɵawa-'ko* need mean nothing more than "branch," used in sentence (a) in a CONCRETE sense and in sentence (b) in a FIGURATIVE sense. Their similarity is somewhat less remarkable if we translate (a) as "I move a branch with my hand," and (b) as "I have a branch on my foot." Because the probability is infinitesimal that any considerable number of Shawnee had extra toes on their feet, it is clear that sentence (b) was made up either to illustrate Whorf's point or as a nonce and humorous way of referring to a highly occasional deformity. It is in any case no more than an illustration of the way human imagination can and does see similarities between otherwise different situations. It is no more surprising or expressive of any special quality of Shawnee or the Shawnee mind than the fact that English "branch" can refer to rivers, pipes, roads, antlers, families, languages, academic fields of study, the houses of Congress, or business establishments, to mention only a few. The striking difference between Whorf's two English sentences is no more than an artifact of his translation-interpretation.

Another of Whorf's examples in the same article is adduced to illustrate the opposite situation, that of close similarity in English corresponding to startling dissimilarity in an Indian language, this time

Nootka. Here sentence (a) is "The boat is grounded on the beach" and (b) "The boat is manned by picked men." Whorf analyzes these grammatically as "The boat is *x*ed preposition *y*" and hence as linguistically and logically identical. One hardly needs to mention in our time that this analysis is faulty, an example of what Chomsky used as the basis for his attack on structuralism and what he accounted for by his distinction between deep and surface structure. It should have been evident even in Whorf's day that the two prepositional phrases stood in wholly different relationships to the verbs, because "on the beach" is a locative with a participial adjective, while "by picked men" is the logical subject of a passive verb.

The Nootka equivalents provided are (a) *tlih-is-ma* and (b) *lash-tskwiq-ista-ma*, in which -*ma*, the only common element, means "third-person indicative." Whorf's main point is that neither sentence contains a word for "boat"; but there IS in each of them a word that suggests activity connected with a boat (or rather, a canoe). In (a) this is *tlih-*, which is glossed as "moving pointwise," hence "traveling in or as a canoe." No evidence is given to show that the highly abstract gloss "moving pointwise" is a valid meaning of the word; one naturally asks from what actual situations this has been abstracted. Whorf compares the word to a "vector in physics" rather than a "thing." But the movement of a boat is not a "thing" in English either, and because the modifier -*is*- means "on the beach," the meaning here can hardly be one of pure motion. We have in English a phrase "to be headed" (in a certain direction), which could also be glossed as "moving pointwise"; but here the metaphor is based on the human head as a director of motion and hence the leading part, for instance of a boat. We can therefore gloss the morphemes of sentence (a) as "boat headed-on the beach-[there] is," with more likelihood of having identified the correct analysis underlying the interpretation "the boat is grounded on the beach."

In sentence (b) the morpheme implying the presence of a boat is -*ista*-, glossed as "in a canoe as crew." The form may be a locative adverbial, as suggested by the gloss, but its analysis of reality is not very different from our noun phrase "boat crew." It is modified by *lash-tskwiq-*, which is glossed as "selected" (litterally "select, pick" plus "remainder, result"). The whole sentence may then be glossed as "select-ed-boat crew-[there] is," which is a step earlier in the translation process than either of Whorf's literal interpretations, "they are in the boat as a crew of picked men" and "the boat has a crew of picked men." And it is quite different from his free interpretation, which

makes use of the peculiarly English verb "to man": "The boat is manned by picked men."

At best these sentences confirm the well-established fact that different cultures talk about different things in nature and have applied
different analogies in expanding their vocabularies from the concrete
to the abstract (or vice versa). These are interesting and important
features in the relation of man to his culture and to his use of language
within that culture. But they do not justify any judgments concerning
a qualitative difference in the way men think. For one thing, similar
discrepancies between the way languages partition nature are not
limited to such major gaps as those between Hopi and what Whorf
somewhat patronizingly called "Standard Average European" (SAE).
Within his SAE there are abundant examples of similar discrepancies,
in spite of the fact that these languages have been "calibrated" through
centuries of cultural-linguistic diffusion. Such differences have been
studied for French and German in attempts to derive some kind of
"soul" characterization of the respective peoples. Anyone who works
with the translation of texts from one language into another knows
how often even the most closely related languages require fudging. I
could cite numerous such examples from my work with Norwegian,
both as translator and as a writer of grammars and dictionaries. We
need not go to the most exotic languages to learn this; but of course
it is easier to find striking examples if we do.

For another thing, Whorf's strongest claims relate to the influence
of the least conscious parts of the language, viz. its categories of grammar. For English (and SAE) these include such categories as number,
gender, and tense. The very fact that these are obligatory categories
deprives them of any great informational value (as was pointed out in
1955 by Uriel Weinreich). The speaker has no choice but to observe
them as conventions implanted in the language long before his own
time. If they reflect any view concerning reality, it is at best one that
was held by our presumably primitive Indo-European-speaking ancestors.

It is simply an incredible naïveté to suggest that the use of grammatical plurals has required us to develop or to function in a world
of numbers and measurement, that the use of the tense forms has led us
to keep records and develop what Whorf calls "historicity," or that the
Hopi system of noun classification (which is analogical to our gender)
required the Hopi to pay more attention to form and shape than other
people. The experiment of the Southwest Project in which Hopi and
American children were tested for their classification of objects by

their shape was an adequate disproof of this hypothesis (Maclay 1958). But it was predictably bound to fail, because the capacity of distinguishing objects by form is surely universally human.

The real test comes when abstracts that have no shape or form are classified by the same categories. Our Indo-European gender classification is simple enough so long as we are dealing with animate sex-marked beings; but when this is extended to inanimate and nonmaterial concepts, there is nothing overtly compelling about it. Even if it may have had a mythological import, as claimed by some, this is secondary to the concerns of most speakers. In Latin the sun is masculine, the moon feminine; in the Scandinavian languages it is the other way around, except that in Danish there is no distinction, both being "common" gender. Even though English retains the three-gender system in the third-person pronouns, English speakers would be hard put to establish the probable gender of nonsex words in those languages that still have the distinction in their nouns.

Whorf makes much of the fact that the plural has a different range of application in Hopi and English, especially in relation to mass nouns ([1939] in Carroll 1956: 140–141). The same is of course true of SAE languages that have plural forms. When Whorf writes that in Hopi " 'water' means one certain mass or quantity of water, not what we call 'the substance water' " (ibid.: 141), it is amusing that the same is true in Norwegian: *vann* (*vatn*) means "water," but *et vann* means "a lake." Similarly, *et brød* is "a loaf of bread," *en saks* is "a pair of scissors," *en kaffe* is "a cup of coffee," etc. This does not prevent Norwegian from also having expressions like those of English, but in neither language does it compel a philosophic distinction between "form" and "content."

Grammatical plurality is itself a poor enough philosophic distinction. All it tells us is that there is a difference between ONE and MORE THAN ONE (or two, in languages with a dual). I am not aware of any language, and I doubt that any exists, in which words for "one" and "many" do not exist. In Indo-European this became an obligatory category, by means of which certain economies of statement were made possible. For one thing it clarified the syntactic relationship between subject and verb, so that one could readily tell which of the nouns in a clause was the subject, in a period when the word order was freer and the place of the noun phrases less fixed than later.

Whorf is even more concerned with differences in the tense systems ([1939] in Carroll 1956: 143–145). He attributes to SAE verbs a "three-tense system," which "colors all our thinking about time." For some reason he overlooks the fact that English does not have a three-tense system; perhaps he confuses tense with time. We have the lexical items PAST, PRESENT, and FUTURE, referring presumably to concepts of time; but at least in English there is no formal expression for "future" in the verb system. As is well known, there is a variety of ways of expressing one's conviction as to what may or will happen after the moment of speaking, including the present tense ("I'm eating at six this evening") or even the past ("If I told him, what would he do?"). The idea that the English (or any SAE) tenses are laid out in a straight line from left to right, with the present as a dot in the middle, is inculcated in many simplistic grammars and verb studies. If we look rather at the information which the tense forms encode, it should not take much reflection to realize that this view is false. A sentence like "he laughed" tells us only that the action took place BEFORE the actual or fictive moment of speaking; it could have been one second or a million years ago. If the moment of speaking is imagined as future, the event could even be in our future; the verb form itself tells us only that the SPEAK-ING is later than the EVENT.

No language I have ever heard of is unable to state this fact, even if it requires using adverbs (which is what Whorf compares Hopi time expressions to). The present tense tells us only that an event is not over at the moment of speaking: it can occur before, during, or after the moment of speaking, but it must at least be valid then. "He laughs" (or its durative equivalent "he is laughing") is timed only in relation to the moment of speaking and, without further modification, to nothing else. According to Whorf, Hopi does not objectify time: "Nothing is suggested about time except the perpetual 'getting later' of it" ([1941] in Carroll 1956: 143). The same is true of SAE tenses, if one looks at the tense meanings themselves and not at inaccurate descriptions of them in grammars. In any case, most of the so-called "tenses" in English grammars are not tenses at all, but aspects or modals. Even the notion of "becoming later and later," which Whorf attributes to Hopi as a peculiar philosophic concept, can be expressed quite easily in some SAE languages, e.g. in Old Norse the terms for the four seasons all have verbal derivatives like *sumra* 'to become summer' (and correspondingly, *vetra* 'to become winter', *vára* 'to become spring', *hausta* 'to become fall').

Even if we put together all the marked differences in grammatical structure between Hopi and SAE, they scarcely support any such contention as Whorf's that "they point toward possible new types of logic and possible new cosmical pictures" ([1941] in Carroll 1956: 241).

The idea that bipartite Greek logic arose from the bipartite Greek sentence has often enough been asserted (ibid.: 237). This overlooks the fact that the formalization involved in logic and mathematics is rather a rejection of the often illogical, if convenient, formulations of natural language. The development of mathematics may be seen as an attempt to overcome the weaknesses of natural languages for the purpose of exact and elegant statement. The terminology of science has been successful to the extent that it has been able to surmount the limitations imposed by natural language and produce an inter- and supralinguistic language.

It is therefore somewhat absurd when Whorf maintains that "modern Chinese or Turkish scientists . . . have taken over bodily the entire Western system of rationalizations, not that they have corroborated that system from their native posts of observation" ([1940] in Carroll 1956: 214). The great discoveries and inventions of Western science have not been expressed in the Western languages at all, but in the special language of mathematics. There is nothing in English as such that enables us to talk about relativity or atomic energy or the double helix. The popular accounts that most of us read are only approximations to the underlying theories, and the English in which we read them is a new terminology which can be translated precisely into any language regardless of its grammar, syntax, or phonology, but which in any language, including English, requires some distortion of the ideas involved because these are not precisely expressible in any natural language.

When Whorf writes, "Formulation of ideas is not an independent process, strictly rational in the old sense, but is part of a particular grammar and differs, from slightly to greatly, as between different grammars" ([1940] in Carroll 1956: 212), he is therefore guilty of a *petitio principi*. We do not know, except by introspection (which is faulty) and by speculation (which is airy) just how ideas are formulated. While the "rational" formulation that Whorf attacks may be false, it is my experience, at least, that many ideas do come in extralinguistic form, as images, patterns, relationships, flashes of illumination. That they are extralinguistic does not mean that language is not involved; quite the contrary. But they are not linguistic until they have been (often laboriously) formulated in a particular language and organized from left to right into the proper syntactic, lexical, and phonological patterns imposed by that language.

In Whorf's statement the "grammar" stands for the whole language, but most of the meanings we wish to convey are not conveyed by the grammar at all. If my shepherd comes running to tell me that a wolf has eaten my sheep, there are three basic facts to be conveyed, and for these he and I need a common vocabulary: "wolf." "eat." "sheep." A statement NP₁ (actor) — V (action) — NP₂ (goal) is merely an empty schema into which he can, if he has the time, fit the words. But he need only cry "wolf!"

Different languages have different ways of expressing such sets of data, but all languages have ways of marking the basic relations, even if they differ widely in the way they apply them to reality. I therefore contend that the grammatical system as such has a minimal connection with any formulation of ideas whatever: the simple and utterly banal contrasts of present with past or singular with plural or definite with indefinite are mostly redundant where they are obligatory and can always be expressed lexically in languages where they are not.

THE CULT OF RELATIVITY

Whorf's one-sided view of the thought-language relationship was not original with him, though one would hardly suspect it by reading his essays. The general ignorance of European linguistic thought by American linguists in the 1940's (on which, see Haugen 1951) kept many from realizing that these views had been debated by European linguists for some two centuries.

Brown (1967) has shown that the men of the Enlightenment were inclined to think of reason as prior to language, making language a mere vehicle of thought. In 1757 the Berlin Academy announced as a prize topic "the influence of opinions on the language and of language on opinions" (Christmann 1967: 463), and the essay that won the prize in 1759 (by David Michaelis) treated both sides of the problem in detail, especially the latter part of it, in terms that proved to have the greatest influence. Coincident with and as a part of the development of literary Romanticism, the emphasis was shifted towards the priority of language to thinking. Wilhelm von Humboldt went so far as to maintain that language was the independent variable: "Language is the formative organ of thought"; "Every language sets certain limits to the spirit of those who speak it; it assumes a certain direction and, by doing so, excludes many others" (Brown 1967: 68, 84).

This idea was most forcefully expressed in Italy (Vico) and Germany (Hamann, Herder, Fichte, von Humboldt) (see Christmann 1967) where the countries and their languages were oppressed and divided. It became, in effect, a weapon in the hands of nationalism, especially in

Germany. Herder proclaimed that "every nation has its own treasury of such ideas that have become symbols, which are its national language: a treasury to which the nation has contributed for centuries ... the intellectual treasury of an entire people" (Christmann 1967: 467). Hamann declared that "every language requires a mode of thought and a taste that is peculiar to it" (Christmann 1967: 466). Von Humboldt carried the idea to the point of declaring: "... so there lies in every language a particular world view (*Weltansicht*)" (Christmann 1967: 445). This idea was particularly welcome as an ideological base for the teaching and cultivation of the native language and the throwing off of classical and French influence. In modern times the idea was picked up again and endlessly varied by the German scholar Leo Weisgerber, whose writings from 1926 on were highly influential in implanting in German textbooks the idea that "man comprehends and organizes physical and spiritual reality through his mother tongue" (Christmann 1967: 3; Basilius 1952: Note 18 speaks of his "cultish" terminology).

By contrast, a more balanced view was presented in the writings of the Swedish linguist, Esaias Tegnér, whose book *Språkets makt över tanken* in 1880 offered a penetrating discussion of the problem. After contributing numerous examples from his native language of the kind of intellectual confusions that could be induced by natural languages, Tegnér rejected all attempts to correlate "national psychology" with features of the grammatical structure (e.g. Lepsius' contention that languages with gender distinction reflected a more elevated moral conception of sex roles in family life!). He did not deny that "grammatical features could be found that exert an influence on the conceptualization of speakers" (Tegnér 1922: 242), and exemplified this with the elaborate Swedish forms of address, which have caused "many, not just social occasions, but also social affairs in a wider sense, to develop differently than they otherwise could and should have done" (1922: 264–265). Of course, it may be questioned whether forms of address are grammatical and not, rather, lexical.

The line of descent from the German cult of linguistic relativity practiced by von Humboldt and his followers (especially Max Müller) to the work of Whorf is clear and unbroken, as shown by Christmann (1967) and others. Boas was German by birth and training, and familiar with this line of thinking. In his well-known introduction to the *Handbook of American Indian languages* (1911), he devoted some space to the problem: "It is commonly assumed that the linguistic expression is a secondary reflex of the customs of the people; but the question is quite open in how far the one phenomenon is the primary one and the other the secondary one, and whether the customs of the people have not rather developed from the unconsciously developed terminology (Boas 1966: 69). While he denied that "a certain state of culture is conditioned by morphological traits of the language," Boas was willing to believe that the metaphorical use of certain terms might have led to the rise of certain views or customs (ibid.: 69). These thoughts were obviously well calculated to lead up to his emphasis on language study "as one of the most important branches of ethnological study," not just for its practical value, but also because "the peculiar characteristics of languages are clearly reflected in the views and customs of the peoples of the world" (ibid.: 69).

Sapir, a student of Boas, is often credited with formulating the relativity hypothesis, but as Hymes has pointed out (Hymes 1964: 118–119, 128), Sapir vacillated on this point. In his *Language*, Sapir denied any correlation between cultural content and linguistic form: "When it comes to linguistic form, Plato walks with the Macedonian swineherd, Confucius with the head-hunting savage of Assam" (1921: 234). But in his famous article of 1929 (and a note in *Science* in 1931, cited by Hymes [1964: 128]) he was concerned with demonstrating the value of "linguistics as a science," and he formulated his expression so as to emphasize the power of language over thought: "The fact of the matter is that the 'real world' is to a large extent unconsciously built up on the language habits of the group" (1929: 209). Sapir's examples are all lexical and leave it open to question just what he meant by "language habits"; but it should not be overlooked that these phrases were part of a special plea for the importance of linguistics.

Whorf's views, which were at least partially shaped by Sapir, bear the same impress of enthusiastic advocacy. In presenting a study of the tenses of Chichewa, an East African language, Whorf concluded: "It may be that these primitive folk are equipped with a language which, if they were to become philosophers or mathematicians, could make them our foremost thinkers upon TIME" ([1942] in Carroll 1956: 266). The fact that Hopi discriminates three kinds of conjunctions all translated "that" in English convinced him that "the formal systematization of ideas" in English, German, French, or Italian was "poor and jejune" compared with that of Hopi: "English compared to Hopi is like a bludgeon compared to a rapier" ([1936?] in Carroll 1956: 85).

In his articles printed in the M.I.T. *Technology Review*, Whorf made it a point to rehabilitate in the eyes of his natural scientist readers "the province of the despised grammarian" ([1940] in Carroll 1956: 211) by showing them "the incredible degree of diversity of linguistic system that ranges over the globe" and so "foster that humility which accompanies the true scientific spirit." The study of Hopi and other Indian languages would prevent us from regarding

... a few recent dialects of the Indo-European family, and the rationalizing techniques elaborated from their patterns, as the apex of the evolution of the human mind; nor their present wide spread as due to any survival from fitness or to anything but a few events of history — events that could be called fortunate only from the parochial point of view of the favored parties ([1940] in Carroll 1956: 218).

In assessing these judgments of Whorf one is reminded that he came to linguistics with a mystic point of view which colors even his most scientific work. One can read about this in Carroll's biographical sketch (1956: 1–33), where we learn that Whorf studied Hebrew because he believed that "fundamental human and philosophical problems could be solved by taking a new sounding of the semantics of the Bible" (for a debunking of this view, see Barr 1961). His early enthusiasm for the French linguistic mystic Fabre d'Olivet was fortunately replaced by the teachings of Sapir after 1928, but the study of Hopi which followed was inspired by his conviction that "the Hopi actually have a language better equipped to deal with ... vibratile phenomena than is our latest scientific terminology" ([1936] in Carroll 1956: 55).

Whorf's last major article and many minor ones appeared in a theosophical journal published at Madras, India. In one of these he pointed out that the West had not bridged the intellectual gulf that separated it from the East and called for an appreciation of "the types of logical thinking which are reflected in truly Eastern forms of scientific thought or analysis of nature. This requires linguistic research into the logics of native languages, and realization that they have equal scientific validity with our thinking habits" (Carroll 1956: 21). In the essay "Language, mind, and reality," published in the theosophical journal in 1941, he found in "the scientific understanding of very diverse languages ... a lesson in brotherhood which is brotherhood in the universal human principle" ([1941] in Carroll 1956: 263). "The Algonkian languages are spoken by very simple people, hunting and fishing Indians, but they are marvels of analysis and synthesis" (ibid.: 265). For Whorf, linguistic research became part of the path to Yoga, with a "therapeutic value" to free patients from "the compulsive working over and over of word systems" (ibid.: 269).

However much we may sympathize with Whorf's goals, his immersion in these ideas clearly distorted his results and left many of them in the state of being little more than cultish hypotheses. The evidence was selected to illustrate rather than prove the hypotheses, and the consequence was an emphasis on those features that agreed with his preconceived views.

It is here suggested that much of the interest that Whorf's one-sided advocacy of the relativity hypothesis aroused was the result of an emotional commitment on the part of anthropological linguists. Like Whorf himself and his teachers Boas and Sapir, they were in the position of needing to justify the effort expended on the study of American Indian languages on grounds better than the mere accumulation of knowledge. In discussion with their colleagues in anthropology they felt obliged to contend that language was not a mere mirror of thought and culture, but an essential factor in shaping the content of both. Whorf himself was something of a sport in linguistics, a genius whose writing skill and infectious excitement over the discovery of new areas of knowledge accomplished something which his more cautious colleagues were unable to do. On the one hand, he had impressive scientific qualifications, and on the other, he applied himself to the precise study of exotic languages. He offered linguists the exciting prospect of making their discipline an "exact science," as the title of one of his essays from 1940 runs, thus answering and reformulating Sapir's earlier essay on "The status of linguistics as a science" (1929).

A TEST OF RELATIVITY

Even if we have now succeeded in showing that linguistic universalism (thought ➤ language) is most congenial to the rationalist thinker, and linguistic relativity (language ➤ thought) to the romantic thinker, we have not established a truth value for either view. It is of course a constant topic of research on the part of linguists, psycholinguists, and sociolinguists seeking to solve specific problems within this area, where no overall solution seems possible. Much that has been written is pure and simple speculation based on superficial acquaintance with exotic languages which have so far not produced native linguists who could check the foreign analyst's intuitions.

I have suggested in earlier writings (Haugen 1956: 87–89; 1973: 81–86; see also Gilbert 1971: xi) that bilinguals ought to be a most valuable resource in the study of this problem. They are the only ones who can personally testify to the differential effect of the "world view" imposed by different languages, at least if their use of them includes actual intimate experience with monolingual speakers of each language. On this point there is some limited evidence. The anthropologist Robert H. Lowie recounted his experiences as an Austrian immigrant to the United States at the age of ten (Lowie 1945). He tried to maintain his German as he learned English, noting both the difficulties and the insights that resulted:

The popular impression that a man alters his personality when speaking another tongue is far from ill-grounded. When I speak German to Germans, I automatically shift my orientation as a social being, I spontaneously adapt myself to the atmosphere characteristic of their status, outlook, prejudices. The very use of the customary formulae of politeness injects a distinct flavor into the conversation, coloring attitudes and behavior. Some of these modes of expression, to be sure, are merely meaningless formulae, but by no means all. The retention of titles, in European fashion for example, colors mutual relations, as does the free and easy American way of dropping them altogether. . . . Language is so intimately interwoven with the whole of social behavior that a bilingual, for better or worse, is bound to differ from the monoglot (1945: 258).

The French-born American writer, Julian Green, has written about the problems involved in writing books in two languages. He found that it was impossible for him to translate one of his books from French into English; he had to sit down and write an entirely new book: "It was as if, writing in English, I had become another person" (Green 1941: 402).

The German-Italian bilingual linguist Theodor W. Elwert has explored in detail his own problems of social and personal adjustment to a succession of early language-learning experiences. He rejects Lowie's formulation out of hand:

On changing languages we do not change our character [*Wesen*], but our behavior [*Verhalten*]. . . . In principle, the process is the same as in changing among two settings [*Milieus*] of the same language. . . . We do not change our behavior (and even less our personality) because we change language, but we change language because we have to change our behavior in a new setting. . . . Language is only a part of a larger behavioral complex (Elwert 1960: 344, fn. 1).

What is evident from these and other accounts is that the learning of a second language requires adjustment to the ways of speaking and behaving that are customary in the new group. This adjustment leaves the bilingual with a keen sense of the difficulty in keeping two languages and the corresponding cultures apart. Lowie gives many valuable examples of his own problems in maintaining equal adequacy in both languages. Because none of the three people here mentioned discusses possible experiences with non-SAE languages (though Lowie knew Crow, as Ives Goddard has pointed out to me), their observations may be considered inadequate. But there is no reason to believe that other memoirs or self-reports would reveal anything different. Thinking in one language is different from thinking in another, but it is reasonably clear that this is largely a matter of vocabulary. One thinks most readily in each language about those topics that one has learned the vocabulary for in that language. Most bilinguals whom I have consulted on this problem have denied that they felt like a "different person" in speaking their other language.

From my own experience I can confirm the views of Elwert: in another language that one feels as an intimate part of one's experience, such that in speaking it one can act as a fully accepted member of the speech community, one does not become a different person or think differently. But one does adopt a different set of expectations. In formulating some ideas one may feel that one language facilitates the formulation while another hinders it and forces a rather different formulation. Each language has its shortcuts and its circumlocutions. But these have nothing to do with the grammar in the usual sense: phonology, morphology, syntax.

Norwegian morphology requires that the English definite article be suffixed on nouns, preposed with adjectives. This placement rule is mostly mechanically equivalent to English "the": *huset* 'the house', *det hvite huset* 'the white house'. A rule of stylistics says that in the latter type of phrase the second article can be deleted for terms normally met only in writing, e.g. *Det hvite hus* 'the White House'. A rule of syntax says that the article usually replaces possessive adjectives when the subject of the clause is the possessor and the thing possessed is intimately connected with the possessor, e.g. *han mistet hatten* 'he lost the hat' = 'he lost his hat'. A lexical rule says that the article is used with abstracts (in a way that is rare in English but well known in French and German), e.g. *kjærligheten* '[the] love', *kunsten* '[the] art'. These (and a host of more detailed rules) require learning and can produce interferences for bilingual speakers.

One has a more than adequate basis for paraphrasing Whorf's statement about the Hopi plural: the definite article is not the same in Norwegian as in English, whether phonologically, morphologically, or semantically. But to claim from this that Norwegians "think" differently with respect to the article is unwarranted. The definite article is not a philosophical concept, however difficult grammarians may find it to formulate rules for its precise use in one or several languages. It is (among other things) a mechanical device for marking identity of reference in a sequence of noun phrases, especially in languages like English and Norwegian, where case and gender markers are virtually gone. For one's "world view" it has no more significance than has the mortar that joins the bricks in a wall for the thinking of those who live in the house.

Macnamara (1970: 25–40) has reduced the cognitive problem to absurdity by describing the bilingual's dilemma if Whorf's ideas should be true: either he uses L_1 or L_2 and is unable to understand the other language or he uses both and is unable to communicate with himself! The answer to this is, of course, that every speaker interprets systems different from his own even if he cannot produce them; a bilingual simply interprets L_1 and L_2 for their intended meanings, and in many cases even forgets which language he learned the meanings in. There simply must be a store of knowledge which is relatively language-free. This may turn out to be the answer to Whorf's problem as well.

Finally, let us not overlook that Whorf himself was aware of this possibility. In a period of linguistic thinking when "mind" was a dirty word, he granted that

... the tremendous importance of language cannot, in my opinion, be taken to mean necessarily that nothing is back of it of the nature of what has traditionally been called "mind." My own studies suggest, to me, that language, for all of its kingly role, is in some sense a superficial embroidery upon deeper processes of consciousness which are necessary before any communication, signaling, or symbolism whatsoever can occur ... ([1941] in Carroll 1956: 239).

REFERENCES

BARR, JAMES
  1961   *The semantics of biblical language.* London: Oxford.
BASILIUS, HAROLD
  1952   Neo-Humboldtian ethno-linguistics. *Word* 8:95–105.
BOAS, FRANZ
  1966   "Introduction." in *Handbook of American Indian languages.* Reprint edited by Preston Holder. University of Nebraska Press. (Originally published 1911 by the Government Printing Office, Washington, D.C.)

BROWN, ROGER LANGHAM
1967 *Wilhelm von Humboldt's conception of linguistic relativity*. The Hague: Mouton.

CARROLL JOHN B., *editor*
1956 *Language, thought, and reality: selected writings of Benjamin Lee Whorf*. New York, London: M.I.T. Press and John Wiley.

CHRISTMANN, HANS HELMUT
1967 *Beiträge zur Geschichte der These vom Weltbild der Sprache*. Akademie der Wissenschaften und der Literatur (Abhandlungen 1966, Nr. 7). Mainz.

ELWERT, W. THEODOR
1960 *Das zweisprachige Individuum: ein Selbstzeugnis*. Akademie der Wissenschaften und der Literatur (Abhandlungen 1959, Nr. 6). Mainz.

FISHMAN, JOSHUA A.
1960 A systematization of the Whorfian hypothesis. *Behavioral Science* 5:323–339.

GILBERT, GLENN G., *editor*
1971 *The German language in America*. Austin, Texas: University of Texas Press.

GREEN, JULIAN
1941 An experiment in English. *Harper's Magazine* 183:397–405.

GREENBERG, JOSEPH
1954 "Concerning inferences from linguistic to non-linguistic data," in *Language in culture*. Edited by Harry Hoijer, 3–19. Chicago: University of Chicago Press.

HAUGEN, EINAR
1951 Directions in modern linguistics. *Language* 27:211–222.
1956 *Bilingualism in the Americas: a bibliography and research guide*. American Dialect Society Publication 26. University, Ala.: University of Alabama Press.
1973 "Bilingualism, language contact, and immigrant languages in the United States: a research report 1956–1970," in *Current trends in linguistics*, volume ten. Edited by T. A. Sebeok, 505–591. The Hague: Mouton.

HOIJER, HARRY, *editor*
1954 *Language in culture*. Chicago: University of Chicago Press.

HYMES, DELL
1966 "Two types of linguistic relativity," in *Sociolinguistics*. Edited by William Bright, 114–158. The Hague: Mouton.

HYMES, DELL, *editor*
1964 *Language in culture and society: a reader in linguistics and anthropology*. New York: Harper and Row.

HYMES, DELL, WILLIAM E. BITTLE, *editors*
1967 *Studies in southwestern ethnolinguistics*. The Hague: Mouton.

LENNEBERG, ERIC
1953 Cognition in ethnolinguistics. *Language* 29:463–471.

LONGACRE, ROBERT
1956 Review of W. Urban, *Language and reality* (1939), and B. L.

Whorf, *Four articles on metalinguistics* (1949). *Language* 32: 298–308.

LOWIE, ROBERT H.
1945   A case of bilingualism. *Word* 1:249–259.

MACLAY, HOWARD STANLEY
1958   An experimental study of language and non-linguistic behavior. *Southwestern Journal of Anthropology* 14:220–229.

MACNAMARA, JOHN
1970   *Bilingualism and thought.* Georgetown University Monograph Series on Languages and Linguistics 23.

MILLER, ROBERT L.
1968   *The linguistic relativity principle and Humboldtian ethnolinguistics: a history and an appraisal.* The Hague: Mouton.

SAPIR, EDWARD
1921   *Language: an introduction to the study of speech.* New York: Harcourt, Brace.
1929   The status of linguistics as a science. *Language* 5:207–214.

TEGNÉR, ESAIAS
1922   "Språkets makt över tanken [The power of language over thought]," in *Ur språkens värld,* volume one, 165–346. Stockholm: Bonnier. (Originally published 1880.)

WEINREICH, URIEL
1955   Review of *Language in culture,* edited by Harry Hoijer (1954). *Word* 11:426–430.

WHORF, BENJAMIN LEE
1950   *Four articles on metalinguistics.* Washington, D.C.: Foreign Service Institute.

Wordless Thoughts

ZENO VENDLER

1.   Plato has the following famous passage in *Theaetetus:*

Socr. ... And do you accept my description of the process of thinking?
Theaet. How do you describe it?
Socr. As a discourse that the mind carries on with itself about any subject
it is considering. You must take this explanation as coming from an igno-
ramus; but I have a notion that, when the mind is thinking, it is simply
talking to itself, asking questions and answering them ... So I should describe thinking as a discourse, and judgement as a statement pronounced, not
aloud to someone else, but silently to oneself.[1]

Notice, Plato does not merely say that thinking is LIKE talking (because, say, it has a structure similar to that of speech) but that it is
talking: silently and to oneself. Consequently, he seems to imply that it
is carried on in a language: Greek for him, English for most of us.

Aristotle does not agree with this view. Just one typical text:

Spoken words are the symbols of mental experience and written words are
the symbols of spoken words. Just as all men have not the same writing, so
all men have not the same speech sounds, but the mental experiences, which
these directly symbolize, are the same for all, as also are those things of
which our experiences are the images (*De interpretatione* 16a, in McKeon
1968: 40).

Subsequent tradition conformed to the Aristotelian rather than the
Platonic account. Throughout the Middle Ages speech was defined as

---

[1]   189e–190a (in Hamilton and Cairns 1963: 895–896). It is repeated with some
changes in the *Sophist* 263e–264a (1963: 1011). I shall call the view expressed in this
passage "the Platonic theory" without making any historical claims about Plato's
"real" theory of thinking.

the expression of thought by means of symbols, i.e. in a language, and not the other way around, namely, that thought is to be considered as the suppression of speech. The rationalists follow the same line. An act of thought, such as mental affirmation, needs no language, claims Descartes (*Replies* III, AT VII, 182–183, in Haldane and Ross 1968: 69), and the *Grammaire générale et raisonnée* insists that there is no similarity between the devices of language and the thoughts they are used to express (in Lancelot and Arnauld n.d.: 27).

Although there are some indications of reverting to the Platonic position in the empiricist writings (particularly in Hobbes and Berkeley), the revival of the "linguistic" view of thought is of very recent origin. If I am not mistaken, it is due to the prevalent behavioristic view of man, to the tendency of trying to explain all human activities in terms of publicly observable manifestations. Now although the processes of thinking are not so observable, nevertheless by representing them as suppressed monologues one at least remains close to public speech, which is not so if one regards thought as something entirely *sui generis*, private and unobservable.

Hence, I think, the attraction of the Platonic account for such philosophers as Gilbert Ryle and Ludwig Wittgenstein. Ryle echoes Plato in saying that "much of our ordinary thinking is conducted in internal monologues or silent soliloquy, usually accompanied by an internal cinematograph-show of visual imagery" (1949: 27), and then goes on to explain the origin of such an activity as follows:

This trick of talking to oneself in silence is acquired neither quickly nor without effort; and it is a necessary condition of our acquiring it that we should have previously learned to talk intelligently aloud and have heard and understood other people doing so. Keeping our thoughts to ourselves is a sophisticated accomplishment (Ryle 1949:27).

Here is the "suppression of speech" theory beautifully expressed. And something else too: the idea that the ability to think presupposes the ability to talk — a natural consequence of the Platonic account. Wittgenstein, too, rejects "wordless thoughts": he is unwilling to accept that deaf-mutes can have thoughts (Wittgenstein 1953: 109); he doubts that animals, say, can entertain a hope or hold a belief SINCE they cannot talk (1953: 174); and he says explicitly: "When I think in language, there aren't 'meanings' going through my mind in addition to the verbal expressions: the language is the vehicle of thought" (1953: 107).

Needless to say, this issue has great importance for the linguist too. I just mention three prominent aspects. If the Aristotelian theory is true, then speech involves the encoding and understanding the decoding of thought. These implications obviously have important consequences for the notions of meaning, paraphrase, and translation. The Platonic view would necessitate a completely different approach to these issues. Similarly, the learning of the first language would require radically different explanations in the two rival positions. Finally, the hypothesis of linguistic relativism would have much greater force given the Platonic theory rather than the Aristotelian.

2.　In this paper I intend to show that what I called the Platonic view is mistaken. I am going to demonstrate that the activity of thinking does not consist in talking to oneself silently, moreover that it is not carried on, *per se*, by means of words or sentences, that is to say, it is not conducted in any natural language. To put it briefly, my claim is that whereas speech essentially involves the use of a language, thought is essentially independent of it.

First of all, I feel I have to explain, in a little more detail, what I mean here by THINKING and THOUGHT.[2] The word THOUGHT is commonly used to denote the object (or, collectively, objects) of somebody's mental acts (such as realization, judgment, assumption, conclusion, decision, etc.) or mental states (such as belief, opinion, intention, etc.), or again, in an extended sense, the object of somebody's speech acts (such as statement, claim, suggestion, advice, etc.). In this sense of THOUGHT the *Little red book* contains Mao Tse-tung's thought or thoughts; in this sense of the word I can wonder about, or ask for, your thoughts concerning a certain matter; and we use the word in this sense in such frames as *Plato's thought about this subject is of Pythagorean origin, Your thought (that p) is not quite original, Then suddenly the thought (that p) struck me, He is thinking bloody thoughts,* and so forth. It is interesting to note that the word IDEA could replace THOUGHT in nearly all of these contexts. Notice, too, that even the form THINKING can function in some of these contexts with the same meaning: we might say, for instance that the *Little red book* sums up Mao's thinking, or that Plato's thinking about that subject is unoriginal or inconsistent.

The word THOUGHT (or THINKING) is a nominalization of the verb *to think*. It is easy to find verbal forms with the same meaning: *Joe thinks (i.e. believes, suspects, etc.) that p, Then I thought (i.e. realized, concluded, decided) that p,* and so forth. The verb-object of THINK in these occurrences is once more a nominalized sentence denoting the

---

[2] This explanation is a brief summary of the theory I offer in *Res cogitans* (Vendler 1972: Chapter 2).

object of one's thought: in philosophical parlance, a proposition, or propositional content.

A little reflection will show that the verb *think* in these contexts hardly admits progressive tenses: *I am thinking that p* or *He was thinking that p* are at best substandard sentences. There is, however, another context for the same verb that admits, and often demands, the progressive tense: *What are you thinking about? I am thinking about your theory,* or again *Last night I was thinking about your theory for more than an hour,* and so forth. Obviously, in these cases the thinking involved is a process, an activity, which goes on in time. Not so in the previous cases: my sudden realization that *p* does not go on in time, and my opinion that *p*, though it may last for a long time, does not go on in any sense either. After all, even if Joe is sound asleep, I still may say truthfully that he thinks that Nixon had known about Watergate. What cannot be said of him, while sound asleep, is that he is thinking about (or thinking of) Watergate. Thinking about (and, sometimes, thinking of) something or other is an activity, thinking that something is the case is not. This latter is either a state (in the cases of beliefs, suspicions, etc.) or an episodic occurrence (in the cases of realizations, decisions, and the like).

Nevertheless the notion of thinking about involves the notion of thinking that. In order to show this relation, I propose to consider another couple of similarly related concepts. Consider talking about something, and saying that something is (or should be) such and such. Quite obviously talking about something is a process that goes on in time, an activity in which a person may be engaged for a while. Thus the "time-schema" at least of talking about is the same as the time-schema of thinking about. But this is by no means the end of the similarity. For what, exactly, does a person do when he is talking about something? The answer is as obvious as it is illuminating: if it is true that somebody is talking about *X*, then it must be the case that he is saying a few things concerning *X*. I cannot possibly be talking about Watergate, or anything else, without performing such speech acts as stating and suggesting, arguing and concluding, questioning and guessing, accusing, blaming, condemning, and so forth. And if the facts I state, the possibilities I suggest, the actions I judge, and the persons I blame, have a relevant relation to the Watergate affair, then I am talking about that affair. Then what about thinking about Watergate? The situation is perfectly analogous. I cannot be engaged in thinking about Watergate without entertaining some thoughts (in the previously described "propositional" sense) about Watergate and related matters. I may recall the facts, realize the implications, consider some possibilities, wonder about the consequences, decide to read the Washington Post, put the blame where it belongs, and so on.

Plato was right part of the way: thinking is LIKE talking, reasoning is LIKE arguing. As one cannot talk about X without saying a few things about X, so one cannot think about X without having some thoughts about X. If I say that John talked about Watergate, you are perfectly entitled to ask what he said about it. And if I say that I was just thinking about Watergate, you are equally entitled to ask what I thought about it.

I do not want to claim that all thought is propositional. The painter may think intensely while staring at the half-finished canvas, the composer while running his fingers over the keyboard, the chess player while brooding over a position. Yet, most likely, they do not engage in propositional thinking: they mentally "see" lines, "hear" music, envision new situations, without being able to articulate in words, even if they wanted to, what exactly they thought. Nevertheless, if their actions are purposeful enough, they are thinking. But this kind of thinking is the exception rather than the rule. The very temptation to see thought as inner monologue indicates that the most common kind of thinking involves propositional thought, thought, that is, which can be expressed in speech.

If so, then our original problem can be sharply focused: in going through the series of mental acts in which thinking about something normally consists, do we actually talk to ourselves silently? Do we use words and sentences? Do we think in a language? Is it necessary to possess a language to be able to think at all?

3.   In arguing against the Platonic position I shall first point out that some of its consequences are highly counterintuitive, bordering in fact on the absurd. Later on I shall produce the technical arguments demonstrating its falsity.

I have mentioned Wittgenstein's qualms concerning the possibility of thought in deaf-mutes. Indeed, if the Platonic theory is true, then not even mature and otherwise intelligent deaf-mutes can think, at least not propositionally, since, as they have no language, they cannot possibly talk to themselves. Let us examine, in some detail, the consequences of this assumption.

To begin with, it would not be necessary to deny all applications of the word THINK to such persons. For, after all, even dumb animals can be said to think many things. The dog barking up the tree thinks that the cat is still there, and the greyhound obviously thinks that the mechanical rabbit it chases with such gusto is a live one. In these cases, however, one would not be willing to assert that these beasts actually HAVE THE THOUGHT that the cat is in the tree, or that the fake rabbit is a real one. One would not say, in other words, that these thoughts, or any thoughts, actually occurred to them. Why is this so?[3]

Suppose somebody is walking and his path takes him over a rickety bridge. "He thinks it'll support him," an onlooker remarks. What he says may be true even if the walker pays no attention to the bridge, has no thoughts about it. Similarly, whenever I, unconcerned, sit down on a chair I may be said to think that it will support me. "He thinks it'll support him," says gleefully and truthfully the villain who, unbeknownst to me, has just unscrewed the legs. His remark, obviously, does not attribute any thoughts to me. Now could he say, in the same situation, "He guesses (assumes or hopes) that it'll support him"? No, since the use of these verbs does indeed attribute some conscious thoughts to the subject's mind. Consider, for example, "He hopes that it'll support him." The truth of this entails, among other things, that I must be aware of some weakness in the chair, yet I am willing to give it a try. And this is contrary to our assumption that I did not notice anything untoward. Similarly, if one were to say that the dog concluded that the cat is in the tree, or that the greyhound pretends that the rabbit is a live one, this would be tantamount to attributing real thoughts to beasts, which we are unwilling to do.

To sum up: our common sense prevents us from speaking of animals in terms of predicates that imply some actual mental acts or mental processes in the subject. Moreover, since, as we saw, thinking about something is a process consisting of real mental acts, we are equally reluctant to say that an animal is ever engaged in thinking about something or other.

But now, what about the deaf-mute? Are we equally unwilling to say that often he wonders and guesses, assumes and deliberates, pretends and hopes? Is it impossible for him to form beliefs, nurture suspicions, find out that he was wrong, change his mind about the matter, and so forth? And, accordingly, should we say that he is inherently incapable of thinking about something or other for a while? I do not see any reason to think so, or to cast doubt on the sincere testimony of past deaf-mutes who later acquired the use of language.[4]

---

[3]   This distinction has been made clear to me by Professor Norman Malcolm.
[4]   Think of Helen Keller and William James's Mr. d'Estrella (1892: 613–624) to whom Wittgenstein probably (?) refers.

There is an even more persuasive piece of evidence. Although we cannot converse with a deaf-mute, we can communicate with him to some extent, via gestures, facial expressions, and pantomime, *no less than with a person whose language is utterly unknown to us*. I do not think that I would find a difference in kind between the difficulty of communicating with a monolingual Tibetan and the difficulty of communicating with a deaf-mute.[5] One can even mistake a weird-sounding language for the mutterings of a deaf-mute, and *vice versa*, at least for a while. Yet, given the hypothesis that the Tibetan can think (since he can talk) and the deaf-mute cannot think (since he cannot talk), the difference should be categorical. For one cannot really communicate with an unthinking being; communication with somebody consists in getting him to understand what I think and what I want, and in coming to understand what he thinks and wants, quite apart from appropriate overt performance, if any. Thus one cannot communicate, in this sense, with a beast, but one can with a stranger and with a deaf-mute equally. It is easy to imagine flattering (or embarrassing) a señorita wordlessly — and whether or not she is a deaf-mute makes no difference. Then think of flattering (or embarrassing) a dog. . . . Thought (real, conscious thought) is required for the uptake of flattery, or for embarrassment.

If so, then the Platonic account must be wrong. How can a deaf-mute have thoughts, i.e. say something to himself, if he cannot say anything to us?

4. "But," you argue, "deaf-mutes CAN say things. True, not in words, but by gestures and the like, as you yourself admitted in granting them the ability to communicate. They have, as St. Augustine puts it 'the natural language of all peoples' at their disposal, to wit 'the expression of the face, the play of the eyes, the movement of other parts of the body' [in Wittgenstein 1953: 2] and so forth."

I grant this, and why should I not? I claim that they do have conscious thoughts and try to express them with the limited means at their disposal. But what follows given the Platonic theory? That they think, if they do, in "mental" gestures, grimaces, and looks? But how can they do that? By imagining (seeing with the mind's eye) themselves performing these acts, as if they were looking at themselves from the outside (in a mirror?)? But suppose they never looked into a mirror, or are blind too (as Helen Keller was). . . . Can they then imagine what they look like in giving, say, a dirty look? (Can you of yourself?) The other

---

[5] Is it inherently impossible for a deaf-mute to understand Marcel Marceau?

conceivable way of doing it would be to mentally recall the muscular and kinesthetic sensations involved in the performance of these gestures, looks, etc. Can we do that? Ask yourself what it feels like to pout or give a dirty look. There is no need to add new gems to the string of absurdities.

But if these things are absurd, is the idea of talking to oneself silently not equally absurd? It does not seem so. We can and we do rehearse poems and speeches in the imagination, look for and mentally try out words and phrases while composing or translating a text, and so forth. It is also true that besides the performance of such explicitly "verbal" tasks, words or even sentences may crop up in the imagination while one thinks about nonverbal matters, too. Introspection shows that in these cases one "hears" the words as pronounced (by oneself?) or, so I am told by some people, one "sees" the words printed, or written down. Notoriously, these experiences are often accompanied by "subvocal" talk (i.e. some not fully executed motions of the vocal organs), which, incidentally, may facilitate the task of "mind readers." Often such "talk" breaks into the open: the thinker "thinks aloud."

This last phrase, together with such expressions as "Stop that noise, I cannot hear myself think" and "Then I said to myself (i.e. thought) ..." may indeed give aid and comfort to the devotees of the Platonic account.[6] Thus although this view leads to absurd consequences with respect to deaf-mutes, it has some initial plausibility when applied to normal people. Accordingly, for someone holding this view, it is better to swallow the lesser absurdity, namely that deaf-mutes cannot think, than the greater one, to wit, that they think in performing mental gestures, making mental faces, and giving mental looks.

5.   Presently I shall turn to the arguments which show that the Platonic theory is not only counterintuitive in some of its consequences, but that it is outright false; I intend to demonstrate that propositional thinking cannot consist in talking to oneself, moreover that it *per se* does not involve the use of a language.

The act of saying something is specifically human (*actus humanus*, not merely *actus hominis*), and as such is subject to the will. This philosophical claim means that the agent performing a speech act must be aware of what he is doing and must intend to do it. This is not the case with all the actions a man can do. We are not aware of our di-

---

[6] Although, as Paul Ziff points out in an unpublished paper, if "thinking" is defined as "talking to oneself silently," then "thinking aloud" becomes "talking to oneself silently aloud" — which result, to say the least, is a bit peculiar.

gesting of food, and we do not intend our heartbeat. Such actions, in fact, are never subject to the will. Some others, such as kicking somebody or breaking the window may or may not be. That they often are is shown by the fact that, first, they CAN be performed intentionally, deliberately, on purpose, and so forth; second, that the agent CAN have reasons for performing them; and third, that he MAY be held responsible for having performed them. There are, finally, kinds of action that by their very nature must be voluntary, i.e. subject to the will: e.g. robbing the bank, murdering the guard, and so forth. One can break the window, but not rob the bank, accidentally; and one can kill, but not murder somebody, unintentionally. Then it is clear that speaking belongs to this last category: one cannot state, promise, or order something, warn, accuse or condemn somebody unintentionally either: the speaker must know what he is saying and must intend to say it.

This claim is not refuted by the fact that often the speaker does not "fully" know what he is saying, or intend all the implications. Granted, one may betray a secret unwittingly, or identify somebody unintentionally (say, by addressing him, using his true name, in front of the detective), but even in these cases the speaker does intend to perform some speech act or other: the "traitor" may just want to make an innocent remark, and the "identifier" may just want to offer a friendly greeting. Such "double effects" are by no means peculiar to speech situations. The child, by eating the candy, may poison himself, and the soldier, by opening the door, may set off the booby trap. They intend the one thing, not the other.

If, therefore, thinking were talking to oneself, albeit silently, then it would follow that all thoughts are intentional, i.e. subject to the will, since, according to the theory, conceiving a thought is saying something, albeit to oneself. And this is clearly false. It is false not only because of the obvious fact that thoughts often emerge ("crop up," "strike us," or "dawn upon us") unasked for, and often keep bothering us to the point of obsession, but because of a deeper and more general reason.

In saying that a certain act (e.g. smashing the window) was done intentionally, we do not merely mean that the agent knew what he was doing, but also that he could have done otherwise (if he wanted to). Now, whereas it is certainly true that in thinking what I think I am aware of what I think, more often than not it is nonsensical to say that I could do otherwise (if I wanted to). Granted, there are certain forms of thought, such as decisions, assumptions, and the like, that are indeed subject to the will, i.e. the agent is free to assume or decide to do something or other. There are, however, other forms of thought which by their very nature preclude such freedom. Think of noticing a similarity, realizing a connection, understanding a problem, discovering a solution, seeing an implication, recognizing a friend, and so forth. In what sense can these acts be intentional, free, or subject to the will? Does it make sense to say: "I suddenly saw the solution of the puzzle, but I could have done otherwise" or "Then I decided to realize the connection between the two aspects"? How unlike it is with speaking: there is nothing wrong with such assertions as "I told him the solution but I could have done otherwise" and "Then I decided to state the connection between the two aspects."

Consequently, if the Platonic theory is true, then it follows that in thinking we "say" things to ourselves involuntarily, unintentionally, in such a way, that is, that we could not do otherwise. Moreover, as the previous argument about "unwelcome" thoughts shows, very often, as it were, we cannot shut up to ourselves. . . . We know, of course, that some people are "compulsive" talkers, cannot indeed shut up. But this is a pathological condition, compulsive behavior or simply lack of self-control. No such explanation is applicable to normal thinkers.

To sum up: talking, saying things, is a voluntary action. Having certain common types of thoughts cannot be voluntary. Consequently thinking in general cannot be talking to oneself. What this argument does not exclude is the possibility that propositional thinking might necessarily involve linguistic entities (words, etc.) in some other way. Later on I shall review this "watered-down" version of the Platonic theory.[7]

6.   We just said that the speaker must intend what he is doing, must "mean" what he says. What does such an intention actually consist of? Well, it depends on the type of speech act he performs. In STATING for instance that he was born in Ashtabula, Ohio, the speaker normally intends his audience to believe, through the recognition of his intention in saying those words, that he was born in Ashtabula, Ohio; in ORDERING somebody to leave the room, he normally intends (via the same kind of recognition) the hearer to leave the room; in PROMISING something he intends (in the same way) to put himself under a specific obligation; and so forth.[8] In other words, he intends to be understood, not merely as to the content of his utterance, but also as to its illocutionary force (see Austin 1962).

In the light of this, consider mental acts against the background of

---

[7]   I am indebted for the original idea behind this argument to Mr. Tom Dimas.
[8]   Here I follow H. P. Grice's theory of meaning (1957: 377–388).

the Platonic hypothesis, namely, that thinking is talking to oneself silently, and having a thought is saying something to oneself. Quite obviously the result is absurd, and, in this case, absurd with respect to any kind of mental act. For, to begin with the first aspect, how can I intend to be understood by myself in saying something to myself, when the very act of saying something presupposes that I understand what I am saying? Or, if I do not understand what I am saying, how can I nevertheless intend myself to understand it?

The second aspect leads to an equal absurdity. Consider such mental acts as coming to suspect, or coming to realize, something or other. If, for instance, my realization that p is the case consisted in my saying to myself that p, then I could not possibly intend myself to come to believe that p as a result of saying to myself that p, since in saying that p, I would already have realized that p. To put it simply: what is the point of telling myself something which I know to be the case in the very act of telling? Or, to make it worse, what is the point of telling myself something which I have to know (if I am sincere) to be able to tell at all?

Then consider a mental act of another kind, a decision for instance. I just decided to go to Paris this summer. What did I say to myself? "Go to Paris!"? Since this looks like an order, it opens up the dimensions of authority in the speaker and voluntary compliance in the hearer. Ignoring the absurdity arising out of the idea of authority over myself, the aspect of voluntary compliance calls for another decision: shall I or shall I not obey this order. Suppose I reply to myself "No, I won't" — did I decide then? Of course, I may have just said to myself "I shall go to Paris." But in this case, what makes this "inner" speech act into the carrier of a decision rather than of a simple forecast, guess, or — to make it worse again — rather than its being just a sentence mentally rehearsed? "Well, you must intend it as a decision; you may even say 'I decide to go to Paris' or 'I shall go to Paris, and this is a decision.' " I reply, first, that even these sentences may crop up in the imagination without my deciding anything and, second, I ask once more what is the point of telling myself what my decision is, and that it is a decision, in the very act of making that decision? In telling you what my decision is I claim your belief, in giving you my orders I demand compliance. Neither of these models works for a decision if construed as saying something to oneself.

It follows, then, that having a thought cannot be viewed as saying something to oneself silently, consequently thinking cannot consist in talking to oneself silently. It remains to be seen, however, whether propositional thought involves words, phrases, or sentences, i.e. elements of a language, in some other ways, which do not amount to the full exercise of saying something.

7.   In reproducing what somebody else has said one usually resorts to the device of indirect quotation, e.g. "He told me that he was born in Ashtabula" or "He ordered me to leave the premises." Nevertheless, in all these cases of indirect reproduction, the hearer still might want to know the original speaker's own words; "What exactly did he say, word by word?" he might ask. Now compare this situation with such mental acts as realizations, recognitions, decisions, and regrets. Suppose I tell you that last night I suddenly realized that it must have been Jones, the janitor, who opened my letters in the office. Would it make sense for you to ask for the exact words of my realizing this? And would it be possible for me to answer? Which of the following sentences "crossed my mind" in the act: "He must have done it," "It was done by Jones," "The janitor did it," or what? Well, suppose I indeed "said to myself" (perhaps even aloud) "It was him!" What makes this into a realization, and the realization of that particular thing? Surely it is not enough if that sentence merely crossed my mind. "No, you must have 'meant' it," you say. But this would make it into an intentional act, which a realization is not. Then, perhaps, it was as if I heard somebody telling me "It was him." We indeed say things like "a little voice told me. . . ." But this would be the description of a hunch rather than of a realization. For one thing, did I believe the "little voice"? We feel that we are, once more, in the domain of the absurd — or the metaphorical.

I do not deny, of course, that that sentence, or some other, may have emerged in my imagination, or may even have been (subvocally or vocally) articulated by me, in making that realization. I may have said to myself "But of course" or "How stupid of me not to have thought of that," or what have you. What I deny is that the act of realization consisted in, or required, the occurrence of any sentence, or word, in my mind. There is nothing surprising about words or sentences being evoked in the imagination while thinking about something; after all they are the normal means of expressing the thoughts we entertain. Some people cannot hum, or mentally hear, a tune without beating the rythm with their hand or foot. So, maybe, some people cannot think without words crossing their minds. Yet these things, though associated, remain distinct: humming is not beating, and thinking is not imagining words.

The same thing applies, incidentally, to imagination in general, to Ryle's "cinematograph-show": images, too, may accompany thinking. In thinking about the law one may visualize dusty tomes, or a courtroom; in thinking about a mathematical problem one may see beads or numerals; this does not mean, however, that then one thinks in terms of dusty tomes, courtrooms, beads, or numerals.

8.   Suppose that my realization that it was the janitor who had opened my letters was indeed couched in the words "He must have done it." Then the problem arises, why is it that the word *he* (mentally pronounced or heard) meant the janitor. In normal speech we select referring devices (names, pronouns, definite descriptions, etc.) which, given the physical setup of the situation and the course of the preceding conversation, enable the audience to understand whom I have in mind. Thus, depending on these factors, I may use *he, the janitor, that man*, etc. to achieve this purpose. If so, then there is something incomprehensible about using any word or phrase in referring to somebody in my thought — there is no need to make *myself* understand whom *I* have in mind. And even if I say to myself, in making that realization, "He must have done it," *he* refers to that man only because I have him, and nobody else, in mind in saying this. But then my having him in mind cannot consist in using *he* or any other phrase. One may talk of or about one thing or another, and to do so one must refer to that thing to be understood; but one thinks of or about one thing or another without referring: there is no appeal to understanding, there is no reference in thought. It makes sense to say that I thought about that man in terms of his being the janitor, but it is nonsense to say that I referred to him in my thought by the words *the janitor*. Consider the contrast: in speaking about that man I referred to him by the pronoun *he*; in thinking about him I thought of him in terms of . . . his being he?

9.   A similar contrast between speech and thought arises in connection with ambiguous sentences, whether or not the ambiguity is due to semantic or syntactic factors. If I tell you that I am going to the bank, you will understand what I said this way (. . . money . . .) or that (. . . river . . .) from the circumstances — if you can decide at all. As to myself, I may "mean" it one way or the other. Now what does it mean to "mean" it, or understand it, in one particular way? Well, as to the first, it depends on what I intend you to come to believe, and — if I am honest — on what I really intend to do: going to the First National or going to the riverbank. As to the second, it depends upon what you

take my words to mean, and — if you think I am telling the truth —
on what you come to think about my intentions. Now is it in the least
believable that these mental acts (i.e. my decision to go to the river, my
intention to tell you the truth, OR TO LIE, your understanding of what
I said, OR YOUR DOUBTS ABOUT ITS TRUTH, and so forth) are all cast in
unambiguous sentences? In sentences, that is, in which the word *bank*
is replaced, or is accompanied, by an unambiguous paraphrase?

Syntactical ambiguities raise the same problems. Think, for instance,
of the mental flip-flop involved in the understanding of *Mary had a
little lamb — and Jane a little pork*. Now how comes that my thought
that Mary had (i.e. ate) a little lamb is NOT ambiguous? Or can one say
"I thought 'Mary had a little lamb' and I meant it in the sense of
eating"?

Then there are metaphors, allusions, ironic remarks, and so forth.
"It was a very nice thing to do," I tell you, meaning that it was an
awful thing to do. Is it possible to think that it was an awful thing to
do in saying to oneself "It was a very nice thing to do"? "He must have
hit the ceiling, I think." Can I ever be in doubt about what I just
thought in this case? Yet the sentence *He must have hit the ceiling* is
ambiguous.

To sum up: the use of language involves all sorts of ambiguities. It
is up to the speaker, therefore, to prevent, and up to the listener to
avoid, misunderstandings due to this source. In doing this both participants have to rely on the circumstances. Now if thought consisted in
the use of language, then, first, there could be, and often would be,
ambiguous thoughts (in the relevant sense of ambiguity), second, the
thinker would frequently face the task of disambiguating (i.e. finding
the correct "reading" for) his thoughts and, third, he would have to
rely on circumstantial clues in doing so. I submit that all these consequences are absurd.

10.   People are not infallible, committing errors in many things they
do, and speech is no exception. They make mistakes of grammar, use the
wrong word, commit malapropisms and make various slips of the tongue.
Thus it often happens that they do not in fact say what they wanted to
say, or even what they think they are saying. Of course both the audience and the speaker may detect such errors, and then the speaker may
come to correct himself. The audience, too, is liable to errors of its
own. One may mishear the speaker, misunderstand him, and so forth.
Errors can occur on both ends of the speaker-hearer relation.

The possibility casts a new pall on the Platonic theory, whether it be conceived actively, as talking to oneself, or passively, as hearing "voices" in the imagination. For, to take the first alternative, it would allow situations in which the speaker could be mistaken about what he actually thought. He might say things like "I thought I thought that p, but then I realized that in fact I thought that q, so I corrected myself" or "I wanted to think that p, but in fact I thought that q," and so on. I forego the pleasure of showing the various absurdities in such reports.

The second alternative, the passive one, fares no better. It leads to the possibility of misunderstanding, or failing to understand, one's own thoughts. "I am not sure what *I* thought," the thinker could report, "it may be understood as p or as q," as if trying to interpret an oracle.

11.   Finally, having given the main arguments showing the implausibility, and the falsity, of the Platonic view, I sketch a few additional considerations to reinforce this conclusion.

Although we do ask the foreigner "In what language do you think?" we do not take this question so seriously as to countenance such answers as "I think in English now, but in bad English. I misuse words in my thought, I commit grammatical errors, and so forth. Moreover, owing to this handicap, I think rather slowly and in primitive sentences." I suppose "thinking in English" means nothing more than the facility of expressing oneself in English directly without first formulating what one wants to say in another language, and then translating by means of some set procedure.

Very often we hear "I do not find the exact word for what I want to say." The most natural assumption is that the speaker does know what he wants to say. For after a while he might exclaim "I have it! It is. . . ." The word fits. Fits what? Fits into the sentence(s) the thinker entertains? Hardly, since many words could do that. But that word alone expresses his thought.

Similarly, in giving paraphrases or translations for a given sentence one does not normally operate on a word-to-word basis. One gets the "sense" of the sentence, and then looks for another sentence (in the same language or another) that expresses the same sense. Now this sense is surely not grasped in terms of another sentence, since that is exactly what one hopes to find. Nor does one, like the foreigner who does not "think" in English yet, follow any set of rules — connecting words to words — in performing the task. Translating is not like projecting another picture from a given picture by some rote; it is rather like drawing another picture, in another medium, of the thing the first picture depicts.

REFERENCES

AUSTIN, J. L.
1962 *How to do things with words.* Oxford: Clarendon.
GRICE, H. P.
1957 Meaning. *Philosophical Review* 66:377–388.
HALDANE, ELIZABETH S., G. R. T. ROSS, *editors*
1968 *The philosophical works of Descartes,* volume two. Cambridge: Cambridge University Press.
HAMILTON, EDITH, HUNTINGTON CAIRNS, *editors*
1963 *Plato: the collected dialogues.* Princeton, N.J.: Princeton University Press.
JAMES, WILLIAM
1892 Thought before language: a deaf-mute's recollections. *Philosophical Review* 1:613–624.
LANCELOT, G., A. ARNAULD
n.d. *Grammaire génerale et raisonnée.* Facsimile edition. Menston, England: Scholar Press.
MC KEON, RICHARD, *editor*
1968 *The basic works of Aristotle.* New York: Random House.
RYLE, GILBERT
1949 *The concept of mind.* New York: Barnes and Noble.
VENDLER, ZENO
1972 *Res cogitans.* Ithaca and London: Cornell University Press.
WITTGENSTEIN, LUDWIG
1953 *Philosophical investigations,* part one. Oxford: Blackwell.

Some Notes on Central Eskimo Color Terminology

ALBERT HEINRICH

INTRODUCTION

Investigations were carried out at Rankin Inlet, Northwest Territories, Canada, during the summer of 1972. Nine middle-aged informants — three women and six men — were interviewed. None of them were color blind, and all seemed to have normal visual acuity.

All understood some English, but their fluency varied from minimal to rudimentary. All were literate in syllabics, but none were literate in English. All of them claimed to be ignorant of French, but some of them listened to the Oblate Fathers talking to each other in French on the radio and seemed to understand some of what was going on. All of them consider themselves to be traditional Eskimos and, in a sense, they are. During their formative years and early adulthood they were part of the semi-migratory, hunting-trapping way of life that focused on various trading posts and missions, but which required and afforded very little interaction with whites.

The culture that these people grew up in was one that had incorporated items such as flour, coffee, tea, sugar, tobacco, Christianity, steel traps, knives, regular visits to the trading center, and the white man as an authoritarian figure, but which had retained many other aspects of the pre-contact Eskimo culture, including the language. They have, of course, borrowed a number of English terms, but I did not — contrary to what is the case in the Bering Strait — run into any borrowed item referring to color phenomena. These people, in fact, seemed to be quite naïve about

Supported by Canada Council Grant S72–0165, *The systematics of Canadian Eskimo colour terminology.*

their color vocabulary; nobody appears to have investigated it before.

The data from the nine informants fall into five categories, which I have termed Systems A, B, C, D, and E. The ultimate validity of this classification might, perhaps, be challenged on the grounds of an insufficient data base. For three of the systems, there is only one informant per system. For one of the other systems there are two informants, and for the other one there are four. It may, therefore, be that consolidations or expansions may be necessary but, regardless of how the data are arranged, each set of responses has internal consistency, and enough internal consistency so that certain statements can safely be made.

All informants were tested on the Ishihara Color Test and found to have normal color vision. Procedure consisted of having informants give their names for the chips of the Munsell Books of Color, following which they were asked to react to the Berlin-Kay Chart, following which they were retested for a certain selection of both the Munsell and Berlin-Kay responses and allowed to discuss color if they chose to do so. Testing sessions were never longer than two hours, and successive sessions were usually carried out on alternate days. Most informants were interviewed only four or five times.

After each session all of the rapidly recorded notes were transcribed into more legible form before they got "cold," a task which required much more time than the original recording. All doubtful responses were checked during the subsequent interview, and wherever possible — when time was available — rough (test) coding and plotting were done to attempt to check the inner consistency of data.[1]

Data manipulation was done at Calgary. It consisted of arranging the responses in various permutations of: native term × hue × light value × chroma value. After much trial and error it was determined that the most productive sorting arrangement was to use the native terms (e.g. *quqsuxtug, quqsuxigtuq, quqsuangayuq*) as set designators (each identifiably different native color word being a separate set) and then to determine the hue range, and the light value and chroma value ranges and averages. This produced meaningful classes from which maps were drawn of the domain of each term for each informant. From this, maps of each individual's color system were made, which were then classified as being of five sorts (below), from which a composite map of (a) each system and (b) each color were made. The latter was possible because there is system and congruence, not random variation, in the responses of the nine informants.

[1]   All informants, regardless of how inconsistent or confusing their responses seemed to be at first, were — it turns out from the results of data manipulation — responding honestly and consistently.

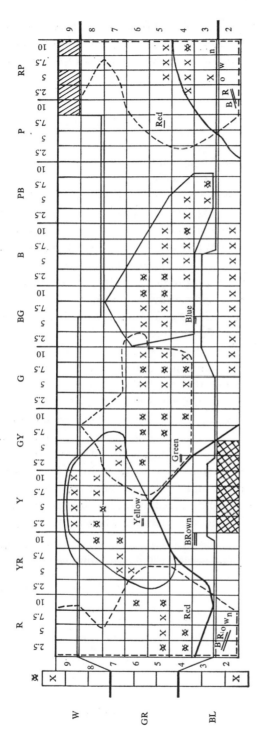

Figure 1. Scale adaptation of Berlin–Kay's "Basic color terms" showing the Eskimo 'responses. Maximum chroma is at each light value of each hue

W = White and Whitish
BL = Black and Blackish
R = Red and Reddish
Y = Yellow and Yellowish
G = Green and Greenish
B = Blue and Bluish

X = White
X = Black
X = Red
X = Yellow
X = Green
X = Blue

✼ = Pure White
✼ = Pure Black
✼ = Focal Red
✼ = Focal Yellow
✼ = Focal Green
✼ = Focal Blue

Termed *kutyuq* by System C informant.

Termed *aqsianayuq* by System C informant.

For the unimorphemic systems, the same Two centers of distribution obtain, as do focal points,

BR = Brown and Brownish. (No responses shown. The entries shown in the right-hand Brown area are off-Reds.)
GR = Gray and Grayish. Chromatic Grays not shown. All 4 light value and most 5 light value chips of 1 or 2 chroma value can be called Gray. Most 3 and 6 light value chips of 1 or 2 chroma can be called Grayish.

The composite map of Figure 1 was produced from the two sorts of maps (a + b) mentioned above. In the process of consolidation some data were lost, but I am convinced that Figure 1 represents a true picture of the essential findings.[2]

THE SYSTEMS

System A, which can be called the Aivillingmiut system, is a consolidation of the data from two informants of Chesterfield Inlet, one of Wager Bay, and one of Baker Lake. These people have terms for White,[3] Black,[4] Red, Yellow, Green/Blue, and Brown.[5] They do not have a term for Gray, but they seem to recognize it as a perceptual category; various Blackish and Whitish terms (as well as Blackish-White and Whitish-Black) are used to designate both achromatic and chromatic Grays.[6] *Qiqnangayuq*[7] [it wants to be black] is consistently used for dark to medium Gray, both chromatic and achromatic. Its mirror image, *qaquangayuq* [it wants to be white], is used for medium to light Neutral Grays and also for Whitish chromatic colors. One informant also gave "flesh colored" for the very light (low chroma, high light value) *RP* chips, the same general area of the color solid for which System C informant gave *qutyuq* (q.v. below). These informants were much more prone than any others to use combinatory designations, e.g. Reddish-blue/green, Brownish-red, etc.

Data for System B were obtained from a person who grew up in the Garry Lakes area. He says his people were called the Senningayamiut, an ethnic group that he says is very closely related to the Utqusiksallingmiut (Chantry Inlet Eskimos). In this system there are terms for White, Black, Red, Yellow, Green/Blue, Brown, and Gray. The latter applies only to medium light value neutral chips and to medium light value, low chroma chips in the *GY*, *G*, *BG*, and *B* range, the same area where higher chroma,

[2]   The writer retains a copy of the complete data manipulations and of the summary and conclusions of the report to the Canada Council, and invites inspection and criticism.

[3]   Unless otherwise noted, a color term listed here subsumes a semantic range, e.g. Red = red, pure red, real red, pale red, off-red, reddish, dark red, imperfect red, etc.

[4]   Where color terms are capitalized, they represent (my) translations of (my perception of) the Eskimo categories. When referring to the stimuli used, the Munsell color chips, I use the designations *R*, *YR*, *Y*, *GY*, *G*, *BG*, *B*, *PB*, *P*, and *RP*.

[5]   No measure of salience was applied, but this is the order in which terms were collected. This is partly the result of using the Munsell Books of Color sequence, but I also have a strong feeling that the informants were responding in terms of some order of salience of this nature.

[6]   Particularly for low light value *BG*.

[7]   The diagraph *ng* is used, for convenience in typing, for the velar (& palatal) nasal.

higher light value chips are designated as *tunguxtuq* (Green/Blue). This system is, as far as I can determine, the same as System A, except that it has a name for Gray.

System C is derived from the responses of a man of Iglulik ancestry who was born at Coral Harbor and grew up at Iglulik. It has designations for White, Black, Red, Yellow, Green, Blue, Brown, Gray, and "Emergent Pink." The base morpheme employed for Blue is *tungu-*, the same as is used for Green/Blue in Systems A and B. The base morpheme *sunga-*, also used for Green by System D and by System E informants, is, for this informant, restricted to a few of the brighter, higher chroma, 6 & 7 light value (a bit above medium) *GY* chips. "Emergent Pink" refers to the term *kutyuq* (or *qutyuq*) and derivatives which the informant consistently uses for light value 9, very low chroma *RP*, and which he also uses for: (a) other Pinkish chips, (b) medium to pale achromatic Grays. For dark Grays and for low chroma, low light value chromatic chips he usually uses Blackish, but for light value 2, low chroma chips in the *YR, Y, GY,* and *G* range he uses a term, *aqsyianayuq*, that is cognate with the System B informant's term for Gray. In addition, the System C informant has a term, *siangna-*, that he employs only for chromatic Grays, i.e. low light value, low chroma chips primarily in the *Y* to *B* range. *Siangna-* responses are not restricted to this range, but they are more frequent there; they occur almost exclusively at light values 3 and 4.

For System D the responses of a husband and wife team were used. These two people do not know exactly when or where they were born, but they agree that their respective parents told them they were born in the same year in two different, widely separated hunting camps in the King William Island-Queen Maud Gulf area. They state that they are just people speaking their own language, not some particular sort of "miut." They claim to have the same speech form, but they do, in fact, sometimes use slightly different terms. This is especially noticeable in color terminology. He and she do sometimes use quite different derivatives of the same basic stem for the same color chip — but without impeding communication. Each understands what the other means. This may be a function of the fact that she is more of a splitter and he more of a lumper; it may also be a function of differential choices from the same morpheme pool; but it probably also entails micro-dialectual distinctions. Despite their disclaimers as to not having any ethnic affiliations other than just plain Eskimo, it is highly probable that the speech form of these people is related to, and that they are one of, the congeries of people who make up the so-called Netsillingmiut to the east of their birthplaces. These people have terms for White, Black, Red, Yellow, Green, Blue, and Brown.

These people do not seem to have a "conceptual focus" for Gray, as the System A informants seem to have. They use Blackish terms for dark Grays (both chromatic and achromatic), and they use various Whitish terms very liberally for high light value and/or low chroma *R, YR, PB,* and *RP* chips. All light value 9 chips are classified by them as functionally White. They have distinct and well-separated focal areas (or perceptual domains/semantic fields) for Yellow, Green, and Blue, but these domains do significantly overlap — Yellow with Green, and Green with Blue. This is also the case with the other two Systems (C and E) that are bi-morphemic for Green/Blue. In Systems A and B, mono-morphemic for Green/Blue, there is no appreciable overlap between Yellow and Green/Blue.

System E was obtained from a man who says he could be called a Pallamiut (Padleimiut), having been born somewhere to the southwest of Padlei, the general area where he spent all of his life until he was past middle age. This man maintains (as do most other Eskimos) that Padleimiut are distinct from other Eskimos — something that may be true at a micro-level. His color terminology system actually is not really different from System D, but his method of responding to the chips of the Munsell Books of Color is different, mostly in that he is a lumper *par excellence.* He gave terms for White, Black, Red, Yellow, Green, Blue, and Brown. Brown was a very infrequent response. This man did not give evidence of having Gray as a "conceptual area." He used Blackish quite liberally for low light value chips and Whitish for low chroma and/or high light value chips.

Some of the informants of the sample sometimes maintain that their system of naming and classifying colors is different from that of Eskimos who belong to another dialectual group. At other times one can get very firm statements to the effect that all Eskimo systems of color naming are the same. Both of these views are correct.

At the particularistic level there are individual, dialectual, and systemic distinctions. Individuals will differ a bit (but not over a wide range) as to where to place the focus of a color area. And there can be a great deal of variation from person to person (and for the same person from one time to another) as to the outer boundaries of general color areas. There are also differences in individual strategies for breaking down the color solid into identifiable entities and classes. There are splitters and lumpers, "God's truth" realists, and relativists, and there are those who define a color domain and then break it down as opposed to persons who focus on the ideal shade and hue and then categorize relatable colors accordingly. At first these differences seem overwhelming, but analysis of the

Central Eskimo data very strongly indicates that these differences are not erratic and do definitely occur within common parameters.

Dialectual differences consist of different lexemes for the same domain (both for root and modifying morphemes), differential usages of allo-morphs, and, of course, systemic differences.

Systems differ mostly as to complexity of named categories. Except for the unresolved question of whether all Central Eskimos "perceive" Gray as a distinct entity, there does not seem to be any significant difference in what these people "see." It seems to be only a matter of some people having (or using) a smaller, and others a larger, list of labels that apply to what they see.[8]

If one turns from perceptual categories and focuses on the systems *qua* systems, a progression from less to more complex is evident. System A is the simplest. It would be Stage IV on the Berlin-Kay scale if it did not have Brown. System B seems to be the next in complexity, having added Gray — again aberrantly according to the Berlin-Kay formulation. Systems D and E would be nice, regular, stage VI systems, and System C would be an "early" stage VII.

Despite terminological and systemic variation, there is a generic unity pervading these systems. This generic unity is manifest (a) in the con-gruence of focal areas and (b) in the fact that the more complex are derivable from the simpler systems by the addition of named categories, not by rearranging of categories. Figure 1 illustrates this; it is a composite derived by: (a) plotting the responses by each informant for each color, then (b) plotting the primary color areas of all of his colors for each informant, and then (c) plotting the primary, peripheral, and focal areas of each color of all informants (combined for each color), and finally con-solidating the results. In producing this combined "map," the peripheral areas of each color had to be eliminated because of extreme overlap, but very little tailoring had to be done to produce the composite shown here. All of the features illustrated in Figure 1 are derived from the data and are observable in all of the systems.[9] The separate Green and Blue areas, though not found as emic categories in Systems A and B, are observable there, too, as etic entities.

[8]   Perhaps also a matter of some having a larger number of basic categories and fewer sub-divisions, whereas others use a smaller number of base morphemes and use modifying morphemes more frequently.

[9]   Except for the shaded areas which apply to System C alone.

COLORS AND COLOR TERMS

When talking about color, the informants of this sample seemed to be referring to three sorts of things — (a) a color generally, (b) a focus, and (c) a peripheral range. I will designate these (for each color) as the GENERAL AREA, the FOCAL AREA, and the PERIPHERAL AREA.[10]

The general area is that range throughout which the informant sees the color as being truly and undilutedly present. For any one color, the range of the general area is fairly constant. This constancy holds across systems, and most individuals agree very closely with most others as to the bounds of any one general area. For an individual from one day to the next, or between individuals using the same system, or between systems, there may be a difference of one or two light or chroma value steps on the Munsell scale, but no helter-skelter inconsistencies. The larger blocks shown in Figure 1 represent the general color areas. The general areas are the ones for which terms are apt to be elicited first, and invariably the simplest term built on that base applies to them.[11] For most colors (Brown being the most exceptional), most responses for any one general area are for chips that are saturated, i.e. the highest chroma value that can be found in that particular hue, at that light value. They are on the surface of the color solid. The general area always encompasses all of the chips of the focal area.

The focal area consists of a very few chips (usually no more than two or three of the more than 1,500 choices afforded by the Munsell Books of Color) that are always the absolutely highest chroma value for the hue in question. The term used for a focal area has *-riq-* (*-xiq-*, *-xix-*) as the penultimate syllable,[12] e.g. *quqsuxtuq* = "Yellow," *quqsuxiqtuq* = "real, focal, Yellow." The focal area is considered to be the best, truest, prettiest, and aesthetically most satisfying representative of the color. Individuals almost invariably chose (only) the same few focal chips on retesting, but there is some slight variation between individuals.

Outside the general area there is always a hazy and vaguely bounded area where the color in question can be perceived, but is perceived as being imperfect — dull, pale, dark, or mixed with something else. The boundaries of peripheral areas are never clear and vary from person to person, and for the same individual with time and according to circum-

[10]   More often than not the really significant colors are found on the "surface" of the "color solid," but this is not always the case; the term, area, as used here, should always be conceived of as potentially three-dimensional.
[11]   In linguistic terms, the general areas are "unmarked."
[12]   Unless preceded by one of the morphemes given above for peripheral terms.

stances. The same chip may elicit different base morphemes and/or different modifications of the same basic term. A medium-low light value unsaturated *RP* chip, for instance, may be any one of several kinds of Reddish, Bluish, Blackish, or Brownish, or any combination of them. The terms used to designate peripheral areas are always more complex than the general term and usually more so than the focal term, e.g. *quqsuanga-yuq* = off-yellow. Non-final suffixes such as *-anga-*, *-aya-*, *-uyu-*, *-lak-*, *-luq-*, *-qayax-*, *-kasaq-*, *-singa-*, *-vallay-*, *-ciaq-* and others (alone or in combination) are used to "bend" the basic meaning by the addition of ideas such as "tend towards, wants to be, pale, obscured, derives from, pertains to, probably, a bit of," etc. Peripheral colors are never chroma maxima for their particular hue and often are unsaturated.

BASIC COLOR MORPHEMES AND THEIR DOMAINS

White: *qaqu-* is the most frequently encountered morpheme, usually actualized as *qaquxtug*. This term was used by System A, B, and E informants for functional (general) White, and the *qaqu-* stem also served as the base for pure (focal) White and for most Whitish terms. They were aware of, but seldom used, the allomorph *quallux-*. The System C informant, on the other hand, used only the latter morpheme. The System D informants employed both these stems, but they most frequently gave responses that were built on some modification of *qat-* (*qataxtuq, qatangasuq, qatsatuq, qatangayuq, qanuatuq*).

As illustrated in Figure 1, Whitish usually reaches down to light value 7 in the achromatic colors and takes in almost all light value 9 chromatic chips. The crowding out by primary (general) Yellow and by secondary (peripheral) Red is characteristic of all systems, as is the tendency to take in light value 8 (and other lower) chips in the *BG* to *P* range. Though most informants will use the general White term rather freely to designate functional White, all of them insisted that only the borders of the Books of Color (and not even the N, 9.5 chip) were pure (focal) White.

For Black only one base morpheme, *qiqniq-*,[13] was found. The domains of Black-Blackish and its characteristics are to quite a large extent the mirror image of White-Whitish. Blackish goes up to light value 4 in the achromatic colors. All light value 2 chromatics can be (and usually are) termed *qiqnixtuq*, functional, (general) Black. The unexplained "hump" at *YR* and *Y* is a general tendency for all informants except for the System C

---

[13] *Qiqniq* → *qiqnix* → *qixnix-* ~ *qixnax* → *qixni-* ~ *qixna-*, depending on environment, and/or dialect and/or free variation attributable to fast versus precise speech.

man who gave *aqsyianayuq* at this place. The tendency for functional Black to crowd in (and replace) Blackish in the *G* through *B* range is evident for all systems. The overlap of Brown and Black is sometimes a matter of one color crowding out the other and sometimes a matter of mixture (Blackish-Brown or Brownish-Black). Two of the informants volunteered that the darkest Munsell chip (N, 0.5) was not pure Black, and, though they applied *qiqnixtuq* to many of the light value 2, chroma value 1 and 2 chips, all informants claimed to be able to detect the chromatic component in even these lowest chroma, lowest light value chips presented to them.

The stems for White and Black terms are opaque to the informants; they cannot etymologize them. That is not the case with the chromatic colors. All the common chromatic color terms are easily relatable to common things of Eskimo life, and usually recognizably so for the informants, viz.: Red ← *auk* = blood; Yellow ← *quq* = urine; Green ← *sungaq* = bile; Blue ← *tunguq* = liver;[14] Brown ← *qayuq* = blood soup; *aksiangnaq*, Gray, is said to be derived from ashes. No information was gathered on the native etymology for *kutyuq*, Pink, or *siangnaq*, chromatic Gray.

Red[15] is given as *aupalluktuq* by System A, B, and E informants. System D informants occasionally use this term but more often use *aupayaxtuq* for general Red.

The System C informant always used the latter term for general Red. For the formation of terms for peripheral Reds, both the *aupaya-* and the *aupallu-* bases are used, but there are no true allomorphs of the term.

The domain of Red is almost equally distributed on the *R* and *RP* ends of the Munsell and Berlin-Kay presentations of the spectrum, and the incursion into *P* on the one hand and *YR* on the other is common to all systems — and expectable in the absence of named purple and orange domains. The overlap with Brown at *P*, *RP*, and *R* is due to the fact that that sort of Brown (q.v. below) is an unsaturated color, underlying[16] the

---

[14]   Here the reference (or parallel) is not so clear or convincing to a native speaker. I have been informed, by separate sources, that the underlying meaning is something that is relatable to (a) death, (b) venous, clotted or intestinal blood, (c) berry juice and/or vegetation.

[15]   Unless stated otherwise, a capitalized color term means the general area.

[16]   The "map" used here is an adaptation of the Berlin-Kay Chart, which was produced by taking the highest chroma value chip at each light value of each of the pages (hues) of the Munsell Books of Color and arranging them into columns and rows. This makes a fairly good heuristic device for plotting and studying the general areas and the foci (both of which are usually saturated) of most colors, but it does not allow for proper representation of the peripheral areas and Brown and chromatic Gray — all of which often are unsaturated.

surface Reds. The "wasp-waist" at light value 7 and 8 is characteristic but is not readily explicable, though evidently relatable to the "Emergent Pink" of System C. Though most informants distribute their Red from P to YR, most of them usually place their focal colors in R.[17]

Yellow is always given as *quqsuqtuq*, or some allophonic variant thereof. It has no allomorphs. Yellow sometimes overlaps a bit with Red and with Green (or Green/Blue), but Yellow and Green are never subsumed together, as is the case with Green and Blue. The left and right downward extension into YR and GY, respectively, are characteristic and are relatable to high chroma content.

Green is termed *sungayuxtuq* (or some other variant of the *sung-* stem such as *sunguyaaxtuq*) by Systems C, D, and E informants. I term these systems bi-morphemic for Green/Blue. Systems A and B use the same stem, in this case *tungu-*,[18] to designate Green and Blue. I call them mono-morphemic for Green/Blue. The *sungu-* morpheme does not occur among the responses of the System A and B informants. For System C, D, and E informants, it seems (intuitively to me) to be subsidiary to *tungu-*. It does appear in the general, focal and peripheral forms. The area shown in Figure 1 is not the constant of all informants, but, rather, the area within which various informants locate general Green. It is also the area within which the mono-morphemic systems find ONE OF THEIR TWO SETS OF FOCAL AREAS FOR *tungu-*.[19] In the bi-morphemic systems there is a marked overlap in the domains of Green and Blue, and also between Yellow and Green. In the mono-morphemic systems this is, of course, also true for Green and Blue, but it is not the case for Yellow and Green. The slightly higher light value location of Green as compared to Blue is characteristic and is relatable to maximum chroma values. There are no allomorphs for *sungu-*.

Blue in all three bi-morphemic systems is represented by terms such as *tunguxtuq*, *tunguyuxtuq*, and/or *tunguyuyuxtuq*. The System C informant used all three terms, in an apparently random manner, but when the data had been coded, it was found that he actually had been consistently applying the terms differentially in terms of light value. Other informants, of both bi- and mono-morphemic systems, showed this tendency, too. Mono-morphemic system informants appeared to be trying to use one of

[17] Though individuals may vary a bit as to which few chips are focal, the chips chosen are usually the absolute chroma maxima for that hue and neighboring hues.
[18] Actually *tung-* plus a vowel, which can be realized either as *a* or *u*. The same is true for *sungu-* ~ *sunga-*.
[19] It should also be added that the *BG* hues, where the Green and Blue of the bi-morphemic systems overlap are (etically) areas where even the saturated chips are low in chroma value.

these three terms for the more Greenish of the Green/Blue range and one or both of the others for Blue, but without much success.[20] There are no allomorphs of *tungu-*.

The most frequent term for Brown was *qayuqtuq* (or *qayuxtuq*). This term was used to identify general Brown by all who did so.[21] Its stem, *qayuq* (*qayux-*) is also the one used more frequently to form the (relatively infrequent) peripheral Brown terms. But curiously, the term usually used to designate "real," focal, Brown is *qatcuRixtuq*, built on the base *qatcu-*, which certainly is not an allophonic variant of *qayuq*. At present *qayuq* and *qatcu-* apparently are allomorphs, but historically this may not be so.

There is nowadays among the Central Eskimos a category of Brown covered by the allomorphs given above. For the informants of this study, this seems to be one semantic domain. But when coded according to factors of light value, chroma value, and hue, this class very evidently breaks up into two entities. The Brown that is found at the lower light values of *P*, *RP*, and *R* usually encompasses unsaturated chips only. On the color solid this color lies "below the surface," underlying dark Red. The other Brown is dark Yellow, i.e. lower light value Yellows, usually saturated, spilling over into *YR* and *GY* a bit.

Informants had little difficulty in deciding whether particular chips were Brownish, or had a Brownish component along with something else, and they were usually also able to decide to their own satisfaction without too much difficulty whether or not something was Brown or not, but most had great difficulty in deciding on focal chips.

The frequency of Brown and Brownish responses was low. The Padlei and Iglulik informants, in fact, gave only one term each. The former used *qayuxtuq* once to identify several contiguous chips of the first kind of Brown and used it a second time to name several contiguous chips of the Dark Yellow sort of Brown. The Iglulik man identified four Dark Yellow chips as *qatcuRixtuq*. The Brown area(s) cannot, in fact, be as neatly delineated as the plotting in Figure 1 suggests.

Gray is definitely a named category for Systems B and C, but in a very indefinite, unsettled way. The System B man used *aksialuktuq*[22] to identify both chromatic and achromatic Grays, and he also, sparingly,

---

[20]   But the two "centers" for Blue/Green of the mono-morphemic systems remained. These centers are the results of coding the data; they are DERIVED from informants' responses, but not given overtly by them.

[21]   See re System C responses.

[22]   The *k*'s (voiceless palatal stops) may, in fact be *q*'s (voiceless velar stops). These are hard to distinguish in fast speech. There may also be inaccuracy in the recording of the similar term, *aqsyianaq*, of System C, which apparently comes from the same source.

used derived *aksialu-* terms to designate Grayish (peripheral Gray) chips. These terms are mostly found in the 3, 4, and 5 light value range, and the chromatic responses usually referred to unsaturated chips in the *GY* through *B* range — an area of overall low chromaticity.

The System C informant used *siangnaq* to designate a number of unsaturated chromatic chips in the light value 4 row, mostly in the *GY* through *B* range. He also used derivatives of this base to name a number of unsaturated chips of adjacent light values and in other hues. This morpheme was never used for achromatic Grays.

For achromatic Grays he sometimes used Whitish and Blackish terms, but he also used *qutyukasaktuq*[23] for medium achromatic Gray and *qutyuxuyuq* for medium to light achromatic Gray. The latter term was also used for high light value, low chroma *R*, i.e. pale Pink.

A term recorded as *aqsyianaq*,[24] undoubtedly the same lexical item as the System B Gray = "ash color," was used by this informant for *Y* and *GY* light value 2 chips — which other informants invariably called Black or Blackish. The term *aqsyianaxuyuktuq* was given for two "outliers" in the light value 2 row of the Berlin-Kay Chart, one of these being in *YR*, the other in *BG*.

Pink seems to form (for want of a better descriptive term) an unconscious emergent named color term for the System C informant. The term *qutyuq* is used by him for very light pale Pink, for chips that would be termed pale or imperfect Red by other informants, i.e. would be designated by them by some term built on the *aupa-* stem.

Purple can hardly be said to be a conceptual category for any of the informants. But one System A informant did give "flesh-like" for the saturated light value 7, 8, and 9 chips of 7.5 *P*, 10 *P*, and 2.5 *RP*, and two other System A informants pointed to light Purple (violet) chips and said they had no name for that color.

LINGUISTIC CONSIDERATIONS

Except for Black and White, Central Eskimo terms are not monolexemic as defined by Berlin and Kay. All of the other principal color terms, with Blue possibly excepted, refer in a very "sensible," common-sense, manner to common and important entities of Eskimo daily life. Red, Yellow, and Green refer to body fluids. Blue may refer to an internal organ, the liver. Brown refers to a common and highly valued

[23] Sometimes recorded as *qutyu-*, sometimes as *kutyu-*. See note 22.
[24] Or *aksyianaq*. See note 22.

food item, blood soup. Gray refers to ashes. Unfortunately no ethno-etymological information was obtained for *siangnaq* and *qutyuq*.

In a descending order of complexity — which would not prove the Berlin-Kay evolutionary hypothesis, but which would add to its acceptability — Central Eskimo color words would seem to fall into an order that goes from etymological obscurity to morphological simplicity, from Black and White, through Red, Blue, Yellow, Green, Brown, and Gray.[25]

This progression is based on the paradigm $\underline{1}$ $\underline{(2)}$ $\underline{(3)}$ $\underline{(4...4n)}$ $\underline{5}$, where 1 represents the base, 2 an assimilated $\overline{\text{bound}}$ $\overline{\text{morpheme}}$, $\overline{3}$ an assimilated $-u-$ element, usually realized as $\underline{-suk-}$, $\underline{-yuk-}$, $\underline{-sux-}$, etc., (but sometimes also by some -a- containing morpheme), $4...\overline{4n}$ a number of penultimately added modifying bound morphemes used (as-*Riq*) for focal terms and for peripheral terms, and where 5 represents the *-tuq* ~ *-yuq* [it is] final verbalizer. Since the analysis can be carried out without reference to peripheral and focal terms, 4 will not be used, leaving the formula as $\underline{1}$, $\underline{(2)}$, $\underline{(3)}$, $\underline{5}$.[26]

For Red, both *aupalluktuq* and *aupayaxtuq* fill the rubric completely. $\dfrac{auk \rightarrow au\text{-}}{1} + \dfrac{p_a}{2} + \dfrac{-ya\text{-} \sim -luk}{3} + \dfrac{tuq}{5}$. The third element here, however, seems to be a very poor, contrived (by me) fit for the required $-u-$ element. But the basic forms in which Red appears do seem to have undergone a considerable amount (long period?) of "linguistic reworking."

The form that I judge to be most representative of Blue is *tunguxtuq*, $\dfrac{tungu\text{-}}{1} + \dfrac{(\text{0})}{2} + \dfrac{-yux\text{-}}{3} + \dfrac{-tuq}{5}$. The very considerable amount of variation that is found for *tungu-* terms may be related to the fact that this morpheme often "controls" such a wide spectral range (and, in fact, has two focal areas), but one might also refer to the case of Red where two forms seem to have developed out of the same base over an apparently long period of time.

Yellow, *quqsuxtuq*, always conforms to $\dfrac{quq}{1} + \dfrac{\text{0}}{2} + \dfrac{-sux\text{-}}{3} + \dfrac{-tuq}{5}$. Its regular occurrence among the Central Eskimos gives the impression that it has been established long enough to be stabilized, but not long enough to have been drastically "reworked" by linguistic processes.

---

[25] The ordering of the elements of the systems, however, does not bear this out. According to the Berlin-Kay formulation Brown should "emerge" only after Yellow, Blue, and Green have been fully differentiated, but in Systems A and B, this is not the case.

[26] Perhaps this should be $\underline{(5)}$. Gray terms sometimes appear as *aksialuq* and *siangnaq* and *aqsyianaq*.

Green is commonly found as both *sunguyuxtuq* (or *sungayuxtuq*) or *sunguxtuq* (or *sungaxtuq*). The first would have the pattern $\frac{sungu}{1}$ + $\frac{\emptyset}{2}$ + $\frac{-yux}{3}$ + $\frac{-tuq}{5}$, and the second would have the (more embryonic?) pattern of $\frac{sungu}{1}$ + $\frac{\emptyset}{2}$ + $\frac{\emptyset}{3}$ + $\frac{-tuq}{5}$.

The *qatcu*-allomorph of Brown is opaque to me, but *qayuxtuq* has the formula $\frac{qayu-}{1}$ + $\frac{\emptyset}{2}$ + $\frac{\emptyset}{3}$ + $\frac{-tuq}{5}$. And both common terms for Gray, *siangnaxtuq* and *aksialuktuq* appear to follow this pattern too, though both of these were often given without the *-tuq* ~ *-yuq* ending, i.e. as 1, $\emptyset$, $\emptyset$, $\emptyset$, a very "defective" (rudimentary?) form.

This has been a summary of my investigations, a presentation of data. Hopefully the theoretical formulations can now follow.

REFERENCES

BORNSTEIN, MARC H.
   1975   The influence of visual perception on culture. *American Anthropologist* 77:774–798.
HEINRICH, ALBERT C.
   1973   "Systematics of Canadian Eskimo colour terminology." Unpublished report submitted to the Canada Council.
   n.d.   "Some preliminary investigations on colour terminology and recognition among an Alemannisch speaking group in Venezuela." Unpublished report submitted to the Research Council of the University of Calgary.
RIVERS, W. H. R.
   1914   The colour vision of the Eskimos. *Proceedings of the RAI* 1914:143–149.

The Terminology of Time in Romanian

PAUL SCHVEIGER

0.1. The question of terminology, particularly that which is related to abstract phenomena, is a function of an ethnic group's conception about the given domain of reality, about the relationship between the denominated OBJECT and its name. The explanations given by a native speaker about his reasons for utilizing one term instead of another are, as a general rule, insignificant and vary with his degree of education.[1] The terminology of time — because of its relation to this essential aspect of reality — represents some language phenomena which reflect fundamental epistemological processes. In this limited field of the process of knowledge the distance between EMITTER and RECEIVER may be considered the most important factor.[2] Golopentia-Eretescu (1971: 289) showed in a recent paper that "stimulated in communication (and transmission), the emitter may not calculate the symptomatic implications (presuppositions) of his messages," and this situation explains — in our view — the peculiarities specified above. Our main interest in this paper is to outline our

The author wishes to acknowledge the great help of Professor Ion Pătruţ, Director of the Linguistics and Literary History Institute of the Academy of the Socialist Republic of Romania, in Cluj, who suggested the topic of this paper and who allowed us to use some of the unpublished materials of the Institute. Without any doubt, full responsibility for any errors must be attributed to the author.

[1] "... one function of culture and society is to provide grammatical norms corresponding to what the mature speaker should know" (Peizer and Olmsted 1969).
[2] In a work of ours (Schveiger f.c.) we tried to demonstrate that from a pragmatic point of view, besides the two poles EMITTER and RECEIVER we must also take into consideration the possibility of the difference between the RECEIVER and the ADDRESSEE, in which case distance may be not the best criterion for an understanding.

view of the analysis of the temporal continuum among Romanians, as this view is reflected by the corresponding terminology.[3]

We will use the following abbreviations:

ALR I: *Atlasul lingvistic român* [*The Romanian linguistic atlas*], containing the material collected by Sever Pop,

ALR II: *Atlasul lingvistic român*, containing the material collected by Emil Petrovici,

N: noun,	V: verb,
Art: article,	sg: singular,
Prep: preposition,	pl: plural,
Aj: adjective,	gen: genitive,
Num: numeral,	refl: reflexive,
Av: adverb,	L: language, and
Pron: pronoun,	T: time.

0.2. A special question is that of language as a twice articulated entity: the conveyance of the abstract notion (TIME, its NATURE and its EVOLUTION) and the analysis of this conveyance in its own development (Žolkiewski 1970: 6).

1.0. The nature of terminology in general (of time especially) is determined by additional elements: the relationship between the *signifié-signifiant* poles of the sign (Voinescu and Schveiger 1971), the conception of time belonging to the given speaker of L_i (a conception which represents in some way the taxonomic code's form for the domain formally determined by this terminology),[4] and the nature of the other terminological subsystems in L_i (in our situation of Romanian).

1.1. A first analysis of the terminology of time, as this terminology is represented by the ALR, allows us to establish the following taxonomic system: $T_1 =$ "terms which denominate units of time" (*lună* 'month', *ianuarie* 'January'), $T_2 =$ "terms for the evolution (modification) of units of time" (*se ivesc zorile* 'the morning is coming'), and $T_3 =$ "nature of time" (*după amiaza* 'the afternoon').

---

[3] It is known that B. L. Whorf thought that the speakers of SAE would have a spatialized vision of time. This idea was also taken into consideration in Bacon's *New organon* as the IDOLA FORI.

[4] See, e.g.: "Le fait est que la dénomination des objets du monde, à l'intérieur d'une langue donnée s'accompagne presque toujours d'une classification, qu'une sémiotique implicite s'est déjà chargée de découpage et de l'analyse de ce lopin du monde qu'elle recouvre" (Greimas 1970: 17).

2.0.   Analyzing the structure of T_1 we will come to the conclusion that it contains a series of forms:

(1) $\begin{cases}(N+Art)\\(N+\varnothing)\end{cases}$
lunia 'Monday', *noapte* 'night';

(2) $(Art+N)+\begin{cases}(Prep+N)\\\varnothing\end{cases}$
o secundă 'a second', *într-o clipă* 'in a second', *o secundă de minută* 'a second of a minute', *o jumătate de oră* 'a half of an hour';

(3) $(N+Art)+Aj$
anul trecut 'the last year';

(4) $\begin{cases}Num\\\varnothing\end{cases}+(N\begin{cases}sg\\pl\end{cases})+(Prep+N)$
un sfert de oră 'a quarter of an hour';

(5) $N+N_{gen}$
timpul anului 'the year's lasting';

(6) $Prep+N$
la prînz 'at noon';

(7) $Av+(\begin{cases}Art\\\varnothing\end{cases}+N)$
mai an, acu an 'last year';

(8) $N+(Pron_{gen}+N)$
luna lui cuptor 'the month of August' (word-by-word translation: 'the month of heat').

The great variation of possible forms to express these notions (with only a few exceptions, very precisely) shows the important stylistic mobility of those speaking Romanian (on the map, for some terms we have three to five different structural variants, to which we also have to add the phonetic variants). In the atlas they do not appear; however, we must mention some terms described by Bogrea (1971), such as *Zoriălă* and *Murgilă* instead of *Luceafărul de dimineață* 'the morning star' and *Luceafărul de seară* 'the evening star' respectively. In actual use, both are connected to the T_2 system.

2.1.   Most terms belonging to T_1 cover approximately the whole territory in which Romanian is spoken. In ALR II *secundă* 'second' is represented in the whole territory — with the exception of cartographic point 872 (*o secundă de minută* 'a second of a minute') and 704 (*într-o clipă* 'in a second') — by the lexical entry *secundă*; *o jumătate de oră* 'a half of an hour' has variants only in cartographic points 29, 141, and 235. (In ALR I the situation is pretty much the same — differences appear only with *timp* 'time', *iulie* 'July', and *august* 'August', etc.) The structural variations mentioned in 2.0. exist sometimes in the same cartographic points in ALR I and ALR II (if they were registered for both atlases).

2.2.   The terms in T_2 may be characterized as having a great semantic-syntactic dynamism (see also 3.2.), a fact which is also reflected by their structure. Analyzing them we found the following structural types:

(9) $\begin{cases} N + V_{refl} \\ V_{refl} + N \end{cases}$

zorile se ivesc, se ivesc zorile 'morning is coming';

(10) V_{refl}

(as a variant of (10)), *se întunecă* 'it becomes dark';

(11) $\begin{cases} V + N \\ N + V \\ V + \varnothing \end{cases}$

crapă zori, zorile ies 'it becomes morning', *răsare* '(the sun) is rising';

(12) $V_{refl} + (Prep + N)$

se luminează de ziuă 'it becomes daylight';

(13) $N + Prep + N$

zori de ziuă 'morning';

(14) $Prep + N + Prep + N$

în vărsat de zori 'in the very morning';

(15) $V + V$

începe a întuneci 'it begins to be dark'.

It was Bogrea who remarked that from the pattern (11), e.g. *a apune soarele* 'the sun's setting', the speakers used *apune* 'sets', and wrote: "For the 'sun's going down' the Romanian terminology is richer than for its rising."[5]

2.2.1.   The distribution of the terms covering the territory where Romanian is spoken and belonging to the system T_2, is less uniform than

[5] "Pentru «apsul soarelui», nomenclatura românească e mai bogată ca pentru răsăritul lui" (Bogrea 1971: 141).

that of the terms belonging to T_1 (see also 2.1), although the structure of T_2 (as a whole) is less varied but more complex. In this terminological group we have very few terms — *se crapă de ziuă* 'the day begins' (ALR II), *soarele răsare* 'the sun rises' (ALR I) — to cover the whole or almost the whole) territory of the Romanian language.

2.3.   Categories T_1 and T_2 also include elements determining T_3: as a general rule the terms in T_1 and T_2 are modified in T_3. Thus *amiază* 'noon' and *seară* 'evening' from T_1 appear in T_3: *după amiază* 'afternoon' etc., but there are also forms which are lexically very different: *după amiază* 'afternoon' is also represented as *cînd toacă popa* 'when the priest makes the bell ring'. As a consequence, the structure of T_3 is varied and sometimes becomes elliptic: *răsalaltăieri* 'two days before yesterday' is represented (in ALR II) as *nailaltă* (approximately 'in the other'). In this category appears an extremely frequent element in the composed terms: the adverb and the adverbial expressions.

2.3.1.   As a consequence of the discussion above (mostly of the facts in 2.3.), we can see that the territorial spreading of terms in T_3 is distinct from the territorial representation of both T_1 and T_2. In ALR I for *după amiază* 'afternoon', there exist nine distinct representations; for *poi-poimîine* 'two days after tomorrow', eleven; etc. In ALR II *răsalaltăieri* 'two days before yesterday' has five representations, and *în zori de zi* 'in the very morning' has four different representations.

3.0.   In order to obtain a better understanding of the phenomenon, we have to make a semantic-syntactic analysis of the terms in T_1–T_3.

3.1.   The category of terms in T_1 is represented in ALR I by lexical entries and expressions which may be considered as being relatively simple; among them we found only one expression with a peculiar stylistic feature: *decembrie* 'December' known in the west of the country also as *luna lupilor* 'the month of the wolves'. In ALR II the situation is even simpler: the very few expressions of T_1 that exist are stylistically unmarked.

3.2.   A similar analysis of the lexicon determined by T_2 shows that this ensemble of the Romanian language (naturally) has a mostly predicative nature and — as a consequence — the stylistic values are more marked: *se lasă soarele* 'the sun sets'. The terms which constitute this category represent the speaker's attitude toward the notion of TIME, mostly in its real function: the running, the display. At the same time the marked stylistic values of these terms show a certain tendency towards personifying some objects connected with TIME: the sun, the stars, and the moon.

3.3.   As we have seen above (2.3.), $t_i \in T_3$ are structurally and semantically the most complicated forms: within the framework of this category both the structural simplicity (isolated words and nonpredicative expressions) characteristic of T_1, and the predicativity characteristic of $t_j \in T_2$ are represented. Within T_3 — a static category — we also find predicative syntagms: *după amiaza* 'the afternoon' is characterized by some speakers as *dă soarele în seară* 'the sun goes into the evening', or *în amurg* 'twilight' is represented as *în amurgu serii* 'in the evening's twilight', etc.

4.0.   In conclusion we have to show that — in general — in the territory where Romanian is spoken in each semantic field of a T_i we have a dominant term T_i. As a general rule, in the territory the dominant T_i is structurally the simplest one and semantically the least ambiguous. We studied fifty-four terms, belonging to the three categories (described in 1.1.), that we found in ALR I and ALR II (there are also terms that appear in both atlases). Twenty-three of them have a nonuniform territory (for a given notion, different lexical entries appear on the map of Romania). In the case of these areas only a few terms determine a more or less close zone in the territory of the analyzed atlases.

5.0.   The above description of facts about the surface structure of Romanian allows us to observe some centripetal forces in terminology of time, forces that are accompanied by some other centrifugal forces, which have predominant stylistic functions. With only a very few exceptions this terminology is precise and the described variants do not impede the understanding of the message based on the utilization of this terminology. The extremely important influence of the standard language upon the speakers of colloquial Romanian greatly reduces the role of geographical (nonstylistic) peculiarities in the terminology of time in Romanian. This fact is probably due to the role of the given NOTION, which is a determining parameter of existence and, as a consequence, of knowledge.

REFERENCES

BOGREA, VASILE
   1971   "Semantism românesc și semantism balcanic [Romanian and Balkan semantics]," in *Paginia istorico-filologice* [Historico-philological papers]. Edited by M. Borcilă and I. Mării. Cluj: Dacia.

GOLOPENTIA-ERETESCU, SANDA
  1971 Explorări semiotice [Semiotic explorations]. *Studii şi Cercetări de Lingvistică* 22:285–289.
GREIMAS, A. J.
  1970 "Sémantique, sémiotique et sémiologies," in *Sign, language, culture.* Edited by A. Greimas, et al. The Hague: Mouton.
PEIZER, D. B., D. L. OLMSTED
  1969 Models of grammar acquisition. *Language* 45:60.
SCHVEIGER, PAUL
  f.c. *Patologia vorbirii* [The pathology of speech].
VOINESCU, I., P. SCHVEIGER
  1971 Receptive aspects in the "signifiant-signifié" relationship. *Revue Roumaine de Linguistique* 16:499–507.
ŽOLKIEWSKI, S.
  1970 "Deux structuralismes," in *Sign, language, culture.* Edited by A. Greimas, et al. The Hague: Mouton.

"Meaning" for the Linguist and "Meaning" for the Anthropologist

YOSHIHIKO IKEGAMI

1.   The discussion of the nature of linguistic meaning seems to revolve around three pairs of contrasting dimensions: (a) psychologism *versus* physicalism, (b) concrete instance *versus* sum *versus* common feature, and (c) something that is meaning *versus* something that stands in contiguous relation to meaning.

a.   PSYCHOLOGISM *versus* PHYSICALISM.   A typically psychologistic position is represented by a view which holds that the meaning of a linguistic item is the "image" that it evokes in the speaker's (or hearer's) mind. This is, for example, a view discussed and rejected by Sapir (1921: 10–12). It is so vulnerable (e.g. through the problems of individual differences, of irrelevant images, of words that evoke no image, of the impossibility of objective testing, etc.) that no scholar seems ever to have supported it with seriousness. Other varieties of the psychologistic approach consider the meaning of a linguistic item as the "thought" or "idea" evoked by it. Although these approaches are certainly capable of disposing of some of the difficulties encountered by the "image" theory (e.g. one can have a "thought" or "idea" about a word that may evoke no particular image), many of the charges directed at the "image" theory remain applicable to the other psychologistic theories as well.
   A typically physicalist position is represented by a view which holds that the meaning of a linguistic item is the "thing" to which it refers. This view, while aiming to attain a degree of objectivity that cannot be expected of the psychologistic one, is itself not free from a number of its own particular difficulties — difficulties which seem to suggest that the

"thing" (or "referent") is not the same as the "meaning": e.g. expressions which have one and the same referent but whose meanings are clearly different ("the morning star" *versus* "the evening star"), expressions whose referents may change while their meanings remain the same ("the largest city in the world"), expressions which have no concrete referent (*the*), and the fact that all the knowledge about the referent is not necessarily relevant in ensuring the correct use of the linguistic item that refers to it (NaCl for *salt*). Other varieties of the physicalist position view the meaning of a linguistic item as the "response" that it elicits in the hearer or as the "situation" in which it is used. In an earnest pursuit of some objective entity that would stand for meaning, all these approaches have ended up by identifying the linguistic meaning with something that it really is not.

b.   CONCRETE INSTANCE *versus* SUM *versus* COMMON FEATURE.   Each of the three choices of this second dimension can combine with either of the two choices of the first dimension. Take the "image" theory, for example. We can first define the meaning of a linguistic item as the particular image that it evokes in the speaker's (or hearer's) mind on a particular occasion. Second, we can define it as the sum total of all the particular images evoked by the linguistic item in all its particular uses. Third, we can define it as the features common to all the images evoked on various occasions.

The first position implies that there will be an infinite number of different meanings for any of the linguistic items in the language; it will lead to a conclusion that there is no such thing as "meaning," thus failing to see something constant behind apparent diversity. The second position turns meaning into something inapproachable, in that any linguistic item can be used again and again, and it will therefore be impossible to reach a stage where we are in possession of all the instances of the use of a linguistic item. Unlike these two positions, which are concerned with surface semantic phenomena, the third position proposes to see some unifying principles behind fluctuating surface phenomena. The problem here, however, is whether it will ever be possible to obtain a "typical image" that would consist of the features common to all of the particular images. Given the possibility of a whole range of individual differences (including possible irrelevant images), it is not very likely that we will be able to arrive at something that we will agree to call the "typical image" (cf. Brown 1958 : 85–89).

The same tripartite division will apply to any of the physicalist views. Recall, for example, an attempt to define the meaning of a linguistic item as "the SUM TOTAL of the linguistic contexts in which it occurs" (Hill 1961 : 466) or as "the FEATURE COMMON to all the situations in which it is used" (Bloch and Trager 1942 : 6).[1] We will later argue that the common features, even if they could be successfully defined, could not possibly be identified with meaning.

c. SOMETHING THAT IS MEANING *versus* SOMETHING THAT STANDS IN CONTIGUOUS RELATION TO MEANING. Among the widely diversified approaches to meaning, we can perhaps distinguish between those seeking to define something that is meaning and those looking for something that is contiguous to meaning and letting it stand for "meaning." An assumption behind the latter approach is that meaning itself can never be identifiable and all we can hope for, therefore, will be to substitute for it something related to it that is more easily subject to empirical observation. This orientation is characteristic of those who try to identify "meaning" with such things as linguistic contexts, situations, responses, paradigmatic semantic relationships (Lyons 1968 : 427), associated linguistic items, etc. On the other hand, those who posit such things as images, thoughts or ideas, concepts, and referents as possible candidates for meaning may be understood as presenting them as something that is meaning.

2. Whence all these diversified approaches and the difficulties confronting each of them? An answer — one which will remind us of a point often missed — is that the functions of linguistic items as "signs" are not uniform. Compare words like *John, dog, idea, large, good, walk, think, can, do* (auxiliary), *he, this, the, a, and, but, on, for, oh,* etc. Some may evoke a mental image, while some others will not. Some again may refer to a concrete thing, while some others will not. Some may elicit an overt response, while some others will not.[2] The important point we have to bear in mind is that the linguistic signs form a rather heterogeneous group in terms of the semiotic functions they perform.

The functional heterogeneity of linguistic signs is what is naturally expected if we consider the uses to which they are put. Suppose we have an (extralinguistic) event that we have to report verbally. We have, of course, to report who or what the participants are, what their

---

[1] The same authors, however, admit that to define such a feature is "obviously an impossible task."

[2] We can also refer to Morris's classification of signs into "identifiers," "designators," "appraisers," "prescriptors," and "formators" according to their different functions (cf. Morris 1946: Chapter 3).

performances are, and in what roles they make their performances. We may also be interested in reporting what the attributes of the participants are or the circumstances under which the event takes place. We may further want to express our attitudes or feelings toward what takes place or, if the event consists of still smaller events, what the relations (logical, temporal) among them are. Which feature to select as "topic" (or "theme") must also be considered. All these aspects will naturally require different kinds of linguistic signs that are functionally diversified.

3.   The foregoing discussion has shown that it would be futile to look for a general definition of the meaning of a linguistic item in such things as "images," "responses," "concrete referents," and so on, which are only uncertain contingencies on the use of a linguistic item. These things may or may not be relevant in defining the meaning of each individual linguistic item. A general definition of linguistic meaning, however, must be made in broader terms, over and above these contingent circumstances.

Perhaps we can approach the problem of the definition of meaning in a profitable way by analyzing what is involved when we say that an ideal speaker "knows the meaning" of a linguistic item. Take the case of a man who is thrown into a society whose language he does not know. At first, although he may well understand that some sort of linguistic communication is going on around him among the native members of the society, he does not understand what is being meant by the linguistic expressions that he hears. He does not even understand which sequences of sounds are the units that carry meaning in that language. In short, he does NOT KNOW THE MEANINGS of the linguistic items used by the native members. He may, however, get used to their language bit by bit and, after a certain period of time, may reach a stage where he not only can understand it but also use it himself in a way that is understandable to the natives. He now KNOWS THE MEANINGS of the linguistic items in the language.

Now when is it that we can say that he KNOWS THE MEANING of a certain linguistic item? Suppose the linguistic item in question is the English word *boy* (in its most usual sense). He cannot be said to know the meaning of the word if he applies the word to a female child, an old male, or a puppy or kitten. If he does so, he is said to use the word incorrectly. The possibility of judging his linguistic behavior in terms of being correct or incorrect implies that "meaning" is something that lies behind the whole rule-governed activity called language. Thus "meaning," like "syntax," which is far better studied as a systematized set of rules, can be thought of as a set of rules (or directions) or, if the words "rules" and "directions" are too strong, conditions as to the use of a linguistic item. If we use a linguistic item in a way which agrees with such rules (or which satisfies such conditions), then we use it correctly and we will be judged as KNOWING ITS MEANING. Such meaning rules differ from the syntactic rules, however, in that they, ideally, involve reference to some part of the whole extralinguistic universe about which we can talk, while the syntactic rules are concerned, ideally, with the relations between linguistic items.

Let us consider some concrete examples and explore the further implications of the above definition. A speaker of English knows the meanings of the words *hat* and *cap*, that is, he knows how to use each of these words in a way that is acceptable to other speakers. Above all, he must know under what conditions he can use the word *hat* but not *cap*, or vice versa. If we want to specify these conditions, we will probably have to make some sort of reference to the physical SHAPE of the object in question (i.e. the existence or nonexistence of a brim). Or if the words in question are *coin* and *bill*, for example, the crucial conditions permitting the use of one but not the other will involve some reference to the MATERIAL of which the object is made. Similarly, in order to state the meanings of such pairs as *foot* and *leg*, and *pig* and *pork*, for example, reference will have to be made to the PART of the human body in which the object is found and to the condition or STATE of having been, or not having been, treated so as to serve as food, respectively.

Notice that the cases we have so far discussed relate to something that is physically observable, but the conditions for use will also very often involve reference to something that may not be immediately observable. Consider the conditions for use of words like *table* and *desk*. It is neither the material, nor even the shape, of the objects that is relevant to their correct use. What has to be taken into account is, rather, the USE to which the object is put: one usually reads, writes, or does business at a desk, while customarily food is served on a table. Or take *smoke* and *steam*. One cannot possibly tell whether it is smoke or steam unless one knows (or believes one knows) how it is CAUSED. If we enlarge the range of our examples to verbs, adjectives, and other parts of speech, we will readily notice that the conditions for their use will cover a very wide range of things which may vary from one case to another.

4.   Whatever the features are that constitute the conditions for use

(identified as meaning) of a linguistic item, they are supposed to be learned by all those who use the language. A fairly long process of learning will be undergone by one who is born into that community as well as by one who is thrown into that society after having acquired a different language as his native language. Because, as we have seen, some of the features that count are not directly observable, we can readily imagine that the process of learning is not an easy one: a number of false starts and wrong conclusions are naturally expected which are to be corrected only at some later stage.

This process of learning the relevant conditions for the use of a linguistic item finds analogues in other aspects of our social life. The situation is similar when we learn the use of a tool. Although we have a variety of cutting tools, each is distinguished from the others in terms of what it is used to cut and how it cuts. Thus, knives, razors, scissors, swords, etc. are all cutting instruments, but we do not usually use a sword, for example, for cutting fried fish (unless in an emergency), and if we do so out of place, there will be some sort of social sanction (e.g. laughs, derision), just as when we use a word in an inappropriate way. The parallelism between a tool and a word is also reflected in the fact that we can say "we USE a word" just as we say "we USE a tool." Just as each tool has its own proper uses defined for it, so each word has its own proper conditions for use defined for it. A tool and a word thus have a "goal-oriented" character in common. Notice, however, we do say the "meaning" of a word, but not the "meaning" of a tool. The reason for this is simple: a tool, unlike a linguistic item, is not a "sign." Not being a sign, a tool cannot have a meaning as a word does.

Another comparable situation involves social manners. For each particular act of social behavior (i.e. a specific "manner") the occasions on which it should be observed are defined, and these occasions may differ from one particular behavioral act to another. In the Western countries, for example, there is a set of definite rules on when and how the shaking of hands is performed; in some Oriental countries, there are various degrees of bowing, which one is expected to be able to perform on appropriate occasions. Note that, unlike in the case for tools, we cannot say "we USE shaking hands or bowing" (unless referring to a perverted occasion like an election campaign), but it is possible to talk about the "meaning" of shaking hands or bowing (which can roughly be characterized as a manifestation of friendliness or respect). The difference stems from the fact that social manners, unlike tools, are "signs," although as signs their functions are severely restricted as compared with linguistic items. The function of social manners may in general be characterized as the expression of certain kinds of feelings or attitudes on the part of the subject, but such an "expression-oriented" function of social manners covers only a part of the far wider range of functions that language is capable of performing.

Thus, although there are obviously both similarities and dissimilarities between words and tools or between words and social manners, the comparison will at least help to clarify the concept of "conditions for use," which, I think, is crucial to defining what linguistic meaning is. One has to learn the conditions for use with respect to words, just as one has to learn the conditions under which a certain tool may be used or certain social manners should be observed.

5.   Now let us consider more closely the nature of these conditions with regard to language. It would obviously not be the case that each new situation in which we encounter a linguistic item would be individually listed and memorized by us as another new condition under which its use is authorized. If such were the case, any linguistic item would be characterized by infinite polysemy, and from this it would then follow that we could never reasonably be expected to master the use of any linguistic item in our finite life span or that we might be unable to guess the meaning of even a familiar linguistic item if it occurred in a situation that was novel to us. Obviously this does not agree with what we know about language.

An alternative view, which is apparently very attractive, is that we extract from what we observe about the situations in which a linguistic item is used a set of features by which they are commonly characterized; these features will be listed as conditions for the use of the linguistic item in question. This view is free from the undesirable consequence of having to posit infinite polysemy for each linguistic item; it can also account for the process of extrapolation we use when trying to guess the meaning of a familiar linguistic item occurring in a novel situation. But do the common situational features (apart from the obvious practical difficulty of defining them) really constitute the necessary and sufficient conditions for the use of a linguistic item (and hence its "meaning")? The answer to this is both "yes" and "no." The point is that some of those features are relevant to linguistic meaning and some are not.

Consider the word *man*. We know a number of features that commonly characterize the creatures to which the word *man* applies: e.g. "having a head," "having two arms," "having a limited life span," "being capable of walking upright," etc. Must a linguist, when describing the meaning of the word *man*, assign to the word a feature like [mortal], for example? We will intuitively feel that something would be wrong with such a treatment. As part of the linguistic meaning of the word *man*, the feature [mortal] would be felt somehow as irrelevant. The feeling of irrelevancy would certainly be still greater with such features as "breathing," "eats food," "needs sleep," and the like. Or to give another trivial example, everyone will agree that trees do not talk as men do. Must we, therefore, assign a feature [incapable of talking] to the word *tree* as part of its LINGUISTIC meaning? Enough examples can easily be quoted to show that the features which are commonly found for a set of things referred to by a word are not necessarily significant as part of the linguistic meaning of the word.

Why is it that some common features are not felt to be relevant as part of the meaning of a linguistic item? What about the feature [mortal] for the word *man*? The feature [mortal] is felt to be irrelevant because it does not function as a DISTINCTIVE FEATURE: that is, there is no word in English whose conditions for use are the same as those of *man* except that it has [immortal] where the word *man* has [mortal]. Let us imagine a case like the following. Suppose in some distant future there should arise on earth a new species of man whose life span is unlimited. Suppose further that a new word X is coined to refer to this new species, which is distinct from the traditional mortal beings referred to by the word *man*. The feature [mortal], then, would have to be mentioned in the statement of meaning of the word *man*, because this feature serves to distinguish the meaning of *man* from that of X.

Or consider the feature [incapable of talking] for the word *tree*. This feature does not carry any distinctive function for the linguistic item *tree* — that is, there is no word in English whose conditions for use are the same as those of *tree* except that it has the feature [capable of talking] where the latter has [incapable of talking]. Suppose, however, that there should arise a strange new type of tree that could talk (whatever "talking" means) and a new word Y were coined to refer to it. In this situation, [incapable of talking] would have to be included in the list of features to be assigned to the word *tree*, because it would then carry a distinctive function for the word.

The meaning of a linguistic item is, then, constituted by those conditions that serve to distinguish its use from the use of any other linguistic item that may contrast with it. It is just these conditions that are to be described by the linguist. To be familiar with these conditions is part of the linguistic competence of the ideal speaker of the language; unless we know these conditions, we will not be able to use the linguistic items in an appropriate way. Notice, however, that these conditions are not exactly the same as the features common to all the situations in which the word is used. The former constitute only a subset of the latter. The rest do not belong to the LINGUISTIC competence in an ideal form; they are rather part of the knowledge that the speaker may have about what is referred to by the linguistic item.

6.   Perhaps a consideration of a hypothetical example like the following will help to make clearer what is meant by the distinction between knowledge about the language and knowledge about the referent. What I propose to do is to give several hypothetical cases in which reference is made to the head of a state and to consider the manner in which each of these four cases is to be described from the linguist's point of view. We will make use of the three English words, *monarch*, *king*, and *queen*, to refer to three possible ways of referring to the head of a state (i.e. for either male or female, for male, and for female) in the hypothetical languages to be considered below, and we will posit three semantic features, [head of state], [male], and [female], in terms of which these words are to be described in each case.[3]

a.   The first language has only one word, *monarch*, to refer to the head of state, and in this country either a male or a female can become the head of state. Then the linguistic description to be given in the dictionary of this hypothetical language will be:

monarch: [head of state].

The fact that a monarch in this country may be either male or female belongs to the extralinguistic knowledge, perhaps to be mentioned in the encyclopedia of this nation.

b.   The second language has only one word, *monarch*, to refer to the head of state, and in this country only a male can become the head of state. Then the linguistic description to be given in the dictionary of this language will be:

monarch: [head of state] (N.B. NOT [head of state] + [male]).

The fact that only a male can become the head of state belongs to the extralinguistic knowledge.

c.   The third language has two words, *king* and *queen*, to refer to the

---

[3]   We will assume that these three words are applied only to the sovereign of the nation in question and not to a foreign sovereign.

head of state. Either a male or a female can become the head of state in this country, and either of these two words is used, depending on the sex of the head of state. Then the linguistic description to be given in the dictionary of this language will be:

king: [head of state] + [male], and
queen: [head of state] + [female].

The feature regarding sex must be specified here, because it serves to distinguish the use of one word from the other.

d.   The fourth language has two words, *king* and *queen*, to refer to a male and a female head of state, respectively. Actually, however, only a male can currently become a monarch in this country. (That is, there may have been a time when a female was able to become one, but it is not customary any longer. The word *queen* is still retained in case it is used in a historical account, etc.) The description to be given in the dictionary of this language will be:

king: [head of state] + [male], and
queen: [head of state] + [female].

The fact that there is currently no possibility of having a queen belongs to the extralinguistic knowledge.

As a series of examples like the above shows, one and the same feature may be distinctive in one case but not in another. The criterion for choosing one decision over the other is "opposition." If the conditions for use of the two words A and B are the same except either for the presence of an additional feature [X] for A and the absence of the same feature for B, or for the presence of an additional feature [X] for A and the presence of an additional feature [X'] for B (where [X] and [X'] stand and contrast on the same dimension), then [X] is a distinctive feature for A (and, for that matter, [X'] is a distinctive feature for B in the latter case). It is only the features carrying distinctive functions that are to be specified in a statement of linguistic meaning. This is "meaning" for the linguist.

7.   Consider what would happen if we did not introduce the notion of functional opposition in defining the meaning of a linguistic item. There would probably be no limit to the number of semantic features that would have to be specified for a given linguistic item. The word *man* would have to be assigned all such various features as we have cited

already (e.g. [mortal]); moreover, the list of assigned features would have to be expanded as new discoveries were made about the nature of man in biology, physiology, anthropology, philosophy, and any other academic fields. This would be a consequence of the misdirected attempt to describe the meaning of a linguistic item without reference to the semantic structure of the language and to substitute for it the knowledge about the object referred to by the linguistic item.

Another undesirable consequence is that without referring to the notion of linguistic opposition it would be impossible to decide whether or not a certain feature could be considered as a legitimate unit in the semantic system of the language. The feature [mortal] obviously can be divided into still smaller units ([destined] + [to] + [die], for example, some of which can be further divided), and it may appear uncertain whether we should keep [mortal] as it is or should further subdivide it. Only a reference to the linguistic structure will give us a reasonable answer. If a certain feature carries a distinctive function in the linguistic structure in question, then it must be cited as a significant semantic unit in the language, irrespective of whether or not it is a minimal element from a logical point of view.

8.   The foregoing discussion has, I hope, made clear what it is that the linguist should aim to describe as the meaning of a linguistic item. A logical question that may arise here is why it is that, apart from those linguistic items whose functions are mainly grammatical,[4] and also from such a lexical field as kinship terminology, many linguistic items seem to be so resistant to semantic analysis. It is certainly not clear, for example, what features we should assign to a word like *water*, even if we know that to define the meaning of *water* in the daily language as H_2O would be misleading.[5]

The explanation for this is very simple. *Water* is a linguistic item that contrasts with so many other linguistic items in so many dimensions. Compare it with the case of the kin term, *father*. *Father* is contrasted with *mother* in the dimension of sex, with *son* in the dimension of generation, and with *uncle* in the dimension of lineality; but this is just about all that needs to be specified to account for (or to predict correctly) the uses of the kin term *father*. The situation is not so simple for *water*. It may contrast with such words as *ice, vapor, wine, oil* and

[4]   There is an analysis of mine of the English verbs denoting locomotion (Ikegami 1970).
[5]   Compare the discussion of the meaning of the word *water* as a chemical term in section 9 below.

less perfectly with many other words (for which it may not even be easy to decide with certainty whether they contrast with *water* at all).

This complexity in the structure of oppositional relationships, together with the vagueness of dimensions of contrast, makes it particularly difficult to define a complete set of semantic features for a number of linguistic items in the language. Notice that the difficulty arises from the inherent characteristics of the semantic system of the language and no theory, however complete, can be expected to produce a clear-cut description.

9.   This difficulty of describing the meanings of many linguistic items has a twofold implication. On the one hand, it accounts for the fact that different individuals may often understand the meaning of one and the same linguistic item in different ways. This does not mean, however, that we have to go back to a traditional subjectivist view of meaning. Notice that what differs is only the degree to which individual speakers are acquainted with the meaning of a linguistic item. Meaning itself "exists," in the sense in which a code for social manners can be said to exist, at a social level over and above individual differences. Meaning, understood in this way, is something "objective," but objective in an entirely different sense from that in which Bloomfield may have meant it.

Asserting the difficulty of describing linguistic meaning, on the other hand, may seem to conflict with the fact that most adult speakers are nonetheless able to use the linguistic items with sufficient appropriateness. The discrepancy here cannot be attributed wholly to the difference between the speaker's "unconscious" control of his linguistic competence and the "conscious" character of the linguist's analysis of it. As we have already hinted, many linguistic items are likely to resist an exact analysis even when the linguist's analytic methodology is much better than it is now. The explanation for this must be sought elsewhere. What is actually happening is that the speaker may substitute certain nondistinctive features for distinctive ones. Of course, a mere substitution of only one nondistinctive feature for a distinctive one will not help to guarantee the correct use of the linguistic item in question; but if a considerable number of nondistinctive features are made use of, it is quite possible that together they will succeed in uniquely identifying the correct referent.

This is exactly what is happening with children in a more or less imperfect way. A child may contrast a man with a woman in terms of the former wearing trousers and the latter wearing a skirt. Wearing trousers or a skirt is by itself clearly neither a necessary nor a sufficient condition on the basis of which to distinguish a man from a woman; but when the child brings in other observable features of either a man or a woman (e.g. differences in dress, in hair style, in the kinds of work they do, etc.), then all these features taken together, even if each one of them is nondistinctive individually, may still serve the purpose just as well as a set of linguistically defined distinctive features. Moreover, certain features may happen to be referentially distinctive. Thus, certain physical shapes and physiological functions can very well serve to distinguish a man from a woman, and children (and, for that matter, adults, too, though perhaps to a lesser extent) may use them as criteria for correctly applying the words *man* and *woman*. (Linguists, however, will not mark the word *woman* as [having breasts], [capable of bearing a child], etc., because they know that there are features that are more GENERALLY applicable and that serve their purpose better.)[6]

If we accept this, we not only will have no need to worry about the discrepancy of the sort mentioned above, but we also will be able to conceive of the process of learning linguistic meaning as a series of gradual stages in which a large number of nondistinctive features (including those which happen to be distinctive within a very limited range of application) of the early periods of learning get replaced by fewer and more select distinctive ones with more general applicability. The former are very often concerned with immediately observable contingent features, while the latter are often abstract ones that become apparent only after the oppositional relationships in paradigmatic structures are considered (and hence require higher intellectual operations on the part of the subject). It is well known that the early dominance of the association through contiguity (e.g. *white – snow*) is followed by a gradual increase in the association through similarity (e.g. *white — black*) in the child's mental development.

10. Consider, on the basis of the notion of meaning set forth above, the problem of the meaning of proper names and technical terms. Either of these two categories of linguistic items has certain peculiarities from a semantic point of view. Is it possible to define a set of conditions

---

[6] Another example. The feature [capable of laying eggs] can serve to distinguish between the use of the linguistic item *hen* and that of the linguistic item *rooster*, just as the feature [capable of bearing a child] can help to distinguish between the uses of *man* and *woman*. Rather than accept these as linguistically significant distinctive features, the linguist, as is well known, sets up a feature like [female], because by doing so he can account for a much wider range of data in a significant way.

under which the use of the linguistic item *John* is distinguished from the use of another linguistic item *Bill* in the language? The answer is obviously "no," because it would be absurd to think that those persons named *John* have some inherent characteristics that make it appropriate for them to be called *John* rather than, say, *Bill*. (Note that we are considering the matter from the viewpoint of the linguistic system as a whole and not discussing a particular situation in which *John* refers to a particular person and *Bill* to another. It is well known that the confusion in this respect has often led to many a fruitless discussion based on misunderstanding.) If we further consider the fact that *John* can be applied not only to a male person (as is its usual use) but also theoretically to just about anything (including an inanimate thing), then we will have to conclude that it is impossible to define a set of conditions on the basis of which the linguistic item *John* is applied to a certain set of objects but not to others. This is the explanation, from our point of view, of the dictum that "a proper name has no meaning."

Next, consider the meaning of the word *water* used as a technical term in chemistry. In this capacity, *water* refers to a compound of hydrogen and oxygen, represented as H_2O. From the chemical point of view, "water" in this sense is distinguished from "nitric acid," "hydrochloric acid," "sulfuric acid," and a host of other substances. Hence, as a technical word, the meaning of *water* must be defined as "H_2O." Here the use of *water* as a technical term is completely determined by the definition given to the substance to which the term is applied. What we have is the convergence of knowledge about the language with knowledge about the extralinguistic object. This is characteristic of what we call "technical terms."

11.   Some discussion will be in order here in considering the implications of our notion. First, there is the problem of its relevance to the relation between language and thought or between language and culture. Distinctive features, in the sense in which we are talking of them, are something that the speaker must learn in order that he may be able to use the linguistic items correctly. They are the features that the speaker cannot disregard with impunity. These features are, therefore, very likely to claim the special attention of the speaker, and to that extent they may control the speaker's way of viewing the world. Thus, a speaker of a language that has one word to refer to an elder brother and another to refer to a younger one will, unlike the speaker of a language in which seniority is not a distinctive feature, always have to pay attention to seniority when talking about a brother. The speaker of

a language that has just one word to refer to either can remain comparatively inattentive to the same distinction.

A distinctive feature, either by itself or in conjunction with some other distinctive features, may constitute a unit of meaning that is realized as one lexical item in the language. Just what feature or features constitute such a unit is also part of what the speaker must learn in order that he may use the language in an appropriate way, and to that extent again the feature may control the way the speaker views the extralinguistic world. It will also be very reasonable to suppose that language provides a lexical item to represent a set of features that it finds culturally worth crystallizing as a unit. Hence the fact that one language has a single lexical item to represent something while another can represent it only by means of periphrasis may have certain cultural implications. (Or even if such cultural implications have been blurred in the historical development of the language, the structural differences between the two languages will still require different ways of getting the attention of the speakers.)

The last argument implies that it is necessary to recognize as legitimate linguistic units those sets of features that can be realized as single lexical items, even though it is theoretically perfectly possible to dispense with such units and describe the meanings in terms of what seem to be ultimate semantic units (just as the phonemes can be done away with in preference to an analysis in terms of phonological distinctive features). The latter treatment would fail to do justice to the cultural implications that might be involved in the structural differences among languages.

12.   We have so far tried to elaborate the concept of meaning from the linguist's point of view. It may very well seem to the anthropologist that the linguist's notion of meaning as set forth in the above is too narrowly constrained. He will probably feel that the distinction between knowledge about language and knowledge about the extralinguistic referent is not essential. He will not be content merely to know what the features are that carry distinctive functions within the framework of the language in question; he will also be interested in knowing everything that the speaker thinks of or feels when he uses a linguistic item. Thus, although the feature [mortal] is certainly irrelevant to the description of the linguistic meaning of the word *man*, the anthropologist will find it very important to know whether or not the members of a given social group believe in the immortality of man. Similarly, the anthropologist would certainly be interested in the "superstitious"

idea of a tribe that believes trees can "talk," even if the capability of talking does not bear any linguistically defined distinctive function in the language of the same tribe.

Let us consider some examples of a different sort.[7] Suppose someone has uttered a sentence, "John cooked" (or, more precisely, its equivalent), in a society in which no male is supposed to cook. What can a linguist say about this sentence? Should he mark the sentence as anomalous in his description? Now suppose that the language has two verbs, *cook* and *X*, the former used for a female and the latter for a male. (Naturally, the verb *X* would occur in exceptional cases, for example, when the taboo is being talked about.) In that case, the sentence would, and should, be marked as linguistically anomalous. But suppose that the language has only one verb, *cook*, and there is no contrast with respect to difference in the sex of the agent. Then the sentence will not, and theoretically cannot, be marked as anomalous by the linguist, because linguistically *cook* is not marked as requiring a female agent. It is only after the interpreter brings in some relevant pieces of extra-linguistic information that he can judge the sentence as referring to something strange.

Compare that case with that of the sentence "John gave birth to a child." If we feel the strangeness of this sentence more readily than the previous one, it is simply because the male's incapability of bearing a child is a biological fact that is established over and above the cultural differences among the various social groups. We have here more readily at hand the relevant information that will help us judge that the sentence refers to something strange.

Between such a biologically determined fact, which counts as something universal, on the one hand, and a culturally determined fact, which applies only to a very small social group, on the other hand, there may be a number of intermediate stages.[8] But the situation is essentially no different. The linguist is interested in the value of a linguistic item as determined by the position it occupies within the whole linguistic system. To the anthropologist, on the other hand, the linguistic structure serves only as a guide to a further understanding of the culture, and he will not, and should not, feel himself bound by purely linguistic considerations. The clear recognition of this fundamental difference will help avoid unnecessary misunderstandings among

[7]   The following examples are adapted from Lyons (1968: 479). We assume that *John* is assigned the feature [male] in the language.

[8]   Consider further a case like *these man*, whose anomaly is apparent without referring to any extralinguistic fact.

linguists, linguistically oriented anthropologists, and socially oriented anthropologists. Thus, for example, consider the controversy over the semantic analysis of kinship terminology (cf. Lounsbury 1969). Those anthropologists who try a "componential analysis" of the kinship terms are applying a purely linguistic technique; they are interested in defining the kin terms strictly in terms of distinctive features. On the other hand, those who emphasize the importance of considering the social functions that a person fulfilling a given kin type is expected to perform are clearly interested in something which lies beyond and outside the linguistic system.[9]

REFERENCES

ANTAL, L.
   1963   *Questions of meaning.* The Hague: Mouton.
BLOCH, B., G. TRAGER
   1942   *Outline of linguistic analysis.* Baltimore: Waverly Press.
BROWN, R.
   1958   *Words and things.* Toronto: Collier-Macmillan.
HILL, A. A.
   1961   Linguistic principles for interpreting meaning. *College English* 1961:446–473.
IKEGAMI, Y.
   1970   *The semological structure of the English verbs of motion.* Tokyo: Sanseido.
LOUNSBURY, F.
   1969   "Language and culture," in *Language and philosophy.* Edited by S. Hook, 3–29. New York: New York University Press.
LYONS, J.
   1968   *An introduction to theoretical linguistics.* Cambridge: Cambridge University Press.
MORRIS, C.
   1946   *Signs, language, behavior.* Englewood Cliffs, N.J.: Prentice-Hall.
SAPIR, E.
   1921   *Language.* New York: Harcourt, Brace.
SØRENSEN, H. S.
   1967   "Meaning," in *To honor Roman Jakobson,* pages 1876–1889. The Hague: Mouton.

[9]   As far as I know, the notion of linguistic meaning as a set of "rules" or "conditions" is found in the following two authors: Antal (1963) and Sørensen (1967).

Linguistic Models in Anthropology

EDGAR A. GREGERSEN

T. S. Kuhn has described the normal activity of scientists as a strenuous and devoted attempt to force nature into the conceptual boxes supplied by professional education (1962: 5). Science is not all of a piece, however, and its various subdivisions have on occasion developed different "boxes." Apart from the basic problems posed by nature itself in such an enterprise, attempts are occasionally made to resolve discipline differences by reduction to more comprehensive categories. Or else a scientist trained in one field straddles another and opens the same boxes in both — often with questionable appropriateness, if not altogether Pandorian overtones.

Here I should like to consider certain boxes — or, more precisely, models — that have diffused from linguistics to nonlinguistic anthropology. (To my knowledge, the direction of diffusion has never been the reverse. And although one might argue for the possibility of models shared because of convergent development, in reality such instances are rare — if they have ever, in fact, occurred.) For the most part, the path of such diffusion has been singularly free of obstacles. There are two basic reasons for this. First, linguistics has achieved a certain preeminence in elegance among the subdivisions of anthropology: the rigor and formalism of linguistics have always been considerably greater than elsewhere in the discipline. It is simply a cultural fact of life that anything even remotely approaching the supposed standards of the natural sciences has considerable prestige in the social sciences. Second, language itself has often been conceived of as an instance *par excellence* of culture, certainly this was the dominant integrating concept of most American anthropology. Among the Boasians, a "linguistic analogy" as Aberle (1960) calls it has been readily admitted for total culture. Certain essential properties of language (over and above the fact that it is learned and shared) were emphasized as also occurring in the total culture. These traits include: (1) selectivity of a small number of potential actualizations in any given language or culture, (2) unconscious patterning, and (3) unique configuration. The notion of pattern that underlies all three traits prompted Sapir to note that because culture patterns are harder to grasp than linguistic ones, language will show the way (Mandelbaum 1949: 164–165). Kroeber even held that ethnographic descriptions should approach "grammars" of specific cultures.

Sometimes identifying the exact provenience of a model is not a clear-cut matter. We shall not be overly concerned with historical niceties here, however. For example, it is of little consequence for the present discussion that the transformational models some anthropologists are experimenting with may have had their initial impetus directly from the work of von Neumann and others in computer programming rather than from the work of Chomsky and his generative grammarians. I assume, however — but without giving detailed proof — that linguistics has here proved to be a mediator for the computer model: knowledge of Chomsky has led to a discovery of earlier work.

We cannot here examine every linguistic idea adopted in general anthropology. A great many minor proposals have been made in an almost offhand manner. For example, Suggs (Marshall and Suggs 1971) mentions but does not develop an analogy between glottochronology and the rate of modification of sexual practices by suggesting that for both one must posit a core relatively impervious to change. This particular example is of interest because the analogy was proposed several years after the virtual demise of linguistic interest in glottochronology. Other instances of such an age-area lag can be found and one example (the taxonomic approach) will be discussed in some detail below.

One probable but unprovable example of model diffusion from linguistics includes the Darwinian theory of evolution. Historical linguistics had set up a family tree for Indo-European decades before the publication of the *Origin of species*. Darwin was undoubtedly familiar with such work if only because his brother-in-law, Hensleigh Wedgwood, was himself a linguist and had even developed his own onomatopoeic theory of the origin of language. It is perhaps unfortunate that, in the controversies over race, subsequent developments in physical anthropology did not involve some of the other analyses provided by linguists, such as the rigorous differentiation of genetic classifications from typological classifications. In Darwin's case, we are perhaps dealing with stimulus diffusion of the subtlest kind, where conscious wholesale importation of linguistic ideas is very unlikely. In the same way, I have always thought, but again without any proof, that the discovery of /ɨ/ in English by Trager and Block was the intellectual heritage of Mendeleev's periodic table, which permitted the prediction of the existence of neon, scandium, radon, and a number of other elements — both discoveries being based on an argument from pattern gaps. At a time when the phoneme was hailed as the analog of the atom, I daresay that many linguists considered the matter in such a light.

In the field of culture history, the *Kulturkreislehre* exploited the linguistic comparative method quite consciously. Gräbner, for example, in *Methode der Ethnologie* (1911), equates his criterion of quantity with vocabulary resemblances. Greenberg (1957: 73) points out quite cogently that Gräbner's analogy is false but that even so "the *Kulturkreis* procedure is . . . the methodological parallel of the genetic method in linguistics."

One could go on and discuss a considerable number of diffused linguistic ideas. But for our purposes it is more valuable to concentrate on the diffusion of what have come to be known as paradigms (following Kuhn 1962). A paradigm is a coherent tradition of research with distinctive laws, theories, applications, and criteria for choosing problems that are important — and solvable — as well as for branding others as trivial.

The paradigms we shall consider are sometimes labeled taxonomic and generative linguistics. At present the generative paradigm is the fashionable one in linguistics, although the taxonomic one has had considerably greater influence on anthropology and continues to do so. Among linguists, the distinctions between the two appear to be considerable. But at least to one outsider, the psychologist Piaget (1968), both represent variations on a more comprehensive paradigm, structuralism.

Taxonomic linguistics is behavioristic in orientation, linguistically particularistic, and antiprocessual in its formulations (although some varieties, e.g. Pike's tagmemics, permit more process statements than others). In Charles Hockett's terminology (1954), its mode of description is essentially item-and-arrangement, involving a model in which the main tasks seen as confronting the linguist are the discovery of language-specific elements (phonemes, morphemes, etc.) and the mapping of their distributions. The whole approach focuses on explicit discovery procedures, the fundamental units being defined in terms of the discovery procedures themselves. The notion of science associated with this paradigm is Baconian induction. A specific analysis is acceptable insofar as it is open to public scrutiny and replication at every stage. Whatever the other limitations of such an approach, one striking fact is indisputable: most work within this paradigm centers on phonology and . morphology; there is little work on syntax, and almost none on semantics. Critics have explained this by insisting that the primary concern is with basic units rather than with relational systems. But clearly this cannot be the whole answer because the units themselves are defined as points of contrasts within a relational system.

Taxonomic linguistics has at least been compatible in orientation with a number of anthropological developments: historical particularism, various schools of culture and personality and, more recently, cognitive anthropology. An extreme example of an ethnographic parallel to the taxonomic approach is given by Metzger and Williams (1963), whose whole methodology is in conscious imitation of neo-Bloomfieldian canons.

In the 1950's, a development of considerable importance occurred for anthropological theorizing. It was then that Kenneth Pike set up his now famous dichotomy of emic and etic approaches and tried to extend emic analysis to nonlinguistic aspects of culture in a way not attempted till then. In his formulation, an etic approach is that of an alien using an objective data language in the study of a culture: an *a priori* analytical grid is imposed by the observer on cultural events he does not really participate in as a culture bearer. The emic approach requires the discovery of the subjective and culture-specific categories of sameness or difference. Pike argues that the emic model — essentially the neo-Bloomfieldian model — can be applied to nonverbal behavior very largely because verbal and nonverbal behavior represent a continuum rather than rigidly separated fields of behavior. This point in itself is an essential flaw and Pike has not lacked critics. Be that as it may, he developed a highly elaborate set of constructs such as actemes, behavioremes, and the like — each with verbal and nonverbal manifestations; thus, a verbal behavioreme is an uttereme. For all the audacity of such a scheme it has been little used by anthropologists, although emic analyses of the same general type have been made of a number of culture traits (divinities, art motifs, and the like). Another problem with the scheme is a difficulty even from Pike's own orientation. As Harris (1964) has pointed out quite vociferously, the behavioreme fails to meet the criterion of operational adequacy because it is defined as a unit of "purposive" behavior and purposes are inaccessible to outside observers. Harris himself argues the need for a more thorough-going etic approach even though in other sciences, as he is undoubtedly quite aware, the search for a true objective data language is generally conceded to be chimerical. Indeed, Lévi-Strauss has recently argued that all etic approaches are a kind of emics (1972). Harris has more and more turned to filming, in the manner, one might say, of Andy Warhol and with perhaps as much success.

Along the same lines as Pike, Birdwhistell and others have tried to determine emic units in body movement. Birdwhistell has defined a basic unit, the kine, as "an abstraction of that range of behavior produced by a member of a given social group, which, for another member of that same group, stands in perceptual contrast to a different range of such behavior" (1970: 193). In direct contrast to Pike, however, Birdwhistell has admitted being unable to discover some higher-level "grammar" of kine assemblages.

Cognitive anthropology (the new ethnography or ethnoscience) was one of the leading currents in the anthropology of the 1960's. It assumes the "linguistic analogy" almost with a vengeance. Some proponents insist that anthropology must be emic, that is, concerned with cognitive maps, or it will be nothing. For all their often brilliant, exceedingly rigorous exercises, the cognitive anthropologists are merely glorified lexicographers. Their definitions were first conceived of in "phonemic" terms, generally with distinctive features (called components), and later with transformational rewrite rules (for this development, see the work of Lounsbury in particular). All their formalism cannot disguise their kinship with the historical particularists. Thus, in a recent statement of the aims of cognitive anthropology, we find an orientation close to classical Boasians: "Rather than attempt to develop a general THEORY OF CULTURE, the best we can hope for at present is particular theories of culture. These theories will constitute complete, accurate descriptions of particular cognitive systems" (Tyler 1969: 14). The cognitive anthropologists may seem to have a kinship with generative linguists because they both seem to have a mentalistic view, but the differences are great if only because the cognitive anthropologists deal in terms of surface lexical items, whereas the generativists have made a strong case for viewing some words, at any rate, as superficial phenomena — hardly isomorphic with an adequate cognitive deep-structure map.

Keesing in a recent paper with the marvelously evocative title "Paradigms lost" (1972) has attacked ethnoscience from the point of view of the generative paradigm, which will be discussed below. But he notes, interestingly enough, that some of the ethnoscientists have pushed the linguistic analogy far beyond what most linguists of either paradigm would consider legitimate. Thus, Keesing quotes Frake, who maintains that a correctly formulated strategy of ethnographic description, "will give us productive descriptions ... which, like the linguists' grammar, succinctly state what one must know in order to generate culturally acceptable acts and utterances appropriate to a given socio-ecological context" (Keesing 1972: 4–5). Keesing argues that a linguists' grammar does not give comparable information, that it does not tell one how to speak a language or how to produce sentences. If his interpretation is correct, both taxonomic and generative linguists would have to take issue with Frake.

The appearance of *Syntactic structures* in 1957 is generally given as the inauguration of the competing paradigm, generative linguistics. Since that time the change in specific generative analyses has approached the frenetic, and an important "heresy" has emerged to challenge the orthodox Chomskyan position. This newer group is usually referred to as the generative semanticists.

The generative paradigm may be characterized as universalist, deductive, rationalist. It approaches Hockett's Item-and-Process model. Whereas the taxonomic paradigm was compatible with the most extravagant notions of the possibilities of human behavior and did not posit a distinction of superficial and more underlying structures, the generative model seeks to construct a computer program as the grammar of a language and in so doing specify the restraints that profoundly limit even the superficial realization of sentences. The pervasiveness of the similarities in the miniprograms thus far produced for a number of languages has suggested that these restraints must be explained as somehow biologically given and as species-specific (see Putnam 1968). As a matter of fact, the generativists have offered what is perhaps the greatest challenge to a *tabula rasa* theory in recent times. But in championing rationalism, Chomsky undoubtedly overstates the classical empiricist position: Locke, for one, admitted certain forms of innate knowledge; what he did deny was the innate knowledge of the truth or falsity of synthetic statements. Chomsky's form of rationalism does not even imply that the "slate" of the mind is NOT clean: rather, merely that its surface cracks and bumps force whatever is written on it to follow inevitable outlines.

One of the remarkable developments in the attempts to apply the generative model in practical situations has been the virtual abandonment of projects for full-scale grammars of any language. Linguistic data have proved to be so complicated that a new sense of awe has emerged, with the result that detailed studies of only minuscule aspects of a grammar constitute the usual output of generative research.

So far the generative paradigm has exerted little influence on anthropology. It is difficult to see any direct application in the offing, although a few attempts have appeared (e.g. Durbin [1970] for religion). Chomsky has himself been skeptical about any direct transfer of the generative model even to such linguistically related fields as text analysis.

In one very significant respect, the Chomskyan model has had serious repercussions in anthropology and will undoubtedly continue to do so. That is, his assertion that a biological basis for language exists. The "linguistic analogy" spoken of earlier persists. If indeed a biological basis for language exists — which of all cultural traits has been held to be unambiguously arbitrary (an esential feature of de Saussure's structuralism) — then biological programming for the rest of human cultural traits seems plausible. This is the thesis of Tiger and Fox's *The imperial animal.* Although their linguistic statements are a trifle off at times, they are correct in their reading of the Chomskyan line that there is a language acquisition device and argue from this that "We have a CULTURE-ACQUISITION device constraining us to produce recognizable and analyzable human cultures . . . however varied the local manifestations must be" (1971: 13). The rest of their book is an attempt to spell out the biological program (in their terms, the "biogrammar") that human beings are wired for. They maintain that they are not trying to bring back a notion of instincts "in any old-fashioned sense." Other anthropologists are. Among them is Robert Paul. He argues for an instinct of aggression largely on the basis of Chomsky's model — together with the findings of ethnologists, the implications of cloning, and Freudian theory.

We have so far failed to mention in any detail the work of Lévi-Strauss, perhaps the foremost vendor of linguistic wares in the anthropological marketplace. The vast literature that has been produced by and about him renders superfluous any but the most general comments here. His variety of structuralism, which he apparently assumes is God's truth rather than hocus-pocus, is couched in terms of distinctive features. Although he has avoided the superficialities of much of cognitive anthropology by going beyond lexical definitions to an analysis of relations in a more underlying sense and almost seeks a joint biological and ecological determinism, the generative linguists have tended to dismiss him. Chomsky's purported demolition of Lévi-Strauss in *Language and mind* says merely that all Lévi-Strauss shows is that people classify — which is indeed only a very small part of Lévi-Strauss's position. If this is criticism, it is repudiation by revelation rather than by reasoned argument. Somewhat fuller are Keesing's comments in the paper mentioned above.

The work of Lévi-Strauss raises a fundamental issue, which has been implicit throughout this paper: what is science? Nutini, for example, has said "Lévi-Strauss is clearly aware of what constitutes good science and yet seems unable to practice it" (1971: 542). Buchler and Selby, on the other hand, maintain that Lévi-Strauss's "orientation to relations rather than terms . . . is much more consonant with the kind of theory that typifies modern science than the constituent analysis of concrete entities on the empirical plane" (1968: 17). Ardener seems to go still further and to suggest that Lévi-Strauss may be heralding a change of mind in science itself (1971; also Prattis 1972).

We mentioned earlier that there are levels of prestige within the sciences. It is usually taken as a matter of course that physics and mathematics are hard-core sciences that soft-core ones should aspire to imitate. Rare is the theoretician who, like Leslie White (1949), grants autonomy and equality to the divergent approaches. On the contrary, throughout the polemics of linguistics or anthropology one finds constant reference to what science is and how woefully opponents' work falls short of it. The invectives of the generative grammarians against the neo-Bloomfieldians, of Harris against the mentalists, and so on, are familiar enough. Boas himself figured prominently in similar disputes and was hailed by his students for making anthropology scientific. Almost mystical reference is made to his training in physics (he received his Ph.D. in physics in 1881 from the University of Kiel for his dissertation "Contributions to the understanding of the color of sea water"). Detractors point out that subsequent work in physics engendered a new philosophy of science that Boas was not even aware of, or did not keep up with. Rather than proving to be a boon to anthropology, Boas's training in physics proved to be quite the contrary by perpetuating an antiquated empiricism abandoned in the science that was unquestionably scientific.

If we return to the question, "What is science?" we find that philosophers of science disagree. Even some of the most cherished traditional notions are being subjected to profound scrutiny and sometimes rejection. Thus, empiricism, positivism, and operationalism have been challenged and such seemingly straightforward matters as the falsifiability criterion are often dismissed as too weak to be useful. The history of science does suggest that certain approaches are more efficient than others. Nevertheless, it is clear that in the long run — as Kuhn (1962), Ackermann (1970), and other historians and philosophers of science have pointed out — science is just a kind of puzzle solving, a creative endeavor that cannot be characterized completely in terms of any one rigid model but rather must be judged in the light of the participants' awareness of the problems.

With this in mind, the wise course would seem to be to try out ideas whatever the prestige of their provenience. If they solve the puzzle, fine. Otherwise, keep an open mind. The vicissitudes of the phoneme concept may prove to be instructive. Vehemently attacked by early generativists as superfluous and worse, its status now is up in the air. Thus King, in *Historical linguistics and generative grammar* (1969), ends his book by suggesting that there may be a need to reassess the role of the phoneme in the competence of the speaker if there are phonological changes that can be reasonably stated at, and only at, the autonomous phonemic level of representation (about which he is not clear). To reject a paradigm in one field, however, probably means it must be rejected in all. But this does not necessarily mean that analytic tools developed in a defunct or unfashionable paradigm must be discarded. On the contrary, the most successful extension of linguistic ideas has been in the nature of such things as elicitation techniques (controlled frames and the like) and other field method procedures developed by the taxonomic linguists. The value of such techniques has been conceded by even the most intransigent generativist. And they have become, like distinctive feature analysis, paradigmatically neutral — the surest sign of intellectual viability.

REFERENCES

ABERLE, D. F.
　1960　"The influence of linguistics on early culture and personality theory," in *Essays in the science of culture*. Edited by G. Dole and R. Carneiro. New York: Thomas Y. Crowell.
ACKERMANN, ROBERT
　1970　*Philosophy of science: an introduction*. Indianapolis: Pegasus.
ARDENER, E.
　1971　The new anthropology and its critics. *Man: Journal of the Royal Anthropological Institute* 6(3):449–467.
BIRDWHISTELL, RAY L.
　1970　*Kinesics and context*. Philadelphia: University of Pennsylvania Press.

BUCHLER, IRA R., HENRY A. SELBY
1968   *Kinship and social organization: an introduction to theory and method.* New York: Macmillan.

CHOMSKY, NOAM
1968   *Language and mind.* New York: Harcourt, Brace.

DURBIN, MRIDULA A.
1970   The transformational model of linguistics for an ethnology of religion: a case study of Jainism. *American Anthropologist* 72(3): 334–342.

GRÄBNER, F.
1911   *Methode der Ethnologie.* Heidelberg: C. Winter.

GREENBERG, H. H.
1957   *Essays in linguistics.* Chicago: University of Chicago Press.

HAMMEL, E. A.
1964   Culture as an information system. *Papers of the Kroeber Anthropological Society* 31:83–91.
1972   *The myth of structural analysis: Lévi-Strauss and the three bears.* Addison-Wesley Modular Publications, Module 25.

HARRIS, MARVIN
1964   *The nature of cultural things.* New York: Random House.

HOCKETT, CHARLES
1954   Two models of grammatical description. *Word* 10:210–213.

KEESING, R. M.
1972   Paradigms lost: the new ethnography and the new linguistics. *Southwestern Journal of Anthropology* 28(4):299–332.

KING, ROBERT D.
1969   *Historical linguistics and generative grammar.* Englewood Cliffs, N.J.: Prentice-Hall.

KUHN T. S.
1962   *The structure of scientific revolutions.* Chicago: University of Chicago Press.

LÉVI-STRAUSS, CLAUDE
1972   "Structuralism and ecology." Gildersleeve lecture, Barnard College, New York.

MANDELBAUM, DAVID G.
1949   *Selected writings of Edward Sapir in language, culture, personality.* Berkeley and Los Angeles: University of California Press.

MARSHALL, DONALD, ROBERT SUGGS
1971   *Human sexual variation.* New York: Basic Books.

METZGER, DUANE, GERALD E. WILLIAMS
1963   A formal ethnographic analysis of Tenejapa Ladino weddings. *American Anthropologist* 65(5):1076—1101.

NUTINI, H.
1971   The ideological basis of Lévi-Strauss's structuralism. *American Anthropologist* 73:537–544.

PAUL, ROBERT
1972   "Instinctive aggression in man." Unpublished manuscript.

PIAGET, JEAN
1968   *Le structuralisme.* Paris: Presses Universitaires de France.

PIKE, KENNETH
  1954   *Language in relation to a unified theory of the structure of human behavior.* Glendale, Calif.: Summer Institute of Linguistics.
PRATTIS, J. I.
  1972   Science, ideology, and false demons: a commentary on Lévi-Strauss critiques. *American Anthropologist* 74:1323–1325.
PUTNAM, H.
  1968   "The innateness hypothesis and explanatory models in linguistics," in *Boston studies in the philosophy of science,* volume three. Edited by R. S. Cohen and M. W. Wartofsky. Boston: Reidel.
TIGER, LIONEL, ROBIN FOX
  1971   *The imperial animal.* New York: Holt, Rinehart and Winston.
TYLER, STEPHEN   GN 29 T9
  1969   *Cognitive anthropology.* New York: Holt, Rinehart and Winston.
WHITE, LESLIE A.
  1949   *The science of culture.* New York: Grove Press.

On Speech and Thought

JOHN W. M. VERHAAR

The problem of speech and thought is one of stupendous proportions. There is, first of all, the task of confining the field to essentials. Furthermore, some clarity is required as to what disciplines are involved. These two questions are related. Finally, I shall have to cut down on essentials even within the limits to be set, and I shall do this as I go on. Inevitably, the pruning will be somewhat arbitrary.

I wish to address myself to the topic mainly from the point of view of linguistics, which to me is an empirical science, distinct from philosophy and from other empirical sciences such as psychology or sociology. However, admittedly much of linguistic theory has originated in philosophy, and it would be unrealistic to suppose that there are no remnants to be removed. Further, one cannot very well study thought, even though for the most part thought in natural language, and hope to avoid philosophy. Therefore, a certain amount of philosophy will be inevitable. The linguistic focus eliminates any thought which is not couched in language: a drastic and convenient limitation of the subject.

Given this, at least two principal approaches to thought in language present themselves. I shall describe these first and then choose, giving reasons for the choice.

If one accepts that meaning is an integral part of language, and that it can and must be studied in the empirical study of language, then it is reasonable to say that what we call meaning from the point of view of language we should call thought from the point of view of the mind. This raises the question whether, inversely, all lingual thought must be confined to lingual meaning. According to its contents, yes; according to its formal structure, no. Therefore, here, lingual thought is substantively meaning and formally certain structures of language, of which the most interesting example is syntax and the most important level within syntax is syntactic functions. The precisions duly made, it follows that anything extralingual is, for my topic, also extramental, even though there must be other factors which are extralingual and which may reasonably be called thought. Let me label the approach described in this paragraph as the "semantico-formal approach" to thought.

It is possible, however, to expand the semantico-formal approach to include a number of data on consciousness given in the concrete act of speech. Such expansion allows of various degrees. As an instance of very wide expansion, some might be tempted to include in the speech act forms of "significant" silence within a coherent series of utterances, assuming that the silence is not merely a pause but is communicative, for example nondirectively to elicit further statements or questions from the interlocutor. From the point of view of the psychologist, such a silence is certainly "meaningful." Yet it is not lingually semantic. We must look, then, for a less comprehensive expansion of the semantico-formal approach which does justice to the structure of the speech act. At this point I wish to phrase, suggestively rather than accurately, such an expansion which includes, beyond the kind of thought taken into account by the semantico-formal approach, all ways of speaking usually discussed in stylistics under the name of tropes or figures of style. Some of them, for example metaphor and metonymy, are based not on the lexical meaning of the words concerned, but on the application of that meaning. Such modes of application also belong to the structure of the speech act and to the domain of the linguist properly speaking. Let us call this more moderate expansion of the semantico-formal approach the "speech act approach."

From these two possibilities I select the speech act approach for the following reasons. First, the speech act is concrete, an actual event, while language (*langage*) as a feature of the human condition is highly abstract and might easily encourage undue speculation. Second, the speech act, far from being merely a starting point for a *linguistique de la parole* or analysis of "performance" is, on the contrary, precisely a point of departure for the analysis of a number of language universals. *Parole* or performance, as it is commonly understood, is the actual exercise of a language user's command of a language (*langue*), while the speech act, as I understand it here, is the concrete speech event, of which only one component, the utterance(s), occurs concretely as language-specifically realized, while other components have features invariable from language to language. This, I submit, is a much safer first, even though surely not exhaustive, approach to language universals than the one confining itself to the utterances only. Third, analysis of the speech act makes it necessary for us to consider the totality within which the speech act fits organically, enabling us to escape the idealizing tendency which has, from the time of Saussure, controlled most of linguistic theory. This totality is what I shall hereafter call "setting" as distinguished from situation.

It is possible to expand the notion of semantics as obtaining in the semantico-formal approach so as to comprise also the kind of thought analyzable in the speech act approach. In itself this would merely be a matter of terminology. But the consequences for the entire theory, and for a number of other terms in it, would be considerable. For example, certain forms of lexical application such as metaphor would no longer be distinct from the lexical meanings that are applied. Also, much of the basis for distinguishing situation from setting would disappear. I shall therefore retain the term "meaning" for what is found semantically in the semantico-formal approach. On the other hand, certain modes of application, such as metaphor, and certain other features of speech, such as intonation and stress, do something to the sentence level (and presumably to the phrase level as well) which may be called "meaning"-full also. In those cases I shall speak about "significance." The term is somewhat arbitrary and chiefly motivated by the need to have a term different from "meaning." But "significance" is not altogether inappropriate either, for most (all?) forms of significance have something to do with performativity, a notion I shall discuss at length below. "Significance," in short, shall indicate all aspects of "meaning"-full-ness not contained in the semantico-formal approach.

I shall ignore intonation and stress, even when they are lingual (it is frequently very hard to determine whether they are lingual or extralingual), simply as a way further to limit the field. I shall also ignore discourse, for the same reason, apart from a few incidental remarks.

Henceforth I shall mean by lingual thought the kind of thought analyzable in the speech act approach. To enumerate, this includes (a) lingual meaning; (b) purely formal lingual structures; and (c) "significance" as provisionally indicated above.

LINGUISTIC THEORY: SOME ESSENTIALS

The following is expository and will be found unsatisfactory by those expecting theory building *ab ovo*. More detailed discussions are found in my "Phenomenology and present-day linguistics" (henceforth PPL, Verhaar 1973a), and a few other items may be checked in Verhaar (1963).

Meaning is distinguished as grammatical and lexical. Lexical meaning needs no further comment at this point. The separate structural positions of lexical and grammatical meaning derive directly from the distinction between lexicon and grammar. A polemical note may here serve clarity. I oppose assimilation of the lexicon into the grammar, because it renounces the proper task of linguistics as an empirical science in favor of a philosophy of mind. I do not recognize Chomsky's "selectional restrictions" as belonging to grammar. Neither lexical nor grammatical meaning entails special features as due to application: meaning is distinguished from use.

By application I mean application of lexical items. These may be applied "properly" and "improperly" — "improperly," when application entails "referential crossover." To explain this, metaphor will do. In a sentence like *That man is a fox* I apply the word *fox*, and therefore its meaning 'fox', not to a fox but to a man. It is not the case that the meaning of *fox* in this sentence is 'sly person', or whatever motivates metaphorical use in the consciousness of the speaker, but, simply, 'fox'. The term "referential crossover" conveys the idea that *fox* is applied to something not a fox. If, then, the meaning of *fox* does not explain its use in the sentence, while the so-called "collocational" rules do not explain it either (for those rules decide that the sentence is well formed in case *fox* is used metaphorically, and deviant in case it is not, but they cannot decide which of the two possibilities obtains), the only theoretical basis for dealing with metaphor is a theory of lexical application.

Grammatical meaning splits up into syntactic meaning and morphemic meaning. Morphemic meaning may range from very abstract (example: third person verbal -*s* in English) to concrete, even close to lexical, meaning (example: -*less* in *sleepless*, semantically very close to *without*, though of course with different structural properties and distribution). An example of grammatical meaning at the syntactic level is the distribution of roles across functions. (Topicalization is grammatical if realized grammatically, for example syntactically by word order, or morphemically by a clitic; and is phonemic if realized phonemically, for example by intonation or stress.)

Syntax has three levels, the highest that of functional structure, lower down that of grammatical categories, and last that of role structure, each of them distributed across the functions in the way "fillers" "fill" "slots," to borrow freely a well-known tagmemic technical device. Categorial filling of functions is mainly according to form and only weakly semantic, while filling by role is mainly semantic and only weakly according to form. (I distinguish "according to form" from "formal(ly)," which term has already been preempted for other use to be further clarified in a moment.) The weakly semantic element in categories comes in by supercategorization. One supercategory has referential meaning, another does not (compare the medieval *categorematica* and *syncategorematica* respectively, which, however, were distinguished according to function-filling capacity — for a language like Latin — and not according to referential meaning); the assumption here is that, though reference does not enter meaning (cf. "application" above), the capacity for reference does. The weak element of form in roles comes in since categorial filling of functions also determines categorial filling of roles, more so in proportion as roles are predominant over functions, as I shall discuss in more detail below. (Categorial filling often adapts, language- and type-specifically, to functions or roles in their interrelational features by morphemic concord.) The distribution of both categories and roles is known to differ from language to language. A theory about functions, categories, and roles constant enough to assimilate language- and type-specific variability of those fillings is thereby language-universal. Such a theory is only barely beginning to be developed. To overcome the one-sided approaches which consider functions (traditional linguistics; Chomsky) or roles (traditional morphemic case semantics; verb focus studies; Fillmore) as the most constant among the three levels, while the study of a universal theory for the categories is still in an extremely confused and provisional stage, what is needed is a theory dealing with all three levels together in a reasonably invariant manner as compared to language- and type-specific realization. The functions themselves are "formal" in two meanings which obtain at the same time. The functions are "empty" of categorial filling and filling by role, "empty," therefore, according to form and semantics respectively; and they are "relational," in that (say) a subject must theoretically be conceived as subject-of (a predicate), a predicate as predicate-of (a subject), and so forth, in such a manner that each and every function is directly related to the predicate (and the predicate to it), and only indirectly, i.e. through the predicate, to all other functions. (Subfunctions, for example an attributive adjective in a noun phrase, are related to the head first and directly, and only then to what the head is directly related to, and so forth until the functional level properly speaking is attained with the predicate; again, as a relational point of reference. Subfunctions, therefore, and functions are hierarchically structured.) Functions form a framework, or structure, itself empty semantically and according to form; roles structurally form a framework as well, only determinable semantically but unstructured formally; and categories are systemic in their interrelations rather than structural.

SITUATION AND SETTING, AND THE COMPONENTS OF THE SPEECH ACT

As explained in PPL, situation should be distinguished from setting. The situation in the speech act is everything we are related to in the utterance, from the point of view of the semantic content of the utterance. "Utterance" may also be read as "utterances," a discourse unity of consecutive sentences. But I am ignoring discourse in this paper, and hence I shall, conveniently rather than correctly, consider the sentence as the basic unit at the level of the utterance. Our relatedness to the situational element is both referential and nonreferential. The setting is more comprehensive than the situation and comprises a number of elements not contained in the semantic content of the utterance. For example, when I talk standing in the snow, the snow enters the situation when talked about, and belongs to the setting only when not talked about. Obviously, in discourse, setting may become situation from one sentence to another. For the principles illustrated here it is not important to develop whether "situation" and "setting" are used in senses mutually exclusive, or whether the setting includes the situation, and I will leave that (genuine) problem (especially for dealing with metonymy) for what it is.

The speech act has three components: the mental component (thought as defined within the semantico-formal approach), the situational component (the "situation" described just now), and the utterance level itself. Both mental and situational components are determined exclusively in terms of the utterance level. The utterance, then, is the ultimate point of orientation in the analysis of the speech act.

Given the principle presented earlier that grammar and lexicon should be kept distinct, the question arises how they compare with mental and situational components. Because words as lexical items used in a sentence are related to situational elements in one-to-one correspondences, the lexicon clearly belongs primarily to the situational component. Because grammar is the concrete way the mental component is entailed in any speech act, it needs little argument to show that grammar belongs primarily to the mental component. However, the qualification "primarily" in both statements is crucial. For obviously, lexical elements also represent elements of thought and thus form part of the mental component. Inversely, certain grammatical properties such as the distribution of roles across functions are based upon certain situational constants and thus also belong to the situational component. It is hypothesized that only the level of functional structure is exempt from the situational component and is therefore mental only, while only certain forms of "referential crossover" at the level of lexical application, i.e. insofar as this crossover needs explanation from the setting rather than from the situation (metonymy is a case in point), are exempt from the mental component. Thus in the cline from the mental component to the situational component there is a vast area of coextensiveness of the two components, which by no means entails their identity however, while few levels at top and bottom are determinable in terms of one of the poles only.

"Significance" as provisionally introduced above does not exceed the analysis of the speech act. All that belongs to significance would be extralingual from the point of view of the semantico-formal approach and genuinely lingual from the point of view of the speech act approach. For, though the setting is wider than the situational component of the speech act, it does show up in the analysis of the speech act as a whole, though not as merely one of its components. While the situational component has only the utterance level for its point of orientation, the setting has the entire speech act for ITS orientation. It is presumably this structural property of the speech act, which is unimaginable without the setting, that has made the distinction between lingual and extralingual so complicated. The setting is the source of significance, which I shall distinguish below as various forms of "performativity," as special "functions" of the speech act as a whole.

THE "FUNCTIONS" OF SPEECH

About forty years ago, Karl Bühler (1934: 28) distinguished three "functions" of speech, i.e. (I add my own glosses) *Darstellung* ("representation"), *Ausdruck* ("expression"), and *Appell* ("appeal"). *Darstellung* concerns what is being talked about, *Ausdruck* is the "subjective" function, and *Appell* is the "intersubjective" function. According to Bühler, these three functions are properly functions of the lingual "sign." It has been suggested, rather circumlocutionally by Bühler himself and more to the point by Reichling (1967), that the only function that matters from a linguistic point of view is the *Darstellung*, but it may be doubtful if a unique "function" can still be called a "function": the nature of speech utterances is that they "represent," and that includes no doubt a great deal, though not all, of *Kundgabe* and *Appell*.

Bühler's attempts at the analysis of the "functions" of speech remind one of those before him by Ogden and Richards (1930), later somewhat modified by Cherry (1957); that triangle of their diagrams, in contrast to Bühler's, is well enough known, and so is Morris's "semiotics" (1946). Morris's "pragmatics" much resembled Bühler's *Appell*, and his "semantics" Bühler's *Darstellung*. Only the German scholar's *Ausdruck* finds no parallel in Morris's system and, inversely, the latter's "syntactics" finds none among Bühler's functions (though Bühler does discuss intrautterance relationships in different contexts).

More recently Austin (Urmson 1962; Urmson and Warnock 1961) has made himself known by his distinction between "constative" and "performative" utterances (in some of their aspects again readily comparable with Bühler's *Darstellung* and *Appell* respectively). The English philosopher has also stirred considerable debate in the wake of his three species of speech acts: locutionary (actually, largely "constative"), illocutionary (what we do "in" performing locutionary acts, for example ordering, warning; very much, therefore, like Bühler's *Appell* again), and perlocutionary (what we do "by" performing illocutionary acts; for example what threatening is, illocutionarily, appears perlocutionarily as intimidating) (see Black 1969). The emphasis on performativity (which Austin had expanded to include even locutionary acts) reminds one of the word *Leistung*, often used by Bühler to indicate the functions, and especially *Darstellung*, in line with the terminology of his time in Germany. *Leistung* and performativity appear as some kind of superfunction, comprising all the other functions: the speech act is an act. There is no need to remind the reader how topical performativity has become in linguistic theory in some nonstandard conceptions of transformational grammar.

The single most important feature of all these (and many more) function analyses of language has been that their point of departure has been some totality more comprehensive than the speech act. In some cases, for example that of Austin, this has consciously been the approach taken. Bühler is not a clear case as far as his own intentions are concerned in this respect, but in actual fact his three functions had to be reduced to one by Reichling, and thus ceased to be functions properly speaking. Ogden and Richards had ambitions which would daunt even a metaphysician, and Morris was after nothing less than a universal theory of sign. In linguistics also, such ambitions have returned with regularity, the stock example being Hjelmslev.

One could, indeed, go on almost indefinitely distinguishing "functions" of speech. Our dealing with certain settings may even be unintentional and even unconscious, with Freudian slips as the example that spontaneously comes to mind. From the viewpoint of the psychologist there is no reason not to speak of a "function" here. One's intention in speaking about the weather may be to do just that, but it may also be to avoid any of a hundred other topics. One may talk politely to be polite, but also to offend; as one may be silent out of discretion or in order to embarrass someone. The last example alone suffices to show that some principle is needed to sort out all these "functions." Some of them cannot reasonably be called "mental," while others which are certainly mental would not belong to lingual thought as described above.

For my topic here, within the limits set, we should perhaps distinguish the functions of language in thought along the following lines. In terms of the situational component we may say that language "represents" things as we experience them, neither including nor excluding claims to ontological validity (this would, among other things, depend upon what type of sentence defines the utterance component). Let us call this function "representation." From the viewpoint of the mental component our thought takes "specified" form, becomes articulate lingually. This function I call "articulation." Note that the idea that our experience gets "represented" and our thoughts get "articulated" entails in no way, and does not exclude either, that the experience may be there previous to lingual representation and the thought previous to lingual articulation; these (important) issues do not fall within the scope of my topic. Lastly I wish to indicate the function of performativity as presenting itself for analysis from the point of view of "significance."

Performatively, the speech act differs from its representative and articulatory functions in that utterances become a tool of practical control through lexical use (given that I do not discuss intonation and stress). The use of words constitutes things in experience and consciousness, and establishes an ontological validity (of the things constituted in experience and of ideas constituted in consciousness) of its own. Further, the use of words constitutes an interpretation due to artistic inspiration and belief. These are three forms of performativity that have to be further explained. (The term "constitute" harbors no mysteries here, let alone idealistic ones; it has been chosen for its neutrality between "evocation" and "mental control" as described below.)

The use of words evokes things as experientially "real," and it does this by the use of words as names. Names are essential features of the things named by them rather than bearers of certain meanings, and name-giving is in that sense creative; this is too well known from the mythical literature to need explanation, and it appears in negative form as lingual taboo. Let us call this "evocative performativity." Then, utterances may become a tool of thought control, so that what we think in the utterances seems to acquire ontological validity merely because we have phrased it. The validity consists in the concreteness our thoughts find in their lingual form as somehow guaranteeing that validity. I consider this feature of performativity as the explanation of the difficulty many people, academic people especially, experience in recognizing that what looks like a substantive issue may be merely or largely terminological: no thinker with a bent for unreflected realism has a natural talent for nominalistic skepsis. More simply, this feature of performativity explains why it is so easy to talk at cross purposes. Let us call the "realistic" tendency that I just mentioned "mental performativity." Finally, our utterances may become an instrument of artistic interpretation and of interpretation through belief; let us call this "interpretative performativity." In evocative performativity, thought has little autonomy compared to utterances; in mental performativity, the utterances have little autonomy compared to thought; and in interpretative performativity, neither situation nor thought has notable autonomy compared to the utterances.[1]

---

[1] The reader with a taste for systematicity will not be slow to see that, given the three components of the speech act, the above three types of performativity do not exhaust all the possibilities. Yet they do, but the reason is subtle. Evocation should give primacy to the situational component, but I am committed to the central position of the utterance level, and thus, as if by sleight of hand, I have characterized words as essentially names, then continued to call them words again. This, of course, is the normal thing to do, as also in discussions of lingual taboo.

I reproduce here the possibilities in diagram form. Square brackets indicate that the component enclosed is nonfunctional in the speech act. Parentheses mean that the component enclosed is functional but not thematically so (not "consciously" so). Italics mean full functionality consciously or thematically. Some such schematization is necessary for adequate critique on the claim, only in part true (for example Merleau-Ponty 1962), that language use makes us forget language and that speech can only function under that condition; or that awareness of language use during that use is irreconcilable with the nature of man (Parain 1942). A consider-

THE REPRESENTATIVE AND ARTICULATORY FUNCTIONS

The representative function is directed towards the things spoken about. Its basis is meaning, lexical and grammatical. The lexical aspect of representation has been well studied in componential analysis. Not surprisingly, anthropological linguistics and sociolinguistics must be credited with most of the work done in this area. It appears that there is no concretely unique way of representing kinship relations, colors, diseases, social relations, assumptions about ownership, and many other networks of lingual determinations of culture particulars. Presumably grammar also needs to be studied with a view to the representative function of speech, such as the experience of time as expressed in tense systems or of speaker-hearer relationship as expressed in pronominal systems. But in this regard linguists have done poorly in many cases, often due to popular conceptions that, for example, the concept of time in a language must be poorly represented because the verb has no tense system, which ignores, however, that time may be expressed lexically in one language and in verbal systems (often redundantly as far as information is concerned) in another.

The coextensiveness of mental and situational components across many structure levels makes it possible to look at many data from either point of view. Thus componential analysis reveals experience in the representative function as much as thought structures in the articulatory function. I believe that very little is known about these matters, but the dual aspects of analyses such as those in componential analysis may well be responsible for much theoretical disagreement in relation to, for example, color names. If there are universal features even in such areas as color naming, should that be based upon physical constants (the existence of which no one can doubt) or upon conceptual universals about the underlying physical facts?

I can only mention the importance of articulatory analysis in learned language as compared to natural language, with the attendant distinc-

---

able number of data analyzed by Vygotsky (1962) would find a reasonable systematic accommodation in a schematization like that below, crude though such schemas inevitably are.

Evocative performativity	Mental performativity	Interpretative performativity
[mental component]	*mental component*	(mental component)
(utterance level)	(utterance level)	*utterance level*
situational component	[situational component]	(situational component)

tion between lexical semantics and conceptual analysis and with the analogous one between unreflective and reflective thought. I have done a certain amount of analysis of the lexical side (Verhaar 1963), although I would now have reservations about some of the things I said in that book. I did not at all discuss then the importance of syntactic structures, and what would be involved would be a comparison between logic as an artificial language and the logic of natural language. The merits of generative semantics in this regard (though not at all in regard to the representative function of language) are impressive enough to stimulate further research.

EVOCATIVE PERFORMATIVITY AND GRAMMAR

I have said that evocative performativity forms the theoretical basis for the word as name and that lingual taboo is the negative side of this name character: language users banish certain realities by not mentioning the names they bear. Data are available, but linguistic theory has reflected on them very little, and philosophers like Cassirer (1952) have done better. I now wish to comment briefly upon evocative performativity of sentences, an issue that has become popular since Austin. In line with that philosopher's analyses, present-day linguistics has tied down performativity to declarative sentences (see Ross 1970; Staal 1970; Thorne 1972). This leads me to remark that, given the theoretical basis accepted here, we must consider every sentence as performative. For if words derive their situation-related character only from the sentence (words with referential meaning are naturally better examples of this [Reichling 1967]), then interrogative sentences also have the same property. However, one may accept this principle and still claim that such performativity does not appear at the utterance level itself. Whether appearance at the utterance level is interpreted speculatively as a feature in deep structure transformationally deleted, or empirically as a matter of either discourse relations or lexical meaning, does not affect the principle illustrated here, which is that evocative performativity of words becomes operative by virtue of sentencehood. If performativity appears at the utterance level, then the analyses do not involve the setting, but only the situation. For example that *promise* must occur affirmatively in the first person if it is to be performative is a matter of the situation, and that *promise* in other forms by reason of concord of tense and person may also be performative is a matter of the situation too. But when, say, the question *When did you see the present king of France?* "presupposes" that there is such a person as the king of France at this time, that presupposition does not appear at the utterance level grammatically (at least not in English), but belongs to the setting (at least when the question is uttered in English). Since every question presupposes something, the grammarian's task will be to investigate whether or not that presupposition is reflected at the utterance level; if not, it is setting-related only. But it would still be performative, even though the sentence is not a declarative one.

MENTAL PERFORMATIVITY: IDEALIZATION

This function is the performative aspect of articulation. Compared with evocative performativity, words no longer function as names but as bearers of meaning: our utterances have become tools of thinking, and the autonomy of speech compared to thought has been weakened, though compared to the situation and the setting it has been strengthened; in the latter sense the language user has become more language-conscious.

One form of mental performativity I wish to discuss here is that of idealization. The obvious way of doing this would be to analyze lingual properties of learned language. But that topic is marginal to this paper, which is concerned for the most part with natural language. I could, therefore, analyze the natural language component in learned language, but that would largely be a matter of the nonperformative aspect of it: the articulatory function, on which I do not want to say anything any more. What is left to be done, then, is a discussion of the role of natural language in mental performativity, and I call this idealization. Finally, I wish to tackle that issue in contrastive typology. I will pick Indonesian, an Austronesian language, as compared with a language like English. My starting point will be English, but, as I go on, it will appear that English is in most respects just a sample of what we find in many Indo-European languages. Instead of "Indo-European languages" I will just use "Indo-European" for brevity and convenience, and when mentioning features of Indonesian widely found in Austronesian languages I will occasionally say "Austronesian." In either case I will ignore the exceptions (which in Austronesian are somewhat more numerous than in Indo-European). The contrastive analysis will in a later section be taken up once more where I deal with much more important issues relating to the typological differences that are important for the analysis of lingual thought.[2]

[2] Indonesian is one form of continuation (another being Malaysian) of older

I have elsewhere tried to capture the problem of idealization under the name of "noumenalization" in natural language (Verhaar 1973b). I define "noumenalization" as the substitution of the "noumenal" (lexical or grammatical meaning) for something the noumenal is not. I summarize briefly the material discussed in the paper referred to. Noumenalization obtains in various forms: (1) mention for use, for example *book* in *Book means what my dictionary says it does* refers not to some book but to the word *book*; (2) words like Latin *seu* 'or' or Dutch *oftewel* 'or', which establish the possibility of a choice not between two objective alternatives, but between intralingual synonyms or paraphrases; (3) words like Dutch *want* 'for' and English *for* (always) or *because* (sometimes) (see Rutherford 1970; de Vries 1971) will indicate not why something is so but why the speaker thinks/says it is so (an English paraphrase is 'and I say so because [. . . . .]'); (4) substitution of the order of thought in lingual form for the extramental order as in *in turn* in *I got it from A., who in turn got it from B.* (but not in *in turn* in *I gave it to A., who in turn gave it to B.!*), or in *primarily* in *In this job I am primarily concerned with politics*, under the interpretation (for this sentence token is ambiguous) that my job really looks like something else and is meant to do so (under that interpretation *primarily* may be replaced, with the same information but not

---

Malay, which occurred in "classical," fairly stable form and in *lingua franca* forms throughout the Indonesian archipelago, one of them being "market Malay." The establishment of Indonesian as the national language of Indonesia in roughly the last generation has been remarkably successful considering the setback of local languages and the developing state of education. The language has, not surprisingly, undergone some instability, within negligible boundaries grammatically and with considerable problems lexically, because of the need for a great many new words, to meet the requirements of technical and economic development. Two factors, i.e. this instability and the inexpert confusion of standard Malay/Indonesian with *lingua franca* forms of it and especially with "market Malay," have led to the inexcusable and in any event wholly erroneous idea that Indonesian is still largely a "primitive" language. The concept of "primitivity" appears to be determined by the impossibility of expressing Western concepts in the language. There is occasionally the suggestion that one aspect of the "primitiveness" of Indonesian is the difficulty experienced by those who wish to express "abstraction." All these rather popular judgments are sometimes corroborated by linguists who claim that the language is "unstable," but this is more often than not due to conflicting judgments of well-formedness on the part of a handful of expatriate native informants. Indonesian is a strikingly rich language lexically, and its grammar exhibits a firm inner consistency, with notable resistance to grammatical interference from Western languages. Naturally, Indonesian is as little equipped to deal lexically with European cultural features, such as those appearing in the history of ideas in the West, as English would be to deal with *kebatinan* 'mysticism', *gamelan* 'music', or *adat* 'law', in the event the world's economic and political objectives were to make such interests widely relevant to the West.

the same meaning, by its antonym *ultimately*, the new sentence then NOT being a case of noumenalization!); (5) in sentences like *One cannot elapse a book*, where *cannot* is associated not with the extralingual impossibility of doing something in particular with a book but with the intralingual, syntactic impossibility of using *elapse* transitively; (6) in words like *linguistic, theological, psychological, sociological*, when occurring in such phrases as *linguistic thought* (meaning not the kind of thought characterizing the linguist, but the kind of thought going into language), *theological problems* (meaning problems not of theology but of faith), *psychological imbalance* (meaning not the imbalance of the discipline of psychology, but of someone's "psyche"), *sociological features* (meaning features not of sociology but of society) — in all these cases (compare also *abnormal psychology*) noumenalization consists in the substitution of an academic discipline for its unacademic object;[3] (7) in sentences like *John is the epitome of efficiency*, or *That is her idea of a nice car*, where John, nonnoumenally, is not an epitome and a car not an idea; and (8) in the substitution of *reason* for *cause*, *mean* for *refer to*; or in the translation of the title of Rudolf Otto's book *Das Heilige* as *The idea of the holy*. ((7) and (8) are in part identical.)

I have checked all these cases for Indonesian, and it turns out that none of them can be said in that language while keeping the noumenalization. (6) may be an exception through simple borrowing of the name of the discipline (from the Dutch), but this is neither necessary nor desirable. Even (1) is unusual in Indonesian. The sentence above would begin with *kata* 'word': '(the) word ["book"]'; however, an Indonesian asking questions to help him solve a crossword puzzle would dispense with *kata*, but that would simply be a case of ellipsis based on constancy of setting clues, and it could not be readily interpreted as a case of noumenalization.

There is some relevance to syntax in (1) through (8), above, but most of it is a matter of lexical application; those items concern the use rather than the meaning of the lexical items involved. (For that reason the expression "mention for use" is not wholly correct, for mention is also a form of use, albeit self-referentially so.) The "significance" of the noumenalizing mental performativity presupposes, it

---

[3] In this paper I use "lingual" in the sense of "relating to language," and "linguistic" in the sense of "relating to linguistic science," to counteract the noumenalization of "lingual" into "linguistic" (see Pap 1951). Thus, also, for obvious reasons, I use "morphemic" and not "morphological" when I refer to the object of the branch of linguistics called "morphology." It is not easy to be consistent in this regard in all cases; thus several times in this paper I use the expression "ontological" validity, as "ontic" would be strange to most readers.

is true, a setting distinct from the situation as defined above (as in the case of the Indonesian asking elliptic questions to solve his crossword puzzle), but the setting coincides with the situation whenever noumenalization takes place; and this is a typological characteristic of Indo-European. That the coincidence of setting and situation may not be considered as an identity appears from an ambiguous sentence token like *John is the same as Johannes.*

Grammatical considerations confirm the absence of the type of idealizing tendencies normal in a language like English and impossible in Indonesian. To illustrate this I pick the subject-predicate relation. Geach (1962: 23) says: "I shall say that a predicate is ATTACHED TO a subject, is PREDICATED OF what the subject stands for, and APPLIES TO or is TRUE OF this if the statement is found to be true" (original emphasis); his example is *Peter was an Apostle*, where "the predicate [. . . . .] is predicated of [. . . . .] Peter, not his name" (1962: 22). I rephrase Geach's claim as follows: the meaning of what occurs in predicate position is applied to the referent of what occurs in subject position.

This is indeed the situation . . . in Indo-European. The name "subject" is explained by it, for it is the "underlying" entity, of which some "property" (or "identity," etc., as the case may be and logic affirms) is predicated by means of a kind of mental superimposition (on the early Greek history of the notion of subject, see Kahn 1973: 46–8) on something extramental and extralingual. Undoubtedly, what occurs in predicate position does have a referent of its own (though, logically, it is not posited by way of a proposition, and that referent need not be a "particular"; however, these problems do not affect the point being made here); nevertheless, it is not that referent but the mental counterpart of it that is applied, and not to the mental content of what occurs in subject position but to its referent. I have called this "predicative application" (Verhaar 1973b) as distinguished from the "referential application" not needing any syntactic functional structure for it to obtain.

In Indonesian this would not be an adequate interpretation of the subject-predicate structure. There the relation between subject and predicate is what I call "juxtapositional," with less of a distinction between the meaning of what occurs in the position of each of those functions on the one hand and the referent of each on the other.[4] In the case of subject AND predicate, referential application of what

---

[4] What I have called "juxtapositional" may be cognate to what Sommerfelt in 1937 called "appositional," or so I would think from Fillmore's reference to Sommerfelt, to whose work I have not had access (Fillmore 1968: 56).

occurs in each of them has a name rather than a word character, in the sense that in Indo-European only what occurs in subject position does. In Indonesian there is not the shift from name to word, from subject to predicate, that there is in Indo-European: the relation from predicate to subject is not that of application if "application" means something moving from lingual to extralingual. No single argument can prove this, but the convergence of arguments is so compelling that the interpretation given here at least cannot be bypassed.

First, the impossibility of noumenalization in Indonesian bespeaks name character rather than word character of the lexical items. Second, one highly prominent sentence type in Indonesian is nonverbal; in Indo-European verbal categorial filling of predicate position is obligatory. This means, at least for the so-called "nominal" predicates in Indo-European, in which a copulative verb is obligatory, that there is an intrautterance link between a predicate and its subject; Indonesian has no verbal copulative words of this kind. There is, between the two language types, no difference between juxtapositional structure: in Indo-European languages it occurs commonly at the phrase level, for example, whenever there is an attributive determination of some word or phrase. Such structures are not only "juxtapositional" distributively but also with the same name character of the attribute which is also found in the Indonesian predicate. Also, in a language like English an attributive adjective does not hold for the constituent modified by it by "application" from semantic to referential level as does a predicate with regard to its subject. The difference, therefore, between English and Indonesian is not the juxtapositional structure considered in isolation but the fact that that structure is possible on functional and subfunctional levels in Indonesian, and only on the subfunctional level in English.[5] Third, a preferred form of the verb in Indonesian is the passive, which is closer to nominal status than Indo-European passives.[6] Fourth, though verbal actives are closer to verbal

[5] From this it appears that for transformational grammar to assign to an attributive adjective sentencehood (though of course in the underlying structure only) is as erroneous as it would be to assign to the underlying structure of a sentence with a nominal predicate in Indonesian (a proposal once made to me informally) a verb which is then deleted transformationally. In both cases the error involved is to think that the mental performativity entailed takes syntactic shape in the manner of an Indo-European predicate in relation to the subject.

[6] This is not to suggest that the Indonesian passive is a noun, but rather that it fits neither the Indo-European noun category nor the Indo-European verb category, while it resembles both. As this qualification would hold for a number of Indonesian regional languages as well, the suggestion has appeared now and then in grammars of those languages that passives are really nouns, for example in van der Tuuk 1971 (originally 1864/67; see Teeuw 1971: xxxi). I have occasionally heard the same

status than verbal passives, even the actives may be interpreted as
more nominal than their Indo-European analogues. One way of recognizing this is to advert to the frequent "absolute" (i.e. objectless)
use of transitive verbs (where object zero is in no way demonstrable);
verbs in such use rather resemble adjectives, since adjectives are also
closer to verbal status (one may come across proposals for categorization which make verbs and adjectives subcategories of a category
"verbals," see Blanche Lewis 1969). Fifth, in (linear) transitivity from
verbs to their objects, a particle interpretable as a preposition is often
optionally possible, and this preposition sticks to the object in its
transfer to subject when the sentence is passivized (in English, verbs
with prepositional objects may be passivized but the preposition stays
with the verb); this confirms the closeness to adjective status of actives
and to nominal status of passives.[7] Lack of space here makes it impossible to supply the material, but the formal characteristics are easy
to check for those knowing the language. My remarks about the categories are in the context of a contrastive analysis and therefore strongly
"translationese." It is generally recognized in Indonesian studies that
the categorization usual in the West is of comparatively little value in
the description of Indonesian.

The fourth and fifth arguments are given confirmation by the way
role determines syntactic structure in Indonesian more than does function. I shall discuss that issue in more detail below.

INTERPRETATIVE PERFORMATIVITY AND SEMANTICS

I have called interpretative performativity a tool of situational control,
and it differs from the practical control of evocation in that it deals
with situational data (and presumably setting data also) artistically,
creedally, and ideologically. The use of literary tropes belongs here,
metaphor being the most frequent example, which also shows that the
interpretative element is not confined to literature, creedal witnessing
and religious experience, or ideological commitment. But all these
genres littéraires are interpretative in a special manner. I will not speak

---

suggestion in discussions; it certainly occurs in published literature apart from
van der Tuuk's Batak grammar, but I have not checked the references.

[7]   As my later interpretation (below) of such passive constructions will be unusual
in assigning to the "prepositional" phrase subject functionality, it will be useful
to give a few examples: *Akan guru itu saya benci*, or *Mengenai masaalah itu akan
saya uraikan nanti*, or *Akan hal itu tidak saya ingat* (the spelling here is the re-
formed spelling effective August 17, 1972).

here about figures of style, or the theory of literature; figures of style have been discussed at some length in PPL. Instead, I wish to point out a few features of interpretative semantics in the language of systems of belief, both in popular and in systematized form.

Semantic problems with the popular form of interpretative performativity have, for almost as long as a generation now, forced themselves on the attention of linguists and especially of philosophers, though studies of them have been rare. As a prominent problem I may mention that of semantic circularity, which may well be as old as language itself. An example: someone at a tense meeting tries to push his proposal by urging that the proposal must be good because all experienced people agree with it and only the inexperienced object. It is clear that the interpretation of "(in)experienced" for the one who is urging the proposal is determined heavily or solely by (dis)agreement with the proposal. Or, the remark "That is not the point" often means that "that" is not what the speaker wants to talk about. A few more examples, well enough known, are where "revisionist" referentially denotes just any Russian, "capitalist" anyone not sharing the particular brand of communism favored by the source of the remark, "communism" or "subversion" any form of critique with regard to established authority, "relevant" only what the user of this word happens to deem important. In weaker form we observe the same phenomenon when technical terms, in more or less popularized usage, become bywords of reproach to taint the adversary: "structuralism" or "taxonomy," to mention two examples in linguistics itself. I do not feel that anyone convinced that he himself is exempt from those interpretative weaknesses in what is supposed to be rational controversy can be sufficiently sensitive to the issues involved. Apart from coincidental metaphoric elements in some such word uses (for example in "taxonomy" as deriving from biology), it is probably incorrect to look at the examples just mentioned as cases of "referential crossover" found in true figures of style.

For referential crossover, being a matter of (referential) application rather than of meaning, presupposes stability of that meaning, but the interpretative variety of performativity discussed here tends to cause semantic imbalance (at least from the synchronic point of view); here, too, is the difference between mental and interpretative performativity even in cases of what ought to be part of a conceptual system. Mental performativity creates imbalance semantically only at the reflexive level in case the language user forgets that terms, as distinct from words, are more arbitrary in meaning while words' meanings are more "natural" (the Saussurean thesis of *l'arbitraire du signe*, quite significant for the way Europeans think, holds for idealized language rather than for natural language, and for natural language only when one's *langue* is no longer unique but just one of many *langues*; again, therefore, reflexively). The confusion frequently wrought by mental performativity is due to lack of reflective detachment (a "nominalistic" attitude), while the confusion wrought by interpretative performativity is due to too much investment of belief. The semantic imbalance of terms/concepts used in mental performativity is in those terms/concepts themselves, unless those are very carefully (and therefore always to some extent arbitrarily) defined; the semantic imbalance attendant upon interpretative performativity is alien to our utterances, and is due to ourselves.

It is at first sight surprising that interpretation of the kind mentioned should hold for systems of thought which are not, as in the examples given just now, popularized with all characteristics of sloppy thinking inevitable in popularized forms, but are presented as methodologically sophisticated and "objective." The hackneyed example is metaphysics. By metaphysics I mean the species of philosophy which, in order to attain a better evaluation of the object that happens to be under analysis (and synthesis), looks to ever more comprehensive totalities as aids for such an evaluation. Historically, this was by far the greater portion of European philosophy until the emergence of antimetaphysical directions of thought at the beginning of this century. (Relevantly for present-day linguistics, this includes traditional rationalism.) Characteristically, one early-twentieth-century trend opposing metaphysics, Moore's "common sense" philosophy, attacked metaphysics not on veridical but on semantic grounds. Subsequently the Cambridge "therapeutical" school advanced the thesis that metaphysical thought is just a provisional way of thinking, from which one may be "cured" by realizing, through semantic analysis, that metaphysical problems are not genuine but only apparent problems, in much the same way as neurotic problems may be cured by one's coming to realize that those problems are not real. That approach was just a modern form of earlier philosophical considerations which (since Auguste Comte) have held that the element of myth is essential to metaphysics, and that the overcoming of mythical thought requires the overcoming of metaphysics. It is still fashionable (and by no means implausible) to say that metaphysics is "rationalized myth," just as, inversely, philosophers like Cassirer and Langer have argued that myth is (positively) inherent in so-called "rational" discourse. What I wish briefly to comment on at this point is the semantic aspect of this set of problems. Semantically there is imbalance because of the investment of belief. Language-functionally this is what I call interpretative performativity as applied to philosophical thought. It would, of course, be an irresponsible simplification to say that all philosophical problems boil down to semantic issues. Convictions of belief, and their irreconcilability in many cases, are obviously more than semantic matters. But semantic sophistication is a potent means of trying to understand, even where one cannot agree.

What is called "myth" from the point of view of the history of ideas, and "vagueness" from the point of view of conceptual analysis, is semantic imbalance from the point of view of interpretative lingual performativity. Metaphysical terms, precisely because of their highly abstract nature, need performative use if they are to function at all. Key concepts in metaphysics are, of course, to a certain extent clearly definable, but, as their semantic content is semantically unstable, one has to be committed to a belief deceptively finding rational paraphrastic form in definitions. Not surprisingly, what is a theory in types of thought largely unmetaphysical is easily called a "doctrine" in metaphysics; this is necessary for ontological validity of the metaphysical system. When thought cedes to belief, semantics becomes interpretative. Curiously enough, the evocative performativity with regard to things people already basically agree upon causes a shift from the situational to the mental pole and becomes interpretative, bringing the metaphysician face to face with what people will never agree upon. Only very few examples here must suffice.

Antonymy is not easily definable semantically because it presupposes a logical theory about contradictories. I now suggest that a definition closer to semantics would be that antonymical relations hold between polar opposites (which, quite acceptably to metaphysicians and not so to their foes, are precisely NOT contradictory). An example is that of "formal" and "material." They are sometimes used in one another's meaning, although never in the same system, so that there is no case here of semantic neutralization. (In medieval logic *suppositio materialis* and *suppositio formalis* sometimes took one another's places with different authors.) The reason is perhaps that reduction to matter is an abstraction as much as is reduction to form. "Form" and "formal" are both terms which may unite in themselves antonymous meanings. "Form" may be opposed to "substance" (as in Saussure), but it may also be identical with it, or at least coincide with it ontologically (as in Aristotle) (because of confusions such as these I was forced above to define "formal" as distinct from "according to form"). Or consider "realism" and "idealism": in the universals issue the "idealist" is the "realist," or even the "ultrarealist," as was Plato because of his "ideas" (!) philosophy. Polarity reversals are, of course, the bane of the historian of philosophy because of the all too easy polarity reversals of the ideal and the real (so that Hegelian dialectics will serve Marx's materialism as promptly as it will Hegel's idealism, or, astoundingly, Merleau-Ponty's phenomenology, which is just about the most anti-metaphysical philosophy this century has produced in Europe). For a natural language parallel, see the note on *primarily* and *ultimately* above.

I will merely mention the problem of analogy, which I tend to consider the systematic source for the possibility of polarity reversals. Analogy makes it impossible to set limits to the comprehensiveness of many concepts in a natural manner, so that limits must be arbitrary and escape the taint of arbitrariness only performatively through belief. For example, to confine myself to a popularized example, when man becomes a "rational animal," this must obscure the fact that man is not an animal, and that an animal is not rational. As it happens, in the present case the polarity is one between the "real" and the epistemological order (prescinding from the possibility, which I am not deciding here, that Porphyry's "tree" may have been intended to reflect the ontological order); reversal of this polarity has presumably been responsible for the ineradicability of the ontological argument ever since Anselm of Canterbury.

A last and more important problem from the point of view of linguistics is that of metaphor. As Reichling has shown, metaphorical application of lexical items is possible in natural language with words, or (equivalently) with their meanings, but not with terms, or (equivalently) with their conceptual contents. However, two factors are of importance here. First, a term still has (usually) a word basis, which may have been the source of the reflective elevation of that word to term/concept status, as in Aristotelian and Thomistic use of "form" for "soul," or in the linguistic functional syntactic name of "subject." Second, genuine terms/concepts always occur in context with words/meanings from natural language, a circumstance that often introduces metaphor in context (this is not so in completely artificial languages such as systems of deductive logic, but even those systems cannot be introduced except through natural language).

Polar domains have always vied for occupancy of the entire ontological domain, at least in metaphysical systems, and where polar opposites cannot be reconciled, "dialectics" will end up by accepting semantic irreconcilables.

IDEALIZATION AND REPRESENTATION: A CONTRASTIVE TYPOLOGY

With the above I have now abandoned performativity, and I propose to return to the articulatory and representative functions, in one particular aspect: how either one of these two functions may take some precedence over the other along language-typological lines. I will do this once more by analyzing Indonesian syntax as contrastive to English, thereby also continuing earlier discussions about these two languages. As English is, in all of the aspects to be discussed, representative of Indo-European languages, I shall often use the term "Indo-European" for short. As before, lack of space precludes listing of the material, which, however, I propose to deal with later (in Verhaar n.d.).

The representative function has been described as the function of speech which is directly related to the situational component. Though representation prescinds from such forms of relevance as ontological validity, this is not to say that the speaker is not concerned, declaratively or nondeclaratively, with that validity, but only that the positing of it is performative, expanding the situation to the setting in various ways. In the representative function the language user's point of orientation is his experience, situationally determined and not (yet) relativized by reflective thought.

I will now select from English and Indonesian the places functions and roles have in either language. I have said that syntax, from a language-universal point of view, has three levels: functions, categories, and roles, in that order from top to bottom. The purely mental character of the functions is clear from their formal character. When prescinding from the categories, which fill the positions in functional structure according to form, and from roles, which do so according to meaning, functions are merely a formal linear framework of sentence (and in part of discourse) organization, without trace of any situational element, let alone elements of the setting, as related to the functional structure. Categorial filling, it may be briefly repeated here, is weakly determined situationally by reason of the possibility of supercategorization according to referentiality and nonreferentiality of lexical items on the assumption that the distinction between them does not run within, but only among, categories properly speaking. There are presumably degrees of referentiality, as I have already suggested by comparing nominal and verbal status in Indonesian, and it is here hypoth-esized that these degrees also accommodate themselves to categorial distinction.

Roles, such as agentive, objective, benefactive, etc. have recently become the focus of linguistic interest, thanks largely to Fillmore's stimulating work in that area (esp. Fillmore 1968). In deviation from the Fillmore theory, I do not accept its transformational framework, and, in particular, I include among roles also those realized categorially as verbs, such as active, passive, medial, inchoative, stative, and so forth. In that manner we are now left with the sole categorial intruder in role structure, the verb, which, one gets the impression, Fillmore thinks is categorially the obligatory filling of predicate position lan-guage-universally.

This, in any event, is not invariably the case in Indonesian. The roles are much more strongly determined situationally than are the categories. Complementation of predicate filling in functional struc-ture frequently presupposes "participants" at the level of the situa-tional component and in one-to-one relationships with the roles: agent, patient, recipient, and the like. On the utterance level such constants appear by role distribution across functional structure. This distribution differs from language to language, according to lan-guage- and type-specific rules.

The study of roles has had a checkered history. In the Western tradition (typologically in Indo-European), functions are more deter-minative of roles than roles are of functions; as a consequence, roles have often been determined in terms of functions. For example, the subject has frequently been determined as characteristically the agent, at least in active sentences (and the Indo-European verb is typically active). In structuralism it has especially been the Austronesian lan-guages that have made linguists aware of the fact that, while in Indo-European languages roles take concrete morphemic form as cases, in languages without morphemic case the verb has taken upon itself the markings assigning a specific role to the functional object: the verb-focus structure. Indonesian is also of that type, as are many regional languages in Indonesia and the Philippines.

There is still no clarity about the role of role, language- and type-specifically. Even Fillmore, whose theory is marked by the significant assumption that roles are more "basic" than functions (which he as-signs to overt structure), has been led, among other things, by con-sidering evidence from ergative languages where there is no categorial subject filling corresponding to the Indo-European "nominative," at least in certain species of sentences. He says that such sentences apparently lack "subjectivalization"; and he explains this as the result of one out of more topicalization options (Fillmore 1968: 57). This means in fact that Fillmore, after having made functional structure generatively later than role structure, still allows functions to be determinable categorially, so that the Indo-European requirement that such filling for subject position must be "nominative" is supposed to apply to non-Indo-European languages as well. One wonders if it is not more consistent to say that, if roles are more "basic" than functions, then functions adapt to roles ALSO in that a subject is not necessarily in the "nominative." Fillmore's hunch that, in certain languages, i.e. in certain species of sentences in them, there is no subjectivalization must then be rephrased as the assumption that such sentences lack "nominative" subjectivalization. The problem is not whether a subject must always be there (if perhaps only in distributionally demonstrable zero form), for there may be many reasons why the subject is absent. Rather, the problem is whether a subject may take "oblique" categorial form. It definitely can in Indonesian. Before I argue this in detail, a few words on ergativity may be in order.

Ergativity has become the subject of rather acrimonious debate. Fillmore's level-headed discussion of that issue (1968: 54ff.; *passim*) suggests there is nothing mysterious in it, that the description should suit all the data and that that is all there is to it. Yet in the background of this there is some impatience with other linguists' interest in the "psychological" approach to language particulars in such cases, and one must hand it to Fillmore that he has picked his examples well enough to make that approach suspect. But then, unfortunately for the "psychological" approach, that is not too hard. I suggest, however, that there is behind Fillmore's critique a too heavy demand for rationalistic clarity, as one would expect from transformational grammar in any of its forms. Fillmore's comments, however, are reasonable enough compared to the badly argued and indignant remarks of Wilbur (1970), who proposes that all the talk about ergativity, as allegedly motivated by inexpert enthusiasm for the exotic, be relegated to oblivion. I wish to show briefly that ergativity, with a slightly altered understanding of that term, is a serious issue, not to be obscured by any enthusiasm for the unenthusiastic, and is important for an adequate analysis of what kind of thinking goes into a language of the ergative type.

A language is usually called ergative if it has one case in the "nominative" (i.e. comparable with categorial subject form in Indo-European languages) for the subject of transitive verbs and another "oblique"

case for the subject of intransitive verbs and the object of transitive
verbs. I think it is reasonable to assume that the categorial identity
of subject of intransitives and object of transitives is determinable in
terms of roles. Then I suggest we take the following theoretical steps.
Terminologically, we distinguish only between "straight" case and
"oblique" case, ignoring other cases, if any. Then we apply the term
"straight" to endocentric phrases as well as to "straight" case, and the
term "oblique" to exocentric phrases as well as to "oblique" case,
provided that in either case where there is a phrase the head is a
noun. In that manner, we shall have transferred a morphemic case
issue to a syntactic framework, which would be valid also, but not
only, for morphemic case. We would then simply speak about
straight subjects and oblique subjects. Now, Indonesian may have
oblique subjects (only phrase-wise), and this would mean that Indonesian is an ergative language. The term "ergative" would also
continue to be a reasonable term from the etymological point of
view, for oblique objects go with actives and oblique subjects with
passives. (So far as I have been able to ascertain, obliqueness and
straightness can be optionally selected with all the verbs — a long list
— that can take oblique objects in active form.) There seems to be no
need to speak about subjectivalization in the case of only straight subjects; for it would hold of oblique ones as well. For from a language-
universal point of view the subject position is empty, in the sense of
neutral, as to categorial form. Oblique filling gives precedence of role
over function, not in the sense that roles are higher up the cline towards
the mental component than functions (which would have to be the
theoretical formula if Fillmore's "case grammar" were to be translated
into the theory followed in this paper), but in the sense that the representative function of a language like Indonesian, and of any ergative
language, takes precedence over the articulatory function. I agree with
Fillmore (1968: 60) that the claim that ergative languages are more
"primitive" than nonergative languages is totally unwarranted, but it is
not without interest to determine why. The reason is not only that
(as Fillmore says) with our present knowledge of intellectual evolution
we cannot know such things, but also that predominance of the representative over the articulatory function of speech in ergative languages entails that the purely formal organization (as apparent in functional structure in syntax) cedes, more than is the case in nonergative
languages, to semantic organization (as apparent in role structure) in
syntax. While this difference cannot be shown to affect intellectual
achievement either way, the charge of "primitivity" is itself evidently

based upon rationalism. Finally, there seems to be no ground for letting topicalization preside over such issues.

I have said that passives (either with straight or oblique subject) approach nominal status in Indonesian. This raises the question whether passivization entails categorial shift or "conversion." If it does, that means that most of verbal morphemic change in passives would not be inflection but derivation. As it happens, however, it is systematically much more consistent to consider the morphemic list of passives as paradigmatic if we interpret the preposed (frequently: prefixed) pronominal agentives as "role flection." Functional flection in the verb is confined to actives, while within the actives there is no flection for subject, and only a few for object. If, then, verbal flection is for the greater part role flection, this confirms the prevalence of role over function in the language. One of the reasons why in Indonesian studies a status approaching nominal status has been accorded to verbal passives is that the preposed pronominal agentives do not (except in a few morphemically bound instances) differ in form from pronouns in any position, while all of them, even the morphemically free forms, are syntactically inseparable from the verb form. Many regional languages in Indonesia have the same structures.

Preference of role over function, then, goes hand in hand with the more strongly "nominal" status of verbs, and especially of their passive forms. If it is true that nouns are more strongly referential than verbs, then what I have just analyzed also serves to confirm the stronger "representative" function of Indonesian as compared to the stronger articulatory function of a language like English.

I must here recall the "juxtapositional" nature of the subject-predicate construction in Indonesian. I have said that such a structure is normal on the phrase level in Indo-European, but not on the level of the highest functions, which is the level where it also obtains in Indonesian. If we now compare role structure with functional structure there appears to be an almost perfect parallelism. I will first suppose that, in a language like English, possessive pronouns, when considered from the point of view of semantics as is natural in role analysis, are "oblique" forms of personal pronouns (indeed, in many languages semantic possessives are categorially oblique forms of personal pronouns). On this supposition, oblique agents of phrases are perfectly normal in English (as in *his attempts*, for example), as are oblique patients (as in *his elimination, his invitation*, etc., with the interpretation that the person possessively referred to by *his* does not eliminate, but is eliminated, does not invite, but is invited). Then it turns out that what is true of functional structure is true of role structure also: roles in Indonesian are "juxtapositional" as much as functions and on the sentence level, while this "juxtaposition" is entirely normal in a language like English also but on subsentential levels only.

CONCLUDING NOTES

It would be tempting to compare the "structural" (as distinct from genetic) kind of typology with another one, also based on syntax, recently brought to the fore by Lehmann (1972, 1973). In that approach VO (verb-object) and OV (object-verb) is taken as matrix of subsentential sequential order, as appearing (in the case of VO) in preposition plus noun (phrase), adjective plus noun, and comparison plus standard. The comparison would lead me to eliminate V in favor of the predicate, to have the sentential order expressed only functionally, then to compare with that functional structure the role structure. Analysis so far has also led me to think that a concept like transitivity would have to be reviewed for both function and role, and that transitivity should be extended to the governor-governed pair in the subsentential levels as well (see Verhaar n.d.).

A last note on the "psychological" approach may be in order. It is unfortunately true that unscientific elements have so far had a great deal to do with attempts in that direction. The examples cited by Fillmore (1968) are the most vulnerable ones as the path of grammar is much more slippery to tread than that of lexical analysis. On the other hand, since the advent of transformational grammar, it has become fashionable to look down even on a much more solid approach like that of the Sapir-Whorf tradition. Many more factors, too, lead one to suspect that mentalism, rationalistic as it is, is not prepared to deal with the vague in natural language. It may be extremely hard to make cultural features available from language, especially in grammar, even without having mentalist critics at the back of one's mind, and it seems certain that a gap like that between mentalism in linguistics and anthropological linguistics concerns much more than just different views of the nature of language.

REFERENCES

BACH, EMMON, ROBERT T. HARMS, *editors*
    1968   *Universals in linguistic theory*. New York: Holt, Rinehart and
         Winston.

BLACK, MAX
1969 "Austin on performatives," in *Symposium on J. L. Austin*. Edited by K. T. Fann. London: Routledge and Kegan Paul.

BÜHLER, KARL
1934 *Sprachtheorie, die Darstellungsfunktion der Sprache*. Jena: Gustav Fischer.

CASSIRER, ERNST
1952 *Language and myth*. Translated by Susanne Langer. New York: Harper and Bros. (Originally published 1925 as *Sprache und Mythos*.)

CHERRY, E. COLIN
1957 *On human communication: a review, a survey, and a criticism*. Cambridge, Mass.: M.I.T. Press.

DE VRIES, J. W.
1971 Want en omdat. *De Nieuwe Taalgids* 64:414–420.

FANN, K. T., *editor*
1969 *Symposium on J. L. Austin*. London: Routledge and Kegan Paul.

FILLMORE, CHARLES J.
1968 "The case for case," in *Universals in linguistic theory*. Edited by E. Bach and R. T. Harms. New York: Holt, Rinehart and Winston.

GEACH, PETER THOMAS
1962 *Reference and generality: an examination of some medieval and modern theories*. Ithaca, N.Y.: Cornell University Press.

JACOBS, R., P. ROSENBAUM, *editors*
1970 *Readings in English transformational grammar*. Waltham, Mass.: Ginn.

KAHN, CHARLES H.
1973 *The verb 'be' in ancient Greek*. Dordrecht: D. Reidel.

LEHMANN, W. P.
1972 Converging theories in linguistics. *Language* 48:266–275.
1973 A structural principle of language and its implications. *Language* 49:47–66.

LEWIS, M. BLANCHE
1969 *Sentence analysis in modern Malay*. London: Cambridge University Press.

MERLEAU-PONTY, MAURICE
1962 *Phenomenology of perception*. London: Routledge and Kegan Paul. (Originally published 1945 as *Phénoménologie de la perception*.)

MORRIS, CHARLES
1946 *Signs, language and behavior*. Englewood Cliffs, N.J.: Prentice-Hall.

NATANSON, MAURICE, *editor*
1973 *Phenomenology and the social sciences*, two volumes. Evanston, Ill.: Northwestern University Press.

OGDEN, C. K., I. A. RICHARDS
1930 *The meaning of meaning: a study of the influence of language upon thought and of the science of symbolism*. New York: Harcourt, Brace. (Originally published 1923.)

PAP, LEO
1951   A note on *lingual* vs. *linguistic*. *General Linguistics* 2:42.
PARAIN, BRICE
1942   *Recherches sur la nature et les fonctions du langage*. Paris: Gallimard.
REICHLING, ANTON
1967   *Het woord: een studie omtrent de grondslag van taal en taalgebruik*. Zwolle: W. E. J. Tjeenk Willink. (Originally published 1935.)
ROSS, J. R.
1970   "On declarative sentences," in *Readings in English transformational grammar*. Edited by R. Jacobs and P. Rosenbaum. Waltham, Mass.: Ginn.
RUTHERFORD, W.
1970   Some observations concerning subordinate clauses in English. *Language* 46:97–115.
STAAL, J. F.
1970   Performatives and token-reflexives. *Linguistic Inquiry* 1:373–381.
TEEUW, A.
1971   "Foreword," in *A grammar of Toba Batak*, by H. N. van der Tuuk. The Hague: Martinus Nijhoff.
THORNE, JAMES PETER
1972   On nonrestrictive relative clauses. *Linguistic Inquiry* 3:552–556.
URMSON, J. O., *editor*
1962   *J. L. Austin: how to do the thing with words*. London: Oxford University Press.
URMSON, J. O., G. J. WARNOCK, *editors*
1961   *J. L. Austin: philosophical papers*. London: Oxford University Press.
VAN DER TUUK, H. N.
1971   *A grammar of Toba Batak*. The Hague: Martinus Nijhoff. (Originally published as *Tobasche spraakkunst*, volume one, 1864; volume two, 1867.)
VERHAAR, JOHN W. M.
1963   *Some relations between perception, speech and thought*. Assen: van Gorcum.
1973a "Phenomenology and present-day linguistics," in *Phenomenology and the social sciences*, volume one. Edited by M. Natanson, 361–464. Evanston, Ill.: Northwestern University Press.
1973b "On noumenalization." To appear in a *Festschrift*.
n.d.   "The role of role." Unpublished manuscript.
VYGOTSKY, L. S.
1962   *Thought and language*. Cambridge, Mass.: M.I.T. Press.
WILBUR, TERENCE H.
1970   "The ergative case and the so-called ergative-type languages," in *Papers from the Sixth Regional Meeting of the Chicago Linguistic Society, April 16-18, 1970*. Chicago, Ill.: Chicago Linguistic Society.

SECTION THREE

Ethnoscience

The Synthetic Informant Model On the Simulation of Large Lexical/Semantic Fields

OSWALD WERNER

This paper follows a simple outline. First, I present a hurried definition of ethnoscience. It is assumed, however, that the reader is generally familiar with the goals of this subfield of anthropology. Second, in somewhat greater detail I discuss the steps that have been found to be necessary for a successful simulation. In particular, I deal with the problem of the ways in which this simulation may differ from other social simulations and from artificial intelligence (AI). My collaborators, students, and staff are engaged in a long-term project to perfect the available models by insights gathered from ethnoscience, microsociolinguistics, generative semantics, computer experiments with large humanlike memory structures, heuristic programming (especially automatic theorem proving), psychiatry (especially abnormal types of speech), and cognitive psychology (especially sources dealing with the content and function of memory).

The "current model" is the summary of our insights up to the end of September, 1973. In a real sense, since the emphasis of this work is

This work was supported by a grant MH-10940 from the National Institute of Mental Health. Various versions and fragments were presented at the Central States Anthropological Meetings, Cleveland, Ohio (1972) and St. Louis, Missouri (1973), at the Conference for Anthropological Theory on the Fringes, Oswego, New York (1972) and the precongress conference at Wingspread, Racine, Wisconsin (Johnson Foundation) of the IXth International Congress of Ethnological and Anthropological Sciences, Chicago, Illinois, 1973. I am grateful for the inspiration of many more people than can be listed in this space. Special tribute is due to Professors Marvin Loflin and James Silverberg, the organizers of the precongress conference at Wingspread, and especially to Ms. Martha Evens, whose checking of every detail with great care improved the manuscript. Remaining errors are due to my obstinacy.

experimental, the model is open and closure in the near future is unlikely.

ETHNOSCIENCE

To be considered a member of a culture makes certain demands on a
human being. One has to be able to function appropriately in many —
thought not necessarily all — sociophysical contexts. One's behavior in
these contexts is based on everything one knows about the world
around him.

The goal of ethnoscience is to invent theories that represent reasonable facsimiles of cultural knowledge. Although we are interested in the
description of the cultural knowledge of particular cultures, the primary
aim is to describe the nature of human cultural knowledge in general.
This paper is an attempt to show how the characterization of human
knowledge may be expanded with the aid of computers. That is, more
precisely, how one can design a complex program system that is capable
of imitating some aspects of the verbal behavior of human beings.

The practical framework for achieving this end is a question-answering device. Such a machine should be general enough to be able to
answer questions that have never been asked before. It should also be
capable of giving appropriate answers of specifiable length, depending
not only on all of its knowledge, but also on context and the amount
of time that is available or specified for answering.

SIMULATION

Current Status

Today, almost all simulation of social and cultural systems by computers is done outside of anthropology, usually by engineers. They are
fast learning the linguist's and anthropologist's trades and will soon
leave us behind. Yet, at the same time, the anthropologist/linguist's
knowledge of "exotic" languages is indispensable for this work.

There are three types of simulation of cognition *qua* question answering today. All three have been conducted by engineers:
(a)   There is (to the best of my knowledge) only one experiment with
explicit aspects of "context." This is Weizenbaum's ELIZA (1966 and
later), which has "scripts" encompassing specialized knowledge and

associated strategies. One such script can imitate a Rogerian psychiatric interview with a live "patient"; another teaches calculus.

(b)   Quillian's (1969) TLC (Teachable Language Comprehender) is a large associative memory system. It is predominantly based on dictionary definitions. However, it can enlarge its store of knowledge by integrating new information with old. Its capabilities are to give just one paraphrase for any lexical item and does not allow for multiple paraphrases of sentences.

(c)   By far the largest group of experiments (e.g. Raphael 1968; Biss, et al. 1971; Schwartz, et al. 1970; Winograd 1967; Slagle 1971; Nilsson 1971) deal with inference-making deductive systems. These are very sophisticated theorem-proving devices. Answering a question can be viewed as the proving of a theorem. If the question can be answered, there is then a valid inference that leads to the answer. These experiments usually have small and simple listlike memories while the deductions may often be called "massive." Chess and other game-playing programs fall into this category. A predominant theme of all these experiments is preoccupation with heuristics. That is, how to select a "best move" among all possible "moves" without having to enumerate and evaluate each and every possible move. In all interesting problems the number of possible "moves" is astronomical — even for computers.

Design Features

According to Naylor, et al. (1966: 23), a simulation consists of the following steps (represented here in a somewhat simplified form).

1.   Formulation of the problem: to imitate human question-answering behavior. This involves: (a) the programming into the device of some initial body of knowledge; (b) the ability of the device to add continuously to this body of knowledge on the basis of newly acquired information; (c) the ability to relate new knowledge to the old; (d) the ability to answer questions of varying lengths that are put to it (that is, it should have full paraphrase power, by which I mean that it should be able to abstract complex or large bodies of information down to their most salient features and/or expand on topics on which the device is better informed than the questioner); and (e) the ability to request supplementary information, or state that such supplementary information is necessary for an adequate answer to some question. The requirements (a) to (e) are generally arranged in the order in which increased difficulties of solutions seem to lie.

2.   Collection and processing of real world data. If we restrict ourselves to English, such collections in various forms and stages of completeness are easily available within existing dictionaries (on the simplest level), encyclopedias (on a more complex level), and a vast technical literature (on the most complex level). For cultures other than English, ethnoscience field techniques provide a method for collecting such information (e.g. Werner and Fenton 1970: Appendix).

The approach is lexical simply because it is assumed that the lexicon of a language (or of a subdomain of language), and the meaning field associated with the lexicon, is an explicit representation of human knowledge. That means that inherently implicit knowledge (knowledge that is implicit for every speaker of a culture) is, at this stage of our model, excluded. This does not preclude later inclusion when we become better informed on the subject.

At present, all preliminary processing of the data is done by hand. This method seems to imply that the complex "actual" speech events or written texts are first reduced to simple sentences by hand because to this day a human being is still the best parsing device. Subsequently, the processing continues with the reduction of the simple sentences to strings of naming units (most simply words) related to each other by a small set of lexical/semantic relations. A few years ago these were essentially the fourteen relations of Casagrande and Hale (1967). I will present later the list of the current set in detail. I have dealt with these relations in previous publications (Werner 1969, 1972, etc.). Although other sets of relations are found in various publications, most, if not all, of these can be compared to the complex relations discussed below.

There are ongoing experimental designs in logic, generative semantics, and artificial intelligence which try to approximate the natural logic of human beings by the extension of the formalism to modal logic (e.g. Snyder 1971), temporal logic (e.g. Rescher and Urquhart 1971), and possibly others. However, I shall not deal with this topic in greater detail here (see below).

3.   Formulation of the mathematical model. The major part of this paper deals with this problem. The term "mathematical" requires some clarification. The mathematics employed is largely a form of graph theory and a subsequent matrix representation of graphs. The mathematics can be called relational and the simulation technique deterministic. Because the interactions of the model vary through time, the simulation is also dynamic.

The structure of traditional ethnoscience models is static. There is good evidence that cognitive behavior as represented for example by question answering is not. One of the difficulties with "context" is its dynamic, changing character which must be taken into account. More on this follows below.

4. Estimation of parameters of operating characteristics from real world data. In a truly deterministic model there is no room for parameter estimation. Given the question "What kind of animals are there?" a totally deterministic device would respond by supplying the entire folk classification of animals. Though this may be useful at times (especially during model building), it imitates human behavior poorly. In the same situation, American English speakers usually name five animals: "horse," "cat," "dog," "cow," and "sheep" are very likely to be among these. Interestingly, these are also the animal names of the highest frequency of occurrence in a corpus of five million words collected in the *American Heritage word frequency book* (Carroll, et al. 1971), in which "animal" occurred approximately 4,000 times; "horse": 2,000; "dog": 2,000; "cat": 700; "cow": 500; and "sheep": 500). This implies that the "associations" (edges, lines) of the graphs connecting the nodes (words) must be weighted: some "associations" are more likely to occur and/or are stronger than others.

A simple word-frequency count, however, is at best a crude approximation because first, the count for "horse" includes the occurrences of "horse" in constructions like "to horse around" and others similar to it, and second, the strength of "association" is related to frequency and possibly some other linkages (e.g. due to positive or negative cathexis of whatever source) between two naming units (words). Such pairwise frequency counts on a large scale are unavailable. Therefore, the raw word frequencies are used as a first approximation.

5. Evaluation of the model and parameter estimates. Some of this can be done by inspection. However, I perceive the major bulk of the simulation to be in this area. It is unwise at this point to plan this research in any other but long-range terms. The most crucial undertaking is to experiment with a wide variety of types of models. Our ignorance about human question-answering behavior or about the nature of human cultural knowledge is profound. Very strong commitment to ANY MODEL is at present premature and not warranted. In fact, the heavy emphasis of this work is on the refinement of the model. The role of the computer is primarily as a device that makes experimentation with huge lexical/semantic fields feasible. Although the current model perhaps still permits evaluation by inspection, some of the characteristics of the model can be clarified only by experimental runs on a computer. Such runs could demonstrate or refute the utility of this particular model for the

representation of very large lexical/semantic fields. This is especially important since human knowledge is vast and complex. No oversimplification will do the job that is proposed as the ultimate goal of this research. I agree with Quillian (1969) — and this is at present largely a matter of faith — that the tremendous size of human memory is in itself a most crucial parameter of a simulation of cultural knowledge. That is, a large machine simulation may result in qualitative as well as any quantitative differences *vis à vis* experimentation "by hand" with minute fragments (50 ± 20 words of lexical/semantic fields).

The experimental nature of this work must be emphasized for still another reason. Almost twenty years ago linguists and computer engineers rushed into machine translation. They eventually found that the major obstacle to success was our ignorance of the nature of human language. It is my aim to make a virtue out of a situation which has not changed substantially. If we assume that we know very little about intelligent behavior and the simulation of it, the only safe approach is to treat every aspect of the work as provisional, exploratory, and experimental. That is, to do basic computer-aided research into the nature of language. Specifically, this means maximum concentration on the improvement of the model and the use of computer programming only to the extent that it is productive in advancing or improving the quality of our insights. In other words, the emphasis is on insights and not on superficially successful but *ad hoc* solutions.

6.   Formulation of a computer program. This should be viewed as a relatively trivial problem, although I do not deny the fact that (a) having to formulate one's model in programmable steps requires much more rigorous statements of the model, and (b) the very process of solving real programming problems can (in the end) contribute to a better solution of problems within the model. What I would like to stress, however, is that the formulation of the model must be as independent as possible from the LIMITATIONS imposed on programming by the state of the art of current computer hardware, by the state of the art of current software, by the state of the art of storage facilities, as well as the computational speeds of current computers. It is premature to talk about efficient programs. Our emphasis must be on efficient models. Let the computer industry catch up with our models if these are accurate pictures of human behavior, rather than let our models become victims of the inadequacies of the current stage of computer engineering.

7.   Naylor, et al. (1966) list three more steps for the conduct of simulation experiments. These are: validation; design of simulation experiments; and analysis of simulation data. Until our question-answering

models can be perfected much beyond their current stage, any discussion of these last three steps remains largely academic.

The ultimate validation of a question-answering device is a three-way interaction between machine, informant, and the anthropologist. Such symbiosis will surely revolutionize anthropology, but is at present not "just around the corner." Crucial questions (analogous to crucial experiments) and the printing out of the steps by which the machine arrives at a given answer (much as Raphael's [1968] SIR program does) and submitting the "reasoning" of the device to the informant will add depth, interest, and intellectual excitement to anthropological fieldwork. It is conceivable that such crucial questions may someday achieve the same relevance to the simulation of human cultural knowledge as crucial experiments did in the development of the physical sciences and biology. Meanwhile, an overwhelming amount of work remains to be done.

CURRENT MODEL

This discussion will include the major features of the model and any resemblances it may have to intelligent humanlike question-answering behavior. There is an important first premise. Since the objective is to imitate as faithfully as possible human capabilities of question answering, every feature of the model must be accounted for by reference to actual skills or characteristics which human beings exhibit.

Lexical/Semantic Field

The model consists of an articulated memory of several levels in which lexical items (possibly also sublexical items) form an associational lexical/semantic field. The units of the field may be simple or complex (chunks — see short-term memory) which are linked by lexical/semantic relations.

The relevant lexical/semantic relations are: Modification or Attribution, symbolized by M; Synonymy, S; and Taxonomy, T. Many properties of lexical/semantic fields can be characterized by these relations. It can be shown that these correspond to different major types of predication (Werner 1972: 290).

1. Attribution(1), symbolized by M(1), is:
   (1a) Reflexive: $(x) M(1) (x)$

(1b) Symmetric: If (x) M(1) (y) then (y) M(1) (x)

(1c) Intransitive: It is not true that if (x) M(1) (y) and (y) M(1) (z) then (x) M(1) (z)

This relation is usually found only in componential analyses and/or cross-classification, e.g. "male parent = parental male = father."

2. Attribution(2), symbolized by M(2), is:

(2a) Reflexive: (see above, 1a)

(2b) Asymmetric: If (x) M(2) (y) then (y) M(2) (x) may or may not be true

(2c) Intransitive: (see above, 1c)

This is the common relation of attribution, e.g. "the blue house."

3. Synonymy, symbolized by S, is:

(3a) Reflexive: (see above, 1a)

(3b) Symmetric: (see above, 1b)

(3c) Transitive: If (x) S (y) and (y) S (z) then (x) S (z)

This represents the exact identity of lexical items or of construction of greater length, e.g. "A physician is a doctor."

4. Taxonomy, symbolized by T, is:

(4a) Reflexive: (see above, 1a)

(4b) Asymmetric: (see above, 2b)

(4c) Transitive: (see above, 3c)

This is the relation of class inclusion (Casagrande and Hale 1967), e.g. "A lion is an animal."

To this we must add two types, each with two subtypes, of relations of linear ordering or Queueing, Q:

5. Queueing(1.1) immediate (strictly ordered), symbolized by Q(1.1), is:

(5a) Nonreflexive: (x) Q(1.1) (x) not part of the relation

(5b) Asymmetric: (see above, 2b)

(5c) Intransitive: (see above, 1c)

This is the relation of immediate ordering and strict ordering, i.e. no repetition. The immediate succession of integers comes to mind as an example.

6. Queueing(1.2) immediate (loosely ordered), symbolized by Q(1.2), is:

(6a) Potentially reflexive: ((x) may succeed itself)

(6b) Potentially symmetric: ((x) Q(1.2) (y) may appear in reverse order (y) Q(1.2) (x)).

(6c) Intransitive: (see above, 1c)

This is the relation of verbal plans (Werner 1966; Topper 1972) for direction, recipes, etc.

7. Queueing(2.1) eventual (strictly ordered), symbolized by Q(2.1), is:

(7a) Nonreflexive: (see above, 5a)

(7b) Asymmetric: (see above, 2b)

(7c) Transitive: (see above, 3c)

This is the relation of eventual succession, for example the larger than (or smaller than) relation between numbers; it may include all comparison of adjectives.

8. Queueing(2.2) eventual (loosely ordered), symbolized by Q(2.2), is:

(8a) Potentially reflexive: (see above, 6a)

(8b) Potentially symmetric: (see above, 6b)

(8c) Transitive: (see above, 3c)

This is the relation of the eventual succession of the relation of provenience (Casagrande and Hale 1967), e.g. "Sheep eventually become mutton."

Of these relations, the Taxonomic T and all four Queueing Q's have inverses, symbolized as T and $Q(1.1) \ldots Q(2.2)$, respectively. The inverse of T ("all a are b") is T ("some b are a"). The inverse of Q ("a and then b") is Q ("b is preceded by a").

In addition, at least all the basic propositional relations of the first-order predicate calculus of ordinary symbolic logic must be included:

9. Conjunction or "and": C

10. Disjunction or "or": D

These apply within predications as well as between predications or sentences.

11. Negation: N

This is the only unitary relation.

12. Implication: F ("if ... then ...")

13. Equivalence: X or the double implication ("... if and only if ...")

The last two link only predications or sentences.

Complex relations can be built out of the primitive ones. Such relations are "part of," "is like," "causes," and others. For example: "(b) is part of (a)" has the structure:

(b)T ((part)M(a)) = (b) (T(part)M) (a) or (b) is an (a)-part

where (T(part)M) symbolizes a complex relation.

Similarly: (b) is like (a)

(b)T ((like)M(a)) = (b) (T(like)M) (a)

(b) causes (a)

(b)T ((cause)M(a)) = (b) (T(cause)M) (a)

(b) is kind of (a)

(b)T ((kind)M(a)) = (b) (T(kind)M) (a) = (b)T(a)

(The equal sign should be represented as the relation X of equivalence, but it is used here instead for greater clarity.)

Associative Memory[1]

The following graphs represent the structure of the basic taxonomic organization of the associative memory network.

Parts of the associative memory network utilizing the relations of the preceding section may be illustrated as in Diagram 1.

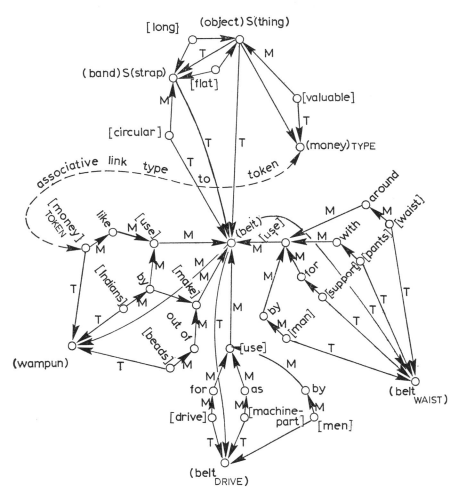

Diagram 1.   Associative memory network with its relations

---

[1]   Because of its relative complexity, some readers may prefer to skip this section and return to it after reading through the section below entitled "The Deductive Component."

The relation of T is represented by downward arrows, the relation of M by upward arrows. Upward M arrows form a unit with the node to which they point. That is, all M relations must be read together with the head noun (naming unit) that is modified, with the label of the node to which M is pointing and from the lower node up in cycles. The union of all cycles represents a "complete" definition. "Completeness" refers to the capacity of the device at one point in time, not the completeness of any particular definition. For example, the graph of Diagram 1 should be read as shown in Diagram 2.

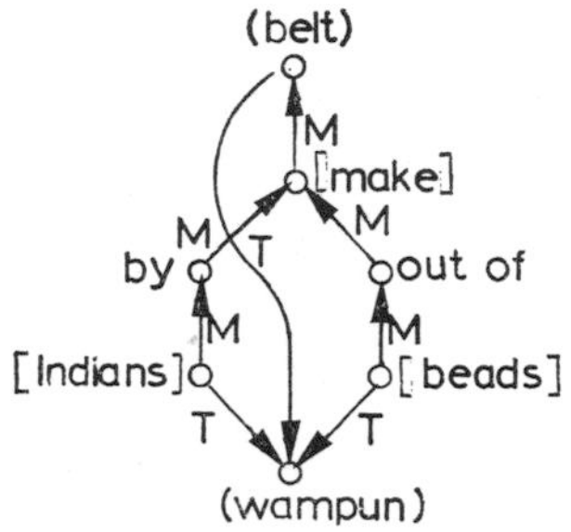

Diagram 2.
    Cycle 1: (wampum) T (belt) or "A wampum is a belt,"
    Cycle 2: (wampum) T ((belt)M(make) M(by) M(Indians))), or "A wampum is a belt made by Indians," and
    Cycle 3: (wampum) T ((belt)M((make)M(out of M(beads)))), or "A wampum is a belt made out of beads"

    Multiple labels per node are synonyms. The prepositions represent a case system (Fillmore 1968). The relation of "deep" to "surface" cases is left open (see representation of verbs). Numbers attached to the arrows or the thickness of the line (not graphed) are measures of strength of association. A useful first approximation of this strength is frequency of occurrence in a large corpus. Because of the transitivity of the relation of taxonomy, all nodes of a taxonomy are connected to every superordinate node by downward T arrows. This is necessary because the strength of association between a higher node and a specific node may be stronger than the strength of either to an intermediate node (e.g., "lion" and "animal" are more strongly linked ["lion": frequency 450; "animal": 4,000; see *American Heritage word frequency book*] than either is to "mammal" [200]). In Diagram 1, the dotted line between (money), the main or type entry of "money," and [money], a token occurrence of "money" (following roughly Quillian's [1968] usage) as a modifier of (belt), represents one of a large number of cross-references to other taxonomies. Thus every token occurrence must have a type-taxonomy to which it is connected.

Before discussing Diagram 1 in detail, it may be useful to draw the graph schematically, as shown in Diagram 3.

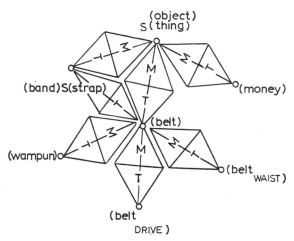

Diagram 3.   Schematic representation of Diagram 1

The triangles pointing upward (with one of their vertices) are marked M for they represent the relations of modification applied to the dominating node. The triangles pointing downward are marked T for the taxonomic relations they represent between the modified superordinate term.

To the question "What is a belt?" the device first partitions out the subtaxonomy in which (belt) is a subordinate node of (band)S(strap) and "reads" downward toward (belt) by following a possible path in the M triangle. For example, "A belt is a strap or band that is circular," or "A belt is a circular band or strap," and others.

Since belt is ambiguous, a possible starting point for the same question is (belt(WAIST)). In that case a possible answer is "A belt is a belt used for support," or "A belt is a belt used for support used with pants," and other possible combinations, given by the four branches of the graph. Since speakers of English tend to avoid expressions like "A belt is a belt . . .," such stylistic constraint is accounted for by requiring the insertion of the next higher node, thus "A belt is a band or strap used for support."

The rule of short-term memory which governs the linearization of parts of the nonlinear long-term and intermediate memory (see below) can be stated as follows: enter at the node about which information is requested; go directly to the most strongly linked superordinate node and take one or more paths back (or . . . and take part of the M triangle or all of it by applying several cycles back to the starting node). With some schizophrenics, as noted by Arieti (1955), psychiatrists have obtained different results. Instead of entering the graph, going up and reading down, speakers with this particular variety of schizophrenic speech disturbance seem to stay right at the node of entry and read down, answering, for example, "It depends what kind of a belt you mean — a wampum, a drive belt, or a belt that supports pants." No more information can be given here as to why this is so. I have addressed myself to this problem in a previous paper (Werner, et al. 1975). Needless to say, many details remain to be worked out.

The "part-whole" relation from the preceding section is represented graphically in Diagram 4.

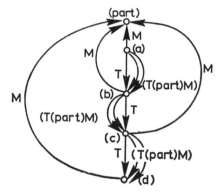

Diagram 4.   Part-whole relations

The interpretation is the same: downward arrows are taxonomic T; upward arrows are attributive M and are dependent on the unit to which they point, that is, the two must be read together. Double arrows are the part-whole relation.

However, care must be exercised in the interpretation of this graph. The apparent chain of T relations between (a), (b), (c), and (d) seems to imply transitivity. That transitivity is blocked, however, by the M relations which cannot be read independently of the nodes to which they point. Thus in such structures the M relation supersedes the transitivity of the T relation.

The part-whole relation is in this case also transitive, and so are "cause" and "kind" relations. The fact that the "kind" relation and the T relation are equivalent is handled by equivalence rules, in this case, $T = (T(kind)M)$, or $T \; X \; (T(kind)M$, where X is the relation of equivalence. Because of the equivalence rule, the apparent chain of T relations must be interpreted transitively. But this is an exceptional case governed by the above equivalence rule.

The representation of verbs is somewhat oversimplified in Diagram 1. Each verb must be accompanied with an associated case system. Rather than deciding at this point on the distinction between deep versus surface case systems, it seems best to list the surface prepositions and hope for deeper generalizations later. The theoretical status of "deep" cases is far from clear today (see Stockwell, et al. 1973). The assignment of the prepositions is based on the nominalization of the sentence in question. It seems that in nominalized form verbs "show" their associated case-marking prepositions more explicitly. The following four sample sentences (shown in Diagrams 5 through 8) are given as demonstrations of the power of the representation for displaying the variations among similar verbs. A more detailed treatment (with examples from Stockwell, et al. 1973) will be offered in a subsequent paper.

"The men loaded the wagon with hay."
"The loading of the wagon by the men with hay . . ."

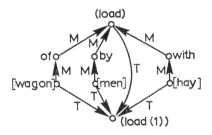

Diagram 5.

Here, (load(1)) is a taxonomic descendant of (load) and acts as a "chunking label" (see below) for the specific mention of the verb, i.e. with wagon, men and hay.

Similarly:

"The men loaded hay on the wagon."
"The loading of hay by the men on the wagon . . ."

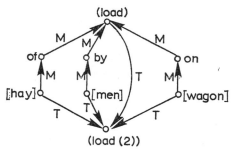

Diagram 6.

"John rented an apartment to Mary."
"The renting of an apartment to Mary by John . . ."

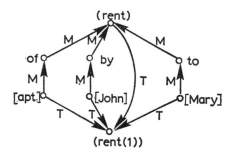

Diagram 7.

"John rented an apartment from Mary."
"The renting of an apartment from Mary by John . . ."

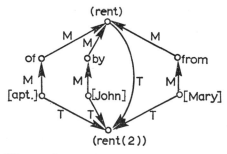

Diagram 8.

With the use of the taxonomic descendants which are indexed for each occurrence i (e.g. (rent(2))) Diagram 1 can be partially redrawn in simplified form, as shown in Diagram 9.

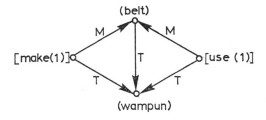

Diagram 9.

In Diagram 9, [make(1)] and [use(1)] are tokens of (make(1)) and (use(1)), shown more fully in Diagrams 10 and 11.

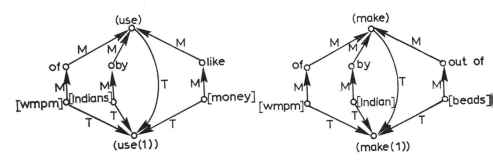

Diagram 10.   Diagram 11.

The terms in square brackets (tokens) are associated with their respective types in other parts of the memory system.

Articulation of Memory

At least since William James, psychologists have agreed on two levels of memory, a short-range, immediate memory and a long-range, permanent memory. For reasons that will become apparent, I will call the latter tacit memory. A few psychologists postulate a third level, which I will call intermediate memory; I hope to show that it is essential to simulation of cultural knowledge and therefore to inference making.

The permanent, long-range, or tacit memory has the following characteristics: it is virtually limitless and its contents are as rich and varied
as human knowledge. There seems to be no fading of traces, i.e. nothing
is ever completely forgotten (Newell and Simon 1967: 245). In our
model this may be viewed as a reduction of the associational link below
a certain threshold, e.g. a frequency value of 1. Repressed associations
may assume negative values. This means that everything is remembered
but that not everything is equally accessible. Frequency of use is at least
one measure of retrievability. Items with positive values greater than 1
are retrievable; 1 and negative values are not retrievable. Varying positive values stand for degrees of retrievability. Retrieval times are of the
order of a few hundred milliseconds. Long-range storage processing
seems to take a young normal adult about 5 to 10 seconds (Newell and
Simon 1967: 245). There is some evidence that some learning may take
even longer. However, ease of retrieval and learning seem closely
related.

The immediate or short-term memory has the following characteristics: retrieval times are about the same as for the long-range memory,
i.e. a few hundred milliseconds; it is very small; its limitations of size
are well captured by the 7 ± 2 chunks that can be contained in it
(Miller 1956); its capacity for active processing is much less; no more
than three items can be maintained at one time (Gregg 1967: 140); its
temporal range seems to extend from a few milliseconds to a few minutes. After that time, memory traces are either passed to permanent
memory or possibly extinguished. Some of the limitations of size can
be overcome by recoding or chunking of information. For example,
taxonomies are ideal structures for chunking. Every superordinate
(more generic) term can stand for the entire subtree it dominates. It
"chunks" (so to speak) the subtree into a single term. Another way of
looking at chunking is by focusing on words rather than individual
phonemes (as the units), on sentences rather than words, on paragraphs (subtitles) rather than sentences, and finally, on discourses
(titles) rather than paragraphs. Different levels of verbal plans, i.e.
instructions on how to do something, also consist of chunks of varying
generality (see Werner 1966; Topper 1972). Even with chunking the
storage capacity of the short-term memory does not exceed a few
hundred bits (Miller 1956). These can at best represent fragments of
taxonomies of plans and associated attributive semantic relations (see
below).

Although psychologists rarely postulate a memory structure between
the permanent and the short-range memory, it can be justified as fol-

lows. Permanent memory is very large. It contains more information than is needed for the sustained interest of both, man or device. Most lexical ambiguities arise across cultural domains. A "pass" is: a clumsy proposition in the relations between the sexes; a ball through the air in American football; a high valley in geography; and a grade better than "fail" in college. Such ambiguity is rarely confusing in ordinary discourse. We must assume that cultural domains or topics are kept separate.

Short-range memory does not hold enough information that is needed to sustain interest in any topic. Furthermore, it cannot hold a large enough part of a cultural domain to disambiguate "pass," for example, by its context. It needs a "back-up memory" small enough so that everything that is remembered does not impinge with equal force and yet large enough to contain most information relevant to a cultural domain or a domain of discourse. That is, it is impossible to think of a context in which all of human knowledge is needed and all of it all at the same time. The human brain must therefore be viewed as a very efficient "partitioner" (subdivider) of information into domains. Not all domains are necessarily definable only taxonomically (more on this below).

Consequences of Articulation

The above brief justifications of the intermediate memory have important consequences on the nature of the long-range memory.

Human beings apparently can maintain contradictory propositions without discomfort. This phenomenon has also been called compartmentalization. Examples are geneticists who are fundamentalist Christians, or social scientists whose day-to-day lives are unaffected by their insights into human nature. Sudden conversions of the Saul-Paul type (as described by Hoffer 1951) may be explainable by compartmentalization. Two independent systems of world-view are maintained. The old one in tacit memory (but accessible to intermediate and surface memory) and another one gradually evolving also in tacit memory. It may or may not be available to intermediate memory at first. Perhaps it is maintained in the form of "false" propositions set up for refutation. As the result of some poorly understood triggering mechanism, the two systems of knowledge reverse positions. This striking reversal accounts for the drama of the (apparent) suddenness of conversion experiences.

Compartmentalization also accounts for observations of "irrational" behavior. Outsiders see an informant in two different contexts in which he uses different partitions of his knowledge. If there are premises in the two sets that are contradictory, some of his behavior may appear "irrational," i.e. different inferences, even contradictions, result from the premises of different partitionings.

Information contained in permanent memory is "packaged" into separate and separately retrievable partitions. To learn various contexts is to learn to subpartition, by taxonomies (e.g. animals only), by attributes (e.g. large African animals only), by context (e.g. formal scientific talk), and others. Partitioning can be viewed as a tree structure. Each branching filters out more and more irrelevant information and sharpens the context. The above example may be graphed, as in Diagram 12.

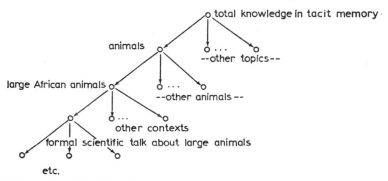

Diagram 12. Partitions in permanent memory

Partitions of the total knowledge must contain the following characteristics (the following list being by no means exhaustive):
(a) partitioning out lexical resources that are necessary for a given discourse or cultural domain;
(b) partitioning out equivalence rules (e.g. if "A is parent of B," then "B is child of A" or the preceding T = (T(kind)M), etc.) in relation to the discourse; this may include plans and strategies, or "scripts" (see ELIZA, Weizenbaum 1966);
(c) some assessment of social "context" and a further subpartitioning in accordance with it (e.g. vulgar versus medical views of sex, formal versus informal discussion of politics);
(d) some assessment of the appropriate length of the response.

On the basis of (d) there is a further subpartitioning of the lexicon by "relevance," or frequency of use up to some measure dependent on the permissible length of a response. For example, when human beings are asked to provide examples of some context, they never provide all

possible examples but just a few salient ones. Saliency may be measured by frequency occurrence and surely by other measures such as
some perception of "importance," positive and/or negative cathexis,
and most likely others. For example, human beings respond somehow
to clues of the social situation as to what constitutes an answer of appropriate length to a question. Given a request "Name some animals,"
one could imagine a relentless retrieval system that would produce an
entire folk classification or the entire Linnaean classification. Most human beings in that situation list about five (± 2?) animals. These are
usually "horse," "dog," "cat," "cow," "sheep," and possibly a few
others. The list may be distorted by likes and dislikes.

Mandler's (1970) evidence seems to imply that although folk taxonomies may be large with many nodes per level (see Werner and Begishe
1970; Werner, et al. i.p.) there exists a "core" taxonomy of at most
$5 ± 2$ items per level. Length of response may well be a function of the
limitation of the "core" taxonomy.

At least five types of partitioning of lexical resources need to be
taken into account:

1. Partitioning by subfield. This can be envisioned in its simplest
form as a taxonomic partitioning. The chemical interpretation of
"radical" is the only one available if the chemistry subtree of a general
taxonomy is brought from the tacit memory to the intermediate memory.
If the subtaxonomy deals with politics, the only available interpretation
in intermediate memory is the political.

2. Partitioning by strength of association. At present, the only available measure is word-frequency counts. This is at best an approximation. One would prefer pairwise associational frequencies, that is, the
association between "animal" and the five named animals in question.
Since "animal" with a frequency of 4,000 is a common term, the raw
frequencies of occurrence may in this case represent a fairly good approximation. Thus, this partitioning can be envisioned as one in which
more and more of less and less strongly associated items are moved
into intermediate memory as the available time for an answer increases.
That is, this kind of partitioning accounts for the range of discourse
from a "definitional" question, "What is an animal?" to "Write me a
fifty-page essay on animals." For more sophisticated movement of subsystems from tacit to focal memory, both topical and strength of associational partitioning is combined by intersection.

3. Partitioning by common attribute. This includes partitions by complex relations. In the proposed model, attributes are always represented
as tokens (square brackets) or addresses which "point" to the taxo-

nomic occurrence of the item as a type. Thus the types can be envisioned as analogous to dictionary entries while the tokens are occurrences of dictionary entries in the definitions of other words. A common attribute, therefore, may be a cross-referencing and retrieval of all token occurrences of an item. An investigation of the vocabulary of personality traits may fall into this category of partitioning. Sociolinguistic contexts, e.g. formal versus informal speech (response) attributes, may also fall under this type. The overused theme of current student papers on "The vocabulary of the marijuana user" is another example of partitioning by attribute field.

4. Partitioning by any one of the four relations of queueing. Any aspect of memory that is sequentially ordered, such as a poem or a process, must be retrievable as a temporal order. With items learned "by heart" the entire sequence must be retrievable as a whole. In the retelling of stories where abstracting of information (reduction of content) takes place, only the most salient (high frequency?) part of the content is retained in retrievable form in memory. Long sequential arrays such as long texts not integrated into the general knowledge system of the memory must be chunked into linear segments about the size of the intermediate memory. This may account for the fact that if a reciter of such a text is interrupted, he must usually return to the beginning. He cannot retrieve the information out of its temporal context because none of it has been dispersed or integrated with the rest of his knowledge.

5. Partitioning by subtaxonomy and attribute field. In many if not most circumstances, a partitioning by both features may be best. In the aforementioned example dealing with chemistry contexts, one would want to retrieve the subtaxonomy of chemistry as well as token uses of "chemistry" as attributes in other taxonomies. In order to avoid the partition and/or retrieval of too much material, the content of the intermediate memory must be restricted. One way of accomplishing this is by a first general retrieval, up to some degree of strength of association only. The cut-off point may vary by field and may ultimately be determined by the absolute size of intermediate memory ("core" taxonomy?). As the discourse focuses on more detailed parts of the chemistry taxonomy for example, other less strongly associated parts, or parts of the memory with recalculated strength of association in reference to some new criteria (common attributes) are partitioned out. This process is dynamic. That is, the partitions are continuously adjusting the content of the intermediate memory by including more information which is appropriate to the continuation of the discourse while concurrently

returning information no longer needed to permanent memory.

Compartmentalization contains a bonus. Following some important theorems of Goedel, Church, and Tarski, a completely formal and consistent logical structure is impossible in principle (Bronowski 1966; Werner 1975). Relatively separate partitions preclude the necessity for completeness and/or consistency.

The three-unit (chunk) limit of active processing in short-term memory seems to be the limit of human focal awareness. That is, three is the maximum number of items one can keep in one's head without external aids. This is supported by the fact that the number of operations we can perform "in our heads" are analogously limited. Multiplications of large numbers, more than two center embeddings, and most logical puzzles are beyond our capacity without extensions of our memory by pencil and paper. Thus it appears that we are aware only of what goes on in short-term memory. In other words, figuratively speaking, short-term memory is in sharp focus, intermediate memory is in soft focus and permanent memory is entirely out of focus, i.e. it is tacit (although parts of it can be brought into focus via the intermediate memory). Phenomena in sharp focus have "tails," so to speak, that reach into the soft focus of intermediate memory. Such "tails" are analogous to connotations or meanings outside of immediate focal awareness. If the totality of a person's knowledge is never available outside the permanent memory, then only a partitioned-out part of information is available for inferential deductive processing. Unless we are willing to limit human inference making to the manipulation of about three units, as seems to be implied by the limits of the short-term memory, the intermediate memory must also be a place for some logical processing.

The size of the intermediate memory depends on the inferential capacity of the model. It should at no time contain more information than can be easily checked for internal consistency. In other words, the partitioning of information first by the reduction from permanent to intermediate memory, then from the intermediate to short-term (which contains the inferential capability) is intended to take the place of the heuristics in theorem-proving devices. By focusing the topic sharply in this manner, only limited sets of propositions are available at one time for inferential processing. Such limitations in size seem to account for the fact that inferences of the complexity of logical puzzles require almost without exception an augmentation of human memory by such aids as pencil and paper. In this context it might be worthwhile to experiment with alternative sizes of the intermediate memory and match the variations in size with variations in the inferential capacity of short-term memory. Such experimentation, especially by a close comparison to human capabilities, will no doubt shed light on the nature of the experimentally elusive intermediate memory.

Since the short-term memory is limited, it must be in the intermediate memory that new information is integrated with old, i.e. it is learned. It must be here because information presented during a discourse is relevant to that discourse and must remain so for future reference while the discourse lasts. Only after a change of topic is the current partition in intermediate memory returned to permanent storage and replaced by a new topical partition. Thus all information passes into permanent memory by way of the intermediate memory. Only after a first-stage integration with the contextual constraint of intermediate memory can it proceed together with this context into permanent memory where it is further dispersed, i.e. placed in relation to any other knowledge to which it may be relevant. My term "dispersal" should be viewed here as implying the destruction of the linear order of most discourses. It applies to most information except that which is temporally ordered, e.g. jokes, stories, poems, songs, recipes, plans, processes, and others.

Similarly, short-term memory controls the influx of information, that is, the chunks that are presented to the focal memory for processing. In addition, the chunks may be recombined by new inferences made at this point.

Recent investigation (Werner et al. 1975) into the nature of the speech of schizophrenics seems to indicate that the short-term memory may be the mechanism for controlling the flow of speech by a linearization of the intermediate memory. The disturbances of some types of schizophrenic speech may be at least in part traceable to disturbances of the sequential ordering of successive short-term memory partitionings. However, this should be interpreted as suggestive at this point, rather than substantive.

Focal Awareness as a Governing Device

This has at least one level of greater depth than other cognitive processes. It is a small window through which can be seen parts of all levels of the processing apparatus. The governor controls partitioning dynamically. As the conditions of the discourse change, as new information is needed, it expedites it from permanent memory to intermediate memory. Material no longer needed is returned. Partitioning is changed continuously as the discourse context changes. This is the dynamic aspect of cognition: the three memories are involved in a constant exchange and interaction. The governor controls by sending and receiving meta-messages, not only gross partitioning dictated by topic, but also sub-partitionings which are dictated by social contexts. It can override the barriers between various levels of the total cognitive organization, i.e. all three levels of memory as well as all other parts of the process. For example, by bridging phonology, semantics, and context, it contributes to the understanding of puns. The governor is in part analogous to, or at least accessible to, the sharply focused part of short-term memory. This focus is, of course, "awareness." However, as such, it can be brought into short-term memory and hence to articulation as statements about the internal conditions of the device.

The Deductive Component

The lexical/semantic field consists of lexical/semantic relations. These relations are language universals that link lexical items which are language specific. Each lexical/semantic relation may participate in some inference making. The relations form the basic structures on all three levels of memory. In the short-term memory they are in focal awareness and participate in explicit deductions. In intermediate memory they are out of focus; there is only vague awareness. Little is known about pro-cesses out of awareness. Some are no doubt analogous to logical pro-cesses in awareness. Some are different; "creative leaps," analogies, similes, and metaphors seem especially, at least in large part, to origi-nate in the soft-focus parts of awareness. Conscious manipulation for reaching inferences takes place only in the focal short-term memory. It is conscious because such "awareness" is equivalent to a report from a higher-order device, the governor, that certain processes are going on in the lower level. The same processes may go on in intermediate memory, but there they are out of sharp focal awareness, i.e. they are not accessible to the governor.

The taxonomic relation T is represented as a tree graph. Such a tree graph contains in its geometry the spatial arrangement of terms, i.e. part of the deductive power of the device is contained in the geometry of the lexical/semantic fields. A traditional representation of a two-level taxonomy as a tree graph is shown in Diagram 13 (using binary branching only for the sake of simplicity).

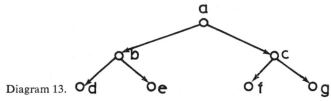

Diagram 13.

A representation with all possible relations due to the transitivity of the taxonomic relation is shown in Diagram 14.

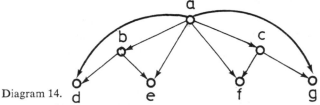

Diagram 14.

One way to represent the taxonomy shown in Diagram 14 in a two-dimensional plane is shown in Diagram 15.

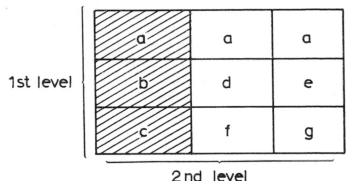

Diagram 15.

The labels on the top row and leftmost (shaded) column are labels of dominating nodes. From any node the perpendicular directions to the top row or to the leftmost row correspond to all possible taxonomic relations (e.g. (g)T(c) and (g)T(a)) that a node may assume. The representation thus contains in its geometry all possible relations contained in a taxonomy. This representation can be easily extended to n dimensions by constructing an n-dimensional hyperplane. The intersection of all possible perpendicular dimensions at a node determines all possible taxonomic relations into which that node may enter (for details, see Werner 1972).

The transitivity of the taxonomic relation establishes a link with syllogistic inference making. This capability is potentially available on all levels of memory (long-term, intermediate and short-term), in and out of focal awareness. Whether it is used on all three levels equally is not known. However, use on the tacit level does not seem likely.

Thus the question which remains is whether syllogisms or the inferential capability belong to the intermediate or to the short-term memory. Assuming, as we must, that deduction is in focal awareness, syllogisms are restricted to the short-term memory. The three chunks available for dynamic processing are precisely what is involved in syllogisms. Before continuing the discussion of valid syllogisms, it is necessary to consider briefly quantification.

Universal quantification is included by traversing the graph from lower node to superordinate node, e.g. "All lions are animals" ((lions)T (animals)). Existential quantification is included by going from top to bottom, e.g. "Some animals are lions" ((animal)$\underline{T}$(lion)).

Intermediate quantification between extremes of the universal and the existential can be viewed as an attributive relation (M) attached to the universal quantifier. Thus, in ordinary English "ten lions" represents a modification of "all lions," that is, a reduction of the extension of the universal quantifier. This follows precisely the definition of the relation of attribution M. (While it expands intension it reduces extension, see, e.g. Lyons 1968). The relation of modification can be envisioned as the replacement of the X in "X of all lions" by the appropriate "intermediate" quantifier, for example, "ten of all lions." This is also congruent with the fact that any and all statements true of all lions will apply to ten lions. It can be given in formula representation:

$\forall$(lion)M(yellow)
"All lions are yellow."
(($\forall$)M(ten))   (lion)M(at Brookfield Zoo)
"Ten of all lions are at Brookfield Zoo."
or "Ten lions are at Brookfield Zoo."

In short-term memory, the deductive capability includes the first ten out of the twenty-four valid syllogisms of classical logic. All ten can be converted by a simple set of rules into the syllogism Mood Barbara, or the transitivity condition of the taxonomic relation. If (b)T(a) is paraphrasable as "All (b) are (a)," and (a)$\underline{T}$(b) is paraphrasable as "Some (a) are (b)," then the traditional first figure of Mood Barbara (Mood AAA) can be represented as:

I (b)T(a)
II (c)T(b)
_____
III (c)T(a)

or: III

Ten of the classical valid syllogisms then correspond to twenty-four valid syllogisms in this notation (N is negation), as displayed below:

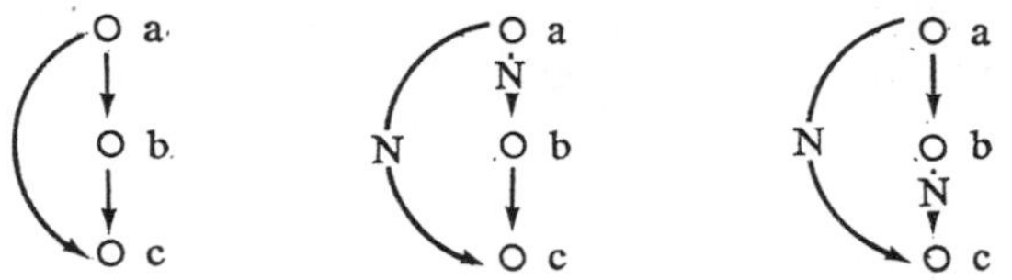

(three circular taxonomy diagrams, left to right:)

Diagram 1: O a → O b → O c

Diagram 2: O a, N→ O b, → O c (with N at left)

Diagram 3: O a → O b, N→ O c (with N at left)

bTa	N(bTa)	bTa
cTb	cTb	N(cTb)
cTa	N(cTa)	N(cTa)
bTa	N(bTa)	bTa
cTb	cTb	N(cTb)
aT̲c	N(aT̲c)	N(aT̲c)
aT̲b	N(aT̲b)	aT̲b
cTb	cTb	N(cTb)
aT̲c	N(aT̲c)	N(aT̲c)
aT̲b	N(aT̲b)	aT̲b
cTb	cTb)	N(cTb)
cTa	N(cTa)	N(cTa)
bTa	N(bTa)	bTa
bT̲c	bT̲c	N(bT̲c)
aT̲c	N(aT̲c)	N(aT̲c)
bTa	N(bTa)	bTa
bT̲c	bT̲c	N(bT̲c)
cTa	N(cTa)	N(cTa)
aT̲b	N(aT̲b)	aT̲b
bT̲c	bT̲c	N(bT̲c)
aT̲c	N(aT̲c)	N(aT̲c)
aT̲b	N(aT̲b)	aT̲b
bT̲c	bT̲c	N(bT̲c)
cTa	N(cTa)	N(cTa)

These syllogisms can all be solved by applying the geometry of taxonomies, that is, by transformation into the Mood Barbara by the following rules:

(1) The relation of T̲ is freely convertible into the relation T by inverting the order of the arguments.
(2) Convert all T̲ into T by applying rule (1).
(3) Only one premise may be negated.
(4) If there is negation remove the negation operator.
(5) Convert all cases to Mood Barbara and conclude accordingly.
(6) Return the operator of negation to the negated premise.

(7)   Apply the operator of negation to the conclusion.

The above rules account for ten of the twenty-four valid syllogisms of classical logic. That is, these and the following rules can be used for the deduction of syllogisms. Five more syllogisms become solvable by adding rules about negation:

(8)   N(aTb) is equivalent to N(bTa).

(9)   N(aT̲b) is equivalent to N(bT̲a).

For the remaining nine classical syllogisms we have to go beyond Mood Barbara. The first five are the result of conclusions that can be made about two separate superordinate taxons of one subordinate term. Without additional information, we know only that somewhere in the taxonomy one of the two must be superordinate to the other. Although the answer appears ambiguous, it is not. Either case holds. I will present here only the formula without negation:

bTa
bT̲c

aT̲c
cT̲a

That is, aT̲c or cT̲a both hold without regard to which of the two (a or c) is superordinate to the other.

The remaining four cases are the inverse of the above: conclusions about two separate subordinate nodes. This is obviously impossible except in negation. Because of rules (8) and (9), there are four equivalent answers.

| N(aTb) | aTb |
| cTb | N(cTb) |

N(aTc)
N(cTa)
N(aT̲c)
N(cT̲a)

For the sake of completeness, I add the "syllogism of metaphor" (Werner et al. 1975) as a final rule. Although it is not considered a valid syllogism in classical logic, it is important in the formulation of analogies, metaphors, and possible "creative leaps."

aTb
cTb
―――
aTc
cTa

The answer in this case is ambiguous. It depends on which of the items is the familiar (a or c) and which is to be explained. The superordinate term b is always the one that explains one of the subordinate terms. For example:

(heart)T(liquid-mover)

(pump)T(liquid-mover)
―――――――――――
(heart)T(pump)

The conclusion is "a heart is a pump" since a pump is simpler and/or better known.
The old relation is shown in Diagrams 16 and 17.

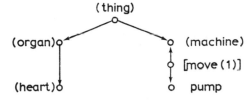

Diagram 16.

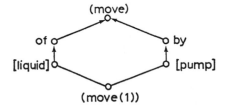

Diagram 17.

In Diagram 17 (move(1)) is associatively related to its token [move(1)]
of Diagram 16 (where 1 is an integer characterizing the above sentence
with the verb "move"). The new relation is then seen in Diagram 18.

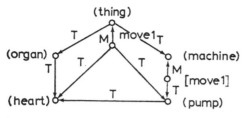

Diagram 18.

The interesting anomaly here is that the relation (heart)T(pump) is
transitively related to (thing) i.e. (heart)T(thing) but not to (machine).

So far I have talked only about the relation of taxonomy and negation N. In many syllogisms the second term of a premise is an attribute
rather than another taxon. The distinction is not significant. In the
notational convention of the lexical/semantic relations developed in
detail above, every taxonomic level consists of an intervening level of
attribution. Schematically this can be illustrated in Diagram 19.

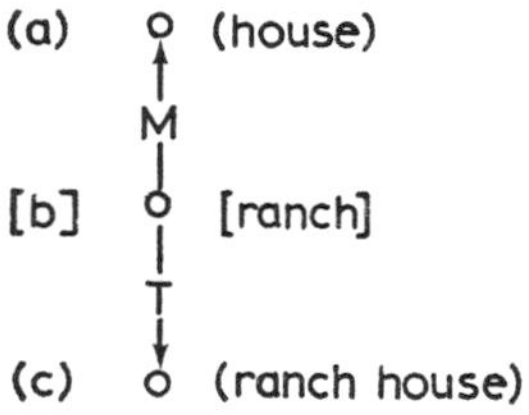

(a)   ○ (house)
       ↑
       M
       |
[b]   ○ [ranch]
       |
       T
       ↓
(c)   ○ (ranch house)

Diagram 19.

Here (a) is a type and a superordinate taxon. This taxon is modified
by [b] which is a token, that is, it is represented by an association that
points to its type in the taxonomy of farms. The modifier and the
superordinate taxon form an intermediate superordinate taxon that is
taxonomically linked to the subordinate taxon type (c). In this manner
every superordinate taxon has a series of modifiers which modify the
superordinate term. A taxonomy consists then of several subordinate
taxons suspended from their superordinate by triangles of modification
that alternate with triangles of taxonomy, as before, see Diagram 20.

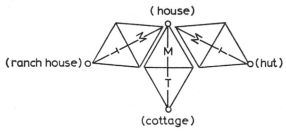

(house)

(ranch house)   M   (hut)

T

(cottage)

Diagram 20.

The flat bottoms of the M triangles represent that aspect of attribute organization that is often called a componential paradigm. However, there are no components in this model. Their place is taken by tokens of actual words (naming units) or modifiers that are linked to their own place (type) in the taxonomic structure. Diagram 21 illustrates this point (see also diagrams of preceding section).

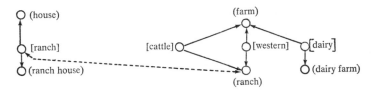

- - - - - - - - - - associative linkage

(ranch) type in "farm" taxonomy

[ranch] modifier in "house" taxonomy which points to (ranch)

Diagram 21.

If some second terms of a syllogism contain only attributes, then it is treated in the semantic network as if it were a modifier of a "dummy" superordinate taxon, usually replaceable by some very general term like "thing." Thus a premise like "All men are mortal" is represented internally in the model as "All men are mortal things." Thus the unity of the presentation is preserved.

It should be noted that at every superordinate node there are two further logically important relations: conjunction (and) C and disjunction (or) D. The branches within the M triangles must be treated conjunctively: ((ranch equals (cattle farm AND western farm)). That is, each and every branch contributes to the definition (paraphrase) of the taxon below it. The triangles themselves, however, are disjunctively connected if viewed from top to bottom (see Diagram 22). Thus, in the previous example, "ranch" is separated disjunctively from the criteria triangles of "dairy farm."

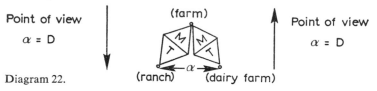

Diagram 22.

There are further uses of conjunction. First, it can conjoin taxons on one level of a taxonomy if viewed bottom to top (see Diagram 22). For example, in Diagram 20, "a ranch house, (and) a cottage and a hut are (kinds of) houses." Second, it can conjoin any elements of separate taxonomies that either belong together or are placed together for reasons of some discourse. Thus, "the doctors and the Indians agreed that the Indians deserve better health care" conjoins doctors (professionals) and Indians (native American, or peoples) in the interest of the above assertion.

The "and" of everyday speech has in addition other functions. In this case, it may represent the lexical/semantic relations of queueing; that is, Q(1.1) and Q(1.2) for immediate succession and Q(2.1) and Q(2.2) for eventual succession, in other words, rather than the simple "and" which is used as an abbreviation in everyday speech for Q(1) and Q(2) which stand for "and then" and "and then eventually," respectively.

Only two more lexical/semantic relations remain to be considered for deductions: Synonymy S which is defined as meaning equivalence, and identity X. It appears at this time that such identities as expressed for example by the syllogistic rules of negation (8) and (9), and equivalence rules, are not synonyms but equivalents.

The building blocks of the deductive component are the lexical/semantic relations. These are independent of partitions of the memory store and are independent of the means or the reasons for partitioning. The relations are available throughout the three levels of the memory. However, humans are consciously aware of their application to inferences only when the logical operations take place in sharply focused short-term memory. Humans may then report that the processes of thought are going on. The same types of processes may go on (possibly in conjunction with others) in intermediate soft-focus memory. However, these processes, though controlled by the governor, are minimally accessible to awareness. They may be totally outside of awareness, though some can eventually be moved to awareness.

SCHEMA AND CONCLUDING REMARKS

Taking into account the discussions of the preceding sections, the current model may be schematized in Diagram 23.

Perhaps the major feature of the current model is that input and output utilize the same route through the articulated parts of the device. This does not appear to be a very likely representation of human question-answering capacity (though there appears to be some counter-evidence from studies of aphasia). However, so far this assumption has not resulted in difficulties; at some point in the evolution of the model it may. To date no one has made a reasonable proposal for the separation of the input from the output channel.

The place of a logical deductive component, as was seen before, is not easily determined. It appears that logical operations could potentially take place on any level of memory, although the long-range memory is a very unlikely place for them to occur. I have argued that logical deductions in full awareness of man or model can only take place in short-term memory. Such focally aware deductive steps are perhaps as short as and no longer than syllogisms. This implies that the basic nature of other cultures' logical systems can and should be investigated through very simple experiments. There is not much point in going beyond the capacity of short-term memory. Deductions in soft-focus intermediate memory are probably analogous to what goes on under full awareness, but we cannot be sure. Both longer chains and other processes cannot be ruled out. Analogies seem to be playing a more extensive role here than in focal memory. Probably a too narrowly empiricist bias has prevented psychologists from seeing the effects of intermediate memory. It became lost between the extremes of short-term and long-range phenomena. More ingenious experiments are needed by both psychologists and anthropologists. Such experiments must be set up so that they are applicable in more exotic languages as well as in English.

Equally important are tests and experiments to determine which aspects of Western logical systems are most appropriate to the modeling of the natural logic inherent in everyday speech. There is a wide choice: traditional syllogisms, propositional calculus, first-order predicate calculus (quantified arguments), higher-order predicate calculi (quantification of functions), many-valued logic (with truth values intermediate between truth and falsehood), modal logic (dealing with possibility and necessity), temporal logic (dealing with "always," "never" and the logic of tenses), deontic logic (dealing with obligations of vary-

MONITOR	TACIT LONG-TERM MEMORY
Content: Control of retention of focus on topic of discourse. Control of inflow and outflow of messages. Control and organization of meta-messages. Control of inflow and outflow of what is in focus in intermediate and in short-term as discourse proceeds. Control and reorganization, integration of new information from short to intermediate and eventually long-range memory. Control of facilitating, repressing and forgetting. Control of style. Control of associations between the levels of the three memories for interpretations of jokes, puns, slang associations, and metaphors.	*Content:* Associative network of lexical/semantic relations representing tacit cultural knowledge. Equivalence rules, e.g. "If A parent of B, then B child of A"; or "If A has B then B belongs to A"; etc. These rules are attached to topics (domains). *Characteristics:* Not necessarily logically coherent. Compartmentalized. Contradictions between compartments possible simply because they do not arise; compartments do not interact and can only interact possibly in intermediate memory, definitely in short-term memory. *Operations:* Probably no inferences made at all. Only movement in and out to intermediate memory, i.e. definition of nature of partitions dynamically by monitor.

INTERMEDIATE "SOFT-FOCUS" MEMORY
Content:
Only partitions of Tacit Memory or "compartmentalized" knowledge related from moment to moment to the flow of the discourse.
Characteristics:
Relatively logically coherent. Contradictions and ambiguity not tolerated, i.e. these lead to requests (questions) for clarification.
Operation:
Some chunking organization accomplished here.
Some inferences, especially the analogic and/or metaphoric kind.

SHORT-TERM OR "FOCAL" MEMORY
Contents:
Items and chunks.
Characteristics:
Linearized input and output in units of 7 ± 2 chunks (surface chunks?).
Operation:
Inferences on the basis of no more than 3 chunks at a time.

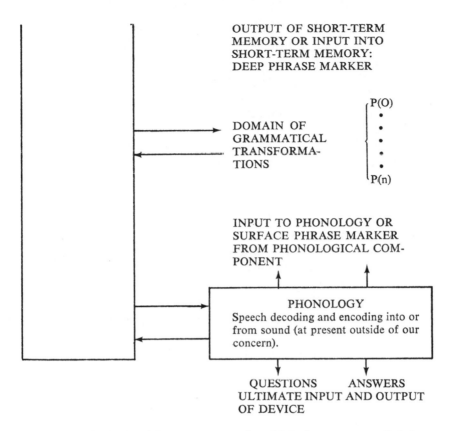

OUTPUT OF SHORT-TERM
MEMORY OR INPUT INTO
SHORT-TERM MEMORY:
DEEP PHRASE MARKER

$P(O)$
·
·
·
·
·
$P(n)$

DOMAIN OF
GRAMMATICAL
TRANSFORMA-
TIONS

INPUT TO PHONOLOGY OR
SURFACE PHRASE MARKER
FROM PHONOLOGICAL COM-
PONENT

PHONOLOGY
Speech decoding and encoding into or
from sound (at present outside of our
concern).

QUESTIONS   ANSWERS
ULTIMATE INPUT AND OUTPUT
OF DEVICE

ing force), the logic of fuzzy concepts (in which the accuracy of deduction decreases as the deductive chain increases), and possibly others. All of these have analogues in all natural languages.

It is not known how much deduction human beings actually use. A logical deductive model's efficiency lies somewhere between brute deduction and brute memory. The fact that humans are fast retrievers rather than efficient calculating machines (i.e. speed over accuracy) seems to argue for brute memory. In artificial intelligence experiments with deduction Robinson's resolution principle looms large (see Slagle 1971: 59ff.). Its inspiration is logical puzzles; it favors brute deduction. Human beings somehow seem to reach a trade-off between deduction and memory though storage seems favored. While a problem may be solved by deductive steps and/or analogies, a problem so solved ceases to be a problem (Polanyi 1964). A calculus is apparently required for problem solving. However, once a solution is successfully calculated, it is relegated to memory. There it no longer presents a problem and the solution is accessible to rapid retrieval.

It is relatively easy to envision a controlling mechanism between short-term focal and tacit (long-term) memory. As the scanning of the short-term memory proceeds sequentially, for example through a text, the intermediate memory changes its content accordingly. An analogy may help. The short-term memory may be conceived of as a small window with 7 ± 2 openings. As the picture in the cells changes (by a kind of scanning) new items from tacit memory must be related to the pictures in the window by being brought into intermediate memory. Thus the intermediate memory is not static but dynamically variable: due to (among others) stimulation from the outside, new unrelated parts of the tacit memory are brought in relation to each other. But since the tacit long-term memory has no inferential capability such information may contain contradictions. There is, as was seen before, no barrier against contradictory propositions in the tacit memory. The short-term memory, on the other hand, contains all necessary logical apparatus. Contradictory information in short-term memory sometimes interrupts "attention"; that is, the information is interpreted as nonsense and no further processing toward the deeper tacit levels can take place. Alternatively the contradiction may give rise to questions of clarification by the device. In any case, the short-term memory cannot tolerate contradictory information. Thus, by bringing two or possibly more formerly unrelated fields together and merging them by making them logically consistent, new boundaries for partitioning are created. This can be viewed as a kind of learning or reinterpretation and reintegration of knowledge.

Different domains of knowledge in tacit memory are probably linked very loosely. This seems to be reflected in the fact (observed in fieldwork, Perchonock and Werner 1969) that the easiest terms to elicit from informants are very specific terms (e.g. terms for actual foods) and the global term for the entire cultural domain (e.g. the term for "food").

The model as it stands codes all information in a semantic notation utilizing the relations discussed earlier. Thus the output of the model is roughly analogous to the deepest available phrase marker in the schema of generative semantics, namely, P(O). Various grammatical transformations then apply and lexical (phonological) insertion rules operate until the surface structure phrase marker P(n) is reached. That is, in quite traditional manner, P(n) is the input to the phonological component of the grammar, which finally provides the terminal string of P(n) with pronunciation (or graphemic representation), thus producing actual sentences of the language.

EPILOGUE

The taxonomic tree and modification triangle approach as sketched in these pages is the basis for the organization of the three memories now in the process of being refined. It is unlikely that the schema will work smoothly without extensive testing on large lexical/semantic fields and without concurrent drastic modifications of the basic structures. The general direction does look promising. Even moderate or qualified success constitutes at this point a significant advance. In all these efforts we need approaches of many different kinds, from speculative exploration of the nature of humanlike devices (as I have done here), and especially the testing of their inevitable shortcomings, to carefully planned empirical experimentation. The experiments must have cross-cultural validity. They will provide answers about the amount of deduction that human beings actually use in human speech.

In anthropology we should rely on our greatest strength: our ingenuity and our eclecticism. We are not constrained by the boundaries of established disciplines to the extent that psychology, linguistics, or logic are. The virtually unlimited and untapped resources of computer simulation could be a breath of fresh air for ethnoscience and could extend it in new directions as well as in scope.

REFERENCES

ARIETI, S.
  1955   Interpretation of schizophrenia. New York: Robert Brunner.
BACH, E., R. T. HARMS, editors
  1968   Universals in linguistic theory. New York: Holt, Rinehart and Winston.
BIERMAN, A. K.
  1964   Logic: a dialogue. San Francisco: Holden-Day.
BINNICK, R. I.
  1969   "An application of an external generative semantic model of language to man-machine interaction." Paper presented at the International Conference on Computational Linguistics, Sanga-Saby, Sweden.
BISS, K., R. CHIEN, F. STAHL
  1971   "R2: a natural languages question-answering system," in Proceedings of the AIFPS Joint Spring Computer Conference, 303–308.
BRONOWSKI, J.
  1966   The logic of the mind. American Scientist 54:1–14.
CARROLL, J. B., P. DAVIES, B. RICHMAN
  1971   The American Heritage word frequency book. Boston: Houghton Mifflin.

CASAGRANDE, J. B., K. L. HALE
1967   "Semantic relations in Papago folk definitions," in *Studies in southwestern ethnolinguistics*. Edited by D. Hymes with W. Bittle, 165–196. The Hague: Mouton.

COWAN, J. L., *editor*
1970   *Studies in thought and language*. Tucson: University of Arizona Press.

D'ANDRADE, R. G.
1972   "A propositional analysis of U.S. American belief about illness." Unpublished manuscript.

FILLMORE, C. J.
1968   "The case for case," in *Universals in linguistic theory*. Edited by E. Bach and R. T. Harms, 1–90. New York: Holt, Rinehart and Winston.

FRAKE, C. O.
1964   "Notes and queries in ethnography," in *Transcultural studies in cognition*. Edited by A. K. Romney and R. G. D'Andrade, 132–145.

FUNK and WAGNALLS
1962   *Standard dictionary of the English language*. New York: Funk and Wagnalls.

GREGG, L. W.
1967   "Internal representations of sequential concepts," in *Concepts and the structure of memory*. Edited by B. Kleinmuntz, 107–142. New York: John Wiley.

HOFFER, E.
1951   *The true believer*. New York: Harper and Row.

KLEINMUNTZ, B., *editor*
1967   *Concepts and the structure of memory*. New York: John Wiley.

LAKOFF, G.
1971a "On generative semantics," in *Semantics: an interdisciplinary reader in philosophy, linguistics and psychology*. Edited by D. D. Steinberg and L. A. Jakobovits, 232–296. Cambridge: Cambridge University Press.
1971b "Presuppositions and relative well-formedness," in *Semantics: an interdisciplinary reader in philosophy, linguistics and psychology*. Edited by D. D. Steinberg and L. A. Jakobovits, 329–340. Cambridge: Cambridge University Press.

LYONS, J.
1968   *Introduction to theoretical linguistics*. Cambridge: Cambridge University Press.

MANDLER, G.
1970   "Words, lists, and categories: an experimental view of organized memory," in *Studies in thought and language*. Edited by J. L. Cowan, 100–131. Tucson: University of Arizona Press.

MC CAWLEY, J. D.
1970   "Syntactic and logical arguments for semantic structures," in *Proceedings of the 55th International Seminar on Theoretical Linguistics*, TEC Tokyo, Japan.

MILLER, G. A.
1956   The magical number seven, plus or minus two: some limits on

our capacity for processing information. *Psychology Review* 63: 81–97.

MINSKY, M.
1968 *Semantic information processing.* Cambridge, Mass.: M.I.T. Press.

MITCHELL-KERNAN, CLAUDIA
1972 "Signifying and marking: two Afro-American speech acts," in *Directions in sociolinguistics: the ethnography of communication.* Edited by J. Gumperz and D. Hymes, 161–179. New York: Holt, Rinehart and Winston.

NAROLL, R., R. COHEN, *editors*
1970 *A Handbook of method in cultural anthropology.* Garden City, N.Y.: Natural History Press.

NAYLOR, T. H., T. L. BALINTFY, D. S. BURDICK, K. CHU
1966 *Computer simulation techniques.* New York: John Wiley. (Revised edition 1968.)

NEWELL, A., H. SIMON
1967 "Overview: memory and process in concept formation," in *Concepts and the structure of memory.* Edited by B. Kleinmuntz, 241–262. New York: John Wiley.

NILSSON, NILS J.
1971 *Problem solving methods in artificial intelligence.* New York: McGraw-Hill.

PERCHONOCK, NORMA, O. WERNER
1969 Navajo systems of classification: some implications for ethnoscience. *Ethnology* 8:229–242.

POLANYI, M.
1964 *Personal knowledge.* New York: Harper Torchbooks.

POPPER, K.
1968 *Conjectures and refutations: the growth of scientific knowledge.* New York: Harper Torchbooks.

QUILLIAN, M. R.
1968 "Semantic memory," in *Semantic information processing.* Edited by M. Minsky, 216–270. Cambridge, Mass.: M.I.T. Press.
1969 The teachable language comprehender: simulation program and theory of language. *Communications of the ACM* 12:459–476.

RAPHAEL, B.
1968 "SIR: a computer program for semantic information retrieval," in *Semantic information processing.* Edited by M. Minsky, 33–134. Cambridge, Mass.: M.I.T. Press.

RESCHER, N., A. URQUHART
1971 *Temporal logic.* New York: Springer-Verlag.

SCHWARTZ, R. M., J. F. BURGER, R. F. SIMMONS
1970 A deductive question-answering for natural language inference. *Communications of the ACM* 13:167–183.

SEBEOK, T. A.
1960 *Style in language.* Cambridge, Mass. and New York: M.I.T. Press and John Wiley.

SLAGLE, J. R.
1971 *Artificial intelligence: the heuristic programming approach.* New York: McGraw-Hill.

SNYDER, D. P.
  1971   *Modal logic and its applications.* New York: Van Nostrand Reinhold.
STEINBERG, D. D., L. A. JAKOBOVITS, *editors*
  1971   *Semantics: an interdisciplinary reader in philosophy, linguistics and psychology.* Cambridge: Cambridge University Press.
STOCKWELL, R. P., P. SCHACHTER, BARBARA HALL PARTEE
  1973   *The major syntactic structures of English.* New York: Holt, Rinehart and Winston.
TOPPER, M.
  1972   "The ethnography of Navajo daily activities." Unpublished Ph.D. thesis, Northwestern University, Evanston, Illinois.
TOULMIN, S.
  1960   *The philosophy of science.* New York: Harper Torchbooks.
TYLER, S. A., *editor*
  1969   *Cognitive anthropology.* New York: Holt, Rinehart and Winston.
WEIZENBAUM, J.
  1966   ELIZA — a computer program for the study of natural language communication between man and machine. *Communications of the ACM* 9:36–45.
WERNER, O.
  1966   Pragmatics and ethnoscience. *Anthropological Linguistics* 8 (8).
  1969   "On the universality of lexical/semantic relations." Unpubl. ms.
  1972   "Ethnoscience 1972," in *Annual review of anthropology*, 271–308.
  1975   "On the limits of social science theory," in *Linguistics and Anthropology: in Honor of C. F. Voegelin.* Edited by D. Kinkade, K. L. Hall, and O. Werner. Lisse: Peter de Ridder Press.
WERNER, O., K. Y. BEGISHE
  1970   "The taxonomic aspect of the Navajo universe", in *Proceedings of the Congreso Internacional de Americanistas, Lima, Peru.*
WERNER, O., JO ANN FENTON
  1970   "Method and theory in ethnoscience or ethnoepistemology," in *Handbook of method in cultural anthropology.* Edited by R. Naroll and R. Cohen, 537–580. Garden City, N.Y.: Natural History Press.
WERNER, O., GLADYS LEVIS-MATICHEK, MARTHA EVENS, BONNIE LITOVITZ
  1975   "An ethnoscience view of schizophrenic speech," in *Ritual, Reality and Innovation in Language Use.* Edited by B. Blount and M. Sanches. New York: Seminar Press.
WERNER, O., A. MANNING, K. Y. BEGISHE
  i.p.   "A taxonomic view of the traditional Navajo universe," in *Handbook of North American Indians.* Edited by W. C. Sturtevant and A. Ortiz. Washington, D.C.: Smithsonian Institution.
WINOGRAD, T.
  1967   Contextual understanding by computers. *Communications of the ACM* 10:474–480.
YNGVE, V. H.
  1960   A model and an hypothesis for language structure. *Proceedings of the American Philosophical Society* 104:444–466.

Tahitian Ethnozoological Classification and Fuzzy Logic

YVES LEMAITRE

The classification of terrestrial animals in Tahiti and the neighboring islands (Society Islands, Eastern Polynesia) will be presented here in a broad outline. Two aspects of this classification will be examined: its evolution during recent history and the type of logic implied by this classification in its present state.

A few points about vocabulary and method ought to be made clear. Organisms are grouped into classes, the taxa (*bird, plant, warbler*). These taxa occupy different levels in the taxonomy, a hierarchic structure established by comparison of the taxa through the means of the relation of inclusion. This relation is one of partial ordering permitting comparison only between nested taxa (*animal, kingfisher*). The procedure needs to be filled out. Insofar as the Tahitian classification is concerned, it would seem that the taxa show characteristics permitting them to be rearranged into ethnobiological categories like those described in a recent article (Berlin, et al. 1973). According to research carried out by these authors, popular taxonomies contain a maximum of 5 levels. At level 0, we find the unique beginner of the taxonomic tree: *plant, animal.* On level 1 are the not very numerous life forms: *tree, mammal, vine.* On level 2 are the very numerous generic taxa: *oak, tit.* These make up the essential part of the classification. On level 3 are the specific taxa, less numerous, subject to binomial designation: *cork oak, coal tit.* Finally, there sometimes exists a level 4: varietal taxa, which are still less numerous. Two categories

I wish to thank Ralph G. White who translated this paper into English and made useful remarks, and J. C. Thibault (EPHE, Paris), who worked out the scientific names of the birds cited.

only, and therefore only two levels, are obligatory: the unique beginner and the generic taxa.

Three periods in the history of Tahiti are representative of successive stages in the Tahitians' ethnozoological knowledge. They are the end of the pre-European era, the missionary period, and the present age. The pre-European era ended in 1767 when the navigator Wallis reached Tahiti; we can study the end of this period through certain written documents available to us. Thirty years later, the missionary period began with the arrival of the first representatives of the London Missionary Society in 1797. Finally, the third period was the end product of a protracted process of acculturation that profoundly transformed Tahitian society.

THE END OF THE PRE-EUROPEAN ERA

Early Tahitian knowledge and beliefs connected with the animal world must be for the most part considered as lost. However, certain texts collected by the missionary, John Muggridge Orsmond (in Henry 1928) make it possible to reconstruct, at least partially, the state of the pre-European taxonomic system. The most interesting in this regard are the mythological texts, at once didactic and poetic, handed down by the great priests of the ancient religion: "Order finally established" and "Division of property" (Henry 1928:395–398, 418–420). They alternate questions and replies on the theme of the creation of the world. Through the usage made of terms denoting animal classes, it is possible to place these classes in relationship to each other. Thus, this study primarily concerns to nomenclature, and not to a hard-to-interpret juxtaposition or similarity of species, which the content of these texts may sometimes suggest. This does not imply in a general way that unnamed groupings of living species may not appear as significant across certain aspects of Tahitian culture: technical knowledge, myths, etc. But, besides the fact that it is relatively hard to come by any certainty on this matter for the historical period, it seems to us that in the present situation the nomenclature reflects the classification of terrestrial animal species.

Tahiti's terrestrial fauna was poor in its number of species, particularly in terms of large animals. Mammals were represented only by the dog, the pig, and the rat. On the other hand, there were dozens of species of birds and small animals such as arthropods and various insects.

Table 1 presents the main divisions of the pre-European classification. There were two kinds of life forms, one of which bears the same taxonomic

Table 1. Classification of terrestrial animals at the end of the pre-European era

Division	Life forms	Generic taxa	Specific taxa
manu terrestrial animal	⋮		
		mo'o lizard	*mo'o 'arara* streaked lizard
			mo'o uri dark lizard
		'iore rat	
		'urī dog	
		pua'a pig	
	manu bird, winged insect	⋮	
		vini species of parrots	*vini rura* black-headed parrot (*vini kuhlii*)
			vini pāuri species of parrots
			vini pātea black-headed parrot (*vini peruviana*)
		rupe carpophage (*Ducula aurorae*)	
		pūrehua moth	
		pepe butterfly	
		pi'ao dragonfly	
	manumanu very small animal	⋮	
		naonao mosquito	

name, *manu*, as the main division of the classification. This characteristic shows up, moreover, in other Polynesian languages and still persists today in certain varieties of the Tahitian language. Perhaps this has to do with the makeup of the terrestrial fauna in which birds were a dominant element. In its general sense of 'terrestrial animal', the word *manu* contrasts with such terms as *i'a* 'aquatic animal', *rā'au* 'plant', etc. In its restricted sense, *manu* may be translated by 'bird, winged insect'; it designates the "flying animal" life form. The second life form is *manumanu* 'very small animal'. The term *manumanu* is formed by doubling the word *manu*, a common procedure in Tahitian in order to give the idea of smallness and great numbers.

These two life forms cover only a part of the "terrestrial animal" domain. The generic taxa *pua'a* 'pig', *'urī* 'dog', *'iore* 'rat', *mo'o* 'lizard', for instance, are not assigned to life forms. The classification extends right up to specific taxa, particularly for birds. These specific taxa are subject to binomial designations; this observation fits into the general model proposed by Berlin, et al. (1973).

THE MISSIONARY PERIOD

Attempts to introduce new species began at the time of the first contacts with the navigators. A procedure commonly utilized to name new species is pointed out by Berlin, et al. (1973:222). In its simplest form, this was applied mainly to plants in Tahiti. The procedure consists of giving the new species the name of a species which is already familiar and which the new species resembles. This name is followed by a qualifying word so that the two species may be distinguished, usually by specifying that one of them is foreign (*popa'ā*) and that the other is native or indigenous (*mā'ohi*), i.e. of Tahiti. Doubling the number of names, however, could not suffice to name the introduced animals. The number of terrestrial mammals that could serve as analogical models was small, and the new classes created had to have more than two elements. A more varied binomial terminology was required (Table 2). The terms *pua'a* 'pig', *'urī* 'dog', and *'iore* 'rat' of the earlier period acquired a greater degree of generality and became names of life forms. This was made explicit in the Davies dictionary of 1851: *pua'a* 'animals that have hoofs', *'urī* 'quadrupeds that have claws, except for the rat'. The binomial appellations thus created are generic names (Table 3).

The terms *pua'a mā'ohi* 'pig', *'urī mā'ohi* 'dog', *'iore mā'ohi* 'rat', although textually attested (Anonymous 1875) were no doubt of infrequent

Table 2. Classification of terrestrial animals, missionary period

Division	Life forms	Generic taxa	Specific taxa
manu terrestrial animal	*'iore* small, clawed animal	*'iore pererau* bat	
		'iore mā'ohi rat	
	'urī big, clawed animal	*'urī ta'ata* monkey	
		'urī pi'ifare cat	
		'urī mā'ohi dog	
	pua'a hooved animal	*pua'a horofenua* horse	
		pua'a niho goat	
		pua'a mā'ohi pig	
	manu bird, winged insect	*'ōma'oma'o*	*'ōma'oma'o uri* lit., dark *'ō.*
			'ōma'oma'o puafau lit., yellow *'ō.*, long-billed warbler (*Conopoderas caffra*)
		vini species of parrots	*vini pā'ura* lit., red *vini*
			vini rehu lit., gray *vini*
			vini tea lit., light *vini*
			vini pāuri lit., dark *vini*
		pepe butterfly	
		pi'ao dragonfly	
	manumanu very small animal	*rō* ant	*rō upo'o nui*, lit., big-headed ant
			rō 'āvae roa, lit., long-legged ant
		naonao mosquito	

Table 3.   Generic names of animals applied to new life forms during the missionary period

---

pua'a 'hooved animal'

    pua'a mā'ohi 'pig' = *pua'a*, pig + *mā'ohi*, indigenous, lit., native pig.

    pua'a horo fenua 'horse' = *pua'a*, pig + *horo*, run + *fenua*, ground, lit., pig running on the ground.

    pua'a niho 'goat' = *pua'a*, pig + *niho*, horn, lit., horned pig.

    pua'a toro 'bovine' = *pua'a*, pig + *toro*, bull (borrowed from Spanish), lit., bull pig.

    pua'a māmoe 'sheep' = *pua'a*, pig + *mā* attenuating prefix + *moe*, sleep, lit., sleeping or sleepy pig (?), or unknown foreign origin (Davies 1851: Appendix).

'urī 'big clawed animal'

    'urī mā'ohi 'dog' = *'urī*, dog + *mā'ohi*, indigenous, lit. native dog.

    'urī pi'ifare 'cat' = *'urī*, dog + *pi'i*, climb + *fare*, house, lit., house-climbing dog.

    'urī ta'ata 'monkey' = *'urī*, dog + *ta'ata*, person, lit., dog man.

    'urī 'aiava 'seal' = *'urī*, dog + *'ai*, dwell + *ava*, pass, lit., dog that lives in the passes (Andrews and Andrews 1944; Davies 1851).[a]

'iore 'small clawed animal'

    'iore mā'ohi 'rat' = *'iore*, rat + *mā'ohi*, indigenous, lit., native rat.

    'iore pererau 'bat' = *'iore*, rat + *pererau*, wing, lit., winged rat.

    'iore popa'ā 'rabbit' = *'iore*, rat + *popa'ā*, foreign, lit., foreign rat.

---

[a]   The standard word is *hūmi*

occurrence, the simple forms *pua'a*, *'urī*, *'iore* being usable under ordinary circumstances without leading to any confusion.

At the same time that new animals were being imported into Tahiti, Bible teaching was being diffused by the missionaries. In order to translate the Bible into Tahitian, the missionaries created great numbers of animal names from Hebrew, Greek, and Latin. With only a few exceptions, such as *'ātini* 'ass' (written *asini*), the names of these animals called up no image for the Tahitians. The Tahitian conception of life forms caused some trouble for the translators who had to find expedients for transposing Judaic ideas about the animal world into Tahitian:

manu 'āvae maha 'quadruped' = *manu*, land animal + *'āvae*, leg, foot, paw + *maha*, four, lit., four-footed animal.

manu pererau 'bird' = *manu*, land animal + *pererau*, wing, lit., winged animal.

manu rere 'āvae maha 'winged four-footed insects' (grasshoppers ...) = *manu*, animal + *rere*, to fly + *'āvae*, foot + *maha*, four, lit., flying four-footed animal.

pua'a 'wild (?) animal' = *pua'a*, hooved animal, pig.

THE PRESENT AGE

Generally speaking, familiarity with nature is now declining in Tahiti. The essential data serving to describe the present state of affairs was gathered from informants from an island neighboring Tahiti where the way of life, still close to nature, is more favorable for the persistence of this kind of knowledge than in Tahiti. This island belongs to the same linguistic and cultural unit, in spite of a few dialectal variations.

The expression *te mau mea ora* 'living beings' or 'living things' may be found both in the old texts collected at the beginning of the nineteenth century (Henry 1962:352) and in the Tahitian translation of the Bible. Informants were asked what meaning they attributed to this term. When consulted, persons between the ages of 45 and 65 gave similar explanations. The domain of living beings extends to the whole creation, everything that was not made "by the hand of man." This includes not only land animals, water animals, and plants, but also stones, the sea, astral bodies, etc. The way in which life manifests itself (movement, respiration, growth, etc.) is considered more or less obvious, according to the case. Insofar as stones are concerned, for instance, it is supposed to be very distinct. Stones live, grow, can have beneficent powers (certain stones can draw fish towards fishing spots) or dangerous powers (stones can be places for supernatural beings to stay), and finally they die by a process of deterioration, like plants. Therefore, the class *manu* 'terrestrial animal' is part of the larger set of *te mau mea ora* 'living things' where myth, philosophical speculation, and biological observation are considered not as separate domains of knowledge, but as integrated. On this subject, one may observe that for a long while zoological treatises in Europe gave descriptions of fabulous animals: the chimera, the unicorn, etc.

In general, the informants were not very much aware of the existence of the extended meaning of *manu* 'terrestrial animal'. This sense appears almost uniquely in such questions as *Eaha terā manu?* 'What is that animal?'. A question of this type is suitable for any kind of terrestrial animal, but not for an aquatic animal.

Three life forms are presented in Table 4. The *manumanu* 'very small animals' include named items (*ra'o* 'fly', etc.) but also organisms that are not designated with any great precision: small flies around fruit, microbes, etc. The class of *manu* 'birds, winged insects' comprises almost one level less than in the preceding era. The specific taxa are hardly represented, except by the two sorts of wasps and the two varieties of reef herons, *'ōtu'u* (*Egretta sacra*), one white, *'ōtu'u 'uo'uo*, and the other gray, *'ōtu'u 'ere'ere*. Certain species of birds have actually disappeared since the nineteenth century and those remaining are less widely distributed as the biological equilibrium has been changed.

A new life form, *'ānīmara* 'big nonflying animal', has taken the place of *pua'a* 'hooved animals' and *'urī* 'big clawed animals'. This class includes

Table 4.   Classification of land animals at the present time

Division	Life forms	Generic taxa	Specific taxa
manu terrestrial animal	*'ānīmara* big, nonflying animal (domestic and exotic animals)	*pua'a pape* hippopotamus	
		taita tiger	
		ruto wolf	
		mīmī cat	
		'urī dog	
		pua'arehenua (*pua'a horofenua*) horse	
		pua'a niho goat	
		pua'atoro cow	
		pua'a pig	
	manu bird, winged insect	*'ōtu'u* reef heron (*Egretta sacra*)	*'ōtu'u 'ere'ere* reef heron, gray variety
			'ōtu'u 'uo'uo reef heron, white variety
		tava'e red-tailed tropic bird (*Phaeton rubricauda*)	
		ma'uroa white-tailed tropic bird (*Phaeton lepturus*)	
		ua'ao red-footed booby (*Sula sula*)	
		noha (indeterminate petrel) (*Pterodroma* species)	
		manu pātia wasp	*manu pātia 'ute'ute* red wasp
			manu pātia 'ere'ere black wasp
		manu hāmani meri bee	
		pūrehua moth	
		pepe butterfly	
		pi'ao dragonfly	
	manumanu very small animal	*rō* ant	*rō māineine* lit., tickling ant
			rō hohoni, lit., biting ant
			rō 'ere'ere, lit., black ant
		'arau'au'a woodlouse	
		hitihiti sea louse	
		ra'o fly	
		naonao mosquito	

domestic and exotic animals, and it is hard to set its boundaries.

The meanings of certain generic names appearing in the missionary era (Table 3) are now obscured. A popular etymology makes the goat *pua'a niho* (< *pua'a*, pig + *niho*, horn, lit., horned pig) a toothed animal because of the only modern meaning of *niho* 'tooth', while there is an old meaning of *niho* 'horn' (Jaussen 1898; Davies 1851). The archaic name of the cat, *pi'ifare* or *'urī pi'ifare* (< *'urī*, dog + *pi'i*, climb + *fare*, house, lit., house-climbing dog), is that of an animal that calls in the house according to a current popular etymology among the Tahitians, as the only remaining meaning of *pi'i* is 'to call' (White 1967:328). Other changed or abridged names include: *mīmī* 'cat' (< French *mimi*), *pārehenua* 'horse' instead of *pua'a horofenua*, *māmoe* 'sheep' instead of *pua'a māmoe*. Among the names of exotic animals, some are borrowed: *taita* 'tiger' (< English), *rāpiti* 'rabbit' (< English); while others have been composed by comparison with familiar animals: *pua'a pape* 'hippopotamus' (< *pua'a*, pig + *pape*, water, lit., water pig or hog), *mo'o taehae* 'crocodile' (< *mo'o*, lizard + *taehae*, wild, savage, lit., ferocious lizard; this name also designates monsters in old texts).

For the sake of completeness, we should mention that the classification just described is among the more conservative. At the other extreme, with the more highly acculturated informants, the Tahitian categories are assimilated with their approximate French equivalents:

manu 'bird' instead of 'bird or winged insect'.

manumanu 'insect' instead of 'very small animal'.

'ānīmara 'animal' instead of 'big nonflying terrestrial animal' (the meaning *manu* 'terrestrial animal' disappears).

THE LOGIC OF ETHNOBIOLOGICAL CLASSIFICATIONS

We would like to draw attention to a difference that shows up between scientific classification and ethnobiological classification, at least at a certain level of the Tahitian example.

In the classifications regularly described that result in a taxonomy, the structure of the tree may be considered as the result of a sequence of elementary operations consisting of successive partitions. A taxon X located at level n of the taxonomic tree is divided into taxa from level n+1 of lesser extent, for example, Y, Z, T which reunite to form X.

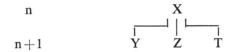

These operations are those of the regular theory of sets. The steps that they entail come from Boolean logic, a true and false two-valued logic. It should be clearly understood that the componential definitions partake of the same logic, even if they include many features.

It cannot be denied that such models produce suitable descriptions in a great many instances. But, when one asks Tahitians about assigning animals to life forms, the most remarkable fact is their hesitations, their contradictions, and the fact that it is sometimes even impossible for them to classify certain animals, even ones that are quite familiar. An attempt has been made (Bright and Bright 1965) to describe a classification by bringing into play "sphere of influence" relationships. The reactions of the informants suggest orientation towards this kind of many-valued logic, which takes into account the fact that the elements or members do not carry the same weight within a class. Within the taxa which have been called life forms, there is a central zone, one might say, containing a certain number of members that are highly representative of the life form concerned, and then there is a marginal zone of less representative or doubtful members. Informants' ideas about the classification of these doubtful members helps us understand their attitude. They themselves specify the characteristics of two of the life forms. The *manumanu* are animals of "small size" and the *manu* are animals "that fly." The third life form, which includes mainly domestic and exotic animals, has no such obvious characteristic. Such propositions conform faithfully to the concept of fuzzy sets (e.g. within the set of men, there is the fuzzy subset of men of great size).

This mathematical theory, called fuzzy sets theory, has been developed during the last few years by mathematicians such as L. A. Zadeh and has recently been presented in French (Kaufmann 1973). It is a generalization of set theory and provides a new way to approach the problems that we are raising. Some explanation is in order.

In the ordinary theory of sets from which the usual taxonomical models derive, a member either belongs or does not belong to a set (or a subset) as has been said above. In order to generalize this theory, it is necessary to introduce the notion of characteristic function. For each subset A (in the usual sense) of a set E, a characteristic function $f_A(x)$ is defined, which, being given any member x whatsoever of E, takes the value 1 when x is a member of the set A, and in the opposite case, the value 0. If E represents the human race, therefore, and A the set of human beings of masculine sex, the function $f_A(x)$ has the value of 0 when x represents a woman and 1 when x represents a man. The logic associated with this is two-valued: a true proposition equals 1, a false proposition 0.

In the fuzzy sets theory, this characteristic function may take values other than 0 and 1, i.e. any values between 0 and 1 (more general many-valued logic). A fuzzy subset is then defined by the values that its characteristic function takes for the various members of the set in which it is included. Within the set of employees of a business, the fuzzy subset of employees of big size would be defined by assigning sizes to the various employees, which would be made up of sizes between 0 and 1. One would have to choose the size of the biggest employee as being 1. The employees of the enterprise would all be members of this fuzzy subset, but in differing degrees.

Let us return to the question of Tahitian classification of life forms. The characteristic feature of the *manumanu* as explained by the Tahitians, i.e. smallness, is a relative notion implying innumerable possible degrees. It may be represented with greater verisimilitude by a characteristic function which includes all values between 0 and 1 than by a function which assumes only two values. The representation of the *manumanu* by a fuzzy subset is therefore preferable to a representation connected with two-valued logic. The "flying" criterion of *manu* would seem at first to correspond to a proposition to which it is possible to reply by "yes" or "no." In fact, such is not the case.

The characteristic features of the various life forms are not mutually exclusive. It does not always suffice to observe that a generic taxon possesses one of them in order to assign it the name of a life form. As a matter of fact, it may possess characteristic features of several forms. The reactions of the informants show that, in this latter case, after comparison, a single one of these features is retained as the most conspicuous for the generic taxon under consideration. Everything occurs as though the classification, which is in the domain of thought, authorizes fuzziness and overlap, while the nomenclature, which belongs to the domain of communication, would like to avoid them. Thus, flies and mosquitoes are small enough to be *manumanu* and/or do not fly well enough to be *manu*. Butterflies fly well enough to be *manu* and/or are not small enough to be *manumanu*. The classification of the cricket, for instance, is uncertain. The chicken is considered rather as an *'anīmara* as it does not fly very much.

In order to put these notions into practice in view of the description of ethnobiological categories, it is necessary to be able to evaluate the characteristic functions. A model where these characteristic functions can take all of the values between 0 and 1 requires the use of elaborate tests.

A three-valued model (0, 1/2, 1) corresponding to a three-valued logic (false, doubtful, true), leads to distinguishing within the classes a marginal

Table 5.   Distribution of a few generic taxa in keeping with the biological forms as fuzzy sets (from four informants, therefore some overlaps)

Generic taxa	Life forms		
	manumanu very small animals	*manu* animals that fly (birds, winged insects)	*'ānimara* large animals (domestic and exotic animals)
vīvī grasshopper	1	0	0
veri centipede	0	0	1/2
vāvā phasmid	0	1	0
'utu louse	1	0	0
'urī dog	0	0	1
tūtūrahonui large-bodied spider	0	0	1/2
tutu'a flea	1	0	0
rō ant	1	0	0
ra'o fly	1	0	0
pūrehua moth	0	1	0
pua'a pig	0	0	1
potipoti cockroach	1/2	1/2	0
pi'ao dragonfly	1	0	0
perete'i cricket (*Grillus oceanicus*)	1/2	1/2	0
pepe butterfly	1	1	0
naonao mosquito	1	0	0
mo'o lizard	0	0	1/2
moa chicken	0	1/2	1/2
mīmī cat	0	0	1
manu pātia wasp	1/2	1	0
'iore rat	0	0	1/2
'arau'au'a woodlouse (Sp. indet.)	1	0	0

zone (1/2) from a central zone (1) (see Table 5).

Within the Tahitian system that has been examined, the Boolean logic of scientific taxonomies does not permit the relations between generic taxa and biological types to be explained in a satisfactory way. The fuzzy set theory and the more general logic associated with it are better adapted to a description of this level of classification. A clue would seem to indicate that this particularity is not restricted to Tahitian: often enough in the ethnobiological classifications, generic classes are not affiliated with biological forms (Berlin, et al. 1973:216, 219). As Kaufmann observes, "The laws of thought that we can introduce into the computer programs are obligatorily formal; the laws of thought in man-to-man dialogue are fuzzy" (Kaufmann 1973:191).

REFERENCES

ANONYMOUS
    1875   *Te tahitan Fabura*. Papeete: Imprimerie des Ecoles Françaises Indigènes.

ANDREWS, EDMUND, IRENE D. ANDREWS
1944 *A comparative dictionary of the Tahitian language.* Chicago: Chicago Academy of Sciences.

BERLIN, BRENT, DENNIS E. BREEDLOVE, PETER H. RAVEN
1973 General principles of classification and nomenclature in folk biology. *American Anthropologist* 75:214–242.

BRIGHT, JANE O., WILLIAM BRIGHT
1965 Semantic structures in northwestern California and the Sapir-Whorf Hypothesis. *American Anthropologist* 67:249–258. (Reprinted 1969 in *Cognitive anthropology.* Edited by Stephen A. Tyler, 66–78. New York: Holt, Rinehart and Winston.)

DAVIES, JOHN
1851 *A Tahitian and English dictionary.* Papeete: London Missionary Society's Press.

HENRY, TEUIRA
1928 *Ancient Tahiti.* Honolulu: Bishop Museum Press.
1962 *Tahiti aux temps anciens.* Paris: Société des Océanistes.

JAUSSEN, TEPANO
1898 *Grammaire et dictionnaire de la langue Maorie, dialecte tahitien.* Paris: Belin.

KAUFMANN, A.
1973 *Introduction à la théorie des sous-ensembles flous. 1. Eléments théoriques de base.* Paris: Masson.

KAY, PAUL
1971 On taxonomy and semantic contrast. *Language* 47:866–887.

LEMAITRE, YVES
1972 La hiérarchie des termes de nourriture en tahitien. *Cahier ORSTOM, Série Sciences Humaines* 9:63–73.
i.p. *Lexique du tahitien contemporain.* Paris: ORSTOM.

WHITE, RALPH GARDNER
1967 "Onamastically induced word replacement in Tahitian," in *Polynesian culture history, essays in honor of K. P. Emory.* Edited by G. A. Highland, 323–338. Honolulu: Bishop Museum Press.

On an African Classificatory System

JEAN-PAUL LEBEUF

Ethnological studies made during the past several decades in the Bas-Chari region have revealed that among the Kotoko people there is an elaborate classificatory system of species.

This system is primarily based upon the elementary division of all Creation into masculine and feminine categories. Secondly, there is great importance attributed to numbers. The system includes five fundamental limitative series: wild mammals, birds, edible grains, wild plant life, and fish. Each of the first four includes twenty-four species, the fish alone containing thirty-six. Twenty-four species of fish live in the river and twelve species inhabit the *marigots* [swamps]. These classes, which represent a large part of Creation, are subdivided into groups of twelve male species and twelve female ones; the exception to this is the class of fish inhabiting the *marigots*, which is subdivided into groups of six each. Items which do not seem to be classified in ordered series include reptiles, insects and arachnids, domesticated animals, edible plants besides grains, and various sorts of plant life.

To each of these series is added a species, always androgynous, which is distinct from all the preceding ones and corresponds to a "counter-order" or opposite order. This is one of the two aspects of a society in which the order is made complete through the inclusion of two complementary orders. These androgynous species are: the dog for the wild mammals, the *Tetraodon bahaka stringosus* and the *Andersonia leptura* for the river- and *marigot*-dwelling fish respectively, the scarlet bee-eater and its eggs for the birds, *Sorghum virgatum* for the edible grains, and the soapberry tree for the bush species. These "added" species are all associated with the metallurgists, the bronze-caster and the blacksmith.

It does not seem that the classes are ordered preferentially among themselves or that certain ones are more important than others. The order in which the species are enumerated can be modified, relatively, to account for deletion, overlapping, or mistakes, without there ever being any confusion.

Within the framework of a general taxonomic system which is fairly elaborate, the wild mammals and the fish on the one hand, and the birds and edible grains on the other, each given a particular sex, are connected with the four elements. The series are grouped as two couples, remembering, of course, that the two varieties of fish form their own "internal" couple. The male wild mammals and the female fish form the male element of another couple in which the alliance of the male birds and the female edible grains represents the female element:

(river fish $\male$ + *marigot* fish $\female$ = $\female$)
Earth $\male$ (wild mammals) + Water $\female$ (fish) = $\male$
Air $\male$ (birds) + Fire $\female$ (edible grains) = $\female$

Due to the fundamental duality of things in the universe, this subdivision appears to be primary since each of the elements is in fact androgynous or, in itself, forms its own couple. In fact, uncultivated land forms a couple with cultivated land, which is female; the water from rain, male, forms another couple with the water from waterways; violent wind, male, and gentle wind, female, constitute a third couple; lightning, male, and fire in the hearth, a fourth. Elsewhere, the water from rain and cultivated land, on the one hand, and the water from waterways and uncultivated land, on the other hand, form two couples, which are not connected to one another. In this perspective, the precise relationship between four of the classificatory series can be set down in the following manner:

uncultivated earth $\male$ (wild mammals) + water from waterways $\female$ (fish)
= $\male$
violent wind $\male$ (birds) + fire in the hearth $\female$ (edible grains) = $\female$

Although, within each classification, the sex attributed to each species expresses its essential nature, in other words, its "principal sex" according to the thinking of the Kotoko, it is clear that each species also possesses to a lesser degree the opposite and complementary sexual traits. However, for the sake of permanence, this notion of androgyneity is not always expressed in the taxonomic system even though it may be quite clearly apparent in certain species.

The WILD MAMMALS are enumerated within their class according to the chronological order of their arrival in the universe. While they are considered to be a male series as a whole and although each element of this series represents a couple, all of the animals appear with a unique sexual aspect; the only exceptions are a breed of horse (le Cob du Buffon), the harnessed antelope, and the red monkey, which each appear twice, once as females and once as males. The dog, the twenty-fifth element of the series, an "added" member, is androgynous. The presence of "leader" animals might be noted, but, with the exception of the elephant which is the first one listed, these group leaders are only placed at the third (lion) and the twenty-second (*hippotragus*) ranks of the classificatory list.

Separate from the rest, the dog is presented here as the intermediary between the world of the wild and the city, an organized world in which a different order was introduced by the primordial blacksmith. The dog is considered to be neither wild mammal nor domesticated animal. His position in the classification system is ambiguous and corresponds to his role, which is dual: on the one hand he is a disseminator of disorder, on the other, he is an intermediary and founder. The animal associated with iron- and bronzeworkers, he is also associated with hunters and is a stranger to fishermen. He must not be connected with the prince, the monitor and symbol of order. The dog is a symbol of thievery, an action that belongs to a counter-order which was, in mythical times, the apparent disorder which preceded political organization. This organization rests in part on a system of exchanges and a complementarity which the dog helped to establish.

In the general classification of the various species, the FISH, numbering thirty-six elements (24 + 12), are considered as a group to belong, along with the wild mammals, to the male portion of the created world (even though they are females in relation to the class of wild mammals). They are subdivided into two series, the one being male and including species which spawn in rivers, the other being female and including only those species which spawn in the *marigots*.

The former group contains twenty-four elements (+ 1) and the latter has twelve (+ 1). Just as the wild mammals are a special class for all sorts of hunters, the fish occupy a preferential position in creation for the fishermen. This special position is determined by the supernatural ties which bind these animals to humans. To some extent, the Kotoko fishermen consider themselves to be fish, and even the prince is required to possess some sort of house on the river in common with the "men of the water."

The classificatory series of the BIRDS includes some twenty-four species (twelve male and twelve female) to which is added an androgynous bird representing the counter-order. As was observed with the wild mammals, the rank attributed to the birds in this classificatory system corresponds to the chronological order of their arrival in the universe, even if there is no information about their place of origin. (The vulture is an exception, it is said to come from two directions, the south and the east.) The rank of certain members of this list does not always correspond to the importance attributed to these members. The fish-hawk plays the same role in the bird family as does the dog among the wild mammals; like the latter he is a thief, but the only victims of his pillage are the river-dwelling fish, which belong to the wilds, whereas the dog steals from humans the product of their fishing.

The series of EDIBLE GRAINS also includes twenty-four species, to which is added a twenty-fifth, *Sorghum virgatum*, which abounds along the shores of the waterways. The series is subdivided into twelve male and twelve female species, the latter including oleaginous grains. Like the wild mammal and bird classes, they are enumerated according to the chronological order of their appearance in the region. Candle millet "the best of all cereals," symbolizes the various types of millet and all the other edible grains. It is placed at the head of the series, whose first seven listings constitute the essence of nutrition from cereals.

WILD PLANT LIFE is also the object of a classificatory list comparable to the preceding ones which includes twenty-five (24+1) species, twelve male, twelve female, and one androgynous. One type alone, *Combretum glutinosum*, is characterized by the two aspects, male and female. These plants unite the terrestrial and the celestial; they are androgynous within a perspective that embraces all Creation.

The Southern Kotoko people, the Lagouans, have established correspondences between wild mammals and fish, on the one hand, and human society, on the other. The population of the area is essentially made up of twenty-four families of hunters, thirty-six (24 + 12) of fishermen, and two of metallurgists: the bronzecasters, the earliest established members of the community, who are "male," and the blacksmiths, who are "female." The twenty-four classes of mammals are the equivalent, in the world of the wild, of as many families of hunters. The fish of the river and the *marigots* correspond to the thirty-six families of fishermen. The disparity between the number of wild mammals and the number of fish thus connected somehow to humans is locally justified by the fact that the fishermen are more numerous than the hunters. The family and the animal corresponding to it are both of the same sex; for example, the family connected to the Nile perch is, like the fish, "male," and the family associated with the civet cat is "female." But while it seems that the hunters "are" these wild mammals, without any intermediary between them, it appears that the fishermen are connected to the fish by way of a bird, the only one whose food is exclusively aquatic, the fish-hawk. The fish-hawk is male in the taxonomic series, but it is androgynous here since it is the intermediary between thirty-six families, some of which are male and some female. Besides, this bird communicates with both the heavens (violents winds), male, and the waters (rivers), female.

An animal or fish as well as the mythical monitor lizard and the serpent correspond to every town founded by a hunter or a fisherman. These towns include only the twenty-four very oldest agglomerations founded by the hunters and the thirty-six primordial establishments of the fishermen who arrived in the country after those hunters. The hunters have some connections (still unclear) with trees: to the twenty-four species of trees are connected just as many hunting families, even though it seems that a given species does not correspond to a specific family (at least, no one seems to remember such an interdependence). To the twelve "male" trees correspond six bow-hunting families and an equal number of assegai hunters, and the subdivision of the twelve "female" trees is similar. Trees and families are subdivided spatially around the center of the Kotoko country — corresponding to the principality of Kousseri — by having twelve species and twelve families which are "male" in the Mandagué area (north) divided equally between hunters who use the lance and those who use the bow; the subdivision is the same in the Lagouané (south) region for the same number of families and tree species which are "female." In the same manner, thirty-six families of fishermen are located to the northwest of Mandagué, those connected to river species living to the right side and those connected to *marigot* species living to the left. The bronze- and ironworkers are placed "farther" to the west, from where they would have originated —"farther" because they are without families and without roots in the towns. This group as a whole is supposed to describe a counterclockwise movement, while in the interior two opposing circles are traced, one counterclockwise for the fishermen, the other clockwise for the blacksmiths.

The hunters and the plant life form, with the center itself, the pivot of a counterclockwise system which represents the entire Kotoko community, made up of the three principalities of Mandagué, Kousseri, and Lagouané. Each principality turns around its capital, in a clockwise fashion for Lagouané, counterclockwise for Mandagué, and both clockwise and counterclockwise for Kousseri. And this spatial representation, since the Kotoko want it to be complete, includes all the species — wild mammals, fish, birds, and edible grains — which are arranged according to the four cardinal directions along with the elements, or more precisely with one of their basic aspects: Water (waterways), Fire (from the hearth), Earth (uncultivated), and Air (violent winds). The fish are in the north with Water, the edible grains are in the east with Fire, the wild mammals are in the south with Earth, and the birds are in the west with Air. In other words, the taxonomic system of the Kotoko people places man in total contact with the universe.

REFERENCES

LEBEUF, A. M. D.
  1952   Aspect cosmogonique de l'organisation politique des Kotoko (Nord-Cameroun). *Comptes rendus sommaires des séances de l'Institut Français d'Anthropologie* 84:16–17.
  1969   *Les principautés kotoko. Essai sur le caractère sacré de l'autorité.* Paris: C.N.R.S.
LEBEUF, A., J.-P. LEBEUF
  1955   Monuments symboliques du palais royal de Logone-Birni (Nord-Cameroun). *Journal de la Société des Africanistes* 25:25–34.
LEBEUF, J.-P.
  1969   *Carte archéologique des abords du lac Tchad* (Cameroun, Nigeria, Tchad). Paris: C.N.R.S.

Ethnoscience as a Research Paradigm

C. GREGORY KNIGHT

Ethnoscience as a paradigm for the study of man requires revision. This statement is prompted by my interest in working with this approach in the context of one aspect of human experience — the interaction of society with its biophysical environment. It is in this realm, at least, where ethnoscience might flourish. If one wishes to take a grandiose view of ethnoscience as contributing to the fundamental understanding of human cultural codes and thought and behavioral processes, the man-environment realm would seem an ideal locus for ethnoscientific research efforts. That society is rooted within and dependent upon environment is universally known. At minimum, environment provides a matrix of material and energy resources essential for sustenance, although few, if any, societies are satisfied with simple, unelaborated subsistence. In exploiting environment for the realization of physiologically and culturally defined requisites for life, societies employ cognitively mediated behavior. Cognitive processes pervade everyday activity and decision making, the discovery and dissemination of new knowledge, and the enculturation of society's new members.

If society-within-environment and the focal role of thought in man-environment interaction are universal, so, too, are the necessary relationships between these phenomena and the environment as an absolute. That no scientific system maintains a monopoly on environmental truth is argued below; nevertheless, we can posit that environment, lying always just beyond the grasp of any scientific system, remains permanent in its

The author gratefully acknowledges continuing discussions with James Blaut and Richard Hansis which have contributed to the development of this communication.

character. This character includes (but is not limited to) flows of matter and energy, systematic behavior, cyclicity, change and evolution. Thus, just as the kinship analyst can "map" varying kinship systems onto a "universal" biologically derived map of possible kinship relations, or the color analyst has his universal Munsell charts, so the researcher, focused on ethnoscience and man-environment interaction, has a similar basis for cross-cultural mapping — basic ecological processes. While not totally explicit, this viewpoint has not been lost on researchers who have devoted considerable effort to the documentation of folk botanical classifications and the like. Thus the universality of man-in-environment, the salient role of cognition in man-environment interactions, and the possibility for cross-cultural mapping on an "absolute" all argue for a strong focus on this realm within ethnoscience. Realization of the promise of early efforts in this direction will require, however, a clear revision of the paradigm. Moreover, this revision must be consonant with the total role of ethnoscience with its multiple subfoci of substantive content.

Revision of the paradigm is also indicated on the basis of less ultimate goals. Focusing in four more pragmatic directions may aid in the larger quests; at a minimum these will require considerable substantive research and will contribute to contemporary human welfare. First, the growth of the ecological movement would seem to provide fertile ground for investigation of the ecology and philosophy of man-environment interactions in other than Western society. Specifically, what are the universals of man's husbrandy of environment? How are environmental management and care cognized, articulated and inculcated in other societies? Is man universally the exploiter? If not, when and how does he become a partner-in-balance? What universals, if any, exist in conversals of man's husbrandry of environment? How are environmental Do cognized processes of population limitation with respect to environment widely exist or did they once exist? This kind of question leads to the second possible direction of ethnoscience, an increment to Western scientific knowledge.

That scientific knowledge is limited by the society in which it is embedded is now achieving universal recognition. Few of us who have worked in Third World social or ecological milieus could not cite numerous examples of incongruence between Western science and local, folk science. Indeed, many of us have further observed empirical validity in the non-Western tradition, a system of thought which could conceivably be overrun by an invalid or marginally applicable Western system with its blindness, arrogance, and power. Whether it be the "discovery" of yet another valuable pharmaceutical from folk medicine or the "validation" of the inherent rationality of a traditional cropping practice, Western science does stand to learn. Specifically it can learn about the environment and its dynamics from other scientific systems. These systems become accessible through ethnoscience. In addition, they provide a perspective from which we can critically view our own ethnoscientific system.

This leads us then to the third pragmatic direction — that of cross-cultural communication. Although it may be most obvious with respect to problems like rural development, difficulties of cross-cultural understanding and the dissemination of innovations pervade the whole of our interaction with (and frequent intolerance of) non-Western systems of thought. In development, experience has sufficiently shown that failure to understand specific innovations within the context of their introduction and to translate adequately their potential within the local terms of reference (the local folk science) means the ultimate failure of the venture (Knight 1971). There must be cases where that failure was applauded by gods who looked down upon our efforts toward "developing" other peoples with schemes that could have been disastrous.

That cognition should play a major role in change is, of course, related to a fourth direction for ethnoscience — understanding of human behavior within environment. Much of environmental behavior is learned and represents the interaction of cultural thought evolved through time, recently disseminated knowledge, and personal experience, all played out within the individual or group. Through a variety of techniques (formal and informal) the scientist can approach understanding the system of knowledge a people brings to some aspect of behavior. Much but certainly not all of this knowledge is articulated verbally. Much but certainly not all behavior can be understood by the investigation of verbally articulated knowledge. Just how much (or how little) is a question we will answer only when we have adequately tested our paradigm. But first we must specify the nature of our strategy and how we might make it operate.

A paradigm for further study in ethnoscience is proposed here. Underlying this proposal is my bias in emphasizing the man-environment focus in ethnoscience. Because the burgeoning literature in ethnoscience is readily accessible, it will not be reviewed here (Colby 1963, 1966; Sturtevant 1964; Goodenough 1970). If my own inclinations are not sufficiently apparent in the following discussion, let it be explicitly noted that, although I believe ethnoscience to hold great promise, I do not see it as the sole route to truth. I lean strongly toward focusing research on both emic and etic levels. Moreover, I see valid explanation residing in both houses; in the specific area of man-environment interaction, in both cultural ecology and ethnoscience. Finally, although I agree almost totally with Keesing's argument (1972) calling for the reexamination of ethnoscience in view of contemporary developments in linguistics, I do not agree that work accomplished to date in folk classifications has been trivial. Rather, I would argue that this work may be a prerequisite for the creation of models of systems of folk science, paying attention most specifically to folk theories and systems of knowledge. It is here that ethnoscience could offer the glimpses into human thought and behavior that would parallel linguistic developments. At a minimum, it will open new perspectives on more immediate and pragmatic matters.

Ethnoscience is concerned with systems of knowledge and belief within and across cultures and through time. Ultimately, it is expected that ethnoscience will result in theorems subject to verification by comparative methods involving the structure of systems of knowledge and their articulation as systems of science specific to individual cultures or reference groups. In addition, ethnoscientific studies may contribute to the analysis of specific cultures and human behavior within a specific social context. The term ETHNO- refers to "the system of knowledge and cognition typical of a given culture" (Sturtevant 1964: 99–100). The general use of the term ethnoscience to refer to both belief systems and to the study of them could be confusing, and suggests the following definitions:

ETHNOSCIENTIFIC SYSTEM: the system of knowledge and belief specific to a reference group.

ETHNOSCIENTIFIC MODEL: a description of an ethnoscientific system, usually expressed as a cross-cultural mapping or translation, often in a language different from that of the reference group.

ETHNOSCIENCE: the study of ethnoscientific systems and models from a cross-cultural perspective.

It would seem reasonable that parallel terminology would be used for specific domains or subsets of the ethnoscience paradigm; for example, in an ethnogeographic system, ethnogeographic model or ethnogeography — all concerned with human cognition of space and resources or geographic knowledge.

These distinctions are more than trivial. Because the investigator cannot replicate the enculturation process experienced by a member of a reference culture, he can at best create a model of that culture's ethnoscientific system. The model can be tested and refined; but it can never totally reproduce the system itself. The term "model" emphasizes that the system is translated and interpreted but never perfectly reflected. Berlin (personal communication) suggested that "folk science" or "folk geography" be used for what I have termed "ethnoscientific system," as the term ethnoscience has had a very specific and limited meaning in anthropology. Nevertheless, words prefixed by ethno- now generally connote meanings parallel to that suggested above (ethnobotany, ethnozoology) and, as value free as we might mean "folk science" to be, this phrase is all too likely to be interpreted pejoratively. I prefer to see the whole notion of ethnoscience broadened to be consonant with the structure proposed here.

The fodder for ethnoscience will be ethnoscientific models. I suspect that we will be doing well if we create a cross-cultural selection of models of even specific subsets or domains of ethnoscientific systems. Focusing across a number of cultures on the ethnoscientific systems underlying traditional agricultural practices, for example, might provide more rapid initial insight into cross-cultural phenomena than documentation of fewer models of whole scientific systems. Nevertheless, specification of domains in this way, although initially attractive, is in fact an etic imposition. Here we are assuming as universal the discrete ordering we see in nature and human activity. I think this assumption needs careful verification. Similarly, we need thorough investigation of the logic of isolating specific domains as well as tools for doing so, from either emic or etic viewpoints. Lacking this, are we satisfied to fall back upon the universal cultural necessity for provision of food as a temporarily adequate delimitation of the core of a domain of analysis? Ultimately, we should be as free to delimit domains as the ecologist is in defining areal ecosystems, with boundaries located to allow accounting for interconnections to and from the domain with relative ease.

Critical for ethnoscience is the nature of the ethnoscientific models from which it will be built. Folk terminologies, taxonomies and limited proto-theoretic discussions are already familiar to us. I think few would disagree that these studies have been interesting but generally unproductive. They have not been linked to specific behavior except in a most general way; they have provided little impetus to cross-cultural analysis; and even the investigators would attest that these studies do not even approach exhaustion of their informants' knowledge. They simply do not go far enough. The next step must be to look at theoretical formulations, empirical relational processes within ethnoscientific systems, and the way in which this theory is used in making behavioral decisions. We have a plethora of methods for working with folk taxonomies (Frake 1964; Berlin et al. 1968; Tyler 1969); we have very few formal procedures for eliciting folk theory. Once we have created models of folk scientific systems as whole systems of knowledge, then tentative answers to questions about processes of logic, thought content, and a myriad of other queries will become accessible. At that stage, verbal models will certainly not suffice, and we will perforce turn to the pregnant world of symbolic logic systems.

The elicitation of theory in ethnoscientific systems may profitably follow the broad structure that has emerged in the documentation of the taxonomic and attributive stages of analysis. In the latter, investigation of taxonomic relationships among and/or attributes within a particular terminological domain have followed a sequence that could be labeled specification, formalization, and generalization. Specification refers to the use of a small and carefully selected group of informants for initial delimitation of the lexical domain of analysis. Frake (1964), Casagrande and Hale (1967) and others have provided formal sets of queries that can be used at this stage of analysis, although informal discussion and participant observation are also used to specify domains of analysis. Formalization refers to the use of formal procedures for documentation of taxonomic structure, attributes or other cognized characteristics of the specified domain. Among these formalized procedures are sorting procedures, the triads test, paired comparisons, and creation of folk trees and/or keys. Here, the sample group will be larger, perhaps randomly selected, and the results will be understanding of aspects of the domain, most frequently its taxonomic structure and the constructs upon which taxonomic distinctions are made. Finally, the distribution of knowledge within the whole reference group may be ascertained by means of formal testing to generalize inferences made from more limited sampling. For example, a semantic differential format might be used with the terms from the specification stage as the stimuli and the constructs elicited in the formalization stage as the evaluative scales. Clearly, some of the formal procedures could be used at any or all stages of analysis; indeed, some of these procedures may also be useful to elicit theoretical or relational statements as well. It is likely that our quest for theory will follow the same broad strategy: specification using a small informal group; formalization with a larger group; and generalization focusing on the reference society as a whole. We will certainly be interested in the distribution of knowledge within societies as well as the structure and content of that knowledge.

Verification of the ethnoscientific model can be approached through one or more techniques. First, the investigator repeatedly translates back to his informants his understanding, seeking confirmation or denial of his interpretation. Second, he attempts to extrapolate beyond his current understanding, formulating inferences using the relationships and logical structure as he understands them. His inferences are confirmed or denied by informants. A model that is productive, able to produce new inferences beyond its present content, is strong evidence for its validity. Third, the investigator compares his knowledge with the verbal and non-verbal behavior of his informants. He may even find artifacts useful—for example, land use patterns as artifacts of ethnogeographic systems can be compared with the decision-making frameworks that underpin them. Behavior or artifacts may confirm our understanding; they may open avenues of query not previously obvious; they may point to idiosyncratic circumstances; or they may point to misunderstandings on the part of the investigator. Fourth, the model must be made accessible to other investigators for confirmation in the same or related cultures; it must be replicable. Finally, the investigator might attempt to behave in a culturally relevant manner using the knowledge he has gained. His performance would be evaluated with the aid of his informants.

Gladwin's analysis of Puluwatan navigational systems provides an excellent example of some aspects of the paradigm suggested here (Gladwin 1970). This interpretation parallels Gladwin's material, although the thrust of his work is not specifically intended for ethnoscientific studies. Here, questions of domain, informants, elicitation, modeling, and verification are implicitly addressed. Navigation is one domain within the Puluwatan ethnoscientific system, a domain defined primarily by the people themselves. This domain is not isolated, however. In the case of Puluwat, navigation strongly overlaps the design and building of canoes, and together canoe building and navigation pervade the whole of Puluwatan society.

In documenting the Puluwatan navigation system, Hipour and other master Puluwatan navigators proved to be Gladwin's main informants. Sailing is a central part of Puluwatan life. Any informant will answer a query, giving the best answer he can rather than admit to having no answer at all. Thus, the notion of random samples and quantifiable results gives way in ethnoscientific research to careful selection of IN-FORMED informants. Only later might we generate formal procedures seeking to understand commonalities distributed across larger groups.

With the aid of Hipour, Gladwin documented a model of the Puluwatan navigation system. Although terminologies and taxonomies might have been appropriate for investigation, Gladwin focused on the body of abstraction and theory that comprise the system. He could not duplicate a lifetime of experience of being around and travelling in Puluwatan canoes, but he was able to benefit from a body of knowledge articulated for formal instruction and to compress the instructional procedure into a short period of time. Unfortunately, only rarely will domains of interest appear in such a serendipitous niche in society, forcing most of our work toward formal elicitation rather than receipt of formal instruction. Gladwin explained the means by which he created his model:

Hipour explained things to me in his terms and I interpreted them back in mine ... The system I present is the one used by Puluwat navigators, described as faithfully and accurately as I can, but the terms in which it is described are necessarily my own, that is, Western. It means that explanations of why and how various elements in the system are effective must be cast in a logical mold familiar to me ... or else they will not make sense ... Therefore the account which follows is a description [model] of a cognitive system organized to make sense to us, not an attempt through words to get inside a Puluwat navigator's head and think his thoughts his way (Gladwin 1970: 143).

Gladwin created a model and cross-cultural mapping of the design and building of canoes in Puluwat compared with sailing craft of the Western world. Here the mapping universal is the problem of design of a wind-propelled water surface vessel, just as the real-world location of ocean islands provides the cross-cultural mapping universal for portions of the navigation system.

Gladwin documented the Puluwatan navigation system in detail, verifying his model through confirmation or denial of his understanding by Hipour. As a further verification, he also appears to have extrapolated from his understanding. In addition, Gladwin's model conforms with reports of other Micronesian navigation systems; I presume that his model is thus consistent as well as replicable and testable by other researchers. The result of Gladwin's report is a fertile, cross-cultural mapping of sailing vessels and navigational techniques, comparing the Puluwatan model with that of Western navigation. The ultimate measure of either system is its ability to arrive at its destination. Gladwin's analysis plus research by Lewis confirms the real-world validity of the Puluwatan ethnogeography — landfall is virtually guaranteed (Lewis 1971).

Gladwin's work thus illustrates some potentials for the documentation of ethnoscientific systems. The critical point here is the focus on systems of thought and on theory within ethnoscientific systems. In this sense, Gladwin's work seems to point in the direction suggested as having great potential for ethnoscience.

It is with no small amount of optimism that I view the future of ethnoscience. The realm of human interaction with the environment allows vast possibilities for cross-cultural investigation of systems of knowledge and belief. Research in this area may profitably expand our perspectives on questions of man and his environment. But in addition to potential, there is also a sense of urgency in ethnoscience. If it is true, as Keesing (1972) reports, that "ethnoscience has almost bored itself to death," then valuable time for the documentation of ethnoscientific models has been lost in an era when an accelerating dispersion of Western science pervades educational systems and promises to its proponents the symbols of modernity. Surely, folk sciences will not disappear in our lifetime. Yet the repository of traditional knowledge diminishes. If cross-cultural understanding is our goal and if our quest has any promise of productivity, the sooner that knowledge is tapped the better.

Equally, if not more, important is the challenge ethnoscience puts before us. This challenge is the step beyond mechanical repetition of taxonomic efforts toward theory — theory in the sense of cross-cultural universals of human experience. Particularly intriguing remains the opportunity to discover, elaborate and structure the new endeavor, one that hopefully will be both interesting and productive.

REFERENCES

BERLIN, B., *et al.*
    1968   Covert categories and folk taxonomies. *American Anthropologist* 70:290–299.
CASAGRANDE, J., K. HALE
    1967   "Papago folk definitions," in *Studies in Southwestern ethnolinguistics.* Edited by D. M. Hymes, 165–193. The Hague: Mouton.
COLBY, B. N.
    1963   Folk science studies. *El Palacio* 70(4):5–14.
    1966   Ethnographic semantics. *Current Anthropology* 7:3–32.
FRAKE, C. O.
    1964   Notes on queries in anthropology. *American Anthropologist* 66(3) Part 2: 132–145.
GLADWIN, T.
    1970   *East is a big bird.* Cambridge: Harvard University Press.
GOODENOUGH, W. H.
    1970   *Description and comparison in cultural anthropology.* Chicago: Aldine.
KEESING, R. M.
    1972   Paradigms lost: the new ethnography and the new linguistics. *Southwestern Journal of Anthropology* 28:299–332.
KNIGHT, C. G.
    1971   Ethnogeography and change. *Journal of Geography* 70:47–51.

LEWIS, D.
  1971   A return voyage between Puluwat and Saipan using Micronesian navigational techniques. *Journal of the Polynesian Society* 30: 437–448.
STURTEVANT, W. C.
  1964   Studies in ethnoscience. *American Anthropologist* 66 (3, pt. 2): 99–131.
TYLER, S. A.
  1969   *Cognitive anthropology.* New York: Holt, Rinehart and Winston.

Australian Kin Classification

H. W. SCHEFFLER

In this paper I present outlines of formal (structural semantic) models of several well-known Australian aboriginal systems of kin classification, and I specify some of the logical relations among the models. This is a working paper; its observations are put forth as hypotheses (which I think are fairly sound), and I do not attempt to exhaust the empirical variation in Australian systems of kin classification. There is no space to present the models in full or the data that were analyzed to yield the models; but I have consulted and attempted to synthesize all of the published data on any system that I mention, and in many cases I have consulted important unpublished material as well.[1] Because virtually all of the various kinds of summary diagrammatic devices that have been used to represent aboriginal systems of kin classification as wholes are seriously defective or misleading in certain respects, I do not attempt to summarize the relevant data by means of such diagrams.

The models are based on the assumption that most Australian kinship terms are polysemous, i.e. that most of them have multiple and semantically related significata. The evidence for this assumption

The research on which this paper is based was carried out in Australia in 1971-1972 and was funded by the National Science Foundation (GS 28091), the Australian National University, and the Australian Institute of Aboriginal Studies. This paper is a brief outline of a monograph now in preparation. It was presented to seminars at the A.N.U. and at Macquarie and Monash Universities where I received many helpful comments from persons too numerous to list here.
[1] I am particularly indebted to Professors A. P. Elkin, W. Stanner, R. Piddington, and L. Sharp, to Drs. L. Hercus, N. Peterson, L. R. Hiatt, and J. Beckett, to Mrs. D. Thomson and Mrs. A. Hamilton, and to Mr. J. R. von Sturmer for permitting access to and use of unpublished data.

has been reviewed elsewhere (Scheffler 1971a, 1972b, 1972c). For an extended discussion of the general theoretical perspective of this paper see Scheffler and Lounsbury (1971).

PITJANTJATJARRA

The system of kin classification of the Pitjantjatjarra speakers (Munn 1965) is fairly typical of a "type" of system found throughout the western desert, though not in all western desert groups or only in western desert groups. The non-Australian systems structurally most similar to the Pitjantjatjarra system are the socalled Hawaiian-type systems (see also Elkin 1939: 214–215). Such systems feature parent, child, sibling, and grandparent and grandchild terms and extend them to all collateral kin of the same generations as the class foci — this by simple neutralization of the lineal vs. collateral opposition, i.e. by the rule (PSb $\rightarrow$ P), etc. (see also Scheffler 1972a: 123–124). The Pitjantjatjarra system differs from these non-Australian systems only in that it features special "mo.bro" and "fa.sis." categories, but these are subclasses of the extended "fa." and "mo." categories respectively. In some Australian systems otherwise identical to the Pitjantjatjarra system, reciprocal "cross-nephew" and "cross-niece" categories are distinguished, but these are subclasses of the extended "ch." category. The subclass distinctions are often neutralized; members of the special subclasses are often designated by the parent or child terms. In the Pitjantjatjarra system and others like it, father's cross cousins (as well as his parallel cousins) are classified as "fa." and "fa.sis."; mother's cross cousins (as well as her parallel cousins) are classified as "mo." and "mo.bro."

MANDJINDJA

In this system (Elkin 1940), also typical of a number of western desert groups, the basic categories are much the same as in the Pitjantjatjarra system; the "mo.bro." and "fa.sis." categories again are subclasses of the extended "fa." and "mo." categories. This system differs from the Pitjantjatjarra, however, in recognizing a "cross-cousin" category (*watjera*); but cross cousins are designatable also as "sibling," which indicates that they are regarded as special kinds of classificatory siblings. There are some indications in the literature that *watjera* or its cognate may not be simply a cross-cousin term; it may designate classificatory siblings in general (including parallel cousins), especially those regarded as too close for marriage.[2] A further difference concerns the rule for determining subclassification as "mo.bro." or "fa." and "fa.sis." or "mo." In the Mandjindja system father's cross cousins (but not his parallel cousins) are classified as "mo." and "mo.bro."; mother's cross cousins (but not her parallel cousins) are classified as "fa." and "fa.sis." This is the opposite of the arrangement in the Pitjantjatjarra system. It would seem that in the Mandjindja system subclassification is a function of relative sex of linking kin within both $G + 1$ and $G + 2$, while in the Pitjantjatjarra system it is a function of relative sex of the links in $G + 1$ only. The difference between the Pitjantjatjarra and Mandjindja systems is similar to the difference between Iroquois- and Dravidian-type systems in general (Scheffler 1971b: 240–247, 1972a: 124–125). The difference is not identical because in the Australian systems we have to deal with a difference in mode of subclassification, and the Mandjindja system, like the Pitjantjatjarra, features the rule (PSb ➤ P), etc.

WIRDINYA

In the region of the upper Murchison and Ashburton Rivers (Western Australia) there are, however, a number of groups whose systems of kin classification are virtually identical to the Dravidian-type systems of Melanesia and south India (for an interpretation of which see Scheffler 1971b). The only apparent difference is that these Australian systems (described in Daisy Bates's unpublished manuscripts)[3] feature two categories of female grandkin — maternal and paternal, or perhaps parallel and cross. There is only one category of male grandkin. There are no indications in the data that $G + 1$ cross collaterals may be designated by the parent terms or $G–1$ collaterals by the child terms; the cross-collateral categories appear not to be subcategories of the parent, child, and sibling categories. Logically, these systems may be derived from Mandjindja-like systems by weakening the rule (PSb → P), etc. to the rule (PPSb. ➤ PP.), etc., i.e. by limiting full collateral merging to the context of grandparents' siblings as designated kin. One consequence of this limitation is that the "fa.sis." and "mo.bro."

[2] This hypothesis was confirmed by a Pitjantjatjarra speaker from the Docker River reserve in June 1972.
[3] These manuscripts are on deposit in the Australian National Library, Canberra.

categories do not have the status of subclasses of the extended "mo." and "fa." categorics, and the "cross cousin" category is not a subclass of the extended "sb." category. The Dravidian-type rule of reckoning the parallel/cross status of third or greater degree collaterals (again, see Scheffler 1971b) then determines simple extension of the cross-collateral and other terms rather than subclassification within the extended "fa.," "mo." and "sb." categories.

KARIERA

It is relatively easy to relate the Wirdinya-like systems to the Kariera system (Radcliffe-Brown 1913) and to others like it reported from all parts of Australia. The similarities may be obscured by the fact that in many Kariera-like systems a terminological distinction is made between male Ego's child and female Ego's child, and the "mo.bro." and "fa.sis." categories are subclasses of the extended "mo." and "fa." classes, respectively (the opposite of the Pitjantjatjarra arrangement). These subclass relations are indicated by the collateral extensions of the child terms and by the alternate designations of FZ as "fa." or "female fa.," and of MB as "mo." or "male mo." (see also Scheffler 1971a: 25–26). But FZ is a special kind of "fa." and MB is a special kind of "mo." only as designated kinsmen; as a linking kinswoman FZ is not treated as a kind of "fa." (though FB is), and as linking kinsman MB is not treated as a kind of "mo." (though MZ is). In the place of the (PSb → P) or (PPSb. →PP.) rule, these systems feature two more restricted rules. These are (1) (FB → F) and (MZ → M), and (2) (FZ. → F.) and (MB. → M.), etc. By the corollaries of (2), female Ego's brother's child is termed "man's ch." and male Ego's sister's child is termed "woman's ch."

The Kariera system itself features four grandparent categories, two male and two female, but in many other systems that are otherwise structurally identical to the Kariera system there are only two or three grandparent categories. Elsewhere (Scheffler 1971a: 27–29, 1972c) I have reviewed the evidence that indicates that this variation (and the further variation in the mode of collateral extension of the grandparent terms, regardless of their number) bears no necessary relation to alleged rules of marriage, i.e. first or second cross cousin (cf. Radcliffe-Brown 1930–1931, 1951; Elkin 1964).

KARADJERI

An interesting variation on the Kariera pattern occurs in those systems that lack distinct "cross-cousin" categories, not because cross cousins are terminologically identified with siblings but because they are identified with cross grandparents, MF and FM. This occurs in the Wailpi system in South Australia and in the Karadjeri, Mirning, and Bibbulman systems in Western Australia. In the Karadjeri system grandchildren may be designated by the grandparent terms used self-reciprocally, or by *telwel*; the distinction between cross and parallel grandchild is optional. Younger cross cousins are designated *telwel*, [gr.ch.], and older cross cousins are designated by the cross-grandparent term, *djambad*. In some discussions and diagrams of this system it has been made to appear asymmetrical (see Elkin 1932; Piddington 1937); according to these accounts matrilateral and patrilateral cross cousins are terminologically distinguished, and MBD is designated by the same term as W, WZ, and BW. But Elkin's unpublished data (see also Jolly and Rose 1943–1945) reveal the pattern described above. MBD is marriageable but FZD is not; as a consequence, MBD may be designated *kabali* [potential wife], as well as *djambad* [gr.mo.] or *telwel* [gr.da.], depending on her age relative to Ego. Since FZD is not a potential wife she may not be designated *kabali,* but she too is *djambad* or *telwel.*

The rule that accounts for the terminological identification of cross cousins with cross grandkin is (δSS → δB), etc., i.e. the structural equivalence of alternate generation agnates. Thus, for example, MBS is also MFSS and therefore equivalent to MFB, which kin type is structurally equivalent to MF by the same-sex sibling-merging rule. Similarly, MBD is equivalent to MFSD and therefore to MFZ. If the classificatory sister of a grandparent (e.g. a cross cousin) is younger than Ego, she is designated by the appropriate granddaughter term; if she is older than Ego, she is designated by the appropriate grandmother term. The rule (δSS → δB) implies that a man calls his SS and his FF "bro." This does not happen, as far as I know, among the Karadjeri but it does among the Mirning. In the Mirning system FF and MMB are optionally classifiable as "bro.," and MM and FFZ are optionally classifiable as "sis." But this difference between the Mirning and Karadjeri systems is just a matter of the relative strength of this particular rule of terminological extension. The rule occurs in both systems; it is weaker or more restricted in its range of applicability in the Karadjeri system than it is in the Mirning.

KUMBAINGERI

This system is similar to the Kariera system and does not feature the rule of structural equivalence of agnatically related kin of alternate generations, but it is somewhat unlike the Kariera system in that it features a number of subclasses within the parental generation. Father's cross cousins are not designated "mo." and "mo.bro." but by one or two other special terms; and similarly for mother's cross cousins (Radcliffe-Brown 1930–1931; Ryan 1964). In some systems like this one these terms are used self-reciprocally, so that the children of Ego's cross cousins are not designated by the child terms but by these special terms; but in others the child terms are used, thus indicating that the special terms in the parental generation designate subclasses of the extended parent categories. The subclass status of these categories is indicated also by the fact that second cross cousins (e.g. MMBDD) are designated by the cross-cousin terms. That is, MMBD, for example, is not designated "fa.sis.," as in Kariera-like systems, but she must be a special kind of "fa.sis." since her child is a classificatory cross cousin.

In some Australian systems, subclass distinctions are made within one of the extended parent categories but not the other. Sometimes, for example, father's cross cousins are designated "mo." and "mo.bro."; but mother's cross cousins are not designated "fa." and "fa.sis." (see Radcliffe-Brown 1913 on the Mardudhunera system). In other systems subclass distinctions are made within Ego's own generation but not in the parental and filial generations. For example, kin types such as FZD and MMBDD may be terminologically distinguished, i.e. a distinction may be made between first and second cross cousins (at least certain types of second cross cousin), but there is no corresponding distinction between FZ and MMBD or between their reciprocals (see Beckett 1959, on the Wongaibon system; Elkin, Berndt, and Berndt 1951, on the Gunwinggu system).

All of these systems are simply variations on the basic Kariera-like pattern. The variation is readily intelligible when viewed as differences in subclassification, but it is difficult to account for in terms of variation in marriage rules (Radcliffe-Brown 1930–1931, 1951; Elkin 1964).

ARANDA

In this system (Strehlow 1907) we find all of the subclass distinctions mentioned in the preceding discussion of the Kumbaingeri and similar systems. That is, there are special subclasses of the extended parent and child classes, and of the extended cross-cousin classes, and there are special subclasses of the extended sibling classes, too. This system also features the rule of structural equivalence of agnatic kin of alternate generations. One of the consequences of this combination of subclasses and extension rules is that cross cousins are terminologically identified with MF and MFZ while second cross cousins are terminologically identified with FM and FMB; certain second parallel cousins (e.g. MMBSS) are terminologically identified with one of the classes of parallel grandkin (MM and MMB).

DIERI

This system (Elkin 1939) is very much like the Aranda system but in it cross cousins are terminologically identified with FM and FMB while second cross cousins are terminologically identified with MF and MFZ (the opposite of the Aranda arrangement). This difference is a simple matter of which is the marked or "special" category and which is the unmarked or "ordinary" category in the opposition between the two kinds of cross grandparents. In the Aranda system the "fa.mo." category is singled out as a special subcategory of "cross gr.par." in general, and the MF term may designate either the "mo.fa." category in particular or the category "cross gr.par." in general. In contrast, in the Dieri system the "mo.fa." category is singled out as special subcategory of "cross gr.par." in general, and the FM term may designate either the "fa.mo." category in particular or the category "cross gr.par." in general.[4] In both systems cross cousins and second cross cousins are classified as cross grandkin, but the second cross cousins are treated as special cases of classificatory cross grandparents and are terminologically identified with the special subcategory of cross grandparents, rather than with the "ordinary" cross grandparents.

SOME OTHER SYSTEMS

A number of Australian systems of kin classification appear not to fit readily into the scheme outlined here, for example, the systems of the

[4] My Dieri informant, Mr. Ben Murray of Farina, S.A., stated that both first and second cross cousins may be called *kami* [FM], that second cousins (*nadada*) are just special kinds of *kami*, and that in the opposition *kami/nadada* [FM/MF], "*kami* is the main word." Mr. Mick McLean of Port Augusta, who speaks the southern Aranda dialect, confirmed the arrangement indicated above for the Aranda system.

Yaralde or Narinyeri of South Australia and of the Worora and Nga-
rinyin of the Kimberley region. There is a fair possibility, however,
that these are little more than rather Kariera-like systems upon which
Omaha-type skewing rules (Lounsbury 1964) have been superimposed
(see also Lucich 1968). That is, instead of alternate generation agnatic
merging there may be consecutive generation agnatic merging in these
systems. But the data are (or appear to be) a bit too chaotic for us to
be very sure of this.

Finally, it may be noted that the Yir Yoront and Murngin systems,
often alleged to be asymmetrical in much the same way as the Karadjeri system, probably are similar to the Karadjeri system. Unpublished
data provided by Prof. L. Sharp (Yir Yoront) and Dr. N. Peterson
(Murngin) reveal that the asymmetry in these systems is, again, a
matter of subclassification and is not a function of asymmetrical marriage rules.

CONCLUSION

I have presented some observations on the structures and relations
among the structures of some Australian systems of kin classification.
I have suggested (but, of course, I have not demonstrated) that these
systems can be understood in terms of a fairly small stock of structural
elements that may be differently combined to yield a fairly wide empirical variety of systems. Although I have not attempted to exhaust the
empirical variety of these systems, I have dealt with the major sources
of variation among them, and it should not be difficult to assimilate
the remaining variation to the general scheme presented here. I have
not attempted to order the empirical variation among these systems
into a single, neat, logically linear sequence with possible "evolutionary" implications (cf. Shapiro 1971) because I do not think that this is
possible. The relations among these systems would be better represented by a sort of tree whose branches (equivalent to relations between structural elements) not only diverge but also converge (cf.
Scheffler 1972a: 120). Nor have I attempted to relate differences in
structure among the systems of classification to differences in other
features of social structure, e.g. alleged marriage rules, except to point
out that certain alleged correlations do not stand up to scrutiny. Thus,
little or nothing has been said about the possible sociological significance of the scheme presented here. It should be clear, however, that
if the scheme presented here is even approximately correct, it supports

the main features of Radcliffe-Brown's (1930–1931, 1951) and Elkin's (1964) theory on the nature of Australian social structure — a kinship and extensions theory — but not the main features of the theory defended by Lévi-Strauss (1969), Dumont (1966, 1970), and others — i.e. the theory of "social categories" and "alliance systems."

REFERENCES

BECKETT, J.
  1959   Further notes on the social organization of the Wongaibon of western New South Wales. *Oceania* 29:200–207.
DUMONT, L.
  1966   Descent or intermarriage? A relational view of Australian descent systems. *Southwestern Journal of Anthropology* 22:231–250.
  1970   "Sur le vocabulaire de parenté Kariera," in *Echanges et communications.* Edited by J. Pouillon and P. Maranda, 272–286. The Hague: Mouton.
ELKIN, A. P.
  1932   Social organization in the Kimberley division, north-western Australia. *Oceania* 2:296–333.
  1938   Kinship in South Australia. *Oceania* 9:41–78.
  1939   Kinship in South Australia. *Oceania* 10:196–234.
  1940   Kinship in South Australia. *Oceania* 10:295–349.
  1964   *The Australian aborigines.* New York: Doubleday.
ELKIN, A. P., R. M. BERNDT, C. H. BERNDT
  1951   Social organization of Arnhem Land 1: Western Arnhem Land. *Oceania* 21:254–301.
JOLLY, A. T. H., F. G. G. ROSE
  1943–1945   The place of the Australian aboriginal in the evolution of society. *Annals of Eugenics* 12:43–87.
LÉVI-STRAUSS, C.
  1969   *The elementary structures of kinship.* Boston: Beacon Press.
LOUNSBURY, F. G.
  1964   "A formal account of the Crow- and Omaha-type kinship terminologies," in *Explorations in cultural anthropology.* Edited by W. Goodenough, 351–393. New York: McGraw-Hill.
LUCICH, P.
  1968   *The development of Omaha kinship terminologies in three Australian aboriginal tribes of the Kimberley division, Western Australia.* Australian Aboriginal Studies 15, Social Anthropology Series 2. Canberra: Australian Institute of Aboriginal Studies.
MUNN, N.
  1965   "A report on field research at Areyonga, 1964–1965." Unpublished manuscript, Australian Institute of Aboriginal Studies, Canberra.

PIDDINGTON, R.
1937   "Karadjeri kinship." Unpublished manuscript.
RADCLIFFE-BROWN, A. R.
1913   Three tribes of Western Australia. *Journal of the Royal Anthropological Institute* 43:143–194.
1930–1931   *The social organization of the Australian tribes.* Oceania Monograph 1. Melbourne: Macmillan.
1951   Murngin social organization. *American Anthropologist* 53:37–55.
RYAN, J. S., *editor*
1964   *The land of Ulitarra: early records of the aborigines of the mid-north coast of New South Wales.* Grafton, New South Wales: University of New England Press.
SCHEFFLER, H. W.
1971a   Some aspects of Australian kin classification: a correction. *Mankind* (Sydney) 8: 25–30.
1971b   "Dravidian-Iroquois: the Melanesian evidence," in *Anthropology in Oceania.* Edited by L. R. Hiatt and C. Jayawardena, 231–254. Sydney: Angus and Robertson.
1972a   "Systems of kin classification: a structural typology," in *Kinship studies in the Morgan centennial year.* Edited by P. Reining, 113-133. Washington, D.C.: The Anthropological Society of Washington.
1972b   "Kinship semantics," in *Annual review of anthropology* 1. Edited by B. Siegel. Palo Alto: Annual Reviews.
1972c   "Afterword," in D. F. Thomson's *Kinship and behavior in north Queensland.* Edited by H. W. Scheffler. Canberra: Australian Institute of Aboriginal Studies.
SCHEFFLER, H. W., F. G. LOUNSBURY
1971   *A study in structural semantics: the Siriono kinship system.* Englewood Cliffs, N. J.: Prentice-Hall.
SHAPIRO, W.
1971   Patri-groups, patri-categories, and sections in Australian aboriginal social classification. *Man* 6:590–600.
STREHLOW, C.
1907   *Die Aranda- und Loritja-Stämme in Zentral-Australien* (5 volumes). Frankfurt: Baer.

Kinship Terminologies:
The Okinawan Case

MASAKO TANAKA

The study of kinship terminology has been centered on egocentric terminology. The statement applies both to formal semantic analysis of kin
terms as they are applied to "genealogical" kin types, and to the exposition
of the view that "kinship terms are category words by means of which an
individual is taught to recognize the significant groupings in the social
structure into which he is born" (Leach 1958: 143). In both cases, the
point of reference is always the hypothetical Ego, from whose standpoint
the entire system is viewed. On the other hand, the fact that in many societies some lexically identical terms are applied not only to formally recognized fictive kin (e.g. blood brothers, godparents, etc.), but to other
nonkin as well, and sometimes not egocentrically at all, has received
little attention. The existence of such a phenomenon, if recognized, is
rather casually interpreted as a self-evident case of the "metaphorical" or
"fictive" extension[1] of the egocentric kinship ideology to wider social
areas. And not without reason.

An earlier version of this paper was presented at a departmental seminar of the
Department of Anthropology, University of Rochester in October 1972. The final
version owes much to the detailed criticisms offered by Dr. Grace Harris, who not
only in a way initiated this line of work by her original comment in an earlier seminar,
but helped me clarify a number of unformulated concepts about kinship terminology.
[1] The word "extension" is not used here as Lounsbury defined it in his 1965 paper,
namely, in the sense that WITHIN THE EGOCENTRIC TERMINOLOGICAL SYSTEM STRICTLY
PERTAINING TO EGO'S "REAL" KINSMEN, each kinship term may have multiple referents,
and that there is a "primary" meaning to each category. I am in complete agreement
with this view. What I am trying to repudiate in this paper is a commonly accepted
vague notion that the use of terms for nonkin whose primary meaning is genealogically
defined signifies the wholesale application of kinship ideology to the nonkinship
sphere, tacitly implying that the underlying principles are the same.

First, these terms, whether they are applied to "real"[2] kinsmen or non-kin, are morphologically indistinguishable. If Ego identifies a nonkin by the same relationship term as the one in which he designates his own elder brother, is it not logical for us to assume that he is extending his emotional and/or status-role relationship with the latter to this particular nonkin, at least in that context?

Second, at least in my own field experience, the natives themselves are often ardent advocates of the extension theory. They are, quite justifiably, very proud of the quality of their interpersonal relationships, which they consider to be "familial," saying that "we are, in this community, if not literally *yaaninz* [members of a single household], all LIKE *yaaninz*." They are sure that when they apply a "kin" term to a nonkin, they feel toward this person some of the same fundamental feeling as they feel toward their "real" kin designated by the same term. Thus, my informants were very unhappy and vehemently disagreed with me when I contended that their calling a nonkin an "elder brother" is solely due to the linguistic structure of their language, nothing more. Under these circumstances, it seemed quite natural and proper to interpret the wider application of "kin" terms as the metaphorical or fictive use of kinship terminology.

Now, if this view is correct, all terminological usages in which so-called kin terms occur must be logically consistent with THE terminological system, supposedly the system of kinship terminology as it is referentially applied to Ego's "real" kin. Unfortunately, my data did not neatly fit into this framework. As is the case with many other peoples in the world, the Okinawans, the subject of my field study,[3] often address a nonkin, even a complete stranger, with a relationship term which can denote a "real" kin category. In fact, Okinawans express and explain nearly every socially relevant human relationship in terms of kinship, using vocabulary apparently derived from the fact of kinship. But sometimes the rules of the terminological application flatly contradict the egocentricity of the supposed kinship terminology. To discern a single system behind all these various usages was impossible.

Spurred on by Dr. Grace Harris' comment on my previous terminological treatment to the effect that maybe some of these terms are kin terms only in appearance, I began to study my Okinawan data anew. I did so on the following premises:

[2]   In this article I use the term "real" kin for those persons to whom Ego is related in SOCIOCULTURALLY defined genealogical and/or affinal relationships. Ego's "real" kin may or may not be biologically or physically related to Ego, as Barnes (1960, 1964) pointed out.
[3]   The fieldwork was supported partly by an NDEA fellowship, a University of Rochester fellowship, and a grant from the University's research funds.

a.   that there may be more than one terminological system in which so-called kin terms occur as classifiers;

b.   that to be a system, component terms in a given context must make up a logically closed and bounded terminological universe;

c.   that kin terms egocentrically and referentially applied to Ego's "real" kinsmen may be defined as "true" in the sense that they LOGICALLY (and only in that sense) come before other usages;

d.   that the application of the lexically identical term to different persons within a system or in different systems may or may not signify the existence of the same social and/or psychological relationship, or the extension of such relationship, diluted, intensified, distorted, or otherwise; and

e.   that, in order to determine whether the use of the lexically identical term in another system is a metaphoric or fictive extension of the "true" meaning, the two usages must be compared in their total environment; that is, not in terms of meaning of the word in isolation, but in terms of underlying classificatory principles.

The specific purposes of this paper are:

a.   to identify and classify various syntactic as well as semantic contexts in which "kin" terms occur, in order to establish the existence of plural terminological systems in the Okinawan case;

b.   to assess the structural interrelationship of component kin categories in each of the identified systems — specifically, how these terms place persons in various categories, and what are the classificatory criteria; and

c.   to structurally compare these systems coexisting in a single society.

I do NOT, in this paper, attempt:

a.   to formulate the rules governing the process in which a primary meaning is "extended" — in Lounsbury's sense (1965) — to more distantly related kinsmen in the egocentric system(s), or the comparable process in the nonegocentric system(s);

b.   to speculate why there are multiple systems in the Okinawan case instead of one, why the number is three rather than two or four or more, or why certain terms are used in two or more systems while others occur only in the egocentric reference system;

c.   to systematically correlate or not correlate each terminological system with features of Okinawan kinship behavior and ideology; or

d.   to fully explicate the underlying structural and semantic principles relating the terminologies to each other.

I regard the following terminological treatment as a necessary preliminary groundwork before attempting to deal with these problems.

The data on which I base my following discussion were obtained through

sixteen months of fieldwork (from August 1969 to December 1970) in
Inoha, a small agricultural village on northern Okinawa. Due to a long
history of official encouragement and spontaneous native effort, most
Inoha residents have become bilingual, speaking standard Japanese quite
effectively as well as their native language, a dialect of Okinawan;[4] it is
obvious, however, that Okinawan is the mother tongue in Inoha. The use
of Japanese is strictly limited to formal sessions at school and in the government, in the press, on television, and in various public speeches. Elsewhere — at home, in the sugar-cane fields, at the town market, at the
playground — the people communicate in Okinawan.

The persistence of the native Okinawan, however, does not mean that
the local dialect is unaffected by the new official language. For instance,
much Japanese vocabulary has been added to or has replaced indigenous
terms. Kinship terminology is no exception. During the last fifty years,
most of the Okinawan kinship terms have been replaced by Japanese
terms. Today many people under forty do not remember indigenous
terms for some of the closest kin relationships, and even older people use
more and more of the Japanese terms.

Of course, the incorporation of a large number of Japanese terms does
not mean that the terminological system itself acquired Japanese structural features. In fact, the difference between the indigenous terminology
and the present one seems structurally insignificant. The only structural
differences I could discern in the indigenous system were: (1) the existence
of two complete sets of kinship terminology, one used by the "peasant"
class and another by the "warrior" class; (2) the optional application
of the seniority principle according to birth order to PG[5] groups; and

---

[4]   Okinawan is one of the four major dialects of the Ryukyuan language, which, in
turn, is part of the Japanese-Ryukyuan family. The separation of the two major
branches, Japanese and Ryukyuan, is estimated glottochronologically to have occurred
between the middle of the third century and the beginning of the sixth century (Hattori
1959). Despite systematic phonological and lexical correspondences, the two languages
are not mutually intelligible.
[5]   Throughout this paper, I use, with slight modifications, terminological abbreviations
developed by the Rhodes-Livingstone Institute and reported by Barnes (1967). The
abbreviations are as follows:

P	parent	F	father	M	mother
G	sibling	B	brother	Z	sister
+G	older sibling	+B	older brother	+Z	older sister
−G	younger sibling	−B	younger brother	−Z	younger sister
E	spouse	H	husband	W	wife
C	child	S	son	D	daughter

The numbers preceding B, Z, S, or D indicate the birth order within the sibling group.
Thus, 1B stands for the oldest brother (not necessarily the oldest child in the family),
2D for the second daughter, etc. The abbreviated signs are used either as the singular
or the plural form; and either as the nominative, possessive, or objective case.

(3) the optional differentiation of the youngest G among Ego's own G and PG groups. To keep the description as simple as possible, I base my following analysis on the currently most prevalent term for each category, whether it is Okinawan or Japanese.

In terms of the manner of designation and persons involved, I could identify three distinct terminological systems, including one with two subsystems, in all of which so-called kin terms occur as classifiers. These are:
TERMINOLOGICAL SYSTEM I: Egocentric kinship terminology pertaining to Ego's "real" kin:
a: Reference terminology.
b: Address terminology.
TERMINOLOGICAL SYSTEM II: Address terminology egocentrically applicable to nonkin.
TERMINOLOGICAL SYSTEM III: Sociocentric reference terminology.

Terminological System Ia

This is the system of reference terms by which Ego IDENTIFIES his genealogical kinsmen including his affines. Terms are given in Figures 1 and 2, and in Tables 1 and 2. The system is egocentric, bilaterally symmetrical, and its applicable range is limited to Ego's PPGCC, although persons outside this range may be descriptively identified so long as the relationship is remembered. Internally, persons are categorized both generationally and lineally. Sex is an important classificatory principle in all categories, but in different degrees.

While the categories of the ascending generation and Ego's own G have two distinct root forms for each of the sexes, as well as inclusive terms, categories 7–14 have terms which do not normally specify the sex. These terms can, however, be sexually specified by adding *ikiga* or *iki* for "male" and *winagu* or *unai* for "female" either as a suffix or prefix. For instance, category 10, GC, is normally identified as *miyui* regardless of sex, but if sexual identification is needed, he or she can be referred to as *ikiga-miyui* (GS) or *winagu-miyui* (GD).

The seniority principle is a crucial criterion for subcategorization of a G group. It precedes the sexual principle, dividing the category first into *shiijaa* (+ G) and *uttu* (— G) before further sexual specification. Very

---

Thus PGCC stands for parent's sibling's child's child(ren), M1B1S is mother's eldest brother's eldest son.

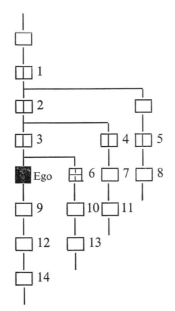

Reciprocal terms for the *unaiki*, male and female full siblings.

iki   *unai*

Categories not included or not numbered are identified descriptively.

Term(s) for each numbered category is (are) given in Table 1.

☐ Two sexes of the category are not normally distinguished. However, sex can be specified by adding *ikiga* or *iki* for male, *winagu* or *unai* for female either as suffix or prefix.

⊞ Two sexes of the category are distinguished in two distinct root forms.

⊞ Seniority and sex are distinguished in distinct root forms.

Figure 1. Terminological System Ia: reference terms pertaining to Ego's consanguineal kin

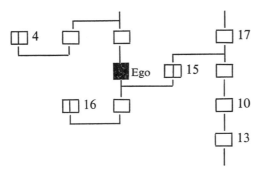

Affinal categories not included or not numbered are identified descriptively (see also Figure 1). Term(s) for each numbered category is (are) given in Table 2.

Figure 2. Terminological System Ia: reference terms for affines

often members of a G group of the same sex are individually specified according to the birth order as described in Table 3. Ego's male children are almost always identified in this manner. The same principle can be applied to Ego's own +G group like *choonan-niisan* (1B), *jinan-neesan* (the second-born +Z), and so on. Syntactically, the terms belonging to

Table 1. Reference terms for consanguineal kin

Category numbers	Kin types	Inclusive terms	Male	Female
1	PPP	*(paapuji)*	*upu-ojii*	*upu-obaa*
2	PP	*paapuji*	*ojii*	*obaa*
3	P	*uya*	*ottoo*	*okkaa*
4	PG	—	*ujasaa*	*ubamaa*
5	PPGC	—	*itsuku-ujasaa*	*itsuku-ubamaa*
6	G	*choodee*	*ikiga-choodee*	*winagu-choodee*
	+G	*shiijaa**	*shiijaa-iki,* or *niisan*	*shiijaa-unai,* or *neesan*
	−G	*uttu*	*uttu-iki* or *otooto*	*uttu-unai,* or *imooto*
7	PGC	*itsuku*		
8	PPGCC	*mata-itsuku*		
9	C	*kwa**		
10	GC	*miyui*		
11	PGCC	*itsuku-miyui*		
12	CC	*nmaaga*		
13	GCC	*miyui-nmaaga*		
14	CCC	*mata-nmaaga*		

* Further specification of these two categories (C and +G) is shown in Table 3.

Table 2. Reference terms for affines

Category numbers*	Kin types	Inclusive terms	Male	Female
4	PGE	—	*ujasaa*	*ubamaa*
10	EGC	*miyui*		
13	EGCC	*miyui-nmaaga*		
15	E	*miitumba*	*utu*	*tuji*
16	CE	—	*muuku*	*yumi*
17	EP	*shiitu*		

* Numbers refer to those in Figure 2.

this system occur in combination with the personal pronoun possessive or, if the referent is a member of Ego's own household, independently. For example, (*wattaa*) *okkaa* 'our mother', *nattaa choonan* 'your eldest son', etc.

Amongst affinal relatives (see Figure 2 and Table 2), only E, CE, and EP are given distinct reference terms, while other categories are either terminologically equated with the consanguineal kin, or identified descriptively. The equivalence rule applies only to categories 4 (PGE), 10 (EGC), and 13 (EGCC). The logic of the equation is based on the limited application of the principle of *miitumba tiichi* 'equivalence of husband and wife' and may be formulated as follows: H = W when one of the marital pair is Ego him/herself AND the referents are EG's descendants; or when

Table 3.   Reference terms for children and elder siblings

Kin types				
9 *kwa* (C)		6 *shiijaa* (+ G)		
Male *kwa* S	Female *winagungwa* D	Male *niisan* +B	Female *neesan* +Z	
1st-born	*chatchi* or *choonan*	*choonan-winagungwa*	*choonan-niisan*	*choonan-neesan*
2nd-born	*jinan*	*jinan-winagungwa*	*jinan-niisan*	*jinan-neesan*
3rd-born	*sannan*	*sannan-winagungwa*	*sannan-niisan*	*sannan-neesan*
4th-born	*yunan*	*yunan-winagungwa*	*yunan-niisan*	*yunan-neesan*
5th-born	*gunan*	*gunan-winagungwa*	*gunan-niisan*	*gunan-neesan*
⋮	⋮	⋮	⋮	⋮

one of the pair is PG. Thus, PGE = PG, EGC = GC, and EGCC = GCC; but GEG ≠ G, PGCE ≠ PGC, etc.

Terminological System Ib

This system consists of kin terms in which Ego ADDRESSES his "real" kin. Terms are given in Figure 3. Like System Ia, this system is egocentric, generational, and bilaterally symmetrical; but there are some notable

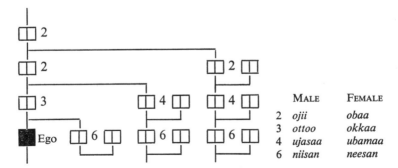

	MALE	FEMALE
2	*ojii*	*obaa*
3	*ottoo*	*okkaa*
4	*ujasaa*	*ubamaa*
6	*niisan*	*neesan*

Figure 3.   Terminological System Ib: address terms pertaining to Ego's "real" kin
General rules:
(1)   All persons who are junior to Ego in generation AND age are addressed in personal names and therefore not included in the chart.
(2)   By the principle of *miitumba tiichi* 'the equivalence of husband and wife', spouse's senior relatives are addressed in the same terms as the corresponding categories of Ego's own kin.

structural differences. (1) Kin terms in this system are applied only to Ego's senior kinsmen. All persons younger than Ego are addressed by their personal names. (2) Lineal separation is only partial, since Ego's line is separated from the collaterals only in the parental generation. Categories in all other generations are lineally merged. (3) Affinal relatives are terminologically equated with consanguineal relatives. (4) In comparison with the seven generations distinguished in System Ia, this system utilizes only four generational categories: one for senior persons of Ego's own generation, the second for persons of the parental generation, the third for persons of the second and more ascending generations, and the fourth for all persons junior to Ego.

The terms in this system occur independently or, if the addressee is Ego's collateral kin, in combination with his personal name. For example, category 3, male, is *ottoo* (F); category 4 (PG, PGE, PPGC, PPGCE, EPG, EPGE, EPPGC, EPPGCE), female, can be addressed with or without her personal name, *ubamaa*, or PN + *ubamaa*.

Terminological System II

The system involves a number of relationship terms morphologically identical with those occurring in System I plus several other terms in which Ego, as a polite gesture or as a means of interpersonal manipulation, addresses a nonkin. The terms are given in Table 4. As is clear from

Table 4. Terminological System II: address terms applicable to nonkin

Categories of Persons Addressed				Terms
"Leaders"	Political office holders Teachers *(sensee)* Other important persons			Office name + *san* (PN* +) *sensee* PN + *san*
"Ordinary People"	Older than Ego	Over 65 AND 15–20 or more years older than Ego	Male Female	*ojii* *obaa*
		15–20 or less years older than Ego, + all persons under 65	Male Female	*niisan*, or PN *neesan*, or PN
	Others		PN	

* PN = personal name

the table, the system distinguishes "leaders," who are not addressed in egocentric relationship terms, from the rest of the population who are. Since the reference terms for "leaders" are the same, I relegate the discussion of this category to the section where I deal with System III. In regard to "ordinary people," this system is, like System I, egocentric; but unlike System I its applicable range is unlimited. Any nonkin, whether he is previously familiar to Ego or not, can be addressed in an appropriate term of this system according to the sex and the age of the addressee. Neither generational nor genealogical relationship of any sort between the speaker and the addressee matters. Apart from the relative age of Ego and the addressee, and the sex of the latter, important factors to be considered here are the addressee's socioeconomic status and the speaker's social as well as emotional relationship with the addressee.

Among the three terminological systems I have identified, this is the only one in which individuals have several options, especially in regard to Ego's senior contemporaries. For instance, a man may call a person *niisan*, or *ojii* (PP in System Ia) if the addressee is over 65, or he may do it without any address term. Individuals thus unconsciously reveal their feelings toward the addressee: affection, respect, willing or feigned acceptance of the latter's authority, etc. Occasionally, they consciously manipulate interpersonal relationships by deliberately choosing a certain term.

Terminological System III

This is the system of reference terms in which all members of the community at a given time are categorized in the same relationship terms occurring in System I plus several other terms. However, in this system classification is not based on personal, egocentric, genealogical criteria but on several objective, sociocentric criteria. Terms are given in Table 5.

It is in this terminology in combination with the household name (*yaan'na*) that all villagers except the "leaders" are identified and referred to. The question "who is that person?" almost always produces the answer that he or she is this or that category of such and such a household. Exceptions are "leaders" (*yuuryokusha* or *shidoosha*) of the community who are identified, both in address and reference, in the manner specified in Tables 4 and 5, but without their household names. Thus, the headman of the village is called *kuchoo-san* 'Mr. Headman'; the school teacher, Mr. Bunyei Nakasone, *Bunyei-sensee* 'Teacher Bunyei'; and the former headman, Mr. Anshoo Nakasone, *Anshoo-san* 'Mr. Anshoo'; and so on. The number of such "leaders" is relatively small. Out of the total village population of 567 in 1969–1970, there were altogether 17 persons who were identified without reference to their household names; all but four of the leaders were male. Everyone else in the village was referred to by his household name and one of the sociocentric relationship terms.

Table 5. Terminological System III: sociocentric reference terms

Categories of persons			Reference terms
"Leaders"	Political office holders		Office name + *san*
	Teachers		(PN* +) *sensee*
	Other important persons		PN + *san*
"Ordinary people"	"Retired" persons		Male: *ojii* Female: *obaa*
	Present heads of households	Over ca. 65	Male: *ojii* Female: *obaa*
		Under 65 "Established"	Male: *ottoo* Female: *okkaa*
		Not "Established"	Male: PN Female: PN
	Persons between 15 and assumption of the head-ship	Heirs Their wives	Male: *chatchi, choonan,* or PN Female: *yumi,* or PN
		Others	Male: *jinan, sannan* ... according to birth order; or PN Female: Before marriage: *winagungwa:* or *choonan-w, jinan-w...* according to birth order; or PN After marriage: *(choonan-)yumi, jinan-yumi,* ... according to the birth order of her husband; or PN
	Children under 15		*kwa*

* PN = personal name.

Although these sociocentric relationship terms are morphologically indistinguishable from those occurring in Systems I and II, the syntactic contexts in which these lexically identical terms occur are, as we have seen elsewhere, unique in each system. To summarize:

In System Ia, relationship terms occur independently or with the personal pronoun possessive. If the referents are Ego's nonlineal kin, they may also occur in combination with the referents' personal names.

In System Ib, the terms occur independently or in combination with personal names if the addressees are Ego's nonlineal kin, but never with personal pronouns.

In System II, the terms may not occur at all, or may be used independently, or in conjunction with the addressees' personal names. The choice is partly based on biological factors (relative age of Ego and the addressee, and the sex of the addressee) but not on genealogical factors.

In System III, the terms for "ordinary people" always occur in combination with their household names; or if the referent is a member of the speaker's or addressee's household, in combination with the personal pronoun possessive plural; but never with the singular form. The terms for "leaders" do not occur in combination with household names or with possessive pronouns.

In the other systems we have studied so far, the category into which a particular individual gets classified depends on the relationship between Ego (the speaker) and the particular referent. Thus in System Ia, a man may be referred to as *ottoo* (F) by one speaker, as *niisan* (+B) by another, as *choonan* (1S), *ujasaa*, (PB, PZH, EPB, EPZH), *itsuku* (PGC) etc., by still others. A person is identified in different terms by different speakers, since the terminology is egocentrically fixed.

In contrast, terminology in System III is objectively, or sociocentrically, fixed in the sense that any dyadic relationship between the speaker and the referent is totally irrelevant as a principle of taxonomic classification. A certain person in a particular community at a given time is identified by all adult members[6] of the community except the present and former members of his own household by a single fixed term. If a person fulfills certain conditions for the category *ottoo* (F in System I), for instance, he is so referred to by adults of all ages and both sexes. That this is not a modified form of teknonymy may be proved by the fact that some men without children may be designated as *ottoo*, while others with children are not. Neither is this a simple terminological age-grading system, since persons belonging to the same age group may be classified differently.

What are then the classificatory principles of this sociocentric system? Age and sex are important criteria here too. All persons except the "leaders" and children under 15 (at which age they graduate from junior high school and most of them begin working) must be sexually identified, and persons over 65 and children are distinguished from the rest of the "ordinary" population solely by the age principle. The persons between 15 and 65 fall into three large categories: those who have not assumed the headship of a household, present heads, and "retired" persons.

The first subcategory is further divided into two classes: heirs to the

[6] Children tend to identify persons of the parental generation and older teknonymically. "Leaders," however, are always and by all members of the community except by the members of their respective households identified in sociocentric terminology.

headship of the existing households and their wives, *chatchi* and *yumi* (1S and SW in System I), and others. Since the Okinawan household is structurally of the patrilineal stem type, the *chatchi* alone among his entire G group succeeds to the headship upon his F's death or retirement. Younger sons, *jinan*(2S), *sannan*(3S), *yunan*(4S), etc., who are collectively called *ji-sannan* and D, *winagungwa*, are, from the point of view of the existing household, structurally irrelevant, since all of them eventually have to leave the household.

The residence rule for a married couple is patri-virilocal for the 1S and his W, neolocal for others; but the principle of *choodee-kasabai* 'incompatibility of brothers' strictly forbids married brothers living in the same household compound. It is thus quite obvious that the most important classificatory principle in this subcategory is the status/role position structurally assigned to the individual within his household.

I would like to emphasize here that, although such assignment is based solely on genealogical criteria of birth order and sex, the assigned status/role itself is neither purely genealogical nor private — in this society the household is a very important unit of social interaction and the continuation or discontinuation of an existing household, therefore, has grave social implications.

That the classificatory criteria in this terminology are social, rather than purely genealogical despite all these kinship-oriented relationship terms, becomes more evident in the second subcategory of "present heads." The ages in the group range from about 20 to 65, but not all persons of this age group fall into this subcategory. Regardless of age, retired persons who have given up the headship to their heirs, and persons who have not set up their own households for any reason are excluded.

Present heads themselves are grouped into three classes. Between 60 and 65, people gradually cease to actively participate in mundane affairs of the village, unless they happen to be leaders, so incumbent heads over 65 form one semi-retired category which is not terminologically differentiated from the "retired persons." The rest of the present heads, who are socially, if not physically, the most active members of the village, consist of those who are identified as *ottoo* (F in System I) and their W, and those who are not. The males of these two classes are not differentiated according to the principles used in Systems Ia and Ib. They are all between 20 and 65 in age, with varied marital status, except that the *ottoo* is never single, though he may be widowed or separated. And although almost all of them have children, some in each group do not. The majority of the *ottoo* are 1S and were therefore *chatchi* before they became *ottoo*, but some are not; some 1S heads never get classified as *ottoo*. The crucial classificatory principle, instead, seems to be mostly sociological: whether a person is an "established" head or not. From my observation of individual cases, the following seem to be the distinctive features of an "established" person:

a. He must be male.

b. He must belong to the 45–65 age group.

c. He must have been an incumbent head of an independent household for some time.

d. He must be mentally and physically capable of regularly and positively participating in village affairs.

e. He must be able to support his family without depending too much upon others including the government.

CONCLUSION

The description and analysis of kinship terminology in a society where morphologically identical relationship terms are applied to nonkin has been unnecessarily complicated and confused due to the failure to distinguish several structurally distinct coexisting terminological systems. In my opinion, this failure is the result of confusing lexical morphology on one hand and of semantics and social context on the other.

In the preceding analysis of Okinawan kinship terminology, I have demonstrated the existence of three distinct terminological systems: an egocentric kinship terminology pertaining to Ego's genealogical kin, with reference and address subsystems (Terminological Systems Ia and Ib in this paper); an address terminology egocentrically applicable to nonkin (Terminological System II); and a sociocentric reference terminology (Terminological System III). I have done so on the basis of my contextual (semantic as well as syntactic) analysis of the terminological data.

Structurally significant features of each terminological system are summarized in Table 6, in which a plus sign (+) signifies the presence or relevance, and a minus sign (—) the absence or irrelevance. It is clear from this table and from the preceding analysis that, despite the occurrence of lexically identical common relationship terms, these three systems are structurally distinct and that the assigned meaning of the same morphological term may differ considerably from one system to another. For instance, the term *niisan* designates in System Ia, Ego's + B. In System Ib, it may mean Ego's real + B, or any male older than Ego and belonging to one of the following kin categories: PGS, PPGCS, E + B, E + ZH, EPGS, EPPGCS. In System II, the term signifies any male who

Table 6. Comparison of the three terminological systems

Structural Features	Ia	Ib	II	III
Point of reference	Ego	Ego	Ego	Community
Range of application	Limited	Limited	Unlimited	Limited
Applicable to	Kinsmen	Kinsmen	Nonkin	All members of the community
Manners of designation	Reference	Address	Address	Reference
Existence of "real" kin relationship between speaker and referent	+	+	−	−
Sex principle	+	+	+	+
Generation principle	+	+	−	−
Number of generations or age groups distinguished	7	4	3	4
Seniority principle	(+)	(+)	+	−
Bilateral symmetry	+	+	−	−
Lineal separation: between Ego's line and collaterals	+	+	−	−
among collateral lines	+	−	−	−
Equation of affines with consanguineal kin	−	+	−	−
Referent's genealogical position within his household	+	+	−	+
Referent's social status	−	−	+	+
Maneuverability	−	−	+	−

+ present or relevant
− absent or irrelevant
(+) partial application

appears to be older than Ego, but the exact meaning can only be inferred from detailed situational analysis. For example, if a person addresses a man not much older than himself by the term, rather than by the personal name, it could signify the existence of considerable respect, or the recognition of the latter's authority, willingness to submit to his will, or affection, etc. on the part of the speaker. The term *ottoo* signifies, in System I, Ego's F; and in System III, as we have seen in detail, this same term designates an established male household head, who is aged between 45 and 65, mentally and physically active, economically independent, and therefore constitutes the politically most significant element of the community.

The existence of "sociocentric relationship terms" was reported first by Service in relation to his treatment of the Australian class system (1960). In a recent article, Kitaoji (1971) also explores the heuristic value of the concept of sociocentric reference terminology which he calls "positional terminology" for the analysis of the Japanese family structure.

What I have tried to do in this paper is to structurally distinguish, as clearly as possible, each independent terminological system from the others. I believe that this kind of terminological analysis is a necessary preliminary groundwork before further attempting to relate kinship terminology with kinship behavior and ideology, or to compare terminological systems found in different societies.

REFERENCES

BARNES, JOHN A.
    1960   Physical and social kinship. *Philosophy of Science* 28:296–299.
    1964   Physical and social facts in anthropology. *Philosophy of Science* 31:294–297.
    1967   "Genealogies," in *The craft of social anthropology*. Edited by A. L. Epstein, 101–127. London: Tavistock.
HATTORI, SHIRŌ
    1959   *Nippon-go no keito* [The genealogy of the Japanese language]. Tokyo: Iwanami.
KITAOJI, HIRONOBU
    1971   The structure of the Japanese family. *American Anthropologist* 73: 1036–1057.
LEACH, E. R.
    1958   "Concerning Trobriand clans and the kinship category 'tabu'," in *The developmental cycle in domestic groups*. Edited by Jack Goody, 120–145. Cambridge: Cambridge University Press.
LOUNSBURY, F. G.
    1965   "Another view of the Trobriand kinship categories," in *Formal semantic analysis*. Edited by E. A. Hammel, 142–186. Washington, D.C.: American Anthropological Association.
SERVICE, ELMAN R.
    1960   "Sociocentric relationship terms and the Australian class system," in *Essays in the science of culture: in honor of Leslie White*. Edited by Gertrude E. Dole and Robert L. Carneiro, 416–436. New York: Crowell.

SECTION FOUR

Ethnohermeneutics

Kachin Social Categories and Methodological Sins

F. K. LEHMAN

1. At the VIIIth International Congress of Anthropological and Ethnological Sciences in Japan, Dr. Edmund Leach presented a brief but provocative paper entitled "The concept of sin among the Kachin of North Burma." In this paper (1970), Dr. Leach advanced the general thesis that if a people can be said to have an idea of sin, it has to be understood as a violation of the society's basic categorial relations and/or premises. He proceeded to try to illustrate this with an analysis of some elements of Kachin ideology and its vocabulary.

The thesis is itself not especially novel. It seems to follow, in the first place, from the basic premises of social anthropology, actually in a rather trivial way, that is to say, by definition. For no concept of sin has any meaning or motivation apart from the underlying idea of DOING wrong. This, in turn, is opposed to "right" action — and rule-governed ACTION is held, in any version of social anthropology, to be systematically struc-

I have to acknowledge my profound debt to Dr. LaRaw Maran, my former student, an active Kachin chief and also a professional anthropologist and linguist. All data that I cite from Kachin other than data from the literature, I got from Dr. Maran, chiefly through questioning him on points of Leach's paper that puzzled and disturbed me. The sources of Dr. Maran's data are twofold, apart from his general expert knowledge of Kachin culture, as an adjudicating chief, deliberately trained in specialized lore of this sort: first, his field notes (e.g. on the *hkăwang măgam* system of marriage) taken during the time that he served as Information Officer, Cultural Affairs Officer, and Commissioner on Customary Law in the Kachin state, Burma; second, his ongoing work in Kachin, comparative Tibeto-Burman, and theoretical linguistics, in particular his extensive revision of Hanson's *Kachin-English dictionary* (Maran, ed. f.c.).

I wish also to thank my student, Mark Woodward, for helping me, in the course of a semester's tutorial work on problems in mythology, cosmology, and social structure in Southeast Asia, to pull together my thinking on this subject, and especially for raising the significant question, why, in Kachin origin myths, the sky is male, the earth female.

tured social action. That is to say, it is action associated with a role, or whatever we wish to call the formal aspects of a social persona (see Keesing 1971), where in one way or another the social structure is taken to be a system of "roles."

Notice that this argument is not defeated if one presumes that the motivations of sin are largely ideological, e.g. that they follow from a cosmological conception. That is simply to argue that the system of social categories narrowly construed is not an ultimate prime; that the social categories are deeply informed by, say, metaphysical considerations. In particular, the argument under inspection is not dependent upon the strictly positivistic view that sees ideology as a hypostasizing of the statistical regularities of behavior, i.e. of social structure defined interactionally. I assume that Needham (1963) has neatly disposed of this view. Let a conceptual order properly underlie the social structure, and the violations involved in sin are still necessarily social violations. Moreover, it can be argued that the general categorial-conceptual system of a culture is "social" not as some sort of reflection of "society" (which has always seemed to me a perfectly circular assertion), but simply in the sense that its functional or practical significance is "knowledge," and cognition is a property of (collectivities of) individuals acting (and thinking) as social personae. I conceive this to be the point of the notion of "practical religion" (e.g. Leach 1968).

In addition, if we consider the possibility of sins of the mind — evil thoughts — we encounter no difficulty in extending the argument above. First, wherever we find such an idea, we see that thinking is to some extent treated as something that can be controlled by will, therefore as something akin to an action. Second, this sort of sin seems to be defined always as a spoiling of the properties of the persona, making it either unfitted for proper social action or prone to improper social action. I do not wish to pursue this line of reasoning. It is enough to concede as strongly as possible Leach's major premise.

Leach applies this view to an elucidation of what he sees as the Kachin idea of sin. That is, he goes on to try to show that certain ideas about what is wicked, terrible to do, abhorrent, morally the worst in Kachin culture — and it is this association of profound moral reprehension that I think makes it possible for Leach to use the word "sin" for his subject — make sense if we look at how these ideas constitute implicit violations of the very premises of the Kachin system of social categories.

However, Leach gets himself into difficulties at once. It is not, as Leach points out, altogether clear that the idea of sin can be successfully applied apart from the Judaeo-Christian ideological context. It is not enough to argue that in some non-Judaeo-Christian systems there is a deep feeling of repulsion against certain acts felt to be profoundly dangerous; in this tradition at least, the idea of sin is, as Leach notices, of course, fundamentally tied up with ideas of retribution, salvation, and the fate of the individual soul beyond his earthly life and death. Note that this means more than our profound feeling of moral reprehension toward acts undermining the very axioms of society. It is easy to argue this point by means of a simple and, I hope, unproblematic experiment in the mind.

Consider a person who may have no religious convictions. He may very well feel that certain acts or even thoughts are so contrary to the axioms of society that society will fall if they are permitted. He may feel this very deeply, and may even fear such acts or thoughts in himself and others to the extent of acting (or advocating acting) against them in a violent manner. He may go so far as to take the position that such acts are "against nature" and immoral, in the sense that, under the influence of such acts, not only will society as he knows it fall, but any other conceivable society also. I can even imagine that some contemporary environmentalists feel this way about acts seen by them as leading without qualification to the extinction of human life. But I do not think that I should want to call such positions conceptions of sin, if only because it is at best not clear whether such persons, who may after all NOT be without religious convictions, conceptualize this evil in the same way that they conceptualize evils explicitly defined in their Christian religion.

In any case, if the idea of sin is worth invoking at all in comparative ethnography, it clearly needs narrower specifications. We might attribute an idea similar to our idea of sin to the case of a society that shows a profound sense of repulsion to certain ideas that it regards as both violating fundamental social structural premises, and involving native ideas about the relation between this world and an "after world" or "other world" such that by virtue of this relation individuals practicing "sinful" acts are subject to retribution.

2. Leach never goes deeply enough into the structure of Kachin ideas about the crucial relations between man and the other world. He relates a sketch of a myth about the origin of death, but chiefly in order to give it an analogical interpretation from the point of view of the ideas informing Genesis in the Judaeo-Christian Bible. Lest this be taken as an unsupported allegation, let me, in view of the undesirability of here recapitulating Leach's whole paper as a prolegomena to my own work, quote two passages from his work:

According to mythology all the evils of mankind, including death itself, derive from Shingnyen[1] who, at critical moments in human history, tangled up the communications between the sky gods and their human descendants. Shingnyen is, in other contexts, *a kind of heavenly gate keeper fulfilling the role of St. Peter, who, likewise had a notable reputation for telling lies!* (Leach 1970:308; emphasis added).

And again in the following paragraph:

The precise relationship between the human beings (*Shinggyim masha ni* 'the people born of pregnancies') and the Sun People is left unspecified, but by implication the situation is the reverse of that postulated in the book of *Genesis*. In the antediluvian world of the Bible the "Sons of God" cohabit with the "daughters of men": in the Kachin schema it seems to be the "Sons of men" who cohabit with the "daughters of God." I infer this because human beings seem to be attending the funeral feasts of the Sun People in the status of *dama ni* (daughter's sons) or as political subordinates of the Sun Deity whose sex is usually represented as female. The human beings take with them the animals and valuables which in real life are appropriate gifts from *dama ni* to *măyu ni* at a funeral. The Sun Deity makes a return gift of magical paddy seed which is intended to have "a stalk as large as a buffalo's leg and ears as large as a pony's tail." The Sun Deity also holds in her hands the *sumri* — the thread of life — by which she is magically joined to human beings. They can only die if she breaks the thread.

Sut wa mădu[2] finds the cost of attending the Sun People's funerals extremely burdensome and hits on the idea of reversing the transaction. He kills a squirrel (*mai chyăhkai*, the giant ground squirrel, or *rùʔ*, symbol of fortuitous good luck!) and pretends that the corpse is that of a human being and he then asks the Sun People to attend the funeral feast which they in fact do.

However, the Sun Deity (*Jan Nat*) discovers the deception and becomes very angry. She then decrees that all men shall die "when their hair turns grey" (Leach 1970:308–309).

Why, apart from his preoccupation with human Kachin marriage as the source of the Kachin idea of ordered relations, and apart from his preoccupation with interpreting the Kachin myth in the light of Biblical analysis, Leach should wish to see this story as saying that death came about because of something analogous to incest (1970:309) is unclear. Obviously what we have here is, as indeed Leach notices on the next page,

[1]   Shingnyen is the trickster-headman of the ancestral-world village, *shingra ga*, which is between *mu ga* [the sky-world of Gods, the ancestors of the hereditary chiefs] and the present world of men.

[2]   Leach calls *Sut wa mădu* "Lord of Merit/Wealth (*sut*)," and this might be a good translation, except that the name clearly stands, as will shortly appear, for the fact that he, the first man to die, established in principle the *Sut Manau* system of grand-merit feasts, which Leach had just finished talking about while motivating a semantics of the word *sut*, but here neglects to see it as relevant. In fact, Leach's meaning would give **Sut mădu wa*.

a repudiation of a certain hierarchical (say, political) order and its implications. By inventing the Feast of Merit, *Sut wa mădu* in effect not only reverses the direction of prestations in the relation with the Sun People, but also replicates among human beings the larger cosmic order, that is, creates a means for differentiating ranks within human society, thus symbolically severing the simple polar relation in which all humans lack merit and are subordinated as a class to all Sun People. He automatically severs this tie, hence the consequence is death, because he creates a complicated and ambiguous relation of MUTUAL dependence between the two worlds (cf. Lehman 1963 on Chin Merit Feasts). That is, death is a flow of persons TO the other world, a counterflow to that of birth, FROM the other world. Now neither party is more or is less dependent than the other in this new relationship. We shall see more of this ambiguous relation later on.

I therefore submit that the wrongdoing here is at least as much hubrsi as anything else. It is quite true that insofar as the *măyu-dama* 'wife-giver/taker' relation is one of SUPERIOR to INFERIOR, a flow of prestations is implicit from the latter to the former. On the other hand, there is no reason to take the first pair as a paradigm of the second. It is merely an important subcase of the second. Indeed, the literature on the asymmetrical marriage systems of the Hill People of the Burma border regions should by now have made it quite clear that there are considerable disparities between the wife-giver/wife-taker (WG/WT) relationship — which is not transitive precisely because it cycles (Lehman 1963) — and the political division into ranks — which, in principle at least, divides people into two nonoverlapping polar sets.

But lest the reader still have doubt that Leach is substituting his knowledge of the Biblical tradition for direct understanding of Kachin ideas, let us see how he goes on. Here the trickster Shingnyen intervenes. He brings it about that the magical paddy given by the Sun People comes to yield just ordinary-size rice. This again, of course, is symbolic of the mutuality rather than the absolute hierarchy of the relation. And he also brings it about that even people who have not got gray hair die:

All this is a very much reduced account of a complex myth in which the original text appears to be full of highly obscure linguistic puns, but the Judaeo-Christian parallels are very obvious: (a) In the Biblical story death is the punishment for sin and the particular sin is that of trying to deceive God, and it is the trickery of the serpent which is largely responsible for all the trouble. (b) In the Kachin story death is again the punishment for trying to deceive God and again matters are made worse by the intervention of the trickster (Leach 1970).

It seems to me that the theme of deceit is relatively minor in the Kachin story, more so by a good deal than in the Biblical.

In the Kachin, the deceit is actually part of a fundamental paradox: death is to be accounted for, yet it is a presupposed condition of the whole structure in which the story is set. Death is accounted for by means of acting out a situation in which the idea of human death is taken for granted. IF there is a funeral and hence human death, the Gods, if invited, must attend and hence bring gifts; for there is no one else to do so (see below). The only trouble is that human death must be simulated, but that hardly seems to be what troubles the Sun Deity. It is rather that the preconditions for a ceremonial act have been falsified; so she decrees, after the fact, a validation for the act. It is less a punishment than a redressing of forces and structural conditions.[3]

What Leach should have said is that in both stories death is brought about because people set themselves up in ways less than perfectly subordinate to God or to the other world and its beings. But this is extremely general, and it must appear to Leach a better course to make use of his knowledge as an educated European Christian, and to presume upon the subtleties of that scholarly tradition in elucidating the theology-cosmology-ideology of the Kachins. This seems to me a most unfortunate way of going about things. I am not at all claiming that useful insights cannot be drawn from comparison. But to make a proper comparison in this case surely requires trying to work out the intellectual position of the Kachin conceptions to start with. The notion, in particular, that one's education in one's own cultural-symbolic tradition gives one PRIVILEGED access to the symbolic processes of a wholly alien people is in itself a hazardous notion. It is downright wrong-headed and presumptuous when it leads, as I shall try to show it has led Leach, to distortions and linguistic absurdities.

In the foregoing story, let us next consider the female sex of the Sun Deity. It is by no means easy to conclude anything about the nature of the relation between men and the Sun People on the basis of the sex of the Sun Deity. For one thing, as I hope to set forth later on, the *mǎyu*

---

[3]   I am reminded here that this sort of mythic paradox seems fairly common in this part of the world. Stories of the origin of this or that, in the end frequently appeal in effect to the prior existence of the thing being accounted for. Thus, in northern Chin: there was once a village that had to go to war with another village, and for the people to get there they had to cross a great stream. In those days there were no boats and the people did not know what to do. Then their leader said: "Let us go to the boat-maker and have him make a boat so we can cross the river." This they did, and from then on boats existed. This is a story told by people who in fact know of but never make, have, or use boats.

'wife-givers' are males, agnates OF the women given, hence it is not at all easy to say that females "represent" wife-givers and/or their status. They do so in a highly complicated and ambiguous way that has confused Leach on another occasion, namely, in his paper (1961b) on marriage and divorce.

There he argued that the stronger the marriage bond and the greater its resistance to divorce, the more the wife is incorporated into the wife-taking lineage and family. However, it is comparatively easy to see that in fact the more she is embedded in her husband's family, the more she "represents" her natal lineage and family, since the very embedding is to be understood as motivated by the following axiom of alliance: the standing of my lineage is a function of the natal standing of its mothers, i.e. of the alliances made with wife-givers of appropriate good standing. The embedding then functions to fix, as nearly as can be, the incorporation of the standing of the wife-giving group in that of the wife-taking group. In the version of Kachin marriage that allows divorce more readily — where dissolution of marriage requires compensation from the wife's natal lineage, rather than, as in many cases of the first kind, from a man who has supposedly seduced her away from her husband — the logic is in fact the same. It is the woman's standing as representing her natal rank that is being preserved and, in particular, preserved for the very purpose of ensuring that precisely this standing gets embedded in her husband's lineage. This paradox — the more she is fixed into her husband's group, the more she represents her own; the more she is fixed in her own, the more that standing redounds to her husband's group — is typical of the thoroughgoing legal and symbolic ambiguity of women in this society.

If we look at the Kachin creation myth (see Gilhodes 1922), we find a related curiosity. When the earth and sky are separated out in the course of creation, the earth is female, the sky male. Yet supposedly the female represents the superior, if we are to take seriously the implicit suggestion of Leach that the basic paradigm of hierarchy is the *măyu-dama* relation. This also, in a way, is the suggestion made by Loeffler (1968) in his important paper analyzing cosmological symbolism and social-ritual structure in a series of hill tribes in Southeast Asia. Roughly, we are told that we ought generally to expect for the patrilineal societies (with asymmetrical alliance) in this region that women will be associated with the sky and symbolically represented as passing downward, while men are associated with the earth and represented as passing skyward, in death as in sacrifice. In such idealized cases, it is hypothesized that the other world is held to be located in the sky. This is no place to go into the logic of Loeffler's treatment, though I believe it is essentially on the right lines.

Therefore Kachin society is thought to come fairly close to this idealization, and yet somehow it is the female that is associated with the earth in the separation of earth from sky. How is this to be explained, in case Loeffler, and to this extent Leach, is correct?

The answer is found in a well-known fact of Kachin ethnography; see, for example, Leach (1961a:13–14, 18–19) and Lévi-Strauss's general treatment of the matter (1969:373–374). In the native theory of heredity, a child is said to get its PHYSICAL FORM from its mother, its more abstract qualities from the father. Now the separation of earth and sky, as Dr. Maran has pointed out to me, amounts exactly to the separation of the domain of physical form and a more abstract realm, respectively. Thus, just insofar as earth constitutes substantial form, it is properly and necessarily represented by the female. Moreover, then, the sky is the analogue not of the female, but of the source of the female among men, namely, yet another group of men, i.e. wife-givers, who are male.

Again — though in this one sense women are symbolically represented as passing downward — birth, which is FROM women, is upward, from the earth/water. Concomitantly, inasmuch as the mutual interdependence of the two realms, through sacrifice and the earning of merit, is to ensure their mutual prosperity in a reciprocating way, and since prosperity is intimately associated in these societies with birth and fertility applicable alike to men, animals, and plants, there is necessarily, e.g. in Kachin, an alternative tie with the other world through the nether regions. This is, naturally, analogous to the paradox of the marriage cycle in asymmetric alliance: rank is not and cannot be transitive, and thus the cyclical principle holds; so, although for Ego his superiors in the system are properly in one "direction" only, and his inferiors in the opposite "direction," one can reach either by proceeding far enough in EITHER direction. There is no doubt a right and a wrong direction in which to proceed in ensuring the circulation of women, for instance, and the measure of this is the prohibition against reversing the direction of the marriage alliance. Yet the directionality is known to depend upon what is passing along. Women and the like pass from WG to WT (sky to earth, so to say), honorable gifts from WT to WG (skyward from earth, as it were).

Similarly, the source of essential prosperity is literally seen as coming from the other world with ambiguous directionality. Rain and such "good" comes from the sky; yet the grain springs up from beneath the earth. And in this society, as in Chin, the other world is held to be skyward only in a special or privileged sense. It is also netherward. People are held to have come from the sky region, but "the" people are also supposed to have come up out of some mountain cave; and, at least in Chin, the spirits of the departed dead, in particular those dying a good death, are said to go skyward at once (in this case represented, as in Kachin, by various bird symbols for the departing spirit) and to travel down to the land of the dead via the netherworld.

These are neither confusions in ethnographic collection and reportage, nor instances of the inchoateness and lack of explicit and coherent system in the thought of the people in question. Rather they are subtle representations of a genuine paradox of cosmic proportions.

There is a very special point in the reversal of prestations as between men and Sun People. With JUST men and Sun People involved, the paradox of cyclical directionality becomes acute. That is, the asymmetry of alliance depends, as has been clearly understood for many years, upon the existence of three substantive units of alliance as a minimum. When there are only two units, each party is simultaneously both WG and WT to the other. That means that the "directionality" is trivialized. In effect, then, just as soon as the relation is SEEN IN TERMS OF the categories of asymmetrical alliance, all paradoxes and ambiguities are seen to follow immediately.

There was, one supposes, just no way that *Sut wa mădu* and his people could have continued to pay prestations without getting the sources of their wealth replenished. The Sun Deity may indeed have been angered by this move and decreed death for men; but, once the point of view of alliance categories and premises of mutual dependence is stated as the context of the relation, death among men follows ANYHOW (hence, as we saw, the idea of it preceded the fact). This, I maintain, is what the myth in question is saying.[4]

[4] A word of clarification. I have written here as if it were unambiguously the case that the relation between men and the Sun People is to be understood as Leach has construed it, on the model of the asymmetrical marriage-alliance system. On the other hand I dispute just this point elsewhere, in section 2, and in section 3, noting that hierarchical rank differences are not isomorphic with status differentiation within the cyclical marriage system and that the relation under discussion in the myth is as plausibly of the one sort as of the other. The evidence suggests that Kachins can look at it both ways. We see elsewhere that there is equivocation on the point of whether or not men married the daughters of the Sun People. Now we have the matter of funeral gifts, and once again the evidence is equivocal. People who are not prescribed WG/WT to each other give these gifts to each other at their respective funerals. But, as Leach notes, a WG never does so when invited to his WT's funeral. The issue resolves itself, however, precisely by virtue of the fact that in this case there are only two parties to the relationship. For, under just these conditions, the difference between linear hierarchy and cyclical hierarchy collapses. A linearized hierarchy, with strict circulation of one of its properties, is reciprocating in its arrangements, and all cases of two entities with circulation between them are simply two-member reciprocating hierarchies. That is, it is only in nonexchanging hierarchies and in cycling systems that adjacent

238 F. K. LEHMAN

3.1. Let us now go back and see what it is that Leach says more particularly about Kachin categories bearing upon the notion of "sin" in Kachin society, and see in particular how he systematically fails to leave room for the Kachin intellectual interpretation.

Leach starts out by pointing to the *mǎyu-dama* relationship and its attendant rights and duties as a fundamental model of ritually right as against wrong social action.

The relationship *mǎyu/dama* is asymmetrical and irreversible. It is implicit in this asymmetry that the *mǎyu* is "superior" to the *dama* and the situation becomes anomalous if, for any reason, a husband belongs to a lineage which is politically or socially superior to that of his wife (Leach 1970).

He goes on to say that "when such 'inversions' of the natural order occur the likelihood of witchcraft accusations becomes very great" (1970:307). He observes then that characteristically *mǎyu ni* are accused by their *dama ni* of witchcraft, and not the other way around. He says, chiefly with respect to the aforementioned myth, that the relation between men and Sun People as a *mǎyu-dama* one is "implicit rather than explicit" (1970: 308), since the first human ancestors do not necessarily figure as marrying daughters of the sky but only as never marrying with sky people in the other direction. In fact they sometimes simply marry princesses. From this I would think it obvious that the *mǎyu-dama* cast to the relation is strictly secondary: IF one marries with a status superior, it must be with the latter as WG. But Leach, of course, has to insist that this is the primary fact of the relationship, since he wishes to demonstrate that death comes to man as punishment for essential sin, violation of this paradigm of social relationship. His argument is tortuous, and ultimately specious, but it goes something like this.

First, sexual relations between a man and an FZD are in some sense evil. They are *jaiwawng*, i.e. of a class that includes sibling incest — including, of course, sexual relations between classificatory siblings, clan siblings. At least some kinds of *jaiwawng*, which Leach, by the way, translates as 'incest', are thought to be quite terrible, bringing punishment and suffering, (*yubak*, see below), of which a salient variety is that thought to be caused by witchcraft. So the salient immediate agency of ultimate suffering is witchcraft; witchcraft is an accusation made of WG; WG are held to

---

pairs can be kept opposed in status. This observation I hold to constitute the basis of the impossibility, for Kachin or anybody, to give a consistent marriage-alliance inter-pretation to the relation under discussion. In any event, at any proper funeral there has to be someone invited who will give the proper gifts. Hence, indeed, the Sun People had no choice but to do so.

sorcerize *dama* for failure of duty; therefore failure of this duty, particularly violation of the asymmetry of the relationship itself, is sin *par excellence*.

But *jaiwawng* as a class is not an especially dreadful wrong, by Leach's own admission. Mere sexual connection with a WT female is not especially important and it leads to *yubak* only in the sense that it predisposes to marriage — it is the latter that is strictly wrong. Moreover, when *jaiwawng*, as marriage, does lead to *yubak*, it is a case of *shut hpyit* (see below), which, unlike the term *jaiwawng*, "implies genuine disgust." *Shut hpyit* is, then, merely the primary candidate for translation as "sin," yet in Leach's argument, as nearly as I can follow it, it is too broad, including as it does such things as mother–son incestuous relationship, having nothing necessarily to do with marriage. That is, the truly sinful violation of the WG/WT relation is not a sexual connection, but a marital one; the other truly sinful relations are, *inter alia*, sexual rather than formal-marital in the first instance. It appears, though I admit he never says so, that Leach would be happy to be able to demonstrate that the focal instance of *shut hpyit* is identical with the worst instance of *jaiwawng* — marriage that reverses an alliance. It should be clear that this cannot be the case. Clearly the class of sins cuts across the various classes of wrong, including the most reprehended instances of each class, and once again, the structure of the marriage system, however focal for social anthropological interests, loses much if not all of its privileged status.

The facts are perhaps even worse for Leach's position than it appears at first glance. The instances of *jaiwawng* comprising relations between real and/or classificatory siblings are treated in equally complicated ways by the Kachin. On the one hand, marriage OR sexual relations between true full siblings or paternal half-siblings is a major offence. It is certainly *shut hpyit*. On the other hand, marriage AS SUCH between siblings, real or classificatory, is indeed just *jaiwawng*. Throughout most of Kachin society it is pretty severely treated if the connection is "close": such a couple are likely to be expelled from the village or villages where they are known and forced to go elsewhere where their true relationship will not be suspected. However, as Leach amply documents, in actuality intra-clan, even intralineage, marriage is not rare if the parties are *lăwu-lăhta* 'remotely related' (1954:74, 138–139, 308), and clans are not in fact exogamous (1961a). Nonetheless, it is possible to show that even the nominal prohibition against intralineage (or -clan) marriage is not a primary condition of the marriage system of the Kachin, just as it certainly is not among the Chin — where cases of marriage between quite close agnates are treated as just not very nice, whereas cases of alliance reversal are met with severe legal penalty.

Dr. Maran recently told me of the existence, among a section of Jinghpaw Kachin of the "Triangle" area (part of the extremely conservative *Gumchying Gumsa* region of old-style hereditary chieftainship — see Maran 1967), of an interesting and hitherto unreported variety of marriage rule. It is called *hkăwang măgam*, literally, "a cycling (*hkăwang*) of aristocratic heirs (*măgam*)." In this system, which in all other respects follows the asymmetrical rules of all the rest of Kachin marriage, among *du ni* 'chiefly families' a son's son's son's son (usually in the direct line of inheritors of a man's status under the rule of ultimogeniture) must marry a daughter's daughter's daughter's daughter (DDDD). During the intervening generations none of the man's direct male agnatic descendants may marry any girl in the direct female line from his wife, which is in fact the way the Kachins interpret the rule. Most of the rest of the details of this interesting system of marriage make no difference to this paper. It is sufficient to remark that the prohibition during the intervening three generations (counting from the man's wife) does not apply to female lines counting from the wife's classificatory sisters. However, the following is crucial.

In the fourth generation, if the only desirable and/or available DDDD happens to be in one's own local clan segment, she MUST still be married! Indeed she may be married even if others are available from other clans. It is enough that she cannot be married if she is of one's WT. The rule against marrying in the female line for three generations, of course, functions to ensure a certain degree of diversification of alliances amongst effective, i.e. fairly low-level, lineage segments and has nothing whatever to do with systematic transitivity of the alliance relation ("the WG of my WG is my WG, and so on"). There is in fact nothing to prevent that a DDDD be in one's own local clan segment, though it is equally obvious that she cannot be in the lineage segment directly descended from oneself. Hence, the rule also functions to define jurally significant lower limits of segmentation in the lineage (and clan). That is, agnates beyond the fourth generation (inclusive from the common ancestor) are "distant," hence positively open for marriage.

Now it could be argued that this legal formalization of the otherwise informal distinction between close and distant agnates is merely a special condition of *hkăwang măgam* with no relevance to the rest of Kachin, but this argument is shown to be untenable. In the rest of Kachin, a marriage in violation of clan and lineage exogamy is held to make the issue of that marriage, where their descent is known, themselves unsuitable at least for a marriage "of state," that is, to this extent their very clan standing is spoilt.[5] However, the *hkăwang măgam* area is a politically and ritually important area for all Kachin. Other Kachin find it useful to make marriage alliances with the chiefs in the Triangle and to be sponsored by them in rituals that raise one's chiefly rank. The fact of *hkăwang măgam* — in particular, the fact that a man or woman from that area is known to descend from a marriage between agnates according to *hkăwang măgam* — is not the slightest bar to marriage with that man or woman on the part of an outsider to this region. It is held to be proper because the local rules made the agnatic marriage proper. Whatever else is true, this shows that for Kachin in general, the rule of clan exogamy is contingent rather than fundamental to the structure of the system of marriage and descent. And the point is that neither in *jaiwawng* (*contra* Leach 1954:138) NOR in *shut hpyit* can we say that focal emphasis is placed upon violations of marriage rules.

3.2. Now, in the hope of being able to prove that violations of marriage asymmetry are the primary instances of evil, Leach proceeds to an excess of bad etymologizing. The way to discover the real Kachin word or meaning for "sin," he says, is to look at pairs of words for the clues to the binary antithesis, good/bad. Presumably that word among the possible candidates that is paired with a term for the bad is the right one.

---

[5] The more usual instantiation of the relation *ləwu ləhtá* is one of pseudo-agnation (*ləwu ləhtá kəhpu kənau*), for instance a relation between persons of different clans or subclans sharing the same lineage as wife-givers. Thus, if X's FM and Y's M are sisters, the children of X and Y are *ləwu ləhtá* to one another though of different clans, and their intermarriage is held to be problematical even though legal. Within the same clan the relation requires that the related parties represent at least different named subclans or lineages. In any case, such a marriage is held to be contracted by those who are, because of their position, able to get away with something less than wholly approved. Generally it was contracted by a son not slated to inherit his father's standing, since such sons are thought to be prone to acts defying social convention (cf. the Haka Chin concept of *mi hrok hrolh*, Lehman 1963:111). Successors to office are hedged round with social and ceremonial restrictions. Nevertheless, such a marriage may be convenient because it cements an otherwise fragile and ephemeral relationship to a family of importance, putting it upon an altered basis of alliance. Pseudo-agnation, unlike the intraclan relationship, lapses within three generations or so from the time of the common marriage with the same wife-givers. That is what makes it "distant." The expression *ləwu ləhtá* applies to a remote INTRA-clan relation only in an extended sense; for these relationships technically do not fade over time. Nevertheless, we can now understand a critical sense in which the expression makes sense when applied within the clan. A relationship within one's own lineage can be so called when the parties are close to becoming (members of) separate lineages or named subclans, especially when they are residing in different territories. Here again, a marriage with a *ləwu ləhtá* has the effect of putting a relationship, INTRA-lineage, that is about to devolve, on the more serious footing of direct marriage alliance!

In Jinghpaw, 'good' is *kăja*, 'bad' *n kăja*, i.e. 'not good'. But, says Leach, *ja* is the same root as we find in the word for wealth, in particular, as in the myth we started out with — property of significance that passes from WT to WG — treasure, riches. We shall see whether this is a correct identification or not. Meanwhile, Leach adds that a man with *ja* 'riches', is said to have *sut* 'merit'.

Sut is the word we encountered in the name of *Sut wa mădu*, and it is present in the name of the great merit-enhancing feast, the *sut mănau*. We have already seen how Leach argues that the ideas of wealth and merit are fundamentally tied to the WG/WT relation and have seen how greatly that connection must in fact be qualified. But he goes yet a step further — a really egregious step as it turns out. *Sut*, says Leach, has as its opposite *shut*, as in *shut hpyit* (see above, section 2): "it deserves note that, from a linguistic point of view, this term [*sut*] differs only by an aspirate from *shut*" (1970:308). Again, we shall see how utterly little there is in this thesis — it reminds me of Trombetti's notorious rule (1923) that in comparative work any sound can be the equivalent of any other. He thus finds himself able to declare, "Where *sut* stands for goodness, clarity, permanence, merit, *shut* represents evil, confusion, impermanence, and that is what Kachins feel to be the essence of 'sin.'"

Finally, it is worthwhile quoting another passage of Leach's paper:

> The New Testament was translated into Jinghpaw around the turn of this century, principally by the American Baptist Otto [*sic*: Ola] Hanson. Where the word "sin" appears in the English text Hanson uses one or other of the following Jinghpaw terms: (a) *yubak* — this word elsewhere means "witchcraft" which is thought of as a metaphysical contamination. As I have explained elsewhere (1954:180), witches are thought of as being able to manifest themselves in the form of rats (*yu*) and *yubak* might be described as "the work of rats." The same root *yu* also occurs in the term *măyu* (1970:308).

The other terms are *shut* (*hpyit*), which we have already encountered, and *num shaw*, which missionaries used to indicate "adultery," but which, as Leach says, surely means just forcible seizure of a woman, rape.

Leach appears to argue here not that *yubak* means sin, since it refers to punishment or suffering, possibly owing to sin, but that it still shows sin to be alliance reversal. That is, he here equates suffering with the use of witchcraft by WG against *dama* who have failed in their duty to *măyu*.

4.   This lapse into wild etymology is a good place to begin our reconstruction of the true facts. Everything depends upon taking care to distinguish different linguistic tones — something that Leach, a perfect

nonlinguist, thinks is not relevant, and upon paying decent attention to the difference between a syllable that does, and one that does not, end in the glottal stop (ʔ).

4.1. First, what about the *yu* in *mǎyu*? The root is *yùʔ* (low, glottalized tone), and means quite straightforwardly 'a source', otherwise 'to encompass, contain, swallow, subsume'. In reference to WG, it can occur without the prefix, *mə-* as in *yùʔ hòʔ* 'a new WG' (*hòʔ* 'to open something'), *yùʔ hsà* 'an old or inherited WG'. There is a Jinghpaw legal couplet,

> *nìŋ hsói n'hsàʔ* 'breath, the substance of life'
> *yùʔ tuŋ yùʔ śà* 'WG, the main (*tuŋ*) source of children (*śà*)'.

This couplet is held to claim that just as breath allows us to live, so WG allow us to get offspring, and hence WG are of as basic importance as the breath of life. Similarly, WG are compared to a source of sustenance (*məyùʔ nìŋtziŋ* 'my WG are the source of reliable fresh, cool water'), while WT is he who puts wealth in my hands (*jà laŋ dàmáʔ — jà* 'gold' *laŋ* 'in the hand' [is] *dàmáʔ* 'WT').

In ritual language the words *məyù* and *dàmáʔ* do not occur, but are replaced, as in the following ritual quatrain, by standard metaphors:

> hkrìŋ tuŋ hkrìŋ yà
> jà lái jà yà
> məhkù məráʔ
> śədó śədai dán hsai

Here, *khrìŋ* is a class prefix for 'sources', *tuŋ* is 'main', *yà* is 'gift' or 'giving', *lái* is 'to get in exchange', *məhkù məráʔ* is a doublet meaning 'interdependent', and the last line reads, "one's central (*śədai* 'navel, center') support (*śədó*) thus is originated." The whole is held to define the meaning of the alliance relationship: interdependent alliance, in which one gets and passes on wealth, is the foundation of one's very being. This quatrain can be supplemented with the following prose explanation or gloss: *dàʔ n'dai gò məyùʔ dàmáʔ* [thus, (*dàʔ*) as for (*gò*) this one (*n'dai*) WG/WT], *ləjèn ləhkàʔ ai nìŋ pòt* [the origin, the beginning (*nìŋ pòt*) is sharing and taking care]; *rai ŋà ai* (thus [*rai ŋà*] it is (*ai*)].

This should serve to make clear the extent to which the alliance relationship is, as I insisted earlier on, one of mutuality of dependence, in spite of its quasi-hierarchical nature. But it remains to point out that the root *yùʔ* continues to have the basic meaning of 'encompass, contain, swallow, subsume,' so that one's standing is thought of as literally encompassed or contained within that of one's WG, which is apparently connected with the idea (also mentioned earlier on) that one gets one's substantial form through mothers, and certainly with the idea that one's position is a function of (is subsumed in) the standing of those with whom one has made marriage alliances.

4.2.   What has this root, *yùʔ*, to do with rats? Nothing. Rat is *əyú*, with the nominal prefix (Lehman 1971) *ə-* and the root on a high, unglottalized tone. Careful examination of the current literature on the relation between tonal variation and morphological derivation (especially Maran 1971 and Matisoff 1972; see also Maran f.c.) shows conclusively that the two forms are not related as members of a word family. Now it is perfectly true that a witch can come in the guise of a rat; any witch can, but there is in fact nothing connecting witches with *məyùʔ*. One's WG can cause one harm, that is curse one, but this does not actually mean that WG are witches — Leach's sweeping employment of the term witchcraft beclouds this issue badly. Actually, the witch comes in this guise insofar as a witch represents the forces of death, and in this case there is no question that death is represented as appropriate to the nether regions, for the rat is a major symbol of just those, and not in fact in and of itself a symbol of evil, which is only loosely and contingently tied in with the nether regions. The situation is obviously that witchcraft proper is thought of in roughly the same way as it is in the whole Burma region, where a witch — that is, a practitioner of bad magic — is called, in Burmese, an *auʔ lan: hsaya* 'a master of the lower or hidden way' (cf. Spiro 1967:23).

Far from being inherently inauspicious, the rat stands symbolically for land-and-water as a domain of wealth. When one goes to sue for the hand of a girl on behalf of some young man, one has to take along gifts symbolic of all the formal domains of the world according to Kachin cosmology, because the suitor is to be represented as a free human being in complete possession of all the rights of that status. A human being is, in principle, lord of these respective domains — or at least a chief is, while those under him may be so only derivatively. He gets his wealth, his sustenance, from all of these: land-and-water (cf. the Shan-Thai domain of nature, with its appropriate presiding spirit, *chao náam chao din* 'the lord of land and water'), the surface of the land, the region immediately above it (the space left when earth and sky were separated), and the sky. We have seen this cosmological axis and something of its meaning earlier in this study. Let us now look at these symbols a bit more closely.

The names of these prestations represent all the creatures and products of their respective domains. Reading upwards, we get: *yúŋá məkài* or *yúŋá məyon*, where *yú* (minus its prefix, as is usual in closed compounds), here with *ŋá* 'fish', is our word 'rat', and *məkài* is a sort of basket, while *məyon* is 'bundle' — this gift being indifferently called a basket or a bundle. Rat and fish go together, representing, respectively, land and water. Then comes *yam-ŋa*, a beast of burden or domestic animal, neither a basket nor a bundle, representing an earnest of the animals (chiefly cattle) that are the major item in bridewealth, and that stand for the focal source of human wealth — that of man's most proper domain, the surface of the land. Then comes *ù məyon*, an elongated oval basket of the kind which contains and carries domestic fowl. Finally, *ləmù səlàt*, literally 'sky-sweat', actually 'liquor', which conventionally represents the sky spirit, the top of the cosmic axis. It has to be added that these are just names for the gifts and not necessarily literal descriptions of items given. Whatever gifts of money or other valuables are given at this time are calculated in terms of four values, with these respective names and meanings. The point is that those who negotiate come with plenary powers of negotiation.

4.3.   What then of *yubak*? First, it is *yù bàk*, or, in slow speech and when the speaker knows its full meaning and thus treats it as a loanword taken just syllable by syllable, *yù pàk*. It is in fact a loanword of profound significance for our argument and has nothing whatsoever to do with either the root meaning 'rat' or the meaning 'to be a source' or 'to subsume'. The origin is the Shan word *yūpaak* — which is Shan Pāli (Pāli is the scriptural Indic language of *Theravāda* Buddhism), or rather dog-Pāli, for the more correct *vi-pāak* (Cushing 1914:541) and means quite specifically 'the consequences of one's acts or actions'. The Pāli is *vipāka*, and my gloss is from Buddhadatta's *Pāli-English dictionary* (1957:240). The *Burmese-English dictionary* of Judson (1953) gives a useful translation derived from Burmese-Pāli scholarship, namely, "The result of any deed, good or bad; the result of an evil deed which remains after the main part has been exhausted through inflictions in a previous state."

Thus, this Kachin word is borrowed from quite sophisticated Buddhist rhetoric precisely about "sin"! We can say, further, that the full expression most immediately relevant to the conception "sin" in Kachin is the Shan loanblend which at least some Kachin understand to be *yūpaak-apyet*, where *apyet* is from the Burmese *pyit* 'to throw aside, neglect carelessly'. Going yet further, one says in Kachin *yùbàk yùbyen* (the syllable *yù* being taken out of context (cf. Lehman 1973:540–541) and preposed to the native Jinghpaw stem, *byen*, meaning 'a burden, something heavy'), and even *yùbàk tsín yam*. In the latter case, *tsín yam* signifies 'suffering'. Notice that both these expressions are typical doublets, the first a loanword, the second an analyzable native gloss.

Now we see that the foregoing is THE basic Kachin reference to the idea of "sin," though not the word for "sin" itself, and that the Kachin conception of sin is in fact a fairly complex and reasonably sophisticated idea. Moreover, we have to understand that these Kachin ideas are directly influenced by the even more sophisticated philosophical ideas of their Shan and Burmese neighbors. We cannot treat Kachin thought as some kind of primitive isolate, and in fact it is Leach who has been prominent above almost all other social anthropologists in putting across this very point, especially for the Kachin (1954)!

Let us go a bit further still. *Yùbàk*, the wages of sin, is not understood primarily as 'witchcraft'. It is understood quite clearly as an inherent burden we bear when we neglect duty, when we are careless in our actions. There is, of course, some lack of clarity for the Kachin about the AGENTS of this retribution. For the general run of less sophisticated Kachin it seems that indeed witches are the basic agents of their suffering, but for others, witches enter the scheme (as indeed they do in Burmese and Shan Buddhism) as merely contingent agencies. The CAUSE is inherent fate. In short, we suffer not because of witches, but because of ourselves. More particularly, the business about sin = witchcraft = metaphysical contamination turns out to be largely nonsense.[6]

The point of all this is simply that Leach's major thesis is entirely supported, but by means of a set of ideas of considerable interest and complexity that Leach almost deliberately avoids. Sin is indeed wrong action; *inter alia*, it at least acts counter to such fundamental orders as the Kachin marriage system. But its wrongness derives from a rather intricate set of abstract cosmological ideas in which the marriage-structure is merely subsumed, however saliently, rather than being the central and originating idea.

---

[6] The matter of witchcraft as metaphysical contamination is a bit more involved than may at first appear. The witches that turn into rats are held to indulge in a self-conscious practice. On the other hand, there is a kind of more or less automatic evil that flows from certain kinds of anger and/or jealousy, and this includes, among others, the "witchcraft" of the presumptively injured WG (cf. Leach 1961a:23). At any rate his "cursing" of his WT in these cases is not always or necessarily self-conscious and deliberate. Again, this distinction is widespread in this part of the world — and elsewhere. For the Burmese, one can refer to Spiro (1967:21–26), for the Chin to Lehman (1963:111–112, where I discuss *hnam ngei*, persons possessing the evil eye of jealousy). I gather, but am unable to confirm, that it is the innate sort of "witchcraft" that Leach intends when he speaks of a kind of metaphysical contamination.

4.4. Let us go on now to some of the other Kachin words adduced by Leach in his argument. Recall that he tries to equate *ja* 'wealth' with *ja* 'good'. But, in fact, the first is really *jà* (low tone), and means quite specifically 'gold' (cf. Benedict 1972:46, etymon 184), while the second is *ja* (mid-tone), as in *kəja ai* 'it is good', *n'kəja ai* 'it is not good'. 'Treasure' or 'wealth' is in fact *jà sùt kàn*, a compound in which *sùt* 'merit, prosperity' figures once again (*sùt mənaàu* = 'treasure celebration'). These two words, *ja* and *jà*, apparently get even further confused in Leach's thinking with the third partial homonym, *ja*, a verb meaning 'to pay a price or exaction, i.e. a bribe'. Thus, *məyùʔ ja:* after a marriage when a WG visits his WT, the latter has to give the former all sorts of gifts. These are NOT part of the marriage price. Rather they are given simply to placate the WG, who, if displeased with the WT, is likely to curse the latter — Leach's "witchcraft." This verb, *ja*, while homophonous with the verb meaning 'to be good', is in fact etymologically related to (i.e. derived from) *jà* 'gold, treasure'.

4.5. Finally, what the missionary orthography writes as *shut* (in *shut hpyit*, for instance) is in fact *śút*. It is in no sense related to *sùt* 'wealth', and, in particular, Leach is wholly wrong when he says the two differ by only an aspirate. Not only are the tones distinct, but the initials are also unrelated — that of the first is not an aspirate but a palatal sibilant, the *h* of the orthography being just the English convention for transcribing this sound. There is, of course, in Kachin a productive system of forming inchoative verbs from adjectives, for example, by aspirating an otherwise surd initial (see Maran 1971:179–180), but this is totally irrelevant to the case in hand. *Shut*, that is, *śút* means 'to err' or 'make a mistake', hence *shut hpyit* is simply 'an egregious mistake'. Its relation to "sin" is fairly obvious. It is a cross-cutting notion, viz., sin certainly derives from a class of mistakes, in fact from a class of heinous mistakes, but, as with ourselves (as observed at the beginning of this paper), not all cases of profoundly reprehensible acts have to be understood as sins.

5. In conclusion, may I somewhat facetiously remark that among the classes of sins in modern Western culture there are those known as methodological sins, and among these is surely the misplaced reliance upon one's own classical training as a motivation and guarantee of one's analysis, to the neglect of evidence of a classical tradition in the cultural system one is studying.

It behooves an anthropologist trying to elucidate matters like conceptions of "sin" to attempt to pay as much attention as possible to what amounts to native intellectual traditions. A classical education is no doubt a great thing and can without question bring a good deal of subtlety and sensitivity to ethnographic theory and analysis. But there must always be the question of whose classical education is particularly relevant. I prefer, in this instance at least, to look at what Kachin intellectual tradition has to tell me about just the collection of facts that Leach and I agree bear upon the Kachin notion of "sin."

REFERENCES

BENEDICT, PAUL K.
  1972   *Sino-Tibetan, a conspectus*. Cambridge: Cambridge University Press.
BUDDHADATTA, MAHĀTHERA A. P.
  1957   *Concise Pāli-English dictionary*. Colombo: The Colombo Apothecaries.
CUSHING, REV. J. N.
  1914   *A Shan and English dictionary* (second edition). Farnborough, Hants: Gregg International.
GILHODES, REV. CHARLES M.
  1922   *The Kachins: religion and customs*. Calcutta: Catholic Orphan Press.
JUDSON, REV. ADONIRAM
  1953   *Burmese-English dictionary* (centenary edition). Rangoon: Baptist Board of Publications.
KEESING, ROGER M.
  1971   "Toward a model of role analysis," in *A handbook of method in cultural anthropology*. Edited by R. Naroll and R. Cohen, 423–453. New York: Natural History Press.
LEACH, EDMUND R.
  1954   *Political systems of highland Burma*. London: Bell; Cambridge, Mass.: Harvard University Press.
  1961a "Rethinking anthropology," in *Rethinking anthropology*, 1–27. University of London Monographs on Social Anthropology 22. London: Athlone Press.
  1961b "Aspects of bridewealth and marriage stability among the Kachin and Lakher," in *Rethinking anthropology*, 114–127. University of London Monographs on Social Anthropology 22. London: Athlone Press.
  1970   The concept of sin among the Kachin of North Burma. *Proceedings of the Eighth International Congress of Anthropological and Ethnological Sciences, Tokyo*, section S-9:307–309.
LEACH, EDMUND R., *editor*
  1968   *Dialectic in practical religion*. Cambridge Papers in Social Anthropology 5. Cambridge: Cambridge University Press.
LEHMAN, F. K.
  1963   *The structure of Chin society*. Illinois Anthropology Series 3. Urbana: University of Illinois Press.

1971 "Wolfenden's non-pronominal a-prefix in Tibeto-Burman: two arguments from southern Chin and some proposed semantic correlates." Paper read at the Fourth Annual Conference on Sino-Tibetan Linguistics, forthcoming as a special number of the *International Journal of American Linguistics* edited by LaRaw Maran.

1973 "Tibeto-Burman syllable structure, tone and the theory of phonological conspiracies," in *Issues in linguistics.* Edited by B. B. Kachru, et al., 515–547. Urbana: University of Illinois Press.

LÉVI-STRAUSS, CLAUDE
1969 *The elementary structures of kinship* (Revised edition). Translated by J. H. Bell, J. R. von Sturmer, and R. Needham. Boston: Beacon Press.

LOEFFLER, LORENZ G.
1968 "Beast, bird, and fish: an essay in South-East Asian symbolism," in *Folk religion and the world view in the southwestern Pacific,* 21–33. Tokyo: Keio Institute of Cultural and Linguistic Studies, Keio University.

MARAN, LA RAW
1967 "Toward a basis for understanding the minorities of Burma: the Kachin example," in *Southeast Asian tribes, minorities and nations,* volume one. Edited by P. Kunstadter, 125–146. Princeton: Princeton University Press.

1971 *Burmese and Jinghpo: a study in tonal linguistic processes.* Occasional Papers of the Wolfenden Society on Tibeto-Burman Linguistics.

MARAN, LA RAW, *editor*
f.c. *Revision and expansion of Hanson's Kachin-English dictionary.*

MATISOFF, JAMES A.
1972 "Tones in Jinghpaw and Lolo-Burmese." Paper presented to the Fifth Annual Conference on Sino-Tibetan Linguistics, University of Michigan.

NEEDHAM, RODNEY
1963 "Introduction" to *Primitive classification* by E. Durkheim and M. Mauss. Translated and edited by Rodney Needham, vii–xlviii. Chicago: University of Chicago Press.

SPIRO, MELFORD E.
1967 *Burmese supernaturalism.* Englewood Cliffs, N.J.: Prentice-Hall.

TROMBETTI, A.
1923 *Gli elementi di glottologia.* Bologna.

"Must" and "Ought": Problems
of Translation in Sanskritic Hindu law

J. DUNCAN M. DERRETT

I do not know of any study of the significance of the use of the optative mood of the third person and of impersonal constructions in stating norms in ancient Indian *dharma* literature. The relevant literature on the interpretation of Vedic, i.e. impersonal injunctions in traditional Hindu, texts is confined to analysis of the types of injunctions, categorized by their effects (Kane 1962:V, 1226, 1228, 1235–1238; see also Sastri 1926: 53–131; Jha 1942: Chapter 13; Ayyar 1952:18–23). *Dharma* is the Indian equivalent of "religion," "morality," and "duty" (combined). *Dharmaśāstra* is the Indian "science of righteousness," and it includes law. To state the problem, I should first illustrate the usages in that literature and then point to the contrast in modern European idiom. The dilemma of the foreign powers who administered law in India is then easily stated, and we may end with a suggestion as to the conclusions to be drawn from the Indian phenomenon.

THE SANSKRIT IDIOM

I have not seen any discussion of this aspect of the problem in Sanskritic logical or *dharmaśāstric* sources. It is enough for them that the injunction is expressed in the optative or by a participle (gerundive). Professors of *dharma* could have been aware of the practical difficulties of the form of expression we are handling, as evidenced by one of the specialized studies of Śaṅkara-bhaṭṭa (A.D. 1540–1600) of which I provided an annotated translation (Derrett 1957). That study, with its abundant documentation, is still the most helpful introduction to the present question. It did not occur to the Indian author that it was the idiom which was at fault, and that the idiom derived from a state of society and a method of legal administration which was peculiar.

The best introduction to the *dharmaśāstra* itself is that of Lingat (1973), but it does not handle this linguistic question (of which Lingat was aware — see p.142), nor its social basis. The vast encyclopedia of the (presumably) unrivalled master of the subject (Kane 1930–1962) does not go deeper than the linguistic point (see above), since the author's attitude to his subject prevented him from considering the possibility that his sources were visionary. The same can certainly be said of other leading secondary authorities (Sen 1918; Sen-Gupta 1953).

It is normal for all injunctions in the ancient Sanskrit texts to be phrased in the optative mood: *syāt* 'it should be' (Manu VI:1); *vaset* 'he should dwell' (Manu VI:I); *gacchet* 'he should go' (Manu VI:3); *cintayet* 'he should give thought' (Manu VII:221); *vivāsayet* 'he should exile' (Manu VIII:123); *prakalpayet* 'let him fix, or inflict' (Manu VIII:322, 324). A verse may contain two optatives, each with a different subject. Sometimes an indicative negative is followed by the optative of positive advice: *sthāvare vikrayo nāsti, kuryād ādhim anujñayā* (a *smṛti* at *Dharmakośa* p. 1589), which may be translated, 'there is no sale in the case of immovable property: he should make a mortgage having taken the (necessary) consent.' Often a gerund is used or a gerundive participle, indicating a precept impersonally: *kāryo 'rdha-pādikaḥ* 'he [i.e. the thief] should be made half-footed' (Manu VIII:325); *na sākṣī nṛpatiḥ kāryaḥ* 'the king should not be made a witness [i.e. in litigation]' (Manu VIII:65). The use of the word *arhati* 'he owes, he ought' and related forms is interesting. It refers to what a person OUGHT to do and what he OUGHT to suffer. At Manu VIII:323 we have an example, and it is extremely common. An example from the *Matsya-purāṇa* (Derrett 1973:14, Note 71) illustrates this: *adravyāṃ mṛta-patnīṃ tu saṅgṛhṇan nāparādhunuyāt, balāt parigṛhāṇas tu sarvasvaṃ daṇḍam arhati* 'one who takes up a widow who has no assets does not sin [or commit an offence]; but one who takes one up by force OWES [i.e. ought to suffer] a fine amounting to his entire property'.

The great problem is how to translate these terms. It is no less a problem when the precept is directed to the king or his delegate. "Sanskrit, with its habitual employment of the optative mood... may lead to translations of a single term as varied as 'he shall not', 'he should not', 'he may not', and 'he must not', [which] directly encouraged ambiguity..." (Derrett 1957:207). The last-quoted article takes up a connected matter, namely the perhaps fortuitous employment of the Sanskrit terms for gift-transactions, *adeya* 'non-giveable' and *adatta* 'ungiven'; the distinction between them is one we can ignore here, since we have enough to do to consider the principle of choosing the optative to cover all types of injunction.

It may be of some help to consider Jewish rabbinical usages. The Old Testament (which vaguely parallelled the Veda as a basic source) freely used the imperative mood and the future: "do," "do not," "thou shalt," "thou shalt not." The rabbinical *halakic* (normative) literature closely parallels the *dharmaśāstra*. Mutual ignorance on the part of the specialists in each is a deplorable thing, possibly due to narrow-mindedness, more probably due to the exhausting character of each discipline. Rabbinical usage emphasizes direct statement, and this is illuminating. A man is "liable" or "free." An action is "permitted" or "forbidden." The proper course of action is indicated by the present indicative "they do"; and an improper course by the simple negative "they do not do." With insignificant exceptions (e.g. "he should make a scroll"; "he should not multiply his wives") rabbinic idiom does not direct precepts to the king (since he has no judicial authority in rabbinical jurisprudence), nor to a court, except in terms "they do this." In other words, the *halakah*, the right path in which to walk, has been determined by decisions (often majority decisions), and those that walk in it are right, those that do not are wrong, and it is sufficient for the rabbis to state what those people do who walk in the right way. The use of the Hebrew participle as an imperative has been noticed by David Daube (personal communication): the participle has the value of an imperfect-imperative or an infinite-imperative, but it does not have the value of an imperative where it denotes a custom (Selwyn 1946: 467–488); this usage, imitated by St. Paul and by the authors of 1 Peter and Ephesians, has until recently embarrassed theologians (Davies 1962:130, 329). Ambiguity at times exists in their law, when of two practices either may be right, and a theoretical choice is indefinitely postponed. But where a decision is known, the answer is always quite unambiguous. WHETHER THERE IS OR IS NOT A COURT TO ENFORCE THE DECISION, the rabbinical law is theoretically certain and binding in conscience. There are evidently points of contact with *dharmaśāstra* and points of difference. The obvious connecting factor is the multiplicity of languages, races, and religions to which the *dharmaśāstra* belonged and to whom, in a peculiarly flexible sense, it "applied." The religious and social solidity of the Jewish people after A.D. 135 had no counterpart in India, and still has not.

An example of how problematical such ambiguities can be is Manu VIII, 167:

kuṭumbārthe 'dhyadhīno 'pi vyavahāraṃ yam ācaret
sva-deśe vā videśe vā taṃ jyāyān na vicālayet

Vicālayet is in the optative 'he should not disturb'; and we note that the immediately preceding half-verse ends with the word *ācaret*, which is a mere subjunctive (though the same part of the verb) 'he should (chance to) transact'. The verse may be translated: 'Should even a wholly dependent person make a contract on behalf of the family, the householder, whether in his own country or abroad, shall not rescind it'. It will be noticed that I have instinctively translated the optative in *vicālayet* as 'shall'. This is not unprecedented since in British statutes the word 'shall' is often judicially construed to mean 'may', and vice versa. Now the practical question is: what happens if a 'dependent' person enters into a transaction which is intended to be for the family's benefit, but which turns out to be the reverse? Such a situation has arisen often in modern India, times (indeed) without number, and it must have arisen constantly in ancient times. In such an emergency, the head of the family invariably seeks ways of recovering the family's property or extinguishing the obligation, and for this purpose he will call upon his own rights (as a non-consenting party) and those of minor or female members of the family. If the text is to be taken seriously — it figures in India's most famous, if not most influential, law book — are we to understand (a) that it would ordinarily lie in the power of the head of the family to annul the transaction unilaterally; (b) if not, could he approach some court to annul the transaction for him; and (c) does this text prohibit his doing this, if the transaction were originally concluded in the family's apparent interest? And why should we be left in doubt? *Dharmaśāstra* encourages the annulment of transactions entered into improperly, fraudulently, or oppressively. The same position is upheld in the *arthaśāstra* [the classical Indian science of "ways and means"], as we may tell from the *Kauṭilīya* III, Chapter 1, and III, Chapter 16 (Kangle 1963: 219ff., 281). In neither science is it made unambiguously clear whether the offending transactions can be considered VOID or merely VOIDABLE in the modern sense of these words.

THE ENGLISH IDIOM AND THE PROBLEM OF FOREIGN ADMINISTRATORS

The words "shall," "may," "void," "voidable," and the like are found in English statutes. The courts have in each case decided whether the rule is mandatory (i.e. an absolute command or requisite) or directory (i.e. it gives or authorizes a discretion as to whether an act shall be done). The distinction between directory and mandatory commands is fundamental to the interpretation of statutes and statutory instruments. The most difficult problems arise (though they arise very rarely nowadays) when an act is prohibited. A prohibition is a good example of a negative mandatory statement. When a statute includes a mere prohibition, without going on to state that the prohibited act is VOID, it is theoretically possible to hold that the act will be valid but that the actor risks punishment. Even in statutes which prohibit an act (e.g. a transfer, in India, by a *de facto* guardian of a Hindu minor) and which go further (which is not the case with the aforementioned example) and prescribe a penalty for the violator, there can arise a doubt as to whether the act itself is void. The difference between a void and a voidable act (as any law dictionary will confirm) is that the latter stands good in law until set aside by a court having jurisdiction to do this. Thus a marriage with a woman whose husband is still alive is void, and no action on anyone's part is necessary to annul it: it can simply be ignored. A marriage of a woman with an impotent man, however, is voidable (in most jurisdictions), and will stand good for all time if one of the spouses does not take action to have it annulled.

When the foreign powers came to India and became acquainted with the content and style of Sanskrit law texts, they were at first in the hands of the pandits, i.e. the traditional Indian doctors of law, who frequently and fairly consistently rendered the optative, and similar modes of speech, as mandatory: "he SHALL do it." In due course, it became evident that not all pandits agreed on every occasion and that differences in social viewpoint were not unassociated with these discrepancies. When pandits could no longer be consulted — their posts as judicial assessors were abolished in 1864 — the British judges, in India and in the Privy Council in London, were forced to decide whether rules in *dharmaśāstra* were to be understood as mandatory or only directory. They reached inconsistent and discrepant results (Derrett 1968:78–80). They made frequent use of the maxim *factum valet* 'a thing which should not (morally) be done may nevertheless be held validly done when actually done', which had Indian (and indeed Jewish) counterparts (Derrett 1958). The French, observing the complexity of native legal sources and the contingent character of injunctions in the Sanskrit texts, adopted a method of administration which left maximum room for maneuvering to the representatives of Hindu castes. The Portuguese enacted a number of codes which, though based on Sanskrit texts as understood by native experts in Goa and elsewhere, produced very different results from their counterparts in British India (Derrett 1969: Numbers 403 424).

A TENTATIVE EXPLANATION FOR THE SANSKRIT IDIOM

A word such as *kartavyaḥ* means 'should be done, *nivartanīyaḥ* 'should be set aside, annulled', *dadyāt* 'he should give', and so on. The precepts are directed to the judge, or to the individual who has discretion to act, and so on. The guiding assumptions of the system known as *dharmaśāstra* could account for this. It sprung from what we may call (for want of a better term) a codification of rules and practices used in religious sacrifices, and the rules of interpretation (called *mīmāṃsā*) which developed out of those needs were taken over without hesitation or apology into legal interpretation; there was a common vocabulary and idiom (Ayyar 1952). It was a religious obligation to apply the rules. A failure to comply meant, in the field of religious actions, that the latter were void; the actor might be liable, in many cases, to a penance for his violation. In the field of non-religious activities, such as were denominated "seen" (i.e. the effects were visible and the rule rational), there was a cultural inducement to obey the precepts of the *dharmaśāstra*, but an adequate reason could overrule them. The religious and moral obligation which supported the whole system would seldom be conclusive *per se*. There were, indeed, some contexts of a combined religious and social character (e.g. occupations reserved for castes, in which the whole concept of caste and class was derived from the *dharmaśāstra*) in which we happen to know that the texts were taken as ultimate authorities (Lingat 1973: 273–274). But the basic presupposition was that there was an option to follow, or to discard, the rules of *dharma* (Lingat 1973: Part 2, Chapter 2), especially in the *vyavahāra* (business) sections of Hindu law, e.g. adoption, inheritance, and the like. Śaṅkara-bhaṭṭa was not content with this solution, recommending that in the *vyavahāra* contexts prohibitory texts should be taken as rendering the action void or at the least voidable (Derrett 1957:214); but it does not follow that his recommendation was ever taken up generally.

An excellent illustration of the outlook is provided by the highly controversial verse, Manu I: 108:

ācāraḥ paramo dharmaḥ śrutyuktaḥ smārta eva ca
tasmād asmin sadā yukto nityaṃ syād ātmavān dvijaḥ

The translation which appealed to administrators in the early nineteenth century was this: 'Custom is supreme law, as is that which is said in *śruti* [Vedic revelation] and *smṛti* [traditional norm-pronouncement]. The twice-born [i.e. male of the three higher classes] concerned for the good of his soul must always be attentive to it' (see Lingat 1973:198). A translation which appeals better to philologists reads: 'The rule of conduct is transcendent law, whether it be taught in the revealed texts or in the sacred tradition; hence a twice-born man who possesses regard for himself should always be careful to follow it' (Bühler 1886:27). The dispute as to the meaning of this verse does not touch the point which interests us: the precept both of custom and of the sacred law was directed to the individual conscience.

But society did not tolerate people in its midst whose consciences did not square with those of the most prestige-worthy inhabitants. This had two effects. One must obey the minimum of conscience-binding rules recognized by one's group, or one goes out, i.e. is excommunicated. On the other hand, there is no support or encouragement to obey *dharma* rules which, remaining in the traditional texts, are no longer regarded as essential by the community. One must not practice that which, being *dharma*, is disapproved by the world (Lingat 1973:189–191). This is the principal reason why, within the same society, we find twin sciences, with conflicting but equally respectable recipes for living, those of the *dharmaśāstra* and of the *arthaśāstra*. The last would have been a great puzzle if its intention, as a corpus of information for those who have decided (on moral grounds) what they want to do, had not been clearly before the critic's mind (Kane 1968:Section 14).

CULTURAL CONTINUITY

A culture which leaves it to the judge whether a disapproved act is void or merely voidable, which leaves it to the influential members of society whether they shall punish, and if so how, an offender against one of a number of rules prescribed in the interest of the public's common supernatural welfare, is likely to have a sceptical view of state-prescribed laws. This transpires in the public's tolerance of visionary legislation. A minor example is the Dowry Prohibition Act, Act 28 of 1961. A major and notorious example is the Indian Constitution of 1950, to which no less than thirty amendments have had to be made. The present writer has commented on the style of Hindu matrimonial litigation, which proves that court law, in the less advanced of Indian social circles, need have no contact with moral standards (Derrett

1968:Chapter 11; 1970: Appendix 4). It seems evident that mandatory legislation, in which the minimum of discretion is left to officials and to persons holding positions of prestige, is contrary to the Hindu genius and, when applied, produces signs of strain and distress. It may even fail entirely. The Sanskrit idiom, which suggests that the only genuine discipline is an internal, not an imposed, discipline, fits a society which evolves its own norms consciously and sincerely, and which makes imported rules (if any) its own by assimilating them. The implications of this run contrary to the trends of the last century of legislation in India.

REFERENCES

AYYAR, A. S. NATARAJA
  1952 *Mīmāṃsā jurisprudence* (*The sources of Hindu law*). Allahabad: Ganganatha Jha Research Institute.
BÜHLER, GEORG
  1886 *The laws of Manu.* Sacred Books of the East 25. Oxford: Clarendon Press.
DAVIES, W. D.
  1962 *Paul and rabbinic Judaism* (second edition). London: S.P.C.K.
DERRETT, J. DUNCAN M.
  1957 Prohibition and nullity: Indian struggles with a jurisprudential lacuna. *Bulletin of the School of Oriental and African Studies* 20:203–215.
  1958 Factum valet: the adventures of a maxim. *International and Comparative Law Quarterly* 7:280–302.
  1968 *Religion, law and the state in India.* London: Faber and Faber.
  1969 "The Indian sub-continent under European influence," in *Bibliographical introduction to legal history and ethnology.* Edited by J. Gilissen, section E/8. Brussels: Éditions de l'Institut de Sociologie, Université Libre de Bruxelles.
  1970 *Critique of modern Hindu law.* Bombay: Tripathi.
  1973 "Dharmaśāstra and juridical literature," in *A history of Indian literature.* Edited by J. Gonda, part four. Wiesbaden: Otto Harrassowitz.
JHA, GANGANATHA
  1942 *Pūrva-mimāṃsā in its sources.* Benares: Benares Hindu University.
KANE, PANDURANG V.
  1930–1962 *History of dharmaśāstra,* five volumes in seven. Poona: Bhandarkar Oriental Research Institute.
  1968 *History of dharmaśāstra* (second edition), volume one, part one. Poona: Bhandarkar Oriental Research Institute.
KANGLE, R. P.
  1963 *The Kauṭilīya arthaśāstra,* part two. Bombay: University of Bombay.
LINGAT, ROBERT
  1973 *The classical law of India.* Berkeley: University of California Press.

SASTRI, C. SANKARARAMA
  1926 *Fictions in the development of the Hindu law texts.* Adyar: University of Madras.
SELWYN, E. GORDON
  1946 *The First Epistle of St. Peter.* London: Macmillan.
SEN, PRIYANATH
  1918 *General principles of Hindu jurisprudence.* Calcutta: Calcutta University.
SEN-GUPTA, NARESH C.
  1953 *Evolution of ancient Indian law.* London: Arthur Probstain; Calcutta: Eastern Law House.

Ethnolinguistic Introduction to Japanese Literature

SAYO YOTSUKURA

If a hippy or someone belonging to today's younger generation were to go back in time to, say, 1860, and meet a rancher in the West, they might converse as follows: [1]

HIPPY: Hi, man.
COWBOY: Howdy.
HIPPY: Got any grass?
COWBOY: Yup, 'bout 100 acres. Why?
HIPPY: Wow man! What do you do with it all?
COWBOY: Well, I got about 100 heads to keep supplied.
HIPPY: Man! You must make lots of bread.
COWBOY: Me? You kidding? My wife does that!
HIPPY: Your wife?
COWBOY: Yea, a whole bundle.
HIPPY: She sounds cool. What else does she do?
COWBOY: Well, her hobby now is raising poppies.
HIPPY: Does she sell dope?
COWBOY: Watch your language, bud! Of course, she sells the flowers.
HIPPY: Cool it!
COWBOY: Why would she cool them? They'd die!
HIPPY: Does she make much bread of them?
COWBOY: Yea, with the seeds.
HIPPY: (points to cowboy's horse) What's that?
COWBOY: That is a lot of horse. Why?
HIPPY: You're kidding.
COWBOY: She's a real beaut she is.
HIPPY: That reminds me, got any speed?
COWBOY: This horse has got more in him than any I've ever seen.

[1] This dialogue was written by Stuart Cook (when he was a seventh grader) as part of his homework for an English class at junior high school.

HIPPY: You shoot up horses?
COWBOY: Only when they're lame. Why?
HIPPY: Then, why did you shoot up this one?
COWBOY: Shoot this baby? You crazy?
HIPPY: Then, how did you get the speed in him?
COWBOY: He was born with it!
HIPPY: Hey, man, that's cool. Next thing you know we'll have trips that last for generations.
COWBOY: That's already happened, friend. There's a man in town who went away twenty years ago hasn't come back yet. Don't know if he will. Any way he's raised a family and has three kids who are twenty and older.
HIPPY: That's freaky, man.
COWBOY: I know. Not many people 'round here like to travel.
HIPPY: You are talking about a town?
COWBOY: Yea, about five miles from here.
HIPPY: What kind of business do they have?
COWBOY: Well, there's a general store which has acid, balloons, candy, chalk, dynamite, flea powder, guns, oranges, peaches, peanuts, rope, sugar, tea, and wheat, plus a whole bunch of other junk.
HIPPY: I can see why you call it a general store! How come there's no pigs around?
COWBOY: This is cattle country!
HIPPY: So?
COWBOY: Well, there used to be some but they interfered with business so we drove them out.
HIPPY: Wow man. What's that? (pointing to the cowboy's gun)
COWBOY: That's my gun.
HIPPY: What can you shoot?
COWBOY: Everything from a bird's eye to a horse.
HIPPY: Can you blast with it?
COWBOY: This gun's like dynamite.
HIPPY: What else can it do?
COWBOY: Well, for kicks I shoot balloons by the hundreds.
HIPPY: Wow man!
COWBOY: Yea, it is fantastic.
HIPPY: It's been nice meeting you. I'm gonna split for this town (leaves).
COWBOY: (to himself) There goes a real nice person. Him and I understand each other perfectly.

Do they really? This conversation would be amusing only to those who know that the hippy and the cowboy are using the same words and expressions to mean very different things. If there were a one-to-one correlation between language and reality, we would not have this kind of fun. And if it were only a matter of having or not having fun, there would be no problem. However, chances are that misunderstanding stems from the very fact that there is no one-to-one correlation between language and reality. Indeed, even when we say "reality" we do not know exactly what it is. All we know is what we think we know, or what we can perceive — what we can see, hear, smell, taste, and feel. That what we can see is not all that actually exists can be easily demonstrated by the simple fact that things in the distance are not visible, or that there are numerous microscopic things that cannot be seen. The human ear cannot pick up sounds which have waves that are too big or too small. It is commonly known that, compared to human beings, dogs can hear better, mice can smell better, cats can see better, etc. That the world we know is the world of perception has been so often stated and discussed by many people at various times in various places that there is no need to discuss it further. The point relevant to our discussion is that there is no one-to-one correlation between language and reality.

One of the reasons for the lack of a one-to-one correlation between language and reality may be that there is no physical contact between them. This results from the fact that we humans are so limited that we cannot know reality itself but only perceive it. We are, as it were, fluctuating or drifting up and down, to and fro, around or above reality, with language not only between reality and us but also between man and man. It is as if we were trying to focus on certain points of reality with the assistance of language. Each of us has his/her own filter to focus, and each tries to find another person who has a filter which is more or less similar. It is like tuning in a station on the radio or focusing on an object with a camera. How many stations you get on your radio or how easily you focus on an object with your camera depends on what kind of radio or camera you possess and use. With recent technology, there are many good radios and cameras that are quite automatically operated. How can this be done, and is it possible, in our operation with language?

Language is said to be a means of communicating thought and/or feeling. It can be thought of as a system of communication filters in which each filter processes and transmits information for succeeding filters; such a system is shown schematically in Figure 1.

The filters in this figure are persons with their language, culture, and experience. The first filter (the speaker/writer) may be compared to an overhead projector which gives a picture of reality on the wall. Language consists of particles which move around aimlessly until they are sieved through the filter of expression. When they are sieved through the filter, they are selected and arranged in certain orders according to the way the filter is made by combining language, culture, and experience. The goal is to give an image as close to reality as possible. However, this goal is not always achieved. While the first filter inevi-

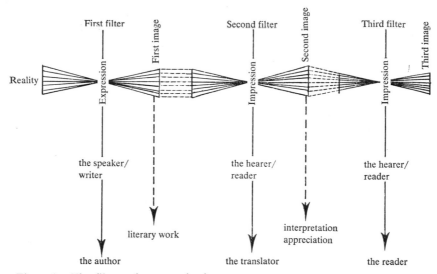

Figure 1.   The filters of communication

tably chooses certain particles and arranges them in certain orders according to the way it is made, the filter (the speaker/writer) has the freedom of doing so within its own frame. Here the creativity of the first filter comes into the picture. The second filter (the hearer/reader) has the role of receiving the image of reality. Again, the second filter may force the first image to go through the second filter by selecting and arranging particles from the first image according to the way the second filter is fixed. In other words, the hearer/reader can interpret the literary work that is being read in whatever way he/she wants.

Some people might say that they are only interested in interpreting literary works in their own way. To these people I have nothing to say. After all, everything we do is limited to the world of perception. As a result, just as "beauty is in the eye of the beholder," value is in the mind of the thinker. What seems to be valuable to one person may not be considered valuable by another. However, if I take the viewpoint that language dictates understanding, then it follows that the role of the hearer/reader is to follow as closely as possible the speaker/writer's intention of reflecting reality in the first image. A writer is considered good when what he tries to convey to the reader successfully brings understanding between the two.

Japanese literature is usually introduced to Americans in English translation since very few Americans can read Japanese adequately. It follows, then, that American readers of a Japanese literary work constitute the third filter, instead of the second filter (see Figure 1). We all know from our own experience — and even youngsters know from their game of "telephone" — that messages change slightly each time they are transmitted from one person to the next. In order for American readers of Japanese literature to be able to appreciate original works, the second filter (the translator) must be delicately aware of this filtering process and flexible enough so that most, if not all, particles sieved through the first filter can go through the second filter. The aim of this paper is to present some aspects of Japanese language and culture which the second filter (the translator) must be aware of in the course of transmitting the first image to project the second. The underlying proposition is that literary appreciation means trying to understand what the original author tried to express.

Compared to English, the Japanese language is characteristically fragmentary. For example, when you say in English "I brought my book with me," we say in Japanese "brought book." Only when it is necessary to specify that it was MY book, not YOURS, that I brought, do we use the word "my" in the sentence. In general, it is customary in Japanese not to state things overtly but only covertly. There is a general understanding that the less expressed verbally the more polite and connotative is the statement. Thus, the skills of expressing and understanding meaning between the lines are crucial for people to get along in the society. Sometimes it is necessary to use more words than usual in order not to be impolite. For example, we would not say overtly and clearly "A is A, and not B." We tend to say "it seems to me quite possible to say that A might probably be A, but . . ." You may expect that something would follow after "but . . ." Actually, "but" in this position is used in place of a period and means "I have nothing further to say." Concluding a sentence in its well-formed shape is simply avoided. We may find similar examples in English. Could you explain when one should say "I could care less" versus "I couldn't care less"? Or why a person was never asked again after she said "I'll think about it" to a person who had asked her to teach him Japanese? Saying "I'll think about it" to mean "no" is simply a euphemism. When a euphemism wears out, then the search begins for another way of saying it. Thus, Japanese has developed a style of "wrapping up" real meaning in several layers of indirectness. One typical example is to add "I think" even when there is no need to say "I think" or "I believe." When an interpreter said, "If you believe in God, He will save you, I think," the pastor, who knew a little Japanese, corrected him and said, "I did not say 'I think'." The interpreter had added "I think" at the end quite spontaneously in order to be polite.

Japanese syntax seems fragmentary to speakers of Indo-European languages partly because the fundamental concept of a sentence is different. It is said that one-third of all sentences in English are subjectless. This includes the imperative construction, such as "Go and get it!" In Japanese, it is not too much to say that as many as three-fourths of all sentences are subjectless. Hockett (1958: 201) says:

> The kernel of an English sentence of the favorite sentence-types is a predicate constitute, ... The most general characterization of predicative constructions is suggested by the terms "topic" and "comment" for their immediate constituents: the speaker announces a topic and then says something about it.

This explanation of topic and comment is quite suitable to describe Japanese syntax. English differs from Japanese in that, as Hockett (1958: 201) continues:

> In English and the familiar languages of Europe, topics are usually also subjects, and comments are predicates: so in *John ran away*. But this identification fails sometimes in formal English, and more generally in some non-European languages.

An example in colloquial English is "I will be only a few minutes." This construction is usually analyzed as [subject + predicate + adverbial]. It is difficult, however, for me to see the difference between this sentence and sentences such as "I will be a teacher." For in Japanese, it is quite grammatical to say "I am beefsteak" or "I am fried chicken" when orders are taken at a restaurant, or to say "I am five cents" when asked how much change you are to receive. Some native speakers of English said that they would accept, colloquially, expressions such as "Were you the soup?" when a waitress forgets which person ordered soup, or "I am the seventy-five cents" when a cashier forgets whose change he has counted. However, this is only peripheral in English, as the tie between the subject and the predicate is so strong that even when there is no need to give the subject, a "formal" subject is given, e.g. "It rains." Seen from this point of view, Japanese is very different, as the subject-predicate construction is only a part of the whole topic-comment construction. Thus, early Japanese scholars had developed grammars that were very different from those written later by Western scholars. One such early grammarian described Japanese sentences as consisting of a name (of a thing) and its attire (clothes), as in Figure 2.

The name or the topic is completely detached from the description of its

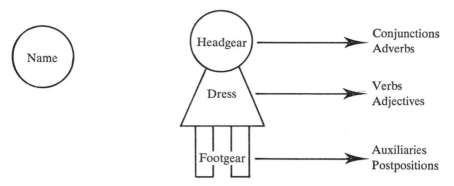

Figure 2.   Early grammatical analysis of Japanese sentences

attire, which consists of (1) the headgear, (2) the dress (or main body of the clothes), and (3) the footgear. A sentence is complete when the headgear, the body, and the footgear are provided. Nouns, which are given as the subject in the construction of Indo-European languages, may or may not be given with the body in Japanese. Thus, as many as three-fourths of all Japanese sentences have no subject.

In the Bible it is said that "In the beginning was the Word, and the Word was with God, and the Word was God." It is difficult to interpret what is meant by these Bible verses. In *Kojiki*, the oldest written document in Japan, it is said that Japan is a country that is blessed with the "Soul of Word," and hence the people need not express themselves in words. That is to say, Japanese have so many things in common that communication can be made without much verbal expression. We could say that Japan is like one family with all her people as the members. It is possible that Japan's isolated location, as well as the closed-door policy of the Tokugawa government for about three centuries preceding Commodore Perry's visit in 1853, enabled the nation to become so homogeneous that it could be considered a family. When it was said in *Kojiki* that Japan was a country where the people need not use too much verbal expression to communicate, we might say that the leaders even at that time (eighth century) might have had in mind such a peaceful country as their ideal. And that ideal has been more or less maintained throughout history until now. That ideal has been realized in the language of a homogeneous people. Subjectless sentences are simply a product of such homogeneity. It may suffice to mention that in writing a diary, a style of writing without using "I" each time, such as "Went to take a walk in the park," etc., is possible and feasible because it is obvious who the agent is. The one-fourth of all Japanese sentences that do have subjects or agents do so simply to avoid ambiguity. When understood under the circumstances or in the context, no subject/ agent is given overtly.

Haiku is a typical product of art that was born out of this homogeneous character of the Japanese people. They have so many things in common that they feel no need to use overt expressions in communication. It is the shortest type of poetry in the world, consisting of only, but precisely, seventeen syllables. It is sometimes compared with Greek epigrams or proverbs. However, there is a big difference between the two: while the latter snap at truth, the former expresses beauty. Thus, for example, if we say "time is money," we all understand the meaning instantly because time is precious in our culture. However, if in another culture money is precious but time is not, or vice versa, the meaning of "time is money" is not known so readily. Let me illustrate with a haiku example:

Old pond, and
    Sound made by a frog
        Jumping into water

What kind of associations do you make? Do you imagine any beautiful scenery in your mind's eye? Which comes to mind by the words "old pond" — clear water or brown water? Does not the word "frog" give you some comic feeling? These lines are a word-for-word translation of a famous haiku written by the most prominent figure in the history of haiku. With this particular haiku, he is said to have raised the status of haiku to an artistic means of expressing beauty. In order to understand how haiku can be the most aesthetic expression of beauty, one must know many things that are shared and hence implicitly understood by the people who produced haiku as a style of poetry. The communication must be clear and complete in only seventeen syllables. When something is spoken or read, 90 percent of the meaning is the listener's own association based on the 10 percent that is expressed verbally or overtly. And if his 90 percent is different from that of other people, he does not understand what is said, nor is he understood in that society.

There was a woman who wrote many haiku that expressed beauty through human feelings. One of her haiku is:

Bitter or not, I don't know
    But I pick up a persimmon
        For the first time in the season.

The translation sounds quite commonplace and prosaic. You may wonder why I said she was good at expressing beauty through human feelings. However, if I explain further that this haiku was written shortly before she married, as an expression of her uneasy feeling as to whether or not the marriage would be a happy one, you would then be able to appreciate the same uneasy feeling common to every young girl who is to marry soon. When I was watching Shakespeare's *Midsummer night's dream* on television, it suddenly occurred to me that the fantasy might have been Shakespeare's description of a similar feeling seen generally in young girls, which he expressed as a scene in Athens. Such human nature, such life, such feeling, underlie all phenomena of the world.

The same Japanese woman also wrote:

Looked at from standing position
    Or lying down, the mosquito net
        Is quite spacy.

Again, the translation is quite prosaic. Is she satisfied with the roomy mosquito net? On the contrary, this is her expression of loneliness after her husband's death. The third haiku by her that I should like to discuss is:

Dragonfly catching
    How far away
        Today?

In more complete sentences of English, this haiku is trying to say that she wonders how far away her boy has gone today for dragonfly catching. Boys are boys, you would say with this much information. However, this haiku was written after her son had died and she was sitting alone in a room on a hot summer day that reminded her of the previous summer when her boy was still running around after dragonflies. The surface calmness of the haiku, which may appear nonchalant, hides her deep sorrow and loneliness. When we reach the depths of human nature, we feel the beauty and truth common to all human beings. When we reach the depths, the harp-string of our soul is struck and resounds with universal compassion. And we share the feeling with the haiku writer regardless of the difference in time and space. A work of literature which strikes the harp-string of our soul is inevitably a masterpiece, because there is deep communication between the author and the reader — communication which is possible only by transcending the gap between language and reality.

In summary, language can be compared to the visible one-tenth of an iceberg, the other nine-tenths of which are submerged under water. The nine-tenths of the iceberg could be said to be the culture of the people who use the language. Literature, which uses language as its medium of expression, belongs to the one-tenth, the visible part. In appreciating literature, if you looked at the visible part only, you would be a *Titanic* in the ocean of literary appreciation. On the other hand, if the nine-tenths, the invisible part, is kept in mind, there would be a peaceful voyage ahead of you.

A problem left unsolved is how to "measure" the invisible part. Linguistic contribution is expected in analyzing language, which is the visible part, but linguists must not forget that language is a medium used to communicate not only thought but also feelings. They must not ignore the need to analyze connotation as well as denotation. Actually, there is no clear line to separate the visible one-tenth from the invisible nine-tenths. If the ocean is rough, then the part which is normally under water may momentarily emerge and become visible. In other words, language and culture are fused as denotation and connotation of words. Thus, when linguists try to analyze language *in toto*, they cannot avoid referring to the culture behind language. Analyzing language requires analyzing culture. In order to accomplish this goal, there must be a unified theory applicable to both language and culture.

REFERENCES

HOCKETT, CHARLES F.
1958   *A course in modern linguistics.* New York: Macmillan.

Ethnohermeneutics: On the Interpretation of Intended Meaning Among the Kpelle of Liberia

BERYL L. BELLMAN

The fact that an auditor is able to interpret a subjective meaning which is the same as that intended by some speaker points to the existence of a hermeneutical methodology. It should not be taken for granted, however, that the procedures which constitute that methodology are the same in every culture. This assertion is supported by the research of Cole and Gay (1967; Cole, Gay, et al. 1971) on Kpelle cognitive structures. They conducted a variety of learning experiments comparing the performance of Kpelle and American subjects and discovered significant differences between the two groups in the way they recalled events from memory, sorted objects, and solved problems. For instance, in one series of experiments they found that the Kpelle treated syllogisms as debatable arguments rather than as having single solutions. The following is an example of what they experienced:

EXPERIMENTER: Flumo and Yakpalo always drink cane juice [rum] together. Flumo is drinking cane juice. Is Yakpalo drinking cane juice?
SUBJECT: Flumo and Yakpalo drink cane juice together, but the time Flumo was drinking the first one Yakpalo was not there on that day.
EXPERIMENTER: But I told you that Flumo and Yakpalo always drink cane juice together. One day Flumo was drinking cane juice. Was Yakpalo drinking cane juice that day?
SUBJECT: The day Flumo was drinking the cane juice Yakpalo was not there that day.
EXPERIMENTER: What is the reason?
SUBJECT: The reason is that Yakpalo went on his farm on that day and Flumo remained in town on that day (Cole, Gay, et al. 1971:187–188).

The fieldwork on which this study is based was conducted over a period of eighteen months from 1967 to 1969 in the town of Sucromu, Liberia. The research was supported by a National Science Foundation grant.

Cole and his associates understood this and similar dialogues to mean that their subjects

... were not responding to the logical relations contained in the verbal problem. Rather they were (or seem to have been) responding to conventional situations in which their past experience dictated the answer. ... In short, it appears that the particular verbal context and content dictate the response rather than the arbitrarily imposed relations among the elements in the problem (1971: 188).

This procedure for evaluating verbal problems obtains not only in the artificial situation of the experimenter-subject catechetical interaction, but also in the most mundane events of everyday life. That is, the Kpelle approach problems as if their solutions were always problematic and reflexive to the social structure of the interaction setting where it was presented. In this study we will examine this practice and explicate several of its features. Because our concern is with the interpretative techniques particular to Kpelle speakers, these descriptions are referred to as a kind of ethnohermeneutics.

THE LOCATION OF MEANING IN RIDDLES

Often the Kpelle, either for amusement or in the context of a palaver, pose riddles which, according to Cole and Gay (1967), is done in order to invoke a cultural rule. The specific cultural rule communicated, however, is not solely the property of the riddle as extracted from its appearance in any localized occasion of talk. Instead, it is as much a feature of the particular meaning context provided by the interaction setting where it was produced. This is evident in the following riddle which I recorded as told by Torkalong, the *Zo* 'shaman-leader' of the Gbo Gbling secret society. Torkalong told the riddle after having first presented a story-like description of how he acquired his *Zo* or shamanistic powers. I shall first present the riddle and then the description to show how both are complementary in function and contain the same intended message. More specifically, we will show how the riddle provides a key for understanding the intended meaning of the story account.[1]

There was once an orphan (*tingong*) that did something that people still argue over. You know something that will always bring an argument out. The orphan was in the bush. There was an old kitchen there. It was in the high bush (*law kene*) where the kitchen was built. His hair grew until it even

[1]   The accounts used in this paper were tape recorded and later translated by two Kpelle informants and myself. The translations are in Liberian English.

went into his mouth. There was a town chief who was very rich. He built a fence in the center of the town and put a lot of kola nut *kinjas* 'baskets' inside of it. He said that if anyone eats any of my kolas that is the end of his life. Anything he said he must do it. A possum came and stole one of the *kinjas*. The possum dropped kola nuts until he was far off in the bush. He met this boy lying down and cut one of the kolas into pieces and put it into the boy's hand while he was asleep. In the morning the people looked at the *kinja* and saw all the kola just lying on the ground. When they saw the kola like that they said to blow a horn.[2] They followed the kola that was scattered about in the bush. The chief said that the thing that took this kola and did this to it you follow and get it. He told the people to kill whatever they found at the end of the kola trail. The people walked until they met up with the young boy who was lying down sleeping. They saw the kola lying in his hand. They tied him up and said let's go. They asked, you are the one who has been stealing the chief's kola? They brought the boy to town and told the chief that this is the boy that stole the nuts. He is the one that always comes in the night to get the kola nuts and carry it away. When we saw him we saw a piece of kola nut lying in his hand. Here is the kola. The chief said to bring him to the center of the town as I must kill him. There was an old lady who told the chief to let the boy mind her rice before killing him. The chief agreed. The boy sat by the rice. When the rice got dry the old lady beat it. The old lady gave the boy the *mawlang nying* 'the last of the beaten rice'. The old lady took the rice and cooked it and gave it to him. When the boy was ready to eat the rice a cat told him to bring the rice and he would save him. He gave it to the cat. The cat brought one rat and gave it to the boy. The boy said, oh the cat told me to give him my rice to save me and he brings a rat to me. At that time a black snake (*tumo*) came. The snake swallowed the rat and told the boy not to be afraid. The snake told the boy to put his hand in his throat (not say anything). The snake told the boy that the chief's head wife who never stepped out before, I will make her take a bucket and go for water, but when she goes I am going to bite her and she will die. It will be something serious in the town and they will even forget about you. He said that if I kill the woman this is the medicine that you will cure her with. If you cure the woman with this medicine the whole town will be yours. When they finished talking, all that the chief's wife said, oh I have been in the fence a long time let me do something outside today. So let me take a bucket and go to the waterside and get some water. They told the woman to stay but she said no. Half of the town even went along with her to the stream. On the way she was the only person that the snake bit and she died on the spot. It was something big. They brought the woman in town and when it was time to bury her the boy stood up and said, as for me I am already dead but I don't like how this woman died like that so you leave her and I will cure her. When he said it more people said to leave. There was the old lady who said a person like that who talks, just don't tell him to go away. Let him come. One other old lady said the same thing. When

---

[2] Horns are blown for major events such as warfare, serious crimes, taxation, and the like.

he came he made medicine one time and the woman got up. The chief was very happy and gave half the town to the boy. They cut his hair and dressed him. They even emptied a whole house for him to live in special. The cat, the rat, the snake, and the old lady who is the main person who made this boy become a man today?

After Torkalong finished telling the riddle a short debate followed:

A: I say it was the old lady. The reason why I say it is the old lady . . .
B: You and I will argue.
A: If the old lady didn't go to the chief and ask him to let the boy mind her rice he couldn't have had the chance to become rich today.
B: What you say is the truth. But the end of her doing was to cook the rice and give it to the boy, but what about the cat that ate the rice and brought the rat?
A: Those are just helpers (*kpong ma kabila*). You only tell them thanks.
B: The person who showed him the medicine to cure the woman and the person that laid the kola in his hand when he was sleeping who would you say gave the most help?
A: If it was not for the old lady all these things couldn't give the boy help but through the lady they gave the boy help.
B: This is something that you have to argue over for a long time.
A: If the old lady didn't start it no one could bring medicine.
B: Yes the old lady started it good but she didn't have any medicine.
A: You that talked this story who do you think gave the most help?
TORKALONG: Oh, me? As for me I told the story, but what I see so far is that you are right it was the old lady that gave the help.

Torkalong began the debate by dichotomizing the riddle events or themes at the point in the story where the boy was first helped. In so doing he established the presence of two groups or sets of categories: (1) those-who-made-this-boy-become-a-man-today, and (2) those who-caused-trouble. Torkalong introduced the member categories belonging to the first set in his original question — "The cat, the rat, the snake, the old lady, who made this boy become a man today?" The first respondent, A, immediately focused on the set division by positing the old woman as the central figure and person responsible for the boy's good fortune. B countered by raising the question regarding the other members of that category set. This led to A's reaffirmation of the woman's primary position through his assertion that the other members of the set were "just helpers." This part of the dialogue, consequently, had the result of both positing the thematic division in the riddle and presenting the rank order of the constituent members of the category set those-who-helped. It is my contention that this outcome was not necessarily accidental. Instead it can be argued that B was not so much debating with A as he was assisting Torkalong in explicating the intended meaning of his riddle and story account of how he acquired his *Zo* powers.

Each time that B asked A a question he presented the opposite to what A said rather than offering an alternative interpretation of the problem. Thus, when B asked, "What about the cat that ate the rice and brought the rat?" he was asking for an explication of A's choice rather than advocating any of the other member categories of the set. A answered by stating that the others were "just helpers." B then immediately changed the topic of the debate from a discussion of the member categories of the set those-who-helped, to a question asking for the rationale of the set divisions in the riddle. He did this by counterposing the woman to "the person that laid the kola in his hand when he was sleeping. . ." (i.e. the possum). A responded by once again stating that the woman was the cause of the boy's obtaining help. At that B reintroduced the category set those-who-helped and raised the question of the order of importance within it.

The necessity of establishing the "main person who made this boy a man today" is consistent with the general Kpelle practice of having to discover the structural arrangement of personnel in all social settings. As I described in another study (Bellman 1975), the Kpelle recognize a variety of social domains or orders of reality (*meni*), each having its own social organization and structure. These orders pertain to and are derived from the various corporate groupings in the community, whether they be ad hoc or enduring over an extended period of time. Examples of such orders are the numerous secret societies, the families or patrilineages (*kala*), the patrilocal compounds (*koli*), farming cooperatives (*kuu*), government (*kwii*) matters, medicine preparations and uses (*sale*), funerals (*nuu saa*), and the like. Whenever a Kpelle speaker enters into an ongoing social interaction he must ascertain which particular order of reality obtains as the organizational basis for that setting. This is necessary because it is in the context of an order of social reality that the speaker decides on his right to talk and on his speaking position relative to the other members present. If he should incorrectly assess his speaking prerogative in the setting he can be held accountable for violating a societal law (i.e. that pertaining to secrecy), or be seen as challenging his consociates' status position in that order and thus be open to a test of power, either through the making of medicines or by his ability to muster adequate political (and medicine) support from others with power.

The importance of this practice to the present discussion is that the location of status or speaking positions provides incoming members to ongoing social interactions with appropriate situational cues for the discovery of the setting's organizational order of reality. This is because the arrangement of speaking prerogatives shifts from one order of reality to another. In this way a speaker may in one situation be able to talk openly while in another, even with the same personages in attendance, he may have to remain silent or speak with great discretion. Consequently, the decision as to "who is the main person who made this boy become a man today" was relevant to the discovery of which order of reality or *meni* the "boy's obtaining help" was a feature of. This is particularly crucial when considering the conversational context of the setting where the riddle was told, viz. Torkalong's presentation of how he acquired his shamanistic powers.

Before presenting that account mention must first be made of the relationship of the personages in that setting to one another. Torkalong was B's wife's brother *'molo'*. This relationship normatively is one whereby the sister's husband shows special respect for the wife's brother.[3] In the case of Torkalong and B the relationship was the basis for a close mutual dependence and friendship. Torkalong had been blind since early childhood. Even though he was very capable and enjoyed demonstrating his ability to work well at tasks which sighted persons usually engage in[4] his *molo* usually accompanied and helped him. Consequently, B was Torkalong's assistant both in his personal life and in his *Zo* work. It was in this latter role that he participated in the riddle debate.

Torkalong presented his riddle in the context of a larger discussion about how he acquired his *Zo* powers. His riddle, as is shown below, was a feature of that description and functioned to provide his listeners with a key to correctly interpret the intended meaning of the following story account.

The reason why is the way my mother got pregnant. My mother's husband (*nee waw surong*) did not like me. When my mother gave birth they all were girls. So she said I can just give birth to so so girls, in the future it will be hard so let me love to see if I can give birth to a boy child. She went and loved one of the family men.[5] So her husband said oh the pregnancy that my wife is in I don't know anything about it. I know the pregnancy is for someone else, so if she happens to give birth to a boy child

[3]   This relationship offers an effective means for cooperative labor on the wife's brother's farms, house building, and the like.

[4]   Torkalong was so capable that he was able to successfully operate a rice farm, have a rum distillery, and cut palm nuts. The town elders finally restricted the latter activity since they said that his climbing palm trees was too dangerous.

[5]   Torkalong's mother was able to do this because a wife is legally permitted to have sexual intercourse with any member of her husband's patrilineage. The husband, therefore, had no reason to reject his wife's pregnancy.

that boy child will be the head of all the children in the future. I will not agree for the next man's child to rule my own children. At that time it was almost time for my mother to deliver. They went to cut the rice and after cutting it they packed it. The sun rose high so he called my mother and told her to sit down and called one of my small sisters (*sawbolo long pene*) to sit also. When he called both of them to sit he went and sat on a big stone and said my mother that died if you are in heaven (*Xala taa* 'God's town') we will be three coming there today. He sharpened his knife and stood it right beside the rock, he took his spear and stood it by the rock. He said that the name of the knife is jumping knife (*surong da bili*), the name of the spear is you who saw it (*yai naakaa*). So he took a walk to the waterside to get some vine (*pali* — which is also used to make sacrifice for the protection of the town). He told my sister to go because he didn't want her to die that day in the same way. The little sister (*sawbolo long*) went straight to the head of our old people (*kung nuua polo*) and they came right away. They took my mother and carried her in town from the farm. That was the time I came on earth as a boy child. There was a big palaver when I started to walk.[6] The man said oh what I said a long time ago if I let this boy walk he will still rule my children because I never borne a boy child, and this is another man's child borne by my wife so I don't want him to rule. He is the one who made witch on me.[7] They set medicine for him and the medicine caught him. I tried and tried until I knew myself only my mother held me by my hand as we walked about the town. She suffered for me until it was once God started helping me and I started walking by myself. So it was like that until one time I went to bed and in my dream I said oh who will I be in this world I am like this. So one of my brains told me to take things easy.[8] Once the Iron Society (*Gbo Gbling*)[9] came here and I joined it. I joined it on Zorzor market day (Thursday). I went to bed again and the society brought medicine to me. The medicine said oh I have come here to help you. I asked how. It said you especially I have come to you to give you this help which is to give you medicines so that if anyone is sick you can make medicine for that person to get well. From that time anytime I go into a dream I must see medicines. One day the *faa sale* 'a society oracle possession medicine' itself came to me. They said oh why should the *faa sale* go to him he is not a *Zo*. They called a lot of *Zos*.

[6] It is a very important event when a child learns to walk as it marks the end of the mother's postpartum taboo. It essentially establishes the child as a living member of the community. Hence, it was necessary for Torkalong's father to act at that time if he wanted to stop his unwanted son from eventually becoming the head of his family.

[7] "Making witch" (*wulu kpete*) means either the making of bad medicines or attacking another in dreams. The Kpelle maintain that they can kill someone by directing their own spirit to the other's house while both are asleep. They then can attack their enemy and cause his death. Both ways of making witch can be stopped by appropriate counter medicines.

[8] The Kpelle believe that each person has two brains (*lii*). One is active while a person is awake, and the other when he is asleep.

[9] The Gbo Gbling society has two names: (1) the Gbo Gbling, and (2) the Iron Society or *Kawli Sale*. The latter is the popular name, while the former is used mostly by the members.

My mother paid all the expenses. When that medicine was coming to me I slept in the bush for four days and never knew how to make the medicine. On the fifth day I just saw myself in town. From that time up to this I thank God (*Xala*) he was the cause of me getting all that. If anyone is sick, if a country man can make medicine for that person,[10] they never brought anyone to me and I failed. From that time until now if anyone asks me for medicine and I don't have it I just go to bed and ask God to give it to me and he gives it to me. That is why if I am doing anything today people like me. My mother is dead. I don't depend on anyone but God.

Both the riddle and Torkalong's story account of how he acquired his shamanistic powers were dichotomized into two component themes: (1) those events which were descriptive of troubles and (2) those which led to help and eventually to status and powers. The first theme was represented in the riddle by the category set called those-who-caused-the-boy-trouble, while in the story account it was found in those events telling of Torkalong's father's malicious behavior (rejecting his son and then causing his blindness). The second theme was represented in the riddle by the category set called those-who-made-this-boy-a-man-today, and in the story by those events that followed God's helping Torkalong learn how to walk by himself (his joining the Gbo Gbling society, the medicine spirit appearing to him in his dream, the *faa sale* speaking to him, and his continued relationship with his dream spirit as an ongoing source of new knowledge). The two accounts, therefore, expressed the same structural relationship of trouble and help. In the story, the relationship was between the father's actions and God's help; in the riddle, the relationship was between the possum's actions and the woman's help. That is, Torkalong's father's behavior was to God's help in his account what the possum's actions were to the old woman's help in the riddle.

Torkalong was thus able through the telling of his riddle to posit the above relationship between positive and negative events and explicate the member categories of the former (the set of those-who-gave-help). In other words, by establishing in the riddle who was the main person responsible in that set he provided the method for locating the particular order of reality or *meni* that governed his obtaining *Zo* powers. Thus, as God was in the same structural position as the old lady in the riddle, He was both responsible for and the source of his powers.

---

[10]   Those illnesses which are the result of someone's having violated the law of some medicine, eaten a taboo food, or committed incest are usually seen as not curable by traditional means. An example of such a malady is elephantiasis of the penis which is caused by a man's coming too close to the women's (Sande) special medicines.

The above is especially significant in that there was an alternate version of how Torkalong became the *Zo* of the Gbo Gbling secret society. I learned of this one afternoon when I was with Torkalong, his *molo*, and another close friend who was also a member of the society. As we were sitting, a man whom I had not seen before stopped and sat down beside us. Torkalong immediately introduced him to me as his older brother *(nia)*. The man then explained that he was actually responsible for Torkalong becoming the *Zo* of the town's Gbo Gbling society. He claimed that he was originally the *Zo,* but decided to teach his younger brother, Torkalong, because he wanted him to have a way of making a living because he was blind. Torkalong made no comment after his *nia* made his speech. I felt it was then inopportune to point out the inconsistencies in what Torkalong had previously told me. When later I asked the others who were present they advised that I not ask Torkalong about his brother, and explained that it was true his *nia* was a Gbo Gbling *Zo* but was currently living in another town some twenty miles away.

When Torkalong presented his story and riddle he was able to communicate that God was responsible for and the source of his powers. In so doing he placed the Gbo Gbling society in the same position as the cat, rat, and snake in the riddle, viz. as the "just helpers." In other words, because he was able to show that God was responsible ("the main person who made the boy a man today" position in the riddle) he established that the role of Gbo Gbling *Zo* was secondary and had only a tangential ("just helpers") relationship to his abilities. Consequently, he presented himself as a *Zo* under *Xala meni* rather than as Gbo Gbling *meni.*

This fact has importance in the context of the Kpelle folk taxonomy for kinds of *Zo* and sources of shamanistic power. I described in another study (Bellman 1975) that the Kpelle essentially recognize three different kinds of *Zo*: (1) the Poro and Sande leaders, (2) persons who have great powers outside the Poro/Sande lineage, and (3) those who purchase the "head of a medicine" *(ngung sale)* belonging to some secret medicine society.

Poro *Zo* are the priest-leaders of the men's secret society. All men are required to join the society. They do this by being captured by a masked dancer or devil *(ngamu)*, taken into the forest to live in an all male age-set community for an extended period of time (traditionally four years, but under government regulation today this period is no longer than a year and a half), washed and scarred with special protection medicines, instructed in the laws of the town's medicines, and then reintroduced to the community by special scarification ceremonies. The woman's society, the Sande, is equivalent to the Poro except the traditional bush school period is for three years. The Poro and Sande are, during their periods of bush school, responsible for the sacred ruling structure of the town. Whenever a major crime is committed (which is defined as a transgression of the town's special medicines) the society functions as both a court and punishing agent. The secular ruling structure as represented by the town chief, his council of elders, and the various compound chiefs then publicly validate the decisions and acts of the Poro and Sande.[11]

In addition to upholding the town's major laws the Poro functions to adjudicate disputes between towns and to constitute the military structure of the community. The leaders of the society are all members of the same patrilineage and reside in the same patrilocal compound. Because the Poro (and for the women, the Sande) is the main society, all other Zo of the various societies must recognize it as an absolute authority. Consequently, the Poro Zo are greatly respected and must be obeyed.

The second category of persons are those with power outside the Poro caste or patrilineage. They are often referred to as "Zo for themselves" as they practice their abilities only for the benefit of their family and themselves. If one should decide, however, to practice his curing (and killing) abilities on those outside his family he will usually announce his willingness by purchasing the head of a medicine belonging to a secret medicine society (the third category of Zo). The head of a medicine or ngung sale is an object which contains a small portion of all the leaves constituting a society's repertoire of medicines. According to several of my Zo informants actually anyone can make such a purchase. Those that do so, however, must possess other medicines obtained either by right of birth or through a dream. This is because the other Zo in the town will test the purchaser by turning their offensive medicines against him to see if he has sufficient protective powers to ward them off. If he survives that test he is recognized as powerful enough to operate a society in the town. It is, however, not necessary for a purchaser to become the leader of a society as he may have bought the medicine solely for his own benefit and protection. In such a case he will keep secret that he owns the ngung sale, except to close friends and family.

Concomitant with kinds of Zo, the Kpelle differentiate between medicines by the way in which they are obtained. They recognize three dif-

---

[11]   The sacred and secular ruling structures discussed here closely resemble Mano social organization as described by Harley (1941).

ferent acquisition techniques: (1) by being "born with the brain" or
inherited knowledge *(kasheng),* (2) learning medicines from a spirit
in one's dreams, and (3) direct purchase, either of an individual medicine or by buying the *ngung sale* of a society. Either the first or second
is a prerequisite for publicly doing the third. Both are seen as powers
obtained under *Xala meni* and are defined as being stronger than any
medicine learned from a living person. The purchase of a head of some
medicine is normally a social or town matter *(taa meni)* because the
purchase is primarily done as a licence to practice the business of being a *Zo,* i.e. having paying patients and clients. It was for this latter reason that the town elders were astonished when the *faa sale* 'spirit possession medicine' of the Gbo Gbling spoke directly with Torkalong.
Such an occurrence only happens to the societal *Zo* or one of his special apprentices. According to Torkalong's account, when that occurred he was only a mundane member of the society. Thus, when the
medicine spirit spoke publicly to him it chose him to be a *Zo* before he
purchased the head of the medicine. Torkalong claims, through the interpretative technique presented in his riddle, that the spirit was obey-
ing God. Hence, his becoming a *Zo* in the society was a feature of *Xala
meni.*

SUMMARY

Torkalong presented his riddle to provide a key to understand his story
account of how he became a *Zo.* Both the story and the riddle made
use of the same essential "cultural rule" or theme, viz. that the first
person who initiates a series of actions is responsible for subsequent actions. Torkalong demonstrated this by pointing to a Kpelle speaker's
practice of locating an ongoing *meni* 'order of social reality' through
the assessment of the speaking prerogatives and status positions within a given interactional setting. In the debate following the riddle, Torkalong's *molo,* B, assisted him in showing this by asking questions of
the first respondent, A, which did not dispute the latter's analysis but
instead led to its explication. By presenting his account in this way Torkalong communicated that his becoming a *Zo* extended beyond the domain of Gbo Gbling society activity and instead was part of *Xala meni*
'God's business'.

The communication of information through indirect expressions, par-
ables, riddles, and story accounts is a common feature of Kpelle rhetoric. This study offered a description of some of the ways Kpelle audi-

tors locate their intended meanings. Both the story account and the riddle were fictitious even though the former may have contained "real" events. What is important in understanding them is not the truth of the events discussed, but rather that the meaning of both narratives is found through the analysis of the structure of their respective presentations. The "cultural rule" that Torkalong made use of in telling his riddle offered the key to making those analyses. This amends Cole and Gay's statement that such talk communicates rules. Instead, the cultural rules are used as mechanisms for the presentation of intended meanings. The relation between rule and meaning, however, is situationally determined since the former is given as a means for locating the latter within a particular meaning context.

REFERENCES

BELLMAN, BERYL L.
  1975   *Village of curers and assassins: on the production of Fala Kpelle cosmological categories.* The Hague: Mouton.
COLE, MICHAEL, J. GAY
  1967   *The new mathematics and an old culture.* New York: Holt, Rinehart and Winston.
COLE, MICHAEL, J. GAY, J. GLICK, D. SHARP
  1971   *The cultural context of learning and thinking.* New York: Basic Books.
HARLEY, GEORGE
  1941   *Notes on the Poro in Liberia.* Cambridge, Massachusetts: Harvard University Press.

Bodily Symbolism in Hindu Ashrams and the Replication of Social Experience

FRANCES N. FERGUSON

Activated by Mary Douglas' recent book *Natural symbols: explorations in cosmology* (1970), in this paper I shall give consideration to the human body as a symbol, the replication of social experience, in the context of the *ashram*, an institution of perhaps 2,700 years' standing in India (Ghurye 1953: 250–266).

Social systems, and especially social experience, generate symbols, says Douglas, the most important and meaningful being bodily symbols. For Douglas, the analysis of symbols need not be confined to patterned relationships in a particular culture group. She is concerned with a formula for classifying human relationships universally.

How to classify relations universally? Douglas does it by group and grid — GROUP being the experience of a bounded universe; GRID being rules which relate one person to another on an ego-centered basis. Conceptualizing group and grid as X and Y axes respectively in a rectangular coordinate system, she attempts to characterize the four quadrants accordingly and to fit selected cultures into the quadrants to illustrate her thesis.

Use of the human body as a symbol, according to Douglas, derives essentially from social relations and the drive to consonance in all layers of experience. The quadrant having the highest positive values for both group and grid is, of course, the first quadrant (the quadrant on the upper right). Eliminating a deprivation-compensation hypothesis, Douglas suggests that religious forms as well as social forms are

Fieldwork in India was supported by a pre-doctoral research fellowship from the National Institute of Mental Health and sponsored by the University of North Carolina Department of Anthropology, 1961–1962.

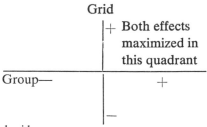

Figure 1.   Group and grid

generated in the same dimension. Her "replication hypothesis" allows for the power of symbols generated in a particular social set-up to control it as well — hence religious symbols are not merely a projection of social life or of psychological needs.

Along with other anthropologists, Douglas considers that the human body is treated as an image of society. Bodily control is an expression of social control. In societies where group is high and grid low, says Douglas, bodily symbols are present, but emphasis is on boundaries, guarding body orifices, and witch hunting. In such societies articulated roles are lacking. In contrast, societies with high grid and low group have rules for reciprocal transactions but no group loyalties and little or no symbolism associated with the human body. In the latter type (societies high in grid and low in group) one finds lack of communication and anti-ritualism. Regarding Western society as belonging to the latter type, Douglas finds in the results of a long secular trend in the West an absence of sensitivity to condensed symbols, a preoccupation with lack of meaning, and an absence of articulation in the depths of the past. Most salutary, she implies, is the situation where both grid and group have plus values — in short, where there are rules governing individual relationships and delineating roles in the larger context of a powerful social identity.

While one may not subscribe to every characteristic which Douglas assigns to the types which comprise her schema, nor agree with her particular assignment of specific cultures to these types, her message is a forceful one and worthy of consideration. Douglas believes that the decline of the use of natural symbols is accompanied by impoverishment of the human spirit, as well as loss of the ability to communicate readily and meaningfully (Douglas 1970).

The present paper is not intended as an examination and testing of Mary Douglas' theory. It merely presents an institution which fits rather spectacularly into Douglas' category of high group (strong group identity) and high grid (complex rules for relating one person to another on an ego-centered basis), with a correspondingly high degree of bodily symbolism.

Let us consider an institution (viable today), which, I believe, is a representative part of traditional Hindu India, as an example of high group and grid. Among large nations, India is remarkable for its linkage between social and symbolic life. Group identity (Douglas' "group"), and rules for inter-relating (Douglas' "grid"), are both prominent. Whether identification with India as a nation is as strong for Hindus as identification with smaller groups such as sub-caste and extended family is questionable. However, in Hindu India one can observe certain general principles, fundamental ideas, or attitudes which give cohesion to rules which vary from one group to another. Therefore, I shall take the risk of speaking of "Hindu society" (Dubois 1906; Srinivas 1952; Basham 1954; Cohn 1955; Marriott 1955; Singer 1959, 1961; Dumont 1970).

However, it would be rash to attempt to approach the problem of grid and group on so large a scope. For this reason, let us look at only PART of Hindu society — an institution which is nonetheless interrelated with Hinduism throughout India. This part is the network of *ashrams* which extend over rural and urban India.

The *ashram* has persisted in India for over two thousand years. Its prototype may have been the forest household of a teacher (and sometimes his wife) (Ghurye 1953: 230, 250–266; Dubois 1906), who accepted pupils seeking wisdom and bringing with them gifts and services. The master-disciple *(guru-chela)* relationship with its nexus in the household is mentioned repeatedly in the Upanishads.[1] The Upanishads tell us that a person without a teacher is like one who is blindfolded (Radhakrishnan 1953: 17, 19, 386–387, 411–415; Raghavan 1956: 503–514; Vidyarthi 1961: 66–71; Ghurye 1953: 4, 20, 30, 51, 52).

The hundreds of *ashrams*, large and small, scattered throughout India, comprise a network of communication and interaction among householders rich and poor, ascetics, politicians, prominent statesmen, wealthy businessmen, and "saints" — those traditional figures not remote in place and time, but present today in the consciousness and active life of India. Gandhi was regarded as a saint and was closely associated with *ashrams* (Kapur 1963: 39). Nehru periodically visited at least one *ashram* of which I know, to pay homage to a saint, as does Indira Gandhi today. A past president of India, Rajendra Prasad, retired to an *ashram*. The teachings from *ashram* life (basically Upani-

---

[1] The Upanishads represent the period 800–300 B.C. and present the highest Vedic philosophy.

shadic and hence Vedic teachings) are found in political addresses today. While some modern "educated" Hindus scoff at *ashrams*, there
are few who are not familiar with the principles taught in *ashrams*, or
who do not have some relative closely associated with *ashrams*.

Ashrams serve a great many functions and offer a diversity of roles.
In spite of the elaboration of some *ashrams*, with their development of
hospitals and other charitable and educational endeavors, and their
many centers, *ashrams* tend to remain homely, simple and intimate —
centers of (often delightfully witty) discourse and dialectic and, concomitantly, of instrumental behavior. Most apparent in this instrumental
behavior is the use of the body as a symbol. In most *ashrams*, bodily
symbolism is very much a part of daily life. In some of them, prayers
and ritualistic offerings are regularly made to deities in various forms,
with the body concept a conspicuous part of this worship. Most often
there will be at least one person in an *ashram* who is in authority and
regarded as a *guru* 'teacher', highly respected and to whom homage is
offered. If the *ashram* leader happens to be a person who is recognized
as a saint, either locally or throughout India, the instrumental use of
the body as a symbol is most apparent. The saint's body represents God
and the entire world, as well as mother, father, child, as one may desire.
Anything associated with the body of the saint, with its inherent qualities, is a powerful "condensed symbol." The attitude toward the saint
is not merely one of respect and pious regard. It is believed that one
GETS something from the saint. What one gets may range from blessing,
solution of a trivial problem, employment, health, wealth, success in
examination, all the way to "God-realization," that state celebrated in
the Upanishads and referred to as "knowing Brahman" (ultimate
reality) — the desirability of which, one hears saints say, is their sole
message to mankind.

The principles and fundamental ideas which, I believe, are common
to *ashrams* and to Hindu India and generally understood by all classes
are (1) special use and beliefs with regard to the human body as a
symbol; and (2) participation in hierarchical relationships. Let us turn
to one *ashram* to examine this symbolic use of the body and, also, the
concept of hierarchy in daily life. While there are many variants of
ashrams, those I visited (eighteen located throughout India and affiliated with various sects) had certain fundamental ideas and identities in
common.

The *ashram* I shall use as an example was in itself a society characterized by group — a sense of group identity coalescing around the
living body of a man regarded as a saint. Grid — rules and underlying

dicta governing behavior among *ashram* personnel and visitors were dictated by the saint and in the main resembled rules and dicta in *ashrams* throughout India. Many persons who visited this *ashram* also visited *ashrams* hundreds of miles away. Dignitaries from other *ashrams* paid visits to this *ashram*. Residents and visitors from many *ashrams* were often known to each other, and yet they represented various levels of status and economic condition. Indian society has been characterized as hierarchical by many students of Indian life (Sinha 1959; Dumont 1970). I shall not enter into the arena of discussion over the caste concept, although it can be remarked in passing that in the Vedas (circa 1,500 B.C.) mention is made of division in terms of bodily symbolism: "brahmin was his mouth, his two arms were made the rajanya (warrior), his two thighs the vaisya (trader and agriculturist), from his feet the sudra (servile class) were born" (Radhakrishnan and Moore 1957: 31). Neither will I linger over the extended family which in those Hindu areas that are patrilineal constitutes a hierarchical structure symbolized by grown children touching the feet of their parents. The *ashram* itself can constitute a reflection of the larger Hindu society — admittedly the more traditional sector but yet having representatives from modern life also and indeed acting not only as a custodian of the traditional but also as a center for modernization of values in the ancient context (e.g. Gandhi's *ashram*, for one; also Vinoba Bhave and predecessors).

Let us examine some of the beliefs about the body of the person in India who is regarded as a saint, or "realized soul," and who in this instance (and in many cases) heads an *ashram*.

At the beginning he "took *sannyas*" — that is to say, he adopted the *gerrua* 'red ochre, actually orange, cloth garment' which symbolizes the flames of the funeral pyre. The person taking *sannyas* may practice austerities — sometimes called *tapas* 'the generation of heat through sacrifice', which may be of many kinds. By *tapas* — and it can also come about through devotion, or by other practices — the body of the saint has become pure. Because the body of the saint is pure (and MIND is included in the body concept here), the saint's body becomes a vehicle for the concentration of spiritual energy which is believed to pervade (and constitute) the universe. Hence persons who "have *darshan* of" 'sight of, or proximity to' the saint are in a position to receive maximum benefits through the saint's body.

When one enters the abode of a Hindu saint, one discards shoes or sandals. Feet in India have a connotation of impurity. Properly, one does not even touch one's sandals when removing or putting them on.

But feet have a wealth of meaning as a condensed symbol. Upon approaching a saint, one touches his feet, just as a Hindu son or daughter may touch the feet of a parent, or a student (in the privacy of the home today) may touch the feet of his teacher. For the European, this gesture may suggest submissiveness. It does indeed symbolize abasement, but at the same time it represents a transmission of benefits from the superior to the inferior. There is also the belief that this is a two-way street. Some saints will not allow their feet to be touched because the ills of the person touching them are believed to be transmitted,[2] one is told. Illnesses of saints are attributed to the touch of a diseased person.

The dust of the saint's feet may be placed upon one's brow — "lower than the dust . . ." Since for those who aspire to holiness, humility is a primary virtue, in India this gesture of touching the feet does not (ideally) represent grovelling.[3]

The feet of a saint are often referred to as his (or her) "lotus feet." Songs are composed and sung about the lotus feet of a saint. This powerful reversal of attitude in the matter of feet is seen most vividly in the value placed on *tirtha,* or water in which the saint's feet have been washed.

On a special occasion, clear water is ceremoniously poured over the saint's feet into a receptacle, sometimes a silver bowl. The disciples of the saint are then offered the water one by one in a teaspoon. *Tirtha* is believed to cure all bodily, including mental, ills. Some Hindus keep a bottle of *tirtha* with them during the year for its therapeutic qualities. *Tirtha* from the feet of a saint is very precious.

A garment which the saint has worn is highly coveted by his followers. Spiritual power resides in anything he or she has possessed. Passed on to another, the spiritual power is also passed on. Followers allowed to massage the saint's legs at the end of the day (a custom in some Indian households, where a daughter-in-law may massage the legs of the mother) consider themselves lucky indeed. Not only when the saint is awake but also when he is asleep, persons consider themselves fortunate to be in his proximity because of the spiritual energy which resides in his body and pervades the area. When the saint at the *ashram* of which I speak (and of which I have given an account of things generally true of *ashrams*) died, he was cremated and some of

[2].   An interesting parallel is found in the New Testament. When a sick woman touched the garments of Jesus, he "knew in himself that virtue had gone out of him, turned him about in the press, and said Who touched my clothes?" Mark 5 : 30.
[3]   Jesus Christ washed the feet of his disciples as an example to them. John 13 : 1–16.

his ashes and small particles of bone were placed in lockets. To have one of these lockets was a great privilege, for in the ashes of the saint the spiritual energy vested in his body still lingers. To this day this energy is believed to linger strongly in the proximity of the *ashram* where the saint's ashes are deposited. This fundamental belief that spiritual energy lingers in the presence of the remains of a saint's body is widespread in India (and, of course, is not confined to India alone).

One sees, then, in the *ashram* situation, a strong emphasis on the body as symbol. It would be difficult to find a more striking example of the use of bodily symbolism. According to Douglas, where bodily symbolism is strong, it is a replication of a social system with a strong sense of group identity. Is there in the *ashram* also, as Mary Douglas would predict, a strong sense of GROUP? While visiting the *ashram*, people are regarded as (and tend to become, temporarily at least) "devotees." This attitude of devotion often brings people back year after year — or so they say — and fosters a sense of identity not only with the members of the *ashram* household, but also with all those who at any time have visited the *ashram*, and particularly with those who visit it regularly. It is not unusual to hear a Hindu say, "I am a devotee of his (or hers) and such-and-such a person is also a devotee" — the implication being that this is a group with which one identifies. Furthermore, this identity with an *ashram* ramifies out into identity with other far-flung *ashrams*, as well as with Hinduism in general. The identity is not necessarily a simple thing (although it can be). Identity at this *ashram* was variously characterized by (1) membership in a particular sub-caste; (2) loyalty to a certain deity (manifestation of Vishnu);[4] (3) being an ardent devotee of the saint; (4) belonging to any Hindu sect; or (5) being an ardent devotee of any saint. Actually (3) can override them all. While identity for all *ashram*-ites is not exactly the same, they share a common identity in being devotees or disciples of the saint, or, if there is no saint in the *ashram*, devotees of a saint somewhere in India, or of a saint-like deity of some sort.[5] Louis Dumont writes, "Now, what one is in the habit of calling Indian thought is for the very great part the thought of the Sannyasi [ascetic] . . ." (1970).

---

[4] In another *ashram* one might find Shiva most prominent, or local deities, perhaps.

[5] Even the saint who is believed to have achieved non-attachment at an earlier period is said to have had a teacher (*guru*) and to have paid his respects to saints in *ashrams*. The brevity of this paper necessitates over-simplification. Devotion is only one of the paths followed by disciples in India. However, all disciples traditionally pay homage to their teacher, particularly if he is regarded as a saint.

While one by no means suggests that all of Hindu India has renounced personal desires in favor of "knowing Brahman," or even that the majority of the population has even heard of the concept, it was my impression that the idea of holiness or spiritual purity, and its contagious and instrumental quality, was generally understood[6] (and indeed, the caste concept is closely allied with it).[7]

Having dealt with the concept of GROUP in the *ashram*, one asks what about GRID, or rules? Rules of inter-relationship which define roles in the *ashram* are in a sense unenforced and played down but very powerful. They are gently conveyed to the newcomer, who may be at first quite oblivious to them. As soon as the newcomer perceives what the rules are, he is not very likely to disregard them, so strong is the attitude of *ashram* visitors and dwellers with regard to them. While there is a good deal of latitude as to how one may seek "realization," the principles of conduct among *ashram* dwellers are firm. (I shall not attempt to delineate them here.)

As in India at large, hierarchy is the order of the *ashram* (Dumont 1970; Srinivas 1952: 205; Sinha 1959: 309). With hierarchy comes a forceful and complex set of rules for inter-personal behavior. In those *ashrams* where a saint resides (as I have said, not all *ashrams* have saints, although they tend to have an incipient saint), the saint is teacher, father or mother, and absolute ruler. According to Upanishadic teachings, whether the pupil thinks his master is right or wrong, the master must be obeyed, and this is true today. The disciple who does not obey is no longer a disciple (Radhakrishnan 1953: 20).

An *ashram* tends to have not one but several leaders. If the *ashram* has a well-known saint at its head, there may also be a disciple who has attained sainthood in his or her own right. Another may be on the way to this spiritual realization which is recognized by Hindus. Further down the hierarchy one finds specially privileged attendants of the saint (or secondary saint), persons who have been particularly dedicated to the *ashram*. They may prepare food for the saintly persons, or take care of their clothes (most often very simple).[8] Then there are others who do the general housework of the *ashram* (which may feed

---

[6] Excluding the tribal peoples, of whom I know little.

[7] The "realized soul," however, is said to be released from the oppositions of purity-impurity. The saint allowed no caste distinction in his *ashram*. Some *ashrams* observe caste distinction stringently.

[8] Among the ancient sculpture at Mahabalipurum in Southeast India one can see a cat preaching to mice. It is well known in India that some spiritual leaders are charlatans. Simple attire and austere living does not tend to characterize the charlatans.

large numbers of guests gratis at times of celebration). There are also old people who have left their families and are said to be seeking "realization" in the *ashram* (the traditional ideal of the fourth stage of life). Lowest in the hierarchy are the neighboring poor, some of whom come to the *ashram* every day, some to do menial tasks, some to receive help in the form of land, housing, and medical care, and all of whom can approach the saint for his *darshan* and to discuss their problems with him. (*Ashrams* have been centers of social reform in India.) Ancient teachings point out that persons of lowly status can achieve knowledge of Brahman (Radhakrishnan 1953: 613) and this is taught in *ashrams* today.

Also part of the *ashram* hierarchy are the wandering mendicants who come there to be fed and sometimes stay a traditional three days. They range all the way from rogues and vagabonds posing as *sādhus* 'ascetics' through orphans and homeless unfortunates to true ascetics, some well known and highly venerated. The saint in this *ashram* was once such a mendicant.

Among the guests there is also a hierarchy. There are the wealthy businessmen who come from the city, doff their expensive European suits, and put on the traditional *dhoti*. Their families are with them and well known to *ashram* staff. These men give large sums to support the *ashram* and its charities.[9] There are political personages and princes who occasionally visit, as well as saints from other *ashrams*. One sees, then, that grid — a set of rules governing inter-relationships and defining roles — is high at an *ashram*.

Each *ashram* population tends to have its own characteristics. Over-riding all idiosyncracies of *ashrams* are the existence of group identity and a set of rules which maintain and regulate a hierarchy. Closely related to the grid and group of *ashrams* is the fundamental idea of "realization" or "knowing Brahman," as the Upanishads put it over 2,000 years ago. For the person who knows Brahman, however, all identities become one. For such persons, it is said, there are no rules. It is believed that saints are persons who have experienced ultimate reality and have returned to society in order to help mankind.[10] Despite the emphasis on bodily symbols in an *ashram*, *ashram* leaders teach that the body is a transitory thing, not to be identified with the self.

---

[9]   Not all of these are known for their ethical behavior. I heard the saint say of one businessman, "He expects to attain realization by the same methods he uses in business!"

[10]   Saints are ordinary people who have become "realized souls"; *Avatars* also help mankind, but they are deities who manifest themselves on earth. In some *ashrams* it is believed the leader is an *avatar*.

(One hears Hindus speak of "dropping the body" when someone dies.) Here is another reversal — the affirmation and yet strong negation of bodily symbolism in *ashram* philosophy. For the average person in an *ashram*, however, identification with the group, as represented by the *ashram*, by *ashram* in general, by Hinduism, and by the body of the saint is strong, and mutually understood rules are compelling.

Suffice it to say, then, that both GRID and GROUP are high in this society, represented by one *ashram* but characterizing traditional Hindu India itself. BODILY SYMBOLISM abounds, and the human body is treated as an image of society — the feet corresponding to the lowest level of the hierarchy and hence disfavored but having the possibility of reversal of attitude (i.e. the feet of a saint are worshipped; the poorest outcaste may become a saint).

According to Douglas, societies high in both grid and group (a type of social experience which she maintains is replicated in rich bodily symbolism) are not apt to suffer from emotional impoverishment and inability to communicate on a meaningful level. I shall not attempt to test her hypothesis with regard to the comparative value of high-group high-grid (as contrasted with low-group low-grid, etc.) in terms of human satisfactions, nor shall I speculate upon the future of the *ashram* system as India undergoes modernization. I merely offer an example of a traditional institution still viable in modern Indian life, an institution characterized by a high degree of group and grid, and accompanying emphasis on bodily symbolism — an *ashram* — which I suggest is representative of a system which extends throughout India and which reflects fundamental ideas of traditional Hindu society.

REFERENCES

BASHAM, A. L.
   1954   *The wonder that was India: a survey of the culture of the Indian sub-continent before the coming of the Muslims.* New York: Grove Press.

COHN, BERNARD S.
1955   "The changing status of a depressed caste," in *Village India*. Edited by Marriott McKim, 53–77. Chicago: University of Chicago Press.

COOMARASWAMY, ANANDA K.
1957   *The dance of Shiva* (revised edition). Noonday Press.

DE BARY, WM. THEODORE, STEPHEN HAY, ROYAL WEILER, ANDREW YARROW
1958   *Sources of Indian tradition*. New York: Columbia University Press.

DOUGLAS, MARY
1970   *Natural symbols: explorations in cosmology*. New York: Pantheon Books.

DUBOIS, ABBE J. A.
1906   *Hindu manners, customs, and ceremonies* (third edition). Oxford: Clarendon Press.

DUMONT, LOUIS
1970   *Religion, politics and history in India: collected papers in Indian sociology*. The Hague: Mouton.
1970   *Homo hierarchicus: an essay on the caste system*. Translated by Mark Sainsbury. (Nature of Human Society Series.) Chicago: University of Chicago Press.

GHURYE, G. S.
1953   *Indian saddhus*. Bombay: The Popular Book Depot.

KAPUR, R. K.
1963   The teacher in Indian tradion. *The March of India* 14:37–39.

MARRIOTT, MC KIM
1955   "Little communities in an indigenous civilization," in *Village India*. Edited by Marriott McKim, 171–222. Chicago: University of Chicago Press.

ORANS, MARTIN
1965   *A tribe in search of a great tradition*. Detroit: Wayne State University Press.

RADHAKRISHNAN, S.
1953   *The principal Upanishads*. Edited with introduction, text, translation and notes by S. Radhakrishnan. London: George Allen and Unwin.

RADHAKRISHNAN, S., C. A. MOORE
1957   *A source book in Indian philosophy*. Princeton, New Jersey: Princeton University Press.

RAGHAVAN, V.
1956   "Methods of popular religious instruction in South India," in The Cultural Heritage of India, volume four. Edited by Haridas Bhattacharya. Calcutta: Ramakrishna Mission Institute of Culture.

SINGER, MILTON
1961   Text and context in the study of contemporary Hinduism. *The Adyar Library Bulletin* XXV, Parts 1-4. Madras, India.

SINGER, MILTON, editor
1959   *Traditional India: structure and change*. Publications of the American Folklore Society, Bibliographical Series, Volume X.

SINHA, SURAJIT
    1959   "Tribal cultures of peninsular India as a dimension of the little tradition in a preliminary statement," in *Traditional India: structure and change*. Edited by M. Singer. Publications of the American Folklore Society, Bibliographical Series, Volume X.

SRINIVAS, M. N.
    1952   *Religion and society among the Coorgs of South India*. Oxford: Oxford University Press.

VIDYARTHI, L. P.
    1961   *The sacred complex in Hindu Gaya*. London: Asia Publishing House.

Prestations and Prayers: Two Homologous Systems in Northern India

R. S. KHARE

Prestations and prayers, both as a system of relationships and as separate systems of parallel significance, require more systematic attention than they have received thus far in South Asian anthropology. If prestations help regulate the sphere of social relations, prayers signify the major relationships that the members of the society posit with regard to the supernatural, the society, and the individual. However, prayers, like prestations, present a wide variety of relationships of the religious sphere and they require systematization in terms of some common logical relationships.

The argument in this essay is that prayers essentially follow a logical paradigm that is characteristic of social prestations, and that this is particularly true for the devotional prayers of Hinduism so widely circulated in contemporary India. These prayers, it is further proposed, are essentially based on the premise of give-and-take, with an explicit idea of both the "quality and quantity of exchange" between the deity and the devotee. The point that the "deities practice exchange" should hardly surprise those who, being acquainted with modern legal practice, know that the deities can formally fight court cases either to retain or to augment the property that their temples hold.

In a more real sense, as we readily understand, a deity's "delegates" (like priests and trustees in a temple) practice exchange and litigate on the deity's behalf. But our treatment will emphasize not only the exchange of THINGS (for which at least two individuals are necessary) but also of IDEAS, where sometimes only the devotee may do the job—"he" may answer himself on behalf of the deity. In the latter cases, the thought that the exchange has occurred is most significant, and it is a

FACT with the devotee. Let us now finish with the preliminaries to reach such a stage of discussion.

In our following discussion, prestations will provide, often only implicitly, a yardstick against which to assess the relative nature, position, and function of prayers. Since the latter are virtually an unexplored field of study in recent social anthropology, we shall concentrate a good deal on their nature under the Hindu tradition of devotion *(bhaktī)*. We will first establish some general homologous points between prestations and prayers to help channel our later discussion of the nature of devotional prayers among the Hindus. We will discuss in some detail forms, functions, and meanings of such prayers, and then return to the underlying idea of exchange in prayers and in prestations. It will be argued that both the structure of contents and the language of expression in prayers are developed to highlight this characteristic. Finally, we will indicate that what prayers display (in thought patterns) is a replica of the entire *bhaktī* movement and that they contain several important contradictions.

PRESTATIONS AND PRAYERS — SIMILARITIES IN STRUCTURE

Mauss, with his celebrated *Essai sur le don, forme archaïque de l'échange* (translation, 1967) and his *La prière et les rites oraux* (in Mauss 1968), remains a pioneer in the field of sociological thinking.[1] Many more recent attempts have appeared that have discussed the topics of gifting and exchange to illustrate further their forms, functions, and cultural meanings under different ceremonial and social situations. However, as Ian Cunnison remarked in his "translative note" to *The gift* (Mauss 1967:xi), the French word *prestation* may be used to mean "any thing or series of things given freely or obligatory as a gift or in exchange; and includes services, entertainments, etc., as well as material things."[22]

The point is important for our present discussion because the broader scope of the term "prestations" will facilitate our task of examining forms, functions, and meanings of prayers. If what is exchanged is not

[1]   While his first work, originally issued in 1925, has been available in English, his writing on prayer, published in 1909, is available only in French.

[2]   The scope of this word is more clearly evident in French usage. Coming from the Latin PRAESTATIO, the meaning of the word varies from ACTION DE FOURNIR [applying, furnishing, stocking] to ALLOCATION DONNÉE AUX MILITAIRES [military pay], to ALLOCATION DE MATERNITÉ [maternity benefits] (Robert 1972).

rigidly tied down to only selected things, relationships, and manners, the field of this study widens considerably, opening up the way for us to analyze certain logical structures that may cut across the usual dis- tinctions inherent in such categories as the religious, the economic, and the political. Certain ideas and actions of give-and-take, to put it as a crude simplification, may run through all the three categories of social relationships, and even what is given and taken — and how, and what for, it is given and taken — may not, after all, differ so fundamentally as we are led to believe under the established classification of social relations.

On closer inspection one finds that not only is the transaction a nor- mal process in the majority of social relations, but even what is trans- acted is not so exclusive to one particular institution. One usual instance given is that of power or influence which may be, either in fact or in essence, transacted through diverse economic, political, religious, and ritual relations, and not only (or exclusively) through the political situa- tions. Hence, if we regard "economic," "political," "ritual," etc., as specific attributes of social relations (rather than as separate classes of social relations), we are on a more realistic ground to examine them.

Ceremonial and ritual prestations, it follows from the above, are also essentially those social relations that carry some distinguishing attri- butes of their own but these attributes, either in form or function, are not exclusive to them. Prayers, as we shall presently see, may have a basic structure corresponding (and similar) to that of ceremonial and ritual prestations. If prestations do not transfer only goods and com- modities but also ideas, then this is even more true of prayers.

Prayers follow a paradigm of social exchange; they are a homologue of social prestations. If prestations keep the social relations alive and connect people with people, then prayers do the same — and more, for they help consolidate a social group around a more symbolic idea — the presence of God. This resemblance between the structure and func- tion of prestations and prayers is neither superficial nor spurious, be- cause it runs through both thought and action patterns — a point that should be more than evident from the following considerations, which essentially deal with the Hindu case.

The basic structure of Hindu prestations, concisely stated here, em- phasizes nine major characteristics: (1) giver-receiver dichotomy, (2) reciprocity, (3) directionality, (4) "ultimate" idea of equivalence, (5) an idea of relative ranks, (6) an idea of "things" transacted, (7) direct/ indirect reciprocity, (8) long-range (circulation) / short-range reciproc- ity, and (9) an idea of part (individual) and whole (collective).

If we examine prayers with respect to these features, we may discover strong similarities. Prayers, like prestations, have inherent giving/ receiving ends: the person who says prayers offers "something" to his deity, which, in return, reciprocates. One static view is that the deity always gives and the devotee always receives. However, on closer inspection, the feature of reciprocity comes to the fore; a deity does not "give" without receiving "something" from the devotee. Further, while in a religious sense, a direction is built into prayers (God always gives more than a human can hope to reciprocate), in actuality, the reverse is more true, where a devotee prays, whether his deity immediately "answers" him or not. (As we shall see below, there are reasons for this attitude, which, as a matter of fact, are sustained by the reciprocity built into prayers.) But this is true only to an extent. According to a priest of the temple of Rāma at Adyodhya in Uttar Pradesh: "Who will pray if it is not answered at all, or more accurately, if there is no idea (or hope) that it is to be answered, even in the remotest way, in the remotest time?"

Here, therefore, once we recognize that the principle of reciprocity is at work in prayers, we should also note its specialized nature. The reciprocity, in a short-range perspective, may here appear to be incomplete, for only one dimension of the action (from devotee to deity) is empirically testable, leaving the other one, the deity's reciprocation, largely an experience of the devotee. Unlike in gifting and exchange, here one often has to depend on the attestation of the devotee to know whether his particular prayer has been answered or not. However, at the same time, it is an equally true social fact that prayers get "answered," and that the belief in this reciprocal dimension is invariably held by members of the society as a mental fact.

However, for a careful social anthropologist, there is another way (at least many a time, if not all the time) to ascertain that the "prayers get answered." Prayers, as acts at a particular time and by particular members of a society, often ventilate needs, anxieties, crises, and calamities. And though they are directed "to the One seated up there" and it is He who is supposed to respond, in fact it is the surrounding individuals and social groups who often answer the prayer. (But for the faithful it, of course, is always his deity.)

In terms of a Hindu's life-aims, prayers offered to obtain something that relates to *dharma*, *artha*, and *kāma* (three out of the four aims) are actually such that the "society must respond to them." It is of course not just a hypothetical postulation but one that can often be verified in the field. While the prayers related to *artha* and *kāma* get answered with the help of those who have these things (which are "gifts" of God, and not simply fruits of one's past *karma*), the prayers for the maintenance of one's *dharma* get answered in a different way — it is protected with the help of others. If *dharma* is essentially a preoccupation of the individual, its protection and maintenance are a societal concern.

It is in the same EXTENDED WAY that the fourth aim — *moksha* — is also ultimately sustained by the social reality, and the prayers connected with this aim, at least in some sense, depend on the society for being appropriately answered. (As we shall discuss below, this classical scheme of ideas is subject to exceptional forces of the *bhakti* movement.)

The above should be sufficient to indicate that in prayers reciprocity is a fundamental idea, once we are able to include in this concept the direct and the indirect, the short-range and the long-range notions of reciprocity. It is important in the context of prayers, which, being as diverse in purposes as they are, are mostly neither directly nor immediately answered. Some prayers of the Hindus are not meant to be answered "either in this life or in this world," others are not meant to be answered at all in the regular sense of the term reciprocity. However, as argued here (and later on), this is not to deny the idea of reciprocity but only to postpone the use of it for a more appropriate occasion.

The ideas of relative rank and of equivalence between what is given and what is received by way of prayers appear together. While no devotee either expects or hopes for exact equivalence between what he does during the prayers and what his deity does in response, there is some definite idea of quantity (as well as quality) attached to prayers. More prayers (usually counted by number) are supposed to accrue more rewards, although beyond this general notion it is hard to specify the measure in any exact manner. Besides, there are notions about the quality and quantity of response that a prayer might invoke from a deity.

Leaving aside some specific considerations until a little later, we might observe here a basic assumption; a devout person's prayers never remain unanswered and God always determines how (and how much) the devotee's wishes should be met at any particular time, "for God always determines only what is in the supreme interest of the devotee." Under the prevalent notions of the *bhakti* sect, one's deity is always generous in his response to one's prayers; if however he seems miserly it is because of the limited — the myopic — view of one's own spiritual interest.

Hence, from God's end, this view continues, prayers are always amply and appropriately answered; only our human interpretation varies "because of the short-sightedness and ignorance of mortals." However, from the human end, prayers do seem to be randomly answered, for the skeptics may sometimes complain that they pray more and receive less (in terms of what they prayed for). In brief, therefore, while exact equivalence (in any quantitative sense) in prayer transactions is unobtainable, there are wide maximum and minimum limits along which the response to prayers may vary.

The idea of rank and the response to one's prayers are also closely related in several different ways, once we do not limit the idea of ranking to caste systemic relations alone (even when such a relevance is not denied). The "politics of prayer" is, if we may make here an association that is not as absurd as it may look at first sight, that one ranking higher can always give as well as receive more, without being accountable to the one who ranks lower. (The relevance of such an observation with regard to the traditional caste system remains obvious.) If follows from the above that the one of highest rank — God — is responsible only to himself. Beside this obvious aspect of ranking between God and his devotee, there are, as we shall see below, numerous rank distinctions recognized within the categories of prayers and devotees that ultimately have an influence on the effectiveness of prayers — or so it is thought.

Finally comes the basic distinction of the part and the whole — of the individual and the collective in current sociological terminology. Prestations and prayers make use of this distinction — or rather it is this distinction that fundamentally necessitates such practices as prestations and prayers. If prestations help link one individual with the other (and one group with another), the prayers help endure human failures and unavoidable crises at one level and link the individual and the group with a supernatural force at another. For the devout, the prayers forge a "living link" with his article of faith. Further, individuals who pray get linked together more because they share their faith rather than other social characteristics. Individuals drawn from different caste groups are known to forge and maintain such a cohesiveness over an extended period of time.

Prestations socially, and prayers philosophically, help a Hindu to announce his identity in relation to a greater totality. It is with the help of prayers that he demonstrates his correct alignment with ultimate values of the culture; and it is with prestations that he correctly recognizes the presence of social collectivities that surround him. The analytical significance of studying such relationships is that they allow us to enter an area of inquiry (individuality *vis-à-vis* collectivity) that has hardly been sociologically investigated in terms of Hindu thought. The interrelationships between the part and the whole, it is here suggested, could be more concretely (and accurately) investigated with the help of an appropriate selection of prestations and prayers.

Elsewhere (Khare 1975) I have discussed some issues and perspectives connected with such an inquiry that suggest the usefulness of the material obtainable from prestations and prayers. Furthermore, they help illustrate criteria that guide the formulation, separation, and merger of the identity of the individual. The point that prayers are a potent means for expressing such urges is well known, but their underlying structure of thought needs to be studied before they can yield those shared criteria that PERSISTENTLY REGULATE the expression of interrelationships between the part (devotee) and the whole (the deity, or God) across situations.

Prestations, when intensively studied in terms of kinship, marriage, and death, afford similar possibilities, for they offer occasions when the individuality is successively developed, differentiated, and lost. In the interim, in various ways they demonstrate the relationships that are forged and maintained (or altered) between the individual and the social collective. This much should be sufficient for making the point that the question of the part and the whole is inherent in the basic structure of both prestations and prayers.

ON THE NATURE OF HINDU PRAYERS

The preceding section, devoted mainly to establishing a linkage between prayers and prestations, prepares us to see some vital resemblances that make prayers an important topic for social anthropological study. Two levels of analysis should be evident in my discussion: one at the level of thought — its structure and its relevance in the Hindu system of ideologies and values (here a direct reference to its sociological significance may not be made beyond the obvious, because I regard its study as rewarding in itself, and for what will be more directly sociological in nature a little bit later); and the other at the level of social reality, either as alleged in the past or as at present.

From now on, prayers will constitute our main focus of inquiry, though we will often draw implicit parallels to prestations; and in prayers, as I see them, thought structures (and their linguistic expressions) are far more significant than the ritual acts (as "technologies") that attend them. A study of the latter is significant (or more informative) in the context of the thought that prompts them. However, we must first suitably channel our inquiry by intensifying our analysis of prayers.

We have so far considered the concept of prayer from a distance, keeping its contents, functions, and varieties constant. Now before we can go any further, we must examine these variations. The term "prayer," as used here, has of course the obvious disadvantage that it carries with it certain traces of Judeo-Christian traditions, and it may be impossible to fully disown these "meanings at the fringe," and maybe this is not necessary as long as the major thrust of the Hindu idea is clearly kept in the forefront during the discussion. (Most desirable would be to use the appropriate Sanskrit and Hindi lexicon, but I shall refrain from it in this attempt to facilitate reading.)

Very briefly, in contemporary POPULAR usage and in my usage here, the lexical entries that are included under the label "prayer" are: *stotra, stuti, vintī (vinaya,* m.) *prārthanā,* and *ārādhanā.* These entries, as explained in any good Sanskrit-English or Hindi-English dictionary, variously emphasize the following minimal dimensions: (a) that something is asked for, (b) that some power or force is being invoked, apologized to, and eulogized, and (c) that an attitude of humility and submission (by the one who prays) is being inculcated.

If the first two dimensions bring out the content and function of prayers, the third one states a necessary valve precondition for it. By implication, therefore, all those attitudes where either a confrontation or a contest or a conflict is espoused with some power or force fall outside the scope of prayers. So one should note here the point that while invocation, exhortation, and activation of power or forces are included within the scope of Hindu prayers, any coercion and contestation, devoid of the spirit of submission, is held outside it. Further, it should be obvious that the idea of prayer is not confined to supernatural forces; it also applies to the inhabitants of the mundane world in a very real sense but again, only the powerful are prayed to, for they alone can answer prayers. (Collectivities of the weak may appear powerful under the democratic system, and they may accordingly be "prayed to" by politicians to derive power to answer the prayers, in turn, of the individually weak.)

However, our concerns here will be quite limited: we shall restrict our attention to religious prayers, primarily directed toward that composite idea in Hindu belief called "God." Although we might occasionally take the liberty to benefit from the width of such a universe, it is still unmanageable. We will therefore further restrict ourselves to the prayers of the *bhakti* tradition, especially because they are more directly relevant to the majority of the contemporary Hindus, whether of the north or the south.

But even so, we will remain at a sufficiently general level to allow us to observe some features of a broad framework that characterizes such prayers. We will therefore, for example, not specify either the deities or the philosophical systems, or the prominent devotees, in terms of whom the structure of these prayers might have originated and developed with time. We will be, instead, content with the criterion that the categories of features discussed below remain a part of the written and/or oral living tradition and knowledge of the Hindus over wide regions. (Such a demarcation of the field of study should greatly allay fears of those who might argue that prayers are too illusive a subject for social anthropological research.)

The General Conception

Once we move into the religious field that is dominated by the idea — and tenets — of devotion *(bhakti)*, it becomes easier to exclude those formulas and prescriptions from consideration here (e.g. such *yantra, mantra,* and *tantra*), that coerce a supernatural god or deity to action, not out of humility and submission but by either threat or command. Such a distinction cannot allow one to dismiss out of hand any specific sect, deity, or body of literature; given the complexity of development of thought about the Hindu pantheon, one has to be more circumspect. Yet the criterion of distinction is neither blurred nor confused in this complexity, as a close study of the material should reveal. However, by the same criterion, there is an enormous body of literature (in Sanskrit and in regional languages), almost with every significant sect, that may not strictly fall in the category of prayers but that goes best with them by criteria of affinity. This body of cognate literature may lay out explanatory schemes in relation to those ultimate values that are clearly spelled out time and again in actual prayers. As a learned devotee recently summarized it to me at Rae Bareli (Uttar Pradesh): "Prayers, as composed by saints after hard and long meditation, encapsulate all those major strands of thought that have taken centuries to develop under exposition and commentary of the learned.

But let us not forget: prayers are real power, while commentaries and philosophical expositions are mere words, for the former are directed to God under the influence of true devotion".

This connection, as it exists today in the minds of the devotees, is useful to note here because, while the philosophical literature may be seen to furnish categories and concepts for prayers, the latter are evidently something more real and potent, and they do not depend on such a literature for their effectiveness and survival. Prayers are supposed to be halos of God.

Finally, the majority of medieval and modern literature that is written expound directly the virtues *(guṇa)*, forms *(rupa)*, divine sports *(līlā)*, etc., of the god (in his numerous incarnations) falls under the category of prayers — some directly and some indirectly. Thus, the contemporary body of literature called *bhajan*s and *keertan*s (for one systematic study of these in Madras, see Singer 1966, 1972), with the help of a devotee's specified purpose and attitude, becomes a powerful and diverse repository of prayers. (It should be more evident a little later in this article why this is so.)

Now let us come to the shared conception of prayers today. Prayers, to be sure once again, chiefly underline the themes of spiritual humility, invocation, eulogy, verecundity, and doxology. (Although the English language carries a number of words that vary in emphasis, there are no easy equivalents to what Sanskrit and Hindi or other regional languages have in India.) Actually, even the current Hindi lexical categories are a poor label for what they are supposed to cover, unless one is prepared to go to numerous prevalent (even if only regionally valid) terms that the *sādhu*s have used to denote and classify shades of devotional attitudes (more correctly called *bhāva*) towards one's deity of worship. Thus appear, for example, in Hindi, such categories of prayers as ones dealing with either union *(milan)* or separation *(virah)* or admonition *(chétāvanī)* or bliss of realization *(darshanānanda)* or renunciation *(samvāsa)* or divine sports *(līlā)*. A systematic study of linguistic categories in this context should be useful, particularly since much regional vocabulary seems to be on the wane, or at least narrowly limited.

Here we of course must also recall the basic classification of sentimental "attitudes" *(bhāva)* towards the deity, ranging from that of a servant *(dāsya)* to a beloved *(mādhurya)*, for they help classify prayers according to the dominant sentiment of the deity-devotee relationship, and they may facilitate comprehension of a set of values that a devotee of a particular *bhāva* can follow in his prayers. Beyond these indications about the formal categories of devotional prayers, the task must be deferred to a more intensive study; here I must now pass on to a more popular conception of prayers.

Prayers are a popular, and yet powerful, avenue to God, open, ideally, to all, even in the face of the exhaustive ranking of individuals and groups in Hindu society. As the preachers these days endlessly argue, they are especially potent for the hopeless, the downtrodden, the meek, and the pure of heart and mind. Sincere prayers, again under the ideal conception, never fail: "When all hopes are lost, prayers do miracles." (Hereinafter, unless otherwise specified, sentences within quotes are taken from the actual religious lectures — *pravacan* — of the contemporary holy men, saints, and priests, which were recorded in substance in 1962 in Lucknow on the premises of the Ramakrishna, Gauranga, and Geeta-Bhawan organizations.)

"Prayers of the helpless are especially effective in the *darbār* [hall of audience] of God, because the devotee has then lost all other mundane props and they become truly sincere and desperate like those of the Gaja."[3] For the devotee who is not under the influence of a specifically acute crisis, the preachers do not forget to make the point that prayers done halfheartedly and without intense concentration remain unanswered. Since praying with heart and soul is everybody's birthright, unvitiated by one's caste, creed, wealth, and learning, the argument is made for its widest practice "in an age when the wants, the sorrows, and the ailments engulf all." Most of such prayers remain unrecorded, and what we find recorded is only the tip of the iceberg.

Beyond their immediate curative use, prayers, as the Hindu devotional thought makes clear, are NATURAL to any soul yearning for God. "It is neither flattering nor bribing the Supreme Being; it is, however, an important indication about the proper journey of one's soul, for prayers are both necessary and sufficient for attaining *bhaktī* as well as, if desired, *moksha*. The glory of God is not an artificial attribute that a mortal can invent at will, and one's participation in it is both natural and inescapable — sooner or later." This is what we may call the long-range view of prayers that is more preventive than curative in function.

---

[3] It is quite frequent that the religious preachers draw upon mythological characters (like Gaja — an elephant who successfully prayed to God [Vishnu] while in distress) for driving home the point. That the preachers advise recitation of such prayers (either in Sanskrit or in one of their regional renderings) to the devotees with some specific purpose in mind is also quite common. Given the scope of our discussion here, however, we shall refrain from drawing in all mythological evidence, for it would invariably draw us to footnote explanations and hence inordinately prolong the discussion. But the ensuing discussion could be easily backed by such data.

All ills, whether physical *(daihik),* or material or "this-wordly" *(bhau-tik),* or supernatural or "other-wordly" *(daivik),* are always curable through earnest prayers, and hence the latter constitute a very powerful preventive step BEFORE such ills have fettered a soul. Mythologies again provide perfect examples to emphasize the point. Thus, in whatever way we look at the general function of prayers, they are RESTORATIVE in both their short-range and long-range functions. This statement must be further qualified to assert that prayers, when directed towards mundane crises, do not lose their long-range benefits to the soul.

Prayers, it is argued, cannot be divested of their spiritual benefits. As a related thought: Whether a devotee prays with a specific purpose in mind or not, prayers automatically bring divine blessings. "The true devotees never ask for results, for they know this fact: 'you get more without asking'." (Consider here the relation between prestation and prayers for the fundamental principle of reciprocation and the maximization of what one can get.)

The above concept may seem to rather unduly exaggerate the utilitarian motive underlying prayers, unless it is also emphasized that prayers, in principle, cannot always be expected to yield immediate results, because even if praying is within human possibilities, its "fruits lie in the hands of God, and if he does not answer them, it is his will." But of course it does not mean the devotee should be disheartened or dejected, "because who knows when God may answer, making up for his past silence all at once." This structure of thought should prompt the devotee to pray again and again, "without losing either patience or faith." It is through such a silence that God tests the faith of his devotee, and in order to avoid frustration during such periods, one should learn to pray without attaching specific desires, i.e. in *nishkāma bhāva,* for the sole purpose of pleasing one's deity of devotion. Alternatively, "he should resign himself to the will of God *(Hari-ékshā),* but without either diminishing his faith or reducing the duration and number of his prayers." Therefore, we may summarize: Successful or unsuccessful, praying with faith must go on undaunted, for it is in contemporary India a major foundation for the *dharma* of the Hindu. The devotional prayer is held to be above the fetters of ritual rules, and of *karma* and *dharma.*

Forms, Functions, and Meanings

Before we continue to discuss other related aspects of the devotional prayer, we must here discuss the structure of prayers — in terms of discernible thought arrangements and of social relationships. The social structure of prayers may differ widely according to the purpose, occasion, and duration of the prayers, as well as varying as a result of the participants. However, the basic distinction is that between the individual and the collective.

Some prayers may be exclusively meant for personal, exclusive use, and the most common, yet forceful, example of this category is provided by one's *guru-mantra*, which only two persons know in this world — the guru and his disciple, who received it as a whisper in his ear when he took *guru-dikshā*, i.e. when he became initiated, for his spiritual welfare. A similar rite may take place during the sacred-thread ceremony of the twice-born, but it can become quite an elaborate separate affair, for a spiritual *guru* is approached once in a lifetime and the *mantra* given by him remains the deepest secret with the disciple; the latter never imparts it to anybody else because it is suited only to "his soul's needs."

Counting the Holy Name *'Nāma japa'* or a phrase eulogizing a deity are other examples of prayers that may be conducted alone while meditating before one's deity. The severity of a crisis may also force a devotee to pray in seclusion, for this way one can really give vent to his feelings and emotions "before the deity whom one adores and who, after all, can help most in distress." Beside these prayers that are meant to be prayed alone, one can of course find many other prayers for either individual or group praying.

As for accompaniments of praying, worshiping remains the most closely associated activity. Very often, while the prayers *per se* may not require a certain ritual state of purity and certain arrangements of objects and accessories of worship, the deities, to whom the prayers are, after all, directed, may invariably require them. Hence, to be able to pray (in a formal sense), a devotee has first to invoke a deity by proper worship (and offerings). These requirements, as the priests and the householders argue, also depend on the nature of the deity. If he is benevolent and omnipotent like Rāma and Krishna, no bars apply — they can be prayed to always in any state of ritual purity. Numerous mythological examples are provided to support this injunction. "One can pray to them even in a most impure state, and they do not need an invocation every time you pray. However, if you worship them daily, it strengthens your faith any way, and it is, at least indirectly, a help in the prayers." However, one has to be very scrupulous with lesser gods and deities, "for they are temperamental, fussy, and more demanding." They require exact preparations every time — all the time — before starting prayers. If it is not done in appropriate sequence, the effect of the prayer may be either nil or even negative, i.e. instead of granting the wish, the deities may cast their wrath and punish the erratic devotee. Examples usually given (at least in northern India, excluding the benign transformations inculcated in, and exported from, Bengal) are those of the goddesses of *navagraha*, astrological starts — as deified in Hindu thought, and of Hanumān. Localized gods usually fall in this same category and require preparations for "proper prestation and invocation" before they can be fruitfully prayed to. Do such gods, as a consequence, fall into disfavor? The answer is "no," because these deities work for quite specified purposes (ailments, crops, efforts, etc.) and, as the people repeatedly argue, "what will a sword [i.e. a bigger deity] do where only a needle [i.e. a lesser deity] is required?" As a result, devotees in search of specific help repeatedly come to these deities, and they remain popular in their own right, despite the deeper urge to be a *bhakta* of the omnipotent Rāma an Krishna "to get away from it all" *(samsāra)*.

Further, some deities work slower and some faster — some only after the accumulation of prayers from the devotees. Some act fast but only after an initial delay, while some slowly guard and supervise all the time during a specific endeavor, if once invoked in the beginning (e.g. the god Ganesha). However, all deities, so to speak, reserve the right to deny a prayer, despite the best human care for their invocation and worship. Such denials may mean either their disposition (at that occasion they may be regarded as displeased) or a signal for further demands, which of course a priest will normally suggest the next time around. Some deities — like goddesses, who are supposed to have awesome control over human affairs — should be prayed to at least twice a year (normally during days set apart for them during the months of October and March) irrespective of any specific purpose. The rich may assign this duty to their priests for a fee, while the poor may do it themselves by setting apart more time for their worshiping hour. This observation should indicate that the nature of deities and their relationship to their devotees are important factors that influence the social and ritual arrangements attending prayers, whether said individually or collectively.

The prayers also can be said directly or indirectly. Under the latter provision, the principle of substitution works with wide latitudes. The rich, the invalid, the diseased, the busy, and the impure may take recourse to it to a considerable extent. A substitution of the actor may be most frequent, but depending upon the necessity and the situation, the substitution may extend to ritual acts, ingredients, contents (of worship and of the prayer) and even gods.

If a certain god is being worshiped but one more effective is later on suggested "by a person who knows about such things," he may be substituted for assuring success in the endeavor. Obviously, such substitutions, as we can readily see, can occur only within the ranks of lesser gods; the supreme ones are kept above such a shuffle. Although "prayers by proxy" may be quite common with many in these times of change, they are left behind in favor of the direct approach if the crisis really deepens, or if it relates to one's near and dear ones. In this ultimate context "everybody knows how to pray, to implore, to beseech the Almighty."

All the above distinctions assume a BASIC two-way relationship between the deity and the devotee. The transaction is completed, in thought at least, when the deity has "answered" his devotee's prayers, or even when the deity has "received and accepted" them. When concerned with the thought structure, there is another interesting dimension. Prayers, very often, especially those in Sanskrit and originated by a renowned saint, or commentator, or philosopher, are a tradition in themselves, and to them are attached, normally as legends and tales, the names of some well-known saints and devotees from various parts of India as an evidence of attestation towards the efficacy and potency of such prayers.

When saying such a prayer, a contemporary devotee feels as if great souls stand behind his prayer because it was their prayer. He then does not feel alone and derives faith and support from the glorious passage of the prayer through time. This diachronic perspective behind certain famous prayers is neither a whim of the few nor is it hard to discover in the field. The devout cite their experiences to claim that such a diachronic company (to invent a bit of sociological slang) is not only real but truly helpful in making their prayers work. Symbolically, therefore, if Po was the original person who invented a particular prayer centuries ago, his following over time could conceivably refer to Po — when praying towards the same deity who was originally addressed. Unless there is some specific reason for somebody to keep such prayers a secret, they are openly shared, advocated, and expounded in detail, leading to a following at any one time.

The same basic phenomenon may be observed in an encapsulated form in another way. Whatever the prayer — if it comes from a famous sage of the past, so much the better — one's *guru* may agree to work as a "catalyzer" (from the viewpoint of the devotee), standing between him and his deity. "One's real *guru* supervises all that transpires between his disciple and the god, and obviously, the former does not do anything without the consent of his spiritual teacher." So, often a *guru* may act to obtain appropriate results for his disciple from the deity. This is of course an act of kindness and piety on the part of the *guru*, which also enhances his spiritual powers.

Another alternative arrangement is that, in an extreme crisis, a *guru* may be moved to grant a prayer directly without apparently going to the deity — or so at least may be the thinking of a devout disciple. It continues to be commonplace knowledge that the GENUINE *gurus* (who are admittedly considered to be rare) carry enormous spiritual powers and that there is NOTHING beyond them: "Actually, they produce miracles."

Still another arrangement is that where the devotee and the deity are interpolated by an additional temperamentally complementary deity to advance the chances of success of the devotee's prayer. Obviously, the intermediary deity should be "heard" by the main deity. The famous examples of such arrangements, the devotees say, come from such teams as Sita-Rama, Hanuman-Rama, Bharat-Rama, and Radha-Krishna. The link evidently can get longer and more complicated in some cases.

Collective praying, let us note here, does not exclude any of the above arrangements as far as the deity-devotee relationship is concerned. Although it cannot be denied that collective praying does produce, in the Durkheimian sense, a feeling of exuberance and solidarity among the members of the group, the identity of the individual, we must emphasize, is not lost under normal circumstances. Only the exceptionally devout are known to be able to do that. The example is of course given of saints like Chaitanya Mahaprabhu in this regard. "Those who claim that they can dissolve their identity frequently and freely [in their devotion to God] are very often fakes who intend to impress the congregation by their artificially induced emotional states," argued a Sangh-Keertan leader of renown from Vrindaban. But, of course, to be able to submerge one's identity while praying is a most desirable goal for the devotee. It is by reaching this state, the devotees argue, that a soul truly stands in communion with the Whole, of which it is, after all, a part. Prayers, therefore help the parts to stand in appropriate relationship to the Whole, according to the *bhakti* idioms.

Collective praying, following essentially the explanation set forth by powerful saints like Chaitanya, is considered to be helpful in many different ways. It draws in the lukewarm and the doubting (who would not pray if they were left alone) to participate in and to realize the significance of praying. The emotional charge that collective participation produces helps shake off the doubts of the devotees on the fringe.

The collective enterprise, at least in modern times, allows for sharing of time, expense, and energy; and the entire *keertan* event is not a burden of a single individual any more. (Earlier, the *rājā*s and the *talukdār*s used to do that, given the conveniences they had at their command.) For the devout, the collective praying (done loudly, even with the help of loudspeakers these days) disseminates the Holy Name to the idle of a whole *mohallā* [neighborhood] or even farther. Also, an active role in collective praying can easily intimate that one is very *dhārmika* — hence "a pious soul in the community." (In most of the towns and villages today such a characterization is helpful; it may have even certain pragmatic advantages in the locality — at least, such a person may wield some extra influence over his *keertan* mates.) The collective efforts can also pull in (or buy in) renowned saints, career-*keertan*ists and expert musicians who adorn and glorify the group's activities at least on such special occasions as Krishna *Janamāstamī*. The size of the crowd, the religious aura created on the podium, and the many hours spent in prayers — either sung, recited, or advocated — combine to make the event a success. The common man in the congregation, then, feels more elated. He gets *darshan* of the holy persons, who can truly, by their mere presence, help him in his spiritual journey. If, however, he has some vexing illness in the family (or the *kula*), he may try to obtain an audience with a holy man, who, in turn may tell him about a special prayer for the purpose. Some may even prescribe certain herbs for the purpose.

The collective prayers may also follow a recognizable sequence of steps to honor the deities and gods of all kinds. For example, a prayer session may begin with an invocation to the god Ganesha (who will protect the sacred event from any accident or disruption), moving next to numerous gods and goddesses that surround Shiva and Vishnu, including astrological stars, mythological figures, and natural elements like earth, sky, water, and fire. The third phase may be to move to chosen devotees of the chief deity. For example, Hanumān for Rāma and Arjun for Krishna may be "invited." An invocation to one's *gurū*s, famous saints of the sect, and other *siddha*s must immediately follow. All of this "introductory" invocation of course helps the congregation to "get in touch with" the chief deity, who is finally prayed to and extolled in a number of ways, mostly by recalling his benevolent deeds towards his devotees. This is, of course, the climax of the event. Once this phase is over, the invoked gods must be appropriately requested to "return in peace" to their abodes. Usually appropriate prayers drawn from a scripture like *Ramacharitmānas* help do it when accompanied by worshiping activities. Once all deities return in peace, their *prasād* [blessed food] is obtained and the group may disperse soon after to join "the world that they had left behind for a while to seek a brief respite."

It may also be mentioned here that recitals of sacred texts, when undertaken for an explicit purpose, work like one long prayer that has to be finished during a specified period (e.g. in twenty four hours, a week, a fortnight, or even a month) by observing some rules of austerity, ritual purity, and seclusion. These recitals may also be undertaken either singly or collectively.

Even *mohallā* committees exist today in towns for such undertakings — some composed only of women (since they have free afternoons) and some mixed. Thus one may volunteer to participate in a sacred recital to help his neighbor in seeking divine intervention in an ongoing litigation or sickness. As a related variation, some prayers may actually be so long that they cannot be recited in a day, but may have to be done in several days to coincide with some auspicious days. An important example of this kind is provided by *Sri Durgāsaptasati Stotra,* which is divided into thirteen chapters with a text of seven hundred verses in Sanskrit. However, since this must be recited during the nine-day period occurring twice every year devoted to the goddess Durgā, the task can be suitably divided either by the devotee or by the substitute whom the devotee may appoint to perform on his behalf. Only the men do it; hence the women cannot be of much help here. Further, since the prayer has to be done with required religious formalities, the task is much more extensive.

Again, these formalities (called *sāngopānga* in Sanskrit) follow a standardized pattern where, besides the regular worship of the deity, a number of preparatory and concluding steps are carried out, called *dhyāna* [invocation by sacred incantations and meditation of the form of the deity], and *nayāsa* [certain ritual steps through which the devotee prepares himself to undertake the actual recital], etc. An idea of such elaborations may be obtained from a Sanskrit-Hindi book published by a well-known press for religious books in northern India (Gita Press, Gorakhpur). While the Sanskrit text of the prayer to the goddess (with special meditation instructions at the begining of every chapter) occupies 118 pages, the introductory and the concluding material occupies approximately 122 pages. These latter categories of pages are there of course "to enhance the effect of the prayer." This same prayer, as the book states towards its end (on page 233), helps one attain all the four major goals of a Hindu's life — *dharma, artha, kāma,* and *moksha.*

Besides, the compiler has produced some thirty incantations that, when singly recited with every verse of the main prayer, grant blessings of the goddess that could work toward anything from collective welfare and easing world crises or controlling an epidemic, to predicting one's future through one's dreams. The book also lists thirty specific "works" that the prayer can perform when it is recited with a specified incantation. Despite these specific assignments, however, the fact that the prayer helps attain devotion to the deity is endlessly emphasized, as it is held to be the most noble aim to work for.[4]

Given the diversity and complexity of the Hindu prayers in different sects, the observations of this section naturally do not exhaust either variety or detail. However, they do bring together some major general features of the prayers, which may be easily comparable at an intercultural level.

PRAYERS AS A "LANGUAGE OF EXCHANGE"

Our aim of accounting for functions and meanings of prayers will be similar in this section as well, but with an altered emphasis.

Varieties

We have so far taken it for granted that all prayers originate in the Sanskritic tradition, and that they may only gradually get translated into regional dialects, keeping their essential cultural elements intact. Obviously it is one side of the coin — and incomplete at that. For example, translations, however well done, do alter the cultural content

---

[4] I compared a publication in English from southern India for the same prayer (Shankaranarayanan 1968). The results were not much different. The prayer, discussesd in greater philosophical detail, has an introductory section of 129 pages, giving the significance of the prayer and all the ritual preparations that are required. The English translation of 700 verses takes 138 pages with spaces for special meditations at the beginning of each chapter. Finally, the concluding section of 47 pages, again given to specialized prayers (for the goddess) that would enhance an appreciation of the glory of the main prayer, also presents appropriate "secrets" about how to use the prayer as a "practical manual" and as a "purposive science." The "works" assigned to the prayer in this book generally conform to those given by the book considered earlier. One could count them over 30 here. One specialized usage: If one wants to remove somebody's wrath, this prayer, in 13 chapters, should be read in the following sequence: chapters 13,1; 12,2; 11,3; 10,4; 9,5; 8,6; and 7,7. The underlying Hindu principle is that sequence of ritual activity determines its meaning and consequence. A reversed order may mean the opposite consequence.

of the original, especially when the translator brings with him the values of the regional subculture. Further, if deities vary regionally (as they do in India) in significance, in form, and in disposition, the prayers assocated with them, wherever translated, should also reflect these differences.

More precise studies of such changes need to be done, and prayers offer a very sensitive piece of thought and writing, where major changes, whenever consciously brought about by a translator or a saint or a commentator, can normally be explained after an intensive inquiry. If prayers tend to resist change to preserve their authenticity and efficacy, there is also a contradictory tendency — prayers are profusely translated in numerous regional languages and local dialects, for it is both religiously desirable and actually essential for wider dispersal. It means that for major prayers in Sanskrit there may be found vernacular translations or renderings for wider understanding, presenting two distinct levels which can be compared for a study.

Popular versions of the Sanskrit original are often obtainable, and they do not have to be either less authoritative or less effective IF the persons responsible for producing such versions are renowned saints and devotees of God. *Ramacharitamānas* in the north is cited as an outstanding example (and, we know, the south, the east and the west have also produced similar regional authorities in India). This rule applies even today with such renowned contemporary saints as Anandmai Mā and Saī Bābā, among several others. Such religious personages are supposed to originate as well as translate prayers, while adding "more special spiritual force" to them. Actually, the devotees may develop a body of prayers just around the miracles of these saints, which append to those meant for deities.

However, such prayers remain secondary in the larger context; they remain group-specific, carrying lore of a religious personage fixed around the enduring values of renunciation, piety, true devotion, spiritual miracles, etc. In popularization of prayers, the language of expression and the religious personage both have very significant parts to play; they reinforce each other, but the role of the latter personage is more crucial, "because prayers, in essence, work through the force of one's faith in, and intensity for, the *bhaktī* of the Lord. Even if a devotee does not understand the meaning of a prayer, and he is not learned enough to keep its linguistic niceties at their places, his faith and spiritual intensity help carry the message to God. Hence the true language of any prayer is the faith that links the devotee to the deity." These observations come from a renowned Sanskritist from an Ayodhyābased Sanskrit school, who was recently honored in New Delhi for his scholarship in grammar.

However, popular renderings of Sanskrit prayers are constantly made, because not all people can become attracted towards something which they cannot comprehend. If a popular version has a stamp of authority from a spiritual leader, so much the better for the common man; but if it does not, many may settle for something that they can make some sense out of. Once this fact is accepted, it is not difficult to realize that even popular versions may belong to different categories of cultural legitimacy. At the top of course stand such works which, as we have already indicated, come from renowned saints like Tulsidās, Meerā, Sūrdās, Kabīr, and Chaitanya (primarily for northern India).

The prayers that they produced are already recognized as *mantra* of immense potency. They are as good as — or even better than — some in Sanskrit. One reason is that not only did these personages produce what illustrates, and even refines, the cherished values of the Sanskrit literature, but they, by their actions, had set an example of the *bhakta* lifeways. This cardinal principle keeps guiding the product that appeared since then, and even today. Higher cultural legitimacy is awarded to those prayers that are backed by an exemplary instance of the *bhaktī* behavior. These are "tested" prayers and hence most effective in the time of need.

Next come the prayers that are popular because they have been examples of either scholarship, musical composition, or prolific — and freely understandable — expression, or all of these. Again, while these features become the carrying force for such prayers, the basic principle of keeping and honoring the sets of ultimate values is assiduously maintained. These may be widely used, but their spiritual test may be often provided by some devotee other than the author. Such a prayer is spread by word of mouth and in this way it gains further popularity. (In Uttar Pradesh, an example of this kind of work is provided by Rādhey Shyāma Rāmāyana and Binduji's *keertan*s.) Other such prayers, if they remain untested for long, may disappear after the initial fascination wears off. They become only a ripple in the pond of popular literature. Since the latter is a very large category, several layers of quality become immediately apparent, at the top of which may stand the acknowledged poets and writers (who are chiefly — or only — appreciated for their literary skill, even when they are writing or composing a "prayer").

The component of faith may be totally lacking here, leaving a question whether they are prayers at all. On the other extreme may appear village bards who compose a devotional prayer to catch the ear of the devout to invoke the sentiment of piety and charity in him. These may snatch a line from a popular film song to weave other parts of the composition around it; but whatever the improvisation, a mention of some ultimate cultural values, an echo of the reflective words of a regionally renowned saint, and a distant image of the *bhaktī-bhakta-bhagvān* trilogy is almost invariably required to gain attention. Sources of borrowings do not matter if these criteria are satisfied.

The rural devout and the rural literati remain two major sources for either producing or bringing in appropriate prayers for the deities of concern. If, however, the rural devotee is also of the rural literati, the effect of his prayers is similar to what we have described earlier for the urban class. Villagers know very well how to retain and incorporate such valuable rural products in their rural ethos for a long time to come. The specific contents may get altered or added to over time, but this is not of much concern, as long as the personage is remembered in terms of some tangible objects (a temple, a hut, a mud platform, or even a place where such-and-such a tree stood before) and the prayers that he asked to be recited in happiness and triumph, and tragedy and failure get recited.

Related to these general prayers is another category. These prayers, mostly event-describing, rather than reflective, are generally more direct in their purpose. Folk deities here would like simple, undisguised, and specific statements from these devotees; if there are some circumlocutions, there must be some evident purpose behind it — for example, making the deity understand some implicit matters that cannot be publicly stated for the fear of offending the violators of specific moral or ethical codes. Such prayers are evidently quite topical and localized, for they are tied to the episodes of one village or several that are situated close together.

In between these two poles of popular prayers, represented by scholars and village literati, there are again several discernible categories which need a more detailed study than I can here provide. But I must refer to them because they constitute a very sizable and significant body. The upper layer here is represented by priests and scholars of traditional style, and the lower one by the women folk who devoutly observe numerous feasts, festivals, and ceremonies the year round.

The priests, and even some religious-minded young university graduates (mostly studying Hindi, Sanskrit, ancient Indian culture, etc.), now increasingly write about the domain that in practice almost exclusively belonged to the women observing *teej* and *teuhār*, following oral traditions and familial practices. Examples from the scores of such titles that I recently came across in Uttar Pradesh, Delhi, and Rajasthan are: *Complete fasts and festivals for all the twelve months* (n.d.) by Bharatiya and Brahmachari (Mathura); same title (n.d.) by Hiramani Singh "Sathi," M.A. (Allahabad); and *Customs and practices of Rajasthan* (1966) by Sukhvir Singh Gahlot (Block Development Officer, Ratangarh, Jaipur).

All of these books provide at least four types of prayers — original in Sanskrit (at least one in every volume that I have seen), original prayers by renowned saints, new prayers written either by authors or by the *gurū*s of authors, and prayers that were until recently orally transmitted by women but are now written down, as known to the authors, after "some consultation" with old women and old priests. The last category of prayers, let us note, often end by saying "As the deity [name given here] blessed so-and-so [a character of the folk tale or a story] with such-and-such things [e.g. progeny, riches, health, wifehood, divine grace, *bhaktī*, etc.], the deity may do the same to all [implicitly to those who are praying at that time]." The published books, however, sometimes drop it, but they always add a paragraph on the significance of a fast or a festival in modern times.

To summarize, in terms of the language of prayers, it could be Sanskrit, Hindi, or a regional language — or any of the dialects of these. But prayers in Sanskrit stand at the top; this language has recognizable cultural legitimacy of its own. It is the ideal language for prayers, as it were, despite its limited popularity at present. Hindi for the north (and southern regional languages) stands as the next most employed medium for Hindu prayers, scores of which have become as — or even more — legitimate as those in Sanskrit. Prayers in these languages cater to the majority with or without interpretation, but they do NOT (for they cannot) replace the ideas inherent in Sanskrit literature.

There is, then, a fairly clear rule-of-thumb about translations: originals are always better and more effective, and they rank higher than their translations. If the language of the original version cannot be understood, the translations serve the purpose. But classics like *Ramacharitamānas*, I was repeatedly told, stand beyond this characterization, "for it is really not a translation of Valmiks' work." Reflective language is more extolled (appreciation of it is another matter) than the descriptive and illustrative, and the emotional over the tersely argumentative.

Then, the standard vehicle of prayers has always been poetry rather than prose. The former can be sung and can be illusively cryptic, leading to alternative interpretations for decades and centuries to come.

Language and the Structure of Thought

Let us now turn to an interesting related problem: how, and how effectively it seems, does the language of prayers convey the idea of exchange lying behind words, and what are some general characteristics in this regard that stand out in the Hindu devotional prayers? To be sure, all prayers are not uniform as far as the moods and the attitudes of the devotees that they inevitably reflect are concerned. Not only are the trials and tribulations of a devotee's spiritual life reflected there, the closeness to and distance from the deity are also evident.

Thoughts are freely "exchanged" with one's deity, mostly in the form of a dialogue, even if the prayers may not often be written in that way. There are certain general notions that guide such expressions. A true devotee is supposed to stand very close to his deity. This closeness brings spiritual power according to those who surround him, but it brings informality for him that is often expressed in prayers. The devotee, then, may fret and frown over his "deity's behavior." He may complain about his deity's "heartlessness" and also about his "indifference and delay"; and he may, when he sees fit, gibe the deity to goad him to action.

In the most intimate hours of the *bhaktī bhāva*, a devotee, I was repeatedly told by the devout, may even rebuke his deity — "a rebuke that arises out of fathomless love for him." Instances were cited of devotees "who took to rebuking their most loved one as a regular mode of prayer, at least in public, although these same persons might have lavished adoration on their *ārādhya-deva* [deity of worship] in secret." Sometimes these are mere façades to conceal the real depth of one's devotion from the surrounding people. Here the culturally valued principle is: if one keeps one's actual depth of devotion a secret from the common crowd, the "fruits" of devotion are obtained faster, as there are few interruptions from the outside.

These intimacies of the devotee are reciprocated by the deity. He "speaks" back in prayers. He settles the position of such devotees in most unambiguous terms: he regards them as the nearest and the dearest ones in his whole creation. He speaks about the influence and the hold that these devotees have on him. In fact, he would do anything for them; he bars nothing from them; and there is nothing that he cannot offer in return to them for their unflinching devotion and dependence. The deity even forsakes his vow to honor his devotee's, as a famous song of Surdas says. Briefly, therefore, a devotee's sincere and complete dependence on his deity brings out a reciprocal response: "the deity feels dependent on his devotee."

Like begets like even at this level, and not only in the social world, allowing us to assert that the basic idea and logic of exchange are squarely (and very often consistently) met in the structure of prayers. They are not merely one-way movements of thought and action, as a hasty look at them might initially suggest. Further, there is graduation of both thought and action that flows back and forth between the deity and the devotee. Prayers record these movements in all their gusto and frustrations. Nothing, as in the social world, is given that is free of the idea of reciprocation sooner or later. The same rule of social relationships applies to the entire world of prayers.

The structure of devotional thought, to be sure, closely reflects the paradigm of social relations. It is actually patterned after it, as we demonstrated above, and not beyond or beside it. If one decides to establish a relationship with God, either as child or friend or servant or beloved, how is one going to behave towards him, except by establishing an homology with the social world. Thus, if the *bhaktī* movement abolishes (at least ideally) caste, creed, and rank distinctions, it maintains and glorifies the most essential social relationships. The joys, emotions, and depressions of these social relationships enchant the devotee and the deity in an equal measure; they both love, reciprocate, and cherish these infatuations "that are beyond the erosion of time." Hence sang Meera about her "eternal" lover and husband (Krishna), mocking the one her parents gave to her for this world (Rānā). The true *bhaktī*, the saint sings, transforms the transient of the social world into permanent bliss.

The above homology has had some pervasive influence on the character and social organization of the entire *bhaktī* movement. Numerous temples, sects of *sādhu*s, their numerous prayers every morning and evening, and the attending congregations endlessly repeat the paradigms of social relationships during every period of worship. They seek the deity either as a child or a parent or a beloved; and while they of course lament that it is not easy, they are almost endlessly bent upon making it true. They draw courage in this task from their saints who proved that it can be done.

Deities in temples and *sādhu*s in sects live, as it were, to reach the same goal. The deities, although immortal, live like mortals (they eat, sleep, and dress), while the *sādhu*s renounce the same family bonds that they are going to seek in the changed, divine, context. (Further similar points can be made on closer inspection.) Although most of such prayers of the millions of Hindus remain unrecorded, they obviously represent (and repeat) a model set by their devout leaders. In this sense, devotional prayers follow an essentially similar structure of thought, the major arrangements of which can be clearly understood through a study of the prayers of saints.

Although the scope of the present attempt precludes a more formal analysis of the thought structure of chosen prayers, it seems perfectly possible — much like Lévi-Strauss' *Structural study of myth* and his other recent studies of mythology. Such an approach can help one check some of the observations made above, particularly with regard to the internal consistency of prayers in expressing primary social relationships and cultural values and in evolving and arranging specified mythological personages and relationships to convey specified meanings and functions. (Moreover, the same approach can also help one observe the underlying "grammatical rules," some which are restricted to prayers and some which in general hold for any mythical narrative.)

Under the prayer-specific category may appear the usage of, for example, Hindi second-person pronouns — *aap*, *tum*, and *tū*. Normally, as we proceed from the first to the third, increasing emotional nearness and informality is indicated. But then, there are other usages as well, where they may begin to reflect increasing grudge, reproach, and insult. Prayers may reflect these — and other — meanings. Prayers, as an index of humility, on the other hand, may play down the FREQUENT (chaste) use of first-person pronouns. This may be particularly true of the prayers written under *dāsya bhāva* (see above).

While answering prayers, the deity may demonstrate the reverse order of the usage of, or preference for, first- and second-person pronouns. His "I" and *tū* (endearing "you") are quite consistent, while for the devotee this sequence will mean hurling an insult at the deity. More such "cross-usages" can be plotted by studying specific prayers. In terms of the gender, prayers, as an offshoot of *bhaktī* (and like it), are characterized as "female." The characteristics of surrender, soft speech, emotionalism (including loud wailing), and abjuring coercion and command — all conform to the Hindu view of femininity.

If mythological material is carefully studied, it also yields clear arrangements that follow syntactic rules of correspondence and concatenation. For the initiated, mythological figures like Yashodā, Hanumān, Rādhā, and Sudāmā stand for such specified kinds of devotional relationships as *vātsalya, dāsyā, madhur,* and *sakhya,* respectively. Similarly, one could prepare a catalogue of mythological events and personages that illustrate how social inequality, impiety, villainy, depravity, and vice are eroded and removed through the grace of God.

Another catalogue could be prepared of the famous devotees who really "conjugate" the divine for the good of the mundane. These catalogues, read as separate columns, illustrate primary categories out of which the content of a devotional prayer is most commonly composed. If the entries in columns are switched, they produce cultural anomalies. For example, if *bhakta* Hanumān is used (instead of Rādhā) in the context of lover-beloved expressions in prayers, the problem becomes obvious. "Even the novice does not make such a mistake." More aspects of such an approach need to be separately considered.

CONCLUDING REMARKS

Prayers, as considered above, reflect only some of the essential features which are contained in the devotional context. As almost a virgin field of study, their many preliminary dimensions need to be charted out in the context of the traditional domains of social anthropological inquiry. We may here remark only on one general aspect.

Prayers, like the entire *bhaktī* movement, point out contradictions that have lingered on without being resolved. Here they move beyond the domain of social prestations. They, for example, espouse social equality in the face of institutionalized inequalities of the caste system, and they have, as yet, not won on any lasting basis. But the ideal lingers on, getting an occasional fillip from religious personages on a regional basis. Prayers, as a part of sincere devotion, decry and aim to cut through the cobwebs of ritualism that pervade all of Hinduism. Thoughts, and not techniques, are important before God, one is repeatedly told in devotional songs; and while rituals become redundant for those who have achieved the *bhaktī,* they are meant to be only minimally followed by the beginners.

More serious philosophical contradictions are brought forth when the prayers repeatedly declare that with God's blessing, one can cut through the bondages of *karma* [action] and *punarjanma* [rebirth]. Mythology provides strong illustrations to support the claim. Not only are the devout members of the lowest caste (and even tribals) accepted by God, but even prostitutes, bandits, and destitutes. And if bondages of *karma* cease to operate in such instances, hope exists for all.

When this "rebellious" thought is further pushed, it is logical to find that a devotee does not care for the fourth ideal of the traditional life — *moksha*. Instead, he craves for the eternal company of his deity (i.e. of the form of God that he fervently worships). Briefly, therefore, *bhaktī* prayers, standing close to the social order, produce a TOTAL, alternative system of thought that exerts increasing influence on the social as well as the philosophical framework of the Hindu society. And the recent political movements toward egalitarianism discover here — often by chance — a strong parallel force that may be popularly tapped in one form or another.

REFERENCES

BHARATIYA, ROOPKISHORE, KRISHNA R. BRAHMACHARI
n.d.   *Vrat aur teuhār* (in Hindi, second edition). Mathura, India: Govardhan Pustkālaya.

GAHLOT, SUKHVIR SINGH
1966   *Rajasthān ké reet-rivāz* (in Hindi). Jaipur, India: Roshan Lal Jain and Sons.

KHARE, R. S.
1975   "Hindu social inequality and some ideological entailments," in *Culture and society*. Edited by B. N. Nair. Delhi: Thompson Press.

MAUSS, MARCEL
1967   *The gift* (Norton edition). Translated by Ian Cunnison. New York: Norton.
1968   "Oeuvres I: Les fonctions sociales du sacré," in *Marcel Mauss oeuvres. Edition critique et présentation de Victor Karady*. Paris: Les Éditions de Minuit.

PANDIT RAMNARAYANDUTTA SHĀSTRI, *translator*
1960   *Durgāsaptasatī stotra* (in Hindi and Sanskrit, eleventh edition). Gorakhpur, India: Gita Press.

ROBERT, PAUL
1972   *Dictionnaire alphabétique et analogique de la langue française*. Paris: Société du Nouveau Littré.

SHANKARANARAYANAN, S.
1968   *Glory of the divine mother: devi māhātmayam*. Pondicherry, India: Dipti Publications.

SINGER, M.
1966   "The Radha-Krishna bhajans of Madras City," in *Krishna: myths, rites and attitudes*. Edited by M. Singer. Honolulu: East-West Press.
1972   *When a Great Tradition modernizes: studies in Madras*. New York: Praeger.

SINGH, HIRAMANI
n.d.   *Vrat aur teuhār* (Hindi). Allahabad, India: Durga Pustak Bhandar.

SECTION FIVE

Oppositions

Correlation of Contradictions:
A Tibetan Semantic Device

ROBERT B. EKVALL

By the stubborn facts and forces of geography the land of Tibet is wedged between the lands of India and China. The glacier and snow giants of the Himalayas, forming a long east-west chain, make a wall of imprisonment or — depending on one's viewpoint — of protection to mark its southern limits. The Kunlun mountains and deserts of the north seal it off from Chinese Central Asia and, although the plateau thus delimited tilts eastward towards China proper, distance and the successive chasms of the "great trench-rivers of Asia" create an almost equally effective barrier or shield. This plateau homeland of the Tibetan people, rock-ribbed from south to north by a succession of snowy ranges interspersed with internal drainage basins, has been given many names, such as "Roof of the World," yet is best described by the Tibetan name "Region of the Glacier-Snow Mountains."

Throughout history a varied assortment of peoples have lived in different parts of the plateau. Some moved on while others left behind

The sources upon which this paper is based — uncited in footnotes but most real — are to be found in: (a) the experiences, memories, and written observations of eight years of living and discussing with Tibetans in northeast Tibet; (b) over one thousand hours of seminar-type discussion with four Tibetan research collaborators, identified and evaluated in "A Tibetan seminar on Tibetan society and culture" (*Current Anthropology*, October 1963); and (c) one year of fact finding among the nearly one thousand Tibetans in Switzerland, which included some rewarding discussion of language, religion, and law with one of the tutors of the Dalai Lama.

I am also grateful to the Wenner-Gren Foundation and the National Science Foundation for various grants; to the Far Eastern Institute of the University of Washington for extensive opportunity which made possible the virtually continuous research cited above; and in particular to a recent National Science Foundation grant for intensive research in Tibetan law — concepts and practices.

remnants or barely discernible enclaves. The ethnic origins or affiliations of the T'ang-hsiang, Yang-tung, Sum-pa, and others are unknown
or only tentatively identified; but those of Hor, Sog Po, Dru Gu, and
A ZHa are traceable with some degree of certainty to Turanian, Mongolian, Turkic, and Uighuric sources. The Ch'iang people, believed by
some to be the true nuclear proto-Tibetans, moved westward and
southwestward onto the plateau, leaving traces at points along the way.
In central-western Tibet, the mysterious ZHang ZHung kingdom com-
peted with the nascent Tibetan empire; as late as the last quarter of the
seventh century it had its own WRITTEN language and books on religion
and philosophy which engaged the efforts of the Tibetan translators of
that time. Yet despite all this, it is mysterious because it vanished completely; it was racially assimilated, its power structure dismantled, and
its language forgotten and replaced by Tibetan.

This process of Tibetanization went on throughout the entire plateau
(and continues to this day in fringe areas) until the unchanging factors
of geography were correlated with and matched by the everchanging
forces of demography. The Tibetan plateau then became, to its very
edges, with spillovers beyond, the habitat of the Tibetan people.

The spearhead and chief strength-factor of this long and successful
process of cultural conquest was language, which, it is true, was linked
to and strengthened by a symbiotic relationship with the Buddhist
religion. In Mongolia, for example, monks learned Tibetan just as
German monks of the Middle Ages learned Latin, and for much the
same reasons. Even now the great majority of Mongolian personal
names are recognizably Tibetan terms of religious significance.

The religious factor, however, is shared with the many peoples of
diverse cultures in the world who believe in Buddhism. The Tibetan
language, on the other hand, belongs solely to the Tibetans. It is thus
the unique instrument (or more aptly weapon) used by the Tibetans in
a one-way acculturative process to Tibetanize their neighbors. How this
process operates may be seen even now in a number of areas in
eastern Tibet inhabited by Mongol, Jarong, Bolotsi, Tsako, and other
enclaves.

Language is felt by the Tibetans themselves to be the important
criterion upon which, in their search for assurance of unity, they base
their self-image and self-identification as a people. On the plane of
BEING, human existence is thought to be a triad of body, speech and
mind; in the plane of DOING, it is a triad of deeds, words, and thoughts.
In their universe of values language is the great fact of man's endow-
ment and his culture. It is thus very natural, yet most significant that

on the occasion of a watershed experience in Tibetan history, when a Tibetan religious leader went to intercede with Godan, grandson of Ghenghis Khan, and sought to halt the invasion of Tibet — then already at full force — he should have represented his mission as being on behalf of "all who speak the Tibetan language." Among the crumbling fragments of the onetime Tibetan empire there remained at that time only the criterion, or bond, of language to symbolize unity.

Having said this much about the geography of a wedge plateau, the demography of a people living on, and mostly limited to, that plateau, and a culture centered to a considerable degree on language, we are tempted to speculate about what might have happened to such a people and culture if their habitat, instead of being a barrier area, had been a passage area similar to the trough along which the Silk Road was routed where the great west-east movements of conquest, trade, and culture change took place. As it is, their self-image and distinct identity are well maintained, even though they are wedged between what they identify as the "land of law/order" on the one side, and the "land of religion/cosmology" on the other. We know them as the two great power structures and cultural systems of Asia which divide a continent between them, the Sinitic and the Indic; one or the other has placed its stamp on all Asian countries. Tibet has been stamped by both yet remains different and in-between; one of the reasons is language.

The Tibetan language is generally considered the lesser moiety of the Sino-Tibetan language family although until ablautism is scientifically demonstrated, some may challenge that classification. However that may be, Tibetan does resemble Chinese in being basically mono-syllabic and strongly idiomatic in usage. Each syllable is very much an isolated semantic unit, lacking intrinsic parts-of-speech differentiation. As such a unit it has a degree of completeness and independence, although particles have lesser autonomy. However, in combination with other such units — all assuming parts-of-speech roles according to need — satisfactory and richly varied communication of phrase and sentence length and content takes place.

An essential element in this kind of communication is the creation and use of compounds. Semantic units, in whatever parts-of-speech roles they are cast, are freely compounded by nongrammatical juxtapositioning into two-syllable forms. There are a few atypical, but very useful, three- and four-syllable forms but they are not treated in this paper. This compounding is not a case of concept *a* plus concept *b*; nor is it a case of concept *a* being grammatically modified by or modifying concept *b*; rather, it is a case of concept *a* being merged with concept *b* to metamorphose into a new concept, concept *c*.

This device gives to language usage an astonishing, even bewildering, fluidity and offers possibilities of virtually unlimited variation of nuance. The nearest analogue to this process is found in the manner and results of a painter when using colors. When he mixes yellow and blue he gets neither streaked yellow and blue nor differing shades of yellow or blue. What he does get is green — a new and true color and not a shade of anything else. There would appear to be no grammar in the handling of colors. This is not to imply that Tibetan does not have a grammar. Indeed, in the seventh century, spoken Tibetan was strait-jacketed within a complex grammar closely modeled on that grammar of all grammars, the Sanskrit one. This process of grammatical hair-splitting by Tibetan grammarians, seeking to outdo Sanskrit itself, coincided with the borrowing of a syllabary derived from Sanskrit for reducing the Tibetan language to writing, and the acceptance of a re-ligion whose books were written in Sanskrit, which made it necessary for Tibetans to learn Sanskrit in order to translate the vast treasure of the Buddhist scriptures.

Under this three-pronged Sanskritic impact the Tibetan language split into two type-forms: *CHos sKad* (religion/cosmology language) and *PHal sKad* (common language). The basic vocabulary of the two is essentially identical; but the grammar and syntax of *CHos sKad* is the form in which the great majority of religious and philosophical books have been written and is, moreover, a copy (labored or un-conscious) of Sanskrit grammar and syntax patterns. *PHal sKad*, how-ever, in spoken and written discourse, maintains the continuity of the old forms: disregard of grammatical distinctions and relationships; use of idiomatic syntax; and a great reliance on compounding.

Compounding is multivariant and, besides its use in the correlation of contradictions, serves a variety of other purposes: the simple one of creating emphasis; the formation of new substantives to match new artifacts; the indicating of different aspects of psychological analysis; and the linking of the general to the particular to sharpen the focus of meaning. In this compounding all parts of speech, not necessarily matched, are used. Examples of the various uses of compounding are: *mTHu-sTob* 'might-strength' i.e. 'power at its greatest' (synonymous noun-noun, simple emphasis device); *rGyang-mTHong* 'distance-see' i.e. 'binoculars' (noun-verb, new substantive to match new artifact); *Sa-ZHing* 'earth-field' i.e. 'cultivated land' (noun-noun, from the general of 'earth' to the particular of 'field'); *rGyug-aDur* 'run-trot' i.e. 'trot as gait' (verb-verb, from the general of 'run' to the particular of 'trot');

Mig-Ser 'eye-yellow' i.e. 'envy/jealousy' (noun-adjective, physio-psy-chological analysis); *NGa-rGyal* 'I-conquer' i.e. 'pride' (pronoun-verb, psychological cause-effect analysis); *Rang-bZHin* 'selfness-face' i.e. 'dis-position/nature' (noun-noun, psychological analysis); *Rang-dBang* 'self-ness-power' i.e. 'freedom' (noun-noun, psychological analysis); *Rang-Don* 'selfness-meaning/interest' i.e. 'selfishness' (noun-noun, psycholog-ical analysis); *gZHan-Don* 'otherness-meaning/interest' i.e. 'altruism' (noun-noun, psychological analysis).

The last two examples in this series of multivariant compoundings are not instances of the correlation of contradictions, but in themselves they do point to and define by analysis the opposing poles of action motivation: the altruistic versus the selfish; the private interest versus the public interest; the individual benefit versus the group (which may be extended to include all) benefit. It is not cogent to the particular theme of this paper to discuss at any length Tibetan attempts to recon-cile or correlate, in any manner, these two fundamental contradictions. Studies of religious observances and, in particular, of pilgrimage and its motivations, do suggest that, by invoking the all-embracing compassion of the Bodhisattva for all sentient beings, sublimation is offered as the causal agent whereby the meanness of selfishness is transmuted into the nobleness of altruism.

Six examples listed below of adjectival compounding of the contra-dictory exemplify the dialectic of the correlation of contradictions and its application in semantics. In each instance, the two components of the compound are starkly contradictory — or at least mutually ex-clusive — yet when merged with each other into one concept their very contrariness demands a conceptualization which will enfold both on equal terms and push towards a higher level of abstraction as a result of the dialectic process.

This dialectic, which is not the Hegelian one of thesis and antithesis, nor the Marxist one which stresses the conflict of contradictions, per-meates much of Tibetan (as well as Chinese) conceptualization and semantics and related aspects of language usage. Its application by-passes the dilemma inherent in a strictly either-or approach, and its indirect influence pervades Tibetan thinking, permitting ambiguities in speech as to person, number, gender, tense, subject-object, etc. The six examples of this dialectic are as follows:

1. *CHe-CHung* 'large-small' i.e. 'size'; adjective-contradiction adjec-tive; conceptualization melding contradictory perceptual characteriza-tions of concrete referents into unity, thereby achieving a more gener-alized higher level of abstraction.

2. *THo-dMan* 'high-low' i.e. 'height'; adjective-contradiction adjective; conceptualization melding contradictory perceptual characterizations of concrete referents into unity, thereby achieving a more generalized higher level of abstraction.

3. *Ring-THung* 'long-short' i.e. 'length'; adjective-contradiction adjective; conceptualization melding contradictory perceptual characterizations of concrete referents into unity, thereby achieving a more generalized higher level of abstraction.

4. *Grang-Dro* 'cold-hot' i.e. 'temperature'; adjective-contradiction adjective; conceptualization melding contradictory sensory characterizations of concrete referents into unity, thereby achieving a more generalized higher level of abstraction.

5. *Yang-lCi* 'light-heavy' i.e. 'weight'; adjective-contradiction adjective; conceptualization melding contradictory experiential characterizations of concrete referents into unity, thereby achieving a more generalized higher level of abstraction.

6. *bZang-NGan* 'good-bad' i.e. 'quality'; adjective-contradiction adjective; conceptualization melding contradictory value-judgment characterizations of concrete referents into unity, thereby achieving a more generalized higher level of abstraction.

The ultimate example of how meaning can be developed by compounding and be refined to abstract and high ethical levels is found in the juxtapositioning of *rGyu* and *aBras*, two words, by themselves, of basic down-to-earth denotations but with far-reaching, surprising and significant connotations and histories. The core meaning of *rGyu*, the first component of the compound, is 'substance' both in the material sense and in the sense that is much more intangible, beyond mere wealth, as when someone is known as a "man of substance." It is 'quality' stemming from its origins as when — to use a marketplace argument — the texture of a piece of cloth is called in question and linked with choice, clean wool, finely spun thread, and appropriate warp; it is 'guts' in a literal sausage-making context, thus showing up in colic identification; it sums up the 'ingredients' in the making of beer; when attached to a verbal root it is the projected promise of the future tense; when compounded with *sKar* 'star', it identifies the constellations through which the moon passes to make them the fate stars of astrology.

Throughout these and many other semantic permutations *rGyu* retains a basic invariant: some aspect or degree of causality, in its active function of CAUSING rather than being caused, and thus fit to stand alone and represent 'cause' in its primary sense of independent first causation (as distinguished from dependent secondary causation).

The core meaning of *aBras*, on the other hand, is simply 'rice' as a particular cereal and, by logical extension, at one remove from a particular crop or yield. The word has virtually none of the associative connotations such as are attached to *rGyu*. Resemblances in color, size, and shape make it do duty as the descriptive word for small saddle-blisters on a horse's back; and it does, indeed, become more generalized in the compound *aBras-Bu* 'rice progeny' meaning 'fruitage', which applies to nuts, berries, fruits, and grain in-the-head. Even in this compound, rice loses its particularity and becomes somewhat of a representative symbol. Except as an imported cereal sold in the markets, rice as a real crop or yield does not belong to Tibet. If grown at all it is found only in small pockets of cultivation of the valley floors of the Salween and Mekong rivers in the farthest southeastern corner of the land. Why should it, instead of barley, which is the true "staff of life" of the land, represent crop and yield? Confronted with this anomaly, the Tibetans hark back to mythic and legendary themes, suggesting that rice was the first grain known to man since, in value, it leads all other grains.

Parenthetically the occurrence of *aBras* 'rice' in place-names is at times tantalizingly suggestive and my own puzzlement is shared (with wry amusement and makeshift explanations) by my Tibetan friends. For example a bench-line plain along the Yellow River, at 34°N with an altitude of approximately 12,000 feet — more than 1,000 feet higher than where even barley is now grown at that latitude — is called *aBras-sKye THang* 'rice-sprout plain'. This is, in itself, something of a contradiction or at least an improbability. Possibly in this and other similar instances rice is either a surrogate name for some other unknown grain or is entirely symbolic.

Unquestionably it is symbolic, and solely symbolic, when it becomes *aBras* 'effect' when it is matched with *rGyu* 'cause' in the compound *rGyu-aBras* 'cause-effect'. In one sense, it is a familiar compound, having its own place in the semantics of English language usage; but in the context of the correlative dialectic and what it can achieve (see earlier discussion), its conceptual meaning, or meanings and disparate levels, is certain to be a quantum jump in conceptualization.

As an illustrative analogy, a case-in-point from the Chinese language is here of some value. In the ideographic writing of that language, the ideograph for the concept of harmony is a compound of two concrete referents with symbolic connotations. Side by side, in balance, and written from left to right, the graphs for 'crop/harvest' and 'mouth' represent resultant 'harmony'. 'Crop/harvest' is relatively self-explanatory when redefined as 'supply'; 'mouth' needs some explanation as to its symbolic use. In many contexts it stands for 'person', e.g. "in my household eight mouths" but those eight do need to be fed and mouth thus can also stand for need or 'demand'. 'Supply' and 'demand' adequately balanced, become 'harmony' — personal and societal.

In the compounded concept of 'cause-effect' and what it signifies, the dialectic of the correlation of contradictions is somewhat modified. Cause and effect are not immutable contradictions; rather, in the entire universe of change of every kind and degree, and at every level, they are semantically opposed yet complementary — as means and ends — in the cyclical and unending process of change. As a concept, the compound has two levels of meaning; it operates on the level of fairness and on the level of justice. It is at the apex of a semantic triangle, yet in Tibetan, it has no particularized name of its own, only the compounded concepts of *rGyu* 'cause' and *aBras* 'effect'. These two base corners of the triangle constitute its semantic surrogate, pointing towards and defining its existence. Yet from its uses and contexts, we can define it and name it in English as 'fairness/justice'.

The dialectic which correlates contradictory or disparate concepts has, in this instance, not only raised meaning to a higher level of abstraction but to the ultimate level of ethical values according to which, in the semantic field of fairness, worthiness or worthlessness, fitness or unfitness, and honesty or dishonesty are defined; in the realm of justice, it is where rightness or wrongness are judged. At both levels, the concept, derived by compounding, is the criterion or standard by which characterization takes place.

The concept of *rGyu-aBras* as 'fairness' is probably the more ancient of the two and more widespread as a necessary accompaniment to an extended range of human interaction. It stands for: fairness in the marketplace — value stated or questioned, and price asked or given; fairness in social relations — decisions made or concessions granted in problems of inheritance, marriage, divorce, assignment of role, cognizance of status fitness, recognition of need, deference to self-image, and much else.

The concept of *rGyu-aBras* as 'justice', which is the final individual and societal criterion of right and wrong is most invoked in the all-important arena of social control. Prior to the Chinese take-over of Tibet, three systems of law (i.e. social-control devices) coexisted, forming an uneven pattern of distribution and effectiveness throughout Tibetan society: (a) the primal law of individual or in-group reprisal; (b) the system of mediated consensus settlement, substituting indemnification for reprisal; and (c) juridically imposed adjudication. Despite sharp differences among all three, they were not mutually exclusive. Reprisal could subside into mediation at any stage in its course, or adjudication might intervene. But reprisal had one fatal defect because, without recourse to mediation, it could not forestall seriatim counterreprisal. Mediation's best pressure leverage towards agreement was fear of reprisal. In at least one well-known instance, adjudication was mediation in disguise — with official posture and mask — to give it the semblance of jurisprudence in action. In each of the three systems, all stages, options, procedures, decisions, and results were scrutinized and characterized, in approval or disapproval, according to the criterion of 'justice'.

For reprisal law to be characterized as "having justice," such reprisal should be in kind: human life for human life; taking of hostages for hostages taken; seizure of livestock for livestock rustled; impounding of possessions for possessions pilfered. It should also be proportionate: the killer killed, NOT his entire family along with him; nor the entire herd of horses driven off for a few cattle or sheep taken; and so forth. It should also not show spiteful or senseless excess: the setting fire to crops, houses, forests or pasturage; ill-treatment of women, children, the aged or the sick; and acts of desecration tempting response from the supernatural. When reprisal "having justice" was carried out, the result — equilibrium in a fair balance of 'cause-effect' — had justice; yet the balance was precarious and did not last for long, because of the inherent defect, previously mentioned, in the law of reprisal.

In the system of mediated consensus, the second social-control device, such matters as selection of mediators, arrangements for effecting cessation of hostile activity by both parties, fixing of time and place, forms and degrees of pressure applied, demonstration of nonbias, arguments used, awareness of real rights (however conflicting they might seem), and the terms of the final settlement — all these were subjected to the same scrutinizing evaluation and characterized as "having" or "not having justice." Only those settlements that met this test, being thus buttressed by consensus opinion, were likely to weather the stresses of time and conflicting interests.

The third system of juridical adjudication — more than either of the two preceding systems — laid stress on cause-effect 'justice' and, congruently, was held even more closely accountable to that justice in all aspects of its application. Arrest and confinement, treatment in confinement, eliciting and/or forcing of testimony, taking and evaluation of evidence, maintenance of official probity, assessment and imputation of guilt, when and how to appeal by ordeal to the supernatural, interpretation of written codes, rendering of a verdict, and determination and infliction of punishment — all of these were aspects of jurisprudence-in-action which might be labeled as either "having justice," or "not having justice." How those labels were apportioned had much to do with the course of jurisprudence throughout the society.

In adjudication, determination of justice was accountable, moreover, in two directions: downwards, in a generalized and diffused sense, to the parties concerned and public opinion; upwards, in the very specific sense of making the required report to higher authority, which in some instances might be at the very peak of the local power structure.

All these aspects and applications of the *rGyu-aBras* 'cause-effect' i.e. 'justice' concept, however high they may rise in the field of public morality, are nevertheless involved solely with mundane (profane, as against sacred) concerns. However, in the sacred-profane dichotomy of the Tibetan world view and universe of values, only the sacred is of ultimate permanence and worth. Moreover, it is in the context of this latter system of values that the concept of *rGyu-aBras* 'cause-effect' became sublimated to the highest sacred level when it found its place in that tremendous transfer-of-concepts undertaking in which the doctrines, rules, and commentaries of Buddhism — originally formulated in an Indic-Sanskrit idiom — were translated into Tibetan and, in the process, reformulated into a Sino-Tibetan idiom.

At this stage, and prior to any descriptive analysis of that undertaking and its results, it is essential to note an important characteristic of the Tibetan language: it is strongly, even stubbornly, resistant to the use of loanwords, though somewhat more receptive to loansemantics which are then articulated in Tibetan quasi-equivalents. Without doubt there are loanwords in fair number, as in all languages. They are mostly words that have come into the culture attached to artifacts and animals, e.g. table, whisky, a special variety of Mongolian felt, motor, chair, horse, stallion, camel, lion, etc. This much being granted, the bent towards resistance — whether because of a built-in linguistic idiosyncrasy or because of cultural awareness of language as a power and/or weapon — still remains. Regarding this bent, a Sanskritist colleague, after long argument, once conceded, "certainly a most inhospitable language." Parenthetically, there are probably more Tibetan words in general common English usage (yak, kiang, lama, for example) than there are English words in general common Tibetan usage.

This inhospitable imperviousness to loanwords and to a lesser degree to loanconcepts persisted throughout the two-centuries-long undertaking of translating the Buddhist scriptures (doctrine, rules, exegetic commentary) from Sanskrit into Tibetan. In the Tibetan text, the results of long labor during a period of great change in Tibetan culture, there are few Sanskrit loanwords of cognitive significance, although some ritual ejaculatory phrases (analogous to "Ave Maria," etc.) occur as salutations; other Sanskrit words credited with mystical sound-power — meaning is secondary because unknowable — are combined in incantatory charms which are retained without translation in the Tibetan text. More Sanskrit key doctrinal terms (*buddha, dharma, sangha, samadhi, bodhisattva, mantra, mandala, vajra, karma,* etc.) are to be found in English writings about Buddhism and related mysticism than in the whole body of Tibetan literature on Buddhism. This is because the terms cited above, together with virtually the entire Sanskritic doctrinal terminology, were translated into Tibetan by using (sometimes singly but more frequently in combination) indigenous and often very commonplace words and the CONCEPTS for which they stood.

What took place when Buddhism was introduced into Tibet and its concepts transferred into the Tibetan universe of values and language is a most revealing example of what happens to concepts — in terms of change and contraction or expansion of meaning — when they are transferred from culture to culture by the process of translation. How that process operated and what its lessons are, is a challenge to scholarship and one of the unfinished tasks in the field of Tibetology. The challenge has been singularly ignored and the task neglected, possibly because of the disparity between Sanskrit and Tibetan in linguistic status, diffusion, and resources. There has also been a somewhat understandable tendency to consider Tibetan words used in translating as mere convenient vocables which have been emptied of their primary Tibetan meanings and then filled with Sanskrit meanings, thus becoming stand-ins for Sanskrit words and concepts, instead of being true translations.

The Tibetans themselves were acutely aware of the pitfalls of translation with its quandaries and misjudgments. They instituted translation schools, attempted to standardize terminology, and set guidelines for the work. One of the reasons given for the failure of an earlier attempt to introduce Buddhism was the lack of qualified translators. In a seeming aside, which nevertheless appears to suggest a grave error, it is stated that the word *bodhisattva* had been rendered *Blo-Sems* 'intelligence-mind'.

The final page of a paper is no place for any attempt to answer a challenge to scholarship or to repair a neglect — such a task requires at least a book, for there are too many examples modified by too many variables. Furthermore, there is only one crowning example which is germane to the theme of this paper. But before analyzing it and showing its relationship to *rGyu-aBras* 'cause-effect', a number of other examples is listed here to illustrate the variety of modifications which do take place in translation.

Sanskrit	Tibetan	English
buddha	Sang-rGyas 'purified-transcended'	the Buddhahood
bodhisattva	Byang-CHub-Sems-dPa 'purged-permeated-mind-hero'	bodhisattva
sangha	dGe-aDun 'virtue/merit-assembly'	the community
triratna	dKon-mCHog-gSum 'rare-perfect-three' (dKon is the common word for 'scarce' i.e. not to be found in the market; mCHog is 'perfect/excellent' as applied to a horse)	The Jewel Triad
samadhi	Ting-NGe-aDZin 'afterglow-real-seize' (Ting names that luminous moment between day and night when light and quiescence merge into peace)	state of meditation
bhavana	sGom 'hibernate/hibernation' (shared deep meditation with marmots, bears, and bats)	
karma	Las 'work'	karma

Las, alone or in combination, is the commonly used word for work of any kind; here, it is a core concept, completely ambiguous as to noun, verb, number, and tense and subsuming the whole of activity throughout all the rebirths in the numberless cycles of existence. It is closest to a definition of *karma*, moreover, when it is compounded with 'cause-effect' i.e. *Las-rGyu-aBras* 'work-cause-effect': the sublimated concept at a transcendental level of final 'justice' to which even the Buddhahood is subject.

Sex, Nature, and Culture in Ponapean Myth

J. L. FISCHER

Probably all cultures express in some form an opposition between nature and culture and an opposition between men and women. It is logically possible, then, to align these two pairs of oppositions, associating one sex with "nature" and the other with "culture." Thus one culture might emphasize the role of women as preservers and builders of the home, which is the seat of culture, and contrast this with the role of men as destroyers in feuding and warring. Another culture might emphasize the role of men in providing the political framework within which culture exists and contrast this with the role of women in drawing men back from the larger society to a concern with satisfying basic animal needs for their families. It is the purpose of this paper to describe briefly the traditional attitudes of the people of Ponape, Caroline Islands (Micronesia) as reflected in their myths and folklore, and to call attention to some methodological implications of the ethnographic data.

The people of Ponape speak a single language with recognizable, mutually intelligible dialects, and think of themselves as sharing a single basic culture, although they were divided into five small independent states at the time of first recorded foreign descriptions. The population was also divided among about twenty exogamous matrilineal clans, which continue to persist to the present day but with somewhat less importance. Most of the clans were found in all five states, their relative rank varying locally.

Ponapeans have no words which directly translate "nature" and "culture" but these are useful labels for the anthropologist to use to subsume a series of more concrete oppositions including "human" (*aramas*) and "beast" (*mahn* — includes fish, insects, birds, etc. as well as mammals);

"cooked" (*leu*) and "raw" (*amas*); "land" (*nan-sapw*) and "sea" (*nan-sed*), "cultivated land" (*nan-sapw*) and "jungle" (*nani-wel*), etc. The first of each of these pairs is, of course, "cultural" and the second is "natural."

People are contrasted with animals in that people live most of the time and ought to live according to social rules, many of which are prescribed or exemplified in myths recounting the behavior of ancestors. People who violate these rules are either said to be crazy or evil or to be acting like animals, or all three. People typically live on land as opposed to sea. Cultivated land as opposed to jungle has largely been cleared and planted with breadfruit trees, coconut palms, bananas, taro, yams, etc. People's houses are in the middle of it, while animals live mainly in the sea or jungle.

Nevertheless the distinction between "nature" and "culture" or "beast" and "human" is blurred at times. Many of the clans have totemic animal ancestors and at times Ponapeans will say that a certain animal species is "not an animal; it is really human." The totemic species are believed to share some human behavior at times even today, and in the totemic myths the ancestral animals are said to have at times performed acts which would require temporary human shape as well as human intent. Thus the freshwater eel, totem of the Great Eel clan (Lasialap), is reported to come out of streams to visit the homes of its human relatives at life crises such as birth and death, and is also said to be able to recognize members of the Great Eel clan and refrain from biting them as they bathe or do laundry in the streams. At the same time the eels are reported to occasionally bite strangers, clan enemies, and even spouses of clan members or children of the men, if the spouses and children are not properly loyal and industrious.

The blurring of the distinction between beast and human shows a certain statistical and logical patterning. If we look at instances of reputed transformation from one category to another in myth it appears that there are cases of animals transforming themselves into humans as babies (e.g. the origin of the Bird Clan from sea slugs who came onto land) and humans transforming themselves into animals as old people (e.g. the first ancestress of the Bird Clan on Ponape, who became an insect in her old age; or the last hereditary ruler of the whole island, who leaped into a stream and became a small brightly colored fish on his defeat in battle) but it appears to me that there are no clear cases of transformations either way involving young to middle-aged adults. This would be consistent with a view that the main bearers and defenders of culture are mature adults, and that the very young and very old both lack full participation in culture, the former not having had time to learn the rules and the latter having lost the physical and mental agility necessary to play a fully cultural role.

If we ask about the sex of animals in myths we also observe a distinct patterning. Where sex of animals is specified the animal is usually, though not always, female. Since the clans are matrilineal the immediate animal forbear of the clan is always female. When male animals appear in the clan myths they are secondary, although human males may be important as actors in the myth along with the animal females.

The principal part of the Great Eel myth, for instance, involves a female eel. Briefly, she was raised by a human couple who planned to eat her when she got big. She ate them instead and then traveled here and there giving birth to the human ancestresses of the various subclans of the clan. She bore her first child after a frightful encounter with a demon eel fisherman, and bore other children after marrying a high chief. Eventually she settled at an estuary and began to eat selected human passersby. A magician lured her out to sea, whereupon she traveled to the island of Kusaie (the easternmost high island of the Carolines) and gave birth to more children there. Finally she swam back to Ponape and beached herself in the state of Net, where she bore her last daughter and expired. Her body now forms a long peninsula.

Nevertheless, preceding the account of the female eel there is another section of the myth which tells about a male eel who was in a sense the father of the female eel. This male eel was also raised by a couple who had a daughter. When the eel grew to maturity it started having a love affair with the daughter, who grew thin because of it. The parents therefore decided to eat the eel. The eel overheard their plans and — unlike the female eel — acquiesced in the plot but told the daughter to request the head for her portion and to bury it and watch what came out of the grave. She did so and two kinds of bananas and one kind of breadfruit sprouted from the grave. The female eel whose career is described above hatched from a small stone or seed in one of the bananas. A bird pecked out the seed and defecated it into the lagoon where the human couple who raised the female eel picked it up.

I have told the two sections of this myth out of chronological order, but this is fairly common on Ponape. The part dealing with the female eel is better known and is more elaborate and more directly relevant to the members of the Great Eel clan. While there are similarities between the two sections of the myth, the differences are interesting. The male who is assigned "beast" status in this myth is engaged too intensely in a premarital romance, while the female who is assigned "beast" status is producing offspring, mostly after marriage.

A review of other Ponapean animal myths tends to bear out the conclusion drawn from the eel myth. Female animals are likely to be engaged in child bearing, while male animals are likely to be involved in premarital or extramarital affairs.

Ponapeans have traditionally placed a high value on children. A woman who produced many children was praised. Abortions were discouraged and infanticide was apparently not practiced, even for defective children, in contrast to some other Oceanic societies. Nevertheless the myths suggest that pregnant and nursing females were somehow identified with animals. I believe this makes sense in view of traditional attitudes and practices concerning food on Ponape.

On the one hand, contributions to feasts were important, and raising food and preparing it for feasts were considered primarily the work of men. The emphasis at feasts was primarily on the display and redistribution of food. Most of the food presented at feasts was taken home by the participants and it was considered bad form for men to eat much, especially in public.

On the other hand, men were also supposed to indulge the appetites of their pregnant and nursing wives in order to produce healthy babies and provide abundant milk for them. A man busy satisfying the food whims of his fertile wife would have less time for feast work, which was traditionally the most important kind of service a man could offer his chief: the "great service" (*tou-lap*) as opposed to the "lesser service" (*tou-tik*), which was bravery in war. It seems safe to say that men also had special appetites for foods at times which they did not satisfy because of the cultural restrictions on male gluttony. From the male view, the pregnant and nursing women, in order to indulge their animal appetites, would appear to be excused from cultural restrictions on eating as well as from the cultural prescription to produce and prepare food.

On the other hand in the case of premarital and extramarital affairs Ponapeans tend to ascribe the initiative to the men, at least in the sense that the men are thought to be generally ready for sex, while it is the role of the women to resist if it is inappropriate for whatever reason. Ponapeans were traditionally fairly tolerant of premarital sex, but parents had definite ideas of who was and was not a suitable potential spouse for their child; infant engagements were sometimes made. Probably parents of daughters frequently disapproved of particular suitors, as they still do today at times. A Ponapean saying, "Men are demons (*eni*) but women make them human," is applied to illicit sexual affairs of various sorts. In this context it is the women who are supposed to uphold the human cultural rules, while men are ready to violate them with the slightest encouragement. Incidentally, there are grounds for regarding demons (*eni*) as halfway between humans and beasts in Ponapean mythology.

In conclusion, it is possible to make alignments between nature and culture, male and female in Ponapean mythology but the alignments differ according to social context and the stage of the life cycle involved. There is the suggestion that infants are somewhat identified with animals regardless of sex and that a similar identification is made for feeble old people. With adults, males are considered more animal-like in the context of pre- and extramarital affairs, while women are considered more animal-like in the context of pregnancy and nursing. Most myths involve only one set of these identifications or associations. Attention to a reasonably large sample of myths is required to develop the complexity of Ponapean traditional thought and attitudes.

Not in Ourselves, But in Our Stars

JEAN-PAUL DUMONT

Among the Panare Indians of Venezuelan Guiana, the word *tyakun* means "star." The stars result from the incestuous union of two siblings: *ecexkun*, the sun, who is male, and *wönö*, the moon, his sister. The informants were not clear about the number of stars thus generated; it was either "star" or "all the stars" which were involved. The sex of *tyakun* could not be clarified by the informants.

Only some of the visible stars are named. Among the stars which do receive a name, a group of them is characteristic of the dry season: Orion's Belt is called *pecka* or *kamawö tyakun* 'the star(s) of the dry season'. Characteristic of the rainy season is Antares (alpha of Scorpio), *tosenpitomunö*, also referred to as *kanokampe tyakun* 'the star of the rainy season'. As such, Orion's Belt and Antares form an axis, opposed not only as stars of the opposite seasons, but also as "lonely" to "accompanied." In the sky of the dry season, the Pleiades are followed by Orion's Belt. In addition, the Pleiades form a galaxy, and different societies recognize in it a different but precise number of stars. The Panare see six stars which are reputed to be siblings, five men and one woman. One of the men has a daughter, Aldebarran (alpha of Taurus), *yoröinkin* 'the child of *yoroö*'. The only female among the Pleiades is married to the man *pecka*. They have a son, Sirius (alpha of Canis Major), *peckankin* 'the child of pecka'. It is noteworthy that one of our informants denied the existence of *peckankin*, saying that *pecka* had no child and that Sirius was nothing but a plain *tyakun*. This discrepancy in information does not affect the point of our argument. Indeed, whether Sirius is named or not, several stars are named in the sky of the dry season, and a whole aspect of social life is reflected here in terms of an astronomical code.

On the other hand, the Panare are explicit about the star of the rainy season: "Antares is lonely." This solitude of the only named star of the rainy season is opposed to the cluster of named stars of the dry season: the latter are close together (in terms of location, that is, of residence) and linked together (in terms of kinship). Hence, the correlation of dry season : togetherness : : rainy season : isolation is stated here in an astronomical code.

But a difficulty emerges: the Pleiades and Orion's Belt are not far from each other. That is to say, they are on the same celestial meridian, and the latter's rise takes place somewhat later than that of the former. Consequently, although the "star of the rainy season" has disappeared when the Pleiades appear, the "star(s) of the dry season" have not yet appeared. As as corollary, a reverse alternation happens at the other end of the year. When the Pleiades disappear, Antares is not yet in the eastern horizon while Orion's Belt is still in the western one; Antares will appear after the disappearance of Sirius (the last named star in the sky of the dry season) and of Orion's Belt.

In fact, the opposition between Orion's Belt and Sirius is neutralized. The latter appears as a weakened combinatory variant of the former, since informants disagreed on the mythical status of Sirius but agreed in emphasizing the role of Orion's Belt. If Sirius is named, it is included in the category of "stars of the dry season." It is opposed to Orion's Belt as appearance is opposed to disappearance. In effect, the appearance of Sirius goes unnoticed at the beginning of the dry season; it is the appearance of Orion's Belt which is noticed. At the beginning of the rainy season, it is the disappearance of Sirius which is noticed (and of Orion's Belt for the informant who did not name Sirius). As we can see, the opposition of Sirius and Orion's Belt is redundant with the opposition of appearance of dry season star and disappearance of dry season star; the former opposition can be suppressed without affecting the structure. In other words, Orion's Belt and Sirius, as signs, do not have the same form (they are not the same stars), but they do have the same meaning and are merged in the category of "stars of the dry season."

The matter is entirely different with the Pleiades, which are not thought of as "stars of a season" but "stars of a year." We are therefore confronted with a contradiction. The Pleiades in their movement mark the change of season, but there is a brief overlap in each season of the stars conceived of as belonging to the opposite season. The contradiction results from the noncoincidence of two axes, represented as diameters of a yearly cycle in Figure 1. The appearance and disappearance

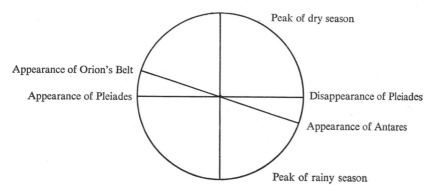

Figure 1.   Remarkable star movements in yearly cycle

of the Pleiades determine a diameter in the circumference of a yearly cycle; the appearance of the stars of the dry and rainy seasons determines another diameter of the same circumference. The Pleiades diameter represents the peaks of the seasons, since it marks the change of seasons. The smallest arcs formed on the circumference mark the two interseasons from rainy season to dry and from dry season to rainy.

This is the astronomical frame within which the structural oppositions and correlations of the yearly cycle will be organized. A simple examination of this frame reveals a major FORMAL opposition between dry season and rainy season. From a strictly formal viewpoint, there are two ways to interpret the length of the seasons: (1) the dry season proper extends from the appearance of Orion's Belt up to the disappearance of the Pleiades, while the rainy season proper extends from the appearance of Antares up to the appearance of the Pleiades; or (2) the dry season extends from the appearance of the Pleiades up to the appearance of Antares, while the rainy season extends from the disappearance of the Pleiades up to the appearance of Orion's Belt. In the first case, the two seasons do not constitute a whole yearly cycle; in the second case, the two seasons overlap. For the moment, there is no way to decide in favor of one rather than the other reading. It is, however, certain that the Panare, in using two axes, conceptualize the change of season as a distinct time period, namely, the duration of the interseasons, which in themselves form an opposition to the seasons proper. While the seasons proper are congruent to the presence of stars, the interseasons are delimited by four movements of stars. From the rainy season to the dry season, *yoroö* and then *pecka* appear; from the dry season to the rainy season, *yoroö* and then *pecka* or *peckankin* disappear. The movement of *tosenpitomunö* itself is not used to conceptualize the interseasons; only its presence, not its movements, are relevant during the rainy season.

We are therefore confronted with a major series of congruent oppositions, such that seasons : interseasons : : star presence : star passage : : duration : moment. Further, each term of the first major opposition may be subdivided in turn into a pair of minor oppositions. We could have easily established the opposition between dry season and rainy season. The interseasons are similarly opposed, such that from-dry-season-to-rainy-season : from-rainy-season-to-dry-season : : star disappearance : star appearance.

We turn now toward the examination of astronomical sexuality, where we discover its social implications as well as further developments in the preceding oppositions. If we are to understand the logic of this sexuality, we have to begin with the shortest time cycle, the twenty-four-hour period, which involves only two elements. Despite its apparent simplicity, this should hold our attention for a while.

Within the daily periodicity, the alternation of day and night is congruent with the alternation of two celestial bodies, the sun and the moon. It has been mentioned that the sun is male and the moon female, which may seem surprising at first sight. If day : night : : sun : moon : : male : female, then this is in flagrant contradiction with what ethnographic observation of daily life has established, i.e. that men : women : : night : day. Such a relation is evidently reversed by the sexes of the sun and the moon. But it should not be difficult to understand why.

The moon and the sun are an incestuous pair of siblings. In other words, through intemperate sexual behavior, they have reversed their kin status into an affinal role. Such antisocial behavior has provoked their astralization. By behaving like animals, i.e. mating naturally and not culturally, they become supernatural beings. This tends to establish that the cultural order (expressed in the present case by the normally expected behavior) mediates between nature and supernature, while its natural transgression leads to a supernatural effect.

In order to understand the involved conceptual logic, we must first discuss the Panare theory of incest. The mere idea of incest provokes a strongly emotional reaction among the Panare. They say *arkon monkay usotnö* 'to have sex like monkeys', meaning by this that incest is essentially natural, not cultural. Interestingly, one informant had a very revealing *lapsus linguae,* saying *arkonya usotnö* 'to have sex with monkeys', which would be equally distant from cultural behavior. Such a slip of the tongue tends to indicate that, in the subconscious of its author, incest as hyperbolic endogamy and bestiality as hyperbolic exogamy, were similarly conceived of as equally deviant from the cultural norm. We would need more than this simple example to draw any conclusions about bestiality. The Panare are not shepherds and do not indulge in bestiality at all, and little emotional response is involved in its discussion, which may merely serve to provoke laughter.

Although the Panare have, of course, a rule for the prohibition of incest, there is a radically different reaction to the discussion of incest, since its eventuality is not ruled out. The Panare are horrified by the very idea of incest. I have neither observed nor been told about any actual case of incest, and therefore could not check whether or not the sanction reserved for those who commit it was ever enforced. But everybody agreed that the guilty couple would be beaten to death, and emphasized that the punishment was absolutely mandatory if the case were to occur within the range of a nuclear family. The corpses of the victims would then be buried as are the corpses of people who die "normally." The informants, however, failed to remember an actual occurrence of such an event; indeed, with a slightly outraged tone of voice, they indicated that no incest case had ever occurred in their settlement.

Whether enforced or not, the penalty is strongly stated. Whatever the case, incestuous individuals are cultural mishaps who behave too naturally. The threatened cultural order reacts violently to reassert itself. In fact, the only way through which those who have strayed into the natural order can be brought back into the cultural one is by being killed. This is so for two reasons: (1) were the incestuous couple to escape before being put to death, they would wander like animals in the forest, die, and be transformed into dangerous spirits, that is, they would reach the supernatural order and escape completely the competence of culture to deal with them; (2) on the other hand, by being killed through cultural channels, those who have committed incest are thereby recovered by the cultural order, and their corpses are then processed culturally, that is, buried. Such a cultural burial leads to the separation of the body, which rots in the tomb, from the soul, which then glows in the Milky Way.

To sum up at this point, an overly natural behavior (incest) has one of two consequences. Either the incestuous couple, without any active participation of culture, escapes into nature (forest) and becomes incorporated into supernature (spirits) or, due to the intervention of culture (clubbing and burial), they rot naturally (in the tomb) while their souls glow supernaturally (in the Milky Way). The first case is unfortunate because culture has been unable to mediate between nature and supernature, whereas in the second case, it has succeeded in doing so. When mediation takes place, it is good because everything happens according to cultural norms; nature and supernature remain separated and under control. The absence of mediation, however, results in the collusion of nature with supernature, which has serious consequences: spirits are to be feared.

Incest is by definition anticultural and it has natural as well as supernatural consequences for its authors, whether they are killed or manage to escape. We are confronted then with a new problem. It is understandable that incest as an overly natural behavior might have either a natural end-result or a supernatural one. But why both? Isn't it because incest is not only too natural but at the same time too supernatural? By being marked as behavior which is maximally removed from culture, incest would therefore necessitate natural as well as supernatural consequences, that is, consequences equally removed from culture.

It is precisely such a collusion of nature with supernature which the cultural order attempts to prevent; this can be shown from the Panare conceptualization of the solar eclipse. The word *towömuku,* which means both "eclipse" and "incest" is revealing in this respect. From such mere linguistic evidence, it can be seen that to commit incest is to participate in the supernatural order to which the sun and the moon belong. Indeed, a solar eclipse is linguistically expressed as renewed sexual intercourse of these two celestial bodies and such recurrence of the natural behavior of supernatural beings threatens the cultural order by provoking epidemics. Although these epidemics have a supernatural cause, they have the most terrible of natural consequences: the death of many individuals. The Panare do not conceive of diseases in general (*a fortiori* of epidemics) as a natural process, but as a supernatural one, although they recognize the natural effects of such supernatural causes.

As indicated linguistically, a solar eclipse is the incestuous behavior of celestial bodies, which does not mean that the latter is the cause of the former. In fact, solar eclipses result from "a bad dance." A bad dance is a cultural mishap, a cultural failure of the group, since dance is a ritual, performed at night, aimed at reaching supernature at the peak of the dry season. Hence, a bad dance is a manipulation of the supernatural in which supernature has not been adequately controlled, so that celestial incest may happen again. In a similar but opposed way, in human incest, two individuals fail to behave according to the cultural patterns and succeed too well in behaving according to nature.

In the same incestuous movement, but secondarily, the celestial pair participates in natural behavior (like monkeys), the human pair in supernatural behavior (like the sun and the moon). In both cases, what should have remained disjoined (day and night, brother and sister) has been conjoined. As we have seen, the same is true for nature and supernature.

Since day : night : : nature : supernature, on the one hand, and since men : women : : night : day, on the other hand, we can say now that day : night : : female sibling : male sibling : : nature : supernature. But again, it follows therefore that the moon, star of the night, should be male, and the sun, star of the day, should be female. To think in these terms would be to overlook the fact that the norms have been reversed in the incest case and in the solar eclipses. As night appears in daytime, as two consanguines mate, and finally as nature and supernature become associated in both cases, we can understand that other reversals can take place. Among the sexualized celestial bodies, the moon and the sun are the only "misfits," so to speak; their sexuality is out of place. The correlation can be written sister : brother : : sun : moon, since they have inverted the norm. It follows that within supernature, the moon is "very" supernatural, while the sun is "rather" natural. This should not surprise us: (1) a parallel ranking can be observed in the structure of the inhabited space, that is, in the domain of culture; and (2) ceremonies are performed at night, not before sunset or after sunrise.

Solar eclipses and human incest both result from a cultural fault, the former through a defective manipulation of supernature (bad dance), the latter through an excessive manipulation of nature (violation of incest taboo). Both have deadly consequences: a solar eclipse leads to the outbreak of epidemics in the group; human incest provokes the killing of the guilty pair by the group. In both cases, the group is confronted with an accident, a contingency, which should have been prevented by "a good dance" and by "incest taboo," that is, by preventions aimed toward supernature and away from nature, respectively. When inadvertently confronted with these "bad" events, the group will actively "remedy" (MEDIATE and MEDIATE AGAIN) the intemperate anticultural collusion of nature and supernature, i.e., their "im-mediation."

Incest and eclipses are both perceived as death threats for and by the group. Incest announces social death, since without its prohibition, no society can last as such. In provoking epidemics, eclipses announce the physical death of the group. In both cases, therefore, the cultural order has been subverted, and the group in self-defense will culturally disjoin what in the first place should never have been conjoined. In order to accomplish this, the culture resorts to a homeopathic treatment of death. In both cases, the group uses a metonymy of death as prophylactic, although not the same one for human incest as for solar eclipse.

To prevent the outbreak of epidemics, the group practices self-flagellation, that is, it inflicts on itself a short-term common painful mistreatment. This external mithridatization, although cultural *par excellence*, uses a natural means toward a supernatural end: natural, since animals are freely tortured in Panare culture while physical violence toward human beings is generally avoided; and supernatural, since, again, epidemics come from supernature. Through symbolic killing of the animality, the Panare are "re-encultured" by flagellation in the same way that the killing of a natural animal transforms it into a cultural food supply. Yet this ritual is, by definition, aimed at supernature. It is efficient only insofar as the cultural order is able to operate the mediation between nature and supernature which it had missed. Flagellation culturally "re-mediates" the duality of nature and supernature.

On the other hand, the incestuous human couple is supposed to be clubbed to death. A technique similar to flagellation is employed, and the Panare say *ötnyepa ipumowon* (which includes the root *ipumo* 'club') meaning "to club the Panare" for both cases. This tends to prove that they do not conceptualize both events differently, and indeed both rituals have the same function. But the incestuous pair is eventually killed; in other words a metonymic substitute of the group is actually killed, while the flagellation is a metaphor of death, self-inflicted by the group. Now the individuals are in turn "re-encultured," which is obvious since (1) they have twice severed themselves from culture in committing incest and need to be relinked (in a religious way, ritually) to culture, and (2) they are culturally buried, and have therefore recovered their culturality. The killing in this case is again a treatment for natural beings and the killing is ritual, that is, oriented toward supernature. The cultural order, in this case as well, has been able to reestablish its balance between nature and supernature which had been "im-mediated." If the couple escape, nothing is done at all, which is understandable since they are out of reach and no longer under the control of the cultural order. By their violent death, the killed individuals are brought back into the cultural bosom and can be buried while the fugitives, of course, would not be.

This burial is what leads us back to the sky, with which we started the present analysis. In the burial process, what culture performs is the mediation as well as the disjunction of nature and supernature. The fugitive pair will live in the forest (naturally) and be transformed into spirits (supernaturally), which is the fate reserved for nonburied people. The buried ones, on the contrary, rot (bodies) in their tomb (naturally) and burn (souls) in the Milky Way (supernaturally). In other words, nature and supernature are disjoined through the cultural mediation of the burial process.

Here it is time to recall that the Milky Way is itself made up of stars. Each star of the sky is called *tyakun* whether it is in or out of the Milky Way. However, we are confronted with a double origin of the stars. On the one hand, all stars, including the stars of the Milky Way, result from the incestuous union of the sun and the moon; on the other hand, the stars of the Milky Way, exclusively, are the burning souls of the dead. No contradiction is involved here. In effect, we have already established the congruence which exists between human or celestial incest, and death. In addition, incest is a sexual union which is the opposite of procreation. The human incestuous couple not only fails to beget offspring as a result of their embrace, but receives death from the group. The incestuous celestial bodies are hardly more fecund, giving birth to asexual *tyakun,* that is, sterile beings wich consequently are social misfits. What could be a better expression of the fact that social life, without incest prohibition, cannot last for long? Incest, in reversing the sexual norms, leads directly to asexuality: the spirits, the souls, and the *tyakun* have no sex. The Panare believe in an afterlife which is not very different from the earthly one, except that it is quite dull — there is no sex after death.

From this discussion of incest and death, we can see that the sexuality of the moon and the sun has been displaced due to their incestuous behavior. It is a male celestial body which appears in the daytime and a female one which appears at night. The latter is accompanied by asexual offspring which are themselves the by-product of an inversion: either normal death as opposed to the continuation of physical life, or incest as opposed to the perpetuation of social life. In fact, there is a supernatural ranking. The ultimate future of the individuals is to reach, as souls, the status of supernatural beings. (But at the same time, dead human beings accede to the supernatural order as asexual offspring of an incestuous union; they accede to a supernatural minus.) In effect, there is a ranking from superior male to inferior female. This ranking continues as sexuality is superior to asexuality. It can be easily established that asexuality is congruent with early childhood. Consequently, during the short periodicity of the day, the relevant celestial bodies which originate from a reversal have either a reversed or suppressed sexuality. The latter case is evidently a modality of the former. At the same time, being reversed, they are "abnormal," so to speak, insofar as incest and death are not "normal." But they are supernatural.

Therefore, the fact that the sun appears during the daytime while the moon and the Milky Way appear at night conforms perfectly to a dialectical logic: all are ambiguous celestial bodies. The sun is a superior male, but reversed as incestuous; "he" appears in the female daytime, and therefore "supernaturalizes" the daytime in the same way as the daytime "desacralizes" him. The moon is an inferior female, but reversed as incestuous; "she" appears in the male night, and therefore enhances and weakens the sacredness of the night. But it is under the condition of being asexual souls that human beings can accede, almost furtively, to the supernatural, humbly glowing in a weakened night.

There is one remaining difficulty which must be examined before we exhaust the structure of daily periodicity. The Milky Way is more often visible during the dry season. If such is the case, the Milky Way is not only marked in the short periodicity of the day, but also in the long periodicity of the year. However, the short mark is undoubtedly primitive, the long one derivative, since (1) the Milky Way is made up of the offspring of the sun and the moon, and (2) it does not appear exclusively in the dry season, only more often. The Milky Way glows at night but also more often during the dry season, the supernatural aspect of the Milky Way is reinforced; indeed, it provides the ultimate access of culture to supernature. At the same time, the frailty of this cultural access is emphasized by the asexuality of the souls.

What is opposed, if anything, to the Milky Way? What would appear during the daytime and mainly during the rainy season? It is obviously the rainbow, *manataci,* the Panare demiurge. While the souls burn in the sky, *manataci* appears only associated with the rain. Consequently, the most supernatural of all beings appears at the least supernatural moment. Moreover, it reveals itself only irregularly, whereas the Milky Way is present (actually or potentially) every night. The most natural is therefore opposed to the least supernatural in every respect since *manataci* manifests its supernatural strength (and simultaneously its distance from culture, of course) in appearing at the most profane time.

This leads us to wonder about the sexuality of the rainbow. In this respect, the rainbow is similar to the Milky Way in that it has none, although rather by excess than by defect. Indeed, I first thought that my inquiries had not been understood, since the questions, "Is it male?

Is it female?" were both answered by "yes." The answers obtained about the sex of the celestial bodies are presented in Table 1. In response to my question whether the sex of the moon, the sun, the rainbow, the Milky Way and the stars in general (the two latter separately) were *apo* 'male' or *wunki* 'female', the answers were either *aye* 'yes' or *cika* 'no'. Although a number of informants answered *tinca pwi yu* 'I don't know', none contradicted the data presented in Table 1.

Table 1. Sex of celestial bodies

	Male	Female
Sun	*aye*	*cika*
Moon	*cika*	*aye*
Star(s)	*cika*	*cika*
Milky Way	*cika*	*cika*
Rainbow	*aye*	*aye*

From the table, it can be seen that there is a major opposition between the sun and the moon, on one hand, and the Milky Way and the rainbow, on the other. Moreover, the rainbow and the Milky Way are themselves opposed, just as the moon and the sun are opposed. The correlation, rainbow : Milky Way : : sun : moon, is fairly obvious; the rainbow and the sun both appear during the day and have a "strong" sexuality (quantitatively for the rainbow, qualitatively for the sun), while the Milky Way and the moon both appear at night and have a "weak" sexuality (quantitatively for the Milky Way, qualitatively for the moon). In addition, while the sun and the moon are at the same supernatural level (they have to meet if they are to mate), the Milky Way is above, the *ne plus ultra* of supernature, and the rainbow is below, the *ne minus infra* of supernature.

These four celestial bodies, apart from being supernatural, share their "abnormality" since they occupy marked positions, either ambiguous (the sun and the moon) or extreme (the rainbow and the Milky Way). For one reason or another, each of these four celestial bodies is displaced: the sex of the moon and of the sun has been reversed in the daily periodicity; and the less supernatural Milky Way appears in the most sacred time (night and dry season), while the most supernatural rainbow appears in the most profane time (day and rainy season). Thus, we can write the correlation, day : night : : rainy season : dry season : : sun : moon : : rainbow : Milky Way. This is important since we can now establish the logical transition between the conceptualization of the short periodicity of the day and the long periodicity of the year that we had earlier abandoned but to which it is now appropriate to return.

The stars characteristic of the year-long periodicity are also sexualized. But their sexuality is, so to speak, "straight," in opposition to both the reversed sexuality of the stars of the day-short periodicity and the ambiguous sexuality of the Milky Way and of the rainbow. The moon and the sun represent a reversed transformation of social life. In a similar but opposite way, the Milky Way and the rainbow represent a reversed transformation of biological life. Both aspects are further linked since we have already established the congruency between incest and death as opposed to socially acceptable sexuality and biological life, as well as to the rainbow, i.e. the demiurge *manataci*.

Manataci does not represent socially acceptable sexuality, nor human life. Doubtless, *manataci* is a principle of life, but it represents its excess, its hyperbole, and this is why "it" is sexually displaced. In effect, *manataci* is a bisexual being who is also fecund since "it" is at the origin (the present shape) of everything and everyone. An androgynous being who is also self-impregnated, *manataci* is therefore located not so much outside of but rather beyond the scope of the social order, of culture.

In addition, while *manataci* represents the excess of life, the asexual stars represent its defect, death. Thus by following a sexual code, when we pass from the rainbow to the Milky Way, we observe a reversed transformation in terms of sexuality: through excess for the former, and through defect for the latter, both equally depart from human sexuality. Still following the same sexual code, when we pass from the sun to the moon, we observe a reversed transformation, this time in terms of sex: as an incestuous being, the sun is, as it were, a *faux-frère*, a "false brother" who behaves as an affine, i.e. the reverse of a brother; in the same way, and for the very same reason, the moon is a "false sister." For having exchanged sex (socially) which they should not have done, the sun and the moon have also exchanged their sexual attributes (biologically).

According to the sexual code which is presently examined, the sun and the moon have been socially excessive, and remain so after their transformation into celestial bodies only when there are eclipses. In this respect they are like *manataci*, who is biologically excessive. *Manataci* in turn is "themselves," so to speak, opposed to the Milky Way which is biologically defective. Let us recall that *manataci* is not excessive socially (indeed *manataci* is quite isolated socially) and that the Milky Way is not defective socially (except for sex, the souls of the dead follow the same "life" as earthly Panare).

For the moment, we have to account for a final transformation of the major opposition between the sun and the moon, on the one hand, and of the rainbow and the Milky Way, on the other hand. In so doing, we shall be able to get rid of a seeming contradiction. We have already indicated that the moon and the sun were at the same "altitude," and that the rainbow was located above, with the Milky Way below. This "vertical" conceptualization contradicts the empirical observation that the moon passes in front of the Milky Way. In fact, the conception exactly reverses perception: the rainbow is an atmospheric phenomenon; the sun and the moon are, with the earth, parts of the solar system; and finally, the stars of the sky are even more distant. The inversion of perception and conception can be perfectly understood once it is grasped that the four elements of this astronomical conceptual system sexually reverse the Panare cultural norm, either biologically or socially, either by excess or by defect. In this process, the rainbow and the Milky Way have exchanged their respective positions while the median pair (moon and sun) has remained in place.

Indeed, the Panare know that during an eclipse (seen, of course, from the earth), it is the moon which passes below the sun and not the reverse. Both are therefore "straight" in their copulation when compared to the favorite Panare technique for sexual intercourse in which the man stands above the woman. The woman lies on her back in her (rather than his) hammock. The man stands up, the hammock passing between his legs. The legs of the woman pass over the arms of the man where elbow and knee can clinch together. The woman lies horizontally and is below the man who stands vertically and is above the woman. Since the Milky Way and the rainbow have commuted along a vertical axis, the moon and the sun should have done the same and . . . the moon should pass behind the sun!

Of course, what has been forgotten is that this opposition is neutralized along this vertical axis, because the transformation has already taken place along a horizontal axis. In effect, the moon and the sun, stars of the diurnal periodicity, are a pair of siblings who copulate, that is they are *par excellence* contemporaneous. Their spatial conjunction causes their disjunction which is expressed in terms of time, as they mark the alternation of days and nights. This transformation into time alternation is correlative of a sexual transformation. The sun and the moon can be represented along a horizontal axis (as in any kinship diagram), along which they have been transformed; this inhibits, by neutralization, their vertical transformation.

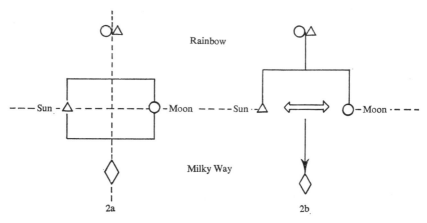

Figure 2. The structure of ill-tempered astronomy

Yet we have also said that there was a vertical ordering of the sun and the moon, as a pair, lying between the rainbow and the Milky Way. Diagram 2a of Figure 2 shows clearly that when the vertical poles commute, the horizontal poles remain unaffected and vice versa. This vertical neutralization of the sun and the moon was already implied when we established, on the one hand, that the moon is very supernatural and the sun rather natural and, on the other hand, that the moon is an inferior female and the sun a superior male. At that point, every effort was made by Panare thought to put the sun and the moon in the same conceptual framework.

But further examination of the kinship relations manifested in this astronomical system is necessary. *Manataci* is the "parents" *par excellence,* and therefore of the moon and the sun, among others. In addition, the sun and the moon are the parents of the stars, including the stars of the Milky Way. In Diagram 2b (which complements Diagram 2a) of Figure 2, the transformations are indicated by double arrows. While the horizontal axis represents alliance and collaterality on the same genealogical level, the vertical axis represents filiation in the succession of genealogical levels. The vertical axis is therefore oriented.

Several points have now been established. While the transformation of the sun and the moon is reciprocal, the transformation of the rainbow and the Milky Way is oriented and dynamic, following the flow of the time. On the one hand, the sun and the moon are used to express, through the periodicity of their alternations, a mechanistic conception of time. On the other hand, the rainbow and the Milky Way are used to express a dialectic conception of time. Repetitive time and cumulative time coexist and mediate one another. By means of an astronomical code, the Panare — excellent philosophers ready to reconcile Zeno and Heraclitus — express the paradox of time. Consequently, two conceptions are involved: one deals with a closed repettitive or cyclic time, in other words, with rhythms; the other one deals with open or cumulative time, in other words, with melodies.

In this structure of an ill-tempered astronomy, all the relations of time are expressed in terms of space: separation of the moon and the sun who have been too close to each other and who are responsible for the diurnal periodicity; and reversal of location (from percept to concept) for the rainbow and the Milky Way who are responsible for the flow of time. Therefore, starting from time categories, we are sent back to space categories.

But, on the other hand, the structure under consideration is not only concerned with astronomy but with sexuality as well. What does it mean? According to the rather complex form of a sexual code, the meaning of the message is, in fact, disturbingly simple: not only does incest generate death mythically and actually, but sexual frenzy, passing through incest, leads to death which itself leads nowhere. In other words, a sexual departure from the cultural norm leads to death. All sexual excesses lead to death since it is the final point in the dynamics of the structure: the sexual frenzy of the rainbow and its subsequent hyperfecundity; the incest of the moon and the sun and the subsequent sterility of their offspring; the asexuality of the unnamed stars (of the Milky Way) and their subsequent sterility — all are essentially anticultural. Only the cultural way is compatible with the perpetuation of life, and androgyny and asexuality are biologically excluded as much as incest is socially excluded. Sexual excesses are conceptually "restraightened" through the reversed transformations that we have just studied, and in the same logical way two processes are guaranteed: the regularity of the alternation of day and night, and the proper progression from birth to death, just as the conjunction of the sun and the moon provokes the catastrophic eclipse, and as the Milky Way above the rainbow provokes the precedence of death over life. In both cases, life would be reversed into death.

It is precisely to avoid this reversal that the Panare conceptualize it as happening outside of them. In such a conceptualization, they attempt to prevent a disruption of their cultural order which maintains its frail balance between two threatening disorders: nature and supernature. Only through their astrosexuality can the Panare make sense

— in opposition to absolute abnormality (and relative nonsense) — of what is hyperbolically outside of them: celestial bodies. In viewing the triumph of the antinorms as far from them as in the sky, they assert nothing but the justification of their norms and the ideological impossibility of the disruption of such norms.

At this conceptual price, the Panare order, cultural order *par excellence,* is established and its negation is prevented, as it is rejected in the infinite distance of the named celestial bodies. Hence, culture has gained, both spatially and conceptually, the security of its own norms since the "abnorms" exert their force not only apart from us, but beyond us — "not in ourselves, but in our stars."

Conceptual Patterns in Yoruba Culture

LUCY JAYNE KAMAU

The Yoruba of southwestern Nigeria are among the most extensively studied groups of people in Africa. There is available a large volume of literature written by European scholars, by missionaries, and by Yoruba writers themselves. The Yoruba have attracted such scholarly interest because they have had an old and indigenous tradition of urban life, an intricate political system, and a complex culture. While much of the literature concerning the Yoruba deals with aspects of pre-European urbanism, a considerable amount of information relating to other aspects of their culture has also been recorded.

The Yoruba today have a population of about five million persons. Historically, they were united by a common language, a common culture, and a belief in a common origin, but, as far as is known, they were never politically united. Rather, they were divided into many small kingdoms or city-states which rose and fell over a period of approximately five hundred years (Bascom 1955). The center of each Yoruba state was the capital town, ruled by an *oba*, or divine king. In the past, many of these towns were quite large, some of them having as many as 50,000 inhabitants. Despite this urban orientation, the basis of the Yoruba economy was agriculture, although trade was also important. Few Yoruba, however, were full-time merchants. Most persons were farmers, those who were city dwellers commuting back and forth between homes in the towns and farms in the countryside.

This paper will attempt to describe the interrelationship between the traditional Yoruba world view, their arrangement of social space, their concepts of time, and certain related aspects of their political, mythological, and divinatory systems. It will attempt to trace out a pattern which ties together many aspects of Yoruba life into a coherent totality. It will not be concerned with changes which may have taken place in recent years, but will try to deal with traditional Yoruba life as much as possible. For the sake of simplicity, this paper is written in the ethnographic present.

While other writers have noted aspects of the relationship to be described in this paper (e.g. Frobenius 1913; Krapf-Askari 1969; Morton-Williams 1960a), they have not investigated it in detail, nor have they dealt with more than one or two parts of the totality. However, it seems that there are patterns in Yoruba culture which are of a much broader and more complex nature than have heretofore been described.

The material for this paper is derived exclusively from secondary sources. The writer has not personally been able to conduct a field study of Yoruba culture. There are certain problems inherent in this approach. First, one is sometimes limited in the availability of complete data, and it may be necessary to make inferences on the basis of only partial information. Second, some writers may be repeating assertions made by earlier writers, but have failed to cite sources of information. Third, there may be difficulty in assessing the reliability of sources, most particularly those which are not methodologically rigorous. However, if original research is to have any enduring value beyond the mere recording of curiosa, it must be usable and used by other scholars. Inasmuch as there is a great deal of material on the Yoruba written by a great many writers, it has been possible in this case to cross-check data for consistency. Those statements which have seemed dubious or inconsistent have been discarded.

The concept of PATTERN as propounded by Ruth Benedict (1934) has been of great use in developing the ideas contained in this paper. While Benedict's writings have fallen into neglect in recent years, largely due to her unfortunate classification of cultures into imprecise psychological categories, there is still a good deal to be gained from her work. The basic idea of pattern is important and useful and should not be discarded merely because other aspects of her work have been shown to be invalid. In analyzing Yoruba culture, the concept of pattern has proven extremely valuable, and indeed, is necessary to such analysis. Yoruba do have at least one pattern which permeates their culture on many different levels. It is this basic idea of pattern which underlies the presentation given below.

Lévi-Strauss (1962:93) has indirectly indicated the importance of patterns in a discussion of myth, when he states that:

The mythical system and the modes of representation it employs serve to establish homologues between natural and social conditions or, more accurately,
it makes it possible to equate significant contrasts found on different planes:
the geographical, meteorological, zoological, botanical, technical, economic,
social, ritual, religious, and philosophical.

This description fits at least certain aspects of Yoruba culture. There is
a logical relationship between different areas of thought, which, taken
together, combine into one system or pattern. A few basic concepts go
through a number of transformations as they are applied to differing
intellectual contexts, but the parts remain in the same relationship to
each other, so that a transformation of one element leads to a corresponding change in another element. The natural world, the social
world, and the cosmological world are seen by the Yoruba as being equivalent: conditions which obtain in one domain likewise obtain in the
others, and differing levels of experience are congruent.

The basic ordering device of the system or pattern to be discussed here
is the numeral two, most particularly when it is duplicated into the
number four. Two and four can be considered "master symbols"
(Wolf 1965:227) or "synthesizing symbols" (Geertz 1970:326), which
link together many aspects of Yoruba life.

The giving of symbolic meanings to the arrangement of space, time,
and society in accordance with cosmological concepts has occurred elsewhere in the world in many places and at many times. For example,
the Oglala Sioux (Radin 1927:276–281) used the circle as a basic ordering
device which gave cosmic meaning to village layout, moral code, and
house form:

Again and again the idea of a sacred circle, a natural form with a moral impact,
yields, when applied to the world within which the Oglala lived, new meanings:
continually it connects together elements within their experience which would
otherwise seem wholly disparate and incomprehensible (Geertz 1970:327).

The Pawnee (Lienhardt 1968:445–446), the Osage (Lévi-Strauss 1962:
143–146), the Dogun (Griaule 1965), and the Aztecs (Wolf 1959), as well
as medieval Europeans (Mumford 1961), to name but a very few, have
all structured portions of their social and physical environments so as to
be in accordance with beliefs concerning the cosmos. In this respect, the
Yoruba are not unique. Their uniqueness lies partly in the coherence,
complexity, and pervasiveness of their metaphysical system and partly
in the fact that they have been so ably and richly recorded by so many different observers, thus enabling one to piece together the parts which
form the whole.

Two is the basic ordering device of the Yoruba system. Yoruba culture is replete with dualisms. Gods are paired, either as united or opposed entities. Time is divided into opposed units. Center and periphery are important conceptual oppositions. The system of divination known as *Ifa* is based upon pairs and upon pairs of pairs. Odd and even, right and left, black and white, are frequently occurring paired oppositions. The Yoruba divide themselves into two types of people, the *ará ilu* or city dwellers, and the *ará oko*, or rural people. Youth and age are commonly opposed. Duality is a constantly recurring theme in Yoruba culture.

Yet it is the duplication of pairs which is perhaps most important, for four is the symbol which stands for order and stability in the universe. It is "the sign of completion and perfection" (Morton-Williams 1960a: 372) in Yoruba culture. Two underlies four, but it is four upon which the world is built.[1]

THE COSMOS

The association of the number four with stability and order is clearly shown in the Yoruba concept of the cosmos. The natural world (*ile aiye*) and the supernatural world (*ile orun*) are believed to be isomorphic, and the former is the reflection of the latter. Ideally, both are four-square.

The supernatural world is believed to be located in the sky (translated as "the heavens" by most writers). It is divided in half by one main road running in an east-west direction. This direction is obtained by referring to the direction in which the sun travels across the sky and is called the "Chief Way" (Frobenius 1913:259; Ojo 1966:199), for the path of the sun is believed to be the most important direction in the universe. East, the direction of sunrise, has higher rank than west. The Chief Way is bifurcated by the "Second Way," a road laid out on a north-south axis, 90° to the right and left of center. Right, or north, has higher prestige than left, or south. The entire supernatural world is surrounded by a wall with four gates, one for each road.

The point at which the roads intersect is believed to be the crossroads

---

[1]   There is some evidence that the number three also has symbolic value for the Yoruba (Krapf-Askari 1966; Morton-Williams 1960a), most particularly with respect to the Ogboni society, many of whose practices are reversals of what the Yoruba consider to be proper behavior. It also seems to have other symbolic associations as well, but the information concerning it is too fragmentary to be considered here. It should be noted, however, that even numbers are generally considered to be good and are associated with the right hand, while odd numbers, particularly three, are considered to be bad and are associated with the left hand (Frobenius 1913:189; Bascom 1969b:47).

and center of the universe (Frobenius 1913:256; Ojo 1966:200). Thus the heavens are divided into four equal parts by a pair of roads and also have four walls, each wall divided by a gate through which one of these roads runs.

The crossroads of the heavens are governed by four different gods, one for each point of the compass. Since the directions are hierarchically ranked, it is therefore possible that the gods associated with the various directions are also hierarchically ranked, but no writer on this subject has stated this explicitly, so that it must remain a conjecture.

The names of these four gods and their directional associations vary somewhat, apparently by locality, but there is nevertheless considerable overlap and agreement concerning which particular gods are crossroads gods. Table 1 lists the names given by Frobenius (1913:256), Dennett (1910:71), Ojo (1966:200), and Odugbesan (1969:200).

Table 1. Crossroads gods according to four authors

	Frobenius	Dennett	Ojo	Odugbesan
East	Ifa/Eshu	Shango	Shango	Ifa/Eshu
West	Shango	Ifa/Eshu	Ifa/Eshu	Shango
North	Ogun	Obatala	Obatala	Ogun
South	Obatala	Oduduwa	Oduduwa	Obatala

Unfortunately, none of these writers has specified the region from which these names were collected. However, only six names occur, out of the possible several hundreds of Yoruba gods' names. These are Ifa/Eshu, Shango, Obatala, Oduduwa, and Ogun. Ifa/Eshu and Shango are consistently named as gods of either the east or the west, while Ogun, Obatala, and Oduduwa are given as names of the gods of the north or south.

These six gods are among the most important deities in the Yoruba pantheon. Ifa is the god of divination, while Eshu, his paired alter ego, controls chance. Ifa and Eshu are frequently conceived of by Yoruba as being two manifestations of one deity, particularly with respect to crossroads domain, and they have frequently been treated as one entity by other writers. They have been so treated in this context by this writer. Obatala and Oduduwa are a set of paired gods associated with the creation of the natural world and of mankind. They were never thought of as dual aspects of one deity, and accordingly have been kept separate here. While Oduduwa and Obatala govern separate domains on two of the above lists, Ifa and Eshu are never found ruling different directions. Ogun and Shango are not paired, although they are similar in that both are characterized as fierce gods. Ogun is the god of war and of iron, while Shango is a deified king of Oyo who is also the god of thunder and lightning, which are fearsome natural phenomena in Yoruba country.

All writers on this subject agree that the four gods of the crossroads are also the four gods of the four gates of heaven and of the four winds which pass through these gates. They are also the names of the four days of the week. When the name of a god changes in one respect, it changes in all others, so that, regardless of the specific deity, a given crossroads god is always a god of a specific day, a specific wind, and a specific gate.

The four quadrants of the heavens are subdivided into four or more parts by two secondary roads in each quadrant, making sixteen sections plus a center. Whether these secondary divisions are also governed by deities is unknown.

Yoruba deities are sometimes divided into gods of the right and of the left (Bascom 1969b: 103), each group presumably on either side of the Chief Way. The number of gods is conventionally given as 200 to each side (Ojo 1966: 184) or 400 gods in the Yoruba pantheon. Sometimes the number given is 401 (Biobaku 1965:25; Lloyd 1965:573; Johnson 1921: 38), the odd one being the supreme god Olorun, who is associated with the center, again presumably on the Chief Way. Gods of the right are said to have higher prestige than gods of the left (Ojo 1966:184) and are beneficent, while gods of the left are malevolent. However, no specific gods' names are associated with this division into right and left and good and bad, while gods of the crossroads associated with north/right and south/ left, do not seem to be classified or classifiable into good and bad. Even such deities as Ogun and Shango have their followers and can be beneficial to those who worship them.

The natural world, *ile aiye*, the world in which men live, is believed to be organized so as to be homologous with the heavens, *ile orun*. The earth and the sky are of the same size (Ojo 1966:196). The sky is curved downward, while the earth is curved upward, their edges meeting at the horizon. They are joined at the center by a chain running from the central crossroads of heaven to the holy city of Ile Ife, believed to be located at the central crossroads of earth. Thus the natural world and the supernatural world are physically linked. Looked at in cross-section, a four-sectioned figure is obtained (see Figure 1).

Like the sky, the earth is said to be surrounded by four walls, with one gate in each wall through which spirits and deities pass on their way into and out of the natural world. The natural world is also said to be divided in half by one great road, the Chief Way, and divided into quadrants by

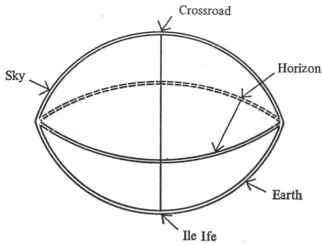

Figure 1.   Oblique view of the Yoruba cosmos

a second road, the Second Way. The city of Ile Ife lies at the junction of these two roads.

The sky and the earth are mirror images of each other. The relationship between them is sometimes symbolized by the relationship between the gods Obatala and Oduduwa. These deities oppose each other and yet are indissolubly linked. In some areas, but not in Ile Ife itself, they are represented as consorts, Obatala being the male and Oduduwa the female (Morton-Williams 1964:250). In Ife, both these gods are thought of as males. As consorts, Obatala and Oduduwa are represented as two halves of a calabash which cannot be broken, the calabash being the symbol of creation (Ojo 1966:196).

Obatala and Oduduwa are also seen as inhabiting the calabash of creation as two persons: Obatala the sky god inhabiting the upper portion, and Oduduwa the earth goddess inhabiting the lower portion. Obatala is also associated with the sun, with light, and with whiteness (Bascom 1969b:103). White is the color of beneficent gods and of the sacred kingship. In one account of his activities, Obatala is said to have created human beings (Bascom 1969a:103), while in another (Dennett 1910:84), he is said to have created the "white" parts of the body: the brain, nerves, and skull. Obatala is always depicted as male. Oduduwa, on the other hand, may be either male or female, depending upon the context. When Oduduwa is seen as a woman, she is known as "the mother of the gods" (Frobenius 1913:232; Dennett 1910:74), and she is symbolized by sixteen snail shells representing the sixteen gods of the sixteen parts of the heavens who assisted Oduduwa at creation. On the other hand, Oduduwa is seen as being male when he is thought of as the ancestor of all Yoruba and as their first *oba*, or king.

Although Oduduwa is not a malevolent god and is not associated with the gods of the left, he/she is associated with darkness and with the color black. It is said that Obatala blinded Oduduwa when they were in the calabash, and for this, she cursed him (Dennett 1910:74), so that in future disputes with Obatala, Oduduwa is inevitably the winner. Oduduwa is said to have created the inhabited world, *ile aiye*, and also the black parts of the body: the flesh and the blood. Insofar as they symbolize the relationship between the earth and the sky, however, these two gods are at once locked together for all time and also are separated, just as heaven and earth are at once joined and separated. Both gods play important roles in Yoruba creation myths, to be described below.

On earth, Ile Ife was the center of creation and of the world. This city is an important unifying symbol for the Yoruba, for it is believed that all Yoruba are descended from the founder of Ife, that is, from Oduduwa. One writer states, with reference to Ile Ife: "All roads in their [Yoruba] religion, history, government, and art seem to lead there" (Smith 1969:15). This remark is apt in more than one way, for the Yoruba believe that all roads literally lead to Ife, the crossroads of the earth. Ife's layout, its governing system, and stories of its origin are shot through with repetitions of the number four and its multiples, and it is in Ife that Yoruba have most consciously striven to make the human world a replica or model of the supernatural world.

To understand the importance of Ile Ife in Yoruba culture, it is necessary to know something of the myths surrounding its origin. These myths vary somewhat, but on the whole they show consistency. The most common creation myth is the following (Lloyd 1960:223): The original impetus for the creation of Ife and of the world was the supreme god Olorun (also called Olodumare). Olorun is a remote creator god who commands other deities but who himself seldom interferes directly in human affairs.

In the primordial existence, there were only the skies above and the oceans below. Olorun decided to create land and to do so he let down a golden chain from the center of heaven to the center of the ocean. He commanded Oduduwa, who in this version is usually male, to descend this chain and to create the earth. Oduduwa descended the chain, threw a handful of sand on the waters, and placed on it a chicken and a palm nut. The chicken scratched the sand, creating hills and valleys, while the palm nut grew into a tree with sixteen branches. The sixteen branches represent the sixteen parts of the world, and the sixteen nuts represent the origin of the divination system called *Ifa*, which uses sixteen palm nuts as counters. The place where Oduduwa landed is Ile Ife.

In one variant of this particular myth (Smith 1969:17; Ojo 1966:194), Oduduwa is said to have taken with him sixteen companions. After creating the world, he settled at Ile Ife and became its first *oba*, dividing the rest of the world into sixteen parts and giving one portion to each of his assistants.

Other versions of the creation myth stress the opposition between Obatala and Oduduwa (Adedeji 1966:89–91; Bascom 1969b:10; Frobenius 1913:283). In one version, Olorun had two sons, the elder being Obatala and the younger being Oduduwa. Olorun sent Obatala to create land, but instead Obatala drank palm wine and fell asleep. Oduduwa was then sent in his place. Oduduwa landed at Ile Ife, created the earth, and ruled it as first *oba*. When he learned of this, Obatala became angry with Oduduwa, and they fought. Obatala first defeated Oduduwa and drove him from Ife, but was himself subsequently defeated by Oduduwa and expelled. Olorun then gave Oduduwa and his offspring the right to rule the earth and Obatala the right to create human beings in their mothers' wombs, thus dividing dominion over human life between these two gods.

In only one version does Oduduwa not figure. This one, recorded by Frobenius (1913:284), gives Olorun the credit for the creation of the earth. An island already existed in the waters and was inhabited by men. These men wandered about in confusion. Then Olorun, together with sixteen deities, came down from heaven and sat in the center of the island on the future site of Ife. He told Ifa/Eshu to sit behind him, Shango in front, Ogun on the right, and Obatala on the left. (These four gods are the gods Frobenius lists as crossroads gods.) The remainder of the gods sat in a circle around him. Olorun decreed that the sixteen gods would rule the sixteen parts of the earth, but that Ife would be the center. A palm tree was planted so that Ife would be the best place for divination. The future Onis (*obas*) of Ife would tell other *obas* the will of the gods. This myth seems to imply that the Onis of Ife are descended from Olorun, which does not seem to fit the commonly held belief that Oduduwa is the ancestor of all Yoruba, all crowned *obas*, and, most particularly, all Onis of Ife. On the other hand, there is some evidence that the Oni of Ife was to other rulers as Olorun is to other gods (Morton-Williams 1964:245).

There is also a conquest version which is an account in historical rather than mythical time. In this myth (Johnson 1921:3; Okediji and Okediji 1966:65), Oduduwa, a human male, is said to have come from the east and settled at Ife. He had sixteen children or grandchildren whom he sent out to colonize and settle other areas. His offspring are believed to be the ancestors of all crowned *obas*, who thus are believed to trace their ancestry in a direct line to Oduduwa.

Although there are differences in content in these myths, certain consistent themes emerge. One is the belief that Ile Ife is the center of creation and the first Yoruba town. A second is the pervasiveness of sixteen and of sixteen plus one. The earth is divided into sixteen parts, that is, the four points of the compass and their three subdivisions, plus the center. Oduduwa brought sixteen companions with him, as did Olorun, so that there would be sixteen crowned *obas* for the sixteen regions of the world, plus the Oni of Ife. Oduduwa had sixteen offspring who founded Yoruba dynasties. The palm tree planted at Ife had sixteen branches and sixteen nuts plus the central trunk. A third theme, excepting Frobenius' account, is that Oduduwa is responsible for bringing the plan of the cosmos to earth and is also responsible for instituting the Yoruba political system. He was the first Oni of Ife and the ancestor of all Yoruba, thus forming a direct link between men and the gods, between historical time and mythical time.

Ife is thus the supposed source of legitimacy for all rulers. Only those *obas* who can trace descent, real or fictitious, to the royal lineage of Ife are eligible to wear the beaded crown of office, the only insignia of legitimate rule (Ojo 1966:126). In theory, the Oni of Ife had divinely sanctioned control over all other *obas*, but in fact, Ife's authority was often disputed by other kings, and its hegemony has more often been spiritual than political (Smith 1969:108). Even so, Ife has remained a potent symbol of Yoruba unity and the sole source of royal legitimacy.

Conceptually, then, the natural world should be a reflection of the supernatural world, divided into four parts and then into sixteen, plus a center, with four walls and four gates at the periphery. The holy city of Ile Ife is the earthly homologue of the crossroads of the universe, for the center is the most sacred portion of both sky and earth. The seventeen crowned kingdoms are the homologues of the seventeen parts of the heavens. The Oni of Ife, together with the sixteen crowned kings are the homologues of Oduduwa and his sixteen assistants or of the palm tree with its sixteen branches. Yet, although they are homologues, earth and sky are still distinct and opposed entities, and the opposition between them is symbolized by the opposition, both in personal characteristics and in contentious behavior, between Obatala and Oduduwa, who, despite their opposition, are eternally linked.

State and Town Morphology

In theory, the world should be laid out and organized according to the pattern originally set down at creation at Ile Ife. In fact, the world is far different from the ideal, but it is evident that the Yoruba have tried on many different levels and as much as possible to create a social world which mirrors the supernatural world. This is particularly evident in the morphology of the capital town, which is the most important town in the state, particularly if it is also a crowned town. In theory, and sometimes in fact as well, the capital town is the geographic as well as the political, administrative, economic, and religious center of the state.

Town morphology varies somewhat between the north and the south, paralleling a difference in kinship structure. Northern Yoruba are organized into agnatic lineages, while in the south cognatic lineages prevail.[2] Southern towns are most often roughly rectangular in shape and are laid out on a grid pattern, the internal divisions or wards being made up of a number of rectangular compounds facing a street and divided from other wards by rubbish heaps in the rear (Lloyd 1960:26). Northern towns, considered "classical" Yoruba towns (Krapf-Askari 1969), are more nearly radial in shape. Krapf-Askari (1969:39) likens them to wheels, the *oba*'s palace being the hub, the town walls the rim, and the main roads leading out of town the spokes. Wards are located along these spokes and divided from each other by footpaths. In both north and south, the town is roughly divided into quadrants, with the center of the town being its most important point, replicating the design of the cosmos.

It is evident that the Yoruba themselves thought of their towns as being replicas of the cosmos. According to Krapf-Askari (1969:39), there exists "a more or less identical morphology which seems to be postulated by the Yoruba themselves," although in fact few Yoruba towns totally conform to this model. Areas around Ife and Old Oyo, the most conservative of Yoruba kingdoms, most closely approximate the ideal, but in any case, it is clear that Yoruba towns are built according to a plan and not haphazardly. Although the contingencies of geomorphology and of history may have altered the final form, the ideal was still to be approximated as much as possible.

Palace layouts seem to follow this blueprint with greater consistency than city layouts. Palaces are more nearly rectangular in shape than towns. Like the town, the palace is surrounded by a thick wall. In this

---

[2] The reasons for the relationship between kinship and town morphology are obscure. This paper will confine itself primarily to a discussion of the northern Yoruba.

wall is one main gate which connects the inner palace with the town. Facing the main gate is the *oba*'s public throne, and the path between gate and throne represents the Chief Way. The palace itself is a compound, and like other Yoruba compounds, it consists of apartments built around a series of multiple rectangular courtyards, one courtyard leading to another. By law in the past, the palace was larger and had more court-yards than other compounds.

Unlike other compounds, the palace itself occupies only a small part of its total area. The remainder is overgrown with trees and shrubs among which are located shrines, ritual groves, and graves of former *obas*. This bush area is closed to outsiders and is highly sacred.

Within the palace proper, the courtyards nearest the gate are for public use, while the inner ones are private. The first courtyard is the location for public ceremonies presided over by the *oba*. Around this courtyard live retainers, servants, and guests — those persons whose contact with the *oba* is minimal. Each successive courtyard leading into the center is occupied by persons successively closer to the *oba*. The innermost ones are occupied only by the *oba*'s closest wives, and it is here that they cook his food, working naked (Ojo 1966:134–138). The innermost courtyard is occupied by the *oba* himself. In addition to being his private quarters, this courtyard is also a shrine, for it is the center of the center and thus the most holy place in the kingdom, corresponding in importance to the crossroads of the universe. The most sacred of all of these is the Oni's private chamber at Ife.

Also in the center of town is a statue of Olori Merin, who is not a god in himself, but a four-headed being representing the four gods of the crossroads (Dennett 1910:70; Ojo 1966:200). This being is believed to protect the town by guarding the four points of the compass at which are located the four main gates of the town. It is believed that without the protection of Olori Merin, enemies, evil spirits, and diseases can enter the town through these gates. Olori Merin is sometimes called the god of the four corners or the wind vane god (Ojo 1966:200). Four times a year in the past, a four-day-old infant was sacrificed to him, one sacrifice for each cardinal point.

Finally, important shrines and the *oba*'s market are located in the cen-ter of town. Ife is an exception to this rule, for in Ife the largest shrines are not in the center of town but near the town walls. Likewise there is no *oba*'s market in Ife, for the Oni is considered to be too sacred to be near such a profane thing as a market. In general, however, the main market is located in front of the palace, where the *oba* can exert his sacred influence on it so as to ensure honest dealings and to prevent disputes.

Shrines dedicated to the patron of the marketplace, the god Eshu, are also located in the central market.

Surrounding this core area are the houses of notables who are within the orbit of the palace. These are persons whose titles allow them to give service to the *oba* and include the Chief Councillor, the Chief Eunuch, the Chief Slave, and the Crown Prince (Krapf-Askari 1969: 44; Ojo 1966: 135).

The palace is located at the intersection of the town's two major roads. These roads divide the town into four parts. Ideally, each quadrant of the town is then divided into four more parts by two secondary roads, creating sixteen sections plus the center. In actual fact, such a neat division is not common. Only Ife and, to a lesser extent, Old Oyo, approximate the ideal (Frobenius 1913:281). In the past, Ife is said to have had seventeen quarters or wards, one in the center around the Oni's palace, four in the cardinal points, and twelve (three each) in between (Frobenius 1913: 279). Oyo had eight wards plus the central precinct. In both cases, the number of wards is a multiple of two plus the central area.

In all towns, each ward is headed by a ward chief or *bale*, whose compound is a smaller version of the palace but much larger and more elaborate than those of ordinary men. As in the palace, ward chiefs live in interior courtyards, surrounded by their wives and their most trusted servants. As in the palace, guests are formally received opposite the main gate, which faces in the direction of the palace. The main gates of ordinary compounds in turn face the ward chief's compound, and the ward chief's compound is the central focus of the ward, just as the palace is the focal point of the town (Krapf-Askari 1969:43).

The smallest dwelling unit in the town is the compound in which lives the lineage or family. Dennett (1910:90) cites the following Yoruba proverb: "A house is composed of four corners and is not otherwise complete." In other words, in order to be considered a proper dwelling, a compound has to be square and fully enclosed, just as the cosmos is.

The head of the compound, who represents it to the outside world and who is responsible for its religious and economic well-being, occupies a relatively larger apartment directly opposite the main gate leading into the compound. The line from his apartment to the gate is the domestic unit's equivalent of the Chief Way. Those persons inhabiting apartments to the right of the head's apartments are of higher status than those living to his left. If the head is a wealthy or important man, he may reside in an inner courtyard, but his apartment is still on a line with the main gate, so that the Chief Way is maintained. On each level — ordinary compound, ward chief's compound, or palace — the layout of

the universe is replicated both in physical structure and in social relations.

Beyond the wards are the town walls, which contain major and minor
gates. Four or multiples of four are the most common number of gates
in Yoruba towns (Ojo 1966:141). The larger and more important the
town, the greater the number of gates it has. Conversely, the greater the
number of gates, the greater the prestige of the town. For example,
Ibadan boasted of having sixteen gates (Biobaku 1965:16). Abeokuta
had twelve gates (Lloyd 1967:6). Old Oyo, though a large and important
town, had only four gates, roughly equal to the points of the compass
(Awe 1967:15). Ikija had six gates, four located in the cardinal points, one
leading to the forest, and one for the king's custom house (Biobaku
1965:16).

Beyond the walls lies forested bushland. This area, in contrast to the
town and its agricultural hinterland, is a polluted area. In it are hidden
Egungun shrines, the *Egungun* being masquerades representing dead
ancestors who are greatly feared. Also in this bush are the unburied bodies
of witches, executed criminals, deformed people and debtors. It is an evil
place, a "bad bush," "a sort of spiritual and moral sewer" (Krapf-
Askari 1969:50), "forbidding and forbidden to the uninitiated "(Ojo
1966:126).

This area of "bad bush" presents certain contrasts and similarities to
the bushland surrounding the palace. Palace bushland is also heavily
forested and contains graves and shrines. It too is forbidden and dangerous to the uninitiated and is heavily invested with an aura of the supernatural. However, its graves are those of sacred persons, former *obas*, who
were properly buried. They are not the repositories of unburied social
outcasts. Palace shrines are those of royalty and hence of divinity, not
Egungun shrines. The palace bush is certainly not a spiritual sewer: in
fact it is the reverse, the location of many of the most sacred and holy
objects in Yoruba culture. It could be termed a "good bush," equally
as potent as the "bad bush," and vital to the well-being of the state. To
add to the polarity between the two, it is noteworthy that the palace bush
is located in the heart of the town, while the bad bush lies beyond its
periphery, thus again repeating the theme of center versus extremity.

Beyond the forested fringe is the countryside, the farming area. Again
there is a contrast between north and south in the relationship of farm-
land to city. In the north, farmlands radiate outward from the town like
spokes of wheels, whereas southern farmlands form a checkerboard
pattern (Krapf-Askari 1969: 25-26). In both areas, however, Yoruba
divide themselves into two kinds of people, the *ará oko* and the *ará ilu*

(Krapf-Askari 1969: 25–26). *Ará oko* means farm people or bumpkins, persons whose homes are not in towns. *Ará ilu* refers to town dwellers who are seen as being more sophisticated than *ará oko*. The word *ilu*, however, means more than just the town. It also defines the area governed by the political institutions of the town, so that *ilu* includes the farmlands beyond the town which are owned and worked by town dwellers, or *ará ilu* people.

Beyond the farmlands of the capital town are the subordinate towns and their lands. Subordinate towns are structured very much like capital towns, with the exception that they have no *obas* but are governed by *bales* whose installation has to be ratified by the reigning *oba*. These towns are divided into market towns, villages, hamlets, and camp settlements.

The morphology of the Yoruba town, and, to a lesser degree, of the Yoruba state, represents an attempt to replicate the scheme of the cosmos. The capital town is the crossroads, the center of the state, and it is in the center of this town that one finds the most important political, economic, and religious institutions. Here is located the palace, the main market, and the major religious shrines, including the palace itself. The *oba*, as divine king and most sacred person in the kingdom, lives in the center of the palace. The central capital town is more important than the peripheral towns, just as the center of the town is more important and more sacred than its peripheries. The pattern is repeated again and again: the center of the earth, located at Ile Ife; the center of the state, located at the capital town; the center of the town, the location of the palace and other important structures representing central institutions; the center of the ward, located at the residence of the ward chief; and finally, the center of the compound, located at the residence of the compound head.

Each of these is conceived of as being square and four-fold, and while not all are walled, the compound, the palace, the city, the earth, and the supernatural world are walled. The larger of these have four gates or multiples of four, while the smaller have at least one gate leading directly to the head's residence and which represents the Chief Way. Thus again one finds dualisms and the repetition of the number four as the quintessential expression of stability and perfection.

POLITICAL INSTITUTIONS

It is not within the scope of this paper to cover the Yoruba political system in detail. Rather, it will confine itself to a discussion of the ways in which the political system reflects the Yoruba world view. As already indicated, Yoruba political institutions were also designed to replicate the Yoruba concept of the cosmos. Their political system represents a transformation into political idiom of the ideal system described above, with its dualisms, its heavy emphasis on four, its distinctions between the center and the periphery, and the importance of the Chief Way.

At the center of the government is the sacred *oba*ship. Although the *oba*'s power in most kingdoms is largely symbolic, this symbol itself is vital to the well-being of the community. Like all divine kings, the *oba* is a mediator between men and the gods. He assures men of peace, prosperity, and a harmonious relationship with the gods, while at the same time he acts to assure the gods that men will treat them properly. In this manner, he preserves the smooth functioning of his kingdom. The *oba* is also the reincarnation of all his ancestors, including Oduduwa, so that he is a physical as well as a spiritual link between the natural and the supernatural, the living and the dead.

The *oba*'s installation sets him off from ordinary people. He loses all personal identity, including possessions, former wives, and family. In fact, he is hardly an individual at all. He exists alone in the remote center of his palace, apart from all men except a very few, appearing in public only on the rare but important occasions when he performs his public ceremonial duties. Not only is he physically secluded, but he is under heavy ritual restraint as well. He cannot be seen eating, and he is not allowed to touch the ground with his bare feet (Smith 1969: 110). His public appearances are confined to the outer courtyard of the palace, where he sits in state upon his throne opposite the main gate. When he does appear in public, he is surrounded by his many retainers, wives, slaves and chiefs. Umbrellas held in front of him screen him from the populace. His body is heavily robed, and his face is hidden by the beaded crown, his badge of office. He holds a white cow's tail before his mouth while speaking, while a specially titled chief repeats his words to the public, for the *oba* is not to be seen speaking or to be heard by ordinary men (Johnson 1921:50).

A new *oba* is chosen from among the royal lineage by the council of chiefs. In the past, he was expected to eat the excised heart of the previous *oba* (Johnson 1921:40; Lloyd 1965:569), thus literally ingesting divinity. He then goes into seclusion until after the third appearance of the new moon after the death of the former *oba* (Johnson 1921:50).

At Oyo (Johnson 1921), the *oba*'s ceremony of installation took four days to complete, but these were not consecutive days. They took place every fifth day, that is, on the day following a four-day interim after the previous ceremony. Thus each ritual took place on successive days of the week, so that each occurred on a different god's day. The total number of days lapsed was sixteen. During this time, the *oba* changed into white clothing, symbolizing his rebirth as *oba*.

In a sense, the *oba* is a living human version of the concentric circles of sacredness in the town. He lives in the center of the state, in the center of the central town, in the innermost reaches of the palace, in the center of ritual prohibitions, and is swathed in heavy clothes, his face hidden by the most sacred symbol of his office, the beaded crown. Physically and spiritually, he is the epicenter of the Yoruba state. Most sacred of all *obas* is the Oni of Ife, who lives in the center of the human world.

Physically and politically, the arrangement of the *oba*'s court resembles the arrangement of the cosmos. The entrance to the ceremonial court is directly opposite the throne, and the line from it to the throne and to the *oba* represents the Chief Way. On either side of the *oba* sit his councillors, those of the Right and those of the Left. Councillors of the Right have higher rank than those of the Left, paralleling the arrangement of the gods into those of the Right and the Left. No moral judgments are made concerning the *oba*'s councillors, however. They are not divided into good and bad, but only into higher and lower rank. Persons from outside the palace who enter the *oba*'s court walk along the Chief Way, kneel, and touch the ground first with their foreheads and then successively with their right and left temples (Frobenius 1913:279), symbolizing the Way, the Right, and the Left. Although at first glance this may seem to be triadic symbolism, in fact it still represents the four-fold division of the world, for there are two axes of orientation, the Chief Way and the Second Way. The Second Way in this case is represented by those councillors who stand to the right and to the left of the *oba*.

A similar but less obvious situation exists when the *oba* is represented by three palace eunuchs. The *oba* himself generally remains secluded in his private apartments, but since his symbolic presence is required on many different occasions, he is represented in public affairs by the Eunuch of the Center, the Eunuch of the Right, and the Eunuch of the Left. The Eunuch of the Center, or the Chief Eunuch, represents him in court and in judicial proceedings. The Eunuch of the Right represents him at religious ceremonies, and the Eunuch of the Left in civil and military matters (Smith 1969: 16). The Eunuch of the Center has the highest rank. Whether the Eunuchs of the Right and Left are also ranked is unknown. If they are, one would expect the Eunuch of the Right to be higher than the Eunuch of the Left. Again, this arrangement appears to be triadic, but it should be remembered that, first, there are actually four persons involved, the *oba* and his three eunuchs; and second, the Eunuch of the Center represents the *oba* in court and apparently his personage also stands for the Chief Way, while the Eunuchs of the Right and Left represent the Second Way. It may be that the symbolism of this arrangement is more complex than the literature concerning it indicates, and it may be that both triadic and quadratic symbolism intersect in this instance. However, it does seem likely in the light of other data concerning the patterns of the *oba*ship and of the Yoruba world view that at least a quadratic scheme is intended to be represented here.

Morton-Williams (1964:245) feels that the *oba*'s council is analogous to the gods who do Olorun's bidding and who are hierarchically arranged as are the *oba*'s councils on earth. The *oba*, he indicates, is the earthly counterpart of Olorun, the supreme god. Like the gods, the members of the *oba*'s council are ranked, the first four councillors of the Right being most important. Of these, the most important is the head councillor, called the *bashorun* (Johnson 1921:47). The *bashorun*, an Ifa priest, is one of the few persons who has access to the *oba*. Most important, the *bashorun* is responsible for determining the quality of the relationship between the *oba* and his *orun*, the *oba*'s spiritual counterpart believed to be resident in the heavens. It is through his *orun* that the *oba* obtains his divinity. Once a year the *bashorun* divines in order to learn whether the *oba* and his *orun* are in harmony. If they are, all is well. If they are not, then the *oba* must perform sacrifices in order to regain harmony with his *orun*. In the past, if he failed to do so, as indicated by the *Ifa* system, the *oba* was forced to commit suicide. The *bashorun* also consults the *Ifa* oracle on behalf of the *oba* every fifth day, that is, on a different god's day each time.

Dennett (1910: 90) claims that the Oni of Ife's council is believed to represent the council of the gods. The *bashorun* represents Ifa, the god of divination, whom Dennett states is believed to be the head councillor and chief advisor to the gods. Dennett also reports a legend to the effect that the first four advisors of the first Oni of Ife were called the "four great ones," and were comparable to the walls of the first Yoruba kingdom as founded by Oduduwa. Furthermore, these walls stood for the four major Yoruba kingdoms of Oyo, Ijebu, Egba, and Ekiti, Ife being the center. The four surrounding kingdoms lie roughly north, south, west, and east of Ile Ife.

Frobenius, who visited Ife in 1911, makes certain observations concerning the ancient court at Ife (Frobenius 1913:279). No other writer surveyed here has discussed this aspect of Ife, and it is uncertain as to whether Frobenius is reporting an actual situation or a situation which his informants believed to have been the case. In any event, it is of some importance that the following account is a Yoruba belief, if not an actuality. Frobenius was told that at one time the Oni of Ife had seventeen advisers. Eight were Councillors of the Right and nine were Councillors of the Left, the ninth councillor representing the central precinct. The other sixteen represented sixteen wards. At some subsequent time, however, a ruling Oni replaced representatives of the four highest offices with members of his own family, who normally would have been ineligible for such positions. He gave his own son the job of administering the central precinct. As a result, at the time Frobenius visited Ife, there were only twelve wards and twelve ward chiefs in the town. Whether or not there were sixteen wards and a central precinct in Ife is ultimately of less importance than the fact the Frobenius informants believed that there should have been, for it is an indication of the Yoruba concept of the ideal government.

Bascom (1955:450), writing about Ife in the mid-twentieth century, notes that five ward chiefs and three other chiefs represent the interests of the people of Ife at court and, together with eight chiefs chosen from the palace retinue, make up the Oni's council. While it is uncertain whether the structure of Ife changed between 1911 and 1955, it is noteworthy that the focus of orientation and the total number of councillors are again a multiple of four.

TIME

Like space and political institutions, time and diachronic events are ordered around the concept of multiples of two, most particularly four, eight, and sixteen. The *oba*'s installation is one example of this orientation, as is the *bashorun*'s weekly divination for the *oba*. The year itself is seen as being of two types. One is the agricultural or natural year, in which seasons pass, and crops are planted, tended, and harvested. This year is not divided into fixed segments. The other kind of year is the ritual year, a series of alternating sacred and nonsacred times, in which segments of time are fixed. These years are cyclical and repeat themselves. In Leach's terms (1965) there are periods of ritually empty time alternating with periods of ritually active time, so that time is an "alternation between contraries," in which the participants, the nature of the world, and time itself alternate between sacred and profane states and are periodically transformed. Normal secular life takes place in the period between abnormal sacred events.

Yoruba ritual time consists of a series of oscillations or pulses. There are four major annual pulses, corresponding with four major annual festivals associated with Olori Merin, the god of the four corners, in which a four-day-old infant is sacrificed to one of the gods of the cardinal points (Frobenius 1913: 304). The most important of these is held in June, when the festival is associated with the east. Another is held in September to the god of the north, one in December to the god of the west, and one in March to the god of the south (Frobenius 1913:258). These festivals last eight days. Interspersed between them are twelve minor festivals, making sixteen in all. The days on which they occur are determined by a pillar located in the center of the town. A circle is drawn around this pillar and marked off into four major and twelve minor sections. When the pillar's shadow falls upon one of these points, the festival begins (Ojo 1966: 202). The pillar itself represents both the center of the natural world, Ile Ife, and the center of the supernatural world, the crossroads.

Daily time is also conceived of as a series of oscillations. The twenty-four-hour day is absent. Instead, there are a series of alternating periods of days and nights, each twelve hours long, from sunrise to sunset and from sunset to sunrise (Ojo 1966:201–202). Night is associated with Oduduwa, while day is associated with Obatala. Each of these periods is bifurcated by noon or by midnight, thus creating four quadrants or classes of time which rotate as the sun or moon travels up and then down the bowl of the sky.

Dawn, noon, and midnight are sacred times. Whether sunset was also sacred is unknown. Dawn is the time at which divination is performed. Both noon and midnight are associated with "awe and fear" (Ojo 1966: 199). At these times it is believed that, as day is transformed into night and night into day, so nature also transforms itself and miraculous events may occur. Animals and trees in the forest around the towns may metamorphose, river spirits may appear in the rivers, and spirits and gods may enter the earth through the four gates of the cosmos. The world reverses itself at these times. It also reverses itself at times of annual festivals, for these are periods when gods and spirits are most active in the natural world.

The Yoruba week is four days long, and the god of a given day is responsible for making that day safe for men. Frobenius (1913:256) claims that in the past each of the four days belonged not to one but to four gods, making a weekly total of sixteen. However, there is no substantiating evidence for this statement, nor does Frobenius make reference to it when discussing the gods of the crossroads, who, as he and other writers have pointed out, are the same gods as the gods of the week. In any event, one finds in the Yoruba week a rotating periodicity around the number four.

Four and its multiples are important ways of marking time, and, as in other aspects of Yoruba culture, the higher the multiple, the more important the event. Eight has higher significance than four, and sixteen is higher than eight. For example, funerals of rich or important men last for eight days, while poor men's funerals last only four days. Most important festivals are of eight days' duration, while less important ones take four days (Ojo 1966:185). Rain-making rituals last for eight days, and meetings of guilds or associations take place every four, eight, or sixteen days, depending upon the importance of the group (Ojo 1966: 215). For example, the powerful Egba and Oyo Ogboni societies meet every sixteen days, as do trade chiefs in charge of markets and as did heads of military societies (Biobaku 1965: 6). *Ifa* priests meet every sixteen days. The installation of a new *oba* of Oyo covers four days, but the total number of days elapsed is sixteen.

The same principle holds true for market days. Yoruba markets are organized as cycles or rings. Each market takes place when it is the only one operating in the ring, and the system works so that no one area is more than four days without a market. Small periodic markets are held every four days, whereas larger and more important ones are held every eight or sixteen days. In rural areas market rings generally operate on four- or eight-day cycles. The order of the cycle seems to be roughly diagonal, beginning in the center, then progressing south, north, west, east, and returning to the center again (Hodder 1962: 105). In towns, the *oba*'s market is generally held every eight or sixteen days. In large towns, there is usually one large market and four small ones located in the four major quadrants of the town. These rotate between the wards, with the *oba*'s market coinciding with one of the smaller ones.

Again one finds that the Yoruba define time as they did space, transforming spatial concepts to temporal ones. Four is the basic ordering device, as the year is divided into four parts and each part is again divided into four. As in other domains, multiples of four have higher prestige than four itself. And finally, underlying the Yoruba division of time is a dual system of alternating periods of sacred and nonsacred time during which the world itself is capable of transformations.

IFA DIVINATION

The Yoruba system of divination known as *Ifa* is extremely complex and cannot be dealt with in detail here. Nevertheless *Ifa* divination is of importance and must be touched upon, for it is the concept of duality which gives *Ifa* its order and form (McClelland 1966: 423).

Yoruba believe in an ordered universe which can be known to man through *Ifa* divination. It is believed that the results are controlled by the god Ifa, who personally supervises all divination, so that if correctly performed, *Ifa* divination gives infallible results.

There are two principal methods of *Ifa* divination, one of which has higher prestige than the other, but both of which are similar (Bascom 1969a). The method with lower status, which is somewhat easier to manipulate, uses sixteen palm nut halves attached to two strings, eight halves on each string. The diviner, or *babalawo*, holds these strings so that four nuts fall on each side. He always uses his right hand in this operation. Even if they are left-handed, diviners do not cast with the left hand, for this is considered unlucky. The strings are then thrown into the air in such a way that the sides fall parallel. The nuts fall into a "heads" or "tails" position, and the resulting pattern is used to select an oracular verse, called an *Odu* (Bascom 1969a: 3; Lloyd 1965: 574). If a nut falls concave upwards the *babalawo* makes one mark on his diviner's tray. If it falls concave downwards, he makes two marks.

The method with higher status does not use a chain. The *babalawo* holds sixteen nuts in his hands, claps his hands together, and tries to grasp as many nuts as possible with his right hand, so that he has only one or two remaining in his left hand (Bascom 1969a: 3; Dennett 1910: 148; Frobenius 1913: 251). If he catches one nut, he makes two vertical parallel lines on his divining board. If he catches two nuts, he makes one mark. If he has more or less than one or two nuts left, the cast does not count. If he repeats this action four times, he obtains one of sixteen basic figures or *Odus*. If he repeats it eight times, he will get one of 256 *Odus*. If he uses a chain, one cast will yield up one of the 256 figures. In either method, the figures or *Odus* are made up of four marks each.

Four marks in a vertical column make half an *Odu* figure. Each half has sixteen possible forms. These forms represent deities, and the deities are ranked in hierarchical order, so that the figures are also ranked. The second half of an *Odu* is also made up of sixteen possible forms which can combine with any of the sixteen forms in the first column, giving a total of 256 possible *Odus* (Bascom 1969b: 70). Each of the sixteen possible combinations of four elements in a column is named, and the name of the *Odu* is the name of the right-hand column followed by that of the left.

There are sixteen possible combinations in which the right- and left-hand columns are identical. These are the principal *Odus*. A further 240 have dissimilar columns, making a total of 256. The principal *Odus* have higher rank than the secondary ones. Each derivative figure has a compound name but not compound verses. Each compound figure forms a separate *Odu* with a separate set of verses (Bascom 1966:41).

The compound figures are seen as paired deities. The relationship between the various *Odus* is metaphorically expressed in the following account (McClelland 1966: 425): Each *Odu* is a king who leaves his own kingdom to visit the *Odu* next below him in rank. The trip takes sixteen days. He stays with his host and then returns. His host then pays a return visit to his guest, also taking sixteen days to complete the journey. Thus there are a pair of visits, then the first *Odu* visits the third *Odu*, and another pair of visits takes place. In all, the first *Odu* makes fifteen visits and is revisited fifteen times, making thirty visits in all.

Then the second *Odu* follows the same process, making fourteen visits and receiving fourteen in return, totalling twenty-eight visits. Each *Odu* in succession visits and is revisited by the *Odu* beneath him in rank. The final *Odu* does not inititate visits because he cannot visit himself, and he cannot visit anyone higher in rank than himself, so here the total is zero. The result is an arithmetic progression totalling 240. This is added to the sixteen single *Odus*, giving 256 or 2^8.

Each *Odu* has a set of myths or verses attached to it which can offer an explanation to a client by referring to an archetypical situation (Morton-Williams 1966:406). The solution to the client's problem is generally a sacrifice made to the *Odu* and possibly to other deities as well.

There is a general Yoruba belief that there are sixteen verses for each *Odu*, or 4,096 verses, "...but as sixteen is a mystical number in Ifa divination, this is only a conventionalized statement and perhaps even an underestimate" (Bascom 1969a:121). Bascom estimates the existence of about 4,000 verses as a conservative guess, since some *Odus* have more than sixteen verses attached to them. The number 4,096 is of importance because it represents a scale of two and can be written as $2^2-2^3-2^4-2^8-2^{12}$ in a geometrical progression (McClelland 1966: 425).

These verses provide clues to the solution of the client's problem. The message given in the verses is further clarified by asking the oracle questions with a yes/no, either/or, or favorable/unfavorable answer (Bascom 1966:51). In other words, answers are phrased in terms of paired oppositions.

Divining paraphernalia are also replete with dual and four-fold symbolism. The divining trays of the *babalawos* are essential elements in *Ifa* symbolism. These trays are generally round or rectangular. Rectangular types are found in the south, while circular ones are common in the north (Frobenius 1913:244). In this, they parallel differences in kinship systems and in town morphology, although why this should be so is not clear. In either case, the periphery of the tray is decorated while the center is smooth. Peripheries are divided into two major sections and two minor, making four in all (Frobenius 1913:244). Major divisions are at the top and bottom, while minor ones are at the right and left sides. These divisions represent the Chief Way and the Second Way. A representation of the god Eshu always appears at the top, and the tray is always held with Eshu facing east. His picture may also be repeated at the bottom and sides of the tray, or the bottom and sides may be demarcated in some other way, but the tray is always divided into four sections.

The divining tray represents the heavens divided into four parts by two "roads." The center of the tray, although it is not marked, represents the crossroads of the cosmos. Frobenius (1913: 254) states that these divisions on the tray are linked with the gods of the crossroads who accordingly govern their respective sections of the divining tray. Odugbesan (1969:200) also states that the divining tray represents the cosmos, its center standing for Ile Ife as well as the crossroads of the heavens, and that the periphery of the tray represents Ife's widening influence on the world.

Eshu is also represented in the nuts which the *babalawo* uses. The *babalawo* divines with sixteen nuts, but he places a seventeenth, sometimes carved in ivory, to the side of the tray, where it "stands sentinel" as a guardian (Dennett 1910:148; Odugbesan 1969: 201). This nut represents the head of Eshu (Frobenius 1913: 251), who is called the "chief of Ifa," or the "chief of the palm nuts." The sixteen nuts themselves symbolize Ifa. Again one finds the pattern of sixteen plus one repeated.

A myth concerning the origin of these nuts as reported by McClelland (1966:424) emphasizes the importance of numbers in the *Ifa* system: A Divine Being who had been taught divination by the god Ifa arrived in Ile Ife. Here he taught *Ifa* to sixteen men, all of whom were twins. A seventeenth man was rejected because he was not a twin. However, he was a son of Eshu and thus was feared, for it was dangerous to invoke Eshu's anger. Since this man could not be ignored, he became a special messenger between men on earth and Ifa in heaven and is the seventeenth nut. All the original sixteen were earthly counterparts of heavenly beings. Each nut therefore stands for four entities, a pair on earth and a pair in heaven, while the seventeenth stands for two entities, one on earth and the other the god Eshu.

Divining bowls also utilize a two-fold division. These are for storage of divining paraphernalia. They are generally divided into a central section with four, six, or eight sections around it. The seventeenth nut and one set of sixteen palm nuts are kept in the central part, while the remaining sections are used for other divining paraphernalia, including other sets of nuts (Bascom 1969a: 33).

Ifa and Eshu

As already shown, Ifa and Eshu figure importantly in Yoruba divination. They are also of interest because of their symbolic roles in the cosmos. The world as it exists ideally should be stable, ordered, predictable, and four-square, based on two paired. This condition is symbolized by Ifa. But in fact the world is not always stable, and the Yoruba take account of this situation by positing the existence of Eshu the trickster/ transformer, whose actions explain events which do not fit the ideal model. The concept of Eshu undoubtedly played an important role in the maintenance of belief in a stable universe during the upheavals of the eighteenth and nineteenth centuries in Yoruba country.

Eshu is a god of reversals, unpredictable and changeable, while Ifa represents predictability and continuity. Like Obatala, Ifa is associated with white and with light. Like Obatala, he is also connected with the sun, with day, and particularly with dawn, the time of divination. Eshu, on the other hand, shares certain characteristics with Oduduwa. Like Oduduwa, Eshu is associated with blackness, with night, and with the new moon. Unlike Oduduwa, however, he is also linked with mischief, evil, and witchcraft. Eshu is responsible for the lack of order and stability in the world, but both Ifa and Eshu are associated with divination, and both must be taken into account when divining. Ifa makes accurate divination possible. Eshu is the troublemaker who can hinder or distort communication between men and the gods. Thus, in every divinatory attempt, he must be acknowledged and placated.

Furthermore, it is Eshu who is sometimes credited with bringing *Ifa* divination to mankind and in one myth for creating Ifa himself (Frobenius 1913: 230–232). In this myth, men had stopped sacrificing to the gods, who as a result had become hungry. Olorun then told Eshu to find sixteen palm nuts and to learn their meaning. If Eshu did this, the gods would have man's goodwill again and would be fed their sacrifices. Eshu obtained the nuts from a monkey, who told him to go to sixteen wise men in each of the sixteen places of the heavens, and these men would teach him the meaning of the nuts. Eshu did so, and he learned that men could avert bad luck and know the will of the gods by using the sixteen nuts. The palm nuts became the deity Ifa, while Eshu returned and stayed with Ogun, Shango, and Obatala. (These, along with Ifa/Eshu, are Frobenius' gods of the crossroads.) The sixteen wise men whom Eshu visited were the children of the goddess Yemaya, and all were born in one birth at Ile Ife (Frobenius 1913:259).

In another myth concerning the origin of divination (Gordon and Lancaster 1961: 23), Ifa, prompted by his hunger, went to Eshu for aid. Eshu taught him divination. Thereafter Ifa could claim offerings made by diviners, but Eshu was to get a portion of every offering as his fee. Therefore Eshu is represented on the divining board.

Ifa and Eshu are sometimes thought of as separate beings and at other times are thought of as one being, each name representing different aspects of the same character. In any event, these two gods are always closely linked and are mirror images of each other. Unlike Obatala and Oduduwa, there are no accounts of rivalry between them. One is the reverse of the other, but they work in harmony, not in opposition. In addition, unlike Oduduwa and Obatala, Eshu and Ifa are never thought of as consorts. Both are indisputably male.

Outside of the spheres of divination and of crossroads, Ifa and Eshu are more frequently thought of as separate beings, and Eshu is the more active god. He is associated with markets and with thresholds of houses. He is said to be the messenger of the gods and represents their anger. He prompts men to disobey the gods, causing the gods to punish them. Men must divine in order to learn the cause of punishment, so that Eshu indirectly brings men into communication with the gods, most particularly Ifa (Wescott 1962:340).

Eshu is perverse and reverse, a god of contraries and hence of dualisms. There are several myths illustrating this aspect of his character. In one (Wescott 1962:340), he persuaded the sun and the moon to change homes thus reversing the order of time. In another (Frobenius 1913:240–242; Wescott 1962:340–341), his role as transformer of order and divider of unity is explicit: Two men owning adjoining farms were lifelong friends and were famous for this friendship. Seeing this, Eshu decided to separate them. He walked down the path dividing their farms, wearing a hat which was black on one side and white on the other. He put his pipe at the back of his head and hooked his club over his shoulder so that it hung down his back. The two friends then quarreled over the direction he had taken and the color of his cap. They ended by becoming enemies. Thus Eshu separated those who had been united.

Even descriptions of Eshu are contradictory. He is said to be both big

and small, firstborn and lastborn, old and young, childless and a
father to all, friendless and a friend to all (Wescott 1962). In his person
he epitomizes dualities and oppositions. He is a homeless wanderer
and yet is associated with the crossroads, the symbol of stability. He
is symbolized by a broken calabash, the opposite of the unbroken calabash of creation. He is also represented by black and white cowrie shells,
which Wescott (1962: 346) feels represent the world of extremes. He
turns day into night, friendship into enmity, right into wrong, and makes
the innocent guilty. In his person he embodies both positive and negative
qualities.

Yet despite the fact that he is a god of reversals, he is also associated
with order and as such he fits the general Yoruba pattern. Frobenius
(1913: 258–259), in describing rituals in temples dedicated to Eshu,
finds a link between Eshu worship and the cosmic scheme. Eshu priests
make offerings in a processional route from east to north to west to
south. This order follows the same order as the sacrifices to Olori Merin,
and the number four is significant:

The processional of prayer, or sacred circumambulation, the symbolic apparatus
of the service, the week-day sequence, the seasonal sacrificial order, and the
turning round of the body during devotion, are in mutual correspondence
down to the very smallest details.

Eshu, along with Ifa, is most particularly associated with the east, the
most important direction in Yoruba thought. He seems to be very closely
connected with the Chief Way, a symbol of stability, order, and authority.
He is also associated with the *oba*'s market and therefore with the center
of town, a sacred location. Yet in his person as troublemaker, he seems
to contradict these qualities. In a sense, this is a contrary of contraries,
and Eshu, more than any other deity, embodies the dualism pervasive
in Yoruba culture. He takes things out of place, disrupts human life,
and transforms qualities. But he himself has his own place in the cosmos,
so that in the long run he only appears to create disorder. In actual fact,
he maintains order by reminding men that all things must have their
place. And proper place is an important quality of sacred things, as
Lévi-Strauss (1962: 10) has pointed out:

It could even be said that being in their place is what makes them sacred for
if they were taken out of their place, even in thought, the entire order of the
universe would be destroyed. Sacred objects therefore contribute to the maintenance of order in the universe by occupying the place allotted to them.

CONCLUSIONS

In the Yoruba world view, all things have their place, which is precisely why they are sacred. Even Eshu, who seems to represent an inversion of all things, comes to have his place within the general intellectual framework. The pattern is repeated on various planes of thought, so that the place of each object is replicated on many levels. Duality and multiples of duality, pairs and oppositions, center and periphery, and the quadratic schemes of the cosmos are reiterated again and again. These concepts undergo transformations as they are applied to various conceptual domains, but the pattern itself and the relations between the component parts remain constant. Objects and events "which would otherwise seem wholly disparate and incomprehensible" are made comprehensible and are seen to be aspects of one grand cosmic scheme, resulting in an extremely complex but comprehensive world view.

The consistency of this world view is remarkable. There is extremely little, if any, contradictory evidence from the many published sources on the Yoruba. The fact that there are so many published sources lends credence to the idea that the Yoruba do in fact possess a complex and consistent world view. Nevertheless, the existence of such an intellectual system raises several questions. One such question concerns the nature of the Yoruba informants who were interviewed and of the nature of the relationship between ethnographer and informant. One wonders whether those Yoruba informants who were interviewed were primarily Yoruba *Ogotemmêlis*, intellectuals capable of seeing conceptual relationships within their own culture and of expressing these relationships in a clearer way than the ordinary Yoruba could. Unfortunately, no writer except Frobenius described his sources of information, and Frobenius' informants were not ordinary Yoruba but were priests and highly ranked titled men. If other Yoruba informants were also such men, it is possible that resulting descriptions of Yoruba culture are more precise and consistent than would be the case if those interviewed were "men in the street."

The complexity of the Yoruba pattern further raises the question of the way in which Yoruba themselves perceive their own culture. Are there some who are philosophers, who spend their time in working out the intricacies of their own system? And are there others, laymen, so to speak, who are not particularly aware of the entire patterns but who merely follow accepted traditions? What is the psychological dimension for individuals living within such a culture? Unfortunately, this sort of information cannot now be obtained in full, for the system as it has been described in the preceding pages is now defunct in many ways.

And finally, the question is raised as to whether there are differences between types of cultures in the way they organize their conceptual systems. Are there some societies like the Yoruba, the Dogun, and the Oglala Sioux who pattern their beliefs more consistently than others? Are there some cultures which are intellectually tightly woven and others which are loosely woven? Could the apparent differences between tightly woven and loosely woven cultures be merely a function of the informants chosen by the ethnographer, or is there a real difference between cultural types? If there is a real difference, what is it that cultures with tightly woven intellectual systems have in common with each other that they do not share with loosely woven systems? A subject such as the one discussed in this paper raises many questions which can only be answered by thorough empirical study, both in the field and in the literature.

REFERENCES

ADEDEJI, J. A.
    1966   The place of drama in Yoruba religious observance. *Odu* 3 : 88–94.
AWE, B.
    1967   "Ibadan, its early beginnings," in *The city of Ibadan*. Edited by P.C. Lloyd, A.L. Mabogunje, and B. Awe, 11–25. London: Cambridge University Press.
BASCOM, WILLIAM
    1944   Sociological role of the Yoruba cult group. *American Anthropologist Memoir Series* 64.
    1955   Urbanization among the Yoruba. *American Journal of Sociology* 60 : 446–454.
    1966   Two studies of Ifa divination: Odu Ifa. *Africa* 36 : 408–421.
    1969a *Ifa divination: communication between gods and men in West Africa.* Bloomington: Indiana University Press.
    1969b *The Yoruba of southern Nigeria.* New York: Holt, Rinehart and Winston.
BENEDICT, RUTH
    1934   *Patterns of culture.* Boston: Houghton Mifflin.
BIOBAKU, S. O.
    1952   An historical sketch of Egba traditional authorities. *Africa* 22 : 35–49.
    1956   "Ogboni, the Egba senate," in *Proceedings, Third International West African Conference.* Lagos: Nigerian Museum.
    1965   *The Egba and their neighbors: 1842–1872.* London: Oxford University Press.
DENNETT, R. E.
    1910   *Nigerian studies.* London: Frank Cass.
FROBENIUS, LEO
    1913   *The voice of Africa*, volume one. New York: Benjamin Blom.

GEERTZ, CLIFFORD
 1970 "Ethos, world view and the analysis of sacred symbols," in *Man makes sense*. Edited by Eugene A. Hammel and William S. Simmons, 324–338. Boston: Little, Brown.
GORDON, TIM, MICHAEL LANCASTER
 1961 Orisha houses in Ibadan. *Ibadan* 9:22–23.
GRIAULE, MARCEL
 1965 *Conversations with Ogotemmêli*. London: Oxford University Press.
HODDER, B. W.
 1962 "The Yoruba rural market," in *Markets in Africa*. Edited by Paul Bohannon and George Dalton, 103–117. Evanston: Northwestern University Press.
IDOWU, R.
 1962 *Olodumare, god in Yoruba belief*. London: Longmans.
JOHNSON, SAMUEL
 1921 *History of the Yorubas*. London: Routledge and Kegan Paul.
KRAPF-ASKARI, EVA
 1966 Time and classifications: an ethnographic and historical case study. *Odu* 2:3–18.
 1969 *Yoruba towns and cities*. Oxford: Clarendon Press.
LEACH, EDMUND
 1965 "Two essays concerning the symbolic representation of time," in *Reader in comparative religion*. Edited by William Lessa and Evon Vogt, 241–249. New York: Harper and Row.
LÉVI-STRAUSS, CLAUDE
 1962 *The savage mind*. London: Weidenfeld and Nicholson.
LIENHARDT, GODFREY
 1968 "Belief and knowledge," in *Theory in anthropology*. Edited by Robert A. Manners and David Kaplan, 438–453. Chicago: Aldine.
LLOYD, P. C.
 1955 The Yoruba lineage. *Africa* 25:235–251.
 1960 Sacred kingship and government among the Yoruba. *Africa* 30: 221–237.
 1965 "The Yoruba of Nigeria," in *Peoples of Africa*. Edited by James L. Gibbs, 547–582. New York: Holt, Rinehart and Winston.
 1966 Agnatic and cognatic descent among the Yoruba. *Man*, n.s. 1:484–500.
 1967 "Introduction," in *The city of Ibadan*. Edited by P.C. Lloyd, A. L. Mabogunje, and B. Awe, 3–11. London: Cambridge University Press.
MABOGUNJE, A. L.
 1962 *Yoruba towns*. Ibadan: University of Ibadan Press.
 1967 "The morphology of Ibadan," in *The city of Ibadan*. Edited by P. C. Lloyd, A. L. Mabogunje, and B. Awe, 35–56. London: Cambridge University Press.
MCCLELLAND, E. M.
 1966 Two studies of Ifa divination: the significance of number in the Odu of Ifa. *Africa* 36:421–431.
MORTON-WILLIAMS, PETER
 1960a The Yoruba Ogboni cult in Oyo. *Africa* 30:362–374.

1960b Yoruba responses to the fear of death. *Africa* 30:34–40.

1964 An outline of the cosmology and cult organization of the Oyo Yoruba. *Africa* 34:243–261.

1966 Two studies of Ifa divination: the mode of divination. *Africa*: 36: 406–408.

1967 "The Yoruba kingdom of Oyo," in *West African kingdoms in the nineteenth century*. Edited by Daryll Forde and P. M. Kaberry, 36–69. London: Oxford University Press.

MUMFORD, LEWIS

1961 *The city in history*. London: Secker and Warburg.

ODUGBESAN, CLARA

1969 "Femininity in Yoruba religious art," in *Man in Africa*. Edited by Mary Douglas and P. M. Kaberry, 199–211. London: Tavistock.

OJO, G. J. A.

1966 *Yoruba culture*. London: University of London Press.

OKEDIJI, F. O., F. A. OKEDIJI

1966 The sociological aspects of traditional African names and titles. *Odu* 3:64–79.

RADIN, PAUL

1927 *Primitive man as philosopher*. New York: Dover.

SCHWAB, W. B.

1955 Kinship and lineage among the Yoruba. *Africa* 25: 352–371.

1965 "Oshogbo – an urban community?" in *Urbanization and migration in West Africa*. Edited by Hilda Kuper, 85–109. Berkeley: University of California Press.

SMITH, ROBERT

1969 *Kingdoms of the Yoruba*. London: Methuen.

VERGER, PIERRE

1966 The Yoruba high god: a review of the sources. *Odu* 2:19–40.

WESCOTT, JOAN

1962 The sculpture and myths of Eshu-Elegba, the Yoruba trickster. *Africa* 32:336–354.

WILLIAMS, DENIS

1964 An outline of the cosmology and cult organization of the Oyo Yoruba. *Africa* 34:243–261.

WOLF, ERIC

1959 *Sons of the shaking earth*. Chicago: University of Chicago Press.

1965 "The Virgin of Guadaloupe: a Mexican national symbol," in *Reader in comparative religion*. Edited by William Lessa and Evon Vogt, 226–230. New York: Harper and Row.

On the Overlapping of Categories in the Social Sciences

FERRUCCIO ROSSI-LANDI

A category is any very general concept used for its power to confer some order to a system, or at least to an aggregate, of other concepts of lesser generality, either in everyday life, or in scientific inquiry, or in both. As shown by Ryle (1971 [1938]: 170–184; 1949), among others, the idea that there exists a finite and very short catalogue of unconditioned categories is pure myth (Ryle 1971:179). Moreover, categories must be understood historically. It is true that the most general categories (such as Aristotle's ten classes or Kant's fourfold division of triads, to give the main European historical examples) are endowed with a special persistency of their own, so much so that persistency may be used as a criterion for generality; however, this does not necessarily involve any reference to metaphysical, i.e. either superhistorical or hypohistorical entities. The stress should be laid on the changes that categories undergo in time and space. Not only do we find that categories differ from culture to culture, we are also able to examine problems from different categorical angles, selecting for ourselves which category must exercise its ordering power upon which others, thereby changing our own categorical system and the level of generality of the categories involved.

Categories are a reflection of reality as operated upon by men in their SOCIAL PRACTICE, and thus they also are HUMAN PRODUCTS. Scientific inquiry is one slice of social practice, and scientific procedures and results are among the most refined human products. The idea that anything which is a human product may be exempt from change is another pure myth; on the other hand, constant features of social practice determine constant categories.

Examples of categories as they are understood here are matter, movement, space, time, connection, relation, totality, part, reciprocal action, contradiction, chance, necessity, regularity, causality, law, structure, system, essence, phenomenon, reality, appearance, and so on. At a level which may, in principle, be described as less general, we find all the basic categories of the social sciences, such as action, behavior, work, exchange, communication, code, message, production, utensil, product, distribution, consumption, money, language, speech, thought, mind, society, nature, culture, person, public, private, tradition, institution, innovation, acculturation, enculturation, education, and so on.

It should be clear that these two lists are only a very rough indication of a particularly wide use of the term "category." However, we may assume that categories of the first roster are necessarily common to all sciences and to all human exchange, verbal or nonverbal; while categories of the second roster, although also widespread, are mainly used in organized groups as fundamental terms of various social sciences.

There is an argument which claims that it is necessary to distinguish each category from all others on its own grounds. If we were to resort to categories other than the category under examination — so the argument runs — it would seem that we would be depriving the category under examination of its very character of being a category proper. A category described by means of another category would simply be an instance of the other category. This is a wrong approach, a leftover of the dual myth that there is a finite (and very small) number of unconditioned categories, and that they are unchangeable.

On the contrary, we maintain that (1) whenever we want to give an adequate account of any category, we do have to resort to other categories; (2) while this is readily granted in some cases (e.g. speaking and language, or tool and product), it is not in others; indeed, the habit of dealing with some categories as if they were entities more or less independent of each other is still common, especially in the social sciences, and constitutes a stumbling block to the advance of knowledge; and (3) when we accept the principle that categories overlap, and deal with two or more categories jointly, nothing like the feared collapse of one category under the rule of some other category need take place; all categories in general, and especially categories used in the social sciences, receive instead full light only if their overlapping is given complete attention.

Here we shall give a brief illustration of this approach.

SOME CASES OF PAIRED TERMS

The ways in which categories are interconnected and overlap may be best introduced through an EXCURSUS on a relatively simple matter, paired terms. These are words (or syntagms, or even phrases) which acquire full meaning only insofar as they involve each other. There is no "right" unless there is a "left," nor is there an "over" unless there is an "under," and so on. We meet the same situation with comparatives: when we say that Charles is MORE fluent in Bulgarian, we refer at least implicitly to the so-called second term of comparison, that is, we assume the existence of someone who is LESS fluent than Charles, or we are implying that at a previous stage Charles himself was less fluent in Bulgarian, or that he is less fluent in other languages. This concerns proper, nonmetaphorical usages.

At a more complex level we meet paired terms of a higher biological, historical, or social content, such as male and female, father and son, husband and wife, king and subjects, master and servant, exploiter and exploited. According to the usage adopted in this paper, these are important categories of the social sciences. A factor of complexity here is that it is more difficult to distinguish proper usages from metaphorical usages. While it is obvious, for example, that there is no father without a son (or daughter), paternal and filial attitudes are also to be found outside of real "father-son" situations. It then remains to be seen whether calling the attitude of a person who never had any child "paternal" is to be considered a proper or a metaphorical usage.

Paired terms, of course, are also interconnected as pairs. For an off-spring to exist, a father does not suffice: you also need a mother. When you speak of a son or daughter, you presuppose both parents. Thus the categorical net enlarges: we have offspring versus parents; both offspring and parents can be male or female. Or, we can distinguish males from females and then proceed to say that both males and females can be parents, and surely are offspring in their turn.

Let us give another example. There is no master without a servant, and vice versa. On the surface the situation appears as simple as that of "over" versus "under." Beyond the paired terms, however, one glimpses a much more complicated situation. "Masterly" and "servile" are adjectives which can also be applied independently of any precise "master-servant" relation. And whenever such a relation does exist, it certainly is not as simple as the relation between "right" and "left." To understand properly what is involved by the paired terms "master" and "servant," or "lord" and "bondsman," one has to examine the dialectic by which, as long as their relation continues, the master becomes more and more of a master and the servant becomes more and more of a servant, up to the final stage where the master is destroyed by the servant and the whole situation collapses (as shown by Hegel 1964 [1807]: 229–240).

One last example: the situation represented by the paired terms "husband" and "wife" is marriage. Now we know that the institution of marriage differs greatly in time and space: it follows that the reciprocal position of the two partners also differs. Polyandry and polygamy, the phenomenology of subordination of one partner to the other in different societies, the recent cases of "marriages" among homosexuals, various forms of cohabitation of two or more persons of the same or of different sex, so-called social sex, many instances of communitarian life, and so on, are all cases in which the properties of being husband or wife cannot be reduced to any simple definition of the pairing of two terms, or where these properties may even disappear.

The overlapping of categories is clear already at this relatively simple level. You would be at a loss, if you tried to explain what being "husband" or "slave" is without resorting, first, to the other term of the pair and, second, to the whole situation to which the pair belongs. As noticed by Vailati (1966 [1908]: 140–141; cf. Rossi-Landi 1967), it is as if words had VALENCES like chemical elements, so that all valences of each word must be satisfied in order to understand it properly.

INSTANCES OF OVERLAPPING CATEGORIES

Let us now examine in a slightly more detailed way a few more cases where the overlapping of categories assumes a more insidious character. There are cases where the categories are more general, or where their overlapping is not indicated by the terms which represent them, or where such terms are not used in pairs and do not even evoke any opposition between them. There are also cases where, at the superficial level, categories present themselves as, and are used as, reciprocally exclusive. Constellations of categories are of course important; but for reasons of space we shall have to limit ourselves here to categorical pairs.

Production and Consumption

Although this typical case is one of the most difficult ones, we shall begin with it for two reasons. The first reason is that it is, indeed, an extreme case. At first glance, it appears that if you are producing, you are not consuming. The activities of production and consumption are not paired in the same way that husband and wife are. Indeed, they do not even creep in from language as joined terms. The second reason is that we possess a classical analysis of the overlapping and reciprocal action of production and consumption, an analysis which can be used as a model for other such analyses. I am referring to Marx's "Introduction of 1857," which up to some years ago used to be published as an Appendix to his *Critique of political economy* of 1859 but which has now been restituted to its rightful place as the general introduction to the immense body of the *Grundrisse der Kritik der politischen Ökonomie* (see Marx 1953 [1857–1858]; McLellan 1971: Introduction; Nicolaus 1968).

There is of course, says Marx, a shallow conception according to which production, distribution, exchange, and consumption exist side by side, as self-contained, independent spheres. But there is also a deeper conception that sees them as belonging to an organic whole. "Not that production, distribution, exchange, and consumption are identical; but they are all members of one entity, different aspects of one unit...; a mutual interaction takes place between the various elements, [as] is always the case with every organic body [*Dies ist der Fall bei jedem organischen Ganzen*]" (Marx in McLellan 1971:33).

While Marx's analysis concerns all four of the aforementioned terms, i.e. production, distribution, exchange, and consumption, we shall limit ourselves to summarizing here what he says about the relation between production and consumption only. In addition to what has been said by economists on PRODUCTIVE CONSUMPTION as distinguished from consumption proper, there is also a CONSUMPTIVE PRODUCTION: as when in nutrition, which is a form of consumption, man produces his own body. More important than this sort of direct unity of production and consumption, however, are the ways in which consumption furthers production and production furthers consumption. Consumption furthers production "by providing for the products the individual for whom they are products," so that "the product receives its last finishing touches in consumption," or indeed it becomes a REAL product only in consumption (Marx in McLellan 1971:24). Moreover, "consumption produces production by creating the necessity for new production": it "provides the ideal object of production, as its image, its want, its impulse and its purpose... No needs, no production. But consumption reproduces the need" (p.25). "Consumption is not only the concluding act through which the product becomes a product, but also the one through which the producer becomes a producer" (p.27).

On the other hand, production (1) "furnishes consumption with its material, its object"; and (2) "it gives consumption its definite outline, its character"; indeed, "the object is not simply an object in general, but a definite object, which is consumed in a certain definite manner prescribed in its turn by production"; and "not only the object of consumption, but also the manner of consumption is produced by production," and in this sense "production creates the consumers." Furthermore, (3) "production not only supplies the want with material, but supplies the material with a want. When consumption emerges from its first stage of natural crudeness and directness..., it is itself, as a desire, mediated by its object. The want for it which consumption experiences is created by its perception of the product" (pp.25–26).

Must we conclude that production and consumption are simply identical, that there is no difference between them? This is by no means Marx's conclusion. Production could be said to be identical with consumption only if we committed the idealistic error of considering a nation ONLY as a whole, or mankind ONLY *in abstracto*. But "to consider society as a single subject is... a false mode of speculative reasoning. For an individual, production and consumption appear as different aspects of one act. The important point to be emphasized here is that whether production and consumption are considered as activities of one individual or of separate individuals, they appear at any rate as aspects of one process" (p.27).

Public and Private

That two categories act upon each other in a way that requires an analysis of the whole situation to which they belong is a general principle. As such, it can be applied to a number of pairs or aggregates of categories. We shall see that the way in which the above action or influence is exercised may be very different from case to case.

If we consider dialectically the opposition of public and private, for example, we will come to the conclusion that being private is a case of being public. To state the kernel of this at the beginning: the proper totality which both categories refer to IS public. INSIDE that totality there is a zone which is private.

Although private and public apply to a number of different situations such as life, behavior, or even language, the most typical case is perhaps that of property, the private or public ownership of material goods. We maintain that the property[1] of material goods can be private only insofar as it is public. For a man abandoned on an island or isolated in a desert it is impossible to claim the property of this or that portion of the island or desert, the reason for this impossibility being that no other such claim is advanced by anybody else. Nor does it make sense for him to claim the private property of the whole island or desert, the reason for this being that nobody else RENOUNCES the possession of that very property. Something arises as private only insofar as it displaces something else which is also private: in other words, inside a totality which is public, at least two parts are distinguished, the one from the other, by the mark of being private. And even after this has taken place, the totality REMAINS public.

Thus, for instance, I am the private owner of my car only insofar as no other member of the community I belong to is the private owner of that very car. To say that all members of a community, or a majority of them, are the private owners of one and the same car would be nonsense. On the other hand, if there are at least two cars and two citizens, a distribution can take place to the effect that citizen A is the private owner of car A while citizen B is the private owner of car B. Similarly, if there are at least two men on that island, they can claim some sort of preference and right to different sectors of the island, and this may be understood as an embryonic form of private property of those sectors.

In all these cases, and in all possible cases, however, the basic fact is that an island and a car ARE public things. Let us take the case of the automobile, of an individual automobile, more specifically, my own automobile which is my private property. Such an automobile IS public for at least the following reasons: (1) it exists under the eyes of everybody; everybody can see it, touch it, hear the noise of its engine and sniff at the smell of its exhaust; (2) it is a PRODUCT, and this means that it has been produced by the joint efforts of several men, according to projects which can be repeated, and using as materials previous products; there is nothing private or individual about the existence of a particular car; (3) every driver can use it; (4) even nondrivers, in another sense, use it whenever they are transported in it. If it were deprived of all of these public dimensions, my own car could not even be sold or given away as a present, i.e. it could never become somebody else's private property.

The common oppositions between private (or covert) and public (or overt) behavior in psychology, and between private and public language in philosophy (especially by the Wittgensteinians) are, I believe, to be

---

[1] Here and in the following discussion, "property" must be used in place of "ownership" because the phrase "private property" cannot be substituted.

dealt with in the same manner. There is private behavior only insofar as behavior is basically public; and the same is true of language.

To conclude, the simple opposition of the terms "public" and "private" does not take us very far. At a superficial level, what is private is NOT public, and vice versa. But dialectical probing shows us that what is private IS but a case of being PUBLIC, while being public is certainly not a case of being private.

Communication and Behavior

A different case is that of categories which do not present themselves as necessarily related, if only because the terms used for them do not demonstrate the same reciprocity as paired terms like "husband-wife" or "public-private." An important example of this is communication versus behavior. A simple splitting of the possibilities inherent in any two-term opposition gives us the following combinations: communication with behavior, communication without behavior, behavior with communication, behavior without communication. We can at least think in terms of these four cases, positive as well as negative; we cannot, however, even conceive of the two corresponding negative cases drawn from the splitting of such pairs as "husband-wife" because the phrases "husband without wife" and "wife without husband" are simply nonsense. (We can of course speak of A husband who is without HIS wife, but this is no argument against the formation of the pair "husband-wife.") However, further analysis shows that while the cases of communication with behavior and of behavior with communication are of course all right, the case of behavior WITHOUT communication does not exist, and the case of communication WITHOUT behavior can be conceived of only if we confer on "behavior" a very restricted sense. We can eliminate this latter case by means of an example: it may be said that even by being immobile and quiet, i.e. without displaying any overt behavior, one does under certain circumstances communicate something. If this were true, there would exist communication without behavior. But "being quiet and immobile" is hardly a good way of excluding behavior in general; the individual action or lack of action consisting of being quiet and immobile at a given moment is nothing but an accidental moment frozen out of its behavioral context. Even by NOT performing any act of overt behavior, one is not escaping the category of behavior. Death may appear to be the only possible exception. A dead man does not act any longer yet his corpse may communicate much information to the onlooker.

Not even this exception, however, is a real one, because a dead man is a man who has performed behavior up to the moment of his death and whose corpse bears signs of it. Death is, among other things, the cessation of behavior, and in this sense the understanding of death must necessarily resort to the category of behavior. There is then no communication without behavior. As for the case of behavior without communication, it is inconceivable that if someone DOES something, i.e. performs some act of behavior, no information whatsoever can be drawn from it.

Behavior and communication always go together. Resistance to this conclusion may come from the identification of communication with VERBAL, or CONSCIOUS, or INTENTIONAL communication. But as soon as one realizes that man communicates with his entire behavior in several verbal OR nonverbal, conscious OR unconscious, intentional OR unintentional ways, then one has to accept the idea that communication and behavior are categories which overlap almost entirely.

What is involved here is a distinction between sign-behavior and non-sign-behavior. We maintain that such a distinction is not really valid or, to put it a better way, that it has to be understood as a distinction between two different sorts of sign-behavior. It is clear that if you assume that a man strolling through a meadow on a lovely springtime morning is not communicating, then what you are actually doing is identifying the category of communication with the subcategories of verbal, or intentional, or conscious communication. But as soon as you realize that our springtime morning stroller, whether intentionally or not, is in fact communicating to the onlooker a remarkable amount of information about himself and his social group by the way he walks and is dressed and groomed, and by the very fact that he IS strolling, then the identification of communication with either verbal or intentional or conscious communication collapses; what remains is the fact that the ONLY possible identification is that of behavior with communication without any further restriction. From this it follows that neither communication nor behavior can be dealt with independently of the other. You cannot really examine behavior unless you are also examining communication, and you cannot examine communication unless you are also examining behavior.

That ALL behavior IS communication, is a major breakthrough of twentieth-century semiotics. This advance has come about by joining, not disjoining, categories, and by taking the overlapping of categories as seriously as possible. It has enriched both the category of behavior and that of communication.

Language and Thought

Quite different is the case of language versus thought. While you cannot act without communicating, you can certainly think without speaking, and in some sense you can also speak without thinking. The attempt has been made by Lenneberg (1967) and others to prove that the acquisition of language is independent of intelligence; this seems to reduce the importance of thought for language. The fact is that the two categories, speaking and thinking, overlap in very special ways of their own. If, as Marx says, "*language* is the immediate actuality [*unmittelbare Wirklichkeit*] of thought" (Marx and Engels 1968 [1845–1846]: 503), it would seem to follow that thought is the mediated actuality of language. This means that one cannot assume thought by itself as something not mediated, as something independent from language. To say this, however, is not to say that no thinking can go on or manifest itself without resorting to language or in the absence of language. Intelligent behavior shows the presence of thinking even when it shows no presence of language. And still, it is principally in the use of language that many of the most important aspects of thought exist; we do much of our thinking through the use of language. It is impossible to imagine that thought developed in mankind as it did without linguistic communication. The two grew together, and together with them grew all the other main factors of social life.

As Wittgenstein (1953 [1945]) and Ryle (1949) — who may or may not have been aware of the fact that they were expanding some principles put forward by Marx and Engels in *The German ideology* (Rossi-Landi 1966; 1968:77–126) — showed in great detail, the main mistake here lies in believing that first THERE IS thought which then MANIFESTS ITSELF linguistically.

The categories of language and thought, of speaking and thinking, and all similar categories, overlap to a great extent, and neither term of any such pair can be properly understood without resorting to the other. Distinguishing various aspects of language from various aspects of thought is an intricate business which itself requires continuous references to both.

Thought and Social Institutions

Social institutions certainly cannot be reduced to verbal activity. Intelligent nonverbal behavior contributed to bringing them into existence.

The same can be said of "material" culture in its entirety: it is the product of human thought, and when we examine any one of its instances we are certainly not content with weighing or measuring it; we try instead to reconstruct the thinking that went into it, its use, its purpose, and the position it held within that culture.

Thus it could be said that while on the one hand thought overlaps to a remarkable extent with language, on the other it also overlaps with social institutions and material culture. It would be impossible to fully assess the thought of any community or culture or society unless we took into account not only its language and literary production, but all the rest of it as well, everything that is NOT language in the proper sense.

This does not mean in the least that thought occupies a central position as traditional philosophers so often used to maintain. On the contrary, the overlapping of language with thought and of thought with social institutions and material culture is there to show that thought, as such, has no central position at all. Thought cannot be understood by itself. To understand it, we have to examine all the various fields in which man has exercised his productive powers.

Social institutions and material culture are nonverbal sign systems, forms of communication. This feature of theirs points to additional dimensions of the general overlapping of categories in the social sciences.

A HINT AT THE DIALECTIC OF ESSENCE AND PHENOMENA

Categories interconnect and overlap to such an extent that the study of any one of them in isolation is impossible and continuous references to many of them are often necessary. Within the limits of a few pairs of categories, we have seen how production and consumption further each other; how being private is but a case of being public; how behavior and communication overlap almost entirely; how language stretches, so to say, to cover a great deal of thought, and vice versa; how thought, however, also covers social institutions and material culture which are nonverbal sign systems, i.e. forms of communication. It is as if there were one common core which expressed itself by means of different phenomena in several fields.

This brings us to a dialectic which has been labelled within a certain tradition as the dialectic of essence and phenomenon; in its turn, it overlaps to a great extent with the dialectic of reality and appearance. The dialectic between mere description and scientific explanation proper may be considered a special case, or a limited application, of the dialectic between essence and phenomenon. Things vary enormously as far as phenomena are concerned, of course; and it is certainly one of the tasks of scientific research to describe all the phenomena of the various fields in the most complete and accurate manner. Underlying the various groups of phenomena, however, there is a unity which alone can account for the overlapping of categories and for the fact that it is impossible to go beyond the level of description to achieve scientific explanation as long as one remains within the limits of any isolated category. We said that semiotics made a breakthrough when it came to "identify" behavior and communication. It was, of course, a dialectical, not a one-to-one static identity; it was an "identity" of essence, not of phenomena, and it was reached by viewing both categories as parts of a wider totality. I believe that this example can be followed in other fields as well, and have myself made an attempt to this effect to give to the usually severed fields of language and material production a unitary treatment (Rossi-Landi 1968; 1975). After all, it is with the essence of things, not their phenomena, that we as social scientists are most intensely concerned.

REFERENCES

HEGEL, GEORG W. F.
1964   [1807] *The phenomenology of mind.* Translated by J. B. Baillie. London: Allen and Unwin. (Originally published 1807 as *Phänomenologie des Geistes.*)
LENNEBERG, ERIC
1967   *Biological foundations of language.* New York: John Wiley.
MARX, KARL
1953   [1857–1858] "Einleitung von 1857," in *Grundrisse der Kritik der politischen Ökonomie.* Berlin: Dietz.
MARX, KARL, FRIEDRICH ENGELS
1968   [1845–1846] *The German ideology.* Moscow: Progress Publishing. (Originally published 1845–1846 as *Die deutsche Ideologie.*)
MC LELLAN, DAVID
1971   *Marx's Grundrisse* [introduction and anthology]. London: Macmillan.
NICOLAUS, MARTIN
1968   The unknown Marx. *New Left Review* 48:41–61.
ROSSI-LANDI, FERRUCCIO
1966   Per un uso marxiano di Wittgenstein. *Nuovi Argomenti* 1:187–230.
1967   "Giovanni Vailati," in *Encyclopedia of philosophy*, volume eight. Edited by Paul Edwards, 224–226. New York: Macmillan.
1968   *Il linguaggio come lavoro e come mercato.* Milan: Bompiani. (Spanish translation 1972; German translation 1974; English, French, and Portuguese translations forthcoming.)

1975 *Linguistics and economics.* Janua Linguarum, series maior 81. The Hague: Mouton.

RYLE, GILBERT
1949 *The concept of mind.* London: Hutchinson's.
1971 [1938] "Categories," in *Collected papers*, volume two, 170–184. London: Barnes and Noble.

VAILATI, GIOVANNI
1966 [1908] The grammar of algebra. *Nuova Corrente* 38:131–157.

WITTGENSTEIN, LUDWIG
1953 [1945] *Philosophical investigations.* Translated by G. E. M. Anscombe. Oxford: Blackwell.

Functions, Structures, and Values

The Semiotic Character of the Aesthetic Function as Defined by the Prague Linguistic Circle

IRENE PORTIS WINNER

This paper will examine some aspects of the concept of the aesthetic function advanced by certain members of the Prague Linguistic Circle and their modern followers, as well as some implications, influences, and applications of the views discussed. The thesis that the aesthetic function is potentially a part of all human cultural behavior, its presence extending far beyond the areas generally defined as the arts or as closely allied to the arts, rests on certain underlying assumptions regarding the nature of cultural behavior, including its dynamic quality, its polyfunctionality, its structuration, and its semiotic character.

I shall not be directly concerned here with the role of the aesthetic function where it is either clearly dominant and specific, or competing with other functions for dominance, that is, in the area of the well-defined arts or in such allied areas as folklore and mythology. The primary focus will be on the less tangible question of the presence of the aesthetic function in domains where it is generally not dominant; but since the aesthetic function is a dynamic aspect of human behavior, it cannot be asserted that a secondary role for this function is in any way a permanent condition of a specific pattern of behavior. I ask: What is the aesthetic function, and what are its underlying assumptions? What is its relation to reality? In what sense is it a part of the areas of cultural behavior traditionally characterized as extra-aesthetic? Are there invariants which define the essence of this function and what are the dimensions of variation which the aesthetic function encompasses?

To set the framework, I discuss briefly the origins of semiotics and the Saussurian view of structure and change. Then, I consider some concepts advanced by the Prague Linguistic Circle relating to structure, change, the polyfunctionality of human behavior, and semiotic approaches to aesthetic function. On the basis of these concepts, I then consider some specific typologies of functions and signs. Finally, I note some influences, parallelisms, and applications of the concept of aesthetic function and its allied theories to cultural behavior.

ORIGINS OF SEMIOTICS AND THE SAUSSURIAN CONCEPT OF STRUCTURE AND CHANGE

Saussure specifically called for a science of signs which had been foreseen earlier. As has been pointed out by Jakobson (1965: 21–23), the ancient Stoic doctrine considered the sign as an entity constituted by the relation of the signifier and signified, defined as the "perceptible" and the "intelligible" (or, in terms of modern linguistics, "translatable"). These concepts were further developed by St. Augustine and, in the nineteenth century, by Charles Sanders Peirce (1839–1914), who attempted to classify signs and called for a study of "semiotics." Peirce's writings, however, remained unpublished until the late 1930's (see Peirce 1938–1958).

At the end of the last century, Saussure advocated a discipline called "semiology." This is stated in the *Course in general linguistics*, based on his teachings from 1906–1911:

Language is a system of signs that express ideas and is therefore comparable to a system of writing, the alphabet of deaf-mutes, symbolic rites, polite formulas, military signals, etc. But it is the most important of all these systems.
A science that studies the life of signs within society is conceivable. ... I shall call it semiology (Śaussure 1966:16).

Furthermore, Saussure concluded:

By studying rites, customs, etc., as signs, I believe that we shall throw new light on the facts and point up the need for including them in a science of semiology and explaining them by its laws (1966:17).

Two important theoretical positions apparently limited Saussure's vision of semiotics, namely, the arbitrary nature of the sign and the sharp dichotomy between synchrony and diachrony. Saussure held that "the linguistic sign unites not a thing and a name, but a concept [the signified] and a sound image [the signifier]" (1966: 66), and that "the choice of a given slice of sound to name a given idea is completely arbitrary" (1966: 113).

Saussure also held that while it is speaking (*parole*) that causes linguistic evolution and while *langue* and *parole* are interdependent, the former being both the instrument and the product of the latter, "their interdependence does not prevent their being two absolutely different things" (1966: 19). "The opposition," Saussure stated, "between the two viewpoints, the synchronic and the diachronic, is absolute, and allows no compromise" (1966: 83). Therefore Saussure held that although a single new element within a system may throw the system out of equilibrium, bring about compensatory changes, and thus give rise to a new system, the intervening changes between different states of a system or diachronic events are accidental and unintentional and have no place in either state (1966: 85, 89). In contrast are the systematic, interrelated, general, and regular synchronic facts. Although they are imposed upon the individual by the weight of collective usage, they are not imperative in the sense of laws, for no force guarantees the maintenance of a regularity once established (1966: 92).

In the later development of structural, functional, and semiotic theories of the Prague Linguistic Circle — which were in large part influenced by Saussurian doctrine, the theories of Karl Bühler, and the approach of Husserlian phenomenology — the Saussurian dichotomies, synchrony-diachrony, *langue-parole*, signifier-signified, were questioned or revised, thus laying the basis for the inclusive view of the aesthetic function which we subsequently examine.

SOME STRUCTURAL THEORIES OF THE PRAGUE LINGUISTIC CIRCLE

Structure and Change

In 1928, in their brief but seminal paper, Jakobson and Tynjanov departed sharply from Saussurian doctrine, insisting upon resolving the dichotomy between synchrony and diachrony, affirming the importance of individual variations in structural studies, and pointing to the dynamic relation between structures. Thus they stated the following:

The history of literature (or art) is closely related to the other historical series. As each of the other series, it is characterized by an intricate complex of specific structural laws. ...

Just as the idea of a mechanical agglomeration of phenomena was replaced by the idea of system or structure in the sphere of synchronic science, it was similarly replaced in the sphere of diachronic science. The history of a system is in turn also a system. Pure synchrony is now turning out to be an illusion. Each synchronic system contains its past and its future as inseparable structural elements of the system. ...

The opposition between synchrony and diachrony was an opposition between the notion of system and the notion of evolution. It loses its principal importance insofar as we recognize that each system is necessarily given as an evolution and, ... on the other hand, evolution inevitably has a systematic character.

Furthermore, in speaking of change, they stated that "the individual expression cannot be considered apart from the existing complex of norms," and "uncovering of the immanent laws of history of literature (or language) enables us to characterize each change of literary (or linguistic) systems." However, the particular tempo or direction of evolution is not necessarily explained, since

... the immanent laws of literary (or linguistic) evolution give us only an indeterminate equation, which admits of the possibility of several — although a limited number — solutions, and not necessarily of only one. The question about the choice of a specific path, or at least of a dominant one, can be answered only by means of an analysis of the correlation of the literary series with the other historical series. This correlation (the system of systems) has its own structural laws which must be studied (Jakobson and Tynjanov 1972: 81–83).

Thus change both within and between systems was held to be a part of both synchrony and diachrony, the conflict between static and dynamic being seen as false. As Jakobson wrote later in relation to poetics and linguistics:

Synchronic poetics, like synchronic linguistics, is not to be confused with statics; any stage discriminates between more conservative and more innovatory forms. Any contemporary stage is experienced in its temporal dynamics, and, on the other hand, the historical approach both in poetics and in linguistics is concerned not only with changes but also with continuous, enduring static factors. A thoroughly comprehensive historical poetics or history of language is a superstructure to be built on a series of successive synchronic descriptions (1960:352).

The foremost aesthetician in the Prague group, Jan Mukařovský (1897–1974), considered not only aesthetic structure but also, by implication — and often by clear statement — all structures pertaining to cultural behavior; his approach, following the Jakobson-Tynjanov theses, ruled out all isolationist or reductionist tendencies. In 1934, speaking of literature but implying other phenomena, he held that structuralism synthesizes two antithetical views, the intrinsic and the extrinsic, because it can support the postulate of autonomous evolution but still not deprive literature of its relations to external phenomena. He stated that:

The area of social phenomena ... is composed of a multitude of sets (structures) each of which has its autonomous evolution; these are for instance, science, politics, economics, social stratification, language, morality, religion, and so on. Over and above their autonomy, however, the individual sets mutually affect each other (1934a:349).[1]

[1]   Throughout this article, Mukařovský's works are cited by the date when they were written. Most of his writings referred to here can be found in two collections, pub-

And in the same year, he also wrote:

We must not forget that the evolving series which are given by the dynamics of the individual structures which evolve in time ... do not run side by side unrelatedly, but form a structure of a higher order, in which they form the components, and that that structure of structures has its own hierarchy and its own dominanta [a dominant series]. Since, of course, this is a live structure and not an immobile system, also this overstructure [highest structure /*vrcholná výstavba*/] is replete with internal antinomies, and is in constant motion and regrouping, the individual components taking turns in the position of the dominantas, and none of them being always in the foreground. ... (1934b:166).

Summing up his views in a lecture delivered during the war, Mukařovský (1943–1945: 229) elaborated on the two antithetical tendencies he discerned in evolution: that of continuity, regularity, and consequent retention of identity of the evolving sequence, on the one hand, and that of the constant disturbance of the identity of the evolving series, which maintains and makes possible the evolutionary movement, on the other hand. The source of the identity of the structure lies in the regulatory power of internal norms, whereas the stimulus for the destruction of the identity enters from without. From the point of view of the regularity of the evolutionary movement, these interventions are accidental; but from the perspective of the external structure from which the intervention emanates, these interventions are lawful results of immanent evolution. Even from the point of view of the series into which these stimuli enter apparently accidentally, the interventions are limited by the demands and intrinsic laws of the evolving structure. The individual as a class is responsible for these interventions which result in innovations.

Mukařovský's several definitions of structure emphasize their dialectical nature. Thus a structure is

... a complex of elements, the internal equilibrium of which is constantly disturbed and is again restored. ... That which endures is only the identity of a structure in the course of time, whereas its internal composition, the correlation of its components, changes continuously. In their mutual interrelations, individual components constantly strive to dominate one another. ... The hierarchy of mutual subordination and superordination of components ... is in a constant state of regrouping (1946:109).

Stressing the structural role of conflicts, he also stated that:

The concept of structure ... is based on an inner unification of the whole by the mutual relations of its parts: and that not only by positive relations — agreements and harmonies — but also by negative relations — conflicts and contradictions (1947:29).

---

lished in 1948 and 1966; one book, written in 1936, appeared in 1970 in an English translation.

Polyfunctionality of Human Behavior

Underlying the Prague Circle's view of dynamic structuralism, and fundamental to the development of the concept of the aesthetic function as a part of ALL cultural behavior, is the assumption of the polyfunctionality of human behavior. The 1929 "Theses" of the Prague Linguistic Circle postulated that in relation to language there are diverse functions in hierarchical relations, one function of which is dominant. Of particular interest was the opposition between the poetic (or aesthetic) function, dominant in poetic structures, oriented on the expression itself, and the communicative function, dominant in a large number of linguistic structures, directed at the object of expression. Consequently, linguistic elements, which are only ancillary and automatic in language in which the communicative function is dominant, obtain partially independent values in poetic language, where these elements and their interrelations become actualized (Prague Linguistic Circle 1929: 43, 47).

The hierarchical relations of language functions posited in the 1929 "Theses" and their nature were later explained and generalized by Mukařovský. Each structure, he held, is defined by a specific (or dominant) function, oriented toward the autonomy of the total structure rather than toward its effect on other structures. The specific function cannot be completely suppressed without causing the structure to cease being itself. In addition, each structure is characterized by various other functions, given by their effect on other structures which, because of constant evolutionary change, are arranged in ever-changing hierarchical patterns, none of which is given *a priori* (1934a: 349–350).

Mukařovský stated that a function is not a characteristic, but rather a means by which the subject exploits characteristics of a given phenomenon (1940a: 114). Furthermore, since the subject is always the live source of the various functions, no region of human activity is limited to a single function. The changing interrelations of types of functions are seen from the point of view of the subject. Only if function is seen as a means of self-assertion of the subject *vis-à-vis* the external world, can we understand polyfunctionality (1942a: 67–69).

Thus Mukařovský disputed such early unifunctionalists as Corbusier, who projected onto the object only its specific function and overlooked the role of the subject (1942a: 67–69). His position would also question such global approaches as that of Radcliffe-Brown, who considered only one universal, general function, the maintenance of the harmonious working and structural continuity of society (Radcliffe-Brown 1952: 180). In Radcliffe-Brown's system, it follows that an activity may have no function or may be dysfunctional as measured against the general criterion of "the contribution which a partial activity makes to the total activity of which it is a part" (1952: 181), whereas in Mukařovský's approach all activities are seen in relation to functions. Nor would Malinowski's functionalism meet Mukařovský's criteria insofar as Malinowski's functions of cultural behavior are reduced to the satisfaction of basic biophysical needs, as well as to secondary, but derived, needs relating to man as a social animal, and insofar as the dynamic, structural organization of these needs was neglected (Parsons 1957: 53–70).

Since functions are dynamic aspects of structures, it follows that a structure itself is meaningful and can be viewed semiotically. From 1934 onward, Mukařovský pointed to the sign character of the works of art and, by implication as well as directly, to the sign character of other structures (Mukařovský 1934, 1936, 1948b). In this view, a structure is a dynamic and energetic unit of meaning, whose energy derives from the fact that every element fulfills a function in it, and whose dynamism derives from the fact that these functions are constantly changing, as are their mutual relations (1948b: 15).

Recently, Jakobson has specifically applied the terms purposiveness and goal-directedness to human functional, structural behavior:

The discussion of goal-directedness in today's biology is of vital interest for all branches of knowledge relating to organismic activities, and the judgements advanced may serve to corroborate a consistent application of a means-end model to the language design, to its self-regulating maintenance of integrity and dynamic equilibrium (homeostasis), as well as to its mutations. ... This purposiveness strikes us as a manifest, perhaps even decisive, difference of living systems from any objects of inorganic nature (1970a: 442).

The implications of these theories, pointing to the functional, dynamic, and goal-directed activity of the subject, suggest Piaget's constructivist hypothesis. Piaget states that:

Structures are inseparable from performance, from functions. ... To be real, a structure must, in the literal sense, be governed from within. ... So we come back to the necessity of some sort of functional activity; and, if the facts oblige us to attribute some sort of functional activity to a subject, it is for our purposes sufficient to define this subject as the center of functional activity (1970: 71).

Piaget concludes that:

The ideal of a structure of all structures is unrealizable. The *subject* cannot, therefore, be the *a priori* underpinning of a finished posterior structure; rather it is a center of activity. And whether we substitute "society" or "mankind" or "life" or even "cosmos" for "subject" the argument remains the same (1970: 142).

In considering the universal motivation for the continual human activity of constructing structures, Piaget (1970: 139–140) states that on the plane of knowledge, and perhaps on that of moral and aesthetic values, "the subject's activity calls for continual 'de-centering' without which he cannot become free from his spontaneous intellectual egocentricity." This "de-centering" leads to the "uninterrupted process of coordinating and setting in reciprocal relations" which is the "true 'generator' of structures as constantly under construction and reconstruction."

Having asserted the polyfunctionality, meaningfulness, and structuration of human behavior, which as we have noted bears a relation to Piaget's approach, the Prague school increasingly paid attention to semiotic problems which they had already suggested in the thirties, namely, the determination of structural principles which facilitate the processes of encoding and decoding of messages communicated, directly or by implication, consciously or unconsciously, by patterned behavior. We turn now to a discussion of some of these concepts and specifically to their relation to the view of the aesthetic function in human behavior.

Semiotics and the Aesthetic Function

In his seminal paper, "L'art comme fait sémiologique," Mukařovský (1934c) called for the application of semiotics to fields beyond linguistics:

All psychic content exceeding the limits of individual consciousness acquires the character of a sign by the very fact of its communicability. The science of the sign ... must be elaborated in its entire scope; just as contemporary linguistics enlarges the field of semantics in treating from this point of view all the elements of the linguistic system, indeed even sounds, the results of linguistic semantics should be applied to all other series of signs and should be differentiated according to their special characteristics (1934c: 85).

In this paper Mukařovský defined a sign as "a sensory reality relating to another reality that it is designed to evoke" (1934c: 86). Since art as a sign is primarily autonomous, the reality evoked is indistinct, encompassing, generally through indirect, metaphoric, or otherwise oblique means, "the total context of social phenomena." All arts, and even provisionally music, are viewed not only as autonomous but also as communicative signs, marked by a dialectical antinomy between these two functions, for "each of the components of works of art, even the most 'formal' possesses its own communicative value independent of the 'subject'" (or thematic content). Thus the entire structure of a work of art functions as the meaning both in the autonomous and in the communicative sense (1934c: 87).

In his 1936 essay, *Aesthetic function, norm and value as social facts*, Mukařovský discusses the role of the aesthetic function not only as a specific function of art but also as a secondary function in extra-aesthetic areas of cultural behavior. The sign is now defined both more specifically and more broadly as "something which stands in place of something else and points to that other thing" (1936: 71). While it is always communicative, it also has other functions. For example, Mukařovský pointed out — as Saussure had noted earlier (Saussure 1966:79) and as Lévi-Strauss suggested later (Lévi-Strauss 1963: 296) — that money is a sign replacing another reality in relation to the function of economic values. Its primary goal is not, however, communication, but facilitation of the flow of goods. Mukařovský concluded that the realm of communicative signs was immeasurably broad and that any sort of fact could become a communicative sign (1936: 71). The aesthetic function itself embraces a much wider area of activity than does art, where it is dominant, because there is no object or activity, whether natural or human, which by its nature is necessarily immune to the aesthetic function. In fact, there is no definite border line between the aesthetic and the extra-aesthetic, their relation being not mutually exclusive but rather one of dialectical antinomy in which the two spheres are in constant contact (1936: 1–5).

In 1937 Mukařovský stated this position more emphatically, holding that the sphere of the aesthetic function outside the boundaries of art is enormous:

This sphere is related to the sum of human activity, as well as to the whole world of things; every activity and everything can become — due to social convention or individual will — vehicles, permanent or transitory, of the aesthetic function, which in relation to the prevailing practical functions is secondary but, nevertheless, effective (1937a: 76–77).

Particularly original was Mukařovský's explication of the social and cultural power of the aesthetic function, which follows from its various characteristics. Thus it may isolate an object or activity by focusing attention on it, for example, in ceremonies and rites. In relation to individuals or groups, its isolating ability may act as a socially differentiating factor emphasizing power and prestige. Moreover, since the aesthetic function evokes pleasure, it may facilitate activities in which its role is secondary. Furthermore, since the aesthetic function attaches to the form of an object or act, it has the ability to supplant some other function which the object or act may have lost in the course of development. In such cases, the aesthetic function may act as a force for cultural conservatism, "in the sense that it preserves for a future period human products and institutions which have lost their original, practical function, so that they can again be used, this time in a different practical function" (1936: 22). Thus Mukařovský concludes that the aesthetic function "significantly affects the lives of individuals and society, shares in the organization of contacts — active as well as passive — of individuals with that reality in which they find themselves" (1936: 23).

Although the aesthetic function can act as a conservative force, it is essentially dynamic, a quality which is understood in relation to Mukařovský's view of the aesthetic norm. In contrast to the dynamism of the aesthetic function, which is frequently responsible for violation of norms, the aesthetic norm strives for unchanging validity which, however, it can never achieve. Its rule may even be challenged by other aesthetic norms applying to the same concrete instance (Mukařovský 1936: 26). Aesthetic norms, like other norms, are frequently formulated as prohibitions, so that the incompatibility between two related norms is frequently accentuated (p. 52). In Mukařovský's terms, the aesthetic norm is "based on a fundamental dialectical antinomy between universal validity and mere regulative or orientational power which implies the conceivability of its violation" (p. 26).

In searching for an empirical basis for the aesthetic norm, Mukařovský points to constitutive principles inherent in the human organism, including rhythm (based on biological processes), symmetry (derived from the construction of the human body), color relations, and — in relation to sculptural forms — stability of the center of gravity, as incomplete examples. Such principles are not in themselves norms because "exact structural rhythm, symmetry of geometric figures, etc., are aesthetically indifferent" (p. 30). They are, however, "a solid basis with respect to which change can only be felt as a violation of order" (p. 31). They constitute motivation for concrete aesthetic norms which are constantly changing as a result of the "interplay of normative principles derived from, but not identical with, constitutive factors and the continuing and changing, individual applications of the aesthetic norm" (Mukařovský 1937a: 77). These changes result not only from necessary adaptations to altering external circumstances, but also from frequent and deliberate violations of the norm. Such violations, which are one of the primary means for achieving aesthetic effect, stimulate aesthetic pleasure which then requires displeasure as a counterbalance. Consequently, within the total work, displeasurable arrangements become positive elements (1936: 32–33, 35). Mukařovský concludes that the aesthetic norm is both regular and changeable, not a law but living energy, based on certain constitutive principles which organize the area of aesthetic phenomena and provide direction for its development (1936: 58–60).

Aesthetic norms have complex relations to nonaesthetic norms which are criteria for other kinds of values in a society. According to Mukařovský, "There is no impenetrable wall between aesthetic norms and other norms, [for] it is characteristic of their mutual proximity ... that the aesthetic norm can turn into some other norm and vice versa" (1936: 52). Yet the aesthetic norm is also seen as being in opposition to other norms which tend toward practical ends, while the aesthetic norm focuses on the object, activity or sign, itself (1936: 3). Furthermore, the aesthetic norm differs from other norms by its less obligatory character. In aesthetic structures, the norm may be conceived of as a point of orientation, serving to make felt the degree of deformation of the artistic tradition by new tendencies (1936: 6). While nonaesthetic norms are also violated, their violation is marked, whereas norm violation is the normal state of affairs in the case of the aesthetic norm (1937a: 75).

It seems that in extra-aesthetic structures where the aesthetic function is not dominant the aesthetic norm behaves more like other norms, that is, its stabilizing qualities are increased at the expense of its dynamic traits. For example, according to Mukařovský (1937a: 76–77), the canons of good taste are characterized by a dominant practical function and a concomitant, but secondary, aesthetic function. Here the aesthetic function approaches the action of a law. More importantly, there is the broad area of folk culture, which he distinguishes from that of urbanized, industrialized societies where innovative changes in aesthetic norms are more frequent. In folk culture, the aesthetic function and norms are usually subordinated to other functions and norms, even in objects which may be designated as art (1936: 58). Thus in the area of folk art, in which "for lack of a distinct delimitation of functions, the predomination of the aesthetic function over others is not completely unequivocal, the aesthetic norm has also a stronger regulative function" (1937a: 77). In folk culture generally, states Mukařovský, all norms are more tightly bound and are so closely interrelated that each prevents the others from changing; consequently, the aesthetic norm fluctuates less and often endures for centuries with no appreciable alteration. However, Mukařovský points out, aesthetic creativity is not absent in folk societies. For the aesthetic norm, which is seen as derived from the dominant class of the larger society, is not automatically interpreted, but exists in many variants. Yet such variants are distinguished from evolutionary violation of norms (1936: 54, 55). We may question whether Mukařovský's opposition of folk to urban culture is not too mechanical an application of the Durkheimian dichotomy. His distinction between variants from the norm in folk societies, as opposed to the more frequent violations of the norm in modern cultures, also seems to imply too sharp a bifurcation. Whether he meant to include primitive cultures under the rubric "folk" is not clear. It should be noted, however, that studies of primitive societies, while taking into account the quite different contexts of the problems examined, have nevertheless established the existence of a degree of independence of aesthetic values, as well as the existence of not inconsiderable aesthetic creativity and freedom of stylistic variation and change (see Crowley 1966: 519–524; Bohannan 1961: 85–94).

Peasant societies, which undoubtedly show great variations in their degree of dependence on the aesthetic traditions of the larger society of which they are a part, could nevertheless hardly be excluded from this general human activity. For example, in their unpublished study of Hungarian folk art, which had its period of florescence during the nineteenth century, Fél and Hofer state that Hungarian peasants "created shapes and forms, color schemes and designs and modes of expression that nobody ever had created before, bearing witness to a particular pattern of human existence" (p. 3). The authors offer considerable evidence of the differing personalities, abilities, and degrees of originality of peasant creators. Pride of authorship is demonstrated by inscriptions marking name and date on numerous articles (p. 55). Various institutions are pointed to which channeled continuous innovation. The dowry, for example, required renewal of a world of objects for each generation. Thus it assured the continuous replacement of old objects by new, allowing for changing tastes (p. 68). The large markets at the end of the eighteenth and throughout the nineteenth century, meeting four times a year and drawing participants from all over east-central Europe, provided another mechanism for change, stimulating creativity and innovation (p. 76).

Various specific examples of peasant originality are fully described. Thus the wearing of the *szur* (decorated frieze coat first worn by peasants in western Hungary) spread widely in the nineteenth century. It evolved from the plain garment to a highly decorated coat with appliqué work and embroidery, expressing original and definitive peasant styles, all of which differed radically from the fashions of the period among noblemen (p. 98). A musical revolution similarly demonstrated originality on the part of the peasants (p. 21).

An underlying theme of Fél and Hofer's study is the two-way influence of urban art upon folk art and of folk art upon urban art. The authors point out that, while the florescence of Hungarian folk art began in the feudal period of the nineteenth century when the influence of the nobility was strong, by 1860 to 1870 peasant tastes began to diverge strongly from urban ones, and peasant art demonstrated its own regional florescence. Stronger colors, more robust design, and finally even simplification, particularly in the style of the *szur*, were characteristic trends. Thus the bourgeois tastes of the later nineteenth century were creatively reinterpreted and original peasant contributions were made.

The dynamic character of the aesthetic function in folk art is implied by the authors in their statement that in the late nineteenth century, when peasant life was being affected by technological modernization, new symbolic expressions in clothes, house arrangements, ceremonies, and festivals all infused energy into peasant forms. Thus the authors believe that the readiness for novelty, particularly in the latter half of the nineteenth century, "is in marked contradiction to the descriptions of peasant character which stress ... aversion to innovation and adherence to strict traditionalism" (p. 155).

The question of the general characteristics which unify all cultural norms, aesthetic and nonaesthetic, as well as the differences between norms, was also considered by Mukařovský. The concept of norm is, first of all, inseparable from that of function, which presupposes an activity tending toward a specific end, whose realization a norm both limits and implements. Secondly, similar to Lévi-Strauss's later differentiation of underlying and frequently nonverbalized structural principles or models from conscious or homemade verbalized models which may disguise the true structure of behavior (1963: 281–282), Mukařovský distinguished norms (Lévi-Strauss's underlying models) from rules or codification (Lévi-Strauss's conscious models). Not only do some norms resist codification or verbalization, but codification may be false, may be in disagreement with a living norm. A norm, in Mukařovský's canon, is a regulative, energetic principle rather than a rule — whether it is applied consciously or unconsciously — which the acting individual feels as a limitation of his freedom of action. The assertion that the aesthetic norm is dynamic, every concrete application being at the same time a change of a norm, is extended to all norms; even the legal norm, the most stable of all, is not excepted, since it is in use and thus subject to change (1937a: 74).

The concepts of aesthetic function and norm are related to a third closely related concept, that of aesthetic value. "Value" is seen as "the ability of something to assist in the attainment of some goal." Such a goal, if it is culturally shared, is governed and stabilized by norms. While the individual may disagree with the norm or try to change it, he must account for it while performing a value judgment (Mukařovský 1936: 26). Aesthetic valuation is a complex process, encompassing at least two fundamental focuses: the ability of the aesthetic function both to fulfill and to violate the norm, and the totality of a phenomenon, for "all extra-aesthetic functions and values are important as components of aesthetic value" (p. 60). Considering the latter viewpoint first, it is notable that Mukařovský held that all the elements of an aesthetic work indicate a certain attitude toward reality (pp. 64, 82). This is true not only of verbal art but also of music, architecture, and the visual arts. For example, although music lacks a specific communicative function, tonal level and melodic and rhythmic structure are, in the total context, carriers of meaning. Music can "very intensively involve the complex material tie to diverse regions of the life experience of the perceiver." Architecture is another example because it contains communication related to a social reality which is closely connected, but not identical, with its practical function. "A building 'means' its purpose, i.e. the acts and processes which are to be carried out within its confines" (1936: 76–78).

The essence of aesthetic value rests, however, not only on a necessary if ambiguous relation to reality, but also on a specific tension engendered by the relation between deviation from, and violation of, the aesthetic norm, on the one hand, and the fulfillment of the norm's strictures, on the other hand. When an object is regarded purely aesthetically, it is viewed as unique and the ACT of evaluation, the perception, rises to the foreground. Yet the aesthetic attitude is contained by the regulatory force of the aesthetic norm. Aesthetic value is thus seen as a dialectical synthesis of normative (stable, regular) and nonnormative (unique, individual, changeable) aesthetics. This struggle, however feeble, between uniqueness and universality, between accident and law, between actualization and automatization, is the psychological equivalent to aesthetic value (1940b: 2). It is important to note that the antinomy, fundamental to aesthetic value, between the unbound quality of the aesthetic function and the regulatory force of the aesthetic norm is held to be potentially universal, although it is brought to its highest intensity in art (1940b: 25).

Here it should be noted that Mukařovský did not limit the source of the regularity of aesthetic norms to psychological and biological universals. Also stressed was the force of "collective consciousness" which opposes "subjective elements" and compels normative regularities in socialized behavior (1934c: 85). As Jakobson noted in relation to language, regulative factors include not only "general laws of thinking" and "the internal logic" of structures, but also the force of social custom. Thus Jakobson states that, "To a considerable degree, the rigor of general laws is due to the circumstance that both language and folklore demand a collective consensus and obey a subliminal censorship." This is illustrated by the fact that the "'alleged strict limits for variations' lose their compulsion in secret jargons and in verbal plays — private or semi-private — as well as in personal poetic experiments or invented languages" (Jakobson 1970a: 436).

TYPOLOGIES AND HIERARCHIES OF FUNCTIONS

The aesthetic function, which we have placed in the framework of Mukařovský's concepts of aesthetic norm and value, and which we have contrasted in general terms to other functions, needed to be set more specifically within the context of other functions characteristic of cultural behavior. In this endeavor, Mukařovský made several attempts to classify functions. In 1938, he put forward the aesthetic function as a fourth to be added to Bühler's three functions of the linguistic sign (Bühler 1933). Besides the representative function (related to reality), the expressive function (related to the sender), and the conative function (focused on the receiver), there is also the aesthetic function, posited as the antithesis of the other three, which are all oriented toward extra-linguistic phenomena, whereas the aesthetic function is directed toward the linguistic sign itself, thereby weakening the relation of the sign to reality (Mukařovský 1938:160).

Later, in suggesting a typology of functions encompassing all cultural behavior, Mukařovský discussed three basic functions, oriented to three differing ways in which the object as "sign" is exploited by the individual. The practical function, which is the most widespread, lays stress on the relation between the acting individual and the object. Here the will of the individual is projected onto the world of objects as a goal of action. Only those characteristics of objects are emphasized that are useful in the attempt to reach the goal of the action; thus the sign is employed as a tool. The second function, the theoretical function, is implemented when the individual's aim is simply the understanding of the mutual relations of phenomena and the establishment of laws for these relationships; thus the sign is a concept. Finally, there is the aesthetic function, which examines the object itself for its own sake, as a unique entity, and as an inexhaustible complex of qualities; thus the sign is self-oriented. Mukařovský continued to emphasize, however, that the aesthetic attitude, and hence the aesthetic function, is present in all human activity, no matter how disguised (Mukařovský ca. 1940: 63). A fourth function, the religious one, posited later, utilizes the sign as a surrogate reality, which acts like the reality it replaces, examples being symbolic signs such as amulets (1942b: 56).

The following general conclusions regarding the nature of the aesthetic function are related to Mukařovský's various attempts to classify and contrast functions. The ambiguous, but essential, connection to reality which characterizes the aesthetic function is always opposed to the more direct communicative and less ambiguous roles of other functions. For the aesthetic region (*estetično*), which denies the external goal of things, makes everything within its grasp the center of self-aimed attention, while nonaesthetic activities turn man's attention to those characteristics which are applicable to a given purpose (1940b: 25). Philosophically, the task of the aesthetic function is the liberation of human discovering abilities from the schematizing influences of life, thereby reminding man that potential postures *vis-à-vis* reality are infinite (Mukařovský 1943). The penchant of the aesthetic function to exploit structural elements in such a way as to distinguish them from common usage (called "foregrounding" [*aktualizace*] in artistic structures) helps realize this philosophical goal (1940b: 25).

In the late forties, Mukařovský saw the role of the aesthetic function as very broad, because it fundamentally affects man's relation to reality by preventing a single function from asserting a one-sided supremacy over the others: "In contrast to all other functions (e.g. cognitive, political, pedagogic), the poetic function, which does not have a concrete aim and does not tend toward the fulfillment of any practical task ... lacks unequivocal content" (1946: 113). Thus "the aesthetic function becomes 'transparent,' does not act inimically to the other functions, but helps them" (1946: 114). While other "practical" functions strive to dominate each other in a tendency toward monofunctionality, the aesthetic function helps man "to overcome the one-sidedness of specialization which impoverishes his relation to reality" (1946: 114). Its transparency, however, is dialectically conceived since, as Mukařovský frequently reiterated, the aesthetic function — which has no external goal, whereas other functions do — does not turn man away from the object or activity which fulfills the aesthetic function, but focuses his attention on that object or activity (1947: 39).

Jakobson's later classification of linguistic and poetic functions has important implications for cultural behavior in general. Jakobson specifically called attention to the role of the aesthetic function in nonartistic structures, where it is not dominant. He noted (1971b [1952]: 557–558) that although Sapir had regarded the cognitive function as primary in linguistic messages, nevertheless, the present emphasis of the message on factors other than its topic was attracting more attention. Normally, he said, there are a bundle of functions, and it is important to know which of the functions is primary and dominant.

In 1960, Jakobson stated that the differing hierarchical ordering of six factors, each focusing on a different function in language, differentiated verbal messages from each other (1960: 353–356). The six functions include Bühler's three functions relating to the sender, the receiver, and the thing spoken of, namely: (1) the referential or cognitive function, oriented toward the factor of context (earlier called topic); (2) the emotive or expressive function, focused on the sender, which aims at direct expression of the speaker's attitude toward what he is speaking about; and (3) the conative function, the purest form of which is the imperative, focused on the receiver. In addition, the three other functions are: (4) the phatic function (Malinowski's term), focused on the contact, as exemplified in the exchanges of ritualized formulae which serve merely to prolong communicative contact; (5) the metalingual function, or speaking of language itself, focused on the code; and finally, (6) the poetic function, focused on the message for its own sake, which is described as

... not the sole function of verbal art, but only its dominant, determining function, whereas in all other verbal activities, it acts as a subsidiary, accessory constituent. This function, by promoting the palpability of signs, deepens the fundamental dichotomy of signs and objects (Jakobson 1960:356).

In 1964, Jakobson proposed yet another function for language, the magical one. Similar to Mukařovský's religious function (Mukařovský 1942b: 56) where an amulet "acts" like the replaced content, Jakobson's magical function substitutes a magical addressee for the context. For example, rain may be personified and addressed with a prayer as though it were a person (Jakobson 1964: 2). Commenting upon the application of Jakobson's scheme to an "ethnography of speaking," Hymes (1962: 35) would put greater emphasis on the ability of a function to participate in more than one factor. Further, he doubts that all messages are characterized by a hierarchical arrangement of functions where one is clearly dominant, since "the defining characteristic of some speech events may be a balance, harmonious or conflicting, between more than one function." While conflict and harmony of functions are clearly basic to Jakobson's as well as Mukařovský's systems, Hymes's suggestion concerning the lack of the clear dominance of one function seems important, particularly in relation to our understanding of "folk" cultures, where patterns are more closely interrelated, even though they may not be as tightly bound as Mukařovský seemed to suggest.

Jakobson has put forward a specific structural principle underlying the poetic function in verbal behavior which would appear to have implications for nonverbal behavior as well. According to him, the empirical linguistic criterion, or the indispensible feature inherent in the poetic function, is based on a reorganization of the two basic modes of arrangement, namely, selection and combination, used in verbal behavior. Thus in ordinary verbal communication, "selection is produced on the basis of equivalence, similarity and dissimilarity, synonymity and antonymity, while combination, the buildup of the sequence, is based on contiguity." However, wherever the poetic function exists, the process of building a sequence is inverted, since this mode "projects the principle of equivalence from the axis of selection onto the axis of combination." Thus in poetry, "equivalence is promoted to the constitutive device of the sequence" (Jakobson 1960: 358). Here a parallel may be noted between Mukařovský's underlying universal factors such as symmetry, rhythm, and balance which govern the generally unverbalized aesthetic norms, and Jakobson's underlying principles of equivalences which govern his subliminal structural principle. Verse-making, Jakobson states, which like music measures sequences by regular reiteration of equivalent units, far exceeds the limits of formal poetry, where the poetic function is dominant. "Apparently, no human culture ignores verse-making" where the poetic function may have only a subsidiary role (1960: 358–359). Jakobson notes that the principle of equivalence of sound in verse "projected into the sequence as its constitutive principle, inevitably involves semantic equivalence" (1960: 368). Thus there is imparted to poetry its "thoroughgoing symbolic, multiplex, polysemantic essence" where "any metonymy is slightly metaphorical and any metaphor has a metonymic tint" (1960: 370).

We return, but with greater power contributed by Jakobson's structural principle isolating an invariant of the poetic function, to ambiguity as "an intrinsic, inalienable character of any self-focused message" (1960: 370–371). When the poetic function is dominant, it makes ambiguous, but does not obliterate, the relation of the message to the referent. Jakobson's structural principle also buttresses Mukařovský's observations pertaining to the conservational powers of the aesthetic function. Jakobson states that:

The repetitiveness effected by imparting the equivalence principle to the sequence, makes reiterable not only the constituent sequences of the poetic message, but the whole message as well. This capacity for reiteration ... this conversion of a MESSAGE INTO AN ENDURING THING, ... represents an inherent and effective property of poetry [emphasis added] (1960:371).

Here one may point to topics which need investigation. What is the significance to other areas of cultural behavior of the structural principle of building verbal sequences based on equivalences, which is seen to underly the poetic function? And, in general, how can the typologies of linguistic functions advanced be applied to the rest of cultural behavior? As Jakobson concluded, the various functions of language and their different hierarchies in diverse kinds of messages "must lead, *mutatis mutandis*, to an analogous study of the other semiotic systems: with which of these or other functions are they endowed, in what combination and in what hierarchical order?" (Jakobson 1970b: 11).

TYPOLOGIES OF SIGNS

Saussure foresaw that his view of the arbitrary nature of the sign would interfere with the integration of some patterns of behavior into the new science of semiotics for which he called (1966: 131–141). For example, could semiotics include modes of expression based on completely natural signs, such as pantomime? In answer to this question, Saussure looked to the organizing rules of such expressive behavior which he saw as arbitrary, being based on convention and being enforced by the collective, even though the relation between signifier and signified in such structures could not be held to be arbitrary. For example, polite gestures, "though often imbued with a certain natural expressiveness, are nonetheless fixed by rule; it is the rule, not the intrinsic value of the gestures, that obliges the use of them." Nevertheless, Saussure concluded that signs that are wholly arbitrary realize best the process of semiosis (1966: 68).

Saussure also suggested, but did not pursue, the view of the relative arbitrariness of some signs within the context of grammatically organized languages (1966: 131–141). Boas has also pointed out that language classifications are arbitrary solely from the perspective of speakers of another language, but for native speakers, no classification is arbitrary (see Jakobson 1966a: 133). Jakobson (1971c [1959]: 275) maintained that the relation between the signified and the signifier, since it is learned by all members of the community, becomes an obligatory habit and is therefore not completely arbitrary. The same view is enunciated by Lévi-Strauss: "The linguistic sign is arbitrary *a priori*, but ceases to be arbitrary *a posteriori*" (1963: 91).

However, there have been advanced more fundamental revisions of the postulate of the arbitrary nature of the sign. Jakobson has called attention to Peirce's three basic classes of signs, distinguished by the differing relationships of the signifier and signified: (1) ICONS, acting mainly by factual similarity between the signified and the signifier, such as a realistic picture of an object (Jakobson 1965: 27); (2) INDICES, acting mainly by factual existential contiguity, such as smoke being an index of

fire; and (3) SYMBOLS, acting mainly by imputed, learned contiguity between signifier and signified, the connection between these two constit-
uents consisting in its being a rule that does not depend on factual
similarity or factual contiguity (1965: 24). Following Peirce, Jakobson
explains that the division of signs into icons, indices, and symbols is
"merely a difference in relative hierarchy within individual signs, since in
each case one of these factors predominates over the others" (1965: 26).

Jakobson later added that music and, to a certain degree, other arts
such as nonrepresentational painting and glossolalic poetry, are largely
based on imputed rather than factual similarity, since the similarities in
these structures are largely learned. Speaking of music, he says: "The
code of recognized equivalences between parts and their correlation with
the whole is to a great degree a learned, imputed set of parallelisms which
are accepted as such in the framework of a given epoch, culture or musical
school" (1970b: 12). Thus a fourth basic type of sign is put forward; in
addition to factual contiguity of the index, imputed contiguity of the
symbol, and factual similarity of the icon, there is also imputed similarity,
which is dominant in the above art forms. Jakobson seems to suggest that
imputed similarity is the basis of "introversive semiosis," a message
signifying itself, "where the referential component is absent or minimal."
Such semiosis plays a cardinal role in all aesthetic structures, but —
except in the arts named earlier — it coexists and coacts with "extroversive
semiosis," in which the referential component is present. According to
Jakobson, the emotive connotation remains important in those arts in
which the referential or conceptual component is scanty (1970b: 12–13).
These highly suggestive insights concerning the imputed, rather than
natural, similarities underlying certain aesthetic structures, and the corresponding heightening of the emotive function and weakening of the
referential one in such structures, seem to have wide implications for
cultural behavior in general. All cultural behavior is, by definition, based
on learning and is, according to the views expressed here, permeated with
an underlying aesthetic component.

By using other criteria for the classification of signs, in addition to the
variable relation of the signified to the signifier, Jakobson has considerably extended the four types of signs discussed (1970b: 9–16). Additional
criteria include the following:
1.   According to the nature of the signifier itself. The five senses are
utilized variously in exploiting time and space. For example, purely visual
signs exploit space, and here icons prevail (painting, etc.), whereas time
is exploited by auditory signs (spoken language, music), in which symbols
predominate.

2.   According to the ways in which signs are produced. We can distinguish directly organic means (speech, gestures, vocal music), instrumental means (instrumental music, painting), and also ready-made objects in which things are used as signs (flowers, etc.).

3.   According to the role of addressor and addressee. In inner speech the two are condensed, while in some cases there is no intentional addressor (as in such sign symbols as omens).

4.   According to whether the semiotic system is pure, such as language, or applied, such as architecture, dress, and cuisine. For example, Jakobson noted (as had Mukařovský), that architecture communicates more than its practical purpose. While we do not dwell in signs, Jakobson suggested nevertheless that the builder's task is not limited to the construction of shelters, for any edifice which requires the organization of three-dimensional space "is simultaneously some sort of refuge and a certain kind of message." Similarly, as the Russian ethnologist Bogatyrev (1971) had demonstrated (see discussion following), any garment has both a utilitarian and semiotic function.

5.   According to factors of selection and combination which underlie all languages. Homogeneous messages use a single semiotic system, while syncretic messages combine different sign systems. The latter are particularly common in primitive societies. For example, primitive poetry is usually sung, and bodily visual signs are usually combined with auditory sign systems (for example, the association of gestures with verbal utterances).

6.   Finally, signals differ from other sign systems because they cannot be combined into novel semiotic constructions. Signals, badges, emblems, coats of arms, warning sounds, etc., are called either indexical symbols or indexical icons.

In considering semiotics itself, which potentially unifies all forms of cultural behavior, and in agreeing with Sapir's perception that "every cultural pattern and every single act of social behavior involves communication, whether in an explicit or implicit sense," Jakobson states that "whatever level of communication we are treating, each of them implies some exchange of messages, and thus cannot be isolated from the semiotic level, which in its turn, assigns the prime role to language" (1970b: 5). Thus Jakobson puts forward three integrated sciences of communication: (1) Linguistics, confined to the study of communication of verbal messages, is narrower than semiotics. Although nonverbal messages presuppose verbal messages, the reverse is not necessarily true; (2) More general is semiotics, or the study of communication of any message, which implies the communication of verbal messages; and (3) Most general is the study of communications where messages are simply implied. This field is seen to encompass two communication levels isolated by Lévi-Strauss (1963: 296), namely, communication of goods and services, and communication of women, or economics and social anthropology (Jakobson 1970a: 425–426). This third most general field would not appear to preclude other cultural levels where messages are simply implied, such as material culture.

APPLICATIONS

We have called attention to the wide areas of cultural behavior where the aesthetic function is present, but not necessarily dominant, nor coequal, nor competing for dominance. In considering some application of this approach, we should note that within the last decade there have been extensive investigations of the relation to cultural behavior of the cognitive function of language by American cognitive anthropologists. The cognitive function, as well as the aesthetic, social, and emotive functions of verbal structures where the aesthetic function is dominant or clearly important (in mythology, folklore, and folk drama and their associated rituals), have been increasingly explored (see Lévi-Strauss 1964, 1967, 1968, 1971; Hymes 1971; Maranda and Maranda 1971; Leach 1969; etc.). Furthermore, in anthropological studies of aesthetic structures where the aesthetic component is by definition dominant, the aesthetic function as well as other functions (cognitive, psychological, social, etc.) have not been neglected (see Maquet 1971; Jopling 1971; etc.).

However, the full implication of Mukařovský's persistent message calling attention to the significance of the aesthetic function in all aspects of human behavior, not only in the areas of the well-defined arts or of folklore and mythology, has hardly been explored. Yet recent developments in semiotics, including refinements of typologies of functions and signs, have all enriched the concept of the aesthetic function and should therefore contribute to a far wider implementation of this concept. Though few in number, there have been some extremely significant applications of the views investigated here, and today there are promising developments. Thus we briefly consider some of these applications, as well as some influences or parallels which may be detected.

A pioneering work of over thirty years ago, which investigated the semiotics of the folk costume in all its functions including, importantly, its aesthetic function, is that of Petr Bogatyrev, one of the original members of the Prague Linguistic Circle, who was a structural ethnographer at the University of Moscow working extensively on folklore. His work, entitled *Functions of folk costumes in Moravian Slovakia*, has recently been published in English translation, accompanied by an introduction by the Russian ethnologist, folklorist and literary scholar, Boris Ogibenin (Bogatyrev 1971). In this and another important essay (Bogatyrev 1936), Bogatyrev showed how the transition of Slovak folk costumes from everyday to holiday to ceremonial and, finally, to ritual uses was related to their changing hierarchy of functions, marked by the weakening of the practical function and the strengthening of the aesthetic and other functions. The other functions discerned were an erotic function, said to be related to a magical function, and sociosexual, moral, holiday, and ritual functions. (The term "ritual" also defined a costume type.) Finally, he noted regional functions, as well as functions held to identify class, occupational, and religious status. In Ogibenin's view, Bogatyrev demonstrated that the opposition between everyday and holiday dress illustrates that "the borderline between both the object and sign may be unsteady and vascillating, depending on the relative strength of individual functions in the whole structure of functions" (Ogibenin 1971: 17; but see also Bogatyrev 1971: 80–85). Although the problem of the relation between sign and object was not completely resolved by Bogatyrev, his basic assumption seems to have been the semiotic role of costumes:

In order to grasp the social function of costumes, we must learn to read them as signs in the same way that we learn to read and understand different languages. ... A costume has a whole structure of functions. ... That functional structure always renders the costume both *object* and *sign* at the same time (1971:83, 84).

In examining the aesthetic function of costumes, Bogatyrev concluded:

Sometimes, in what appears to be the most eminently practical object, an aesthetic function may come to predominate, transforming the object into a sign devoid of practical use (1971:103).

Exemplifying such an extreme change is the altered function of beating stones, once employed in Slovak areas to wash linen. Later, these objects were decorated with broken bits of mirror and included among gifts traditionally given by the groom to the bride. Because of their decoration, they could no longer be used for practical purposes (1971: 103).

In addition to the hierarchy of special functions, Bogatyrev posits a "general function" which is the function of the "structure of functions" (1971: 95–98). Such concepts as "our costume," "our language," "our culture," which are always associated with an emotional element, are held to mark the general function. Such a general function is characterized as an organic whole and a unique system. "Thus the loss or change in intensity of one of the functions, or addition to the structure of a new function, will cause a change in the whole structure" (1971: 100). One wonders whether the "general function" would not have been more felicitously conceptualized simply as the "expressive or emotive function" with which, as Bogatyrev states, the general function is always associated, since the general function refers to that which is closest to the speaker (1971: 97, 99). In this view, the expressive function, rather than the "general function," would share with the aesthetic function certain organizing qualities which pervade the whole.

Although there may be reservations concerning some of the conceptualizations in this early study, one must agree with Ogibenin that this monograph testifies to the heurism of insights of structural linguistics and poetics, which may inspire new interpretations applicable to the humane sciences contiguous with linguistics and poetics, such as popular customs and beliefs (Ogibenin 1971: 9).

Among the concepts which Ogibenin believes were fruitful in Bogatyrev's study are the following:

1.   The polyfunctionality of language and the variability of the hierarchical arrangements of functions, as well as the opposition between the poetic (or aesthetic) and communicative functions and, in general, the semiotic approach to functions, in which functions are seen as "roles or tasks fulfilled by costumes or their parts which confer the value of signs upon objects" (Ogibenin 1971: 17): while we have already noted some examples of these functional principles in Bogatyrev's work, we may add a further one, showing that the same stock of clothes may be used differently for various functions. Thus an item which in one community signifies an unwed mother is worn in another community by virgins (Bogatyrev 1971: 30, 84).

2.   The distinction between *langue* and *parole* and Bogatyrev's implicit anticipation of the opposition between nature and culture (made later by Lévi-Strauss), in which logical rules are seen as imposed upon natural phenomena: in relation to the latter assertion, which may be somewhat forced although of interest, Ogibenin holds that even though Bogatyrev did not explicitly state it he surmised that wearing clothing is a universal constant, since where clothing is not ritualized it is differentiated only by the factors of age and sex. Only by a secondary intervention of the human mind does clothing acquire new significant functions. Thus clothing is both a natural system and a cultural system which becomes significant of more than itself (Ogibenin 1971: 13–14). Ogibenin concludes that "human body appearances, including clothing ... are used in human societies as signs," thus constituting boundary areas which provide "illus-

trations of transitional phenomena between nature and culture" (1971: 14).

3. The detection of unconscious, patterned regularities which govern customs relating to the function of clothing (Ogibenin 1971: 19): because Bogatyrev relied in part on museum collections and information gathered by other ethnographers, this claim appears somewhat exaggerated; yet it is suggestive. For example, the erotic function of clothes receives only limited treatment but it is not neglected, in spite of the fact that, as Bogatyrev himself states (1971: 74), he could not find definite reference to that function in the data of other ethnographies pertaining to Moravian Slovakia, and in spite of the fact that his own informants usually denied the existence of such a function.

4. The force of collective censorship: it is the collective which upholds the authority and obligatory character of ritualized rules which may be arbitrary. However, Ogibenin notes that Bogatyrev does not treat the structural roles of deviations, such as the breaking of conventional usage in relation to clothes at carnivals and masquerades (Ogibenin 1971: 29).

The recent unpublished study of Hungarian folk art by Fél and Hofer, alluded to earlier, bears some relation to Bogatyrev's work, but the treatment reaches beyond the folk costume to the entire world of folk art. Moreover, this world is seen as structurally related to all aspects of peasant behavior. The aesthetic as well as the traditionally conceived extra-aesthetic becomes an interrelated whole. The authors' approach seems clearly to suggest the multifunctional, dynamic, and semiotic quality of folk art, whereby folk art becomes an overreaching concept, imparting meaning to all aspects of the culture.

Stressing the close interrelation between the practical and the aesthetic in peasant culture, the authors point out that there is no clear boundary between art objects and nonart objects, nor between artist and craftsman, and peasants making objects for their own culture (p. 3). The aesthetic realm is interrelated with the whole material environment of peasant culture and each practical object, to varying degrees, has an artistic meaning. Therefore the authors assert that "it is only the body of objects as a whole, cohering and supplementing one another, that is able to reveal the struggle of aesthetic principles which weld them into an integrated whole " (p. 3–4). Suggesting various functions for an object — practical, ritual and ceremonial — the authors state that "various factors combined to raise an object from something in daily use to the rank of a ritual object for festive uses." An object may be transformed from everyday into ceremonial, ritual and festive by its aesthetic value in form and decoration (p. 17). The realm of aesthetic objects is conceived as a broad one in this study. The communicative aspect of aesthetic objects is viewed as fundamental, leading Fél and Hofer to suggest that the complicated system of beautiful objects existing within a certain village may be considered as a ritual language" (p. 24). Rites here refer to all repetitive formal actions connected with ceremonies or festivals where social relations are expressed (p. 23).

An interesting and important example of the semiotic quality of the aesthetic function is the peasant ornamental bed and the most varied rites associated with it throughout the life of the girl, bride, wife, and mother. The degree of elaboration of the bed, and its possession, is itself a sociodifferentiating factor communicating considerable information about its owner. The many different roles of the ornamental bed and its various furnishing in different situations impart a wealth of concealed associations and implicit information. Such observations led the authors to suggest not only that the world of peasant folk art objects should be viewed as an expressive language of objects (p. 40), but that, furthermore, the structural unity of the peasant world be seen as symbolically communicated by the entire assemblage of such objects. "The systematic possession of beautifully shaped objects was a reminder for each single person and for the whole community of the proper way to be a peasant "(p. 45).

The authors' view of the structural interrelations between the aesthetic and the extra-aesthetic levels, and their semiotic qualities, led them to reject the traditionally posed contradiction between the social and economic reality of peasant life with its conflicts, miseries, and tensions, and the idealized ceremonial, festive, and aesthetic level. For it is suggested that the structural opposition of the two levels, both viewed as realities, is essential to the full meaning of the message communicated by the aesthetic realm (p. 49). This conclusion is supported by the observation that when the socioeconomic structure begins to disintegrate, local costumes, traditional gestures, etc. all are lost "like lights out after a play" (p. 45). Traditional objects are frequently rejected, or retained only in one room of the house. Old crockery may even be destroyed. Finally, objects taken out of context of this total reality and way of life lose their former unity and are relegated simply to being mere ornaments in a bourgeois existence.

I now turn to a related problem. Although the primary emphasis of this essay is on the role of the aesthetic function in the areas of cultural behavior traditionally conceived of as extra-aesthetic, mention should be made of some aspects of Lévi-Strauss's applications of allied concepts to the study of myth, which seem to demonstrate clear parallels or close relations to the Prague Circle's view of aesthetic function.

In his introduction to *The raw and the cooked*, Lévi-Strauss states that he sees myth as based on secondary codes, the primary codes being drawn from language (1969: 12), and that he has tried to transcend the contrast between the tangible and the intelligible by operating from the outset at the level of the sign, the function of the sign being to express one level by means of another (1969: 14). Mythology, however, has no obvious practical function, for "it is not directly linked with a different kind of reality, which is endowed with a higher degree of objectivity than its own" (1969: 10). Myth, like music, lies somewhere between aesthetic perception and exercise of logical thought (1969: 14). Both operate on a two-fold continuum, external and internal. Thus myth is composed of a theoretically infinite series of historical events from which each society selects a limited number of incidents with which to create its myths. (In relation to music, this continuum is the infinite series of physically producible sounds from which a scale is selected.) The internal part of Lévi-Strauss's continuum suggests Mukařovský's constitutive factors which govern aesthetic norms. Situated in the psycho-physiological time of the listener are elements which include "periodicity of cerebral waves and organic rhythms, the strength of memory, and the power of attention." In mythology, such internal criteria make demands on "length of narration, the recurrence of certain themes, and the other forms of back references and parallels which can only be correctly grasped if the listener's mind surveys ... the whole range of the story as it unfolds" (1969: 16).

Similar to Mukařovský's system in which tensions between normative and nonnormative aesthetics create aesthetic value, in Lévi-Strauss's system, aesthetic pleasure is produced in music when expectations are disappointed or fulfilled beyond anticipation, reactions which are brought about by musical exploitation of organic rhythms and normative relations between the elements of the scale (1969: 17). Analogies are implied to mythology, which appeals to psychological, if not physiological and visceral, time, "since the telling of a story may be of 'breathtaking' interest," although this reaction is not held to be as essential as it is in music (1969: 16). Jakobson's suggestion that imputed similarities are an aspect of the introversive semiosis of aesthetic messages which signify themselves seems to be foreshadowed in Lévi-Strauss's comparison of myth to music since, as Lévi-Strauss reminds us, contemporary musical thought seems to reject "the hypothesis of the existence of some natural foundation that would objectively justify the stipulated system of relations among notes of the scale" (1969: 21). "Nature," writes Lévi-Strauss, "produces noises, not musical sounds; the latter are solely a consequence of culture, which has invented musical instruments and singing" (1969: 22). Thus "the sequences of each myth and the myths themselves in respect to their reciprocal interrelations may be compared to the instrumental parts of a musical work" and can be studied "as one studies a symphony" (1969: 26). The polysemantic ambiguity that Mukařovský attributed to the aesthetic function is also implied in Lévi-Strauss's invocation of Baudelaire: while each listener reacts to a work in his own particular way, music also "arouses similar ideas in different brains" (1969: 26).

In an illustration of the frequent syncretism of messages in primitive cultures (upon which Jakobson has also commented [1970b: 13]), Lévi-Strauss tells us that while myth mediates between culture and nature, the force of myth is not as strong as that of music. But myth is frequently sung, thus enhancing its powers, because singing is a particularly clear union of nature and culture (Lévi-Strauss 1969: 28).

Lévi-Strauss asserts that music must be able to fulfill the same functions as speech, because it is in itself a complete language. Thus he applies Jakobson's six functions, although they are differently organized. Since mythology lies on the same axis as music, analogies are again implicit. The phatic function, insofar as it applies to music, is said to be subjectivized, giving pleasure to the performer who does not necessarily have to have an audience. The phatic function is often accompanied by a conative one — implying the reversibility of sender and receiver, noted by Jakobson and Mukařovský (Jakobson 1971b [1952]: 558; Mukařovský 1937b: 223) — since the conative function may be focused on the performing group and not on a separate receiver. Thus a group performance may create a harmony of gesture and expression as one of its aims (Lévi-Strauss 1969: 19). In other words, the message is focused on the sender who is also the receiver.

The above functions (phatic and conative) are seen by Lévi-Strauss as polar opposites of the cognitive function, which itself is broken down into three functions: metalinguistic, referential, and poetic, each corresponding to a particular kind of message. As we have seen, Jakobson and Mukařovský have held that although the poetic or aesthetic function does bear meaning indirectly, it is not subordinate to the cognitive function. Rather, its orientation on the message itself brings it into opposition to the cognitive function. Finally, the emotive function in music is seen by Lévi-Strauss as pervading the whole. As Lévi-Strauss states, "Theoretically, if not always in practice, emotive function and musical language are coextensive" (1969: 30).

While Lévi-Strauss seems to limit the poetic function to one aspect of the cognitive, the implications of the fundamental analogy of myth to music — the aesthetic structure *par excellence* — and of the discussion of aesthetic pleasure, as well as the emphasis on the pervasiveness of the emotive function, all seem to imply a generalized, organizing quality for both an aesthetic and emotive function throughout the entire structure of myth. Relations are implied to Jakobson's later concept of "introversive semiosis," where the aesthetic and emotive functions are strengthened at the expense of the referential (Jakobson 1970b: 12–13). As we noted earlier, Lévi-Strauss's view was that myth has no obvious practical function since it is not directly linked with a different kind of reality. Thus the referential function would appear to be weakened. One is reminded of Jakobson's earlier impressionistic comparison of the aesthetic function to the function of oil when used in cooking. They are similar because both are elements *sui generis* which cannot be reduced to other elements yet they can reorganize other elements within a polyfunctional structure. Thus oil, which is not a special dish nor a mechanical part of a special dish, changes the taste of the entire dish (Jakobson 1971a [1933–1934]: 30).

In a similar vein, stressing the organizational abilities of the aesthetic function, Lévi-Strauss stated that in art objects the important factor relates to the arrangement, pattern, or relationship between objects. Aesthetic emotion is the way "we react when a non-significant object is promoted to the role of signifier," thus bringing out "certain fundamental properties common to both sign and object." Thereby the structure, normally latent in the object, suddenly emerges "thanks to its plastic or poetic representation" (Charbonnier 1969: 95, 123).

I conclude with a few remarks about some Soviet linguists and literary structuralists (grouped in the section on structural typology at the Institute of Slavic Studies of the Soviet Academy of Sciences in Moscow and around Jurij Lotman at the University of Tartu in Estonia) whose interpretations and applications of semiotic approaches developed by the Prague Linguistic Circle extend not only to folklore and mythology but also to other areas of ethnology. For example, the Moscow scholar, T. V. Civ'jan (T. V. Tsiviane) has examined systems of etiquette from a semiotic point of view (Civ'jan 1962, 1965, 1970). In a recent discussion, Civ'jan (1970) says that such simple semiotic systems, where signs enter into only a few combinations, form a syntax of the pragmatic type. Etiquette is defined as "rules of ritualized conduct of the individual in society" which reflect social criteria and demand particular ceremonials (1970: 390). Using the traditions of modern Europe as her field of study, she defines four universal oppositions, one having precedence in each case (masculine/ feminine, old/young, high/low, self/other). Civ'jan also applies Jakobson's six factors and functions without, however, clearly determining a dominant function, except insofar as she states that etiquette consecrates relationships and ties within the group (1970: 391). The social aspect is later defined as the referential function. The poetic function, she holds, often distinguishes a particular conduct of etiquette from nonetiquette. The level of expression (signifier) is composed of a vocabulary consisting of formulae within the natural language, gestures, and objects which have ritual significance within an etiquette situation, all of which are combined according to certain rules which in turn form a grammar of etiquette.

A difficulty in Civ'jan's approach seems to be her attempt to construct too general a model, applicable to the whole of modern European society; as a result, the analysis tends to approach a list of traits whose obligatory relationships are too varied to contribute to a clear structural analysis. Secondly, there may be valid objections to so automatic an application of linguistic terminology and methods, since it would seem that the appropriateness of theory to facts requires translation or reinterpretation when moving from one semiotic system to another.

Jurij Lotman's discussion of intersemiotic translation directs us to a key problem which semiotics must attack if it is to be a unifying discipline. Lotman has called for the extension of semiotic methods to general ethnographic studies encompassing all of cultural behavior. Material culture is not excepted, since even material products play a double role. In addition to their practical aspects, they condense the experience of work, acquired in the course of a long past, in order to finally become instruments able to conserve and transmit information (Lotman 1971: 46). Structures of cultural behavior are seen as secondary modeling systems, or "communication structures, built up as superstructures over the level of the natural language." "Secondary" here does not mean that the new structure uses natural language as material, nor that all aspects of natural language are reproduced, but rather that such secondary systems are built along the lines of language (Lotman 1970a: 16). Following this position, a culture can be viewed as a semiotic system, or bundle of semiotic systems, which is a symbiosis of individual systems; it also forms a hierarchy composing a superlanguage. "Texts," in Lotman's terminology, are conceived of as the totality of communications in these languages (1970b: 8). A culture is viewed on two levels, the communication itself and the code needed to decode the communication. Because types of cultures are thus viewed as special but complex languages, a complex system of codes is needed, one of which is seen as dominant (1970b: 12).

Lotman has usefully pointed to the problem of meaning in the study of secondary modeling systems, such as cultural systems (1965: 22–23). The very concept of the sign as a unification of signifier and signified implies its inclusion in more complex systems of features, since both signifier and signified are a part of systems of their own. As Lotman noted, while it is generally recognized that one can transcode the material aspect (or the signifier) of a sign into other systems (for example, sound systems into graphic systems), the transcoding of the signified (the level of content) is equally necessary. Since meaning is the possibility of transcoding from one system to another, where one element in a system is conceived of as equivalent to an element in another system at some intersecting point, then it follows that when one transcodes a sign, the original sign acts as signifier for a new signified found within the intersecting structural chain.

Jakobson had written earlier (1966b: 223) that the meaning of any linguistic sign is its translation into some further alternative sign. Three kinds of translation were set forth: intralingual translation, interlingual translation, and intersemiotic translation or transmutation; that is "an interpenetration of verbal signs by means of signs of non-verbal sign systems." Here, it would seem, one may understand intersemiotic translation as also including those between nonverbal sign systems when messages are simply implied.

I conclude by calling attention to the importance of studying the semiotics of aesthetics and, most particularly, implicit aesthetics, which is posited as an underlying aspect of those areas of cultural behavior which are traditionally conceived of as extra-aesthetic. I further suggest that the close relation of the aesthetic function to the emotive function, and its ambiguous relation to the cognitive or referential function, as well as its underlying organizing ability and its dynamic and conservative character, all warrant investigation.

REFERENCES

BOGATYREV, PETR G.
  1936 Kroj jako znak: funkční a strukturální pojetí v národopisu. *Slovo a slovesnost* (Prague) 2: 43–47.
  1971 *Functions of folk costumes in Moravian Slovakia.* The Hague: Mouton.
BOHANNAN, PAUL
  1961 "Artist and critic in an African society," in *The artist in tribal society.* Edited by Marion W. Smith, 85- 95. London: Routledge and Kegan Paul.
BÜHLER, K.
  1933 *Die Axiomatik der Sprachwissenschaft.* Berlin: Kant Studien 38. Berlin.
CANCIAN, FRANCESCA
  1960 "Functional analysis of change," in *Theory in anthropology.* Edited by Robert A. Manners and David Kaplan, 204–212. Chicago: Aldine.

CHARBONNIER, C.
1969   *Conversations with Claude Lévi-Strauss.* New York: Grossman.

CIV'JAN, TATJANA V.
1962   "K opisaniju ètiketa kak semiotičeskoj sistemy," in *Simpozium po strukturnomu izučeniju znakovyx sistem.* Moscow.
1965   "K nekotorym voprosam postroenija jazyka ètiketa," in *Trudy po znakovym sistemam,* volume two. Tartu.
1970   "Contribution à l'étude de certains systèmes sémiotiques simples (système de l'étiquette)," in *Sign-language-culture.* Edited by A. J. Greimas, et al., 390–400. The Hague: Mouton.

CROWLEY, DANIEL J.
1966   An African aesthetic. *The Journal of Aesthetics and Art Criticism* 26: 519–524.

DE SAUSSURE, FERDINAND
1966   *Course in general linguistics.* New York: McGraw-Hill.

FÉL, EDIT, TAMÁS HOFER
n.d.   "Hungarian folk art." Unpublished manuscript.

HYMES, DELL H.
1962   "The ethnography of speaking," in *Anthropology and human behavior.* Edited by Thomas Gladwin and William C. Sturtevant, 13–53. Washington D. C.: The Anthropological Society of Washington.
1971   "The wife who 'goes out' like a man/ reinterpretation of a Clackamas Chinook myth," in *Essays in semiotics.* Edited by Julia Kristeva, Josette Rey-Debove, and Donna Jean Umiker, 296–326. The Hague: Mouton.

JAKOBSON, ROMAN
1960   "Closing statement: linguistics and poetics," in *Style in language.* Edited by Thomas Sebeok, 350–377. Cambridge, Mass.: M.I.T. Press.
1964   "Minutes of study group in linguistics and psychoanalysis." Mimeographed manuscript. The New Psychoanalytical Institute, New York.
1965   Quest for the essence of language. *Diogenes* 51:21–37.
1966a   "Franz Boas' approach to language," in *Portraits of linguists,* volume two. Edited by Thomas Sebeok, 127–137. Bloomington: University of Indiana Press.
1966b   "On linguistic aspects of translation," in *On translation.* Edited by Reuben H. Brower, 232–239. New York: Oxford University Press.
1970a   "Linguistics," in *Main trends in the social and human sciences,* part one, 419–463. The Hague: Mouton.
1970b   "Language in relation to other communication systems," in *Linguaggi nella società e nella tecnica,* 1–16. Milan: Edizioni di Communità.
1971a [1933–1934]   "Co je poesie?" in *Studies in verbal art.* Ann Arbor: University of Michigan Slavic Contributions 4.
1971b [1952]   "Results of a joint conference of anthropologists and linguists," in *Selected writings,* volume two, 554–567. The Hague: Mouton.
1971c [1959]   "Diskussionsbeitrag," in *Selected writings,* volume two, 272–279. The Hague: Mouton

JAKOBSON, ROMAN, JURIJ TYNJANOV
1972 [1928]   "Problemy izučenija literatury i jazyka," in *The structuralists from Marx to Lévi-Strauss.* Edited by R. deGeorge and F. deGeorge,

81–83. New York: Doubleday.

JOPLING, CAROL F.
1971 *Art and aesthetics in primitive societies.* New York: E. P. Dutton.

LEACH, EDMUND, *editor*
1969 *The structural study of myth and totemism.* London: Tavistock. (Originally published 1967.)

LÉVI-STRAUSS, CLAUDE
1963 *Structural anthropology.* New York: Basic Books.
1964–1971 *Mythologies*, four volumes. Paris: Plon.
1969 *The raw and the cooked: introduction to a science of mythology.* New York: Harper.

LOTMAN, JURIJ M.
1965 "O probleme značenij vo vtoričnyx modelirujuščix sistemax," in *Trudy po znakovym sistemam*, volume two. Tartu.
1970a *Struktura xudožestvennogo teksta.* Moscow: Iskusstvo. (Reprinted as Brown University Slavic Reprint 9. Providence: Brown University Press.)
1970b *Materialy k kursu teorii literatury, I: Tipologija kul'tury.* Tartu.
1971 "Problèmes de la typologie des cultures," in *Essays in semiotics.* Edited by Julia Kristeva, Josette Rey-Debove, and Donna Jean Umiker, 46–56. The Hague: Mouton.

MAQUET, JACQUES
1971 *Introduction to aesthetic anthropology.* Reading, Mass.: A McCaleb Module.

MARANDA, PIERRE, ELLI KÖNGÄS MARANDA, *editors*
1971 *Structural analysis of oral traditions.* Philadelphia: University of Pennsylvania Press.

MUKAŘOVSKÝ, JAN
1934a "K českému překladu Šklovského teorie prózy," in Mukařovský (1948a(1):344–350).
1934b "Polákova 'Vznešenost přírody'," in Mukařovský (1948a(2):91–176).
1934c "L'art comme fait sémiologique," in Mukařovský (1966:85–88).
1936 *Aesthetic function, norm and value as social facts.* Translated 1970 by Mark E. Suino. Ann Arbor: University of Michigan Slavic Contributions.
1937a "Estetická norma," in Mukařovský (1966:74–77). (Originally published as "La norme esthétique.")
1937b "Individuum v umění," in Mukařovský (1966:223–225). (Originally published as "L'individu dans l'art.")
1938 "Básnické pojmenování a estetická funkce jazyka," in Mukařovský (1948a(1):157–163).
ca. 1940 "Úkoly obecné estetiky," in Mukařovský (1966:62–64).
1940a O jazyce básnickém. *Slovo a slovesnost* (Prague) 6:113–145.
1940b Estetika jazyka. *Slovo a slovesnost* (Prague) 6:1–27.
1942a "Místo estetické funkce mezi ostatními," in Mukařovský (1966:65–73).
1942b "Význam estetiky," in Mukařovský (1966:55–61).
1943 "Umění," in Mukařovský (1966:127–139).
1943–1945 "Individuum a literární vývoj," in Mukařovský (1966:226–235).

1946   "O strukturalismu," in Mukařovský (1966:109–116).
1947   "K pojmosloví československé teorie umění," in Mukařovský (1948a
(1):29–40).
1948a   *Kapitoly z české poetiky*, three volumes. Prague: Nakladatelstvi
Svoboda.
1948b   "Strukturalismus v estetice a ve vědě o literatuře," in Mukařovský
(1948a(1):13–28).
1966   *Studie z estetiky*. Prague: Odeon.

OGIBENIN, BORIS L.
1971   "Petr Bogatyrev and structural ethnography," in *Functions of folk
costumes in Moravian Slovakia*, by Petr Bogatyrev, 9–32. The Hague:
Mouton.

PARSONS, TALCOTT
1957   "Theory of social systems," in *Man and culture: an evaluation of the
work of Bronislaw Malinowski*. Edited by Raymond Firth, 53–70.
New York: Harper.

PEIRCE, CHARLES SANDERS
1938–1958   *Collected papers*, four volumes. Cambridge, Mass.: Harvard
University Press.

PIAGET, JEAN
1970   *Structuralism*. New York: Basic Books.

PRAGUE LINGUISTIC CIRCLE
1929   "Téze předložené prvému sjezdu slovanských filologů v Praze 1929,"
in *U základů pražské jazykovědné školy*. Edited by Josef Vachek,
35–65. Prague: Academia.

RADCLIFFE-BROWN, A. R.
1952   "On the concept of function in social science," in *Structure and function in primitive society*, 178–187. New York: Free Press.

SAUSSURE, FERDINAND, DE (see DE SAUSSURE)

Interrelationships of Individual, Cultural, and Pan-Human Values

C. R. WELTE

1.   Twenty years ago the study of values was given much attention at the Wenner-Gren Foundation International Symposium on Anthropology. Prominent anthropologists of the day discussed the two inventory papers (Tax et al. 1953: 322–341), and A. L. Kroeber devoted the last four pages of his "Concluding review" to the subject. Throughout the decade of the 1950's value studies were actively pursued.[1] In England their relation to social structure was emphasized (Firth 1953). In America Kroeber and Clyde Kluckhohn wrote extensively on values and culture and tied the two concepts closely together (Kluckhohn et al. 1951; Kroeber 1952; Kroeber and Kluckhohn 1952; Kluckhohn 1953; Kroeber 1953; Kroeber 1956; Kluckhohn 1958). A massive fieldwork project, the "Comparative Study of Values in Five Cultures" of the Laboratory of Social Relations, Harvard University, lasted for six years and generated over fifty publications (Vogt and Albert 1966: 299–305). There seemed to be widespread agreement that value studies were important, and that, as Kroeber had said, "it follows that if we refuse to deal with values, we are refusing to deal with what has most meaning in particular cultures as well as in human culture seen as a whole" (1952: 137).

Nevertheless, in the 1960's there was a general turning away from

---

[1]   Except for American and British studies, there has been little theoretical development of the concept of values as an analytical tool in anthropology. Recent European work has been on the philosophical side and often deals primarily with the metaphysical concepts of the people being studied. For a survey of the work in sociology, and of its limitations, see Hutcheon's recent article in *The British Journal of Sociology* (1972: 173-177).

value studies. Firth noted that they "are perhaps less fashionable now" (1964: 180). Vogt and Albert, in their summing up of the Harvard "values study" in *People of Rimrock* (1966: 1–21), identified many unresolved problems that the study had brought to light and could only hope that developments in componential analysis might provide solutions. Theodore Graves, in a review of *People of Rimrock* (1967), added charges of circular reasoning and opportunistic stretching of definitions. Manners and Kaplan, in their *Theory in anthropology* (1968), left the subject of values to an article from a sociology handbook which denigrated both values and culture as explanatory concepts (Blake and Davis 1964).

No one had responded adequately to the fundamental need for a classification of values. Commenting on a presentation by Kluckhohn, William L. Kolb said, "I am appalled at the number of systems of classification of values... that are running loose today, each claiming... to be exhaustive at the same or similar level of abstraction; and each failing to give a full-scale logical ground for its claim" (1961: 52). Ethel Albert, in her article "Value systems" in the *International encyclopedia of the social sciences* (1968), found no classification systems that had improved on those of the 1950's. At the end of the decade a philosopher published *Value theory and the behavioral sciences* (Handy 1969). He found the theories wanting and even, at times, incoherent.

The unresolved problems of value studies are still with us. Neither developments in componential analysis nor in other kinds of cognitive studies related to values (Wallace 1962: 354–55) have proved to be effective. I think, however, that a clue to a fruitful approach has been given to us by Kroeber and Kluckhohn. They wrote, in their monograph on culture, "culture change seems to be due to the ceaseless feedback between factors of idiosyncratic and universal human motivation, on the one hand, and factors of universal and special situation, on the other. Unfortunately, we lack conceptual instruments for dealing with such systems of organized complexity" (Kroeber and Kluckhohn 1952: 111). In this paper I develop a taxonomic classification of values — based on distinctions between, and interrelationships of, the individual, the cultural, and the universal — and show how this provides a basis for attacking the problems that have arrested value studies. I also analyze the diachronic and synchronic interactions of major classes of values and thus provide a new view of the value factors in the "systems of organized complexity" with which anthropologists must deal. This view is based on the assumption that the calculi of culture describe only one area of the cognitive processes that must be investigated in the study of cultural differentiation and change.[2]

2.   Semantic considerations must be faced at the beginning of any study of values. The widely varying meanings of "culture" are well known. When they are combined with the ambiguities of "universals" and of "values" immediate clarification is called for.

As for "culture," suffice it to say that I use it as equivalent to "social heritage" and place culture in the ideational order of reality. "Universals" cannot be dealt with so easily. In addition to the many meanings of "cultural universals," the association of "universals" with "values" has caused ambiguity because the term "universal values" is often used as equivalent to "universal cultural values." In his "Concluding review" Kroeber entitled the last section "Universal values" but he discussed universal cultural values (Tax et al. 1953: 375–376). Investigations of universal cultural values have been unsatisfactory because of the few universals found, because of the almost contentless level of abstraction of most of them, and because of lack of agreement on what is proved about a value if it is found to exist in all cultures.

In investigating the factors of "universal human motivation," that Kroeber and Kluckhohn referred to in the clue that they gave us, we must make a place for the possibility that there are values that are not part of the social or the genetic heritage; values that are rooted in experience, but which interact with cultural values in motivating the choices men make; values that, if they do exist, radically change the interrelationships that have been assumed to be operative in the field of values. This possibility will be investigated, but to avoid the confusions apparent in the use of "universal values" I shall use the term "pan-human values."

The term "values" itself has proved to be a stumbling block in value studies. As Vogt and Albert comment in *People of Rimrock,* "descriptive studies of values usually either offer no definition at all or adopt a verbal definition that does not make effective contact with the data. Any other definition might have been cited without affecting the description. Such 'ritual' use of a definition of values does not contribute

[2] Roger Brown, in his summation of the conference "Transcultural Studies in Cognition," spoke of the contrasting views of mind as categorical grid or template, and as operating agency or transformer. He said, "We need comparative studies of mind in all its aspects and not of the categorical grid alone. Eventually someone is going to have to nail together the template and the transformer" (1964: 252). In value studies the transformer metaphor is apt, particularly if extended to include the interrelationships of rules for behavior in a wider-than-cultural context and the interactions of sets of these rules in decision making.

to stabilizing the concept" (1966: 6). Kluckhohn had tried to stabilize it with a definition that restricted it to concepts of the desirable (as opposed to the desired), but this was the very definition that has been subject to "ritual" use. Furthermore, it has been rejected as too narrow, in the article "The concept of values" in the *International encyclopedia of the social sciences* (Williams 1968), and, as Albert writes in her ensuing article, "it is doubtful whether a definition of values can be produced that embraces all the meanings assigned to the term and its cognates or that would be acceptable to all investigators" (1968: 288). Kluckhohn saw the problem when he reviewed the literature on values and found "values considered as attitudes, motivations, objects, measurable quantities, substantive areas of behavior, affect-laden customs and traditions, and relationships such as those between individuals, groups, objects, events. The only general agreement is that values somehow have to do with normative as opposed to existential propositions" (1951: 390).

I think it clear that an attempt to reconcile the definitions that are in use is not the way to approach the problem. If we were to make a semantic analysis of the domain of values in the usage of social scientists, the results would be startling but hardly useful. "Values" has usefulness only as a collective term to group kinds of values. When a particular kind or class of values is meant, a distinctive term must be used. We need a vocabulary of terms as part of a taxonomic classification.

3.   In order to develop a logical classification, the locus of values must be decided upon. We are concerned with cognition, so our approach should be from the point of view of human symbolic processes. An objective symbol may be said to be "valued" and thus may "have value" for a person, but it is on the subjective side of the valuing process that choices are made, so I place values in the realm of cognitive elements with symbolic significance.

Before proceeding we must investigate the various usages of the term "symbol." A symbol can be anything that stands for something else, or has a meaning. The symbol itself may be an idea (notion, conception, mental image, element of cognitive structure) or an objective representation (a word, object, or sign). The meaning may be conventionally assigned, may develop through association, or may lie in the felt importance of an experience to the subject's scheme of life which includes future possibilities as well as present requirements. It is the last of these three kinds of meaning or significance that is applicable to values. They are symbolic in the sense of having this special kind of significance.

Values are not words or verbal propositions. The entanglement of values with the verbal level has been one of the causes of difficulties in value studies. The importance of the distinction between values and the terms or labels (conventional symbols) used to express them will become apparent as we progress.

For a formal definition, values must be assigned to a class and then differentiated from other members of the class. In conformity with the locus chosen, let us call the class "elements of underlying cognitive structure." In addition to values, this class includes beliefs (in the broad sense of the existential ideas: those that pertain to what exists or what is considered to be true). Values are distinguished from beliefs by virtue of being affective and symbolic. Thus, values are defined as affective symbolic elements of underlying cognitive structure.

A definition such as this is useful only if we proceed to specify subordinate levels of classification and thus bring down the level of abstraction to where contact can be made with descriptive data. This procedure will form our taxonomy.

The first subordinate level of the taxonomy is that *of categorisch.* The three categories, *individual values, cultural values,* and *pan-human values,* designate the taxa at that level. Differentiation between them is to be made on the basis of the genesis of each category. The next subordinate level is that of *major classes.* Differentiation will be made on a functional basis by means of a cognitive model of the making of a choice. Further subdivision will produce the levels of *classes, subclasses,* and *types.* In the case of cultural values, 120 types will be specified for the ordering of descriptive data.

As a clarification of the nature of the categories, I wish to contrast them with *levels of discourse.* Three levels of discourse are sufficient for our purpose. The *universal level* is with reference to all men: mankind as a whole. The *group level* is with reference to all members of a specified society or subsociety: all the bearers of its culture or subculture. The *idiosyncratic level* is with reference to a particular member of a society: one flesh-and-blood culture-bearer. The values in each of the categories can be described at each level of discourse. Ambiguity is avoided by using terms for the categories that are distinct from those used for the levels of discourse. For example, individual values at the universal level of discourse are discussed in terms of the hypothesized processes of the human ego. Furthermore, a discussion of the interaction of individual and cultural values at the group level can be readily distinguished from a discussion of their interaction at the idiosyncratic level. Whether we study a person, a society, or mankind, all three categories of values are applicable.

4.   The ontogenesis of each category of values is the basis for differentiating the three categories. The values in each category are rooted in experience but they are learned in different ways. Only the cultural values are part of a social heritage.

The ontogenesis of cultural values is through the special kind of learning called enculturation. During enculturation the beliefs and values of the culture are learned as the result of instruction or example. They make up the social heritage. The beliefs form existential patterns for behavior and the values form normative patterns for behavior. Behavior includes thinking, feeling, and acting. The distinction between the existential and the normative relates to the distinction between fact and value rather than that between real and ideal.

In the case of pan-human values, it is my thesis that their ontogenesis lies in the application of rudimentary powers of symbolization to experiences that all infants must undergo in some measure in order to survive. These are of two kinds: (1) experiencing satisfaction of biogenetic needs, and (2) experiencing activities which provide for satisfaction of those needs. When symbolization is applied to such experiences, values are formed that include the affect due to the relation of the experiences to self-preservation. In Section 7 the content of pan-human values will be discussed and the subordinate major classes (*primate needs*, based on satisfactions of needs shared with the anthropoid apes, and *pan-human standards*, based on experience of essential activities) will be differentiated.

In the case of individual values, we must turn to the psychologists for an hypothesis concerning their ontogenesis. The challenge given by Kroeber, when he wrote "we can hardly forever leave the psychic equipment of man a blank except for a few reflexes, no instincts, and a faculty for symbolization; at least not without a try" (1956: 295), has not been taken up by anthropologists. There is certainly no consensus among psychologists, but there are psychologists (sometimes referred to as the "ego psychologists") who have developed a view of man's psychic equipment that provides a basis for an hypothesis concerning individual values. As Gordon Allport wrote, "to such writers the ego-ideal is no longer, as it was with Freud, a passive reflection of the superego, which in turn is conceived as a mere legacy of the parent. The ego through its ideals reaches into the future, becomes an executive, a planner, a fighter" (1960: 75).

In the process of maturation, as the ego becomes the executive, the planner, and the fighter, individual values are learned. They develop from the experiences of mediating between the environment, internal tensions, value conflicts, and the struggle to develop and maintain identity. When Ego is able to resolve the conflicts, the values learned in the process become the standards, norms, preferences, and goals of the ego. These *ego values* are guides for future decisions.

The conflicts that Ego cannot resolve, and which it views as threats, may result in the development of *neurotic needs*. These neurotic defenses, obsessions, compulsions, etc., and the related anxieties, can become strong enough to override all other values at times. The ego values and the neurotic needs are the subordinate major classes in the category of individual values. I will not go further into personality structure, but will accept the view of the relative autonomy of the ego that sees Ego as attempting to resolve (among other problems) internal conflicts between values when confronted with a choice to which it must respond.

5.   The major classes of values (the taxonomic level next subordinate to the categories) are the ego values and neurotic needs within the category of individual values; the pan-human standards and primate needs within the category of pan-human values; and the cultural values (the category of cultural values is not subdivided at this level, so the term "cultural values" will designate a major class as well as a category). The genesis or source of each of these major classes has been indicated in the previous section. It will be assumed that, by virtue of their common source, the values in each major class form a set of values that function together when brought to bear on a problem. For instance, we can think of situations in which cultural values are opposed to primate needs, or in which other combinations of the major classes interact.

Now let us analyze the elements involved in the making of a choice, in order to provide the basis for functional distinctions that will supplement the genetic distinctions we have made. The analysis will also relate the major classes to one another, and distinguish values in general from beliefs, capacities, responses, and objects of interest. Figure 1 represents the steps involved in the making of a single choice by an actor. This synchronic model assumes that the choice is an important one (a considered choice) in which all elements are active, but that questions of whether certain elements are rational or irrational, conscious or unconscious, strong or weak, are not essential to the relationships and distinctions with which we are concerned. The model presents an ideal case, but one that is useful to us.

The elements of a choice, as numbered in Figure 1, are:

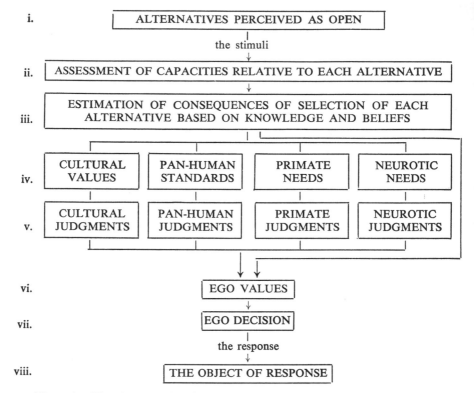

Figure 1.   The elements of a choice

i.   Perception of open alternatives. (These are the alternatives as perceived by the actor. The processes of perception are prior to this and
are not included.)

ii.   Assessment of personal capacities relative to each alternative. (This
involves considerations of how well, and at what expenditure of time
and effort, the alternatives could be executed.)

iii.   Estimate of the consequences of selecting each alternative. (Beliefs
about what is, or can be, or can be expected, are used to make the
estimate. Beliefs include what the actor considers to be "knowledge,"
so that is included in the model.)

iv.   Consideration of the applicable values in each of four of the major
classes with reference to each estimate of consequences.

v.   The forming of a judgment or evaluation of the desirability of each
consequence in terms of each of the four sets of values.

vi.   Application of ego values to the various judgments, and to the
estimates of consequences of the alternatives.

vii.   Decision by Ego that issues in a response.

viii.   The object of interest. (Whatever the response is directed toward.)

The model provides the basis for a functional definition of values: values function to assess the desirability of estimated consequences when choosing between alternatives. In this process the values in each major class provide *guides for behavior*. That is to say, the elements of underlying cognitive structure group together to indicate, with reference to a particular problem, the pattern for behavior that is valued. Thus, the relation of values to motivation is twofold: (1) they motivate choice by providing judgments of desirability which operate to determine the direction of the response, and (2) once the choice has been made, they provide the impulse to act in accordance with the choice.

To supplement the distinctions that have been made by means of the model, some axiological discriminations are needed. These will permit us to move to the next subordinate level — the taxonomic level of classes. Here are the terms and definitions we will use:

Standards are guides for behavior that are widely applicable and per-during; considered to be justified and justifiable; subject to deep commitment and affect; measures for other values, giving them orientation and direction. They are to be lived up to, to be striven toward, and to be defended.

Norms are guides for behavior that are bases for rules, roles, or ways of behaving that are necessary or expedient for implementing standards, achieving goals, or satisfying needs. They are particularly useful for routine decisions.

Preferences are guides for behavior involving simple likes or dislikes that are taken for granted, or guide choices in the absence of other values. Some preferences are minor variations in modes of fulfilling needs. They are all lightly held or optional.

Goals are guides for behavior related to a planned ocurse of action or change in a situation that are formulated by focusing applicable standards, norms, preferences, and needs on an area of interest.

Needs are guides for behavior which aim to satisfy biogenetic drives or neurotic anxiety reactions. They are related to deficiency motives, but because of their symbolic nature they function even when the drive is not active.

The foregoing definitions, and the groupings of values that they imply, are arbitrary. In the face of general lack of agreement on terminology we can only adopt the criterion of usefulness and construct a vocabulary that provides an adequate range and whose terms we can distinguish relatively clearly. Using these terms we can specify eleven classes of values and arrive at a level where we can dispense with the term "values" except in its collective usage. Thus we establish that the classes of values are: (1) cultural standards, (2) cultural norms, (3) cultural preferences, (4) cultural goals, (5) ego standards, (6) ego norms, (7) ego preferences, (8) ego goals, (9) neurotic needs, (10) pan-human standards, and (11) primate needs.

6.   I not only wish to show the importance of values in the generation of behavior, but also wish to stress that, in addition to cultural values, individual and pan-human values are involved. Nevertheless, I wish to keep in view the importance of cultural values within the cultural patterns for behavior, and that the behavior generated by values in interaction is an important source of culture change. This complex of relationships is shown diagrammatically in Figure 2.

In Figure 2 the large upper left hand box, labeled "the culture-bearer as actor," is a simplification of Figure 1. Those items that are not part of the social heritage are labeled "the non-cultural." The box represents the actor making a response which results in behavior. This becomes part of the total behavior of the society (labeled "raw behavior"). From perceptions of this raw behavior all culture-bearers abstract patterns *of* behavior that become their views of "what is going on." Through a little understood complex of processes, a consensus is arrived at that results in the selection of some of these patterns of behavior to become patterns *for* behavior (guides) and to be passed on through processes of enculturation. Thus, behavior generated by the interaction of the five major classes of values (as in Figure 1) has become a basis for new cultural patterns.

I have not yet mentioned the two boxes that are enclosed in double frames. These are labeled "processes of cultural development and change" and "culture." They represent scientific abstractions made by anthropologists. In regard to these abstractions, I wish to point out that culture as an explanatory concept must be regarded as patterns *for* behavior (a design for living, a guide). If culture is regarded as patterns *of* behavior (an abstraction from raw behavior), any attempt to use culture to explain behavior is bound to involve circular reasoning. So, the anthropologist studies culture as an abstraction, but one viewed as patterns for behavior to be passed on by the processes of enculturation. But, the processes of enculturation are not abstractions. They are going on all the time; most of them can be observed and, in some cases, participated in by an ethnographer. Here is the prime source from which to abstract a view of culture, including cultural values, as patterns for behavior.

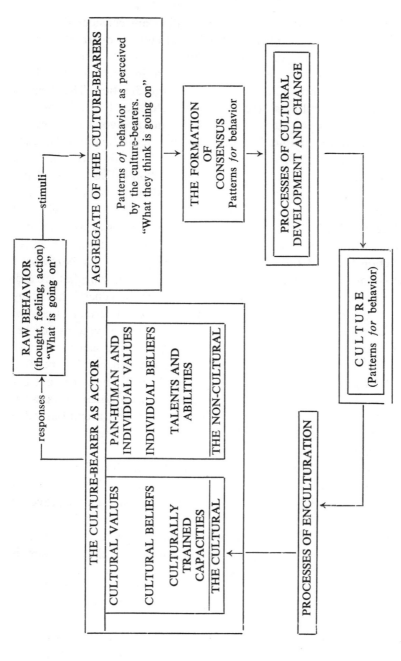

Figure 2.   Culture and behavior

In Figure 3, the processes of enculturation are considered in more detail, and culture is divided into traditional culture, operative culture, and subcultures. These divisions of culture are usually sources of conflicting values, and each has its own measure of integration. In studying enculturation all three must be taken into consideration. The diagram shows the three cultures "feeding" their values and beliefs into the enculturation process. Many kinds of selection are involved as they are passed on to the culture-bearers. The internalized culture of each culture-bearer results from the selections made in his particular case.

I use the terms "traditional culture" and "operative culture," not because of particular accuracy or aptness of their connotations, but to avoid other distinctions such as overt/covert, implicit/explicit, and ideal/real which include considerations of the patterns *of* behavior that I have excluded from my view of culture. The traditional/operative distinction is based on a division within the patterns *for* behavior. I conceive of the traditional culture as patterns for behavior that are old, idealized, formal, venerated. Verbal support may be general, but many of them are followed out only when convenient or in certain situations. The operative culture usually consists of alternative patterns for behavior that are operative when the traditional culture can be circumvented. The nature of the division between the two can be specified only with reference to a particular society. The distinction is not between lip service and practice or between norm and mode, but between two designs for living. The two cultures coexist, and a cultural value system exists in each. In addition there may be one or more subcultures with their own value systems.

Four types of selection are shown in the enculturation processes (Figure 3). There is selection by the culture-bearer when, as a result of temperament, physique, particular experiences, or even the sequence of enculturation, the individual accepts certain items and rejects others. There is selection by enculturators when differences in roles and personalities of the enculturators result in varying emphases. There is selection by "groupings" in which the patterns transmitted depend on the age, sex, class, etc., of the enculturee. Finally there is selection by roles and specialties. The end result is the complexity of the internalized culture shown at the right side of the figure.

The foregoing rather lengthy discussion of matters that are usually taken for granted has been necessary because neglect of essential distinctions and details of processes has resulted in views of culture that tend to discredit value studies. If cultural values are viewed as abstractions, their place in human motivation and processes of culture change

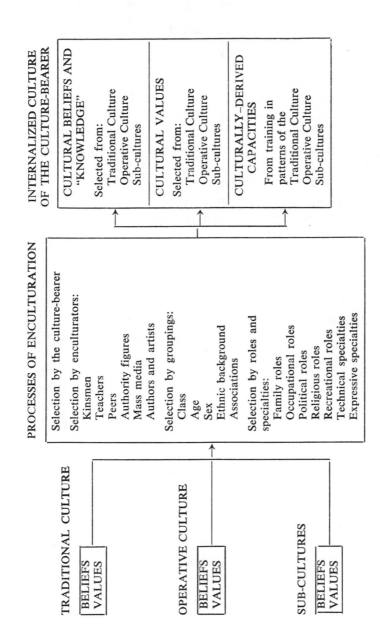

Figure 3. Enculturation

will be misunderstood. If they are viewed as elements of underlying cognitive structure, their importance becomes evident, but a full analysis of the cultural processes we have reviewed is required to assess their content and functions.

7.   Before proceeding with the consideration of cultural values, we must work out descriptions for the taxa that constitute pan-human standards and primate needs. How may they be described, and what are the observations on which descriptions can be based? These questions must be answered now because cultural values are to be typed, as will be shown in the next section, on the basis of their relationships to the pan-human standards and the primate needs.

As we have seen, the pan-human standards are assumed to have their genesis in symbolizations of infant experiences that have brought satisfaction of genetically transmitted needs. These experiences vary in degree, but not in kind, from one society to another. Erik Erikson and Charlotte Buhler are prominent among those psychologists who consider that the experience of a feeling of "trust" is of fundamental importance. Buhler refers to "that 'trust' with which the infant, almost immediately after it is born, opens its mouth and itself to the world" (1962: 158–159), and Erikson refers to "a sense of basic trust, which is a pervasive attitude toward oneself and the world derived from the experiences of the first year of life" (1968: 96). Buhler emphasizes that trust is revealed in the behavior of all normal infants. Although Erikson is concerned with the development of trustfulness by the reward of trust that prevents it from converting into a feeling of "basic mistrust," some measure of the reward of trust is essential to the survival of the infant, and the mistrust that is experienced is felt as a threat to self-preservation. In addition to trust, conative and exploratory activities on the part of the infant are required for the satisfaction of its needs. All infants that survive will have experienced them.

The essential experiences can be described as trusting (in a mutually open relationship), willing (forming intentions), and exploring or searching (motor activity and sensing). When these experiences of activities and relationships take on affect and symbolic significance, further experiences of the same sort will be sought. Such additional experiences will reinforce the affect and symbolic significance of the elements of underlying cognitive structure, and their meanings will become more generalized, covering the variations in successively wider experiences. The trusting will extend to trusting in other people, to trusting in the physical environment, and to trusting in oneself. The willing or conation will extend toward the taking over of direction of wider areas of one's life and of the consequent decision making. The exploring and searching will extend to use of the full range of one's talents and abilities.[3]

At the universal level the standards can be briefly described as: (1) trust in others, (2) trust in environment, (3) trust in self, (4) use of talents and abilities, and (5) self-direction. Observation of the mothering of infants in a society will give an indication of the degree of early reinforcement of the pan-human standards, and thus an indication of the strength and breadth to which they will develop, but, regardless of the cross-cultural variation in mothering practices, the standards will be formed and will develop to some degree.

The primate needs, in man, take on symbolic significance through symbolization of experiences of actual satisfaction of the genetically transmitted needs. On the symbolic level the needs are part of the value system, however manifestations of the genetically transmitted needs are observable in the behavior of the other primates, particularly the anthropoid apes. Ethological studies are available to provide descriptive material. How they are to be grouped is not critical, but the following designations are useful: (1) physiological requirements, (2) safety–security, (3) affection–belongingness, (4) activity–competence, (5) recognition–esteem.

It must be recognized that the words or phrases that I have used to describe or label the subclasses of the pan-human standards and the primate needs are not the values themselves. The values are the taxa so designated. Words are used to describe the taxa, but understanding their content derives from observations of behavior and analyses of processes of development — not from analyses of the semantics of the descriptions.

In order to avoid undue reliance on verbal labels, and for convenience in tabulations (which will be made in the comparisons with cultural values), I shall use the following letter or letter-number indicators for the subclasses of pan-human values: PHS-A (trust in others), PHS-B (trust in environment), PHS-C (trust in self), PHS-D (use of talents and abilities), PHS-E (self-direction), PN-1 (physiological requirements), PN-2 (safety–security), PN-3 (affection–belongingness), PN-4 (activity–competence), PN-5 (recognition–esteem).

8.   We are now ready to complete our classification of cultural values.

---

[3] The assumptions related to the symbolization of essential infant experiences and the generalizing of their symbolic significance as a result of further experience are considered to be warranted by virtue of their adaptive nature. Seeking satisfactions in a successively wider range of experiences leads to the finding of new sources of support for survival.

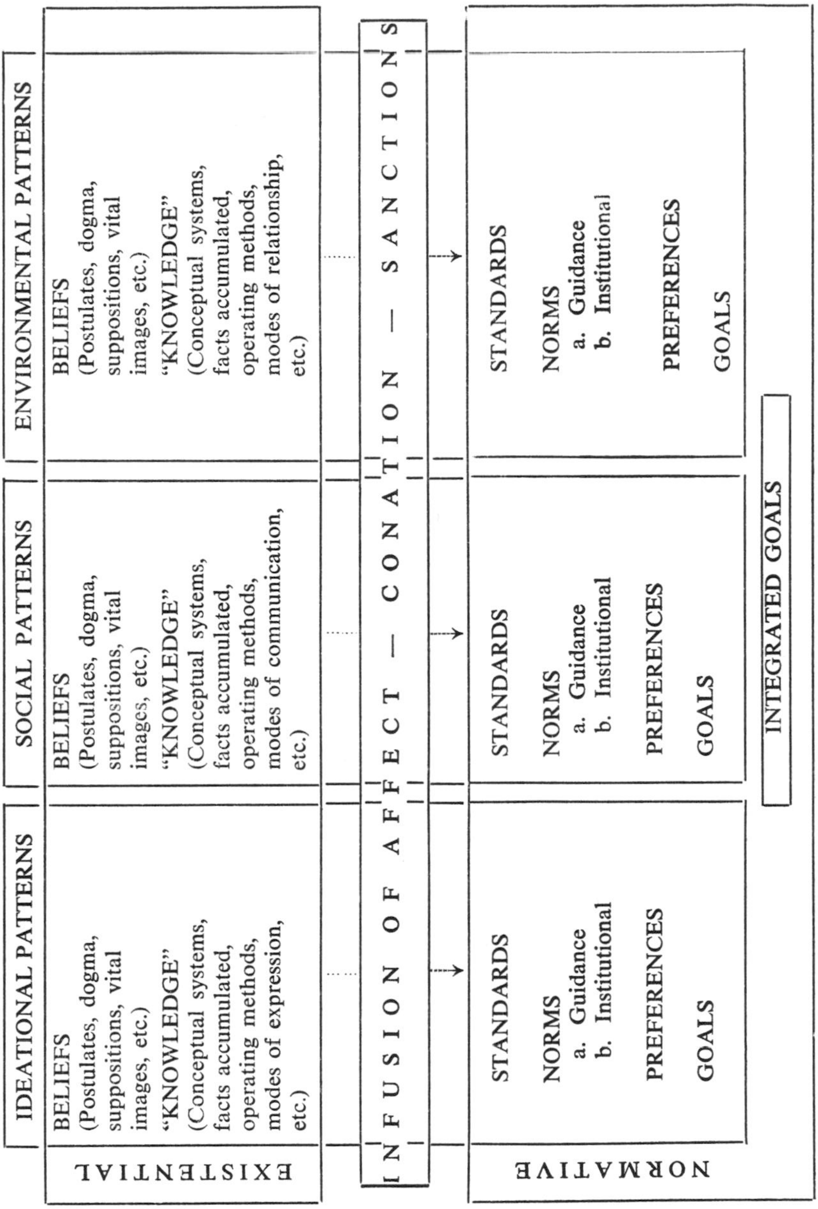

Figure 4. A terminology for cultural "patterns for behavior"

The first step will be to divide the culture as a whole into three sets of patterns for behavior as shown in Figure 4. The terms "ideational," "social," and "environmental" indicate the nature of the problems or the objectives toward which each of the sets of patterns is directed. Ideational patterns (patterns for ideation) are for dealing with ideas or abstractions; social patterns are for dealing with other people or with social organizations; environmental patterns are for dealing with the natural or artifactual environment. There have been a number of other threefold divisions of culture proposed (see summaries in Kroeber 1952: 154–157, and in Kroeber and Kluckhohn 1952: 98), but all of them either concentrate values in one sector of culture or omit areas that are of significance to values — such as nonexploitative relationships to the natural environment. In Figure 4 the three sectors, or sets of patterns, are arranged in vertical columns with the existential/normative division cutting across them horizontally. Values are given equal prominence in each sector. We now have twelve divisions of cultural values formed by the tripartite division of the standards, norms, preferences, and goals. We have arrived at the taxonomic level of subclasses.

Further subdivision will be necessary to lower the level of abstraction to that of useful descriptions. First we will drop the preferences from consideration. They have been defined as lightly held or optional and their extent may be almost limitless. Now we will use the ten subclasses of pan-human values, set forth in the foregoing section, as a cross-culturally valid basis for defining taxa of cultural values below the level of subclasses. These taxa are at the taxonomic level of types. The subclasses of cultural values are to be divided into types by arranging their component patterns for behavior in accordance with their relevance to the subclasses of pan-human values. Such an arrangement is shown in Figure 5 in which 120 types are provided for by dividing the standards [S], norms [Ng and Ni], and goals [G] in each sector of cultural patterns — ideational [I], social [S], and environmental [E] — into 10 types (20 in the case of norms) in accordance with their relevance to the subclasses of pan-human values listed in the left-hand column. A letter and number designator for each type indicates the sector (I, S, or E), the class (S, Ni, Ng, or G), and the last character of the comparable pan-human value designator (1 to 5; A to E). Separate designators are assigned to norms that provide guidance for conduct [Ng] and those that are primarily oriented toward the maintenance of institutions [Ni]. This is done to facilitate description and in recognition of the importance of institutional support for values. A description of

Sectors of Culture	IDEATIONAL PATTERNS — *STANDARDS*	IDEATIONAL — *NORMS* Institutional	IDEATIONAL — *NORMS* Guidance	IDEATIONAL — *GOALS*	SOCIAL PATTERNS — *STANDARDS*	SOCIAL — *NORMS* Institutional	SOCIAL — *NORMS* Guidance	SOCIAL — *GOALS*	ENVIRONMENTAL PATTERNS — *STANDARDS*	ENVIRONMENTAL — *NORMS* Institutional	ENVIRONMENTAL — *NORMS* Guidance	ENVIRONMENTAL — *GOALS*
Pan-human culture Subclass PN-1	Type I-S-1	Type I-Ni-1	Type I-Ng-1	Type I-G-1	Type S-S-1	Type S-Ni-1	Type S-Ng-1	Type S-G-1	Type E-S-1	Type E-Ni-1	Type E-Ng-1	Type E-G-1
,, ,, PN-2	Type I-S-2	Type I-Ni-2	Type I-Ng-2	Type I-G-2	Type S-S-2	Type S-Ni-2	Type S-Ng-2	Type S-G-2	Type E-S-2	Type E-Ni-2	Type E-Ng-2	Type E-G-2
,, ,, PN-3	Type I-S-3	Type I-Ni-3	Type I-Ng-3	Type I-G-3	Type S-S-3	Type S-Ni-3	Type S-Ng-3	Type S-G-3	Type E-S-3	Type E-Ni-3	Type E-Ng-3	Type E-G-3
,, ,, PN-4	Type I-S-4	Type I-Ni-4	Type I-Ng-4	Type I-G-4	Type S-S-4	Type S-Ni-4	Type S-Ng-4	Type S-G-4	Type E-S-4	Type E-Ni-4	Type E-Ng-4	Type E-G-4
,, ,, PN-5	Type I-S-5	Type I-Ni-5	Type I-Ng-5	Type I-G-5	Type S-S-5	Type S-Ni-5	Type S-Ng-5	Type S-G-5	Type E-S-5	Type E-Ni-5	Type E-Ng-5	Type E-G-5
,, ,, PHS-A	Type I-S-A	Type I-Ni-A	Type I-Ng-A	Type I-G-A	Type S-S-A	Type S-Ni-A	Type S-Ng-A	Type S-G-A	Type E-S-A	Type E-Ni-A	Type E-Ng-A	Type E-G-A
,, ,, PHS-B	Type I-S-B	Type I-Ni-B	Type I-Ng-B	Type I-G-B	Type S-S-B	Type S-Ni-B	Type S-Ng-B	Type S-G-B	Type E-S-B	Type E-Ni-B	Type E-Ng-B	Type E-G-B
,, ,, PHS-C	Type I-S-C	Type I-Ni-C	Type I-Ng-C	Type I-G-C	Type S-S-C	Type S-Ni-C	Type S-Ng-C	Type S-G-C	Type E-S-C	Type E-Ni-C	Type E-Ng-C	Type E-G-C
,, ,, PHS-D	Type I-S-D	Type I-Ni-D	Type I-Ng-D	Type I-G-D	Type S-S-D	Type S-Ni-D	Type S-Ng-D	Type S-G-D	Type E-S-D	Type E-Ni-D	Type E-Ng-D	Type E-G-D
,, ,, PHS-E	Type I-S-E	Type I-Ni-E	Type I-Ng-E	Type I-G-E	Type S-S-E	Type S-Ni-E	Type S-Ng-E	Type S-G-E	Type E-S-E	Type E-Ni-E	Type E-Ng-E	Type E-G-E

Figure 5.   Frame for the classification of cultural values

a cultural value system would consist of a description of the normative patterns for behavior that make up each of the 120 types. They can then be compared with the subclasses of pan-human values in order to assess their effect on individual values and on behavior.

Now that we have reached the level of description we are faced with the problems of etics and emics. I think that we are justified in passing directly to an etic frame because of the purpose of the classification, and because we have the hypothesized pan-human values to provide a cross-cultural base. Our purpose is to see how cultural values, pan-human values, and individual values interact. To do so, we need an analysis of cultural values that shows their significant relationships to pan-human values (in the sense of fostering or frustrating them). Therefore the differences that are significant in this classification are not the distinctions made by the culture-bearers but the differing relationships of cultural patterns for behavior to pan-human values.

In the domain of values, unconscious processes play a large part, the lexicon is more limited than it appears to be, and there are large unverbalizable areas. Furthermore, some of the distinctions that are important to members of the society are due to elaborations in a particular area of culture — elaborations that are of little relevance to pan-human values. Even if a componential analysis could uncover all the primitive elements of a cultural value system, we would have to group them differently than the culture-bearers group them. We want to know how they impinge on pan-human values, not how they are grouped in the calculus of the culture.[4]

The linguist can describe the sounds of a language he does not know by using the symbols of a phonetic chart. The botanist describes and groups plants regardless of their local names or uses. He employs a taxonomy unrelated to the semantic domain of plants in the language of the people who use them. The ethnographer who is following our system finds in Figure 5, along with the definitions and analyses on which it is based, a frame for classifying and describing types of cultural values in accordance with his interests. The taxa are made up of

---

[4] As will be pointed out later, the relationships that cause conflicts of interest to us are not to be found in emic categories or in their interaction. We are interested in conflicts that are seen most clearly when the emic categories are disregarded. Furthermore, we do not find the kind of etic frame we need by "passing through" the emic categories. The type of "etic kit of possibilities" that is developed by doing so, and the kind of general theories to account for variance among cultures that Goodenough speaks of (1970: 110) are for application to subject matters that are cultural. In such applications the objective is to see each subject matter in the terms of the culture. In contrast, we wish to explore conflicts for which the culture has no terms.

components of the affective patterns for behavior that he sees being taught, has explained to him, or constructs from his analyses of motivations of behavior. For example, in any society the great variety of acts that are prescribed through instruction, example, or sanctions are grouped as patterns for behavior, and some of these are verbalized as values. The ethnographer is concerned, not with the patterns or the labels, but with the component acts themselves. These he classifies in accordance with the 120 types of Figure 5. He does not label them but describes them with at least a paragraph for each type.

The number of descriptions required may seem excessive, especially when it is remembered that a full set will be required for the traditional culture and another for the operative culture. However, the normative system of a culture, even within the limits that we have imposed, cannot be described adequately at the level of abstraction at which ethnographers are wont to present "the cultural value system." As Kluckhohn said of a differently based, but methodologically similar, descriptive system, "the next step is to organize data and write an ethnography within the framework of the invariant points of reference. The first serious trial will not be easy, but it should be rewarding" (1953: 522).

9.   Our taxonomic classification system for values is now complete. Starting with the three categories, we have moved to the successive subordinate levels of major classes, classes, subclasses, and, in the case of cultural values, to types. The resulting classifications are shown in Figure 6. At the level of the subclasses we begin to make contact with descriptive data, and here the diagram makes use of the levels of discourse that were set forth in Section 3. The subclasses of the pan-human values were described in Section 7 at the universal level of discourse. That level is considered to be the *base level* for describing pan-human values. This is indicated in the diagram by the use of a double frame to enclose the ten subclasses. The base level for describing cultural values is the group level of discourse. The base level for describing individual values is the idiosyncratic level of discourse. The base levels are those from which descriptions in the same category, but at other levels of discourse, are derived.

The levels of classification and of discourse shown in Figure 6 should also be viewed as levels of abstraction. Values are elements of underlying cognitive structure, and it is these that compose the taxa and are being classified. The idiosyncratic level is the lowest level of abstraction at which we can attach verbal descriptions to taxa whose nature we infer by methods appropriate to the category. Even at that level we arrange our descriptions of cultural values in accordance with the 120

Categories	INDIVIDUAL VALUES		CULTURAL VALUES	PAN-HUMAN VALUES	
Major classes	EGO VALUES	NEUROTIC NEEDS	CULTURAL VALUES	PAN-HUMAN STANDARDS	PRIMATE NEEDS
Classes	EGO STANDARDS EGO NORMS EGO PREFERENCES EGO GOALS	NEUROTIC NEEDS	CULTURAL STANDARDS CULTURAL NORMS CULTURAL PREFERENCES CULTURAL GOALS	PAN-HUMAN STANDARDS	PRIMATE NEEDS
Subclasses and descriptions at *universal level* of discourse	Nature of EGO STANDARDS EGO NORMS EGO PREFERENCES EGO GOALS	Nature of OBSESSIONS COMPULSIONS DEFENSES ETC.	The nature of each class (above) within the IDEATIONAL PATTERNS SOCIAL PATTERNS ENVIRONMENTAL PATTERNS (forming 12 subclasses)	PHS-A PHS-B PHS-C PHS-D PHS-E PN-1 PN-2 PN-3 PN-4 PN-5 (The 10 subclasses described)	
Descriptions at *group level* of discourse	Modal EGO STANDARDS EGO NORMS EGO PREFERENCES EGO GOALS	Modal OBSESSIONS COMPULSIONS DEFENSES ETC.	Description of each of the 120 TYPES (Fig. 5) of values of a culture	The modal profile of pan-human values developed in a group	
Descriptions at *idiosyncratic level* of discourse	Descriptions of the ego values and neurotic needs of a particular person		Description of the cultural values internalized by a particular person	The profile of pan-human values developed in a particular person	

Figure 6. The classification and description of values

types of the group level of discourse, since that is the base level for description of cultural values. Similarly, the pan-human values are described at the idiosyncratic level with reference to the ten subclasses of their base level. Descriptions at the group level and at the universal level are at higher levels of abstraction. The diagram indicates the type of description at each level of discourse.

In constructing the classification system we started at the level of the categories and worked downward. If we had been classifying objects such as plants we would have started at the level of particular plants and moved to higher levels of abstraction. This is not possible in the case of values — the units of the taxa are not observable — so the classes must be constructed in accordance with the hypothesized system of relationships that we seek to investigate. Once the system is set up, however, the descriptions and designations within it are considered as abstractions from lower levels. In this system the primary divisions of the *summum genus* "values" are not concepts such as "honesty," "justice," or "freedom," but are taxa designated by the category names "individual values," "cultural values," and "pan-human values."

The interrelationships of the three categories are our special concern because therein are found neglected sources of conflicts pertinent to the understanding of intragroup conflicts and culture change. At the universal level of discourse the potential conflicts between pan-human and cultural values can be considered by comparing their subclasses shown in adjacent boxes in Figure 6. Then we can investigate the nature of the ego values and neurotic needs that might result, using the hypothesized interactions discussed in Section 4. At this level we get a general view of the potential problems. At the group level the interrelations would be between the cultural values of the society, the modal profile of pan-human values as they developed in that society (the "profile" refers to the relative strengths of the subclasses), and the modal individual values (a part of the modal personality). Here we would get a society-wide view of the conflicts. At the idiosyncratic level one person's profile of pan-human values, his internalized cultural values, and his individual values are in interaction. Here we find the sources of the conflicts as they affect our informants.

Particular note should be taken of the part that individual values play at the group level. They mediate the interaction of cultural and pan-human values and directly influence behavior as well. As a result, behavior may change in ways that neither the pan-human nor the cultural values can account for. The interactions are as shown in Figure 1 and include those discussed in the last paragraph of Section 4. The effect on the behavior observed in the society and on the formation of consensus is outlined in Figure 2. The modal ego values and neurotic needs that are developed in a society eventually contribute to change in cultural values, and are thus partly absorbed by them, but synchronically they are distinct. They may override the cultural values at times and provide unexpected sources of conflict. The action of the pan-human standards should also be noted. They may seem to be a negligible factor since direct manifestations in behavior are rare. This is so because the power of the cultural values and the action of the ego values and neurotic needs combine to submerge them. But, submerged or not, the pan-human standards are involved in internal conflicts, and sometimes are the governing influence on behavior.

The symbolic factors in pan-human, cultural, and individual motivation can be related to one another and to behavior, both synchronically and diachronically, and at all levels of discourse, by means of values.

10.   The outline of a theory of values and their interactions that has been presented bears directly on problems of culture change, and culture change in its many aspects — micro and macro, voluntary and directed, planned and opportunistic — bears on most of the problems of anthropology. The traditional view of the part played by values in culture change has been rather limited. Felix Keesing wrote, "It has been said metaphorically that the values of a culture, particularly the 'basic' values, act as 'watchdogs' or 'censors' permitting or inhibiting entry and exit of cultural elements. Values, in other words, have a screening effect on stability and change" (1958: 400). The dynamic aspects of value conflicts as sources of change have been slighted, and values other than cultural values have largely been ignored. A purely cultural calculus may explain customs, but explanation of change in customs requires a wider calculus that "transcends" culture. That is, one that includes the psychological capacities that provide the potentialities for culture change as Hallowell has explained them (1960: 361). It is the prediction of culture change rather than of behavior that is characteristically the anthropological problem.[5]

---

[5] Cultural determinists contend that culture change is to be explained without reference to individuals. My view follows that of Morris Opler: "This idea, that man manipulates and uses his culture for his own ends quite as much as he is subject to it, the cultural determinist resists and ignores. And because he does so, much of the richest data of anthropology passes by him, unrecognized and unappreciated" (1964: 525). Hallowell specifically points to the psychological basis for culture change: "The psychological basis of culture lies not only in a capacity for highly complex forms of learning but in a capacity for transcending what is learned; a potentiality of innovation, creativity, reorganization, and change" (1960: 361).

Pan-human values set up requirements that each culture must fulfill in some measure. All cultures fall short of complete fulfillment. Cultures develop values that tend to frustrate the pan-human requirements and conflicts are produced. As men strive to cope with the resulting shortcomings and frustrations, ego values and neurotic needs are produced that may lead to behavior that intensifies conflict, and this behavior may, through the formation of consensus, lead to the development of cultural values that further aggravate the frustrations. Only with full understanding of the part played by values can one work out measures to break the vicious circle.

When working at the level of the five major classes of values, it is obvious that the synchronic and diachronic interrelationships are complex and introduce many variables. In my view, these five major classes of values act as if they were five "grammars" simultaneously at work in determining behavior. Such complexity precludes a behavioristic analysis and requires the positing of hidden underlying mechanisms. Theories that include such constructs are useful if they account for a wider range of behavior than do those now in use. The models that I have presented are designed with this idea in view and they appear to have heuristic value. They can generate or suggest hypotheses that have a place in a meaningful whole and can guide empirically based studies. The studies needed include studies of infancy to determine the degree to which pan-human standards are fostered; ethological studies of the anthropoid apes to refine concepts of the primate needs; extensive enculturation studies to apprehend cultural values at their source; psychological studies of ego autonomy, ego strength, and neurotic needs; and studies of symbolization to clarify the processes of symbol formation.[6]

In these studies, research that is less than elegant may have to be accepted. Elegant research is desirable, but those who are doing it now cannot assure us that their detailed studies can ever be combined into a significant whole. René Dubos has given us a microbiologist's view of this problem: "There is a more honorable, though fallacious, reason for the reluctance of the scientific establishment to initiate, encourage, or support the study of the complex problems of human life. It is the strange assumption that knowledge of complex systems will inevitably

6   Studies of symbolization usually concentrate on conventional symbols or on those whose meanings derive from historical associations. These are important in the study of culture, but symbolization in the sense used in this paper — recognition of meaning in relation to a scheme of life — is also a requirement for cultural development. Some in-depth studies of symbolization in psychology are useful but studies that are more broadly based are needed.

emerge from studies of much simpler ones" (1968: 216).

In setting forth my views on values, many assumptions have been required. It is not my purpose to defend these as the best that can be worked out, but rather to insist upon the need for an integrated set of concepts and assumptions that covers the possibilities envisaged here and that has explanatory and heuristic usefulness. We must be willing to investigate unconventional views whenever they hold promise of shedding new light on problems of man and culture.[7] As Sol Tax wrote in concluding his article "The integration of anthropology," "an essential value in the case of anthropology is its historic reaching for new ideas, tools, and subject matters that may further the study of man" (1956: 326).

11.   Culture is man's great creation. It has largely freed him from the bonds of instinctual behavior. But cultural development has been mostly a process of trial and error. Opportunistic solutions have been perpetuated; the values attached to even the best solutions have often outlived their usefulness. These cultural values have become new bonds, and attempts to break free of them have caused dire conflicts. The conflicts themselves have become roots of culture change, and often this has been change toward values of intolerance, dominance, and violence.

Anthropologists are involved in culture change, and not just in the study of it. This has been obvious in applied anthropology, but the inevitability of political implications in almost any kind of fieldwork is now recognized. Our involvement is reflected in the call for a "profound critique," not only of the cultures we are studying, but of the culture we are representing. Cultural relativism has served its purpose by exposing the stumbling block of ethnocentrism; now it should give way to a search for a scientific basis for a profound critique of all cultures. Value studies can provide such a basis, but they should be aimed at cross-cultural comparability and be based on an holistic view of pan-human requirements and capabilities — not just those of "social man," or "economic man," or "man the primate."

A holistic view of human requirements and capabilities implies a model of man. An analysis of values as sources of human motivation and culture change is an essential part of such a model, but many different models should be formulated, and hypotheses derived from

---

[7]   Insistence on a concept of culture that views it as man's only guide is one way of shutting off inquiry. An example is the statement by Geertz: "Without the guiding patterns of human culture, man's intellectual life would be ... buzzing, booming confusion ... Without the guidance of the public images of sentiment found in ritual, myth, and art we would, quite literally, not know how to feel" (1964: 47).

them should be tested. We are already confronted with a number of models that, in view of the violence and destructiveness all about us, have been developed to tell us that such is the nature of man. An alternative is to hypothesize that violence and destructiveness occur because the nature of man is being violated by the cultures he internalizes — by cultural values that cause unacceptable internal conflicts.[8] We are being unscientific if we do not investigate both alternatives. We are being shortsighted if we do not realize that, as Leon Eisenberg pointed out in a recent issue of *Science*, "the behavior of men is not independent of the theories of human behavior that men adopt" (1972: 123).

REFERENCES

ALBERT, ETHEL M.
    1968   "Value system," in *International encyclopedia of the social sciences*, volume sixteen, 287–291. New York: Macmillan.
ALLPORT, GORDON W.
    1960   *Personality and social encounter: selected essays*. Boston: Beacon.
BLAKE, JUDITH, KINGSLEY DAVIS
    1964   "Norms, values, and sanctions," in *Handbook of modern sociology*. Edited by Robert Faris. Chicago: Rand McNally. (Reprinted, abridged, in Manners and Kaplan, 1968: 465–472.)
BROWN, ROGER
    1964   "Discussion of the conference," in *Transcultural studies in cognition*. Edited by A. Kimball Romney and Roy Goodwin d'Andrade, 243–253.
BUHLER, CHARLOTTE
    1962   *Values in psychotherapy*. New York: Free Press.
DUBOS, RENÉ
    1968   *So human an animal*. New York: Scribner's.

8   An hypothesis such as this requires a view of the nature of man that admits a "human nature" that is more than "primate nature" and is sufficiently independent of the culture in which it develops to provide a point of reference for evaluation of that culture. Redfield pointed out that the phrase "human nature" has been used in recent psychological and anthropological literature to mean at least three different things. One of those things is that which all men inevitably have as human beings regardless of their particular biological or social heritage (1962: 443-444). This usage is applicable to our hypothesis. The hypothesis also requires a view of culture that admits that it can develop in ways that are contrary to some of the needs of man. This is not necessarily in conflict with the view of culture as "adaptive." Cultures can be viewed as adaptive in the sense of providing for man's physiological needs in a given environment, and yet be in conflict with many of the other human requirements that make up human nature.

EISENBERG, LEON
1972   The *human* nature of *human* nature. *Science* 176:123–128.
ERIKSON, ERIK H.
1968   *Identity: youth and crisis.* New York: Norton.
FIRTH, RAYMOND
1953   The study of values by social anthropologists. *Man* 53:146–153.
1964   *Essays on social organization and values.* London School of Economics, Monographs on Social Anthropology 28. London: Athlone.
GEERTZ, CLIFFORD
1964   "The transition to humanity," in *Horizons of anthropology.* Edited by Sol Tax, 37–48. Chicago: Aldine.
GOODENOUGH, WARD H.
1970   *Description and comparison in cultural anthropology.* Chicago: Aldine.
GRAVES, THEODORE D.
1967   Review of E. Z. Vogt and E. M. Albert, *People of Rimrock.* *American Anthropologist* 69:751–752.
HALLOWELL, A. IRVING
1960   "Self, society, and culture in phylogenetic perspective," in *Evolution after Darwin,* volume two: *The evolution of man.* Edited by Sol Tax, 309–371. Chicago: University of Chicago Press.
HANDY, ROLLO
1969   *Value theory and the behavioral sciences.* Springfield, Illinois: Thomas.
HUTCHEON, PAT DUFFY
1972   Value theory: towards conceptual clarification. *The British Journal of Sociology* 23:172–187.
KEESING, FELIX M.
1958   *Cultural anthropology: the science of custom.* New York: Rinehart.
KLUCKHOHN, CLYDE
1953   "Universal categories of culture," in *Anthropology today.* Edited by A. L. Kroeber, 507–523. Chicago: University of Chicago Press.
1958   The scientific study of values and contemporary civilization. *Proceedings of the American Philosophical Society* 102:469–476.
KLUCKHOHN, CLYDE, *et al.*
1951   "Values and value-orientations in the theory of action: an exploration in definition and classification," in *Toward a general theory of action.* Edited by Talcott Parsons and Edward A. Shils, 388–433. Cambridge: Harvard University Press.
KOLB, WILLIAM L.
1961   "Values, determinism and abstraction," in *Values in America.* Edited by Donald N. Barrett, 47–54. Notre Dame, Indiana: University of Notre Dame Press.
KROEBER, A. L.
1952   *The nature of culture.* Chicago: University of Chicago Press.
1953   "Concluding review," in *An appraisal of* Anthropology today. Edited by Sol Tax et al., 357–376. Chicago: University of Chicago Press.

1956   "History of anthropological thought," in *Current anthropology: a supplement to* Anthropology today. Edited by William L. Thomas, Jr., 293–311. Chicago: University of Chicago Press.

KROEBER, A. L., CLYDE KLUCKHOHN
1952   *Culture: a critical review of concepts and definitions.* Papers of the Peabody Museum of American Archaeology and Ethnology, Harvard University 47–1.

MANNERS, ROBERT A., DAVID KAPLAN, *editors*
1968   *Theory in anthropology: a sourcebook.* Chicago: Aldine.

OPLER, MORRIS E.
1964   The human being in culture theory. *American Anthropologist* 66: 507–528.

REDFIELD, ROBERT
1962   "The universally human and the culturally variable," in *The papers of Robert Redfield*, volume one: *Human nature and the study of society.* Edited by Margaret Park Redfield, 439–453. Chicago: University of Chicago Press.

TAX, SOL
1956   "The integration of anthropology," in *Current anthropology: a supplement to* Anthropology today. Edited by William L. Thomas, Jr., 313–328. Chicago: University of Chicago Press.

TAX, SOL, *et al., editors*
1953   *An appraisal of* Anthropology today. Chicago: University of Chicago Press.

VOGT, EVON Z., ETHEL M. ALBERT, *editors*
1966   *People of Rimrock: a study of values in five cultures.* Cambridge: Harvard University Press.

WALLACE, ANTHONY F. C.
1962   Culture and cognition. *Science* 135:351–357.

WILLIAMS, ROBIN M., JR.
1968   "The concept of values," in *International encyclopedia of the social sciences*, volume sixteen, 283–287. New York: Macmillan.

The Nature of Value and the Experience Entities

GEORGE G. HAYDU

Value is a word that has a great variety of content in it, a great many diverse referents. It is used constantly in anthropological literature (Parsons and Shils 1952). Not only is there wide divergence as to what referents are included, there is wide disagreement as to its importance. Depending on the persuasion of the scholar about the nature of cultural activities and transformations (one might say about sources of the existence and constitution of culture), values are either given a central place or a merely marginal role in the factual scheme of things.

A commonly used definition of value is that quality or condition or even object which is desirable (Kluckhohn, et al. 1953). Others define value as those qualities or objects that members of a culture designate as valuable (Rockeach 1968). Some speak of cultural values and individual values. When cultural and individual values are placed in one dimension for comparison or for the purpose of elucidating their relationships, then both varieties are taken to be of the same modality. Much confusion has resulted from these attempts.

Past thought has been keen in the analysis of values (Dewey 1929; Ortega y Gasset 1931; Perry 1926; Rickert 1934; Scheler 1921; Whitehead 1938). Scholars spoke of aesthetic values or ethical values or historical values. This constitutes the scholarship of axiology (Urban 1929). Historical research has been most often descriptive, certainly more so than some recent comparative studies on values of smaller and better-defined peoples (Vogt and Albert 1966). The study of the problem whether values were truly operative and really functioning structures convinced most students that value was something that must become desirable to people, desirable to individuals. People of a culture can easily say that a condition or quality or object has such and such value; they can even appraise it on a scale of valuations. Yet at the same time they will admit that such a condition or object is not desirable as far as they as individuals are concerned.

It appears that desirability must be an internal condition of the person in order to establish value for him. The individual must have some experience, some experiential event, that will create in him a functional locus for establishing the desirability of anything. We all need carbohydrates, proteins, and other alimentary substances, yet some of the most desirable foodstuffs like meat can produce intense dislike and revulsion in cultures where they have negative value. Obviously something happens in enculturation such that a very harmless and indeed nourishing substance can acquire a negative value. The desirability or undesirability of a thing is what makes value in the axiological-anthropological and functional sense, and not some calculation according to an abstract scale or a scale of easily establishable monetary worth. This latter we could call VALUATION. Often value and valuation are similar for objects. But valuation (an appraisal of worth) is not value in the axiological or anthropological sense.

These questions, unfortunately, are more than merely interesting to a theoretician. In our present world, these problems are highly practical. In some parts of our present world these are questions of life and death. By mere fiat or by a pamphlet of a chief of state, thoughts on what are the required value qualities and value objects are laid down for all to follow. Most people in such a culture acknowledge these required values in order to save their lives. In a strikingly similar manner, the Orwellian phraseology in our own culture makes short shrift of naïve attempts to establish by questionnaire (and similar statistically manipulatable but otherwise inadequate methods) what is desirable. We must see how qualities and conditions desired are actually pursued, how their pursuit (or avoidance) originates in enculturation, how they are nourished, and what happens when value pursuit is obstructed. When violation of value pursuit occurs, the consequences may be negligible, a mere shrug of the shoulder, a mere feeling that after all we are all erring human beings. Or they may arouse righteous indignation, a rage to suffer or inflict punishment, or to destroy someone else.

We have learned a good deal in the last decades about how qualities and conditions become desirable under experimental conditions (Pavlov 1940; Renner 1972; Skinner 1938). These trustworthy and controlled studies seem not to run counter to careful observations in man about the way things become desirable to him (Freud 1917). New knowledge on desire and fulfillment is bound to affect our conceptions of those processes that lead to value. In this paper, I will attempt to elucidate this and will try to illustrate it with an example or two chosen from the description of the Desana people. We have some descriptive outline of this culture from an encultured source with true "native" acquisition of its cultural values (Reichel-Dolmatoff 1971).

A huge array of things can become desirable to people: possessions, power, family, individual status, respect, good health, physical characteristics (like slenderness), general attitudes (like compassion), ideals of excellence, types of activity (like business success), creative potency, other-worldliness, and so on. But we must be careful not to take lip-service for fact. We know that many people "subscribe" to the so-called value of COMPASSION, and yet their behavior is one of cruelty. Truly, nothing can be called value unless it is an aspect of the behavior pattern of a person or a group of people. We must ascertain what kind of events make it stable or durable and what happens when it is violated by the self or others. The dynamic locus, the functional context where desirability becomes a living fact, must be observed before the nature of value can be understood or its expression and transmission be considered. The primary fact of aliveness (in the present, or having been so in the past) is the touchstone that enables us to differentiate value from a label or a symbol.

Drive objects, needs, motives, attitudes, and expectancies are all related to what makes things desirable. Every one of these constructs is a pattern of intention, having some goal-directedness. One aspect of these has been generally established: any present deed or goal-pursuit is the result of past outcomes of similar strivings. Experimental psychology, through modifications of the environment and events, shows conclusively that outcome, awareness of past success or failure, decisively affects the pursuit and desirability of an object or condition. So we have to look at the site where the event of a need-pursuit results in the establishment of a new desirability.

It was found by Penfield (1952) that individuals record events of their life activities most comprehensively. By administering a mild electric current in the temporal lobe, he could activate patterns of events that had all the facets and completeness of a total experience: interaction of people, feelings of interaction, sounds, speech, neighborhood noises, cars passing in the street, the subject's own state of awareness at the time, etc. When the current was discontinued this unitary recall stopped; when the current was renewed, this experience entity reappeared. Only one such entity could be aroused at a time. It seemed as if one's experiential life consisted of discrete entities. Yet many aspects of such an experience entity are separately grouped by the experiencing person.

Here we must say a few words about recent psychobiological knowledge on feature selection which underlies the phenomenon we call abstraction. Since the work of Hubel and Wiesel (1965), we have ample evidence that the central nervous system is so constructed that it is able to select features of a large experiential event and store them, move them, or combine them with others. Thus what in psychological literature is called concept formation, or the storing of affectively similar aspects, or the amassing of almost any aspect of the total event, is done by very flexible specific neural structures which can select (abstract) particular features. Concept formations, or the formation and later recall of particular affect aspects, or the discovery of particular pattern features, are not something unsubstantial and chimerical. They are as solidly real patterns of activity as any inborn need that is programmed prior to birth (Haydu 1972).

For the past dozen years we have tried to separate and study the experience entities of persons as they contrast with conceptual structures (Haydu 1961). We found that the conative, affectional, and configurational (form) aspects of productions correlate well as contrasted with the conceptual, discursive, logical aspects (Haydu 1962). This agreed with the findings of Penfield. Bindra (1969) offered data which led to similar conclusions in a very different setting. We think of experience as that contexture in which the individual's needs and desires meet and transact with available tools and instrumentalities of the environing world. An experience entity is a unitary portion of a person's experiential life, the smallest unit that contains simpler drives, their modifications in past experience, obstacles to be avoided, and many other influences and elements. It is nonconceptual and imageless, although it can be translated or conveyed (no matter how partially) through images or even concepts. It is somewhat akin to dream entities which can represent and condense many diverse ingredients and vectors into one powerful configuration (Durkheim 1965). The experience entity is not a vague emotional tone; it is more like an affect-integral that can be conveyed by body posture, by dance, by the words of a poet, or by dream image. If the psyche is that coordinating structure of a person through which he as an outcome of experience perceives and performs in his world, then the smallest unit that still has the essentials of a full psychological happening, the experience entity, could be called a PSYCHEME. The model of the psycheme is a need in search of fulfillment looking for its congenial "object" or "action" and receiving back in the process the awareness that the going is good or bad or any variety in between.

The psyche as defined above is a sequential, historical product. The common human needs are variously met right from birth onward, according to the ways of the particular culture: psychogenesis is enculturation. When the need for protection from cold is fulfilled by swaddling, then we have a very different experiential development of a basic human need than when the same kind of need is fulfilled by an air-conditioned cubicle. And so in every aspect of life one continually gains an extension, a qualification, an enrichment of one's experiential system that was valid and regnant before. It is worth noting that we do not own these experiential structures; we are constituted by them.

Looking at the psyche (a coordinating system) and experience in this manner, a new reinforcing object (or love object) becomes so in the process of need fulfillment, in the contexture of experience. But we have learned that there are different ways in which an object becomes valuable. Punishment produces very different dynamics from persuasion or attraction. The former will produce a sharp DEFRACTION from the hitherto established goal. The latter will produce an easier DEFLECTION from it. This is not a negligible difference. In defraction, the new goal object is strongly contrasted to the old one: the old way is bad or horrible. In deflection, the old one is natural but inadequate, commonly human, even if incompetent. When one violates a defracted need, then the original punishing force will be reactivated; it will cause feelings of guilt and an urge to undergo suffering. When one violates a deflected need, then a feeling of shame or inadequacy may arise. When others violate a defracted need, then these persons appear to be alien and wicked, and must be hurt or destroyed. When others violate a deflected need, then they appear to be erring fellow creatures.

These somewhat exaggerated examples of the dynamics of drive modifications illustrate my point: the contexture of experience is the site where the value resides and not in the object itself. The original notions of Parsons (1965) which identify values with something cathected, internally energized in the psyche, is unexceptionable. But to identify this internal structure with the Freudian superego is not tenable. In some examples it may very well be true. But the Freudian superego is close to the concepts the person has of dangers in the environment which have to be minded. These do enter the contexture we call experience, just as objects, instrumentalities, knowledge, and all manner of external conditions are elements of this unitary entity. But what counts is the quality, texture, final tastes, and terms of the integrated configuration itself (Haydu 1972).

Let us note that experience entities are conative structures (Haydu

1962; Terry 1971). Whatever new desire-form should arise, it will become an executive force by changing older experience patterns that inform it as to past satisfactions, past obstacles to be avoided, proper ways, effective ways. That is why similarly charged or colored psychemes form a more or less common network or, as Schilder (1920) put it, a particular sphere. Many experiential particular events merge and color one another (Spitz 1965); similarly toned experience patterns stick together. So will the experience of a mothering, nurturing figure emerge in development, for example (Kernberg 1972). Often, as in the case of important persons with whom we have had most intimate and formative relationships (like one's mother), the similarly colored experience events concern the same person or objects. And so objects, conditions, and interpersonal relations acquire the quality of value. But we must realize that these objects are not the value itself. The value resides in the similarly colored system of experience entities. Objects are not value. They are not alive until they become the energized experience pattern of an individual's psyche. Yet this individual pattern of a person can be expressed (in fact if you believe Confucius, you cannot avoid expressing it although you do not profess it), can be conveyed, can be communicated. It is a form of communion.

Here we ought to realize that this is not a kind of electrochemical happening in the central nervous system exclusively. The central nervous system coordinates the tensions, the wants, the needs of the whole body. An experience entity has its individuality that unites not just so many hundred thousand neural cells in one individual action (Eccles 1958), but also unites and patterns the tensions, wants, and functions of the rest of the person. Each experience pattern is an individual quality of the whole person which can appear in his stance, in his voice, in his kinetic individuality. It can be expressed in paint or song or dance, if the expressive means and their mastery are available. That is why the so-called aesthetic expressive field is not something negligible, merely added to a culture or a way of life. The participants realize that it is an essential activity. And values, both in axiology and anthropology, are essentially related to aesthetic activity. In fact, it is safe to say that one who is untrained or insensitive to aesthetic activity is impotent in the study of these matters, just as a man without practical manual skill is unfit to do plastic surgery.

As outlined above, experience entities have conative functions. It must also be stated that they have their distinct individuality. Experience patterns can be grouped according to certain qualities and the typology of values is a very common and fruitful way of studying these matters (Allport 1961). Yet one can often go into this world of valuation and by choosing larger and fewer types of valuations one can develop a system of comparatively few general types. The danger in this sort of study is that one loses the basic individuality of value that constitutes its true final function, as it is the site of similarly constituted experiential patterns. This is not only a theoretical loss but it leaves out those quasi-compulsive activities which attend the modifications or transformations of particular value events. Typology often leads to the exclusion of the study of individuality. We now realize that even the most special individuality can be studied adequately (scientifically, if you please) as it appears in its various manifestations.

With all our care about functional individualities, the study of smaller cultures shows how common certain varieties of experiences are and how value as an internal configuration of the psyche is expressed in so many ways, in so many activities, and in so many objects of use and objects of art. Redundancy is the rule in the cultural world — which is another way of saying that the way of life of a people in its different aspects and different institutions and instrumentalities must make ample sense (Mead and Métroux 1953). Redundancy is the rule and comfort. It affirms the rightness of each culturally interrelated experiential event unless, of course, there should be severe contradictions at a particular time. The result of the latter is beyond our present topic, but it is quite evident that the signs and effects of disintegrative forces can also be seen redundantly, as we are regretfully learning in our present world.

The third aspect of viewing values as the system of similarly modulated experience entities is their tendency to form a tolerably integrated system with other values. The question of the integrated nature of values of a culture (Hoyt 1961) is not a matter of their logic, or some other way of stringing them together. The pressure for integration resides in the nature of value as part of a person's life. A person must have order in his needs and in their transaction, not merely for the sake of efficiency but also, for want of a better term, of sanity (Haydu 1958). This requirement for a large measure of order in the experiential self is the root of the integrated nature of values of a culture (Mannheim 1952).

It is the contention of the foregoing that only through seeing (even isolating in its various realizations) experience patterns can value be understood. This is one reason why reconstruction of value from practices and objects of a culture, although quite feasible, must elucidate how a live experience pattern was its fullest and proper source. This does not claim that new modes of production, climatic changes, new knowledge, new sources of energy, new discoveries, new dangers are not causes of culture change and thus cultural evolution. But before any such forces requiring change can become part of a way of life they must first become an integral part of the experiential patterns of lives lived and thus attain the status of true values. These are then exhibited, realized, transacted in the activities of the members, and in the transmission of the way of life as a continuum. Thus causes of change are not the final explanation or description of cultural transformations. Only the nature and quality, indeed the individuality, of the achieved experience patterns can do that. That is why value theory cannot be bypassed by cultural studies. There is also the reason why a culture, apart from the enumeration of its techniques, artifacts, particular practices, particular family and property arrangements, and so on, can be most appropriately described as a value structure — as long as this value structure is not a system of valuations, not a system of appraisals, but an integrated structure of experience patterns.

We can define culture as that system of skills, instrumentalities, and certainties through which a particular people at a particular time form and fulfill their wants (Haydu 1970). I think such a description is quite adequate and it can be put in even more operational terms. Yet to grasp the quality of life that culture grants (or requires), to grasp the movements of transformations (their adequacy or competence), one must see a particular culture as an integrated structure of experience patterns, as a structure of value patterns. The symbolic and factual ingredients of any culture are the necessary elements for the re-creation of something alive. These elements alone are truly nonliving "artifacts" essential for the cultivation and creation of the live configurations which can work with them and use them in their pragmatic functions. So value, once sequentially (historically) conceived, is the site where man's genetically programmed wants blossom out into culturally fostered, culturally sanctioned practices and desires. The genetic wants and cultural requirements are not opposed (usually), but find integration in the psychemes.

Cultural values are often spoken of as semiotic structures. To my mind these structures are the expressive means for the development of values, for value communion, for value transformations. Strictly speaking semiotic structures are not values. We must constantly check back in the study of cultures, or in the study of the historical past, and refer to the experience patterns which constituted live value — as we study professed or institutionalized semiotic patterns. Cultural values are those live values which are energized and which can be detected in a large number of people. It is quite natural that the professed and institutionalized semiotic structures should be close to them. To accept for value a direct subscription to this or that semiotic construct is a serious mistake. Such expressions of desire, for example, for love or charity or achievement of sorts, may contain the most dissimilar and contradictory live values. There was a time when one burned one's fellow creatures at the stake in order to exhibit one's concern for their salvation. Yesterday one scarcely considered such statements for their love-value or for their value of compassion. In today's world similar atrocities have been attempted for professions of similar values.

Man's environment of instrumentalities and semiotic structures embedded in his culture form the environment of which he will become an integral part. The semiotic instrumental elements can be conceived as expressive means of experience entities that can be communicated to others. They are expressive means of communion. They are work-doing pragmatic products. The culture's semiotic and instrumental forms of art, science, and religion are repositories of some form of knowledge, some form of understanding, some point of view achieved and communicated. When vitally fused with man's genetically programmed wants, they become a huge realm of enrichment, empowering and enhancing the biological organism. The mandatory experiential establishment of the human being confers upon him a huge extension of his biologically stable needs. This can be contrasted with all previous forms of biological life. In man alone practically all his preexperientially programmed wants must FIND THEIR DEFINITION through the interpersonal activities of his culture. We cannot even walk upright without the pattern being seen and encouraged by our fellow human beings. In fact, without speech and the special solicitude of his fellow beings — with all hygienic and alimentary requirements granted — the developing child suffers stunting, anaclitic depression, and death (Bowlby 1969).

Man cannot be conceived of as a human being without this huge extension and enrichment. If biology deals with structures as they develop mainly by genetic programming, then man's culture is suprabiological. But if we realize that cultural entities become alive (that is, functionally existent) only in individuals, then culture is just a means to extend biological nature into a new functional world. Culture conceived only as a semiotic realm is dead; it becomes alive when it is the formative and transactive means of the biological abilities of man. Through enculturation as experience, the basic human needs and abilities fashion their definition and become the particular values of the individual.

In the welter of daily activities of a people one discovers certain processes which seem to be sought after, which are prized. This is usually the starting point of studies which concern values. One can ask the people why they pursue a thing, why they prefer a thing or a condition, why they find it pleasing and desirable. One will get answers, usually stereotyped which are a cultural coding for the significance and desirability of a quality or a condition. To be satisfied with the explanations of the cultural coding will not grant insight in the nature of the value. A rational answer or description of use and meaning can serve the scholar only if it is congruent with the functional nature of the value for individuals in their daily existence and with the functional nature of value in the process of transmission and transformation.

The Desana people consider hunting activities very desirable. And yet they are a sedentary people whose food, at least 75 percent of it, comes from fishing and agriculture. Hunting is done by men. They say, "only a pregnant old woman eats fish," yet fish is a staple element in the diet of all. Meat and fish are never mixed. That is not only inconceivable but it produces revulsion and nausea. Meat is a male food and hunting is a male activity. It becomes apparent that hunting has a place that involves experience connected not so much with alimentary needs but with sexuality, but sexuality as developed by Desana experience. As conceived by them, sexuality is an aspect of fertility and life energy. To hunt is to "make love to the animals." The hunter tries to achieve sexual attractiveness by Desana norms: sexual abstinence, high level of excitation, cleanliness, a pleasing odor through aromatic herbs, etc. They speak of the sexual attractiveness of the animals, their perfume, the caresses between them. The deer and certain rodents "whistle" and incite the hunter sexually just as the sustained whistling sounds of the Desana flutes do. "To kill is to cohabit." The hunter expresses his regret for having killed "such a pretty beast." He feels he has diminished life energy. So the value patterns residing in hunting are of an entirely different order than the plain drive to satisfy hunger. We must find out what experience patterns are the final expression of sexual and related interpersonal needs. Without those elements (like continence, certain repressions, strong flirtatiousness, and many other ingredients) entering into the confines of individual experience patterns, the cultural valuation of hunting would be completely inadequate. It could not properly delineate its function, its perseverance, its resistence to transformations, its role, etc.

Or let us consider the aesthetic evaluation of yellow color by the Desana, the intense pleasure and satisfaction in viewing and touching things that are yellow. In the cosmogony of the Desana, the life energy that pervades the world and whose circulation impels and makes fruitful all living things originates with the sun. The "Creation" myth details how this happened and how it continues. But this codification cannot tell what the quality and final taste and term of yellow constitute in the life of the Desana. To us yellow might be bright and comforting. To the Desana it represents experience of strength and recovery from illness. It is connected with purposeful action-experience. It is like the jaguar roaring and procreating, like the gentleness of the *tinamou* (which is a yellow bird) or the active beauty of the hummingbird (also a yellow bird and the ancestral animal of the Desana). The *kumú* (a kind of illumined person who is not a shaman but an achiever of inner wisdom, a highly respected person of very desirable qualities) imparts his beneficial influence as he identifies himself with this yellow experience. He is the yellow beam (central beam of the house) and the yellow bench (a ceremonial resting place of stability and protection) who gives comfort and strength to others through his power and wisdom, through the luminous energy of his "penetrating glance." Without the use of all of the above elements of a Desana experience, the valuation of yellow makes very little functional or aesthetic sense. In fact, an alien value, no matter how easily it can be seen as some sort of overt pursuit, cannot be perceived or fathomed as an experiential configuration or even as a concept of an entity desired. One has to patiently re-create an alien value through a great many aspects and activities of an alien people and give resonance to it; but it is a re-creation that is bound to stay deficient.

A value pattern is seen, in its purest and most concentrated form, in a successful work of art. A poem, a prayer, or a painting is able to transmit a unified pattern, a seamless web (Burnshaw 1970). It must resonate with one's experiential system in order to be understood, in order to have its "content" grasped. This content is not a discursive or prescriptive statement although that may be part of it. It is an experiential state which in this instance is successfully communicated through the semiotic construction of the poem or song. It is a stance of the psyche which can actually be danced. No wonder that in many preliterate societies, and in the Desana too, the dance is a very important activity of communion. Those who cannot express the values of the culture in dance are considered considerably inferior to the rest.

A culture could be considered a net of value patterns. It is so only if the skills, instrumentalities, activities, and themes that we students discover can be used to re-create those structures which fuse them in order that members may become functioning beings in the process of enculturation. Over and above this process, the MAINTENANCE of one's potent experiential patterns, as expectancies of what is reasonable, natural, and just in one's life, requires a constant cultivation of these structures. To exercise and cultivate what keeps our experiential self-system harmonious, active, and serviceable is a vital activity. It is pragmatic; it is also in service of growth. Without going into that aspect, let me just indicate that new conditions, both internal and external, require for competence, and indeed for sanity, the transformation of a person's experiential system in the process of living (Haydu 1958). In order to stay tolerably at ease within one's internal and cultural ambiance, the value system suffers (or enjoys) constant transformations. This is the site where new ways of seeing and seeking arise and where new values come into being. Creativity, the creation of constructs in pigment, words, and bodily movement, has its locus at this juncture. But the bare maintenance of one's experiential self (this system of tolerably harmonious experiential structures through which the individual sees and seeks in his world) is a constant activity. It has its own needs, requires periodic use and confirmation, periodic exchange and communion with others. Religion (the "rebinding" in the original sense of the word) apart from theology or conceptual world views has its pragmatic work anchored here. For the basic aspect of religion is not a cosmology or a philosophy of gods and spirits, but those worshipful activities through which a people can bind and rebind their experiential system and remain tolerably harmonious within themselves and within their cultural world.

In the light of the foregoing, value seems to be the focal point where the individual's psyche meets with cultural opportunities and constraints, where old ways change into new ones, or where old ways are maintained stubbornly. This is the locus where desirable attitudes and expectancies dwell and are energized, and from which they are expressed and communicated. The view of value as an integrated structure of similarly toned experience entities is not denying the causative or impelling force of economic necessity or that of new knowledge, new opportunities, new dangers, new disharmonies, or new discoveries. All these are or can be elements of experience entities. The experience patterns preserve them in a sense-making structure and each ingredient is essential to THAT particular pattern. This is the reason why values cannot be easily exported or imported, or conjured up at will. Perhaps we ought to be thoroughly grateful that it should be so.

REFERENCES

ALLPORT, G. W.
  1961 *Pattern and growth in personality.* New York: Holt, Rinehart and Winston.
BINDRA, D.
  1969 A unified interpretation of emotion and motivation. *Annals of the New York Academy of Sciences* 159:1071–1083.

BOWLBY, J.
1969   *Attachment and loss*. New York: Basic Books.
BURNSHAW, S.
1970   *The seamless web*. New York: Braziller.
DEWEY, J.
1929   *Experience and nature*. New York: Norton.
DURKHEIM, E.
1965   *The elementary forms of the religious life*. Glencoe: Free Press.
ECCLES, J. C.
1958   The physiology of imagination. *Scientific American* 199:135–146.
FREUD, S.
1917   *Introductory lectures on psychoanalysis*. London: Allen and Unwin.
HAYDU, G. G.
1958   *The architecture of sanity*. New York: Julian Press.
1961   Event-experience patterns and conceptual structures: an experimental approach. *American Journal of Psychotherapy* 15:619–629.
1962   Schizophrenic behavior and aspects of psychopharmacology. *Annals of the New York Academy of Sciences* 96:160–169.
1970   Interrelated transformations of Rousseau's life and of Western culture of his time. *American Journal of Psychoanalysis* 30:161–168
1972   Cerebral organization and the integration of experience. *Annals of the New York Academy of Sciences* 193:217–231.
HOYT, E. E.
1961   Integration of culture: a review of concepts. *Current Anthropology* 2:407–426.
HUBEL, D. H., T. N. WIESEL
1965   Receptive fields and functional architecture in two non-striate visual areas of the cat. *Journal of Neurophysiology* 28:229–289.
KERNBERG, O. F.
1972   Early ego integration and object relations. *Annals of the New York Academy of Sciences* 193:233–247.
KLUCKHOHN, C., H. A. MURRAY, D. M. SCHNEIDER
1953   *Personality in nature, society and culture*. New York: A. A. Knopf. (Originally published 1948.)
MANNHEIM, K.
1952   *Essays in the sociology of knowledge*. New York: Oxford University Press.
MEAD, M., R. MÉTRAUX
1953   *The study of culture at a distance*. Chicago: University of Chicago Press.
ORTEGA Y GASSET, J.
1931   *The modern theme*. London: C. W. Daniel.
PARSONS, T.
1965   *Social structure and personality*. Glencoe: Free Press.
PARSONS, T., E. SHILS
1952   *Toward a general theory of action*. Cambridge: Harvard University Press.
PAVLOV, I. P.
1940   *Conditioned reflexes: an investigation of the physiological activity of the cerebral cortex*. London: Oxford University Press.

PENFIELD, W.
1952   Memory mechanisms. *Archives of Neurology and Psychiatry* 67:178–198.
PERRY, R. B.
1926   *The general theory of value*. New York: Longman, Green.
REICHEL-DOLMATOFF, G.
1971   *Amazonian cosmos*. Chicago: University of Chicago Press.
RENNER, K. E.
1972   Coherent self-direction and values. *Annals of the New York Academy of Sciences* 193:175–184.
RICKERT, H.
1934   *Grundprobleme der philosophischen Methodologie, Ontologie, und Anthropologie*. Tübingen: Mohr.
ROCKEACH, M.
1968   *Beliefs, attitudes and values*. San Francisco: Jossey-Bass.
SCHELER, M.
1921   *Der Formalismus in der Ethik und die materielle Wertethik*. Halle: Niemeyer.
SCHILDER, P.
1920   Über Gedankenentwicklung. *Zeitschrift für Neurologie und Psychiatrie* 59:250–263.
SKINNER, B. F.
1938   *The behavior of organisms*. New York: Appleton-Century.
SPITZ, R.
1965   *The first year of life*. New York: International Universities Press.
TERRY, R. L.
1971   Expectancy, confirmation and affectivity. *British Journal of Sociology and Clinical Psychology* 10:228–233.
URBAN, W. M.
1929   *The intelligible world*. New York: Macmillan.
VOGT, E., E. M. ALBERT, *editors*
1966   *People of Rimrock: a study of values in five cultures*. Cambridge: Harvard University Press.
WHITEHEAD, A. N.
1938   *Modes of thought*. New York: Free Press.

SECTION SEVEN

Discussion

Summary of Discussion

S. A. WURM

The central issue emerging from the totality of the discussions of language in anthropology, and in fact one of the major subjects to which much discussion was devoted, was the importance of studying language in its social and cultural setting and of recognizing the paramount role of sociolinguistic approaches in studying language in its function as a means of intercommunication, and also in studying the nature of language itself. Approaches widely regarded as valid, especially transformational-generative approaches, came under severe criticism. Their artificially restrictive approach of dissociating the subject matter which they study from the social and cultural background in which the subject matter functions was regarded as a severe drawback which made the value of their findings questionable. It was argued that the subject matter of linguistics has a real existence only in the social and cultural settings in which it appears, i.e. it can function only against the background of these settings. It was pointed out that approaches to the study of language which ignore these settings and backgrounds in the light of their orientation can only produce results of doubtful validity, or results which lack relevance. In other words, they may indicate WHAT is going on in language, but not HOW it relates to the world.

Other views put forward admitted that a distance exists between the transformational-generative approach and sociolinguistics (which was increasingly being hailed as THE linguistics), but it was suggested that the transformational-generative approach could be extended to include sociolinguistic factors in its system of description. This was countered by holders of the opposite view, who felt that the sociolinguistic approach involved the utilization of methods which basically belong to realms lying outside the field of linguistics.

In general, there was wide agreement that it was necessary to include in the study of language a fundamental tenet of sociolinguistics, namely, the study of variation and sociocultural setting, but there was disagreement as to the nature of the approach. The essence of the opposition was the view that (a) such an extension required the utilization of methods which came into linguistics from other disciplines, whereas (b) the adherents of the transformational-generativist school argued that it could be achieved from within linguistics through an application of linguistic methods to the study of social factors impinging on language.

In the subsession on "Language and Thought," the opening discussion was provided by four formal discussants, Professor Einar Haugen of Harvard University, Professor Harold W. Scheffler of Yale University, Professor John W. M. Verhaar, S. J., of the University of Indonesia, and Professor Oswald Werner of Northwestern University.

Haugen started his comments by saying that the themes represented by the papers in the session were too diverse to summarize briefly in a few minutes. He found that the study of tightly structured referential fields continued to be a popular one, citing the papers on kinship (Tanaka), color (Heinrich), time (Schveiger), and heavenly bodies (Dumont). Several papers were concerned with this establishment of semantic structure in terms of ethnoscience (Knight), ethnohermeneutics (Bellman), or ethnolinguistics (Yotsukura). Haugen regarded as major theoretical papers of considerable complexity those by Verhaar, which was concerned with speech and thought; by Welte, dealing with the definition of values; and by Gregersen, on linguistic models in anthropology. He said that he had some difficulty in accepting Verhaar's concept of "noumenization," which seemed to cover much the same ground as Roman Jakobson's concept of the metalingual function, treated in Winner's historical rather than critical survey of the aesthetic function as defined by the Prague Circle. Haugen said that he found it hard to believe that the "noumenization" should be absent from Indonesian, since the activity as described was largely one of learned men in English.

Haugen continued by saying that in glancing through the papers, he picked up a few thought-provoking expressions, e.g. Heinrich's characterization of his Eskimos as "splitters" and "lumpers" — Haugen felt that "analytic" and "synthetic" might be appropriate terms for this — and the claim by Gregersen that "cognitive anthropologists are merely glorified lexicographers." Since this was clearly intended as a put-down, Haugen said that he would like to ask in a pugnacious tone, "Well, what's wrong with being lexicographers?" One could just as well say, "Linguistic theorists are merely glorified grammarians," with negative associations for grammarians as dried-up pedants. Otherwise, Haugen said, he found Gregersen's paper a balanced, thoughtful assessment of the role of linguistic theory, without the hysterical demand for *a priori* theoretical models as the *sine qua non* of all linguistic research.

Haugen continued by saying that Ikegami's paper on "meaning" was particularly interesting to him because Ikegami came to the same conclusion that he [Haugen] had reached many years earlier in his essay on "Terms of direction in modern Icelandic," namely, that the meaning of a word was the feature that distinguished it from other words in given contexts: the criterion was opposition. However, Haugen added, when Ikegami concluded that the feature [mortal] was not part of the definition of *man* because there was no word in English whose conditions on use were exactly the same as those of *man* except that it had [immortal] where the word *man* had [mortal], he seemed to have overlooked the word *God*.

Haugen then turned to his own paper and said that in it he had discussed three possible aspects of linguistic relativity with a view to expressing the uneasiness which he had felt for many years towards the Sapir-Whorf hypothesis, because, like so many generalizations, it was merely a half-truth. In the first section, entitled "Pitfalls of Relativity," Haugen said, he had tried to point out some of the weaknesses of Whorf's arguments. He felt that basically, the thinking, as thinking, was the same with the Indians from whose languages Whorf quoted as with ourselves. The second point that he dealt with in his paper was the "cult of relativity," i.e. the question of why people went in for the notion of relativity with such eagerness. He concluded that the emphasis on the view that language forced thought into certain patterns was essentially due to a desire to promote certain languages. This led to a one-sided emphasis of the effect of language on thought, and to a neglect of the reverse. The third point in his paper, Haugen continued, was concerned with the "test of relativity"; here he suggested that one might look to bilinguals and their own accounts of their feelings regarding their shifting from one language to another to try to solve the problem of the world views that were inherent in different languages. Haugen felt that so far the evidence on this point was relatively negative. Bilinguals obviously had to shift their personalities to some extent when switching from one language to the other, but this was not necessarily a shift of true cognition or deeper patterns of thinking. In thinking about language and thought, language might very well be defined as "linguistic formulation," i.e. the process of turning thought into linear sequences, and this was the result of mental processes of grouping and distinguishing (i.e. analysis and synthesis) for purposes of interpersonal communication of information. The formulation was based on shared phonological, grammatical, and semantic patterns, but was individually initiated for each utterance and would be shaped by momentary needs and novel experiences. We might, said Haugen, call all such mental activity "thought" and ask how this "thought" was in turn shaped by the formulation that was all the listener heard or the reader read. The double translation was bound to lose information, but it was usually adequate for practical purposes. The problem was how different language formulations were related to reality and to each others' formulations, and the extent of influences of these formulations on the behavior of the speakers.

Haugen continued by asking what were the LIMITATIONS and the OPPORTUNITIES of formulation in each given language, and what differences and similarities did different languages show in this respect. Could we say anything about language in general or, phrased otherwise, were there language-universal features of formulation, beside the obvious language-specific ones?

This remark led Haugen to his last comment, on universals. He said that one of the unresolved issues of linguistics and anthropology today — one which was not unworthy of our endeavors — was the delimitation of the particular and the universal. When he had entered linguistics a generation ago, most of those whom he had met in the field were people who knew or had studied many languages and were interested in their differences. They were concerned with establishing general principles for the analysis and description of languages, but they were too modest to venture generalizations about linguistic universals. Nowadays, Haugen continued, he found a great many linguists who knew virtually no other language besides English, yet who were all too ready to discuss linguistic universals with the greatest freedom. It was as if the key to linguistic universals could be found in every language and one's confidence in these solutions were inversely proportional to the number of languages in which they had been demonstrated. The change was exemplified by the popularity, in the early days, of Whorfianism, which in effect declared that each language was unique, compared to the present-day neglect of his ideas in favor of the notion that all languages are alike.

Haugen felt that no empirical solution was possible between these two extreme positions. Anyone who had life competence and not just linguistic competence knew that all men were alike in being men and as such had brains that could communicate through their larynxes and their auditory nerves. That all men were created equal was even written into the American litany. But that languages were different just as men were different was equally obvious, and that each language and dialect embodied a different but still human culture was undeniable. After childhood, people learned new languages only with some effort and for the most part reluctantly and, if sufficiently goaded, they would fight for the right not to have to learn a new language imposed on them by their masters.

In one sense it was right that every language mirrored the universals of language, for by definition they had to be there. But this was only because the entire universe that was knowable and much that was unknowable could be expressed in every language. Every language offered endless riches for the one who lingered with it long enough to really learn it. A linguist could spend a lifetime and not learn all that could be known about one language. But the kind of universals that were now being extracted mostly from the study of English or a few other languages were either trivial or vacuous. They depended heavily on the use of logic and semi-mathematical symbolism, which corresponded to certain aspects of natural languages, from which they were ultimately derived. They offered ways of talking about language, even ways of manipulating language through computers and other machines. But languages were not logical, Haugen said; they were conventional, traditional, historical accretions of arbitrarily concatenated signs by means of which specific groups of men had learned to interact. Haugen illustrated this by saying that the difference between "one" and "more than one" was a logical, mathematically definable quantity. But the difference between singular and plural was a wilderness of wildly illogical and often quite undefinable entities, e.g. why was "information" singular in English and plural in all Western European languages, but "pants" and "scissors" plural in English and singular in the rest of the world?

One did not have to look far to see the thrust behind the search for universals: in a world torn by war, revolution, crime, and general social unrest, one emphasized that which all men had in common. We were looking for the common denominator, the touchstone that made us all kin, even if it be on a high intellectual level, out of the reach of most of those who needed to learn about it. But in moving to this extreme, we were neglecting the individual languages that we studied. We treated our informants as digits in a computer, our languages as materials for dissertations and research grants, and our grammars as mere illustrations of nth-level abstractions. Before our eyes, languages were dying and their speakers were being macadamized into the airstrips and the freeways of our brave new world. Anything that smacked of applied linguistics we referred to as performance rather than competence and so pretended that the linguistic problems of the world did not exist.

Haugen concluded by saying that he realized that he had strayed from his theme. But in trying to redress somewhat the balance between particular languages and general linguistics, he was merely asking that we considered not only the infinitely great, but also the infinitely small. Perhaps it was just a passing phase: one age found languages infinitely varied, another found them infinitely similar. Both views were partly true and partly false, and he hoped that linguists and anthropologists would reject the false and retain the true.

Scheffler began his comments by saying that the general topic for discussion in the session at hand was semantic possibilities in human cognition. He said he would like to comment briefly on this, and on some of the papers in the session, from the point of view of an anthropologist concerned with the possibility of finding some universal cultural constructs in terms of which, or by reference to which, human social systems might be compared and contrasted. The possibility of doing this, in his view, was made quite unnecessarily difficult because of two related factors. First, exotica was the anthropologist's most valuable stock-in-trade item. Anthropologists had a vested interest in making things, peoples, thoughts, and so on appear to be different, strange, weird. Had Malinowski returned from years in the Trobriand Islands only to write: "They think about sex and kinship pretty much as we English or Poles do!" Who would have bought his books? Anthropologists are, as a profession, predisposed to believe "odd things about odd people."

The other factor related to this was, in Scheffler's opinion, the willingness of some anthropologists these days to imagine that there was something culture-bound about ordinary Aristotelian logic and about class logic. It had seriously been argued that "we need more powerful formalisms" than are provided by these old standbys, when we attempted to describe other people's cultural constants. However, Scheffler added, this was not what we required. What we did need was greater awareness of just how powerful most of our simple, elementary semantic concepts really were, concepts like signification versus connotation, polysemy, metaphor, and so on, all of which rested, of course, on elementary Aristotelian and class logic!

Scheffler remarked that some of the papers in the session utilized and developed some of these concepts to considerable advantage. He was thinking particularly of Haugen's eminently sensible review of the "linguistic relativity" hypothesis, of Ikegami's discussion of meaning for the linguist and meaning for the anthropologist, and of Fischer's paper on Ponapean myth.

But there were others, he said, in which there appeared to be some confusion or doubt about the value of these elementary semantic concepts and their logical foundations. For instance, Tanaka on Okinawan kinship purported to be dealing with "three distinct terminological systems." Although many of the lexemes were the same in all three systems, Tanaka said that they were structurally independent. For this to be true it would have to be the case that the three systems shared no features of meaning in such a way as to suggest derivation of one from another. But given the evidence presented in Tanaka's paper, Scheffler felt that the several systems were interrelated. Scheffler quite agreed with Tanaka that it was important to realize that the same expressions might be used in systematically different ways in different social contexts, and thus their use in the three contexts constituted several different systems of use and classification. But the very use of the same terms, he said, implied some semantic continuity from one context to another. And, he concluded, this was structural dependence rather than independence.

Scheffler added that similar comments could be made about some of the other papers. He felt that his main point was that, in trying to contrast and compare various cultural systems, one should be more aware that a useful body of elementary logical concepts of apparent universal applicability was available, as well as a number of rather elementary semantic concepts based upon these. What appeared to be different modes of thinking and of conceptualizing the world was often simply made to appear different due to the failure of the anthropologist or the linguist in question to make adequate use of these rather elementary bits of logic and semantic apparatus.

Verhaar began his comments by saying that he too had found the papers to be rather diverse, but he was trying to find some basic principles by which this diversity could be reduced. Digressing for a moment, he mentioned the frequent disagreements between transformational grammarians about the grammaticality or otherwise of sentences. He felt that at the bottom of such difficulties was not really a judgment of grammaticalness, but the very content of the sentences, which might be at variance with certain kinds of philosophies, i.e. the question of what could be thought or not be thought.

Verhaar then raised the question of whether or not we could think without words. In searching for the few common lines of approach underlying the papers of the session, Verhaar said, it was noticeable that some dealt with lexical studies such as componential analyses of kinship terms, color terms, etc., whereas others were concerned with grammatical data in very divergent ways. He felt that the two types of studies were not only distinguished as to whether they were lexical or grammatical, but that the lexical studies had much more to do with denomination, i.e. naming things, than the grammatical ones. When one focused one's attention on things, then this constituted an experiential or situational approach, and thinking might be defined or analyzed on such an experiential or situational basis. This kind of thinking might be determined as a mode of consciousness which was not the same as systematic thinking. The other approach which was more exemplified in studies pertaining to grammatical analysis was the mental or rational approach. This could, in extreme form, become rationalistic in the sense that anything not clear was not worth looking at, as was the case in modern rationalism and mentalism in all forms of transformational grammar. If we distinguished thinking to be analyzable on two kinds of bases, the experiential-situational one, on the one hand, and the intellectual-rational one, on the other, and confined ourselves to words as something through which we were related to some situational element, then this seemed the way in which an anthropologically oriented linguist would prefer to deal with these matters. In the light of this, Verhaar felt that the split between anthropological linguistics and a trend like present-day mentalism, for instance, should be explained on a basis much more complicated and profound than theoretical *a prioris* or even philosophical ones. Verhaar thought it was more a question of attitudes than of anything else. This consideration, he added, entered into the problem of the great split between those who were interested in language particulars and played down universals, and those who were interested in language universals and relegated the interest in language particulars to "romanticism."

As a final remark, Verhaar mentioned that the experiential-situational approach was the one that figured often in language and culture studies. Verhaar thought that a word was a name when it was thought of as belonging to something that was named by it; but a word was a kind of thought when it was considered as some bearer of meaning. These two approaches were very difficult to reconcile, and this might well be the reason why in present-day linguistics the splits were so insuperable.

Werner, in his capacity as formal discussant, addressed himself to the question of language and thought in general terms. He referred to the Navaho, whose ethnoscience had been for years a major concern of his study, pointing out that in the Navaho language, which contained numerous classificatory verbs used to refer to different types of objects, the one used in connection with "thought" was the one which referred to objects of a mixed sort which were in themselves disorganized. Werner felt that this highlighted matters quite well: language was linear, whereas thinking was nonlinear. This was intrinsically linked with the question of definition: all definitions were open-ended and the system of differentiating created the nonlinear complex network of thought.

Werner continued by saying that this led him to the problem of memory. He felt that any semantic theory of some explanatory power that did not come to grips with memory was not a proper theory. In his opinion, thinking and memory were closely related. He felt that contextual problems were linked with memory context which constituted templates in memory against which perceptual experiences were compared and according to which the total memory was partitioned. Werner said that when people talked to each other, they were not at any time using their entire memories. For instance, with a sentence such as "the bill was large," which could refer to money or to a bird, the appropriate subcontext was taken out of the total context of memory to refer to money or to a bird.

Werner then turned to the Whorfian theory and said that he thought that part of the problem arising with it stemmed from the different views that anthropologists and linguists had of language — what he called the grammaticalist stance and the lexicologist stance. Anthropologists were lexicologists, and they did not think, as linguists often did, that the lexicon was not part of the language. This led to many misunderstandings between them.

Werner mentioned that perhaps in some way the Whorfian theory could be right. It had been argued by a Hungarian mathematician that in attempting to solve anything through mathematical formulation, the initial selection of the symbol system was not a trivial matter. It was important for the possible solution of a problem that the symbol system was properly picked, because if this was not done, the problem might be insolvable. Undoubtedly, different languages constitute different symbol systems, and cut up reality in different ways; what applied in mathematics might apply to languages too.

Werner also said that it was very important to study bilinguals, though the difficulty with them was that they mixed semantic systems and had "semantic accents" which were very difficult to detect. One point of interest was the situation of two bilinguals who lived in close proximity and tended to mix the two languages; in such a case, it would be very important to study *when* and on which occasions they switched from one language to the other.

Werner pointed out that he disagreed with Verhaar's view that lexical studies were studies of naming. He thought that lexicographical studies were not really just concerned with naming, and pointed out that any good dictionary was expected to contain some pictures, and that the meaning of one word was explained through another word. Therefore, dictionaries and lexicography were concerned with paraphrase relationships, and the possibilities of paraphrasing were almost infinite. Werner said that if ethnoscience was looked upon by some as glorified lexicography, that was all right with him. He felt he wanted to deal with semantics and the lexical field in a way which led to better paraphrase definitions.

Regarding universals, and referring to Haugen's criticisms, he said that one trick of referring to universals in the way which transformationalist-generativists did was to overstate things so that they were easily vulnerable.

Werner concluded his remarks by saying that in linguistics, the study of language particulars was leading us to learning about language in general, and from this the ultimate goal was the understanding of the nature of man. In anthropology, the study of culture was leading to the understanding of the nature of man. Unless linguistics and anthropology led us to understanding human beings better as they functioned in this world, he said, there was no point in doing what we were doing.

Following delivery of the above prepared remarks by the formal discussants, comment was invited from the authors of the papers in this subsession. The comments could be in direct response to the formal discussants, or be based on previous discussions already held during a presession general planning conference, or on other informal exchange of views between authors and other interested Congress members.

Ikegami said that his first comment concerned Haugen's comment on his paper, "'Meaning' for the linguist and 'meaning' for the anthropologist," in which Haugen suggested that the feature [mortal] be assigned to the word *man*, because there was a contrast in this respect between the meaning of the word *man* and that of the word *God*. He was not quite sure how seriously Haugen was proposing this treatment, but in any case this was exactly what he did not want to do. Such a treatment would make sense only if it were the case that *man* and *God* were characterized by exactly the same set of features [mortal] where the other had [immortal]. But this was clearly not the case. There were other respects in which *man* and *God* were distinguished. Thus if one gave the feature [immortal] to *God*, there was nothing which prevented one from assigning a feature like [almighty] as well. He would rather assign a more general feature, say, [divine] as subsuming the notions of "immortality," "almightiness," and so on. How general the feature to be asssigned should be could only be determined by referring to the structure of opposition in the language. This point was discussed in Sections 7 and 9 of his paper, where consideration was given to the problem of why a linguist, in defining the meaning of the word *woman* in contrast to *man*, would have to assign the feature [female] rather than a feature like [being capable of bearing a child].

His second comment had to do with the question whether there was no *a priori* reason why we should follow the binary principle in semantic analysis. Under this principle, if one assigned the feature [divine] to the word *God*, then one would have to assign the feature [−divine] to the word *man*. He would rather claim that the feature [divine] be given to the word *God* and the feature [human] to the word *man*, and that there could only be a partial and by no means complete overlapping between the feature [human] and the feature [−divine] or between the feature [divine] and the feature [−human]. The unary rather than the binary principle would be more realistic in analyzing so complex a structure as that of meaning.

Ikegami's final comment concerned the status of semantic features with regard to the problem of universality. Werner had remarked, in a pre-Congress conference which they had attended together, that componential analysis was a failure because many of the semantic components that were set up were clearly not universal. Again, Ikegami thought that there was no *a priori* reason to suppose that the semantic components or features should be universal. He would rather claim that a semantic component which happened to be labeled in the same way in different languages might have different implications in different languages. Thus a feature like [divine] or [female] might have a quite different set of notions associated with it in one language than in another. And this was exactly the point which the anthropologist would be more interested in. Finally, he said he would also argue against the position taken in Werner's paper in which componential analysis was rejected in favor of the theory of the semantic field. He thought there was nothing incompatible between the two approaches; it could easily be demonstrated that the theory of the semantic field could profitably be reformulated in terms of componential analysis.

In response to Scheffler's comments, Tanaka said that he did not claim that there was no semantic continuity, since a lexically identical "kin" term was used in several terminological systems. However, the purpose of his paper was NOT to find transformational rules for individual terms, but to examine the total terminological configuration of each system. He still felt that it could be claimed that the three systems identified were structurally or configurationally distinct, if not semantically independent, since classificatory principles in each system were distinct.

Secondly, Tanaka was fully aware that many people had noticed the existence of sociocentric terms. However, even if the fact was known, such terminological usages were explained in terms of genealogical and/or status role relationship within the household. The point made was that the structural principles of the sociocentric terminology were different, though not totally unrelated, from the principles of genuine kinship terminology, or kinship, or family system of the society, for that matter. Finally, Tanaka had to point out that at least in the kind of society he was referring to, it was essential to recognize the distinctiveness of these systems, because it was closely related to the social organization of the village and the neighborhood.

Cecil Welte pointed out that, since his paper was on values, one might be wondering why it appeared in the linguistics session. This was because we were all concerned with cognitive processes. The study of cognition covered a wide spectrum, and in recent usage included decision making. This gave values a prominent place, as they formed the heart of the decision-making process. Furthermore, the relation between language and thought had been the focus of the subsession, and the relation of beliefs and values to the words used to express them was an interesting aspect of this problem.

In his view, Welte said, the basic units of cognitive structures were beliefs and values and lay at a great depth below the verbal level. Many of them were partially reflected in verbal expressions, but others were not at all. And since words were not the units of cognitive structure, he thought it was misleading to consider them to be the units of cognitive processes in any exclusive sense. There were two situations that illustrated this: (1) when we, as students of culture, used words to designate the values of a people, we were describing classes of cultural values, while the values themselves (the taxa of the classes) could not be reached; and (2) when, on the other hand, the people themselves said that certain words "were" their values or represented their values, the status of these words in their cognitive processes was highly problematical.

As a last point, Welte wondered about the fact that values had to do with emotion. How could we reconcile this with their place in cognition? He said he thought that values cut across the conventional classifications of mental functions. They were involved in cognition, in emotion, and in conation. Thinking, feeling, and willing all had their part in decision making; values were used to assess the desirability of alternatives, they were the basis for the act of will in the decision to move, and they provided the emotional impulse to go ahead with it. They were symbols with power.

The formal subsession on "Language and Thought" adjourned after these comments from authors, but a subsequent open discussion on language and anthropology at large provided an opportunity for any interested Congress member to speak on the topic of language and thought, and several individuals did so.

M. Guboglo criticized Haugen who, in his opinion, lumped socio-linguistics and ethnolinguistics together, or subsumed ethnolinguistics under sociolinguistics. Formerly, these two approaches were kept separate and Guboglo felt that this separation ought to continue. He illustrated the validity of his arguments with examples drawn from the U.S.S.R. McCormack expressed agreement with Guboglo's views, and it was mentioned that dictionary making was connected with ethnolinguistics, not with sociolinguistics.

Jane H. Hill gave some comments on Haugen's paper and said that she thought that the people present might want to hear a brief report on what linguists working within Uto-Aztecan were finding with reference to Whorf's work, which Haugen had discussed in his paper.

First, Carl and Florence Voegelin, working with a Hopi grammarian, Masayesva, have restudied the "vibratile" verbs of Hopi, which Whorf had discussed in a famous paper. They found that the Hopi did not accept many of Whorf's glosses on the forms he presented, that many other ways of discussing vibrating and pulsing phenomena existed which were not in Whorf's paradigm. In short, this small group of verbs could not make the contribution to Hopi "physics" that Whorf had claimed for them. Hill reported that although the Voegelins' paper was not published, it was probably available from them.

Second, Hill reported that work by Roderick Jacobs and herself on Cupeño and Cahuilla (Uto-Aztecan languages closely related to Hopi) shed light on Whorf's claims about the relationships between the aspectual system in the Hopi verb and the Hopi world view. In his article, "An American Indian model of the universe," Whorf built an enormous philosophical edifice on the fact that the Hopi verb distinguished only "realized" versus "unrealized" instead of past, present, and future, the latter set of distinctions supposedly characterizing "Standard Average European," and having repercussions on the SAE notion of time and space.

Apparently, Cupeño and Cahuilla used to have the Hopi system as well; in Wanikik Cahuilla, the system was retained. But in other dialects of Cahuilla, and in Cupeño, in main clauses and in relative clauses where the head noun of the relative clause was the subject of the verb in the relative clause, the "realized" had split into past and present, and the "unrealized" had in turn become a future. However, in relative clauses where the head noun was the object, and in complement clauses, the earlier realized/unrealized "Hopi" system remained unchanged. The upshot of this was that Hill and Jacobs found it extremely difficult to believe that the Cupeño and Cahuilla had TWO world views, one for main clauses, and another for most types of subordinate clauses.

Emanuel Drechsler said that he could only agree with Haugen's suggestion that in linguistics and anthropology the two phenomena of relativity and universality should not exclude each other, that in fact both had to be taken into account if we were to provide an adequate picture of language and of culture.

He said he would like to go a step further and suggest some armchair inferences concerning a model where both relativity and universality were included. In recent years, universals had been referred to with respect to the deep structure in generative-transformational terms, whereas specific language features often had not been dealt with explicitly in the lately predominating universalistic trend. However, if we did not want to completely discard the Whorfian hypothesis, at least its nondeterministic version, then we should also try harder to account for "relativity" in our linguistic models. Clearly, the surface structure in generative transformational terms was relative but, he said, he wondered whether a surface structure would be relevant enough to have some influence on the way one spoke. In fact, he added, we would be too naïve to assume any direct and simple correlations between what we now call linguistic surface structure and thought, as Whorf and his followers had stressed on several occasions. Rather, such possible correlations had to be expected to be of "underlying form," which he thought had already been proposed in Sapir's and Whorf's writings.

This "underlying form" would be interpreted as nothing else than a sort of deep structure, not the universal deep structure, but some intermediate one, analogous to Henrik Birnbaum's "shallow deep structure" or "infrastructure." Since we thus had to assume several layers of structures, not only two, inferences from language to thought and vice versa would have to be made on an intermediate level and not on the surface structure, assuming that thought itself had to be assumed as a deep structural cultural phenomenon. The surface structure evidently could not reveal too much in this regard.

To promote further research into such possible correlations, he would moreover propose that we referred to deep structural conceptions such as Wallace Chafe's "semantic structure," or George Lakoff's "logic structure," even if both Chafe and Lakoff would not necessarily agree with his proposition. Such a theoretical framework could be particularly revealing in studies of pidginization and creolization as well as in bilingual and multilingual language acquisition, where two or more languages and thought systems clashed together. Thus, for example, black English was surface structurally so similar to standard American English, but it turned out to walk hand in hand with a thought system rather different from the one of white middle-class Americans. If we could establish that black English shared a deep structure with African languages, we might also be able to find possible correspondences with respect to the thought world. As far as bilingualism was concerned, he said that he would not exclude some correlations between language and thinking, judging intuitively from his own experience.

Finally, Dreschler once more emphasized that even assuming such a model, we should not expect simple correlations. But even though such possible correlations might be hard to prove, this was no reason to turn away from the hypothesis of linguistic relativity. As long as it was not disproved — and he thought it was not — it still had some "explanatory" value.

Biographical Notes

BERYL L. BELLMAN (1941–   ) is Assistant Professor of Sociology and Coordinator of the Communications Program at the University of of California at San Diego. He received his B.A. in 1964, an M.A. in 1966 (both from the University of California at Los Angeles), and a Ph.D. in Social Sciences from the University of California at Irvine in 1971. He taught at the California State University in Los Angeles, the California Institute of the Arts, and the State University of New York at Stony Brook before joining the Sociology faculty at the University of California at San Diego. His special interests include the use of video recording in research and analysis, and the application of ethnomethodological and phenomenological procedures in cross-cultural research.

JOHN DUNCAN MARTIN DERRETT (1922–   ) was born in London. He served in India during 1942 to 1945. From 1947 to 1949, he studied for his Ph.D. in Ancient Indian History at the School of Oriental and African Studies, University of London, and since 1949 has taught Hindu law and other aspects of Indian law there. His main interests include the adjustment of the traditional society to the modern world, in particular the cosmopolitan concepts of duty and obligation. Besides numerous works intended for practicing lawyers, he has written on religion and law (1968) and has authored a basic critique of the Hindu personal laws in their then state (1970). His *Bhāruchi's commentary on the Manusmṛti* (1973) has made available the earliest commentary on Manu. His secondary interest is "law and interpretation" in the New Testament: *Law in the New Testament* (1970), *Jesus's audience* (1973).

He received the D.C.L. of Oxford in 1966 and the LL.D. of London in 1971.

JEAN-PAUL DUMONT (1940–   ) was born in France and has been a resident of the United States since 1966. He received a Licence ès-Lettres from the Sorbonne in 1964 and, after two years of fieldwork in Venezuela and Guiana (1967–1969), a Ph. D. in Anthropology from the University of Pittsburgh in 1972. Since 1975, he has been Assistant Professor of Anthropology at the University of Washington. His publications include *Le foetus astral: essai d'analyse structurale d'un mythe cinématographique,* written in collaboration with Jean Monod (1970) and *Under the rainbow: nature and supernature among the Panare Indians* (1976).

ROBERT B. EKVALL.   No biographical data available.

FRANCES NORTHEND FERGUSON (1925–   ) was born in Hartford, Connecticut. She received an M. A. degree (1959) and a Ph. D. (1972) in Cultural Anthropology from the University of North Carolina at Chapel Hill. Study in India (1961–1962) was undertaken with an NIMH pre-doctoral fellowship and was followed by work with Navajo Indians (1964–1968) in northwestern New Mexico. During the summer of 1975 she taught at the University of Kentucky. Her current area of interest is in modes of personal adaptation to modernization.

JOHN L. FISCHER (1923–   ) is Professor of Anthropology and Chairman of the Department at Tulane University, New Orleans. He received the degrees of B.A. (1946), M.A. (1949), and Ph.D. in Social Anthropology (1955) from Harvard. He has conducted field research in Micronesia, a New England village, and a Japanese city, studying folklore, child rearing, and language. His most recent field research concerns the oral poetry of Ponape, Caroline Islands.

EDGAR A. GREGERSEN.   No biographical data available.

EINAR HAUGEN (1906–   ) was born in Sioux City, Iowa, studied at Morningside and St. Olaf Colleges (B.A., 1928), and did graduate work at the University of Illinois (M.A., 1929; Ph.D., 1931). He was Thompson Professor of Scandinavian Languages at the University of Wisconsin in Madison from 1931 to 1964, Victor S. Thomas Professor of

Scandinavian and Linguistics at Harvard University from 1964 to 1975, and since then emeritus. He is the author of several textbooks on Norwegian, a *Norwegian-English dictionary* (1966), *The Norwegian language in America* (1953), *Bilingualism in the Americas* (1956), *Language conflict and language planning* (1966), *The ecology of language* (1972), *Studies* (1972), *A bibliography of Scandinavian languages and linguistics 1900–1970* (1974), *The Scandinavian languages: an introduction to their history* (1976), as well as articles in *Language, PMLA, Word*, etc. He is a past president of the Linguistic Society of America and of the Permanent International Committee of Linguistics; he was president of the Ninth International Congress of Linguists (1962).

GEORGE G. HAYDU (1911–) studied humanities, medicine, and philosophy. He is a Fellow of the American Psychiatric Association and Head of the Clinical Sciences Division, Creedmoor Institute for Psychobiologic Studies. His present interest centers on the dynamics of integrative transformism.

ALBERT C. HEINRICH (1922–) was born in Columbia, Illinois. He studied at the University of Alaska, the New School for Social Research, Columbia University, Cornell, and the University of Washington (Seattle). He has degrees from the New School (B.A., 1951), the University of Alaska (M.Et., 1955) and the University of Washington (Ph.D., 1963). He has taught at the University of Alaska, the University of Montana, and the University of Calgary, where he is now Professor of Anthropology. He has done fieldwork in Alaska, Canada, South America, and India.

YOSHIHIKO IKEGAMI (1934–) was born in Kyoto, Japan. He majored in English at the University of Tokyo and in linguistics at Yale University, where he obtained his Ph.D. Since 1963 he has been teaching at the Department of Foreign Languages, College of General Education, University of Tokyo. From October 1974 to March 1976 he was a research fellow of the Alexander von Humboldt Foundation in the Seminar für allgemeine und vergleichende Sprachwissenschaft, University of Hamburg. His special interest is in linguistic theory, especially semantics and poetics. His publications include, among others, *Middle English DIGHT: a structural study in the obsolescence of words* (1964), *Eishi no Bumpo* [Grammar of English poetry] (1967), *The semological structure of the English verbs of motion* (1970), *Noah Webster's grammar: traditions and innovations* (1972), and *Imiron* [Semantics] (1975).

LUCY JAYNE KAMAU (1938–   ) was born in Albany, New York. She received a B.A. from the University of California at Los Angeles in 1961, a M.A. from Washington State University in 1963, and a Ph.D. in Anthropology from the University of Chicago in 1971 with a dissertation on the relation between belief and ritual in Christian Science. She was a Research Fellow at the University of Nairobi from 1971 to 1973. She has been an Assistant Professor of Anthropology at Northeastern Illinois University since 1973. Her research interests include symbolism and systems of thought.

R. S. KHARE (1936–   ) was born in India. He studied at Lucknow University (B.Sc., 1955; M.A., 1957; Ph. D. 1962) and did postdoctoral work at the University of Chicago (1963–1964). He has taught at Kanya Kubja College, Lucknow, the University of Wisconsin–Green Bay, the University of Virginia, and the Ecole Pratique Des Hautes Etudes, Paris. He has been a Senior Fellow of the American Institute of Indian Studies, a guest member of the Indian Institute of Advanced Study in Simla, and a member of the Institute for Advanced Study at Princeton. He has been Professor of Anthropology at the University of Virginia since 1971. Recent publications are: *The Changing Brahmans* (1970); *Culture and reality: essays on Hindu management of foods* (1975), and *The Hindu hearth and home: culinary systems past and present in north India* (1975).

C. GREGORY KNIGHT (1941–   ) is Associate Professor of Geography at the Pennsylvania State University. Born in Buffalo, New York, he studied geography and mathematics at Dartmouth College (B.A., 1963), receiving his M.A. and Ph.D. (1970) in Geography with a minor in Anthropology from the University of Minnesota. He served as Assistant Professor of Geography at the University of Kansas from 1968 to 1970. His primary research interests are cultural ecology and human use of environment, particualrly in tropical Africa. Among his publications is *Ecology and change; rural modernization in an African community* (1974).

JEAN-PAUL LEBEUF (1907–   ) was born in Paris, is a Docteur ès-Lettres, and an officer in the Legion of Honor. He is a Director of Research in the Centre Nationale de la Recherche Scientifique and a Professor at the University of Paris V (Réné Descartes). From 1936–1976 he directed scientific expeditions in the fields of ethnology and archaeology for the C.N.R.S. to the African countries of Cameroon,

Chad, Congo, Mali, and Nigeria. He holds a membership in the Académie des Sciences d'Outre-Mer and has founded the Institut National pour les Sciences Humaines in N'Djaména, Chad. His principal publications include: *L'habitation des Fali du Nord-Cameroun* (1961), *Archéologie tchadienne. Les Sao du Cameroun et du Tchad* (1961), *Carte archéologique des abords du Lac Tchad* (1969), *Devinettes peules* (1972), *Etudes kotoko* (1976), and *Les Arts des Sao* (1976).

FREDERIC K. LEHMAN (1925–) grew up in India and Burma. He studied anthropology under Heine-Geldern following the Second World War and took a Ph.D. in Anthropology and Linguistics at Columbia University in 1959, having also studied Indology and linguistics at the University of Pennsylvania in 1953–1954. He has done fieldwork in several parts of Burma and Thailand, has published extensively on the ethnography and linguistics of the Tibeto-Burman and Thai-speaking peoples, is editor of the *Occasional Papers of the Wolfenden Society* on Tibeto-Burman linguistics, and Professor of Anthropology and Linguistics at the University of Illinois, Urbana.

YVES LEMAITRE (1936–) took his degrees in mathematics, linguistics, and ethnology at the University of Paris and the Ecole Normale Supérieurs de l'Enseignement Technique. He served for seven years as a teacher of Mathematics in a secondary school system and entered the Office de la Recherche Scientifique et Technique Outre-Mer in 1968 as a linguist at the Center of Papeete. He has devoted his time to the study of the Tahitian language (Phonology, lexicography) and is now preparing a work on the lexico-semantics of technical vocabularies in Tahitian. He has been Maître de Recherche at the O.R.S.T.O.M. since 1973.

NGUYEN DANG LIEM (1936–) was born in Saigon. He received his Licence ès-Lettres d'enseignement de français from the University of Saigon, his M.A. in English Language and Literature and his M.A. in Linguistics from the University of Michigan, and his Ph.D. in Linguistics from the Australian National University. He is Professor of Southeast Asian Languages and Literature at the University of Hawaii. He has authored fourteen books and numerous articles on Vietnamese, English, French, and other Southeast Asian languages and linguistics, and he is currently Editor of the South-East Asian Linguistic Studies Series at the Australian National University.

WILLIAM C. MCCORMACK (1929–), a Canadian, is Professor of Anthropology and Linguistics at the University of Calgary. Born in the U.S.A., he received a B.A. in Liberal Arts from the University of Chicago in 1948, a B.A. with distinction in Psychology from Stanford University in 1949, an M.A. in Anthropology from Stanford in 1950, and, after also studying at the University of California (Berkeley, 1950–1951), a Ph.D. in Anthropology from the University of Chicago in 1956. Having studied linguistics, he took part in a Summer Institute at the University of Michigan (Ann Arbor, 1956), then taught and researched in linguistics during 1956–1958 at Deccan College, Poona, India, with special reference to Kannada ethnolinguistics and sociolinguistics. He is author of *Kannada: a cultural introduction to the spoken styles of the language* (1966) and of many articles on language in relation to society, religion and identity in India. Since his fieldwork in Friesland and Scotland in 1967–1968, his research orientations have been directed towards comparing forms of religious communication among Lingayats of South India and selected Calvinists of the West.

FERRUCCIO ROSSI-LANDI (1921–) is Professor of the Philosophy of History at the University of Lecce, Italy. He studied at the Universities of Milan, Pavia, and Oxford. In 1953 he published a monograph on Charles Morris which was the earliest semiotic inquiry in postwar Europe (reprinted, with other material, in 1975: *Charles Morris e la semiotica novecentesca*). His publications concern general semiotics, Marxist theory, linguistic production and alienation, the relationship between semiotics and ideology and the circulation of goods both in the material and the linguistic field. His most recent writings include *Il linguaggia come lavoro e come mercato* (1968, 1973), *Semiotica e ideologia* (1972), *Dialektik und Entfremdung in der Sprache* (1973), *Ideologies of linguistic relativity* (1973), and *Linguistics and economics* (1974, 1975). He is currently working on the position and function of sign systems within social reproduction.

HAROLD W. SCHEFFLER (1932–) was born in St. Louis, Missouri, and studied anthropology at the University of Missouri (B.A., 1956) and the University of Chicago (M.A., 1958; Ph.D., 1963). He has taught at Yale University since 1963, where he is now Professor of Anthropology and Chairman of the Department. Major publications include *Choiseul Island social structure* (1965) and, with F. G. Lounsbury, *A study in structural semantics: the Siriono kinship system* (1971).

PAUL SCHVEIGER (1932–) graduated from Cluj University in 1955 and has received a Ph.D. in Speech Pathology. Since 1959, he has been Assistant Professor of Russian and Linguistics at the Babeṣ-Bolyai University in Cluj and in 1968 became an Associate Professor there. His main scientific interests are in normal and pathological communication. He has published more than 50 papers and review papers in Romanian and foreign linguistics journals.

MASAKO TANAKA (1933–) was born in Yokohama, Japan. She received her B.A. in German Area Studies from the University of Tokyo in 1956, and a Ph.D. in Anthropology from the University of Rochester in 1974. She won the 1974 Yonina Talmon Prize for her essay on Okinawan ancestor worship. Her present research interest is in kinship, religion, and semantics. She is currently a Visiting Assistant Professor of Anthropology at the University of Rochester.

ZENO VENDLER (1921–) was born and educated in Hungary, received his S.T.L. in Maastricht (the Netherlands), and his Ph.D. in Philosophy at Harvard (1959). He taught at Cornell University, the University of Calgary, and Rice University, and is at present Professor of Philosophy at the University of California, San Diego. His publications include *Linguistics in philosophy* (1967), *Adjectives and nominalizations* (1968), and *Res cogitans* (1972).

JOHN W. M. VERHAAR (1925–) is Professor of Linguistics and Philosophy in the University of Indonesia, Jakarta, Indonesia, regularly lecturing also in other institutions in Indonesia. He studied English Language and Literature at the University of Amsterdam (1946–1951) and later obtained M.A.'s in Philosophy and Theology, meanwhile continuing his specializations in linguitics. He obtained his Ph.D. at the University of Groningen (the Netherlands) in 1963 with a dissertation entitled *Some relations between perception, speech and thought*. Over the years he has lectured in Europe, the United States, Australia, and various countries in Southeast Asia. He is the Managing Editor of the journal *Foundations of Language* and of the series *NUSA, Linguistic Studies in Indonesian and Languages in Indonesia*. He is currently writing two books, *The speech act and language theory* and *The function of theology in the Church*. His interests are phenomenology and structuralism, for the most part in interdisciplinary application, as well as the relationship between theology and spirituality.

CECIL R. WELTE (1915–) was born in Philadelphia, Pennsylvania. After an engineering education he spent twenty years as a linc officer in the U.S. Navy. He then took an M.A. degree in Mesoamerican Anthropology at Mexico City College, with the thesis "Aztec value orientations" (1962). His primary theoretical interest is in the varieties of values that are involved in human motivation, and in relating them to the development of the indigenous peoples of southern Mexico. Since 1964 he has resided in Oaxaca, where he established and now mainains the Oficina de Estudios de Humanidad de Valle de Oaxaca. He is a member of the Consejo Ejecutivo of the Museo Frissell de Arte Zapoteca.

OSWALD WERNER (1928–) was born in Rimavska Sobota (Rima Szombat) in Czechoslovakia. He studied at the Technische Hochschule in Stuttgart, Germany, and at Syracuse University, where he received an M.A. in Anthropology. His Ph.D. in Anthropology and Linguistics is from Indiana University. He has been a Professor of Anthropology and Linguistics at Northwestern University in Evanston, Illinois since 1963. His interests and publications deal with the exploration of systems of cultural knowledge or ethnoscience and the application of theoretical insights to the study of Navajo ethnomedical knowledge and ethnographies of Navajo education. He has conducted extensive fieldwork with Navajo Indians and more briefly on Easter Island (Rapa Nui).

IRENE PORTIS WINNER (1923–) received a B.A. from Radcliffe College, an M.A. in Cultural Anthropology from Columbia University, and a Ph.D. in Cultural Anthropology from the University of North Carolina at Chapel Hill. She has taught anthropology at Wayne State University, Tufts University, and is presently Associate Professor of Anthropology at Emmanuel College in Boston. She also holds a research appointment at Brown University and is an Associate of the Russian Research Center at Harvard University. She specializes in peasantry, ethnicity, and anthropological theory. Her recent publications include works on East European peasantry, East European ethnicity in the United States, problems of anthropological semiotics, and aesthetic theory.

STEPHEN A. WURM (1922–), an Australian, studied linguistics, anthropology and Oriental languages at the University of Vienna where he received his doctorate. He held teaching and research posts at the

University of Vienna, the Central Asian Research Centre (associated with St. Antony's College, Oxtord University), Sydney University, and the Australian National University, and visiting appointments at Northwestern University, Indiana University, and the University of Hawaii. Since 1958, he has been in charge of the extensive research program in Pacific Linguistics at the Australian National University and was appointed to the Chair of Linguistics in the School of Pacific Studies of that university in 1968. He has been editor of the serial publication *Pacific Linguistics* since its inception in 1963. His major research interests are concerned with the Papuan, Australian, South Western Pacific Austronesian, and pidgin languages of the Pacific as well as with sociolinguistics (formerly he also studied Turgic languages). He has published widely in these fields.

SAYO YOTSUKURA (1921–) was born in Tokyo, Japan. She received her B.A. in English from the University of Tokyo in 1950. Her M.A. (1955) and Ph.D. (1963) are both in linguistics and from the University of Michigan. From 1963 to 1970 she headed the Japanese program at Georgetown University, Washington, D.C. Her primary concern has been to theorize analytical methods of language and thought by adopting and expanding Kenneth L. Pike's theory of "Language as wave," on which she delivered a paper ("Tagmemics as wave grammar") at the IXth International Congress of Linguists, Bologna, Italy, in 1972. She has been engaged as a consultant in organizing and supervising the language service of Ketron, Inc. (Arlington, Virginia).

Index of Names

Aberle, D. F., 88
Ackermann, Robert, 95
Adams, P., 4
Adedeji, J. A., 367
Albert, Ethel M., 441–442, 469; *People of Rimrock,* 442–443; "Value systems," 442, 444
Allport, Gordon, 446, 474
Andrews, Edmund, 176
Andrews, Irene D., 176
Anselm of Canterbury, 120
Antal, L., 85n
Ardener, E., 94
Arieti, S., 143
Aristotle, 30–31, 119, 120, 391, 490; *De interpretatione,* 29
Arnaud, A., 30
Augustine, St., 35, 408
Austin, J. L., 38, 106, 110
Awe, B., 372
Ayyar, A. S. Nataraja, 251, 256

Bacon, Francis, 92; *New organon,* 62n
Barnes, John A., 212n, 214n
Barr, James, 22
Bascom, William, 359, 362n, 364, 365, 367, 377, 380–381, 383
Basham, A. L., 285
Basilius, Harold, 20
Bates, Daisy, 203
Baudelaire, Charles, 434
Beckett, J., 20ln, 206
Begishe, K. Y., 150
Bellman, Beryl L., 6, 271–282, 486, 501

Benedict, Paul K., 247
Benedict, Ruth, 360
Berkeley, George, 30
Berlin, Brent, 171, 174, 182, 194–195
Berndt, C. H., 206
Berndt, R. M., 206
Bharatiija, Roopishore, 317
Bidney, D., 4
Bindra, D., 472
Biobaku, S.O., 364, 372, 379
Birdwhistell, Ray L., 91
Birnbaum, Henrik, 498
Biss, K., 133
Bittle, William E., 12
Black, Max, 4, 106
Blake, Judith, 442
Blaut, James, 191n
Bloch, B., 71, 89
Bloomfield, Leonard, 80, 90, 94
Boas, F., 20–21, 23, 87, 91, 94, 425; *Handbook of American Indian languages,* 20–21
Bogatyrev, Petr G., 427, 428–433; *Functions of folk costumes in Moravian Slovakia,* 429
Bogrea, Vasile, 63–64
Bohannan, Paul, 418
Bowlby. J., 477
Brahmachari, Krishna R., 317
Bright, J. O., 5, 180
Bright, W., 5, 180
Bronowski, J. 152
Brown, Roger Langham, 19, 70, 443n
Buchler, Ira R., 94

Index of Subjects

Abeokuta (Yoruba town), 372
Abstraction, 6, 197, 450–542, 460–462, 472
Aesthetic function, 6, 407–409, 412, 434–435, 486; communicative function, 412, 414–415, 420, 422, 424, 430, 432, 436; dynamism of, 415, 419; functions of, 407, 408, 412–414, 415–416, 430–431, hierarchy, 421–425; poetic (aesthetic) function, 412, 422–424, 430, 434; and reality, 407, 421–422; role of, 415–416, 422, 424, 428; semiotics and, 414–421, 432, 437; structures, 410–414, 417, 422, 424, 428. *See also* Behavior, cultural; Language functions: Prague Linguistic Circle; Semiotics
Aesthetic function, norm and value as social facts (Mukařovský), 415
Alliance systems, 209, 235, 243; asymmetrical, 208, 233, 235–237, 241; reversal of, 239–240, 242. *See also* Marriage systems
American Heritage word frequency book (Carroll, et al.), 135, 141
American Indian languages, 11–17, 22, 23, 487. *See also* Hopi language
"An American Indian model of the universe" (Whorf), 497
Analogy, 120, 154, 159, 163, 165
Anandmai Mā (Indian saint), 314
Anthropology: cognitive, 5, 90–91, 93, 489, *see also* Ethnoscience; diffusion of models, 88–89; linguistic models in, 87–89, 91, 93, 486–487; structural, 5
Antonymy, 119
Application: lexical, 102, 103, 105; predictive, 114; referential, 114–115, 117
Approaches to language, 4
Aranda system, 206–207
Arjun (Indian deity), 311
"L'art comme fait sémiologique" (Mukařovský), 414
Artha and prayer, 298, 312
Arthaśāstra, 254, 257
Ashram: guru, 285–286; origins of, 285–286; saints, 285–292, devotees of, 289–290; social system, 283, 287–292. *See also* Body; Saints
Atlasul linguistic român (Petrovici), 62–66
Atlasul linguistic român (Pop), 62, 64–66
Australia, kin classification in, 201–209
Axiology, 469–470, 474
Aztecs, 361

Bas-Chari region, 185
Behavior, cultural: and aesthetic function, 407, 412–414, 415, 428, dynamism, 407, 410, 413, 415, polyfunctionalism, 407, 408, 412–414, 422, 430, 435, semiotic character, 407, 414, 415, 425–428, 432, structuration, 407, 410–414, 419, 424; and belief, 446, 447; and hierarchy of functions, 421–425; and semiotics, 436–437